**PERGAMON INTERNATIONAL LIBRARY**
of Science, Technology, Engineering and Social Studies

*The 1000-volume original paperback library in aid of education,
industrial training and the enjoyment of leisure*

Publisher:  **Robert Maxwell, M.C.**

*Towards the Elimination of Racism*

**Publisher's Notice to Educators**

## THE PERGAMON TEXTBOOK
## INSPECTION COPY SERVICE

An inspection copy of any book published in the Pergamon
International Library will gladly be sent without obligation for
consideration for course adoption or recommendation. Copies may
be retained for a period of 60 days from receipt and returned if not
suitable. When a particular title is adopted or recommended for
adoption for class use and the recommendation results in a sale of
12 or more copies, the inspection copy may be retained with our
compliments. If after examination the lecturer decides that the
book is not suitable for adoption but would like to retain it for his
personal library, then our Educators' Discount of 10% is allowed on
the invoiced price. The Publishers will be pleased to receive
suggestions for revised editions and new titles to be published in this
important International Library.

# PERGAMON GENERAL PSYCHOLOGY SERIES

*Editor*: Arnold P. Goldstein, *Syracuse University*
Leonard Krasner, *SUNY, Stony Brook*

---

## TITLES IN THE PERGAMON GENERAL PSYCHOLOGY SERIES
### (Added Titles in Back of Volume)

The terms of our inspection copy service apply to all the above books. A complete catalogue of all books in the Pergamon International Library is available on request.

The Publisher will be pleased to receive suggestions for revised editions and new titles.

# Towards the Elimination of Racism

Phyllis A. Katz
*Editor*

Sponsored by the Society for the Psychological Study of Social Issues

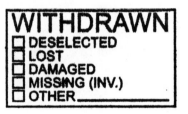
PERGAMON PRESS INC.

New York / Toronto / Oxford / Sydney / Braunschweig / Paris

*Pergamon Press Offices:*

U.S.A.  Pergamon Press Inc., Maxwell House, Fairview Park, Elmsford, New York 10523, U.S.A.

U.K.  Pergamon Press Ltd., Headington Hill Hall, Oxford OX3, OBW, England

CANADA  Pergamon of Canada, Ltd., 207 Queen's Quay West, Toronto 1, Canada

AUSTRALIA  Pergamon Press (Aust.) Pty. Ltd., 19a Boundary Street, Rushcutters Bay, N.S.W. 2011, Australia

FRANCE  Pergamon Press SARL, 24 rue des Ecoles, 75240 Paris, Cedex 05, France

WEST GERMANY  Pergamon Press GmbH, 3300 Braunschweig, Postfach 2923, Burgplatz 1, West Germany

**Library of Congress Cataloging in Publication Data**

Katz, Phyllis A.
    Towards the elimination of racism.

    (Pergamon general psychology series; no. 54)
    "Sponsored by the Society for the Psychological Study of Social Issues."
    Includes bibliographies.
    1.    United States—Race question—Addresses, essays, lectures.    I.    Title.
    E185.615.K3        301.45'0973        74-28030
    ISBN 0-08-018316-6
    ISBN 0-08-018317-4    pbk.

Printed in the United States of America

This volume is dedicated to Martin and Alice who let me pursue my own thing in spite of contrary stereotypes, and to Aron, Martin 2, and Margaret who are equally understanding.

# *Contents*

**Part IV — Change in the Real World**

# *The Editor*

Phyllis A. Katz (Ph. D., Yale University) is currently a Professor in the Education and Developmental Psychology doctoral programs at the City University of New York. Her major areas of professional interest are the development and modification of children's inter-group attitudes and behavior, and she has published papers in a number of professional journals in this field. She serves on the editorial boards of several journals in developmental psychology and consults for a variety of governmental and private agencies. She is a Fellow of the American Psychological Association, and a member of a number of other professional organizations in psychology and education.

# Contributors

Dr. Yehuda Amir
Department of Psychology
Bar-Ilan University, Israel

Dr. Richard Ashmore
Department of Psychology
Livingston College of
    Rutgers University
New Brunswick, N.J.

Dr. Mark A. Chesler
Sociology Department
University of Michigan
Ann Arbor, Mich.

Dr. Frances K. DelBoca
Rutgers University
New Brunswick, N.J.

Dr. Samuel L. Gaertner
Psychology Department
University of Delaware
Newark, Del.

Dr. Bradley S. Greenberg
Department of Communication
Michigan State University
East Lansing, Mich.

Eric Hirschhorn, Esq.
Cadwalader, Wickersham and Taft
New York, N.Y.

Dr. Phyllis A. Katz
Graduate Center
City University of New York
New York, N.Y.

Sherrie L. Mazingo
Department of Communication
Michigan State University
East Lansing, Mich.

Eleanor Holmes Norton, Esq.
Commissioner
New York City Commission on
    Human Rights
New York, N.Y.

Dr. Myron Rothbart
Department of Psychology
University of Oregon
Eugene, Ore.

Dr. T.A. Weissbach
Department of Psychology
Pomona College
Claremont, Cal.

# *Preface*

My need to participate in a volume of this kind began with an experience I had on the Chesapeake Bay Ferry when I was eight years old. I was thirsty and walked over to the water fountain marked "colored," eagerly anticipating the green, purple, and orange streams of water. The shock and outrage I felt upon being rudely informed that the sign did not refer to the water have still not diminished.

The issue of how such outrage towards inequitable treatment of individuals because of their membership in particular ethnic and racial groups has been transformed into social science research is the underlying theme of this book. Social scientists have exhibited considerable fascination with the problem of racism for at least four decades. This volume seeks to assess what can be distilled from these efforts, and to indicate where future research is leading. The emphasis throughout is on the question of how negative interracial attitudes and behavior can be changed.

The effort that went into this undertaking was truly a joint one, and invaluable assistance was received from many sources. The Society for the Psychological Study of Social Issues generously supported the preparation of this volume both financially and emotionally. Although many individuals were involved, I would especially like to thank Marcia Guttentag, Bert Raven, Richard Schmuck, and Caroline Weichlein for their help in seeing it through. Gratitude is also extended to the many individuals who served as critical advisors for portions of the manuscript and provided many useful ideas. The participation of Chester Pierce, Claire Selltiz, Hylan Lewis, Charles Thomas, and John Robinson is gratefully acknowledged. Particular thanks are extended to Irwin Katz for his thoughtful overall review, which was extremely helpful in revising earlier drafts of the manuscript. Finally, I wish to express my deepest appreciation to Karyl Robbins for the preparation of the book. Her secretarial skills and patience are both unsurpassed.

P.K.

# *Foreword*

This volume forces a focus on changes in American racism, for so long the country's most changeless phenomenon, and on the role of the social scientist in measuring, assessing, and accelerating the pace of change. In effect, this compilation helps us measure the tasks bequeathed us by the civil rights movement of the 1960s.

Racism was the central issue of the sixties, as it should have been for decades before. A social movement of genuine mass proportions attacked American racism head-on and finally began to work profound changes in the nation's attitudes, laws, and institutions. Even as it forged impressive legal and political tools, the movement dared the generation of the seventies to convert them to lasting advantage. This is a task that will surely exceed the limits of a decade as it encompasses the fruit of centuries of oppression. But it is a task that must be resolutely pursued if we are to ensure that the events of the sixties were more than a show of style and passion and that the changes they wrought will be real and enduring.

Many who were actors in the movement events of the last decade have embraced the challenges their own efforts created. Some, of course, are dead and martyred; others were personally devastated by the struggle itself. But thousands have turned their talents to new and not unrelated objectives. Some have entered politics and government to work for the enforcement of the laws they forged. Maynard Jackson, the young black Mayor of Atlanta who is one of these, has even called politics "the civil rights movement of the seventies." But many others of my old movement colleagues—people like Vernon Jordan, Fannie Lou Hamer, Floyd McKissick, and John Lewis—have taken the movement to its next logical step, scattering themselves to places where they can do some good and even wield some of the power they helped create through struggle.

What is clear to us all is that the issues of the seventies are far more defined, and in their own way more difficult, than those of the sixties. The goal is no longer the broad "Freedom Now," but the complicated and demanding effort for affirmative action in employment and housing, for a guaranteed annual wage, for an equal share of educational allocations, and the like.

The danger always is that the recalcitrance of American racism will make too many weary and will tempt the country to give up. Like those who rightly "don't want to study war no more," many would prefer to leave the progress and problems in eradicating America's oldest sickness unexamined. But we must continue to study racism, as those who have contributed to this book have done. For study, and the education that results, are among the best weapons we have to fight racism. Those who have studied and acquired knowledge are the least bigoted and most vigilant against the racial myths that have held the nation back. These thoughtful chapters represent the kinds of efforts that are indispensable to durable and steady progress. Let us continue to study, to learn, and to fight.

Eleanor Holmes Norton, Esq.
Commissioner
New York City Commission on Human Rights

# Part I
# Introduction

# 1

# Racism and Social Science: Towards a New Commitment

PHYLLIS A. KATZ

Racism—the unequal treatment of individuals because of their membership in a particular group—appears to be alive, well, and thriving in the United States. As Martin Luther King so aptly stated in 1968, white America is "poisoned to its soul by racism." Evidence that we are indeed a racist society, as noted in the *Report of the National Advisory Commission on Civil Disorders* (1968), is continuous. Scarcely a day goes by without new documentation. The dynamiting of school buses to be used in a new integration program; the shooting of a black off-duty policeman who is mistaken for the thief; the involuntary sterilization of young, black, teenage girls; the use of a black, untreated "control" group in a longitudinal study of syphilis—such reminders are, sadly, too familiar.

Discussions about racism, however, tend to be analogous to discussions about sin. There is general agreement that it is bad. Its existence is loudly decried, often with great piety and occasional protestations of guilt, but more frequently it is perceived as a problem associated with other people. Moreover, like sin, racism has been with us for a long time.

Long before civil rights commissions and today's continuous media commentary, astute observers of the American scene noted the paradox of our expressed egalitarian ideals on the one hand, and our racist practices on the other. The victims of the discrimination have, of course, for centuries been continually conscious of the schism between the words and the behavior of the white community, and have repeatedly stated their case with eloquence and passion. Until recently, however, whites have preferred not to listen. Although many were probably shocked to hear H. Rap Brown describe racism as "American as apple pie," even the most cursory venture into our history supports his statement. The inequality of the races was woven right into the original fabric of our society and clearly reflected a cultural heritage of long standing (Knowles and Prewitt, 1969). Moreover, as the last chapter of this book documents, political and legal rights for racial minorities were extremely long in coming, and grudgingly given only when great pressure was applied. Our very Constitution, a document we are taught to revere in school, recognized slavery in many of its provisions.

3

Thus, the practices and beliefs of racism have been an integral part of our culture. What is relatively new over the past decade, however, is the growing awareness of the problem, the widening polarization of groups, and the increased militance of the victimized minorities. This latter factor introduced a new element into race relations in the mid-sixties, and the psychological and societal effects of this are still being explored.

Racism is clearly one of our greatest domestic problems. It has been described by some as a social disease of epidemic proportions. Unlike comparable social problems such as drug addiction, however, there has not yet been any unified, national effort to counteract its negative effects. Congress has not appropriated massive funding for projects designed to eliminate racism in children and adults. The President has not shown any particular leadership in this area. There has been no call for the establishment of a National Institute for Social Health to study the issues and recommend changes. So, despite the piety, and the guilt, our national commitment toward dealing constructively with the psychological and sociological sources of racism has been surprisingly minimal.

This may well be because, as King (1967) noted: "The problem is deep. It is gigantic in extent and chaotic in detail." Nevertheless, there are many who feel that solutions are not impossible to find. Comer, in his recent book, *Beyond Black and White* (1972), offers a beautiful analogy of the various strategies that can be taken:

> When a problem is long-standing, complex, and painful, everybody wants an immediate solution. Most people expect a dramatic solution. Concerned people want to be personally involved. "What can I do?" they ask.
>
> When a bathtub is overflowing and the faucet is still on, there are a number of things you can do. You can wring your hands in despair or turn away. That's what complaining and copping out are all about. You can curse and abuse the person who left the faucet on. That is what so much anti-establishment action is all about. You can take a thimble and begin to dip water from the flooded floor. That is what so many programs to help the victims of inadequate social policy are all about. You can blow up the bathtub. That is what violence and instant and dramatic proposals are all about. You can turn off the water faucet, pull the plug, and then begin to dip water from the flooded floor.
>
> The solution to black and white conflict and other fear- and anxiety-producing social problems will require turning off the water of those who are failing to produce a solution now. The action is not dramatic and resolution will not be immediate. But there is no faster feasible way. (p. 239)

It is clear that the major thrust will be, as it has been in the past, political in nature. Furthermore, pressure for change will continue to come primarily from the minority communities. As the victims of an unjust system, they have both more knowledge regarding the effects of racism and a greater emotional commitment to seeing it halted.

Thus, a volume of this kind can offer no substitute for needed and concerted action in the political arena. It can, however, provide useful information as to how change can be accomplished most effectively. The primary question to be addressed in the following pages is whether social science, and psychology in particular, has helped towards this goal in the past. A second question is whether the new directions now being taken in psychological theory and research may be useful in future change efforts. Katz and Gurin (1969) state that "There is no field of intellectual inquiry with as much potential value for dealing with racial problems as the social sciences" (p vii). How, then, has psychology fared? Does it, in fact, have anything of value to offer? Does the knowledge obtained from 40 years of research efforts contribute more to the problem (as suggested by the author of Chapter 2) or to its solution?

With such questions in mind, the chapters in this book review some of the major scholarly contributions concerned with the theories and practices of race relations. Viewed against the social and historical backdrop of institutional racism and injustice, many have recently questioned whether a scientific approach can contribute anything useful. It is sometimes easy to empathize with those who throw up their hands in despair, since scientific efforts, although voluminous, still seem minor in contrast to the problem. Our attempts at "relevance" may seem to some like incredibly puny drops in an enormous bucket.

Are we to conclude, then, that psychologists may be more valuable when they don't utilize their training? Are they indeed more useful when they devote their efforts to political action, as has been suggested by a number of recent observers? To many concerned individuals, these appear to be valid and cogent questions. To a new generation of impatient youth, the very notion of objectively studying a disturbing social phenomenon, rather than manning the barricades, may seem particularly difficult to comprehend.

In view of such attitudes, and of the rapid societal changes taking place over the last decade, a decision to do a book of this kind may require justification for some. Let us begin, then, with the assumptions underlying this volume. Scientific studies offer no substitute for effective political, economic, and legal action aimed at bringing about meaningful change either on an individual or a collective level. The authors represented here are in agreement that such societal restructuring remains the most potent avenue for eliminating racism. Having said this, however, it is equally clear that gaps frequently occur between legislation, judicial decisions, and people's behavior. Our political leaders have often not kept pace with legitimate minority group aspirations. On the other hand, there are times when both institutional and individual change lag behind contemporary judicial and legislative accomplishments.

Why these discrepancies occur, and how change might be facilitated, are issues that appear central to social science concern. Psychologists and sociologists should, in fact, have a great deal of information and expertise to offer in these areas. Thus, the reasons for the current academic defensiveness are not immediately apparent. Indeed, in a time of rapid change, institutions may be more in need of such knowledge and applicable principles than ever before. Do we have anything to offer? This is the major question towards which this volume is addressed.

Some investigators have concluded that we do not. Conger (1973), for example, noted the social scientist's general reluctance to "invent" things instrumental to change and their preference for an analytic role. He suggests further that,

> Each social system comprises a series of social inventions. Some systems are relatively well developed—such as education—while other systems—such as intergroup relations—have so few methods to rely on that the system is more of a constellation of problems than of solutions. (p. 216)

Since psychologists have devoted considerable attention to the problem of racism for over 40 years, it appears to this writer that such a conclusion is both overdrawn and hasty. The various chapters in this volume will examine earlier findings to assess which, if any, may still be relevant and to suggest and delineate promising new directions in research. The reader may then judge the issue for him/herself.

There are many substantive questions that appear relevant. What factors must be present before successful attitude change may occur? Must attitudes be changed prior to behavior, or might behavior change influence attitudes? What are the major determinants of negative intergroup attitudes in children, and can they be changed? Why does integration sometimes result in positive and sometimes negative change? What factors must be considered in overcoming political resistance to change? What problems does the contemporary investigator of racism encounter? These are some of the issues that the ensuing chapters discuss.

Most earlier books about racism have focused upon documenting the pernicious effects of racism upon minorities (e.g., Goldschmid, 1970; Kovel, 1970; Wilcox, 1971). In view of the number of recent publications on this subject, plus the more frequent communication of these effects by the popular press and television, a decision was made not to duplicate these efforts in the present volume. Instead, the emphasis throughout is on the modification of white racism. Each of the research reviews included in this volume attempts to extract the essential principles underlying successful change efforts. Theory and research relevant to attitude and behavior change have not been previously addressed in depth; the present volume will provide this coverage.

A number of basic and recurrent themes emerge in evaluating changes in race relations. One controversy has to do with whether meaningful change has occurred at all, and along what dimensions. In the economic sphere, for example, Eleanor Holmes Norton, Commissioner of Human Rights for The City of New York, reports (1973) some very positive statistics for the decade of the 1960s:

> Blacks and whites come close to parity in job distribution, particularly in white collar jobs in the city. Measured in current dollars, the proportion of non-white families with income below $7000 declined from 80% to just under 50% between 1959 and 1969 in New York ... Results from my agency ... show stark progress among the city's minorities in breaking employment barriers. Companies under compliance standards enforced by the New York City Commission doubled minority employment from 6.8% to 13.7% in an average period of three years beginning in 1969. More dramatic than this escalated rate of minority employment is the fact that it occurred when these companies were experiencing a 39% decrease in total employment because of economic recession. Thus the syndrome of job advancement only to be followed by inevitable cutbacks in hard times has been broken in this city. (p. 6)

Comer's interpretation (1972) of similar statistics reveals a different conclusion:

> Despite educational and job advancement, black are like the weary runner trailing the field in a long-distance race. Every step uses up more energy but often results in losing ground. Because blacks were kept so far behind prior to 1960, a disproportionately large number of them are still at the bottom of the labor force and have the least amount of training and education. The pace of scientific and technological change destroys the lower rungs of the economic ladder just as most blacks begin to reach them. (p. 109)

Although the above-cited authors address themselves to interpreting change in the economic area, a similar diversity of opinion is reflected in the current volume with regard to psychological change as well. This issue is not a simple one, as Professor Rothbart's discussion in Chapter 10 points out.

A second major issue in evaluating change research is whether modification attempts directed at the individual level have been more successful than those directed at the institutional level. Again, there exist many differing perspectives on this issue. The traditional psychological view, for example, typically assumes that institutional practices are an expression of individually held values and beliefs. The recent work of Pettigrew and Riley (1972) offers some support for this view. They found that a sizable proportion of the variability in desegregation practices could be predicted from knowledge about expressed community racial attitudes. Nevertheless, citing earlier work, these same investigators conclude that "Contrary to conventional wisdom, social psychological research in race relations has shown repeatedly that the racial attitudes of white Americans typically follow rather than precede actual institutional alterations" (p. 184). A similar view is expressed by Triandis (1972), who suggests that if we "create institutional arrangements in which exploitative behaviors are no longer reinforced" we will then succeed in changing attitudes (p. 132).

Since the relationship between behavior at the individual and collective levels is such a complex one, an attempt was made in the present book to present the data from as many vantage points as possible. Thus, some of the chapters consider the theoretical aspects of the problem, others review experimental evidence pertinent to individual attitudes and behavior, and the latter chapters are addressed to what may be more appropriately considered institutional racism, including the legal changes that have occurred.

## HISTORICAL TRENDS IN RESEARCH ON PREJUDICE

The study of race relations has occupied a prominent place in social science, and particularly in psychology. It may seem paradoxical to the reader, therefore, that these efforts have not been more fruitful. Since most of the reviews in the present volume concentrate on current research, it may be instructive at this juncture to look at some of the trends in previous research. This earlier literature has been comprehensively reviewed elsewhere (e.g., Harding, Proshansky, Kutner, and Chein, 1969; Simpson and Yager, 1972). What this chapter will do, therefore, is to attempt to analyze the major types of research included in the lengthy and fairly representative bibliography presented by Harding *et al.* (1969). Five decades of research efforts spanned by this review were examined and its citations were categorized. It should be noted that although the Harding *et al.* review is not an absolutely complete one—e.g., it does not adequately cover behavioral and change studies in the 1960s—it remains the most authoritative one in the field. The results of this analysis are presented in Table 1. This survey suggests that there are four discernible periods.

1. *Rulers Come First.* The earliest citations of scientific work on racism are from the late 1920s. Of the nine references from this decade, almost all of them are concerned with the direct measurement of attitudes. This early

**Table 1.** Content Analysis of Bibliography in Harding *et al.* (1969) Review Article

| Decade | Theoretical Articles | Attitude Measurements Direct | Indirect | Behavioral Measures | General Descriptions of Prejudice | Experimental Manipulations | Attitude Change Studies | Total Number of Citations |
|---|---|---|---|---|---|---|---|---|
| 1920-30 | | 7 | | | 2 | | | 9 |
| 1931-40 | 3 | 14 | 3 | 3 | 4 | 7 | 3 | 37 |
| 1941-50 | 27 | 34 | 3 | 4 | 2 | 4 | 4 | 78 |
| 1951-60 | 14 | 45 | 8 | 19 | 4 | 9 | 14 | 113 |
| 1961-70* | 1 | 13 | 4 | 10 | 1 | 8 | 4 | 41** |

*Latest: 1967.
**Prorated to 1970.

interest received its impetus from the work of Bogardus and his measure of social distance. Interestingly, some of this very early work is still relevant in that the basic social distance technique remains a frequently employed index of ethnic and racial attitudes.

More generally, however, the period of the late 1920s in race research was analogous to that of inventing a thermometer. Racial attitudes could now be studied legitimately since they could be measured. Succeeding investigators, in fact, exhibited a continuing fascination with the direct measurement of attitudes. The techniques continued to proliferate so that direct measurement of attitudes still constitutes the bulk of studies cited for all decades.

The period of the 1930s witnessed a fourfold increase in the number of articles. The content of these contributions also began to vary. Although almost half of the studies were still concerned with direct attitude measurement, several investigators explored indirect measures of attitudes (e.g., Horowitz and Horowitz), whereas several others were concerned with emerging theoretical issues. Psychologists were beginning to branch out.

2. *The Theory Decade.* The period immediately following World War II might well be labeled the heyday of ideas regarding prejudice. Of the 78 articles cited in the Harding *et al.* review (representing twice as many as the previous decade), 27 of them are either theoretical treatises or studies attempting to test theory.

It is tempting to compare research in this area with the intelligence testing movement. Both clearly began with a measure, and subsequent theory followed from studies of the measure. The analogy breaks down upon further analysis, however. For one thing, the intelligence testing movement did, in fact, produce several reliable and valid indices, even in the absence of theoretically guided efforts, whereas the status of attitude measurements still remains a topic of debate (e.g., Scott, 1968). Another significant difference is that early efforts in intelligence testing were instigated because of need. Whether a child scored high or low on these early instruments could have a distinct and very real effect upon his future. Attitude tests, on the other hand, were never intrinsically tied to consequences for the test-taker. Indeed, this latter difference may partially account for the continuing controversy with regard to the empirical status of the attitude construct.

3. *Manipulation Is the Thing.* Although measurement and theoretical concerns were still of importance to social scientists working in the 1950s, a perusal of this literature indicates that a new and important element was added—the attempt to change prejudicial attitudes. There are four times as many change studies cited for this decade as for the preceding one. In some ways, the decade of the 1950s is a flowering one for race relations research. The bulk of investigations cited in the Harding *et al.* review were conducted during this decade. In reviewing some of these investigations, moreover, a tremendous sense of optimism and productivity is evident. Social scientists behaved during this period as if their work might actually make a difference.

They began to pay attention to behavioral indices as well as to verbally expressed attitudes. Indirect measures were more commonly used. Tests of theories were frequent, and psychologists of widely differing persuasions were offering their versions of how attitudes could best be changed. There seemed to be a general sense of excitement and hope.

4. *Consolidation—or Decline?* Then came the 1960s. The number of references from this decade drops to 41 from the 113 of the previous period. Even allowing for the fact that the dates of these references only go through 1967, there is still, proportionately, an unquestionable decline in the volume of research during this decade. It should be pointed out that the number of behavioral studies is somewhat underrepresented in this review. There is clearly, however, a decrease in the overall number of research studies, as well as surprisingly few new theoretical efforts.

Why this should be is somewhat puzzling. One possibility may be that as sophistication increased, productivity decreased. Or perhaps a degree of complacency was becoming evident. We already had enough theory and research to fill our textbooks. Another possibility is that a certain degree of pessimism was beginning to set in. Investigators may have begun to feel that the complexities of the problem were beyond their reach, or that the tremendous societal changes that were occurring rendered their efforts insignificant. For whatever reason, it is clear that what was happening in race relations during the 1960s was occurring outside the arena of the social scientist. Research had not kept pace with social reality.

## CURRENT TRENDS

This historical overview leads to the issue of where we are headed—a question to be examined in considerably more detail in the chapters to follow. Some researchers have returned to their laboratories to pursue professionally safer and perhaps more trivial areas. The reward structure for social scientists is, after all, still based upon a "publish or perish" philosophy. Others, however, have recently exhibited renewed interest in race relations research, despite (or perhaps because of) the challenges involved.

The social context for race relations in the late 1960s and early 1970s was a very different one, thereby rendering some of the earlier research obsolete. In some areas, sophistication seemed to increase substantially. Group self-definition became an important theme. Within some intellectual circles, being a member of a minority group automatically made one more "interesting." The fashion world seized upon "ethnicity" as a keyword, and conferred high status upon it. The number of magazines aimed at helping people define the meaning of their group membership increased considerably. Talk shows presented more ethnic variety, and suggested that everybody was becoming both healthily vociferous and more positive.

How such a picture meshes with the continuing instances of both individual and institutional racism is difficult to understand. Concomitant with the new-found liberalism were new surges of resistance to school busing and increased strength for conservative candidates, for example. The use of labels such as "backlash" and "polarization" became more popular as attempts to reconcile the discrepancies increased.

These disparate trends lead us once again to the question of whether intergroup attitudes and behavior have actually changed, or whether what we are witnessing is simply an increase in their variability. Studying the impact of such changes represents one fruitful avenue for current and future research efforts. There are three different interpretations of the effect of contemporary events upon race relations that can be discerned among present researchers.

1. *Things Are Now Better than Ever.* This is the message of some of the survey researchers. Campbell (1971), for example—in a comprehensive survey of 15 major cities in 1964, 1968, and 1970—concludes that "that on many questions of principle and policy, white and black attitudes moved closer together" (p. 6). He also reports increased contact between blacks and whites, which he predicts will lead to a gradual easing of tension.

Simpson and Yinger (1972) concur in this judgment when they state, "By most measures, prejudice in the United States has declined quite sharply in the last generation." In support of this, they cite responses such as: 60% of the population were in favor of integration in 1968, compared with 30% in 1942; 65% of whites surveyed in 1968 maintained that a black moving next door would not upset them, as opposed to 35% making such a response in 1942. Professor Rothbart examines survey research in depth in Chapter 10.

Another line of evidence in support of this position comes from studies of social stereotypes. Karlins, Coffman, and Walters (1969) found, for example, that white college students in 1967 were much less inclined to choose adjectives like "lazy" and "happy-go-lucky" to describe blacks; they attribute this to a generally positive shift in the content of stereotypes of minorities.

2. *Things May Look Better, But Under the Magnifying Glass* .... Clearly, the evidence cited as demonstrations of "improvement" in attitudes can be dismissed by some as extremely superficial. People (and especially college students) have learned that certain feelings are not to be expressed directly. Thus, it is argued by some, basic attitudes have not actually changed—only the verbalization has.

Support for this view derives from investigators such as Sigall and Page (1971), who (like Karlins *et al.*) also studied stereotypes. Sigall and Page, however, included an additional condition in their experiment that other investigators had not used before—a manipulation referred to as the "bogus pipeline." They wired students up to electronic equipment, which subjects believed elicited a direct physiological measure of their attitudes. Control subjects (i.e., those not hooked up to the "bogus pipeline") evaluated blacks more favorably than in past studies, thus replicating the previously cited Karlins *et al.* finding. The group that believed their physiological responses were monitored, however, gave considerably more negative evaluations. Thus, when there appeared to be an external "check" on the truthfulness of their attitudes, even liberal college students expressed negative attitudes. The attitudes of "liberals" are explored in more detail in Chapter 6 by Professor Gaertner.

Another instance of the "no basic change" belief can be found in a study by Williams, Tucker, and Dunham (1971), which attempted to assess whether connotations of color names had changed from an earlier investigation (Williams, 1963). In the earlier study, both blacks and whites, employing a semantic differential technique, rated "white" as good and active, whereas "black" was more frequently rated as bad and passive. The 1971 study found changes—but only in the scores of the black college students. The color connotations of the white students did not change.

A last example that all may not be as rosy as it appears can be found in a study by Rubovits and Maehr (1973). These investigators assessed differential teacher expectations for black and white students. In an attempted replication of the Rosenthal (1966) "Pygmalion" technique, student teachers interacted with groups of two black and two white children. One child of each race was labeled in advance as "gifted." In actuality, all children were matched for intellectual achievement. These investigators found that white student teachers responded quite differently to the white and black junior high school students who were labeled gifted. Blacks were ignored more, criticized more, and praised less. It might be argued that if white attitudes towards blacks had indeed become more positive, this should certainly have been evident with young college students who were interacting with intellectually gifted black children. If only a verbal measure were used in this study, the outcome might have appeared to be very different.

3. *Things May Be Better Now, But There's Still a Long Way to Go.* This is an intermediate viewpoint that holds that, although changes in verbal statements cited in the surveys may not be truly indicative of the magnitude of change, they still suggest that something significant is taking place. Thus, the fact that white people do indeed feel more guilt and ambivalence about directly expressing prejudice may in itself be taken as evidence of some progress. If such attitudes are no longer overtly reinforced, they ultimately may be extinguished.

If one examines the roles portrayed by blacks and whites in the media (reviewed in more detail in Chapter 9), one can find evidence for this belief. A study by Cox (1969-70), for example, surveyed changes in six general magazines in 1949 and 1968. In the earlier period, blacks were pictured in menial roles 93.9% of the time. In the later year, such pictures constituted 28.7% of the total. This would certainly seem to be "progress" viewed in and of itself. Nevertheless, the 28.7% figure is still considerably higher than the comparable one of 2.7% for whites depicted as menial laborers.

How one wishes to interpret these results may reflect a temperamental difference of whether one looks primarily at the doughnut or the hole. Moreover, if one is a minority group member, the hole may be much more salient.

## ORGANIZATION OF THIS VOLUME

The major purpose of the present volume is to present a picture of where current theory and research about racism are, and in what directions they are heading. The focus throughout will be upon attitude and behavior change. The authors have attempted to present the research issues without oversimplification, so that the information can be used by practitioners as well as non-researchers. We hope that the reader will be willing to share with us some of the intriguing complexities and differing interpretations involved.

This book is organized into three sections. The first summarizes the various theoretical viewpoints that have been offered to account for the acquistion and maintenance of negative racial attitudes and behavior. The second section reviews research relevant to the modification of racial attitudes and intergroup behavior on an individual level. Finally, the last section considers some research germane to the modification of institutional racism.

It is difficult to describe current status and extrapolate to the future without some knowledge of the past. Accordingly, the first section of this text examines the more salient theories of intergroup attitudes, behavior, and change. Professor Chesler, in Chapter 2, presents an overview of both past and present sociologically oriented approaches—specifically those that refer to institutional racism. The various theoretical viewpoints are discussed and ordered along a number of dimensions, including: (a) whether "blame" is placed predominantly on the victim or the system, and (b) how embedded in the culture racist practices are perceived as being. In addition, the role of the social scientist as a possible perpetuator of the status quo is discussed and elaborated. In the third chapter, Professors Ashmore and DelBoca provide an extensive review of both the older and more contemporary psychological approaches offered to elucidate the origins of intergroup conflict. The theoretical status of variables such as competition, conformity, defense mechanisms, and frustration are considered in detail. Several new theoretical concepts and their supporting evidence are discussed and evaluated. These include: (a) perceived racial threat, (b) symbolic racism, and (c) tokenism. They exemplify new directions being taken in current psychological research on racism. The fourth chapter, by the present author, examines the onto-genesis of racial attitudes in children. Theories delineating the various mechanisms assumed to underlie the development of racial attitude are reviewed, including instructional factors, personality variables, child-rearing practices,

and cognitive, perceptual and reinforcement components. The relevant supporting evidence is evaluated for each position, and a new theoretical synthesis
is offered to account for racial attitude development.

The second major section of the book, comprised of Chapters 5 through
8, concerns itself with contemporary research on individual attitude and
behavior change. These chapters represent updated reviews of the most significant research in this area by psychologists. Professor Weissbach, in Chapter 5,
reviews the status of laboratory studies aimed at change. He reviews the
various techniques employed, as well as some recent controversies such as the
issue of whether race or belief similarity are more salient. Studies stressing
cognitive structure changes and the inhibition of interracial aggression are also
discussed, and several particularly promising trends in new research are noted.
Chapter 6, written by Professor Samuel Gaertner, explores the research relevant to change in more naturalistic types of situations, with a particular focus
on individuals who are generally characterized as politically liberal. Psychologists have been concerned with the applicability of their findings beyond the
laboratory; one way to increase such generalizability is to utilize a more
natural environment to elicit change. This chapter discusses these efforts,
particularly as they apply to dominative, ambivalent, and aversive types of
racism. Chapter 7 investigates the various techniques that have been used in
attempting to modify negative racial attitudes in children. It reviews the many
indices that have been utilized to measure attitudes in children, and evaluates
the effectiveness of various intervention techniques. Both frequently employed
measures (e.g., education and desegregation) and relatively experimental
approaches involving perceptual and learning procedures are considered. The
last chapter in this section, written by Professor Yehuda Amir, examines the
attitudinal effects (in both children and adults) of intergroup contact. It
summarizes the very extensive literature in the area (over 250 references) and
evaluates it in terms of theory, scientific orientation, practical application, and
future directions.

The final portion of the book considers change as it is relevant to
institutional racism. In Chapter 9, Bradley Greenberg and Sherrie L. Mazingo
analyze the kind of role minorities have played in the growth and development of the major mass media (particularly television) and how they have
been portrayed. A number of basic issues are examined, including the quality
and quantity of minority employment patterns within the media, key regulatory efforts to aid minority representation, the nature of minority markets,
and the social effects of exposure. Professor Myron Rothbart, in Chapter 10,
discusses areas of resistance to social reform. Survey data assessing white
people's attitudes towards minorities over the past three decades are examined
and the implications of these studies for social reform are discussed. The
status of several contemporary hypotheses regarding white resistance (e.g.,
hostility, fear, economic and status threat) is explored, and ways of organizing
social reforms in a manner that maximizes white acceptance are presented.

Changes that have occurred in the legal status of minorities since the Civil War are considered in detail by attorney Eric Hirschhorn in the final chapter. In the first portion of this chapter, Mr. Hirschhorn traces the historical development of American law relating to slavery and racial discrimination, pointing up the parallels between law and social traditions. The latter portion of the chapter covers the federal civil rights laws as they exist today, together with the interpretations that have been given by the courts. The categories covered include general civil rights statutes, public accommodations, education, employment, voting, and housing. Included at the end of the chapter is a list of agencies that can provide assistance to individuals who believe themselves to be victims of institutional racism. This chapter may initially appear disparate from the others to the psychologically oriented reader. We believe, however, that its inclusion is important for several reasons. First, a study of change with regard to race relations could not possibly be comprehensive without an accompanying consideration of the legal matrix within which such change occurs. Second, as noted earlier, the legal and political spheres remain the most potent avenues of change for discriminated against minority groups. Finally, when this volume was originally conceived, we hoped that it might be instrumental to individuals who believed themselves to be victims of institutional racism. In this regard, the legal remedies outlined in Chapter 11 have more immediate implications than the scholarly contributions of researchers.

At the outset of this introductory chapter, an attempt was made to justify this text to those who believe that social scientists may better devote their energies to the political realm. In closing, however, it appears that an analogous justification may be required for readers at the other end of the scholarly continuum—i.e., those who believe that answers to our practical problems will necessarily come primarily from "basic" rather than "applied" research. An ideal embodied by this view suggests that research on social change be firmly tied to well-delineated etiological theories and relevant basic psychological and sociological research on the underlying processes of group interaction. Such an ideal is a laudable one, but it may not mirror reality. If, for example, treatment for cancer were withheld until the causes of the disease were fully understood, many more people would have died. The proper balance between basic and applied research may be a hard one to find, but the pressures of the real world upon discriminated against minority groups make it incumbent upon us to explore all possible routes to a solution. As Calvin Hernton* reminds us:

> A Genocide so blatant
> Every third child will do the
> junky-nod in the whore-scented

---

*"Jitterbugging in the Streets," by Calvin C. Hernton. In L. Jones and L. Neal (Eds.), *Black Fire*. New York: Morrow, 1968.

night before semen leaps from his loins—
And Fourth of July comes with the
    blasting bullet in the belly of a teenager
Against which no Holyman, no Christian
    housewife
In Edsel automobile
Will cry out this year.

It is time now to use our resources to help ameliorate racism. It is time for a new commitment.

## REFERÉNCES

Campbell, A. *White attitudes toward black people.* Ann Arbor: Institute for Social Research, 1971.

Comer, J.P. *Beyond black and white.* New York: Quadrangle, The New York Times Book Co., 1972.

Conger, D. S. Comment on: How scientific are the social sciences? *Journal of Social Issues,* 1973, **29**, 215-218.

Cox, K. Changes in stereotyping of Negroes and whites in magazine advertisements. *Public Opinion Quarterly,* Winter 1969-70, **33**, 603-606.

Goldschmid, M.L. *Black Americans and white racism.* New York: Holt, Rinehart and Winston, 1970.

Harding, J., Proshansky, H., Kutner, B., and Chein, I. Prejudice and ethnic relations. In G. Lindzey and E. Aronson (Eds.), *The handbook of social psychology.* Second edition, Volume 5. Reading, Mass.: Addison-Wesley, 1969.

Karlins, M., Coffman, T. L., and Walters, G. On the fading of social stereotypes: Studies in three generations of college students. *Journal of Personality and Social Psychology,* 1969, **13**, 1-16.

Katz, J., and Gurin, P. *Race relations and the social sciences.* New York: Basic Books, 1969.

King, M. L., Jr. The role of the behavioral scientist in the civil rights movement. Initial address, American Psychological Association, September 1967.

Knowles, L. L., and Prewitt, K. (Eds.). *Institutional racism in America.* Englewood Cliffs, N. J.: Prentice-Hall, 1969.

Kovel, J. *White racism: A psychohistory.* New York: Pantheon, 1970.

National Advisory Commission on Civil Disorders. *Report of the National Advisory Commission on Civil Disorders.* New York: Dutton, 1968.

Norton, E.H. New York at the watershed. Doctoral commencement address, Graduate School of the City University of New York, June 1973.

Pettigrew, T. F., and Riley, R. T. Contextual models of school desegregation. In *Attitudes, conflict, and social change.* New York: Academic Press, 1972.

Rosenthal, R. *Experimenter effects in behavioral research.* New York: Appleton-Century-Crofts, 1966.

Rubovits, P. C., and Maehr, M. L. Pygmalion black and white. *Journal of Personality and Social Psychology,* 1973, **25**, 210-218.

Scott, W. A. Attitude measurement. In G. Lindzey and E. Aronson (Eds.), *The handbook of social psychology.* Second edition, Volume 2. Reading, Mass.: Addison-Wesley, 1968.

Sigall, H., and Page, R. Current stereotypes: A little fading, a little faking. *Journal of Personality and Social Psychology,* 1971, **18**, 247-255.

Simpson, G.E., and Yinger, J.M. *Racial and cultural minorities: An analysis of prejudice and discrimination.* Fourth edition. New York: Harper & Row, 1972.

Triandis, H. C. The impact of social change on attitudes. In *Attitudes, conflict, and social change.* New York: Academic Press, 1972.

Wilcox, R.C. (Ed.). *The psychological consequences of being a black American.* New York: Wiley, 1971.

Williams, J. E. Connotations of color names among Negroes and Caucasians. *Journal of Perceptual and Motor Skills,* 1964, **18**, 721-731.

Williams, J. E., Tucker, R. D., and Dunham, F. Y. Changes in the connotations of color names among Negroes and Caucasians. *Journal of Personality and Social Psychology,* 1971, **19**, 222-228.

# Part II
# Theories of Prejudice Acquisition
# and Reduction

# 2

# Contemporary Sociological Theories of Racism *

## MARK A. CHESLER

## INTRODUCTION

My purpose in this chapter is to review some contemporary sociological explanations and theories of American racism. The current literature on race relations contains a spate of empirical descriptions of people's attitudes and opinions, and of economic and political patterns. Further, we have numerous case studies of community organization, neighborhood dynamics, and local change processes. But seldom are these data organized into coherent theoretical and broadly explanatory systems. Even more rarely have those systems been put to work describing the integration of prejudiced attitudes, discriminatory patterns, and inequitable outcomes that comprise American racism. Blalock (1967) noted this same state of affairs several years ago, reporting: "...it is a commonplace criticism of the field of minority groups, as an academic discipline, to note that there is relatively little knowledge of the subject that can properly be called theoretical" (p.1).

Part of the problem of theory generation in sociological studies of racism undoubtedly lies in the difficulty of agreeing on definitions of terms. Concepts such as prejudice and discrimination have been much easier to define, agree upon, and utilize over time. "Racism" was first given broad usage in the *Report of the National Advisory Commission on Civil Disorders* (1968). For some, it is a term with very little fruitfulness—a conceptual truism that appears to lead either everywhere or nowhere; for others, it leads to certain specifications and eventual use. In the recent literature, racism has been defined primarily in terms of three different forms of evidence: (a) effects or outcomes—as evidenced in racial group differentials in economic, political, and social rewards; (b) institutional procedures or personal acts—as evidenced in the identification of racially discriminatory mechanisms providing differential advantage and privileges; and (c) personal attitudes or cultural values—as evidenced in symbol systems and in reports of racial opinions and information held by the public. These are three quite different forms of

*In preparing this essay I have benefited enormously from the comments Dr. James Crowfoot. Dr. Burgan Bryant, Darnell Hawkins, and Diana Wright also have been very helpful.

evidence, varying in their levels of analysis, assumptions, and causal implications or concerns. In many cases, the complexities of our social institutions make it difficult to determine institutional procedures and personal values, and we must rely upon the inference of discriminatory behavior or prejudiced attitudes from obvious effects—inequalities in rewards, resource allocation, and life opportunities.

To further complicate the problems of agreement among scholars, some definitions of racism focus upon personal or institutional ideology and the attitudes, norms, and myths that support racist practices. Other definitions focus upon powerful institutional procedures that diminish the life chances of minority members. Tumin (1969) connects these two themes as, "an ideology of entitlement, that is, what members of one category are believed to be entitled to; [and] ... the capacity of a dominant group to enforce this ideology in concrete terms" (p. 15). This delineation seems to us a good combination of the power and ideology definitions, and is one that only now is being utilized broadly by scholars.

In our own use of the term racism, we mean whatever acts or institutional procedures help create or perpetuate sets of advantages or privileges for whites and exclusions or deprivations for minority groups. This usually requires an ideology of explicit or implicit superiority or advantage of one racial group over another, plus the institutional power to implement that ideology in social operations. Thus, it should be clear that in this chapter we are concerned primarily with what has been called by others "institutional white racism" (Carmichael and Hamilton, 1967; Knowles and Prewitt, 1969).

Sometimes it is hard to see the concrete meanings of such a definition. To speak of institutional white racism does not mean that everyone who is white consciously or unconsciously believes that all whites are innately superior and that all blacks or minority group members are innately inferior. Nor does it suggest that persons believing or acting in ways that maintain white privileges are operating on conscious and evil intentions. In some cases racist policies, acts, and attitudes are fairly actively and overtly pursued; in other cases they may be more passive responses awaiting articulation and mobilization. But in whatever way persons or institutions contribute to the social condition wherein minorities receive lesser social and economic rewards, they help maintain racial injustice and racism.

It is clear that the American society by and large does fit this definition; it does operate in racist ways, ensuring continuing unmerited distinction between majority whites and minorities of color.[1] Our question in this essay is: How does American sociology explain this state of affairs? The data we

---

[1] The assertion that we live in a racist society is the starting point for this essay, as indeed for the entire volume. Among the broadest documentations for this perspective are: *Report of the National Advisory Commission on Civil Disorders* (1968); Knowles and Prewitt (1969); and Schwartz and Disch (1970).

review to answer the question are basically the explanations offered by contemporary American sociologists and the theories they have generated to connect the evidence of logic and experience to broad interpretations of the workings of the American society. Literature reviewed here spans several decades, including ones in which the term "racism" was never in vogue, let alone clearly agreed to. So our preferred definition will not organize everything, and we will often work from other scholars' terms, including prejudice, discrimination, and the like.

The range of sociological theories explaining racism is quite broad, both in historical span and in terms of the variables usually covered. Our focus will be upon relatively contemporary theories; while we will try to cover a range of sociological thinking, time and space limitations require our review to be limited in depth and detail, and primarily focused upon blacks as the target of racism.[2]

## CATEGORIES OF THEORIES ABOUT RACISM

Theories of racism can be divided into several major categories. For purposes of simplicity, we have established a pair of dichotomies, although it should be clear that these really are continua along which scientific thought varies. We recognize that these two categories are not independent; they co-vary and reinforce each other in important ways.

The first category system we use to review theories of racism is their degree of "victim-system control." This category system describes the extent to which a theory locates the root or cause of racial injustice: as within the environmental control of its primary victims—the poor, black, brown, yellow, and red minorities—or within the larger social structure. The high end of the victim-system continuum stresses the minority's ability to control, order, or alter its own life chances—including personality, skills and attitudes, and family or community patterns and culture. The low end of the continuum stresses the controls exercised by the larger social system through authority relations, resource allocations, institutional structures and processes, and cultural norms and symbols. Myrdal (1962) provides a pithy statement of this difference in stating that the Negro problem is really "a white man's problem," and the major reason is because "practically all the economic, social and political power is held by whites" (p. lxxv). Thus, whites have the power to

---

[2] The struggle to be clear about racism is not just a scientific problem; it is a major part of our continuing human struggle to be clear about ourselves—who we are and what the nature of the society is in which we live. As a white, Jewish male operating from a middle-class base within an established university, my own reflections in this essay are of course suspect—from race, ethnic, class, and sex bases. My attempts to be clear, incomplete as they are, are part of the data for this essay, just as is the literature produced by others.

determine the shape, maintenance, and intensity of the "Negro problem."

The concept of "victim-system control" in social theory is developed in a particularly interesting way by Ryan (1971). In a cogent and often brilliant analysis, he documents a number of theories of social organization that seem to blame the relatively powerless victims of social injustice for creating their own problems. He notes:

> The new ideology attributes defect and inadequacy to the malignant nature of poverty, injustice, slum life and racial difficulties. The stigma that marks the victim ... is an acquired stigma, a stigma of social rather than genetic origin. But the stigma, the defect, the fatal difference—though derived in the past from environmental forces—is still located *within* the victim, inside his skin.... It is a brilliant ideology for justifying a perverse form of social action designed to change, not society, as one might expect, but rather society's victim. (p. 7)

For instance, Ryan argues that theories of cultural deprivation seem to locate the reasons for different or inadequate educational performance in the inferior early training provided to poor children. These theories do not thoroughly explore possible alternatives—for example, that the school and its staff ask for irrelevant or inappropriate performance, or are invested in maintaining educational failure, or are unprepared for cultural variation. Ryan finds another excellent example of what he calls "victim blaming" in the Moynihan report.[3]

Theories that explain differential allocation of economic rewards or life opportunities in terms of minority groups' family or cultural pathology clearly blame aspects of the victims' social system for the state of their injustice. One important result is that social treatment or change designs focus on altering the family or family members rather than mainstream institutions of the larger society. As Caplan and Nelson (1973) note,

> The way a social problem is defined determines the attempts at remediation. ... If matrifocal family structure is argued to be the basis for deviancy, non-achievement and high unemployment, then opportunity structure, discriminatory hiring practices, and other system defects would appear less blameworthy as the causes of poverty. (pp. 200-201)

Alternative social theories, of course, would seek not only to locate the societal sources of such presumed pathology (which the "Moynihan Report"

---

[3] That report, and portions of Ryan's critique, can be found in Rainwater and Yancey (1967).

does), but would place responsibility for the nature and change of this situation on those aspects of the social and economic order that create conditions of family pathology. Efforts at treatment or change, then, would focus on the larger system—the apparatus of economic and social discrimination—rather than the victims—the minority family and culture.

To the extent that whites are in obvious control of the larger American social system, it is they who administer, if not control, patterns of injustice and racist advantage and disadvantage. Theories of white prejudice and discrimination tend to stress the control and responsibility of members of the majority group. Thus, they, too, are steps in the direction of a focus on systemic controls of minorities' or victims' lives, and are examples of the lower end of the victim-system control continuum.

The second category we will use to review theories of racism is their "degree of embeddedness." This category system describes the extent to which a theory interprets racism as an isolated and peripheral element of the American social system or as a root characteristic involved in and perhaps defining much of our way of life. Myrdal (1962) again illustrates this issue and his own reading of it, as he states that "The Negro problem is an integral part of, or a special phase of, the whole complex of problems in the larger American civilization. It cannot be treated in isolation" (p. lxxvii). Social theories that reflect Myrdal's sense of high embeddedness represent the high end of this continuum; theories that treat racism as a minor or peripheral issue in American life represent the low end of the embeddedness continuum.

Studies of individual prejudice often have depicted prejudiced persons as deviants, or as having aberrations. Such individuals often are seen not as acting upon basic American principles, well embedded in and rewarded by the social structure for their views and actions, but as individuals running against the mainstream of American life. Similarly, studies focusing upon the racism of one or another social group often isolate these groups as the main purveyors of a sick or maladaptive social ideology and set of discriminatory practices. The focus upon a particular "out-group" suggests that racist values are not deeply embedded in our culture, and are held strongly only by certain groups—most particularly those least representative of our "liberal" tradition. For instance, the historic-scientific stress upon the white redneck Southerner often blinded us to the underlying attitudes and values of Northerners or Westerners; and the focus upon the racism of working-class whites has clouded our understanding of the conflicting racist ideologies of affluent and educated whites. Thus, these theories all tend toward low embeddedness.

The stress upon aspects of the dominant white culture and its embracing views of the inferiority of black people and people of other minority groups turns this focus around. Attitudinal studies of the prejudiced views held in some degree by all or most Americans (and the reflection of these views in the white dominated media and in cultural symbol systems such as art and the movies) awaken us to the overall attitude structure of our society, not merely to its expression or location in a few special groups of intolerant persons.

Another example of low embeddedness can be found in theories that see our society as divided primarily by social class and that seek to place racial injustice solely within that framework. An alternative of a highly embedded character would see racism and racial caste systems ordering class relations. To the extent that theories treat racism as stable and continuing parts of our usual institutional conduct, they are envisioning it as normal and central rather than as peripheral or ephemeral. Van den Berghe (1967) emphasizes the need for highly embedded theories of racism, stressing that "race relations must be placed within the total institutional and cultural context of the society"; he objects to the way the current theories have created a "high degree of analytical isolation of race from its general social context" (p. 6).

Are "victim-system control" and "degrees of embeddedness" differences that make a difference? To the extent that social science helps determine what is normative and what is deviant, surely they do. To the extent that sociological theory helps focus our treatment of change efforts on peripheral or malfunctioning persons or institutions, or on the basic character of our moral and social structure, it makes a great deal of difference. The difference theories make may not be with respect to truth and untruth, for truth about American racism may be multiple and undeterminate, resisting any single theory. But the differences in our theoretical preferences and priorities make a difference in our orientation to social policy or program—e.g., what we decide must be funded or what are social fringes. They make a difference in the way we interpret and support various change efforts. And they also make a difference in what social scientists see as important to study, in what we elect to report and not report, in how we relate to research content, in who we recruit and support into our ranks, and in what we implement as policies of our profession.

Thus, it is important to look at the range of theories sociologists have utilized to explain racism, and to examine the meanings of their differences. In the next section of this essay we group theories into relevant families or clusters, and examine them and their assumptions especially with regard to "victim-system control" and "embeddedness." In a concluding section we speculate further about some of the issues raised here, about the role of social theory in general, and about theories of racism in particular.


## THEORIES OF RACISM

With these definitions and categorizations in mind, we can proceed to a review of some theories and families of theories about American racism. Essentially, we are concerned about the ideas social scientists utilize to explain the evidence of continuing racism within the American society.

## Theories focusing on characteristics of minorities

Several theories and research traditions appear to explain American race relations in terms of various social characteristics of minority groups and their members. Some of these theories begin with the assumption that patterns of discrimination and injustice have created certain conditions, perhaps even intolerable ones, for minority groups. They then focus upon the adjustment patterns minority groups make to these conditions as causative agents in another round of injustice.

One general theory proceeding along these lines is that of cultural deprivation or cultural disadvantage, most commonly implemented by social workers and educators seeking to understand the differential institutional performance between black or brown people and whites, or between affluent and poor people. In the field of education, for instance, studies documenting differential school performance by white or black or brown students may be the starting point. Differential performance often is real; the questions are what to look at next and how to interpret the differences. One possibility would be to focus on intragroup differences or on the unique factors accounting for the performance of each group. But when the focus is on gross differences between groups, the differences often are translated into better and worse performance, utilizing some set of "commonly agreed upon" criteria. Terms such as "underachievement" and "learning difficulties" then begin to be used to characterize minorities' differential performance.

Once these research traditions identify differences as deficiencies, they attempt to explain the "inadequate" performance of the minority group vis-a-vis the majority. In the sociological and social-psychological literature this performance inadequacy is not typically interpreted as the result of genetic inferiority.[4] Rather, it is presented as the result of sociogenic factors, which disable black or brown students from performing up to the level of their white peers. Perhaps, it is argued, there is little uncrowded time and space in the home for the student to do homework and study; perhaps mother and father do not truly value an education and do not help motivate the young student or do not support his working on schoolwork; perhaps a lower-class anti-intellectualism in the family or peer group establishes anti-schoolwork norms; perhaps it is a result of a cultural unfamiliarity with reasoning in abstract terms, and a preference for concreteness in experience and symbol manipulation; perhaps it is due to an unwillingness to delay gratification—to think about, plan for, or learn for the future (Riessman, 1962; Passow, 1963; Bloom, Davis, and Hess, 1965; Heller, 1966; Carter, 1970). Some of these

---

[4] Social theorists generally are heated in response to colleagues who argue thusly; witness the controversies surrounding Jensenism. *(Harvard Educational Review,* 1969a; *Harvard Educational Review,* 1969b; Jensen, 1969).

hypotheses have not been well substantiated and their existence is the subject of continuing debate and controversy. However, they have been used as building blocks for those theorists who do believe in their presence.

Theories of cultural deprivation or disadvantage suggest that social and economic conditions in the minority (and often poor white) community and culture create these lifestyles and school orientations that make it difficult if not impossible for the student to develop and learn in a "normal" manner.

To be sure, the criteria for success are not necessarily "commonly agreed" to, and the criteria are seldom equally relevant or responsive to different cultural patterns and priorities in multiethnic or multiracial communities. The white majority historically has set and still agrees to certain universal standards of school performance, and these criteria are the basis for "commonly agreed upon" standards. Thus, theorists are making universal assumptions about performance, which are not tuned to cultural pluralism or conflict (Gordon, 1965; Baratz and Baratz, 1970; Vaca, 1971; Valentine, 1971).

Stein (1971) and Banks (1972) suggest that sociogenic theories contribute a great deal to the reinforcement of racial and social class stereotypes by preparing educators to expect and accept inadequacy from classes of students. Kenneth Clark (1965) puts the matter quite succinctly when he argues that "cultural and economic backgrounds of pupils do not constitute a barrier to the type of learning which can reasonably be expected of normal children in the elementary grades" (p. 139). Rather, he feels that schools' loss of faith in their students and in their own potency lets these background factors become a barrier. Other barriers that need to be explored include: low levels of curriculum diversity and quality, minimal options for bilingualism or biculturalism, teacher incompetence, the professional culture of educators, styles and values of whites running urban and largely black schools, educational leadership as political control, and the social function of black school failure for white advantage. In later sections of this essay we review a number of theories that do adopt some of these alternative foci and explanatory systems.

Another example of the victim-blame type of theory is found in a variety of reports on the status of the minority family. We may note in the Moynihan report, for instance, the same liberal theory that focuses on historic and sociogenic factors making it hard for people to behave in ways normal for middle-class white Americans. But then historic conditions fade into the background, and the black family and culture are portrayed as inadequate, failing its members, and ill preparing them for life in America.[5] The theoretical approach that proceeds from viewing the Negro family as a victim of social forces to victimizer of the Negro—from the low to the high end of the victim-system control continuum—is especially clear in a comment by Parsons (1965):

> Even as the *victim* of the most radical discrimination of any group, the Negro has not only been forced to be subservient, but has also *failed to develop*, or bring with him from his Southern rural past, sufficient ingredients for socially effective self-help—a question not merely of individual qualities and initiative but of collective solidarity and mutual support at many levels, particularly the family and the local community. (p. 1038) (Italics added.)

Thus, characteristics of victims (the minority family, community, or culture) are utilized to explain racial differences in economic and educational rewards, in health care patterns, etc.

Given these theorists' enumerations of racist social and economic conditions affecting the minority community, their focus of concern could have explored those societal conditions rather than the family's allegedly pathological adjustment to them. In fact, as Sizemore (1972) points out,

> Moynihan could have as well reported the facts in a more positive light to demonstrate that black families have maintained a remarkable measure of stability despite the discrimination against blacks and females. (p. 151)

Rainwater (1966), whose diagnosis is similar to Moynihan's, does discuss and appreciate this adaptive strength in "toughened" Negro families. He also argues clearly that the "responsibility for the disadvantages Negroes suffer lies squarely upon the white caste which derives economic, prestige and psychic benefits from the operation of the system" (p. 174).

The approaches taken by Rainwater (1966) and Valentine (1969) do not promote a doctrine of complete cultural relativity, nor do they espouse irresponsibility. Rather, they seek to fix attention on the environmental forces that surround and constrain the cultural and community situation of minorities. This kind of view reverses the focus of inquiry and posits the need to study and alter the majority community.

[5] The complexity of scientific issues and political controversies surrounding these theories are too extensive to explore in detail here; the specific case of the Moynihan report and this element of social theory are dealt with further in Rainwater and Yancey (1967) and Billingsley (1968), as well as elsewhere. A number of scholars have argued that these images of minority life are not accurate, and that, as Ten Houten (1970) puts it, "the stereotype of lower class black families as matriarchial, pathological and 'approaching a state of complete breakdown' may in reality constitute social mythology" (p. 171). And Monteil (1970) deplores the way a focus upon "inappropriate" cultural values and exaggerated "machismo" has distorted views of the reality of life in the Mexican-American family.

A third major example of explanations of racism that focus upon characteristics of minorities can be found in recent reports of the causes of urban riots. Some studies of urban violence have investigated "aggressive" black responses to injustice and have interpreted riots primarily in terms of "impulsive" expressions of black frustration and anger (Berkowitz, 1968; Gurr, 1968). Others, primarily not scientists, have developed a "riffraff" theory that posits the lawless, criminal, and most deviant portions of the urban minority community as responsible for outbursts. Both views deemphasize, while not necessarily ignoring, the nature of the social order that establishes or maintains patterns of inequitable resource allocation and social reward. Both Berkowitz (especially, 1972) and Gurr indicate the potential roles of economic and political exclusion in creating deprivation and frustration, but their concentration on personal characteristics of rioters does stress the minority's lack of adjustment to those conditions. While not discounting the importance of personality characteristics of rioters, some other critics of the above-cited approaches have explicitly connected their analyses of riots and riot participants to the institutional dynamics of the larger, white-controlled social order (Caplan and Paige, 1968; Fogelson and Hill, 1968; Tomlinson, 1968; Blauner, 1969).

Most of the theories reviewed in this section include substantial descriptive material on minority life. Part of their concern appears to be to create understanding of minority peoples and especially of their problems. The apparent assumption seems to be that if the liberal white majority understood better the reasons for the "unfortunate" or "unavoidable" behavior of minority group members, they might be more tolerant of it and less likely to engage in and support further injustice and degradation. Another concern appears to be to identify minorities' dysfunctional behaviors—i.e., the way in which they fail to adapt "successfully" to mainstream middle-class institutions and standards. From this analytic base, social policy formers could consider ways of changing minorities' behavior so that they may be more successful. The assumption appears to be that if blacks (and members of other minorities) could alter these behaviors or cultural patterns, racism would be substantially reduced. Whites would be more tolerant of their behavior, minorities would be more successful, and economic and social justice might prevail.

Thus, it should be clear, and appreciated as such, that these theories have roots in some of the best liberal traditions of American social thought. But, as in other theories of assimilation and adaption, these are distinguished by their relative emphasis on the minority rather than the majority group. Rather than focusing upon majority criteria for success, and majority control of the environment within which the minority acts and adapts, these theories focus upon the behavior of minority groups and individuals. Racist outcomes are explained as largely a function of inappropriate minority adaptations. Thus, these theories are on the high end of the victim-system control continuum; they concentrate on the minority group's ability to control the environment.

With regard to the category of degree of embeddedness, the situation of these theories is not clear. On the one hand, patterns of racism are seen as deeply embedded for long periods of time. On the other hand, these patterns are seen as embedded primarily within the minority community (although the majority is often noted as the original or primary genesis), and not within the broader American society. Thus, while these theories see racism as sustaining and real, they may not interpret it as a necessary or structural feature of the larger American society and culture.

## Theories focusing on personal and/or social characteristics of prejudiced persons

A number of social theories explain racism as a product of the attitudes and personality characteristics of certain white Americans. One central tendency in this family of theories is to interpret racial prejudice as part of a personality syndrome involving rejection of a variety of ethnic groupings. Allport and Kramer (1946), for instance, suggested that a person's prejudices were deeply ingrained in his personal philosophy and were reflections of a broader belief system and personality system. Adorno *et al.* (1950) went even further to propose the concept of an authoritarian and ethnocentric personality, replete with a variety of neurotic or potentially neurotic tendencies and personality disorders.[6] Most of the more recent literature on personality and ethnocentrism (some reviewed in this volume) supports these central conclusions:

1. Prejudice is often the result of early socialization practices that scar the development of a healthy personality—especially authoritarian, inconsistent, neglectful, or rejecting child-rearing practices.

2. Prejudice can be related to a variety of forms of mental illness or poor adjustment patterns.[7]

3. Prejudice is often held toward not just one group but a variety of out-groups or minority groups, thus legitimizing the ethnocentrism label. economic & status self interest.

4. Prejudice or ethnocentrism is integrated into the personality and

---

[6] Christie and Jahoda (1954) provide excellent guidelines for reviewing this work and the large amount of follow-up and extended research related to it.

[7] At one point, in fact, Allport (1958) suggests that prejudice *is* a mental illness.

affects a variety of cognitive understandings about the world, a variety of affective orientations and consequent value judgments.

Various theories of attitude structure are utilized to explain the connections made in points 3 and 4 between racial views and other aspects of one's cognitive, perceptive, or emotional orientations. Consistency and balance theories are among the most widely used paradigms for integration; concepts such as compartmentalization and short-term inconsistency or imbalance often are used to explain conditions whereby individuals do not have well-integrated attitudinal systems.

A somewhat different theoretical orientation to personality factors and racial prejudice is presented by Doob and Sears (1939) and Berkowitz (1962). These and other scholars link prejudice to a generally low tolerance for frustration and a tendency to focus aggressive reactions onto outsiders. If aggression cannot safely be targeted on the real sources of frustration, the individual will seek release or displacement onto others—scapegoats. In order for outsiders to be scapegoated as the target of aggression, they must be easily identified and weak, or visible and vulnerable (Williams, 1964). Of course, if societal norms have already identified particular minority groups as deviant and objectionable, they are especially good bets as scapegoats. The role of aggression is used here to explain whites' prejudice in ways similar to its use to explain blacks' reactions to racism, particularly in psychopathology or "rioting" behavior. In both cases the assumptions of deviance, anger, and inappropriate targeting are critical.

Welsing (1970) has developed a personality theory of prejudice that explains whites' behaviors in terms of their fears and deep-seated inadequacies and inferiorities regarding people of color. Although there are several psycho-analytically oriented theories of this sort, Welsing's explanation is unique in that it roots the sense of inferiority in whites' genetic inability to produce sufficient melanin for adequate skin coloration. This abnormality (relative to the more normal states of color that predominate among the world's peoples) is made more frightening by whites' existence as a small numerical minority. According to Welsing, various psychological defenses, especially ones focused upon sexual issues (the arena within which one's melanin capacity is transmitted), are used by whites to compensate for or rationalize their situation. In addition, whites utilize economic and political forms of oppression to dominate and "inferiorize" people of color who can produce significant skin pigment.

The characterization of prejudice as integrated into an often disordered or frustrated personality, and the generalization of the prejudiced attitude toward a variety of sometimes arbitrary groups clearly suggests that the root of racism lies within the prejudiced individual and not in characteristics of the minority group member or members. This is a clear distinction from the class of theories noted earlier and locates them somewhat lower on the victim-system control continuum.

The location of racism in aspects of individuals—as opposed, perhaps, to cultures or social structures—stresses individual white responsibility rather than that of institutional or societal systems. Moreover, the emphasis upon prejudiced persons' instability or mental illness implies that they are aberrant or abnormal. Thus, these theories generally do not see racism as deeply embedded in American society and culture (although it is as widespread and dangerous). On occasion, these theorists do examine the sources of individual racism in the context of family or community life. For instance, Adorno *et al.* (1950) discuss the especially important role of harsh, discipline-centered child rearing as a condition for the maximum expression of aggressive and prejudiced feelings. Parsons (1965) notes even more broadly that family socialization must be full of imperfection and tension in a society itself filled with hostilities, conflicts, potential destruction, and the like. Of course, Welsing's theory is even more fully embedded in the total genetic pool of whites and of white's institutional reactions. However, to the extent that these linkages are noted rather than fully explored, and to the extent that the major theoretical focus is on the white individual rather than on the culture, we have grouped them here on the rather low-embedded end. Later sections of this essay treat other theoretical efforts that more explicitly stress the role of the larger American culture in family socialization and individual attitude formations.

Another tradition within this general theoretical family focuses upon the social roles and statuses of individuals rather than upon their intrapersonal characteristics. This research has led to a theoretical stress on the relationship between prejudiced belief systems and social or occupational roles and statuses. Bettelheim and Janowitz (1964) summarize much of this research; in this and later sources it has been reported that more prejudiced persons are:

likely to be less educated and/or to have lower status occupations,

likely to experience inconsistency between level of income and level of education (status inconsistency),

likely to be downwardly mobile in a time of social change (sometimes reported for upwardly mobile as well),

likely to be somewhat isolated and alienated from peers,

likely to be members of more fundamentalist religious sects, and

likely to engage in more extreme political associations and activities.

Obviously, these studies have much in common with the foregoing material, although they start from a different place. Some of the studies reviewed here and elsewhere (cf. Westie, 1964; Hyman, 1969) stress the psychological problems of adjustment to downward mobility or to status inconsistency and then reconnect these issues to personality factors. Others stress the ideological justifications and rationalizations involved in religious and political extremism and connect to the ideologies of prejudice in that fashion. Still others focus on the personal and social coping mechanisms involved in living with alienation and with its probable (although not necessary) correlates in low status.

These theories relate individual attitudes to parts of the social structure via concepts of status and role. The central explanatory themes appear to be threefold. The first is that persons in these lower social roles and statuses are more likely to be deviant from the mainstream of American life and more likely to be alienated and/or mentally unhealthy. Thus, generally speaking, the less educated, more fundamentalist church-going, lower status people may be seen as ignorant, confused, and disordered. Second, location in these political and socioeconomic roles may be primarily a function of education. If low education is seen as low exposure and commitment to professed American norms of equality and justice, it is easy to see how this would fit. Third, persons of whatever status may be protecting themselves from the threat of association or competition with lower status people—minorities. Persons of lower status have the least distance from this threat and are most likely to come into contact with low-status Negroes; thus, they have the greatest need for mechanisms of status protection—discrimination and prejudice. Whether and how all these positional elements are tied together and ordered is not undertaken very systematically by these theories.

The theories dealing with persons' social characteristics clearly suggest that racism is a function of the white individual's response to his or her social role and status rather than a function of minority group members. Like the personality theories, they are lower on the victim-system control continuum than those theories focusing upon characteristics of the minority.[8]

The degree of embeddedness of these theories is uneven. To the extent that racism is seen as embedded in responses to social role and status, rather than in individual's personalities, the level of embeddedness is increased. However, according to these theories, racism often remains a characteristic of individuals. Thus, racism may not be embedded in the total society, but only in that portion of the white population that is more or less peripheral to the

---

[8] But since the control of racist conditions and practices may not be in the hands of lower status or deviant whites, the personality and social characteristics theories may require consideration of another element in the victim-system control category. Since these whites also may be victims of an environment controlled by white elites not included in the research, the theories that focus on them may be rather high on a displaced form of victim-system control. These dilemmas in theorizing about the white population are analyzed further in the section dealing with economic and status self-interest theories.

well-educated and successful mainstream. On these terms the degree of embeddedness would be fairly moderate.

Prothro (1952) and Pettigrew (1959) have taken the lead in extending these orientations toward white attitudes and roles and in creating several potentials for alternative theorizing. Their research failed to confirm that low status is positively related to prejudice across the board. They suggested that more prejudiced Southern whites are more likely to be in positions of high social status and leadership in local communities; the overt expression of prejudice is more likely to be associated with higher status and social partici-pation in the South than in the North. Just as Allport made some room for the white conformist who feels no overt antipathy to blacks but only loyalty to whites and white traditions, Pettigrew argues that strong social norms at work in the South seem to reinforce prejudice or racism and support and advance those persons who subscribe to such attitudes. Norms against preju-dice, or at least against its overt expression, may be more potent in the North. Several other theorists have utilized the reference group concept to explain the sources of white attitudes on racial matters (Sherif and Sherif, 1953). Others have attempted to specify the ways in which referent groups and social constraint systems operate in racism (Ewens and Erlich, 1972), the role of ideology and perceived social distance of situational characteristics (Raab and Lipset, 1962) and reference groups (Sherif and Sherif, 1953) in the expression of prejudice (Pettigrew, 1964, 1965).

These last theories of referent systems in white attitudes continue to maintain the focus on whites rather than on characteristics of minority members. Further, they suggest that individual whites, too, may not be able to fully control their racism; control may lie in the situations of norms and rules of the game embodied in referent group dynamics. Although the focus here is still on the individual, the full implications of these theories suggest a greater embeddedness of racist norms and values in the dominant culture. In the next two sections of this essay, we review theories that do focus more explicitly on the social and cultural framework of American racism.

## Theories focusing on networks of social relations

Several sociological theories attempt to explain the character of American racism in terms of the network of social relations that define, constrain, and/or support the behaviors of white Americans, and that regulate the interaction patterns between whites and members of minority groups. Some of the more familiar theories within this tradition include those that examine the naturalness of distinctive groups, "contacts" between racial groupings, and demographic or institutional isolation and segregation.

One example of this sort of theory appears as an extension of reference group theory examined previously. The starting point is evidence and theory about separateness between referent groups of whites and minorities. In this theorectical context it is seen as a mark of one's membership in a social group of whites to believe certain things about minority members and to act in certain ways toward them (and, presumably, to act in certain standardized and approved, although different, ways toward whites). Rokeach and Mezei (1966) suggest that whites' separateness leads them to assume that blacks have different values, and that this phenomenon helps explain prejudicial attitudes. Unless confounded by obvious class or sex differences, the corollary assumption is one of shared values—especially about race—within the white population. Based on patterns of group identification and assumed normative consensus, Daniels and Kitano (1970) cite evidence for the theoretical view that "the normal person, strongly identified with his own group, will tend to limit social interaction with other groups" (p. 7). Accordingly, only the poorly adjusted or marginal group members would cross group boundaries and engage in social interaction with others—in this case with minority group members. Clearly, this is a different perspective on normality and deviance with regard to discriminatory behavior than that expressed in earlier sections focusing on personality disturbance.

Patterns of group identification and differentiation are not accidental; they are created and sustained by societal systems of social segregation and stratification. Several theorists suggest that the roots of racism may lie in the network of segregated social relations that keeps equal status contacts between members of different racial groups to a minimum.[9]

For instance, contact theories of racism popularized by Deutsch and Collins (1951) and Williams (1964) propose that white Americans tend to become less prejudiced when they have an experience of equal status inter-racial contact, and that this is especially true when the contact is positive or when it occurs in an organizational environment low in tension and relatively high in morale. Ford (1974) reaffirms this line of theoretical development, stating that "the greater the amount of previous equal-status contact, the less racial prejudice is manifested" (p. 1436). We would expect then, that the reverse is true as well, and that a lack of equal status contacts is a source factor in racism.

Research in this general tradition is reviewed in detail in Chapter 8. Trends indicate that our social relations are structured so that it is atypical for whites to have sustained equal status contacts with members of minority groups. In residential organization, for example, there is documentation for several communities (e.g., Duncan and Duncan, 1957; Tauber and Tauber, (1965) of a high degree of racial segregation in urban and suburban residential

---

[9] Cross group contacts of an unequal character are common in a stratified but not completely segregated society—e.g., housewives and maids, foremen and line workers, office managers and secretaries, farmers and farm laborers or migrant workers, diners and waiters or busboys, etc.

patterns (as well as in patterns of residential transition). The picture is one of largely separated racial areas, usually further complicated by the location of more Negroes and poorer people in high density sections nearer the central city. Negroes are well removed from the suburban areas, which are populated in general by whites and more affluent peoples.

Most authors in this tradition underscore the conclusion that differential economic resources is not a sufficient explanation for such urban segregation (Molotch, 1972; Hermalin and Farley, 1973). Some of the other factors beyond financial status are apparent in urban and suburban whites' behavioral commitments to maintain segregated living conditions. As the Taubers (1965) argue, any individual's behavior in the housing market is a complex outcome of his "position in the social structure and the groups to which he belongs" (p. 19). Once again, the concept of group membership, with its psychoreferent group, social structural, and now even demographic components, is seen as crucial.

Theories about the workings of the housing market are also utilized in explaining these residential features and the institutionalization of discriminatory group behaviors. Tauber (1969) indicates that the dual market system works to restrict available housing supply for blacks, resulting in higher prices charged for scarce minority housing; this pricing mechanism further restricts the effective supply. Molotch (1969) extends the characterization of this system, and see the problems of differential housing supply, as well as whites' maintenance of favorable spatial locations vis-a-vis employment opportunities, as more important than individual attitudes about racial matters. These authors' theories are good examples of the way social group networks and impersonal market systems based on them can be seen as more relevant than individual attitudes in determining racist outcomes.

As we have indicated, a community is not merely a geographic entity; it is a social entity constructed out of its members' images of social reality. In this view, physical separation and distance leads to psychological isolation and the invisibility of others in different communities (Jeffries and Ransford, 1969; Warren, 1970; Johnson, Sears, and McConahay, 1971). As Warren indicates, "Not only do these communities (white suburbs) reflect racial segregation, but the existence of perceptual distance that is super-imposed on the lack of face to face interracial contact" (1970, p. 325). Although all three of these studies were conducted in connection with urban insurrections of the late 1960s, their theoretical approach is broader and connects to the other issues we have been exploring in this section. Racism is explained in terms of groups' isolation from each other—physical and psychological—and in how that isolation prevents contacts, supports ignorance and misconception, and erodes the possibilities for collaboration.[10] Johnson *et al.* and Warren stress the role

---

[10] Clark (1965) has suggested that there is an element of conscious or unconscious self-interest here, and that the privileged white community endeavors to blind itself to get to realities in order to escape guilt and responsibility.

of the press or the mass media in failing to aid accurate communication between white and black communities and in reflecting only the social reality of dominant economic and political powers. For Johnson *et al.*, biased news coverage of insurrections and other racial events not only fails to combat white ignorance in itself, but it embodies racism.

There are numerous by-products of residential segregation. One of the outcomes of community racial demography that has been well documented and studied is school segregation. Moreover, numerous studies of school segregation and desegregation indicate the role that schools may play in furthering racial isolation and racism (*Racial Isolation in the Public Schools*, 1967). The report indicates—as did Ford (1974) in another context—that persons with interracial schooling experience themselves were more likely to be positive toward such future experiences, both for themselves in other settings and for their children in school. Pettigrew (1969) indicates that one of the reasons desegregated schooling experiences are vital is that they provide an opportunity to erode cultural mythology through processes of cross-racial self-evaluation. Crain (1969) suggests that, through interracial school contacts, a form of trust is built that translates into shared information about employment and career opportunities.[11] These processes of positive evaluation and sharing are seen to occur within a situation of equal status contact between white students and members of minority groups; the *quality* of interracial interaction is what matters.

Although there continues to be some uncritical support for school desegregation, several scholars have taken pains to point out that positive outcomes are not guaranteed (Katz, 1964; Chesler and Segal, 1968; Pettigrew, 1969). In desegregated schools where students are retracked on racial lines, or where white staff members constantly deride or create anxiety for minority members, or where curriculum and administration do not reflect pluralistic concern, the context of student contact is not equal, and one can expect racist outcomes comparable to those of segregated schooling or perhaps even exacerbated conflict (Chesler, 1972).

The theories in this section appear to be relatively low on the victim-system control continuum in that minorities are not perceived as being in control of the social network and the racist conditions that flow from these networks. Although there have been suggestions that some minority group members may have a vested interest in segregation, the factors that maintain separated patterns of group location and interaction clearly are controlled by community powers, members of the majority and the majority-run institutions, and impersonal system dynamics.

---

[11] In this way Crain connects school integration processes to a potential rise in the occupational achievement of minority members. This may occur, of course, without a rise in academic achievement.

These theories also appear to assume a fairly high degree of embeddedness of racism in the fabric of American communities. Theories discussed above that focus on individual attitudes note that more prejudiced individuals are likely to be well identified with and integrated into the majority group—not deviants from it. The contact theories indicate that equal status interactions are not common, primarily because of other factors in the organization of the society—its productive sectors and service systems as well as its residential patterns. And if equal status contacts are rare, those unequal contacts most likely to maintain and advance racism are common. The theories of residential location and interaction clearly assume that these patterns are rooted deeply in the bases of social structural organization as part of the ecology of the human community.

## Theories focusing on cultural values or ideologies

Several theories of American racism primarily contend that a cultural and ideological commitment to racism underlies the basic value structures of our social system. The focus upon systemic values and ideologies can be seen as an attempt to understand and explain the nature of attitudes and beliefs as well as norms and symbol systems from a macrocultural viewpoint. Values individuals hold are seen as more than aspects of individuals; they are basic properties of social systems, and individuals derive their personal values from these ruling ideologies. Institutional goals and norms also are generated and maintained within the context of societal goals and ideologies. Weber made this point with regard to Protestant ideologies of achievement and rationality in the development of Western capitalism; others have used the same theoretical approach in investigating racism as a key element in the American value system. Many authors who vary considerably in the concrete phenomena they investigate and in the general theories they use to explain racism do point to or note the operation of a broad and culturally based ideology of white supremacy and superiority.

The central theme of *An American Dilemma* (1962) focuses precisely at this level of analysis of social ideology or cultural value systems. Myrdal emphasizes the role of the American Creed, and the gap between the Creed and other belief systems and priorities in the American society. As he sees it, the "dilemma"

> is the ever-raging conflict between, on the one hand, ... the American Creed, where the American thinks, talks and acts under the influence of high national and Christian precepts, and, on the other hand, the valuations on specific planes of individual and group living where personal and local interests; economic, social and sexual jealousies; considerations of community prestige and conformity; ... dominate his outlook. (p.lxxi)

Myrdal feels that Americans are committed deeply to the basic principles expressed in the Creed; but in much of our national practice he sees the expression of racism. He interprets this as an inability to live up to and implement the Creed in practice. Whatever the explanatory value of the "American Creed," it is clear that its meaning certainly is not fixed—not in time, place, or subcultural commitment. Alternative interpretations and competing creeds—for instance, ones of innate white superiority—have operated and still do so.

Schuman (1969) reports a steady decrease in white Americans' belief in the doctrine of innate racial superiority. However, he also indicates the potency for racial matters of an alternative American creed—the doctrine of individual free will and choice. According to this ideological principle, every person should be held responsible for his own fate; it is assumed that people could "make it" on their own if they really tried and worked hard. Schuman's research shows that this strongly held view interacts with whites' growing understandings of the reality of racial injustice to create confused and ambivalent value stances. Perhaps this theory helps to explain other empirical findings that report that many white Americans appear to be pro-black but continue to advocate social actions and policies that foster racism.

Myrdal and others who agree with him have been convinced that we will catch up to our Creed; it is so powerful, it must prevail, partly because men are rational and want to do what they feel is right and good. However, other scholars within this family of theories contend that racism is not necessarily ideological and institutional deviance or slippage from the American Creed, but that it is an ideology that competes with the Creed and may even predate it. Lyman (1972) argues this position forcefully in his summary of early research on slavery and antebellum society:

> both prejudice and the caste system are features of a large and prior phenomenon—racism, a value that arose at a particular time and became embedded in complex ways in the fabric of Western social organization. (p. 95)

Similar conclusions have been drawn by historians working with diverse sociological perspectives (Handlin, 1951; Genovese, 1956; Jordan, 1968).

Kovel's (1970) theory of racism also treats our cultural values—our system of shared meanings and visions—as the source of much societal practice. He feels that the cultural system reflects our view of nature and the social order, and takes form in language, literature, art, and other symbol systems. The specific concept of racism changed over time, as has our society, but generally, "racism served a stabilizing function in American culture," especially in our conceptions of property, humanity, order, and national unity (Kovel, 1970, p. 4). Jordan (1968) illustrates the operation of the national unity principle in noting that early American whites tied themselves together despite their diversity by contrasting or distinguishing themselves from blacks (and from native-Americans as well).[12] Conceptions of private property that included slaves as elements of that property also helped distinguish humans from nonhumans, the civilized with rights from the savages without rights, or the heathen from the God-fearing.

Whereas orthodox Marxists contend that values flow from economic and productive arrangements, the cultural theorists generally reject that material determinism. Myrdal (1962) argues that ideological forces operate independently to influence behavior and cannot be reduced "solely to secondary expressions of economic interests" (p. 72). Genovese (1972), primarily a materialist-oriented historian, suggests an integration of the roles of value systems and material forces as follows: " ... once an ideology arises it alters profoundly the material reality and in fact becomes a partially autonomous feature of that reality" (p. 32). According to this view, debates about whether productive forces or moral ideologies are primary may continue endlessly; however, we might all agree that established ideologies do profoundly affect consequent moral and material forces.

Patterns of cultural belief thus affect social practice in various ways: they filter throughout the society, finding implementation in governmental policy and economic hiring patterns and in the programs of secondary institutions such as schools, welfare agencies, service organizations, and the like. Westie (1964) indicates that, "Prejudice is part of the normative order of the society in which it occurs ... The normative order is, of course, part of the culture" (p. 582). From norms, people learn current expectations about "oughts"—about what ought to be and how they ought to feel and act. Learning these orientations occurs throughout life, but in many scholars' views it is centered in childhood socialization. A wide variety of theories about the socialization of children's racial attitudes take off from this sort of view of the genesis of racism.[13] Studies of school systems that document and explicate the preeminence of white cultural standards in the education of an interracial populace are other examples of this general theory (Green, 1969; Ortega, 1970; Wilson, 1970; Cuban, 1972).

Theories of cultural racism in communities and schools cluster at the other end of the victim-system control continuum than theories discussed in the section on minority group characteristics. Theories in that section explain school "failure" in terms of minority group characteristics and patterns; here those same differences or "failures" would be explained in terms of majority control of the culture and the programs, standards, and operating procedures

---

[12] Of course, many black writers have made the same point in works of fiction. And this is not merely an historic issue; to this day, inquiries to whites as to the meaning of their whiteness continue to call forth the response of "nonblackness."

[13] Westie (1964) provides an excellent summary of some of these theories.

of its major institutions. Theories that stress culture and ideology explain racism in ways that are representative of the low end of the victim-system control continuum. They all stress racism's roots within the total community or the community as controlled by the white majority.

The several theories reviewed here vary somewhat with respect to their view of the embeddedness of racism in the American culture. Myrdal implies only moderate embeddedness—largely reflected in his optimism regarding the power and ultimate prevalence of the Creed. Other theorists, such as Kovel, (1970), indicate that white racism in America is no aberration but an ingredient of our culture which cannot be understood apart from the rest of our total culture" (p. 3).

Scholars who have connected racism to other treasured American ideologies that support and advance stratification, segregation, and injustice would seem to agree with this statement of deep embeddedness.

### Theories focusing on normal institutional practice, "business as usual," or vicious cycles

A significant and growing tradition of theory suggests that the American society now operates in ways that feed upon the historic injustice done to minority groups so as to reinforce and maintain their lower status and lesser rewards. It is argued that this is so embracing an operating principle that it no longer requires conscious or even overtly racist acts to sustain it. Thus, racism is explained in terms of the normal operations of our institutions that are laid on top of patterns of historic injustice/racism. As Tumin (1969) suggests, " . . . starting with differential power and privilege, the advantaged group creates effective discrimination that . . . once put into motion . . . endures often without much formal enforcement" (p. 16).

One example of this theory can be found in Myrdal's (1962) discussion of the vicious cycle of discrimination and injustice. If education prepares people for jobs, and if good jobs lead to successful economic rewards, and if these rewards lead to other opportunities for enhancement and success, and if these opportunities lead to a supportive and healthy sense of self, and if fulfilled selves lead to healthy families and community members, and if positive community membership leads to youngsters' success in schools, we have a cycle of positive effects. The cycle can be made negative by breaking it anywhere; segregated and unequal schooling may lead to poor job preparation, thus poor jobs, and on goes the cycle. Once the negative cycle is established, social policies of apparently equal treatment or meritorious reward will keep it going.

Arguing that apparent equal treatment is in fact discriminatory or racist may sound absurd and offensive at first; it clearly challenges contemporary white efforts to have the best of both worlds—a superior position and the feeling that it has been meritoriously earned. However, the anti-universalism position is put quite reasonably by Willhelm (1971),:

> By enforcing uniform standards regardless of race, "no" discrimination against a person's race is involved. But the impression of fairness is achieved only by overlooking the fact that Negroes are not just like whites at the time of promotion. To be judged by criteria applicable to all persons irrespective of color when the Negro is extremely different can only mean the Negro will receive unequal treatment. To enforce equal standards to unequal individuals is to perpetuate inequality in the name of equality. (p. 91)

The alternative would be to adopt particularistic criteria and advance minority members especially fast in ways that combine individual merit with collective or societal need—sometimes called compensatory action or quota implementation.[14] Gilbert and Eaton (1970) elaborate on this possibility, suggesting that favoritism in the form of preferential treatment or discrimination may be an appropriate response to racism. Coleman (1968) has raised the question of equal opportunity even more provocatively, suggesting that at least one definition of the term is "equality of results given different individual inputs" (p. 17). Since we are predisposed to see evidence of racism in outcomes as well as in processes or mechanisms, the direct commitment to altering outcomes seems to us more important than insuring nondiscriminatory mechanisms, that may not alter patterns set by historic injustice.

Some scholars find the root of normal institutional practice in our cultural values as well as in economic stratification systems. Mercer (1971), for example, provides documentation of the flow of unjust institutional practices based on culturally biased standards of behavior and educational performance. Once "ethnocentric definitions of 'normal' behavior" (p. 317) are made, these definitions are implemented in ways that impersonally and universally promulgate racism in the education of black and Chicano students. She finds that clinical psychological testing procedures, and subsequent interpretations of student pathology, constitute the "primary factor in the disproportionate placement of Mexican-American and Negro children in classes for the mentally retarded" (1971, p. 321). This example undoubtedly can be repeated for a variety of institutional sectors; it is illustrative of a cycle of unjust or racist institutional practices that flow from a partisan or particular cultural standard that has been accepted as universal or "commonly agreed" to.

---

[14] We cannot even begin here to summarize the arguments for and against quota systems, etc., but it does appear that they stem largely from this theoretical approach to racism.

A further development of this theoretical approach suggests that public knowledge and acceptance of images and reports of minority inferiority may set into place new institutional cycles. For instance, such "validation" of inadequacy or pathology as Mercer found in schools may justify prejudiced persons' expressions of their views, and even others "without initial racial prejudice may essentially adhere to what has been known in the past as the 'earned reputation theory'" (Daniels and Kitano, 1970, p.23). The earned reputation theory operates a bit like the notion that "where there's smoke there's fire!"

Another way these mechanisms of institutional practice can be established, and earned reputations created, is through the paradigm of the self-fulfilling prophecy. Dramatized and popularized for the field of education by Rosenthal and Jacobsen (1968), these theories suggest that when powerful people behave in certain ways towards others, they tend to reinforce certain types of behavior. For example, when teachers behave toward their students as if these students were inadequate, students begin to adopt this definition of themselves and they perform in inadequate ways. A good deal of research on the self-fulfilling prophecy in schools has been conducted in recent years, and some of its specific methods and findings are suspect. But the general theory is alive and well; it stands as one more useful explanation for the maintenance of racist patterns.

In industrial systems, Whitehead and King (1973) comment on the workings of this social phenomenon with regard to interactions between white managers and Mexican-American workers:

> When managerial attitudes are translated into behavior relative to Mexican-American employees, their work environment can tend to evoke the set of behaviors which confirm managers' initial expectations and perceptions. (p. 769)

These examples of self-fulfilling prophecy theories locate the primary maintenance of racist practices in three places; first, in the white manager's or teacher's or other's attitudes and expectations; second, in the interactional or cultural or economic setting that permits transmission and legitimation of these expectations in an authority relationship; and third, in the minority group's adoption of those expectations as conditioners or generators of their own performance.

The theoretical emphasis upon explaining racism through the normal workings of major institutions also has important implications for our earlier discussions of prejudice and discrimination. Merton (1949) pointed out that prejudice (as a state of mind) and discrimination (as an act or behavior) are not coterminous and do not always operate together. At the individual level, a person may be both prejudiced in attitude and practice discrimination in his/her behavior. But a person also can be prejudiced and not have an opportunity to discriminate. Of importance for this discussion, Merton argued that a person may behave in ways that are discriminatory without harboring prejudiced attitudes.[15] A substantial amount of research has continued to explore these distinctions and to specify the conditions of such disparity between prejudice and discrimination (e.g., DeFluer and Westie, 1958; DeFriese and Ford, 1969).

At the institutional or societal level, this issue is far more germane than a general statement of the distinction between attitudes and behavior, especially when we consider institutionally normal and accepted ways of doing things based upon apparently nondiscriminatory standards. The personnel manager impersonally implementing a quota, or impersonally administering a company requirement for a specific level of education, may be discriminating against whole classes of people without conscious intent. So may the psychologists discussed by Mercer, or the teachers Banks noted as operating on assumptions of cultural disadvantage. Kovel (1970) had developed a concept of *metaracism*, intended to apply to just such situations where values and practices are so deeply ingrained in the social order that the individual does not personally have to "be bigoted at all for racist degradation to continue" (p. 223). Thus, the normal operations theories permit us to focus on organizational or institutional practices and outcomes without necessarily connecting to the minds and hearts of individual white Americans.

In some ways, these theories have much in common with the logic of the first family of theories—those focusing on sociogenic characteristics of minority members. Both sets of theories suggest that decisions made on the basis of apparent underqualifications or deprivations of minority members promote patterns of racism that constitute the basis for further discrimination. But the normal operations' theories are either different or more explicit in three ways: (a) they stress that minority members or communities developed these characteristics under conditions of prior injustice; (b) they emphasize that the maintenance of these conditions of injustice or deprivation is unfair and racist; and (c) they focus most of their attention on the practices and programs utilized and controlled by the white majority and white institutional settings. Thus, their focus on the workings of a racist system of cultural values and institutional procedures carries quite different implications, and they are rather low on the victim-system control continuum.

This family of theories generally suggests that racism is deeply embedded in our society and that it continues to operate whether we "want" it to or not.

---

[15] These must be relative matters, because it is extremely unlikely that someone could live in a society fraught with the racist value patterns discussed in the prior section and not harbor at least some components of that ideology. And, that the same person in a racist social structure would not, passively or actively, discriminate by complying with at least some institutionally racist procedures. Of course, we may not be aware of all we believe and all we do!

Its institutional weight appears so great and omnipresent that we are hard pressed to identify its operating dynamics, except to say that it appears to be everywhere—everywhere things operate as normal or as usual.

## Theories focusing on economic and status self-interest

A number of theories and research studies have focused on the role of white economic and status self-interest as the root of racist attitudes and institutional practices. One of these general types of theories primarily views the relations between lower- or middle-class whites and Third World groups, and stresses racial threat and competition in a scarce employment market and in a status-conscious social system. Another general type of theory primarily views the relation between white economic elites and both white and Third World workers, and stresses capitalist elite control of all workers through labor-market manipulation and the creation of racial divisions and antagonisms.

Theories of white worker antagonism toward blacks and minority groups discuss white racism in terms of the economic and status self-interest of the white worker. As van den Berghe (1967) argues, "in such a dynamic industrial society [like the United States] ... mechanisms of subservience and social distance break down to be replaced by acute competition between the subordinate caste and the working class within the dominant group" (pp. 29-30).[16] One central notion in such theories is that jobs, especially good jobs, are scarce. When blacks compete with whites for these jobs, a natural antagonism is established between white and black workers; since good jobs heretofore have been the prerogative of whites, strenuous black competition threatens the economic status whites have already achieved. Glenn's (1966) investigation of this theory confirms that "many whites in Southern urbanized areas benefit occupationally and economically from the presence and subordination of a large disadvantaged Negro population" (p. 177).

Tobin (1965) is representative of several economic analysts who suggest that an expanding labor market would make jobs plentiful and thus lessen the threat of economic competition and ensuing white racism. But this appears to be only a temporary palliative, eradicated when the job market shrinks and labor is plentiful. Willhelm (1971) also feels that such views of the role of the labor market are simplistic and treats racism as solely determined by economics. In his view, racist patterns are maintained by sets of economic and

---

[16] In an excellent and rare effort at a multisocietal analysis of racism, van den Berghe drew the distinction between paternalistic and competitive models of race relations. The paternalistic model fits preindustrial and slave societies (the early US South, for example), while the competitive model is more appropriate for industrialized and urbanized societies (like Britain and the modern US).

racial values, as well as by objective market circumstances; this explains why black income does not vary consistently with labor-market conditions. Glenn also indicates the broader cultural forces suggested by Willhelm suggesting that in some cases whites' subjective self-interest may be more potent than their objective economic circumstance: "Even those whites who are unaware of the benefits they receive may act in accordance with their self-interest, since they may adhere to a racial ideology shaped by the interests of earlier generations of whites" (Glenn, 1966, p. 178).[17] The results conform to Genovese's (1972) discussion of the emergent power of culture and ideology to shape material circumstance.

Blalock (1967) has conceptualized the process of economic competition and threat in ways that integrate the roles of several other key variables.[18]

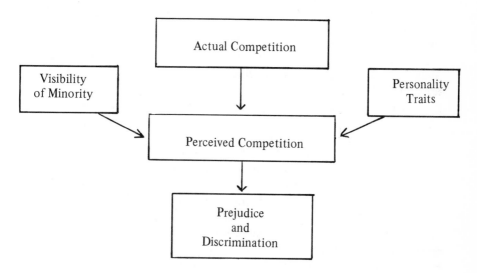

This diagram emphasizes that the perception of economic competition is not necessarily related directly to the actual state of competition. The size and visibility of minority groups represent an additional factor—one which is used to help explain the connection between contact or increased contact and

[17] Important questions may indeed be raised regarding what is or is not really in a person's or a group's objective self-interest. Balbus (1971) draws some powerful and clarifying distinctions between the concepts of objective and subjective self-interest that are quite relevant to the issues discussed here. In his view, people can be "interested in" things (subjective) they are really not "affected by" (objective), in which case they have false consciousness; or they may not be "interested in" things they are "affected by," in which case they lack consciousness. When the two come together accurately, the ground is laid for true consciousness and political mobilization.

[18] This diagram is adapted from Blalock (1967, p. 102, Fig. 11).

feelings of economic competition (Roof, 1972; Vanneman and Pettigrew, 1972). The minority's vigor or success in attempting to enter the job market represents another important factor, and white workers' personality traits (or attitudes and values) also affect how whites may feel about the situation.

There is not always agreement among scholars regarding the data on white workers' attitudes on which some of these theories are based. Campbell's (1971) report of a national attitude survey indicated that lower-class white workers did not have significantly more negative views toward blacks than did others sampled.[19] But, as he himself indicates, "The exclusion policies of many of the craft unions still provide a convincing illustration of the determination of advantaged white workers to protect themselves from black competition" (p. 51). A similar position has been presented by Blumer (1961), who notes that collective self-interest "transcends the feelings of the individual members of the dominant group, giving such members a common orientation that is not otherwise to be found in separate feelings and views" (p. 221). Lohman and Reitzer (1952) also argue for attention to the socially defining role of organized collectivities of an interest group character—in this case especially, workers' unions.

This competitive threat theory also attempts to deal with whites' reactions to current efforts by the government and some segments of industry and labor unions to more rapidly advance blacks into good jobs, perhaps even to engage in "compensatory hiring." White workers, and that includes persons in previously restricted unions and safe white-collar and professional roles who have benefited from the "normal operations" of the economic system, often feel that this is biased and discriminatory behavior (in reverse). In this connection, Ransford (1972) and others oppose the conception of white working-class people proposed in earlier sections of this essay dealing with prejudiced personalities. There, such workers are presented as prejudiced primarily because of low education or high alienation; rather, Ransford finds a clear class interest underlying "blue collar anger to be rooted in the actual or perceived social situation" (1972, p. 345). The situation he identifies is one of a lack of influence in decisions at work, high taxation and apparent aid for blacks only, and an unresponsive political power structure.

Closely connected to theories about white workers' protection of their economic self-interest are theories of status interests. In this view, whites who see their privileged status being challenged may also engage in racist acts to deny opportunities or resources to minorities. Vanneman and Pettigrew (1972) draw attention to these two different interests, utilizing the terms "contact"

---

[19] This is notably deviant from other findings reported by numerous scholars and treated earlier in this paper. It is not clear whether changing times have altered values (nor whose in which direction), whether Campbell asked better or worse questions, or whether white people reported differently, regardless of their attitudes.

(a status-connected aversion to some intimacy with people different from oneself) and "competition" (a resentment of special programs to advance others' economic resources) to highlight the differences. Blumer (1961) notes that the dominant group is concerned with its group position and the notion of the "place" of subordinate groups. Economic competition may be relevant, but for Blumer it is only one example of the general theme of potential "encroachment at countless points of proprietary claim" and privilege (p. 222).

The stress on the workability of equal status group contacts, treated in an earlier section of this essay, also implies that racism occurs as a function of high interdependency in the face of unequal status contacts. Racism is presumably a reaction to the threat to one's sense of privileged group identity and position brought about by close interaction with people of different status.

Theories of white elite control of the social system as the source of racism emanate from socioeconomic data and principles rooted in views of corporate capitalism. Rather than starting with the self-interest of the white worker, these theories start from the self-interest of the white elite manager or owner—the capitalist class controlling economic opportunities and rewards. The main thrust of this theoretical orientation focuses on two labor-oriented needs of the capitalist system: (a) to preserve cheap and stable labor pools and (b) to keep working masses from organizing to take control of the workplace and the economic system. The first need involves a practical exploitative relation—one supported not only by economic power but by a social ideology justifying and legitimizing it. As Cox (1959) points out,

> Racial prejudice ... is a social attitude propagated among the public by an exploiting class for the purpose of stigmatizing some group as inferior so that the exploitation of either the group itself or its resources or both may be justified. (p. 393)

Because cheap labor is essential for effective capitalism, exploitation of blacks is seen as just one example of exploiting all proletarian peoples—which includes some whites and all blacks. In this context, the exploitative class uses racism to promote images of the inferiority of blacks so that white workers will not object to minorities' obvious exploitation.

A similar analysis is proposed by Ofari (1970), who attempted to discover whether and how all whites benefit from corporate capitalism's dominance and exploitation of blacks. His response:

> No, it is monopoly capitalism that has prospered from the exploitation of white workers, as well as the super-exploitation of black workers. It is here that the onus of blame must be placed. This is not to negate the fact that white workers, primarily through their racism,

have nearly always uncompromisingly supported the corporate structure in the economic rape of black America. (p. 55)[20]

The second of capitalism's labor needs requires strategy to insure that
the working masses do not organize together in ways that could seriously
threaten owner equity, relatively low worker wages, and general elite control.
Thus, Cox (1959) suggests:

> Both the Negroes and the poor whites are exploited by the white
> ruling class, and this has been done most effectively by the mainte-
> nance of antagonistic attitudes between the white and the colored
> masses. (p. 473)

The strategy of exacerbating racial tensions keeps elements of the proletariat
off balance, fighting each other, while also keeping any pressure for economic
reform off the white elites. Tabb (1971), Glascow (1972), and Reich (1972)
also see capitalism's need to transfer all workers' potential resentment away
from corporate exploitation onto black scapegoats. Thus, "struggling whites
blame their binds and pressures on the blacks' rise, failing to see that the
power-wielders have permitted them to have only a circumscribed and
precarious existence" (Glascow, 1972, p. 63). White workers benefit from
racism by their greater material advantages and by subjective comparisons with
Third World peoples; thus, they aid in further subjugation and exploitation
(Boggs, 1970). The capitalist system benefits by maintaining a marginal working class that can be used as a wedge against the organized laboring class, that
can be used as an emergency pool of reserve labor, and that prevents the
formation of large interracial organizations of poor people, which might
advance a socialist alternative to corporate capitalism.

Willhelm (1971) objects to much of this line of analysis, arguing that
racism existed prior to capitalism historically. In this view, Cox's stress on
class exploitation regardless of race incorrectly "transforms race relations into
purely economic relations; racism is at best epiphenomenal" (Willhelm, 1971,
p. 172). Moreover, Willhelm does not absolve the working class of responsibility for its own actions by blaming corporate elites alone; he sees white
workers as more than pawns of corporate myths. The American economic
system obviously is discriminatory, he argues, but the economic system imple-
ments racist values, not the reverse.

Economic interest theorists also utilize analyses of corporate capitalism
to assess the relevance of labor-market operations and the potential of black

---

[20] Glenn (1966) disagrees, reporting, as we noted earlier, that neither lower-class
whites nor elites appear to benefit most from Negro subordination; rather, it is the
middle-class white worker and some professionals who appear to gain the most.

capitalism. In their view, it may seldom matter whether there is a real labor shortage: if white economic elites can foster the conviction that there is a shortage market for jobs and job advancement, they can heighten all workers' perceptions of competition. This process can be conceptualized by returning to Blalock's diagram. Without altering actual economic conditions, perceived worker competition may be increased in the following ways: manipulating information about the labor market (threat of competition), about minority demands and likelihood of challenge (visibility), or about other white workers' reactions (referent groups and attitudes). Therefore, manipulation of the labor shortage myth supports exploitative control over whites and minorities; it also triggers white workers' general reactions to minorities in other social arenas.

The maintenance of white capitalist dominance assumed by these theorists as essential also explains probable white resistance to meaningful ventures in black capitalism.[21] Ofari (1970) argues that white corporate capitalism, which now controls and exploits black workers, will still control the fledgling efforts of black capitalists. And even if they did not, he feels that "There is no value in trading white corporate exploitation for black exploitation" (p. 85). This priority is echoed by Boggs (1970). These authors clearly are concerned with the implication of their analysis for a socialist alternative to the racial and economic divisions of capitalist structures. In contrast, numerous advocates of black capitalism see it as a useful way to support black economic advance, even if it may be somewhat limited by the surrounding white corporate structure. If capitalism does continue to define the American way of life, they feel black entry into it and stabilization of it may be the only long-run alternative.

Since the exploitative character of the capital structure must not be overt in a democratic society, the covert cooperation of other institutions must be employed in preserving the privileged and manipulated marketplace and in maintaining the appearance of a meritorious and just society. It could be argued, then, that there is capitalist advantage in educational systems that ensure minority failure, police and public control systems that ensure arrest records (which disqualify minorities for certain careers), union apprentice systems that ensure inadequate minority skills, and the like. In these ways the capitalist theories of racism provide an economic-structural explanation for the racism in schools and service agencies that was explained by the cultural and normal operations theories in prior sections.

These economic/status interest theories vary somewhat in the degree of embeddedness they portray. Those stressing the economic or status self-interest of white workers focus attention on this particular portion of the

---

[21] Except, of course, where it is obvious that black capitalism is really a cover for white control of conglomerates, financing systems, investment agencies, ghetto or barrio outlets, etc.

American public and national society. However, unlike other theoretical treatments of similar white worker phenomena, they do root white reactions in the collective workings of the economic system—a system that establishes racial group interests in apparent competition with one another. The group of theories concerned with the role of capitalist elites perceives racism as deeply embedded in the total American system. The relations of corporate capitalism to managers and workers and to various primary and secondary institutions are seen as crucial. Tobin's (1965) claim that economic racism is an "aberration from the principles of our society, rather than a requirement of its functioning" (p. 878) is a single exception to this trend. Most other theorists see racism as so tied to economic stratification systems and other elements of capitalism that it would take the same socialist-proletarian revolution to do away with them both.

While the various theories of economic and status self-interest differ in important ways, almost all agree that corporate capitalism supports racism and racism supports capitalism. Control of racism clearly lies in the politico-economic system exploiting minorities, with the minority victims playing only a minor role in generating racism or in controlling their life opportunities. The theoretical emphasis on worker competition highlights the role of white workers operating out of a sense of economic threat and insecurity; but the capitalist interest theories portray these white workers as almost as much a fellow victim as an oppressor. It is suggested that a manipulated and distorted sense of economic reality gets white workers to degrade minorities. The implication is that if they could see clearly, they would turn against the real sources of control over their situation—capitalist elites. Thus, according to these theories, racist ideology is rather deliberately used, although perhaps not created, by these elites to help confuse white workers about their real interests and consequently serve capitalism's needs for economic control and advancement. The explanatory system utilized by these theories range from moderately low to quite low on the continuum of victim-system control.

### Theories focusing on colonialism

Recently, several theories have been generated that interpret American racial relations with the theoretical paradigm of internal colonialism. Some of these theories have drawn heavily from historical accounts of racism and African colonialism (e.g., Fanon, 1963; Memmi, 1967). Many of the essential elements appear similar to these theorists (Blauner, 1972): (a) forced entry or conquest, (b) economic exploitation, (c) political control, (d) cultural alteration and control, and (e) a self-justifying ideology.

The colonial theoretical approach argues that there are two (at least) separated societies in the United States; indeed, black, Mexican-American, and native-American communities geographically appear to be almost separate ghetto, barrio, or reservation nations. These separations were initiated when members of the black minority were coercively brought to this land, and set down (later reinforced by "natural" economic and demographic forces) and maintained in carefully prescribed geographic areas. The conquest of the West and Southwest forcibly included large numbers of indigenous Indians and Mexicans into the domestic American empire. All these groups' internal locations in America are seen as still ruled by external political and socio-economic forces. As Tabb (1971) explains with regard to the black ghetto, it is an "internal colony set off from the rest of the society and systematically exploited in a consistent manner to maximize the well-being of the 'mother country' (white America)" (p. 431). In referring further to the black community, Carmichael and Hamilton (1967) note that, "exploiters come into the ghetto from outside, bleed it dry, and leave it economically dependent on the larger society" (p. 17).

Most bases for the economic aspects of colonial theory already have been summarized in discussions of capitalism's economic self-interest, and colonial theorists echo that thinking. However, the present theories extend the analysis further to emphasize relationships between economic exploitation and political control from the outside of the colonized group (Carmichael and Hamilton, 1967; Blauner, 1969, 1972; Tabb, 1971). Baron and his associates (1968), for example, convincingly demonstrate how the black community in Chicago lacks control over its internal decision making. According to their data, blacks were underrepresented in positions of control of economic enterprises, professional associations, voluntary organizations, religious and welfare agencies, and political offices. When represented, minority members were less influential than those offices would ordinarily demand. Flaming et al. (1972) report similar findings for the black community in Milwaukee, Wisconsin, and Moore (1970) documents the problems of Mexican-American political organization and influence in the colonized areas of New Mexico, Texas, and California. Clark's (1965) views of the power of the external white community in the very fact of ghetto isolation and impotence sums up these studies in the following terms:

> The dark ghetto's invisible walls have been erected by the white society, by those who have power, both to confine those who have NO power and to perpetuate their powerlessness. (p. 11)

Here Clark connects some of the earlier material on social contacts and networks to the realities of power—the power that the white society has to create and sustain separated ghettos and institutions.

In time, the maintenance of economic and political control outside the minority community may create some secondary problems for effective capital development. Christoffel (1970), for instance, argues that many capitalists now are concerned about the negative effects of unbridled capitalism and racism. In order to deal with low consumer resources and disruptive riots (both effects of and challenges to the efficient workings of monopoly capitalism), "the first thing corporate imperialism must do in the ghetto is develop more efficient local political control" (p. 337). Christoffel also implies that locally credible political stability within ghettos is more efficient and preferable in maintaining the image of American democracy than would be overt domination from outside corporate interests. The solution, then, is to support the appearance of local, internal control, perhaps even with token gestures, but to retain control in the hands of the corporate elites. Covert political dominance also is vested in bureaucracies administered by whites, even when these systems provide needed health and welfare services and resources to minority communities. Through such welfare colonialism, the white society is able to rule other societies that exist in its midst without making that rule obvious. Failing to control relevant economic and macropolitical forces that inevitably determine the destiny of urban scenes, apparent political independence in urban centers masks real dependence on ruling white political and economic systems.[22]

Fanon and others point out that another essential component of colonialism is cultural control and/or eradication of the indigenous culture: "Cultural and social organization are important as vessels of a people's autonomy and integrity; when cultures are whole and vigorous, conquest, penetration, and certain modes of control are more readily resisted" (Blauner, 1972, p. 67). However, even where minority social and cultural organizations remained fairly strong, as Moore (1970) suggests they did for Mexican-Americans in New Mexico, Anglo political conquest occurred along colonial lines. Her view is that the focus upon weak and inadequate minority cultures as explanations for internal colonial conquest often masks the real application of superior and oppressive white power. Here, again, we can see how colonial theorists could utilize data generated by the sociogenetic theorists (earlier discussed in the section on "minority characteristics") and apply it as evidence for their own views.

The focus on cultural issues is another of the major features of colonial theory that sets it apart from economic self-interest theories; colonial theory agrees that white as well as Third World workers are exploited, but that the latter are exploited differently. For a colonial power must seek to justify its control by embedding in the colonized "country" the people's belief in the colonizer—his right and duty to rule. This is not merely a matter of generating new myth systems that justify political arrangements; these myths must seep down through the schooling and family and media systems so that they

---

[22] Obviously, this view parallels reports of the preparation and legitimization of "native" leaders in various internationally colonized systems who are actually stabilizing agents of external powers.

pervade the mind and consciousness of children as well as adults. For instance, Carmichael and Hamilton (1967) argue that "the social effects of colonialism are to degrade and dehumanize the subjected black man [with] ... assumptions of white superiority" (p. 31). Under such conditions, "black people begin to doubt themselves, their worth as human beings" (*ibid.,* p. 29; Clark, 1965; and many others).[23] Thus, all minority persons who seek knowledge of their state or community as part of the process of self-identification must wrestle with the colonizers' unilateral definitions of what is the culture and what is not. Oppressed people must create new realities in order to be human, and this requires resocialization and the generation of new ideologies to redefine self and society. Fanon's (1967) description of the resultant dilemmas of understanding and appreciating blackness under white rule rings true to many black Americans; it explains not only his personal popularity but the American relevance of the culturally destructive aspects of colonialism.

Control of the subordinate group is seen as a central fact of life in a colonized society—one that takes precedence over other traditions such as justice, egalitarianism, and the like. One way to justify such precedence in our "egalitarian" society is to see the minority as not able to appreciate or not deserving of full membership in the larger society's cherished traditions. Boggs (1970) argues that in order to justify this economic, political, and social exploitation, the American people invented black inferiority—"they had to believe that the only reason why the Negroes continued to remain outcasts from the American way of life was because they were racially inferior" (p. 10). To believe otherwise, he notes, would be to recognize that equal opportunity itself did not exist. Another alternative is for the majority to be ignorant of minority conditions (Myrdal, 1962)—a state that is often supported. Our review of contact theories of racism indicated some of the ways such ignorance is maintained, and how that ignorance and distance has further consequences of a racist character. Both tactics help preserve the majority's positive image of itself and its own culture, while maintaining control of minorities.

Of course, no attempt at cultural and political control is completely successful. The human person and social system are too complex for a preexisting culture ever to be completely eradicated or made over. And so we see distinct elements of minority cultures and interests continuing to sur-

---

[23] There is substantial debate about this conclusion now. While not overlooking the deleterious effects of cultural control, Yancey, Rigsby, and McCarthy (1972) find that differences between self-evaluations of whites and blacks vary, depending upon the traits queried and on other aspects of social role and status. They object to gross assessments and pronouncements regarding racial self-esteem that focus solely on racial comparisons in much the same way other authors have objected to the use of gross measures of school success and solely racial or social class comparisons of school achievement.

face... and now to surface as deliberate weaponry in the fight against white colonial hegemony.[24]

Central to the notion of colonial control is the maintenance of superior white status and privilege. Blacks are controlled by economic, political, and cultural forces operating together. Whites gaining privilege are less inclined to see, let alone object to, the racist oppression in their midst. Some of the privileges involved in racism are political—i.e., having the power to elect representatives that protect white interests primarily, and generating a governmental system that serves whites with priority. Others are related to social status (e.g., having higher social status assigned to whiteness, regardless of merit or style), cultural priorities (white domination of various artistic and expressive media), and superior self-identification. For the minority groups, of course, the reverse is true—political powerlessness, inferior social status, cultural exclusion, and dilemmas in socialization and self-identification.

The colonial theories represent extreme points on the two categories initially advanced: very low on the continuum of victim-system control, and very high on embeddedness. The oppression of minority peoples is a necessary part of colonialism—internal or external—and control of racism is located in the oppressing system. Moreover, the argument that political, economic, and cultural controls operate together in maintaining colonial oppression indicates how deeply racism is embedded in the entire fabric of the American society.

### A graphic summary of theories of racism

Our review of these theories of racism has focused on descriptions of the central tenets of each family of theories, as well as a few of their divergencies. Moreover, we have analyzed each major theory in terms of two prespecified categories: (a) degree of victim-system control in the location of sources of control over racist processes and outcomes; and (b) the degree of embeddedness of racism in the overall structure and operations of the American society. Figure 1 graphically represents each theory with respect to its position on these two (nonindependent) continua.

## THEORIES OF RACISM AND RACIST THEORIES

The range of theories we have discussed represents the work of a number of sociologists and other social scientists operating over several decades. Some appear to illuminate our understanding of the complex phenomena of racism and point the way toward meaningful change in our

---

[24] For instance, they have surfaced in resistance to wars of conquest and in slave rebellions of the 18th and 19th centuries, in minority attempts to build insulated cohesive communities of their own in ghettos, barrios and reservations, in minority studies programs in white institutions, and in urban and rural insurrections of the 1960s and 1970s.

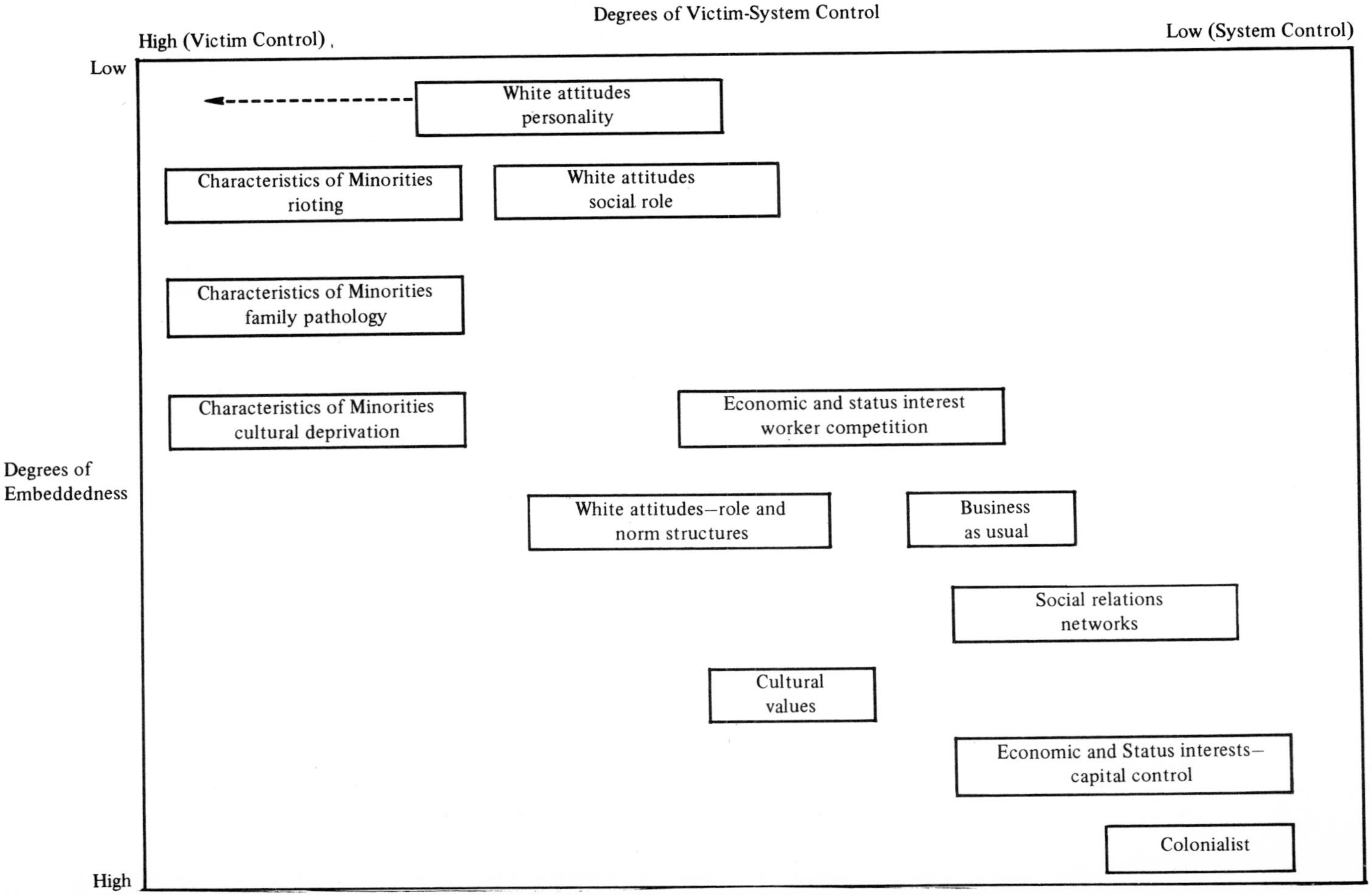

**Fig. 1.** Representation of theories with regard to two major categories

57

society. Others fail to deal with important structural realities in the control of racist mechanisms and effects, and fail to attend to the deeply embedded racist procedures and value systems in our society.

Two general conclusions can be drawn about the state of theorizing and the relative prominence of the different viewpoints reviewed here. First, there are few theories that are comprehensive and that encompass the full range of individual and systemic variables that appear to be involved in American white racism. The colonial theories come closest to such comprehensiveness but, even here, there are few fully developed perspectives on how the internal colonial paradigm actually operates. Second, the first two types of theories reviewed seem to be the most popular, both within the profession and among the public at large. Much more research and theory has been developed on minority adaptations and attributes and on white attitudes than on the other approaches. Both approaches downplay the roles of group dominance, political and economic conflict, and cultural pluralism. In their policy implications, then, they tend to encourage a focus upon individual and subgroup changes for minorities and certain whites; this distracts attention from the potential modification of structural characteristics of our society. Moreover, both types of theories cluster towards the high end of the victim-system control continuum and towards the low end of the embeddedness continuum.

Questions can be raised of why these two types of theories are so prominent. Are they "better" theories? Do they explain more? Is their relative popularity an example of fad and fashion in social research? Are the theories suited to the kinds of public views that protect and advance the role of social science? Do they lead to policies and programs that could advance social justice concerns? Are they designed (consciously or not) to support racist myth systems and social structures popular in the white society? There may be many sociological explanations for their prominence and also for why so many theories fail to unlock the complex sets of issues involved in white-controlled and deeply embedded racism.

In our view, theories that fail to focus on the interrelated and systemic roots of racism contribute to our public ignorance and to continuing injustice and exploitation of minority people. In the section of this essay on "normal institutional operations" we reviewed theories of racism that suggest how the conduct of business as usual works to maintain prior patterns of racist advantage and disadvantage. The same dynamic occurs with regard to the operations and effects of social theory. Theories of racism that do not help to clarify our racist social system priorities help maintain ambiguity about racism; theories that do not lead to innovative anti-racist programming help maintain traditional racist programs.

As we indicated in the introduction to this essay, we feel that social theory does make a difference. Sociology can be a key link in either generating, rationalizing, and maintaining racism or in attacking, exposing, and delegitimating it. There are three major ways in which such effects can be achieved: (a) by direct information needed to develop social policies concerning urban reform, family planning, affirmative action programs, etc., (b) by indirect information obtained through the collection and publication of certain kinds of data that could highlight selected issues and forces, and (c) by directly or indirectly affecting norms and program agencies such as schools, universities, social welfare bureaus, police and judicial establishments, and industrial management systems.

Sociology, as a scientific enterprise, not only conducts scholarly studies of racism; it also is itself an obvious and potent actor in a racist social system. As Gouldner (1970) notes succinctly, "social science is part of the social world as well as a conception of it" (p. 13). Several prominent historians argue that early American social theory on race relations blatantly contributed to the social processes underlying elite white control through the promulgation of theories of white superiority and black inferiority.[25] As one critic of social science has suggested:

> Even before the Civil War the Southern ruling class had inspired a pseudo-scientific literature attempting to prove the Negro inhuman and thus beyond any moral objections to human slavery. (Ellison, 1973, p. 83)

More recent scholars of the sociology of knowledge have argued that all or most modern sociology has been wedded to priorities involving order, assimilation, and consensus around legitimate authority, and that this is especially true when it comes to race relations and other "social problems." Horton (1966) suggests that commitments to "working within the system" have led scholars to a concern for "the expansion of opportunities for mobility within the society and socialization of the deviant (the Negro and the anti-Negro) to expanding opportunities" (p. 167). The expansion of opportunities represents policy derived primarily from theories about racism and the expanding job market (see economic competition theories); programs and concerns for the socialization of deviant Negroes derives from theories about racism rooted in minority characteristics; and concerns about socialization of the deviant anti-Negro derives mainly from theories about racism rooted in individual white prejudice and discrimination. These are the popular themes in the literature of race and racism; as noted, they downplay the operations of caste systems and the majority's uses of power and control. These theories also have difficulty explaining conflicts of interest as legitimate and appropriate; pluralism and conflicts in values and interests would be seen primarily as potential threats to order and to the prevailing consensus.

Van den Berghe (1967) agreed with much of Horton's analysis, indicating that:

[25] Such theories are reviewed by Jordan (1968), Genovese (1972), and Lacy (1972).

> ...much of the work done by North Americans in the area of race has, until the last three or four years, been strongly flavored with a great deal of optimism and complacency about the basic "goodness" of American society and with the cautious, slightly left of center, reformist, meliorative, gradualist approach of "liberal" intellectuals. (p. 7)

According to Metzger (1971), this convergence of political liberalism and sociological theory also leads to an assumption of eventual minority assimilation and an expectation that the American Creed will persevere to whither away vestiges of prejudice and discrimination. The theoretical and ideological convergences suggested by van den Berghe, Horton, and Metzger may offer one potential explanation of the prevailing biases in theory construction.

It appears to us that the specific societal context has a very significant influence upon the social scientist. It is not simply that sociologists mirror the prevailing assumptions of the social order; obviously that is too simple an explanation to be very helpful. The society itself employs the resources of social science in ways that are useful to system order and maintenance. Any society can be expected to seek and publicize theories of social organization congruent with its central ideologies and organizing principles. This may well be one of the purposes of social theory. The sociologist needs a theory for at least two purposes: to guide the search for relevant variables, and to help tie together empirical findings and conceptual interpretations. The society at large needs social theory for another purpose: to provide an understanding of how aspects of persons and social systems operate so that we have coherent images of the nature of our world. In this way, we discover how to behave in relation to social objects or systems and how to manipulate them to our self-interest or to our definition of the common good.

In a pluralistic society, any single explanation or image of social reality helps different groups reinforce or provide justification for certain preferred states of affairs. In a society where some groups are more powerful than others, it is likely that "every group in power ... tells its story as it would like to have it believed, in the way it thinks will promote its interests and serve its constituencies" (Becker and Horowitz, 1972, pp. 54-55). When powerful social elites can engage social science in conducting research that serves their interests, they gain great help in the preparation and legitimization of their partisan images of the world. In this way, some theories of racism feed into white elites' needs or plans to control minority people and poor people.

One rather clear example of this partisanship can be found in the theories of minority inadequacy, which were believed by some minority members as well as many whites.[26] New generations accepted portions of

---

[26] The concept of partisanship we are employing does not necessarily indicate conscious or intentional bias on the part of sociological actors. Their work may be partisan

these theories as public ideologies and acted in ways that eventually provided new and self-confirming data. The theories we reviewed that explained racism in terms of cultural norms and values indicated the covert power of such thought forms and myths to help define social reality and legitimate social control. In response to such theories and implications of minority inadequacy, Bailey (1973), quoting Clark, justified black studies' programs partly on the basis of the need to resist the white "official version of social reality." In a similar vein, Padilla (1972) argues that the views of scholars often negate "the authenticity of his [the minority group member's] own reality" (p. 6). What is called for is a sociology that can express the partisan views and needs of minorities more adequately and one that can more effectively authenticate the versions of social reality that minorities feel they experience.

The problems of authentication illuminate not only the relationships of scientific institutions to cultural systems and ideologies; they also emphasize how the status location of a person in the social order may affect his or her knowledge. The social class origins, racial and sex role backgrounds of scientists, as well as the general cultural and economic framework of the professional may contribute to the nature of the theories developed. According to this reasoning, a social scientific enterprise made up primarily of white males from middle- and upper-middle-class backgrounds—96.7 percent to 98.4 percent, according to Glenn and Weiner (1969)—can be expected to mirror much of the society's conscious or unconscious white racism (and sexism and class biases as well). As Billingsley (1970) states rather strongly: "American social scientists . . . reflect all the prejudice, ignorance and arrogance which seems to be endemic to Americans of European descent" (p. 127). Ellis and Orleans (1971) come to similar conclusions in their own review of research on urban race relations. They note that:

> Many social scientists, and especially those from minority back-
> grounds, have begun to question the assumptions embedded in the
> research and writings of their (usually white) predecessors . . . In the
> past the predominant perspective in the social sciences was cast by
> those who, though often sympathetic with the underclass and the
> racial and ethnic castes were nonetheless not a part of them. (p. 17)

It would seem, then, that another explanation of the nature of current theory is that the social scientific enterprise is overwhelmingly monocultural, and thus likely to be racist.

But it is not just that it is difficult for individual scientists to escape their own racist backgrounds and socialization. The current membership of the

---

because of unconscious personal biases; because of collective professional assumptions, standards, and norms, or because of the nature of the using system that sees, receives, and translates social theory in social policy and program.

profession, university selection and admission criteria, the character and content of training programs, positions of leadership in the profession, and role models of professional lifestyles and political priorities all affect the conduct of sociological work. Both Mills (1943) and Hughes (1963) warned against overlooking the influence of these factors in noting that increasing professionalism could reduce the sociologists' capacity to empathize and identify with the nonwhite, nonaffluent, and nonintellectual classes of society. Thus, the specialized training, technical ideology, and high-status professional and social roles of social scientists establishes them as a social group with some clearly identifiable special interests and goals. We could then expect them to maintain racism in the profession in ways similar to the self-interest operations of other white occupational and social groups.

The heavy dependence of social science and the university on governmental and elite funds for research and general support creates a reciprocal relationship between the profession and the polity. One result is a natural (although not universal) tendency for research evidence to fit or be used by the main currents of social policy and program makers. Becker and Horowitz (1972) support the contention that "agency sponsorship tends to put conservative limits on the search for necessary conditions" (p. 63). The influence is subtle, they suggest, and operates through definitions of the problem, pressures for feasible results, and the like. Katznelson (1971) argues that one result in the area of race relations is that most riot commission reports have used sociel science "to discover the means to secure the greatest level of black docility at the lowest cost to the wider society" (p. 55). He does not thereby criticize all the studies done on riots, but the interactions between scientists and public commissions that result in certain kinds of public reports.

Rainwater and Pittman (1967) discuss several examples of the way social research on minorities had been or could be used in ways that maintained racism, and share their own confusions about whether and what findings they should have published from their studies of lower-class Negro life. Brazziel (1973) cites some specific internal and external pressures that operate on the large number of white researchers working in race relations, especially focusing on pressures to distort or omit references to racism in their published works. Our own review certainly confirmed the relative absence of the term racism. Although we can only speculate upon whether the other specific constraints Brazziel cites are accurate, it is clear that the reporting-production apparatus is a key element in the overall picture of social theory on racism.[27]

There are other issues related to reporting results as well. One is who should determine or control the use of research products. Rainwater and

----

[27] In the context of comments on Project Camelot—a not completely unrelated scenario—Blumer (1967) provides excruciating details of overt and covert agency pressures on scholars' considerations of reports of their work.

Pittman (1967) discuss the problems of ethics and data confidentiality, although the issue of confidentiality is phrased primarily in terms of protecting individuals, not groups. In their concern about collectivities of the poor and black, accountability is typically not to the groups being "researched" but to "the public in general." Who is the effective public? Who are the readers, judges, and users of scientific research? The nature of professional training, colleagueship, and dissimination usually means that most social researchers are accountable (if at all) to white peers, white academic superiors, and white funders. This system helps reinforce racist tendencies, since white knowledge-makers are not accountable to minorities, poor people, or the general citizenry who provide the data for research on social problems. In light of these tendencies, Brazziel (1973) explicitly suggests that "A black parent advisory panel should review and monitor all research involving black children" (p. 43). However it works, more and more scholars—mostly minority members—are urging that public accountability systems should be established to protect minorities' interests (Thomas, 1971).

Some explanations of the character of theories we have reviewed may originate in the methods typically used in sociological research. Blauner and Wellman (1973), for example, note the social inequality that occurs when the researcher is in a position of power over the subject. When the researcher is white and the subject a minority member, such situations are exacerbated and may be exploitative. Several investigators have discussed the technical problems of social-psychological and sociological data collected in this context (Lenski and Leggett, 1960; Katz, 1964; Ledvinka, 1971). And Forsythe (1973) documents blacks' increasing political reluctance to give accurate answers to white researchers.

Research on whites may be just as problematical, especially if it depends on self-report data. Adequate answers by whites rely on white scholars' abilities to ask the right questions. In addition, we must assume that white respondents know what they feel about racism and can articulate it; it appears to us that in many cases white racism is so buried that we aren't even aware of some of our feelings. Even if awareness is present, many respondents will not go against prevailing social norms and will not verbalize their true feelings. On these grounds it is increasingly unclear to us just what white subjects' answers may mean.

Thus it appears that—for reasons rooted in the social context of American race relations, in the structure of the profession, and in the methods of sociology—white scientists can be expected to have difficulty discovering the complex character of minority life and the complicated nature of relationships that exist between minorities and whites. By themselves, whites can have only an incomplete understanding of racism, racist behavior, and its effects. As Ellis and Orleans (1971) argue:

> Undoubtedly white social scientists are as capable of engaging in race research as their non-white colleagues, even though their everyday

experiences differ. However, because they come to their task with different backgrounds they are likely to see different problems and pose different questions. (p. 18)

Merton (1972), however, reacts to this position negatively and vigorously, characterizing it as a doctrine of "insider knowledge" and taking pains to demonstrate its error and futility. But Merton himself resorts to exaggerations of this view in an attempt to destroy it. Also, he addresses only the methodological and technical aspects of contemporary studies of racism and downplays their political contexts, impacts, and uses. Nevertheless, his article is an instructive piece in the important debate over who can (epistemologically) and should (ethically) conduct what kind (methodologically) of research on whom (politically).

In our view, the study of racism and racial relations walks the thin and confusing line of all interactions between the races in America. White scholars embedded in the society may be careful, but hardly "value-free" or "objective" in their treatment of the subject matter. As Hamilton (1973) points out, it just is not "possible for a white social scientist, who has benefited directly or indirectly from racial oppression, to be 'objective' about his position of preference, whether he admits it or not" (p. 472). Obviously, Hamilton views the issue of benefit in very broad terms, for he includes whites' advantages of living in a supportive culture with a wide net of social relations and with access to many political as well as economic life choices.

Our central concern here is not that sociologists are racist, or more racist or less racist than others; in a racist society that is a fact of life people of various races and positions may argue about. But as America (1970) points out, "The problem here is that the consultant and researcher who is racist is also represented as an expert and a scientist, an objective and dispassionate analyst who presents findings and conclusions backed by data and evidence" (p. 13). Moreover, sociologists themselves often are unaware of the liberal and order-serving biases of their work (Horton, 1966).

Thus, the most dangerous outcomes occur when sociologists refuse or are unable to recognize the white cultural and professional context within which they exist. Most discussions and concerns about bias are highly individuated, focusing on the technical operations of scientific work, and occasionally on the individual moral and political biases of individual scholars. Relatively little attention has been paid to the issues we have just noted, to the collective cultural biases of a whole class of social theorists and to the problems of doing racially relevant research in a racially unjust society that is well organized and seeking means of maintaining social control. The results, in our view, have helped make most of American sociology a covertly racist enterprise and an exceedingly effective instrument of white racial control.

In summary, we have argued that one of the major societal functions of the sociological enterprise is the generation of social mythology—sets of understandings of how the social system works and should work. Therefore, social theories that have strong racist components are keys to maintaining the rationale for much social practice, providing the intellectual base of much white social power. We do not suggest that this is intentional or deliberate; given the nature of the social order, to do anything different would require a conscious effort to swim against the tide. We have attempted to locate some of the roots of this phenomenon in the nature of the interaction between social science and society; some in the internal membership, training, and norms of the profession; and some in the traditional methods of gathering information and disseminating it. Undoubtedly there are other factors at work, and we hope that serious research can be undertaken on this critical problem in American social theory.

Finally, it is important to remember that theories change over time. They change as our knowledge changes, as our values change, and as our social structures change: they both reflect and help create the state of our science and our politics. What seemed reasonable and fashionable at one time may appear outrageous at another. The problems of changes in theory are more potent in the area of race relations and racism than in other areas of social investigation. The issues are more deeply hidden in our white psyche and group loyalties. The issues have highly visible political ramifications, and public events and conditions are changing very rapidly. Therefore, no one who constructs or reviews theory in this area can afford much personal chagrin when it no longer is useful or sensible.

# REFERENCES

Adorno, T., Frenkel-Brunswik, E., Levinson, D., and Sanford R. *The authoritarian personality.* New York: Harper, 1950.

Allport, G. *The nature of prejudice.* New York: Doubleday-Anchor, 1958.

Allport, G., and Kramer, B. Some roots of prejudice. *Journal of Psychology,* 1946, **22,** 9-39.

America, R. The case of the racist researchers. *Black World,* May, 1970, 10-15, 91-94.

Bailey, R. Black studies in historical perspective. *Journal of Social Issues,* 1972, **29,** 97-108.

Balbus, I. The concept of interest in pluralist and Marxian analysis. *Politics and Society,* 1971, **6,** 151-177.

Banks, J. Racial prejudice and the black self-concept. In J. Banks and J. Grambs (Eds.), *Black self-concept.* New York: McGraw-Hill, 1972.

Baratz, S., and Baratz, J. Early childhood intervention: The social science base of institutional racism. *Harvard Educational Review,* 1970, **40,** 29-50.

Baron, H. Black powerlessness in Chicago. *Trans-Action,* November 1968, **6,** 27-33.

Becker, H., and Horowitz, I. Radical politics and sociological research: Observations on methodology and ideology. In *Varieties of political expression in sociology.* Chicago: University of Chicago Press, 1972.

Berkowitz, L. *Aggression. A social Psychological analysis.* New York: McGraw-Hill, 1962.

Berkowitz, L. The study of urban violence: Some implications of laboratory studies of frustration and aggression. In L. Massoti and D. Bowen (Eds.), *Riots and rebellion: Civil violence in the urban community.* Beverly Hills: Sage, 1968.

Berkowitz, L. Frustrations, comparisons and other sources of emotional arousal as contributors to social unrest. *Journal of Social Issues,* 1972, **28,** 77-92.

Bettelheim, B., and Janowitz, M. *Social change and prejudice.* New York: Free Press, 1964.

Billingsley, A. *Black families in white America.* Englewood Cliffs, N.J.: Prentice-Hall, 1968.

Billingsley, A. Black families and white social science. *Journal of Social Issues,* 1970, **26,** 127-142.

Blalock, M. H. M., Jr. *Toward a theory of minority-group relations.* New York: Wiley, 1967.

Blauner, R. Internal colonialism and ghetto revolt. *Social Problems,* 1969, **16,** 393-408.

Blauner, R. *Racial oppression in America.* New York: Harper & Row, 1972.

Blauner, R., and Wellman, D. Toward a decolonization of social research. In. J. Ladner (Ed.), *The death of white sociology.* New York: Vintage Books, 1972.

Bloom, D., Davis, A., and Hess, R. *Compensatory education for cultural deprivation.* New York: Holt, Rinehart and Winston, 1965.

Blumer, H. Race prejudice as a sense of group position. In J. Masuoka and P. Valien (Eds.), *Race relations: Problems and theory.* Chapel Hill: University of North Carolina Press, 1961.

Blumer, H. Threats from agency-determined research: The case of Camelot. In I. L. Horowitz (Ed.), *The rise and fall of Camelot.* Cambridge, Mass.: MIT Press, 1967.

Boggs, J. *Racism and the class struggle.* New York: Monthly Review Press, 1970.

Brazziel, W. White research in black communities: When solutions become a part of the problem. *Journal of Social Issues,* 1973, **29,** 41-44.

Cambell, A. *White attitudes toward black people.* Ann Arbor: Institute for Social Research, 1971.

Caplan, N., and Nelson, S. On being useful: The nature and consequences of psychological research on social problems. *American Psychologist,* 1973, **28,** 199-211.

Caplan, N., and Paige, J. A study of ghetto rioters. *Scientific American,* 1968, **219,** 15-21.

Carmichael, S., and Hamilton, C. *Black power.* New York: Vintage Books, 1967.

Carter, T. *Mexican-Americans in schools' a history of educational neglect.* New York: College Entrance Examination Board, 1970.

Chesler, M. Desegregation and school crisis. *Integrated Education,* 1972, **10,** 54-63.

Chesler, M., and Segal P. Southern Negroes' initial experiences and reactions in school desegregation. *Integrated Education,* 1968, **6**, 20-28.

Christie, R., and Jahoda, M. (Eds.). *Studies in the scope and method of "The authoritarian personality."* New York: Free Press, 1954.

Christoffel, T. Black power and corporate capitalism. In B. Schwartz and R. Disch (Eds.), *White racism.* New York: Dell, 1970.

Clark, K. *Dark ghetto.* New York: Harper & Row, 1965.

Coleman, J. The concept of equality of educational opportunity. *Harvard Educational Review,* 1968, **38**, 7-23.

Cox, O. *Caste, class and race.* New York: Monthly Review Press, 1959.

Crain, R. School integration and occupational achievement of Negroes. *American Journal of Sociology,* 1969, **75**, 595.

Cuban, L. Ethnic content and white instruction. *Phi Delta Kappan,* 1972, **53**, 270-273.

Daniels, R., and Kitano, H. *American racism: Exploration of the nature of prejudice.* Englewood Cliffs, N.J.: Prentice-Hall, 1970.

DeFluer, M., and Westie, F. Verbal attitudes and overt acts. *American Sociological Review,* 1958, **23**, 667-773.

DeFriese, G., and Ford, W. Verbal attitudes, overt acts, and the influence of social constraints in interracial behavior. *Social Problems,* 1969, **16**, 493-504.

Deutsch, M., and Collins, M. *Interracial housing: A psychological evaluation of a social experiment.* Minneapolis: University of Minnesota Press, 1951.

Doob, L., and Sears, R. Factors determining subject behavior and the overt expression of aggression. *Journal of Abnormal and Social Psychology,* 1939, **34**, 293-313.

Duncan, O. D., and Duncan, B. *The Negro population of Chicago.* Chicago: University of Chicago Press, 1957.

Ellis, W., and Orleans, P. Race research: 'Up against the wall' in more ways than one. In P. Orleans and W. Ellis (Eds.), *Race, change and urban society.* Beverly Hills: Sage, 1971.

Ellison, R. An American dilemma: A review. In J. Ladner (Ed.), *The death of white sociology.* New York: Vintage Books, 1973.

Ewens, W., and Erlich, H. Reference other support and ethnic attitudes as predictors of intergroup behavior. *The Sociological Quarterly,* 1972, **13**, 348-360.

Fanon, F. *The wretched of the earth.* New York: Grove Press, 1963.

Fanon, F. *Black skin white masks: The experiences of a black man in a white world.* New York: Grove Press, 1967.

Flaming, K., Palen, J., Ringlen, G., and Taylor, C. Black powerlessness in policy making positions. *The Sociological Quarterly,* 1972, **13**, 126-133.

Fogelson, R., and Hill, R. Who riots: A study of participation in the 1967 riots. In *Supplemental studies for the National Advisory Commission on Civil Disorders.* Washington, D.C.: US Government Printing Office, 1968.

Ford, W. Interracial public housing in a border city: Another look at the contact hypothesis. *American Journal of Sociology,* 1974, **78**, 1426-1447.

Forsythe, D. Radical sociology and blacks. In J. Ladner (Ed.), *The death of white sociology.* New York: Vintage Books, 1973.

Genovese, E. *The political economy of slavery.* New York: Random House, 1956.

Genovese, E. *In red and black.* New York: Vintage Books, 1972.

Gilbert, N., and Eaton, J. Favoritism as a strategy in race relations. *Social Problems,* 1970, **18**, 38-52.

Glascow, D. Black power through community control. *Social Work,* 1972, **17**, 59-65.

Glenn, N. White gains from Negro subordination. *Social Problems,* 1966, **14**, 159-179.

Glenn, N., and Weiner, D. Some trends in the social origins of American sociologists. *The American Sociologist,* 1969, **4**, 291-302.

Gordon, E., Characteristics of small, disadvantaged children. *Review of Educational Research,* 1965, **35**, 377-388.

Gouldner, A. *The coming crisis of western sociology.* New York: Avon, 1970.

Green, R. (Ed.). *Racial crisis in American education.* Chicago: Follette, 1969.

Gurr, T. Urban disorders: Perspectives from the comparative study of civil strife. In L. Massoti and D. Bowen (Eds.), *Riots and rebellion: Civil violence in the urban community.* Beverly Hills: Sage, 1968.

Hamilton, C. Black social scientists: Contributions and problems. In J. Ladner (Ed.), *The death of white sociology.* New York: Vintage Books, 1973.

Handlin, O. *Race and nationality in American life.* New York: Doubleday-Anchor, 1951.

*Harvard Educational Review,* 1969a, **39**, 3.

*Harvard Educational Review,* 196b, **39**, 2.

Heller, C. *Mexican-American youth: Forgotten youth at the crossroads.* New York: Random House, 1966.

Hermalin, A., and Farley, R. The potential for residential integration in cities and suburbs: Implications for the bussing controversy. *American Sociological Review,* 1973, **38**, 595-610.

Hill, H. The racial practices of organized labor. In B. Schwartz and R. Disch (Eds.), *White racism.* New York: Dell, 1970.

Horton, J. Order and conflict theories of social problems as competing ideologies. *American Journal of Sociology,* 1966, **71**, 701-713.

Hughes, E. Race relations and the sociological imagination. *American Sociological Review,* 1963, **28**, 879-890.

Hyman, H. Social psychology and race relations. In I. Katz and P. Gurin (Eds.), *Race and the social sciences.* New York: Basic Books, 1969.

Jeffries, V., and Ransford, E. Interracial social contact and middle class white reactions to the Watts riot. *Social Problems,* 1969, **16**, 312-324.

Jensen, A. How much can we boost IQ and scholastic achievement? *Harvard Educational Review,* 1969, **39**, 1-123.

Johnson, P., Sears, D., and McConahay, J. Black invisibility, the press, and the Los Angeles riot. *American Journal of Sociology,* 1971, **76**, 698-722.

Jordan, W. *White over black: American attitudes toward the Negro, 1550-1812.* Chapel Hill: University of North Carolina Press, 1968.

Katz, I. Review of evidence relating to effects of desegregation on the intellectual performancy of Negroes. *American Psychologist,* 1964, **19**, 381-399.

Katznelson, I. Power in the reformulation of race research. In P. Orleans and W. Ellis (Eds.), *Race, change and urban society.* Beverly Hills: Sage, 1971.

Knowles, L., and Prewitt, K. (Eds.). *Institutional racism in America.* Englewood Cliffs, N.J.: Prentice-Hall, 1969.

Kovel, J. *White racism: A psychohistory.* New York: Pantheon, 1970.

Lacy, D. *The white use of blacks in America.* New York: McGraw-Hill, 1972.

Ledvinka, J. Race of interviewer and the language elaboration of black interviewees. *Journal of Social Issues,* 1971, **27**,155-197.

Lenski, G., and Leggett, J. Caste, class and reference in the research interview. *American Journal of Sociology,* 1960, **65**, 463-467.

Lohman, J., and Reitzer, D. Note on race relations in mass society. *American Journal of Sociology,* 1952, **58**, 240-246.

Lyman, S. *The black American in sociological thought.* New York: Capricorn, 1973.

McCarthy, J., and Yancey, W. Uncle Tom and Mr. Charlie: Metaphysical pathos in the study of racism and personal disorganization. *American Journal of Sociology,* 1971, **76**, 648-672.

Memmi, A. *The colonizer and the colonized.* Boston: Beacon Press, 1967.

Mercer, J. Institutionalized anglocentrism: Labelling mental retardates in the public schools. In P. Orleans and W. Ellis (Eds.), *Race, change and urban society.* Beverly Hills: Sage, 1971.

Merton, R. Discrimination and the American creed. In R. MacIver (Ed.), *Discrimination and national welfare.* New York: Harper, 1949.

Merton, R. Insiders and outsiders: A chapter in the sociology of knowledge. In *Varieties of Political Expression in Sociology.* Chicago: University of Chicago Press, 1972.

Metzger, L. American sociology and black assimilation: Conflicting perspectives. *American Journal of Sociology,* 1971, 627-647.

Mills, C.W. The professional ideology of social pathologists. *American Journal of Sociology,* 1943, **49**, 165-180.

Molotch, H. Racial change in a stable community. *American Journal of Sociology,* 1969, **75**, 226-239.

Molotch, H. *Managed integration: Dilemmas of doing good in the city.* Berkeley: University of California Press, 1972.

Monteil, M. The social science myth of the Mexican-American family. *El Grito,* 1970, **3**, 56-63.

Moore, J. Colonialism: The case of Mexican-Americans. *Social Problems,* 1970, **17**, 463-472.

Myrdal, G. *An American dilemma. The Negro problem and modern democracy.* New York: Harper Torchbooks, 1962.

National Advisory Commission on Civil Disorders. *Report of the National Advisory Commission on Civil Disorders.* New York: Bartam, 1968.

Ofari, E. *The myth of black capitalism.* New York: Monthly Review Press, 1970.

Ortega, P. Montezuma's Children. *El Grito,* 1970, **3**, 38-50.

Padilla, R. A critique of Pittian history. *El Grito,* 1972, **6**, 3-44.

Parsons, T. Full citizenship for the Negro American? A sociological problem. *Daedalus,* Fall 1965, 1009-1054.

Passow, H. Ed.). *Education in depressed areas.* New York: Teachers College Press, 1967.

Pettigrew, T. Regional differences in anti-Negro prejudice. *Journal of Abnormal and Social Psychology, 1959,* **59** 28-36.

Pettigrew, T. *A profile of the Negro American.* Princeton, N.J.: Van Nostrand, 1964.

Pettigrew, T. Complexity and change in American racial patterns: A social psychological view. *Daedalus,* Fall, 1965, 974-1008.

Pettigrew, T. The Negro and education: Problems and proposals. In I. Katz and P. Gurin (Eds.), *Race and the social sciences.* New York: Basic Books, 1969.

Prothro, E. Anti-Negro attitudes in the deep South. *Journal of Abnormal and Social Psychology,* 1952, **47**, 105-108.

Raab, E., and Lipset, S. The prejudiced society. In E. Raab (Ed.), *American race relations today.* New York: Doubleday-Anchor, 1962.

*Racial isolation in the public schools.* Washington, D.C.: US Government Printing Office, 1967.

Rainwater, L. Crucible of identity: The Negro lower class family. *Daedalus: The Negro American,* Winter, 1966, 172-216.

Rainwater, L., and Pittman, D. Ethical problems in studying a politically sensitive and deviant community. *Social Problems,* 1967, **14**, 357-365.

Rainwater, L., and Yancey, W. *The Moynihan report and the politics of controversy,* Cambridge, Mass.: MIT Press, 1967.

Ransford, E. Isolation, powerlessness and violence: A study of attitudes and participation in the Watts riot. *American Journal of Sociology,* 1968, **73**, 581-591.

Ransford, E. Blue collar anger: Reactions to student and black protest. *American Sociological Review,* 1972, **37**, 333-346.

Reich, M. Economic theories of racism. In M. Carnoy (Ed.), *Schooling in a corporate society.* New York: McKay, 1972.

Riessman, F. *The culturally deprived child.* New York: Harper & Row, 1962.

Rokeach, M., and Mezei, L. Race and shared belief as factors in social choice. *Science,* 1966, **151**, 167-172.

Roof, C. Residential segregation of blacks and racial inequality in southern cities: Toward a causal model. *Social Problems,* 1972, **19**, 393-407.

Rosenthal, R., and Jacobsen, L. *Pygmalion in the classroom.* New York: Holt, Rinehart and Winston, 1968.

Ryan, W. *Blaming the victim.* New York: Pantheon, 1971.

Schuman, H. Sociological racism. *Trans-Action,* 1969, 7, 44-48.

Schwartz, B., and Disch, R. (Eds.). *White racism.* New York: Dell, 1970.

Sherif, M., and Sherif, C. *Groups in harmony and tension: An integration of studies in intergroup relations.* New York: Harper, 1953.

Sizemore, B. Social science and education for a black identity. In J. Banks and J. Grambs (Eds.), *Black self-concept.* New York: McGraw-Hill, 1972.

Stein, A. Strategies of failure. *Harvard Educational Review,* 1971, **41**, 158-205.

Tabb, W. Race relations models and social change. *Social Problems,* 1971, **18**, 431-443.

Tauber, K. Negro population and housing: Demographic aspects of a social accounting scheme. In I. Katz and P. Gurin (Eds.), *Race and the social sciences*. New York: Basic Books, 1969.

Tauber, K., and Tauber, A. *Negroes in cities*. Chicago: Aldine, 1965.

Ten Houten, D. The black family: Myth and reality. *Psychiatry,* 1970, **33**, 145-173.

Thomas, C. Introduction. In C. Thomas (Ed.), *Boys no more: A black psychologist's view of community*. Beverly Hills: Glencoe Press, 1971.

Tobin, J. On improving the economic status of the Negro. *Daedalus,* Fall 1965, 878-898.

Tomlinson, T. The development of a riot ideology among urban Negroes. *American Behavioral Science,* 1968, **11**, 27-31.

Tumin, M. Introduction. In M. Tumin (Ed.), *Comparative perspectives on race relations*. Boston: Little, Brown, 1967.

Vaca, N. The Mexican-American in the social sciences, 1912-1970: Part II—1936-1970. *El Grito,* 1971, **4**, 17-50.

Valentine, C. Culture and poverty. Chicago: University of Chicago Press, 1969.

Valentine, C. Deficit, difference and bicultural models of Afro-American behavior. *Harvard Educational Review,* 1971, s,41, 137-157.

van den Berghe, P. *Race and racism: A comparative perspective*. New York: Wiley, 1967.

Vanneman, R., and Pettigrew, T. Race and relative deprivation in the urban U.S. *Race,* 1972, **13**, 461-487.

Warner, L., and Dennis, R. Prejudice vs. discrimination: An empirical example and theoretical extension. *Socail Forces.* 1970, **48**, 473-484.

Warren, D. Suburban isolation and race tension: The Detroit case. *Social Problems,* 1970, **17**, 324-340.

Welsing, F. *The Cress theory of color-confrontation and racism (white supremacy)*. Washington, 1970.

Westie, F. Race and ethnic relations. In R. Faris (Ed.), *Handbook of modern sociology*. Chicago: Rand McNally, 1964.

Whitehead, C., and King, A. Differences in managers' attitudes toward Mexican and non-Mexican Americans in organizational authority relations. *Social Science Quarterly,* 1973, **53**, 760-771.

Willhelm, S. *Who needs the Negro*. New York: Anchor, N.J.: 1971.

Williams, R. *Strangers next door*. Englewood Cliffs, N.J.: Prentice-Hall, 1964.

Wilson, C. Racism in education. In B. Schwartz and R. Disch (Eds.), *White racism*. New York: Dell, 1970.

Yancey, W., Rigsby, L., and McCarthy, J. Social position and self-evaluation: The relative importance of race. *American Journal of Sociology,* 1972, **78**, 338-360.

# 3

# *Psychological Approaches to Understanding Intergroup Conflicts*

RICHARD D. ASHMORE and FRANCES K. DEL BOCA

Race relations have long been of interest to psychologists, particularly social psychologists. During the 1930s and early 1940s, most research attention was directed at measuring anti-Negro prejudice and its demographic correlates. The period from approximately the end of World War II until the 1954 Supreme Court ruling on school segregation was marked by a large number of studies concentrating on the prejudiced individual—how he got that way and what could be done to make him change. The late 1950s and 1960s witnessed a significant decline in research on prejudice.[1] During the mid-1960s, psychologists interested in black-white relations shifted their attention to the prejudiced-against individual and his environment and produced a considerable body of research on minority group aspirations, achievements, and adjustment (e.g., Deutsch, Katz, and Jensen, 1968). Over the past three or four years there has been a small but significant return to research on the prejudiced individual.

This chapter is concerned with the prejudiced individual. Our basic goal is to critically summarize psychological research and theory on how negative intergroup attitudes and behavior are developed and maintained. Two points should be kept in mind about this "summary." First, our attention will focus primarily, though not exclusively, on the anti-black attitudes of white Americans. Thus, generalization to other groups within the United States and particularly to different societies, must be made with caution. Second, and more important, we have definite preferences ("prejudices"?) for and against various explanations of prejudice and these preferences certainly color our interpretation and evaluation of the extant data. This interpretive bias could have been minimized by presenting all theories and empirical studies on an "equal time" basis. However, we feel that an approach that simply reviews the

---

[1] There were, of course, exceptions to this generalization, the most prominent were the work on conformity and prejudice (e.g., Pettigrew, 1958), the scapegoat theory of prejudice (e.g., Weatherley, 1961), the self-insight method of prejudice reduction (e.g., Katz, Sarnoff, and McClintock, 1956), and—most significant of all in terms of the number of studies—the race vs. belief prejudice controversy stimulated by Rokeach, Smith, and Evans (1960).

"facts" merely pays lip service to the notion that prejudice is multiply determined, and it perpetuates the continuation of research and theory that examines potential individual causes of prejudice in an isolated fashion rather than considering seriously the interactions among such causal factors. Thus, we will be clearly evaluative in reviewing the research literature. Where our interpretation of the data conflicts with others, we will reference these alternative views and attempt to suggest research strategies that will clarify conflicting interpretations.

The major concept in psychological approaches to intergroup relations is "prejudice," which we define as "a negative attitude toward a socially-defined group and toward any person perceived to be a member of that group" (Ashmore, 1970, p. 253). Psychologists don't study this internal, mediating variable for its own sake but because they feel that it helps to account for negative intergroup behavior. A number of social scientists (e.g., Deutscher, 1966) have argued that the study of prejudice is not a good way to understand intergroup behavior and have cited research indicating a lack of correspondence between racial attitudes and racial discrimination (for a recent summary, see Wicker, 1969). Although this is not the place to get into this controversy in depth, several points about the attitude approach to intergroup relations should be made clear. First, all social psychologists agree that attitudes are just one determinant of overt behavior (see, for example, Cook and Selltiz, 1964). Second, attitudes are associated with beliefs and feelings, which may imply various—and in some cases contradictory—behaviors (e.g., a prejudiced white might be angered by and yet fearful of blacks), and a particular stimulus person may engage several different attitudes (e.g., a young black, male college student wearing a *dashiki* may engage not only racial attitudes but also attitudes toward college students and attitudes toward those who wear unconventional clothes). Finally, the empirical evidence against a link between attitudes and behavior is not as strong as is often thought (see Collins, 1970, pp. 79-87; Dillehay, 1973). Rather than advocating the abandonment of the study of prejudice, we urge more precise conceptualization of the variables relevant to the attitude approach, while at the same time acknowledging the importance of other approaches to understanding hostile intergroup relations.

We begin our psychological analysis of negative intergroup relations by distinguishing two levels used to explain hostile individual attitudes and behavior: societal and individual. Societal-level explanations of prejudice delineate how the attitudes of individuals are shaped by the nature of relations between groups, or, more generally, how norms of prejudice develop within a society or community. Individual-level explanations are concerned with how an individual living in a particular culture acquires prejudice and when this prejudice is acted out. Most psychological research has been on individual-level explanations. The research conducted in the late 1940s and early 1950s (and continued on a limited basis thereafter) provides us with a set of "principles" that we will discuss under the rubric "Individual-Level Explanations of Prejudice." The recent renaissance in race relations research has yielded a number of suggestive findings that have not yet been fully tested, thus we consider them under the heading "New Directions in the Psychology of Prejudice." The final section of this chapter will summarize the present state of knowledge regarding prejudice and will provide some suggestions for future research and theory.

## SOCIETAL-LEVEL EXPLANATIONS OF PREJUDICE

Except for a small number of hermits, living in groups (families, neighborhoods, nations) is a significant fact of life for humans. Societal-level explanations seek to account for how properties of relationships between groups shape the attitudes of the individuals comprising these groups.[2] Two major societal-level explanations have been offered for the anti-black prejudice of whites. One views prejudice as a justification for exploitation; the other sees it as the result of negative intergroup interdependence.

Cox (1948), the most noted proponent of the exploitation theory, feels that, "Race prejudice is a social attitude propagated among the public by an exploiting class for the purpose of stigmatizing some group as inferior so that the exploitation of either the group itself or its resources may both be justified" (p. 393). While Cox focuses on economic exploitation, other observers have traced racist attitudes to sexual exploitation as well (e.g., Dollard, 1937). There is little direct evidence supporting the exploitation theory premise that conscious propagation of racism by elites is a significant determinant of individual attitudes. This is not to say that political and business leaders do not, in many instances, use intergroup conflicts to further their own ends, thus serving to perpetuate such conflicts (McWilliams, 1944; Secord and Backman, 1964, p. 421).

A second societal-level theory explains prejudice in terms of negative relationships between social groups. In its most general form this explanation can be stated as follows: both the direction and general content of intergroup attitudes are determined by the nature of intergroup interdependence. (For related formulations, see Sherif, 1951; Bernard, 1957, p. 38; Boulding, 1962; Secord and Backman, 1964, p. 413; Campbell, 1965, p. 288; Ehrlich, 1973.) Positive intergroup interdependence (e.g., allies in wartime) promotes favorable intergroup attitudes, while negative intergroup interdependence leads to hostile

[2] This is not to say that all societal- or group-level variables that influence race relations are mediated by individual behavior and attitudes. Of particular importance is "institutional racism"—the built-in discrimination in industry hiring practices, housing for the poor, etc. (Knowles and Prewitt, 1969, especially pp. 134-176). Thus, the special methods and insights of nonindividual-level disciplines are necessary for fully understanding and alleviating black-white conflict.

intergroup attitudes such as prejudice. This generalization, particularly that aspect dealing with the effects of negative interdependence, has been supported by a large body of historical, sociological-anthropological, and psychological research (see Ashmore, 1970, pp. 258-263, for a review) and consequently is the most solid "principle" of the psychology of prejudice.

While we know that prejudice develops out of negative intergroup interdependence, we need a more precise knowledge of the nature of negative interdependence in order to explain the beliefs and feelings accompanying prejudice. In his anthropological-historical analysis of black-white relations in Brazil, Mexico, South Africa, and the United States, Pierre van den Berghe (1967) identified two major stages of interdependence: paternalism and competition.[3] In the paternalistic stage, blacks were enslaved and an exaggerated dominant-subordinate interdependence existed. The image of blacks most congruent with this relationship was that of the child (an inferior form of adult human), a person who needed to be enslaved because he couldn't take care of himself. In the competitive stage, which van den Berghe feels began shortly after the Civil War, blacks and whites compete for economic and political power. This competition produces images of blacks as threatening and aggressive.

*As applied to the US*, the van den Berghe model is a good start, but it oversimplifies the nature of black-white interdependence both before and, particularly, after the Civil War. (It is important to note that we do not disagree with van den Berghe's history of black-white relations in the United States, only his interpretation in terms of "types," which we feel tends to obscure some important "within-type" differences.) Although the relationship between blacks and whites during the slavery period was largely one of dominance and subordinance, there were a strikingly large number of slave revolts and other aggressive actions by blacks (see Aptheker, 1969), which created, at least for a short time and in a limited area, a conflict or competitive relationship. Such flare-ups help us to understand why the image of blacks as threatening and forceful could exist though certainly not predominate during this period (Boskin, 1970).

A more significant problem with the van den Berghe formulation is the oversimplification of the period after the Civil War. The Thirteenth Amendment and the Civil Rights Act of 1866 brought about a formal end to white dominance; in some Southern states there was open black-white competition for economic and political power. This competitive relationship, however, was abridged through Jim Crow laws, the exploitation of sharecroppers, and intimidation by the Ku Klux Klan. While theoretically blacks and whites were in open competition, by 1890 whites had regained a clearly dominant position

---

[3]More precisely, he identified two "ideal types" of negative black-white interdependence. Since, however, the paternalistic type preceded the competitive type in all cases studied, we will use the term "stage."

in practice. This state of competition is quite different from open competition, and we feel that it should be seen as a distinctive stage in the history of black-white relations in the US. (van den Berghe, on the other hand, includes this time period in the competitive stage and would probably distinguish it from the Reconstruction period and the 1960s in terms of "social control" variables that regulate intergroup interaction.)

This state of defused competition allowed the paternalistic image of blacks to continue well into the middle of the present century. In the late 1950s, however, blacks began to challenge the racial status quo. During the Civil Rights years—roughly bounded by the Montgomery, Alabama, bus boycott of 1955 and the Watts riot of 1965—black strategy concentrated on ending the *dejure* discriminatory practices of many Southern communities through the use of nonviolent protest. Such goals and methods were not a threat to most white Americans (although Southerners were quite angered and responded with much resistance). However, the urban riots of 1964 to 1967, and the rise to prominence of the term "black power," ushered in a stage of open black-white competition on a national scale. The black demands for equal power and shared decision making were clear threats (either directly or indirectly) to a large number of whites. Although the open, large-scale violence of the mid-to-late-1960s is no longer in evidence, blacks and whites continue in a competitive relationship. This new stage of black-white relations has had a significant impact on white attitudes toward and beliefs about blacks. These changes will be discussed in depth in the section on "New Directions in the Psychology of Prejudice."

## INDIVIDUAL-LEVEL EXPLANATIONS OF PREJUDICE

In order to facilitate our discussion of how individuals acquire prejudice, we distinguish two general classes of explanations—those stressing intraperson factors and those based on interpersonal relations. While recognizing that individuals never function in a social vacuum, proponents of the former view feel that prejudice can, in part, be explained by basic cognitive, motivational, or personality processes. By far the most prominent psychological explanations of prejudice have been in terms of personality variables, and most of these have been stimulated by Freudian psychoanalytic theory. These explanations, discussed below under the heading "symptom theories," are united by the assumption that prejudice can ultimately be traced to some intrapsychic or personality conflict. Other psychologists, while agreeing that prejudice has significant intrapersonal roots, disagree with the psychoanalytic flavor of the symptom theories. These psychologists account for prejudice in terms of either self-concept, basic cognitive processes, or cognitive consistency motivation; a section is devoted to each of these below.

There is yet another group of psychologists that also rejects the symptom theory approach. Instead of calling on basic psychological processes of cognition or motivation, they focus on interpersonal factors in accounting for prejudice. Such explanations assume that prejudice is acquired in much the same way as other attitudes—that it is learned through interaction with the social environment.

### Intrapersonal factors in prejudice acquisition. I: Personality processes

*Symptom theories of prejudice.* A key aspect of Freudian psycho-analytic theory is the assumption of complete intrapsychic determinism (Rapaport, 1959). That is, all behavior can ultimately be traced to intrapsychic conflicts between the id, ego, and superego. In this view, the behavioral predisposition of prejudice can be seen as an indicator or symptom of underlying personality conflict. Three major symptom theories of prejudice have been advanced. The first two to be discussed—projection and displacement—account for prejudice in terms of a single Freudian defense mechanism, while the final one—the "authoritarian personality"—is a fuller theory that actually subsumes the previous two.

Although there are three identifiable forms of projection (Allport, 1958, Chapter 24), only direct projection has received much attention from psycho-analytic writers concerned with explaining prejudice. In direct projection, an individual protects himself from an anxiety-arousing id or ego impulse by saying *"I don't* have those feelings (or desires), *they do."* The most common projection theory of anti-black prejudice is that whites, who see sex as evil, project their natural yet tabooed sexual drives onto blacks (Halsey, 1946; McLean, 1946; Seidenberg, 1952).[4] Once blacks are seen as sexually uninhibited and insatiable, they are justifiable targets for scorn and degradation.

Unfortunately, there is very little research dealing with the projection theory. Projection of sexuality by the English who first contacted Africans may have been one basis for their initial anti-black prejudice (Jordan, 1968, pp. 32-40). Also the sexual exploitation of black females during slavery seems to have contributed to the image of the "rapin' Nigger" (Nash, 1970, p. 20). Though projection may have played some role in the original development of anti-black prejudice in this country, there is little evidence that it continues to be an important factor in shaping white attitudes toward blacks. In the only methodologically adequate investigation, Pompilo (1957) found no support for a link between projection and prejudice.

---

[4] Bettelheim and Janowitz (1950) provide a similar but more elaborate projection theory of anti-minority prejudice. Also, Pinderhughes (1971) and Wadeson (1971) have recently offered different projection theories of white racism; the first is based on self-hatred, while in the second, projection serves to maintain in-group solidarity. Neither of these latter explanations has stimulated any systematic empirical research.

The defense mechanism of displacement has also been employed to account for the acquistion of ethnic prejudice. The displacement explanation (popularly known as "the scapegoat theory") goes something like this: (a) growing up in society of necessity involves some frustration (i.e., social organization requires the curbing or delaying of id instincts); (b) this frustration often cannot be expressed against the actual frustrators because they are bigger and might retaliate (e.g., parents), or the actual frustrator can't be identified (e.g., social norms embodied in such parental prouncements as "Nice little boys don't do that."); (c) the aggressive feelings against the actual frustrator are repressed, thus creating a pool of "free-floating aggression"; and (d) the anxiety aroused by the frustration and the repression of affect is partially relieved by displacing it onto an out-group in the form of prejudice.

The research findings generated by this formulation yield a confusing picture. On the positive side, there is evidence of a correlation between various indices of self-reported dissatisfaction with one's condition in life (which presumably indicates "free-floating aggression" due to frustration) and ethnic prejudice (Gordon, 1943; Allport and Kramer, 1946; Campbell, 1947; Rosenblith, 1949). A number of studies have indicated that people who experience downward social mobility are higher in prejudice than those who move up or are stable in social status (for a review see Bettelheim and Janowitz, 1964, pp. 29-34). Parents of high prejudiced children are more likely to report using harsh, punitive discipline than parents of children scoring very low in out-group hostility (Frenkel-Brunswik, 1948; Harris, Gough, and Martin, 1950).

There are, however, a number of negative findings. Though they are most often discriminated against (which we assume is frustrating), Jews are lower in anti-black prejudice than Protestants or Catholics (Allport and Karmer, 1946). Morse and Allport (1952) found no consistent pattern of correlations between self-reported feelings of frustration and measures of anti-Semitism. Although the studies reviewed by Bettelheim and Janowitz support the proposition that downward social mobility increases prejudice, the only relevant national survey does not (see Sears, 1969, pp. 405-406). And, mothers of highly prejudiced children were not less permissive (amount of child aggression allowed) than mothers of high tolerant children (Harris et al., 1950). Finally, children who were highest in prejudice reported that their parents used intermediate not high levels of punitiveness (Epstein and Komorita, 1965a, 1965b, 1966).

The scapegoat theory of prejudice acquisition is further undermined by the fact that all of the supportive research cited above is correlational, and in none of the studies were efforts made to rule out alternative explanations. This is particularly important in the studies demonstrating a correlation between parental punitiveness and child prejudice; child prejudice may not be caused by the parental punitiveness. Parental punitiveness and parental prejudice are also correlated, as are parental prejudice and child prejudice.

This suggests that child prejudice may be caused by parental attitudes rather than punitiveness.

While there is only scant evidence that frustration is a significant cause of the development of prejudice, there is a great deal of support for the notion that frustration, together with societal norms, determines when prejudice will be acted out. Experimental induction of frustration has been found to increase ethnic prejudice (Miller and Bugelski, 1948; Feshbach and Singer, 1957; Cowen, Landes, and Schaet, 1958), although there is at least one failure to replicate (Stagner and Congdon, 1955).[5] Correlational studies using aggregate data provide additional support. Hovland and Sears (1940) obtained a correlation of -.6 between the annual per-acre value of cotton and number of lynchings per year in the South for the period from 1832 to 1930. (Using a more appropriate statistical procedure, Mintz [1946] found the correlation to be -.3.) Raper (1933) computed the equivalent correlation for the period 1900 to 1930 and obtained a -.5 correlation. These correlations suggest that it is during hard times that anti-black feelings are most likely to be acted out, in this case in the form of murder. Frustration can also evoke other kinds of anti-black behavior. The economically depressed regions of the South are more likely to vote for strongly pro-segregationist politicians than areas that are better-off (Pettigrew and Cramer, 1959).[6]

Frustration helps in predicting when prejudice will be acted out, but social norms are involved in this process in two important ways. First, norms specify what types of aggressive behavior are allowed. Brazil has a large black population and certainly has as much economic frustration as the United States, yet no lynchings of blacks are reported (Klineberg, 1950). Second, and even more significant, social norms dictate which group is to be the scapegoat. The displacement theory does not specify which group will become the object for displaced aggression, only that it should be visible and relatively defenseless (Zawadski, 1948). Social norms perform this specification function— scapegoats are groups against which prejudice is felt and this prejudice is

[5] There have also been a number of studies concerned with individual differences in hostility displacement. Lesser (1958) obtained a significant correlation between prejudice and a measure of extra-punitiveness, and Genthner and Taylor (1973) found anti-black attitudes correlated with the Buss-Durkee Hostility Inventory. Also, in experimental settings high-prejudice subjects show more displacement of hostility under frustrating conditions than do low-prejudice subjects. Unfortunately two points cloud the picture: (1) In only one study (Weatherley, 1961) was this displacement specific to a minority-group target, while in two others (Berkowitz, 1959; Genthner and Taylor, 1973) there was no target specificity. (2) In the Weatherley study, the difference between high- and low-prejudice subjects was due to low-prejudice subjects decreasing in hostility under frustration, not to increases by high-prejudice subjects.

[6] There are, however, alternative explanations for this correlation. The economically retarded areas, for example, tended to have higher proportions of blacks and the voting for pro-segregation candidates may have resulted from whites' perception of economic and political threat.

acquired through socialization. A laboratory experiment supports this idea that displacement is determined not only by frustration but also by learned attitudes toward the potential target. Berkowitz and Green (1962) found that following a frustrating experience subjects displaced aggression more often onto a target whom they had earlier been led to dislike than onto a neutral target.

The single most influential work on the psychology of prejudice is *The Authoritarian Personality* (Adorno, Frenkel-Brunswik, Levinson, and Sanford, 1950), which offers a rather full theory of prejudice acquisition together with a large amount of supporting research. The authoritarian personality theory can be summed up in three assertions: (a) intergroup attitudes are part of ideologies (organized systems of beliefs, attitudes, and values); (b) ideologies are determined by "deep-lying trends in personality"; and (c) the personality sources of ideologies (and, by implication, of prejudice) are the result of parental child-rearing practices. (For a complete discussion of the nature of the psychodynamic mechanisms implicated in the formation of prejudice see Adorno *et al.*, 1950, pp. 385-389.)

Adorno and his co-workers began by developing self-report measures of their central theoretical constructs. The Political and Economic Conservatism (PEC) scale assessed degree of attachment to the US political and economic status quo (e.g., *laissez faire* economics). The Ethnocentrism (E) scale measured a generalized rejection of seven ethnic groups, while the Anti-Semitism (A-S) scale was concerned with prejudice against Jews. Finally, the Implicit Anti-Democratic Trends (F) scale was designed to capture the meaning of the personality syndrome that was presumed to underlie prejudice. More specifically, it was theorized that the authoritarian personality syndrome is comprised of nine central variables: Conventionalism, Authoritarian Submission, Authoritarian Aggression, Anti-intraception, Superstition and stereotypy, Power and "toughness", Destructiveness and cynicism, Projectivity, and (exaggerated concern with) Sex.

Over 2000 people responded to the various forms of these scales and the correlations obtained provided some support for the first two parts of the theory. All of the scales were significantly intercorrelated. That is, those who scored high on the PEC also tended to score high on the E, A-S, and F scales, thus indicating that general ideological conservatism, ethnocentrism, anti-Semitism, and the authoritarian personality syndrome go together. (This research did not however provide a direct test of the psychodynamic mechanisms that presumably underlie the personality syndrome.) The third tenet of the theory was supported by interviews[7] with a sample of very high and very

---

[7] The interviews also provided additional support on the second proposition since the highly ethnocentric subjects differed from the low scorers in several aspects of personality functioning. The high scorers more often repressed and externalized conflict, they were more concerned with status (rather than personal qualities) in relationships, they were more dependent on group norms, and they were high in cognitive inflexibility.

low scorers on the E scale. The highly ethnocentric respondents more often reported that their parents used harsh, arbitrary discipline, defined parent-child roles clearly as dominant and subordinate, and required strict adherence to conventional middle-class values and mores.

Although *The Authoritarian Personality* is an impressive work, it suffers from a number of methodological flaws. These flaws have been discussed elsewhere (Christie and Jahoda, 1954); here we will mention only three of the major problems. First, all E and F scale items were positively keyed (i.e., an agree response indicated greater ethnocentrism and greater authoritarianism), thus both are contaminated by "acquiescence response set" (Kirscht and Dillehay, 1967, pp. 13-29). Second, while the F scale items were originally written to tap the various hypothesized components of the authoritarian personality, items were retained or discarded during the item-refinement stage on the basis of their ability to discriminate high and low scorers on the E scale (Hyman and Sheatsley, 1954). The authors did this in order to make the F scale both a measure of personality authoritarianism and a disguised measure of prejudice. Unfortunately, their scale construction strategy made it a poor measure of both. And third, interviewers were aware of the prejudice level of the people they interviewed and were allowed a great deal of freedom in asking questions. Such a procedure would seem to maximize the possibility of interviewer bias in the direction of the hypothesis.

*The Authoritarian Personality* stimulated a vast quantity of research; some facets of this personality theory of prejudice have been clarified by this research, while in other cases it has simply made the overall picture more confusing. First, the role of parental child-rearing practices in predisposing one toward authoritarianism and prejudice is still unclear. (Other reviewers have tended to regard the relationship between parental child-rearing practices and prejudice as more firmly established—e.g., Harding, Proshansky, Kutner, and Chein, 1969, p. 39.) As noted above, high ethnocentric children differ from very tolerant children in being more likely to have parents who use harsh discipline; Lyle and Levitt (1955) obtained this result even when the effects of IQ were partialed out. The parents of prejudiced children, however, are no less permissive than those of relatively more tolerant children (Harris *et al.*, 1950). Also, McCord, McCord, and Howard (1960) found no correlation between any of 11 family background variables (which included aggression, disciplinary techniques, consistency of discipline, dominance) and ethnic prejudice in a lower-class sample. Similar negative results were obtained with a college student sample (Richert, 1963) and an upper-middle-class sample of mothers and their children (Mosher and Scodel, 1960). Another group of studies suggested a link between parental domineering behavior and child prejudice but produced equivocal evidence regarding the possible effects of parental possessiveness and ignoring behavior (Kates and Diab, 1955; Dickens and Hobart, 1959). Probably the best summary for this research is to say that harsh parental discipline and dominance may predispose children to be prejudiced, but that the weakness and inconsistency of the relationship suggests that it depends on a number of other variables (e.g., parental prejudice, community norms).[8] The relationship between prejudice and other child-rearing practices must at this point be regarded as unsupported.

Second, the personality traits comprising the authoritarian personality syndrome have been somewhat clarified, although the accumulated research evidence requires considerable revision of the initial theory. The notion of an authoritarian personality *syndrome* composed of nine coherent and unified dispositions is questionable in light of the extant data (Kirscht and Dillehay, 1967). Cognitive rigidity seems to be a significant part of authoritarianism, though again the research results are inconsistent enough to warrant searching for interactions with other variables (see Kirscht and Dillehay, 1967, pp. 42-46; Ehrlich, 1973, pp. 143-146). Generalized hostility and distrust are significant components of authoritarianism (Martin, 1964, pp. 52-63), but the evidence suggesting a personality type that has a negative attitude toward mankind and rejects all out-groups has been vastly overplayed (see Ehrlich, 1973, pp. 128-130). In addition, it has been clearly demonstrated that social and situational factors influence variations in prejudice (Simpson and Yinger, 1965). A number of studies have shown that social class and education are negatively correlated with prejudice, and, in fact, these variables have been offered as alternative explanations to account for prejudice (for a review, see Kirscht and Dillehay, 1967, pp. 37-41). Thus, the authoritarian personality is hostile and distrusting, but whether he will be prejudiced against one specific group or many groups depends on a number of factors beyond his personality structure.

Finally, the Freudian interpretation of the authoritarian personality and prejudice is open to many counterexplanations. Much research indicates that the F scale assesses American right-wing conservatism (Christie, 1954; Shils, 1954; McClosky, 1958).[9] Other work indicates that such conservatism is part of a cultural configuration that often involves anti-minority attitudes (Sears, 1969, pp. 399-414). Thus, it may be that authoritariansim and prejudice are independently passed on from parent to child, and not that prejudice is a

[8] Also, it seems that harsh parental discipline may be most important in producing extreme bigots (i.e., those who hate all out-groups) but less important for the development of less extreme negative attitudes. The major research supporting the connection between prejudice and harsh parental discipline involved comparisons between children who scored extremely high or extremely low on the E scale, which measures generalized anti-minority attitudes (Frenkel-Brunswik, 1948; Adorno *et al.*, 1950; Harris *et al.*, 1950).

[9] Rokeach (1960) developed a measure of "dogmatism" that assesses the personality predisposition to prejudice independent of right-left ideology. Although the Dogmatism scale does correlate with ethnic prejudice, interpretation of this correlation is made ambiguous by two qualities it shares with the F scale: (1) It is composed of items tapping a number of different personality "traits" (i.e., dogmatism is not a unitary construct). (2) All Dogmatism items are positively keyed, thus introducing the possible confound of acquiescence response.

secondary derivation of parental child-rearing practices that creates a personality need for prejudice (Rhyne, 1962). A related possibility is that conformity needs, which are a rather important part of authoritarianism (Lindzey, 1950; McCandless, 1961), may predispose individuals to acquire the prejudices of their culture during socialization. A final possibility is that authoritarian child-rearing practices may lead the child to have a negative self-concept, which, via generalization and the need to promote self-esteem, may cause him to dislike others and reject minority groups (Ehrlich, 1973). This possibility will be discussed in depth in the next section.

*Self-concept and intergroup attitudes.* Ehrlich (1973) has proposed an intimate link between prejudice and low self-esteem. The nature of this association is captured in his "principle of self-congruity," which states:

> The more favorable are a person's self-attitudes, the greater the number of acceptable targets and the more positive their attitudes toward them; the more negative the self-attitudes, the greater the number of unacceptable targets and the more negative are attitudes toward them. (p.130)

Ehrlich asserts that parental child-rearing practices, particularly rejection, cause the child to develop a negative self-concept (low self-acceptance), which in turn predisposes the child to negative other-attitudes and ethnic prejudice.

Parts of this formulation are well supported by the available data, while others are not. Ehrlich presents only one study (Rosenberg, 1965) to support his view that parental indifference is a primary determinant of low self-esteem. Research by Coopersmith (1967) indicates that other variables, particularly inconsistent discipline, may be more important. While Dickens and Hobart (1959) obtained a significant correlation between parental ignoring behavior and child prejudice, Kates and Diab (1955) found no correlation between authoritarianism and willingness to endorse items reflecting the ignoring variable. (These studies did not assess the presumed intervening variable of negative self-concept.) The correlation between negative self-concept and negative other-attitudes and ethnic prejudice is better documented. Ehrlich (1973, pp. 131-133) reviews a large number of studies all demonstrating a strong relationship between negative self-attitudes and rejection of others. He also cites three studies indicating a negative correlation between self-esteem and anti-black prejudice (pp. 134-135). In one of these (Tabachnik, 1962), however, the relationship was not strong—eight of the ten self-esteem measures were significantly (negatively) correlated with prejudice but the correlations were not large (ranging from -.13 to -.27). In addition to the studies discussed by Ehrlich, there is one other (Rubin, 1967) that supports his formulation. Prior to a sensitivity training session, there was a significant negative correlation between self-acceptance and anti-black prejudice (see Rubin, 1967, footnote 12). In sum, a negative self-concept does seem to predispose an individual toward ethnic prejudice, although the relationship may not be particularly strong and the exact mechanisms underlying the effect are not well known. Also, as is true of all personality factors as causes of prejudice, one must carefully evaluate possible confounds. Particularly relevant to the self-esteem/ prejudice link is the role of social class. Porter (1971) found strong social class differences in self-esteem among preschoolers, with middle-class children having more positive self-images and less anti-black prejudice than lower-class children (see Porter, 1971, p. 150, Table 20).

*Suggestions for improving research on personality processes and prejudice.* Since the publication of *The Authoritarian Personality* (Adorno, *et al.* 1950), personality-based explanations of prejudice have stimulated a voluminous quantity of research. Although many of the findings have been suggestive, much of the literature has tended to confuse rather than clarify the role of personality factors in the acquisition and maintenance of prejudice. Three factors appear to account for this. First, conceptualization of the relevant variables (independent and dependent) has been vague and imprecise, both on a literary and operational level. Different investigators have focused on variables that appear to be conceptually similar. However, a closer examination of the various methods employed to assess these constructs has made it clear that they cannot always be logically equated. For example, cognitive rigidity has been hypothesized to be an important feature of the authoritarian personality (Adorno,, *et al.*, 1950). Research has indicated, however, that it is not a unified characteristic, and it may in fact have several separate components (e.g., inability to make cognitive shifts, intolerance for ambiguity), which may relate to prejudice in different ways (Kirscht and Dillehay, 1967, pp. 42-45).

Second, theorists have frequently been unclear and incomplete in specifying how different variables are theoretically related within a conceptual framework. While *The Authoritarian Personality* provides a rather complete theory of the personality-prejudice link, most subsequent work on this topic has been restricted to demonstrating some empirical relationship (generally, a particular child-rearing practice correlates with a particular kind of personality trait or a particular personality trait correlates with a particular negative interpersonal attitude). Little attention has been devoted to placing such relationships into a larger "model" or "theory." Greater concern with conceptual questions *prior to doing research* seems essential in this field where there are many "facts" (as represented by written-up studies demonstrating some relationship), some general "models" or "theories," but no clear "principles." Third, the relationships among specific aspects of child-rearing practices, personality dispositions, and interpersonal attitudes have not been explored systematically. Research efforts have been piecemeal, focusing on single, isolated factors believed to be important in the formation of prejudice. Frequently

## Table 1. Preliminary Schema for Conceptualizing Personality-Prejudice Relationships

| Antecedent Child-Rearing Practices | Intervening Personality Variables | | Consequent Interpersonal Attitudes |
| --- | --- | --- | --- |
| | Underlying (intrapsychic) processes | Personality Dispositions | |
| Adorno et al. (1950)<br>Discipline: harsh, threatening, arbitrary, intolerant of nonconformity<br>Values: rigid, externalized, conventional, status-oriented<br>Interrelationships: dominant-subordinate, role-determined, emotionally distant | Adorno et al. (1950)<br>Structural Adaptations<br>Ego properties: narrow, circumscribed; constriction of fantasy, concreteness of thinking, undifferentiated emotional experience, extrapunitiveness<br>Superego properties: punitive, poorly internalized<br>Conflict Resolutions<br>Underlying trends (e.g., sex aggression, dependency) are rendered ego-alien<br>Countercathetic ego defenses:<br>projection<br>denial<br>reaction formation | Adorno et al. (1950)<br>Conventionalism<br>Authoritarian submission<br>Authoritarian aggression<br>Anti-intraception<br>Superstition and stereotype<br>Power and "toughness"<br>Destructiveness and cynicism<br>Projectivity<br>(exaggerated concern with) Sex | Misanthropy<br><br>Ethnocentrism<br><br>Specific prejudices<br>(e.g., anti-Semitism, misogyny, anti-black prejudice)<br>1. Strong cultural support<br>2. Weak (or no) cultural support |
| Kates and Diab (1955);<br>Dickens and Hobart (1959)<br>Dominance<br>Possessiveness<br>Ignoring | | Rokeach (1960)<br>Dogmatism<br>Subcomponents: e.g., the perception of irrelevance, beliefs regarding the uncertainty of the future (fear of future, a feeling of urgency, self-proselytization), paranoid outlook on life, authoritarianism (beliefs in positive and negative authority, belief in the cause) | |
| Lyle and Levitt (1955)<br>Punitiveness | | Ehrlich (1973)<br>Low self-esteem | |
| Ehrlich (1973)<br>Parental rejection | | McCandless (1961)<br>Conformity proneness | |
| | | Kirscht and Dillehay (1967)<br>Cognitive functions:<br>cognitive rigidity,<br>intolerance for ambiguity<br>Dogmatism and anxiety<br>Psychopathology | |
| | | Kutner (1958)<br>Rigidity<br>Overgeneralization<br>Categorizing and dichotomizing<br>Concretization<br>Simplification<br>Furcation<br>Dogmatism (omniscience)<br>Intolerance of ambiguity | |

variables such as social class and education level are given insufficient attention. The schema presented in Table 1 is proposed so that we may begin to improve research on personality processes by correcting the problems discussed above.

The major antecedent, intervening, and consequent variables that have been of interest to psychologists concerned with personality and prejudice are listed. (It should be noted that this list is not intended to be exhaustive.) Two levels of personality functioning have been distinguished: (a) deep underlying structures and processes (e.g., ego defenses) and (b) specific personality traits and cognitive tendencies (e.g., conformity proneness and cognitive rigidity), which are more directly linked to overt behavior. Different types of dependent variables are also distinguished as the various antecedent and intervening variables may be related to different types of interpersonal attitudes. Particularly important are the distinctions between global and more specific rejection of social groups and, within the latter category, between prejudices that are culturally approved and those that are not. Within this framework, we can trace the various hypothesized relationships between the different types of variables. The first entries in each column present the authoritarian personality model of prejudice. Adorno *et al.* (1950) contend that certain styles of parental behavior (e.g., harsh, threatening discipline) cause children to develop distinct personality tendencies (both underlying and surface), which produce blanket rejection of out-groups (certainly ethnocentrism and perhaps misanthropy). Nonpsychodynamic personality formulations leave column 2 completely out of Table 1. For example, Ehrlich (1973) hypothesizes that parental rejecting or ignoring behavior produces low self-esteem in the child, and this in turn results in a generalized rejection of others, thereby increasing the likelihood of ethnic prejudices. McCandless (1961), on the other hand, seeks to explain how children acquire the specific prejudices of their culture by drawing on the personality trait of conformity proneness.

The schema above suggests a two-stage empirical strategy that might untangle the relationship among the various antecedent, intervening, and consequent variables. In the first phase, social class and educational level would be held constant. A multivariate design (i.e., one that measured as many of the variables listed as realistically possible) would be employed to assess the relative importance of each of the antecedent and intervening variables and their interactions in producing the different varieties of intergroup attitudes. (The inclusion of different operationalizations of seemingly identical constructs would allow the empirical establishment of equivalence.) The data produced by this research strategy would allow us to make valid comparisons among the alternative theories. The second phase of research would involve the same multivariate design, now making contrasts among groups that differ in social class, educational level, and other related variables. A research strategy of the type outlined above would begin to clarify the manner and extent to which child-rearing practices, personality processes, and demographic variables are related, and their relative importance in the psychology of prejudice.

## Intrapersonal factors in prejudice acquisition. II: Cognitive processes

Tajfel (1969) proposes three cognitive processes—"categorization," "assimilation," and "search for coherence"—which are implicated in the formation of social attitudes. Categorization refers to those cognitive activities that shape the perception of groups of physical and social stimuli. The process of assimilation denotes the manner in which individuals are taught the relevant social values and norms that provide the content (particularly evaluations) of social categories. The search for coherence describes how individuals make attributions regarding the causes of changes in intergroup relations. The tendencies inherent in categorization are most relevant to a consideration of cognitive functioning per se, and they have been the major research interest of Tajfel and his associates. Therefore our discussion will focus on research that bears directly on this process.[10]

Categorization tendencies arise from the need to introduce simplicity to a highly varied and complex environment. (There is considerable support for this assumed need; see Hastorf, Schneider and Polefka, 1970, Chapter 1.) Tajfel makes three assertions about the important features of social categorization. First, judgments of personal traits implicitly involve comparisons along continuous dimensions. That is, an individual is perceived as having some characteristic (for example, "laziness" or "intelligence") only in relation to other people. Second, through personal and cultural experience, some traits come to be associated with certain classifications or groups of people. Thus, when individuals have little specific information concerning a given person, they will tend to ascribe to him characteristics that are derived from knowledge of some kind of class membership. Third, and most important, when a continuous dimension is related to a classification or group, differences between individuals belonging to *different* groups will tend to be exaggerated, while differences among persons within the *same* group will tend to be minimized (the "enhancement of contrast" effect).

Tajfel and Wilkes (1963) demonstrated the operation of these cognitive tendencies in an experiment on the perception of physical stimuli. They presented subjects with a series of eight lines, which varied in length by a constant ratio. In one condition, the label A was assigned to the four shorter lines in the series, and the label B to the four longer lines. In the second

---

[10]Assimilation is quite similar to the idea of the socialization of ethnic attitudes, while search for coherence is concerned with causal explanations or attributions regarding the nature of intergroup relations and the social position of groups. Both of these topics are covered below in the section on interpersonal factors.

condition, half the lines were randomly labeled A, and half B; in the third—no labels were used. Subjects were then asked to estimate the length of each of the lines in the series. Those in the first condition consistently exaggerated the differences in magnitude of the lines labeled A and B, and they tended to minimize differences between lines within the same group. These effects were not present in the other two conditions, illustrating the importance of a correlation between a dimension (in this instance, line length) and the labeling of groups.

Stereotyping behavior, which occurs when general psychological characteristics are attributed to large classes of individuals, is an important consequence of the categorization process. An early study by Secord, Bevan, and Katz (1956) demonstrated the effects of this process in racial stereotyping. Ten photographs of blacks and five of whites were used to construct a rough continuum of individuals displaying Negroid physiognomic traits. White subjects were required to rate each pictured individual on a series of personality traits and to categorize each as Negro or Caucasian. Subjects tended to assign stereotypic personality traits to all of the individuals whom they perceived as Negro. That is, assignment of a given photograph to the Negro category resulted in the attribution of the complete stereotype.[11]

Tajfel, Sheikh, and Gardner (1964) demonstrated the minimization of within-group differences in a study of stereotyping behavior in a more naturalistic setting. Canadian college students questioned two Canadians and two Indians about their views concerning films and books. After the interviews, subjects rated the four individuals on a series of descriptive scales. This set of judgments was compared with stereotyped descriptions of the two ethnic groups obtained from an independent student sample. Subjects tended to minimize differences among members of given ethnic groups but only on those traits that were stereotypic of the groups. This study suggests that this tendency is present even when subjects acquire some specific information about target individuals. (However, since little effort was made to control the content of the interviews, the results are open to the alternative explanation that the members of each ethnic group did, in fact, express rather similar views and that these views were consistent with the cultural stereotype of this group.)

A series of studies with American youngsters further supports the idea

---

[11]The photographs used in this study varied only in physiognomic characteristics. There is no a priori reason to suspect that such variations (within the range that allows respondents to classify the face as that of a Negro) should be related to personality judgments. A more demanding test of the effects of categorization would be to vary facial expression, attractiveness, or some other variable that should produce variations in personality judgments. If all the blacks pictured are still seen as possessing stereotyped personality traits, there would be evidence that categorization is a powerful mechanism since it would have to overcome cues that should produce differences in personality judgments.

that perceptual factors may be quite important in prejudice acquisition. Since the studies are discussed in depth in Chapter 4 of this volume, we will mention only two here. Katz (1973) had preschool children learn a task requiring discrimination of shades of skin coloring under one of three conditions: Negro faces, Caucasian faces, Green faces. The task was most quickly learned by white children with Caucasian faces, and most slowly with Negro faces, and only the Caucasian-Negro differences were significant. That is, by age 3, white children already had learned to perceptually group Negro faces such that within-group differences (i.e., skin color shade) were not discriminated. Katz, Sohn, and Zalk (1974) required grade-school children to make judgments (e.g., "Which child is winning a trophy?") about ambiguous interracial slides and were categorized high or low prejudice on the basis of their responses. They then viewed slides of faces which varied in terms of skin color, skin shade, facial expression, and in other ways. Those children highest in anti-black prejudice tended to use racial cues (i.e., skin color) in making their judgments to a significantly greater extent than did low-prejudice children. These studies suggest that the "enhancement of contrast" effect identified by Tajfel may have a significant role in the development of negative intergroup attitudes.

A series of more recent studies by Tajfel and his associates indicates that categorization is implicated in negative intergroup relations in yet another way. Simply dividing individuals into groups and applying labels allowing the identification of "in-group" and out-group" can produce discrimination against the out-group, even in the absence of intergroup competition or other conditions known to facilitate hostility. In the first study (Tajfel, 1970), English schoolboys were presented with 40 clusters of dots and asked to estimate the actual number of dots on each of a number of trials. Subjects were randomly assigned to groups and were given code numbers reflecting their group assignment. They were then asked to dispense monetary rewards and penalties to the other boys on the basis of code numbers. (Subjects did not know the identity of the person that corresponded to a given number, only the group that a given number signified.) Intergroup discrimination was the dominant strategy adopted by a large majority of the boys; subjects gave more money to boys in their own group than to boys in the other groups. The general finding that social categorization causes discrimination has been replicated several times (Tajfel, Flament, Billig, and Bundy, 1971; Doise, Csepeli, Dann, Gouge, Larsen, and Ostell, 1972; Doise and Sinclair, 1973; Billig and Tajfel, 1973) and the plausibility of two alternative explanations—categorization effects are due to assumed similarity or experimenter effects—has been reduced (Billig, 1973; Billig and Tajfel, 1973). Although the exact reason for this intergroup discrimination is not clear, Tajfel feels that it is due to a social norm specifying that the in-group should be favored and that this norm is rooted in the need to establish one's social identity (see Billig and Tajfel, 1973). That this effect holds even when this norm is not made explicit (or conveyed by other group members), suggests that it is a firmly internalized norm that approximates a basic cognitive process.

Although the findings of the studies by Tajfel and his co-workers are very consistent, several aspects of this research should be noted. First, all of the reported studies on social categorization have used the same general paradigm, and, as a consequence, the results may be paradigm specific. Two studies suggest that this might be the case (Rabbie and Horwitz, 1969; Rabbie and Wilkins, 1971). Both of these experiments used controls similar to those employed by Tajfel. Subjects were arbitrarily divided into two groups and asked to make personality judgments of the other subjects. No own-other group differential was obtained in the favorability of the personality ratings. Second, Tajfel has confined his research to studies of English subjects and generalizations of his findings to other cultures must be made with caution. Finally, while Tajfel feels that the norm of in-group bias is rooted in the need to establish a social identity in a given situation, there are alternative explanations. For example, subjects may expect that they will be more handsomely rewarded by members of their own group and may be responding to a norm of reciprocity rather than attempting to establish a clear social identity.

## Intrapersonal factors in prejudice acquisition. III: Cognitive consistency motivation

Milton Rokeach and his associates have advanced the theory that race prejudice is a consequence of perceived group differences in beliefs and values—i.e., members of disliked out-groups are perceived as having beliefs that are dissimilar and incompatible with one's own. This assumed belief incongruence is considered to be a much more crucial determinant of evaluations and behavioral intentions than race or ethnic group membership per se. Essentially, this theory explains prejudice in terms of cognitive consistency motivation: rejecting another who is assumed to have dissimilar beliefs produces a balanced or consistent relation. If it is learned that this other has beliefs that are congruent with one's own, the individual will be motivated to evaluate the other more positively.

This belief theory of prejudice has been supported by a large number of investigations using subjects of widely differing ages and backgrounds (Rokeach, Smith, and Evans, 1960; Byrne and Wong, 1962; Byrne and McGraw, 1964; Stein, Hardyk, and Smith, 1965; Anderson and Cote, 1966; Rokeach and Mezei, 1966; Insko and Robinson, 1967; Smith, Williams, and Willis, 1967; Willis and Bulatao, 1967). In most of these studies, subjects were asked to indicate the degree of friendliness they felt toward hypothetical stimulus persons. These individuals were described by statements such as, "A black boy believes in God," "A white boy believes in God," "A black boy is an atheist." In general, race was manipulated by a single word—"black" or "white"—while belief similarity was induced by a number of statements of attitude. These experiments were criticized for their artificiality and the apparent inequality of the race and belief manipulations. Triandis (1961) found that race was more important than belief when the belief system was manipulated by a single sentence, and Byrne and Nelson (1965) found that attraction increased as the number of similarity items increased.

Three more recent experiments by Rokeach and Mezei have examined the effects of race and belief prejudice in more naturalistic situations with race and belief manipulated more equally. In two of these studies (see Rokeach, 1968, pp. 66-68) college students engaged in a discussion of controversial issues with two black and two white confederates. Belief similarity-dissimilarity was manipulated by having one black and one white agree with the subject's viewpoint and one black and one white disagree. Following the discussion, each subject was asked to select two of the confederates to join him for a coffee break. In a third study, persons seeking jobs at two state mental hospitals were engaged in a conversation by two black and two white confederates who posed as job applicants. (Discussions focused on techniques for handling problems that might arise in the work setting.) Again, one black and one white confederate agreed with the subject, while the other two disagreed. Following the discussion, subjects were asked to indicate which two of the other applicants he would prefer to work with. In all three studies, choices were most frequently based on similarity of belief. Hendrick, Bixenstein, and Hawkins (1971) have reported similar results using a videotape discussion between two black and two white graduate students. Belief similarity was found to be generally more important than race when subjects were asked to respond to social distance questionnaires regarding the participants in the discussion. Race, however, was found to be more important than belief on the item, "Would you be willing to have this person date your sister?"

Although subjects responded to "real" stimulus persons in these latter studies, it should be noted that the actual behavioral consequences of their decisions were relatively minor. More recent efforts in this area have focused on the behavioral intentions of subjects in situations that imply varying degrees of intimacy and publicness. Stein (1966) reported that value similarity was a more important determinant of willingness to "sit next to in class" and "eat lunch with" but found that teenage subjects tended to respond in racial terms to items such as "invite home to dinner," "live in my apartment house," and "have a close relative marry." Race was found to be more important than belief for marriage acceptance by Filipino subjects (Willis and Bulatao, 1967). Mezei (1971) reported that race prejudice was more important than belief prejudice in three social interactions—"marry," "date," and "accept as kin"—and that there was a greater amount of perceived social pressure regarding these interactions. Thus, while belief congruence has been shown to be an important determinant of friendship acceptance, it is clear that race becomes the more important criterion as the intimacy and publicness of social interactions increases. Rokeach and his associates have tended to explain these variations in terms of perceived social pressure and institutionalized racial prejudice and generally to regard these more intimate behaviors as exceptions to their theory. That race relative to belief increases in importance as intimacy of the dependent variable increases is however a nontrivial complication for the belief theory of prejudice.

The proposition that perceived belief dissimilarity causes prejudice raises yet another question. There is virtually no research on the developmental implications of this model. While there is some evidence that prejudice and assumed belief dissimilarity are correlated (Byrne and Wong, 1962; Stein *et al.*, 1965; Stein, 1966), these studies offer little support for the idea that assumed belief incongruence causes prejudice. An equally plausible interpretation of the data might be that prejudice causes people to assume belief incongruence. The literature on prejudice acquisition suggests that this is indeed the case. According to this research, majority-group children first learn affective, good-bad reactions to out-groups, and only later acquire specific beliefs about them.

Thus, assumed belief incongruence seems not a cause of, but rather a supporting mechanism for, prejudice. Dienstbier (1972) takes a very similar position in arguing that prejudice (as a negative affective response) and assumed belief dissimilarity exist in a mutually causative relationship.

The extant literature also fails to answer another important question about discrimination on the basis of race or belief—which determines behavior *in vivo*? In all of the foregoing studies, subjects were forced to learn both the race and belief system of the stimulus persons. While in everyday interaction it is difficult to avoid cues as to racial group membership (since they are external and highly visible), this is not true of beliefs and values, which are internal. Thus, it may be that whites *in vivo* may reject blacks on the basis of their race without taking the trouble to ascertain whether these blacks have belief systems that are congruent or incongruent with their own.

As in most cases where social scientific debates are phrased in either-or terms, the race vs. belief controversy (after almost 15 years and much research) has yielded no firm answer to the original question: Is it race or belief dissimilarity that causes social discrimination? It has, however, raised several issues that are quite relevant to a full understanding of the psychology of prejudice. Among the more important are: (1) How does assumed belief dissimilarity develop in children and adults? (2) How does the acquisition of cultural stereotypes interact with the learning of assumed belief dissimilarity? (3) What kinds of belief information about blacks do whites "learn" in various types of direct (i.e., face-to-face) and vicarious (e.g., television) contact with blacks? (4) What is the nature of various behavioral choices that makes race or belief a more potent determinant of the choice? (That is, is it simply heightened intimacy that increases the importance of race or is it some other variable such as specific cultural proscriptions?) (5) What individual differences are there (and how do they develop) in the use of race vs. belief in social discrimination? (Goldstein and Davis, 1972, have made a preliminary step in answering this question by empirically identifying what they call "race" and "belief discriminators.") We agree with Dienstbier (1972) that rather than continuing research aimed at establishing the greater importance of race vs. belief (recently described as the search for the "fair test") studies should be directed at systematically attempting to answer the above, more specific questions.

## Interpersonal factors in prejudice acquisiton. I: Socialization and conformity

In this and the following section, we will discuss two interpretations of prejudice that stress interpersonal relations rather than the more purely psychological processes covered in the preceding sections. The explanations to be covered are united by the assumption that ethnic prejudice is learned in the same way that other preferences, beliefs, and values are learned—through interaction with one's sociocultural environment.

Socialization is the process by which a child is trained in the ways of his culture. During this process the child learns the language appropriate to his culture (and subculture), the "right" political values, and the expected patterns of behavior for his or her biological sex. The socialization explanation of prejudice asserts that the child also learns to differentiate various social groups and to attach positive or negative valuations to these groups.

If prejudice is acquired much as any other aspect of culture, then there should be consistent and rather lasting differences among cultural groups with respect to ethnic attitudes. As one moves from one society to the next, there is wide variety in the groups against which prejudice is directed, but there is much consistency through time in the pattern of intergroup relations within a particular society (cf. Rose and Rose, 1965, Part II). If we look specifically at the United States, we note both a national pattern of prejudice and a number of local variations. The national pattern reflects the fact that the United States is a "mass society" with powerful media and a broad educational system, which allow the wide diffusion of cultural values, attitudes, etc. The local patterns reflect the unique historical factors (e.g., slavery, Jim Crow laws, racial etiquette in the South) and context variables (e.g., urban decay, crime, etc. due to the reduced economic importance of center-city areas) of different geographic areas.

The American pattern of prejudice specifies the "good guys"—e.g., English, (white) Americans, Canadians—and the "bad guys"—e.g., Turks, Chinese, Koreans, Indians (see Table 2). Not only is this pattern relatively stable (ranks haven't changed much in 40 years), but it is highly diffused within American society. Of particular interest is the fact that even groups rated low tend to accept the general pattern with just one exception—they rate themselves high. For example, Jews and blacks produce rank orders similar to those listed in Table 2, but each puts itself at the top (see Ashmore,

1970, pp. 283-284). There is, however, little evidence for "sympathy" effects—
blacks rank Jews near the bottom and Jews return the favor.

**Table 2.** Social Distance Rankings of 28 National and
Ethnic Groups by White Americans, 1926-1966

| Target Group | 1926 | 1946 | 1956 | 1966 |
|---|---|---|---|---|
| English | 1.0 | 3.0 | 3.0 | 2.0 |
| Americans (U.S., white) | 2.0 | 1.0 | 1.0 | 1.0 |
| Canadians | 3.5 | 2.0 | 2.0 | 3.0 |
| Scots | 3.5 | 5.0 | 7.0 | 9.0 |
| Irish | 5.0 | 4.0 | 5.0 | 5.0 |
| French | 6.0 | 6.0 | 4.0 | 4.0 |
| Germans | 7.0 | 10.0 | 8.0 | 10.5 |
| Swedish | 8.0 | 9.0 | 6.0 | 6.0 |
| Hollanders | 9.0 | 8.0 | 9.0 | 10.5 |
| Norwegians | 10.0 | 7.0 | 10.0 | 7.0 |
| Spanish | 11.0 | 15.0 | 14.0 | 14.0 |
| Finns | 12.0 | 11.0 | 11.0 | 12.0 |
| Russians | 13.0 | 13.0 | 22.0 | 22.0 |
| Italians | 14.0 | 16.0 | 12.0 | 8.0 |
| Poles | 15.0 | 14.0 | 13.0 | 16.0 |
| Armenians | 16.0 | 17.5 | 18.0 | 19.0 |
| Czechs | 17.0 | 12.0 | 17.0 | 17.0 |
| Indians (Amer.) | 18.0 | 20.0 | 19.0 | 18.0 |
| Jews | 19.0 | 19.0 | 16.0 | 15.0 |
| Greeks | 20.0 | 17.5 | 15.0 | 13.0 |
| Mexicans | 21.0 | 23.5 | 26.0 | 26.5 |
| Japanese | 22.0 | 28.0 | 24.0 | 23.0 |
| Filipinos | 23.0 | 22.0 | 20.0 | 20.0 |
| Negroes | 24.0 | 27.0 | 25.0 | 26.5 |
| Turks | 25.0 | 23.5 | 21.0 | 24.0 |
| Chinese | 26.0 | 21.0 | 23.0 | 21.0 |
| Koreans | 27.0 | 25.0 | 28.0 | 25.0 |
| Indians (India) | 28.0 | 26.0 | 27.0 | 28.0 |

Source: Ehrlich, 1973, p. 74
Original Source: Bogardus, E. Comparing racial distance in Ethiopia, South Africa
and the United States. *Sociology and Social Research,* 1968, **52,** 149-156.

On top of this national pattern, however, must be projected significant geographical differences. Anti-black prejudice, for example, is higher in the South than in other regions (e.g., Kelly, Ferson, and Holtzman, 1958). And, as we shall see in the section on perceived racial threat, there are also differences in racial attitudes between those who live in the innercity and the suburbs.

How are these cultural and subcultural patterns of prejudice converted into the attitudes and beliefs of individuals? Socialization is achieved through four major channels: (a) parents, (b) peers, (c) schools, and (d) mass media. We will put off discussion of the effects of schools and mass media for a moment and briefly cover now the influence of parents and peers.

That parents play a role in the transmission of prejudice is supported by the consistent correlation obtained between parent and child ethnic attitudes (Bird, Monachesi, and Burdick, 1952; Frenkel-Brunswik and Havel, 1953; Mosher and Scodel, 1960; Epstein and Komorita, 1966). Particularly noteworthy is the Mosher and Scodel study: there was a significant correlation between mother and child prejudice even when the possible confounding effects of mother's authoritarian child-rearing practices were partialed out. It should be noted, however, that although these correlations are consistently positive, they are frequently rather low and it may be that the influence of parents has been somewhat overplayed. (For a further consideration of this issue, see Chapter 4 of this volume.)

The data concerned with how parents transmit ethnic attitudes to children is somewhat surprising. There is little evidence that direct verbal instruction plays a major role. However, indirect methods of conveying attitudes prove quite effective. First, parents shape prejudice through rules that forbid the child from playing with blacks and through punishments when these rules are broken (Horowitz and Horowitz, 1938; Bird, Monachesi, and Burdick, 1952). Second, most parents are ill-equipped to answer their children's naturally occurring questions about group differences. When such questions arise, they either "change the subject," thereby conveying to the child that race is an anxiety-arousing topic, or they fall back on derogatory stereotypes (Radke-Yarrow, Trager, and Miller, 1952; Goodman, 1964). Third, children "overhear" the race-related conversations of their parents, thereby learning the vocabulary of prejudice (Quinn, 1954). And finally, there is some suggestive evidence that imitation and identification are implicated in the process of parental socialization of racial prejudice (see Ashmore, 1970, p. 286).

As the child grows up, the relative importance of peer groups in socialization increases greatly. Grossack (1957) found a significant correlation between an individual's racial attitudes and the "perceived group norm" on this topic for a group of ninth- and tenth-grade children. Wilson (1963) provided further evidence of individual movement toward the group norm. On several different prejudice measures there was significantly less variance in the responses of older, as opposed to younger, high school students suggesting that as the students moved through adolescence their racial attitudes were converging on the group norm. There is also evidence that individuals change their attitudes to accord with their new reference group when they attend college (Sims and Patrick, 1936; Eddy, 1964), especially if ties with the former reference group are broken (Pearlin, 1954).

Two studies by Pettigrew (1958; 1959) provide further evidence for the influence of group norms on individual prejudice. In the first, South African college students completed measures of authoritarianism (F scale), conformity-proneness, and anti-black prejudice. Although these subjects were higher in anti-black prejudice than a comparable American sample, their F scores were virtually the same, which argues against an authoritarian personality explanation. On the other hand, there was a significant correlation between conformity-proneness and prejudice, thus suggesting that group norms (which in South Africa are explicit and strongly anti-black) can influence individual attitudes. A series of subgroup comparisons provided further support for prejudice based on conformity to group norms—e.g., students born in Africa (thus more socialized into the South African pattern of prejudice) were more prejudiced than those born elsewhere. A second study—involving comparisons between a sample of Northern and Southern adult Americans—turned up similar results. The Northerners were significantly lower in anti-black prejudice but their F scale scores were no different from those of the Southern sample. Those people highest in prejudice were most likely high in conforming tendencies (e.g., church-goers) and lived with group norms explicitly denigrating blacks (i.e., in the South). These data are, however, correlational and cannot be regarded as conclusive.

It seems clear that socialization factors and conformity to group norms can explain a large proportion of the variance in prejudice. Consistent cultural (and subcultural) patterns of belief are well documented. However, much of the evidence in this area is correlational, there are conflicting results (e.g., regarding the role of parents), and some topics have not received much research attention (e.g., schools and the socialization of prejudice). Thus it is not clear exactly how these cultural patterns are transformed into the prejudice of individuals, and the relative importance of the various agents of socialization (parents, peers, television, other media) is not known. More research directed specifically at these issues could explicate the role of socialization more fully.

## Interpersonal factors in prejudice acquisition. II: Attribution theory

The perception of persons or groups differs from the perception of nonhuman objects in one important respect: person-perception involves the search for the cause(s) of behavior. For example, if we see someone strike another person, we don't walk away saying "He hit him." Rather, we attempt to explain the action by asking ourselves, "Why did he hit him?" Attribution theory is a loosely organized set of propositions about the "rules" used by humans in perceiving other humans (see Jones, Kanouse, Kelley, Nisbett, Valins, and Weiner, 1971). Of particular relevance to the present topic are the rules by which we infer internal dispositions (e.g., attitudes, values, personality traits) from overt behavior. In the above example, under what conditions do we conclude that the person who strikes another is "violent" and "aggressive?"

Before discussing these inference rules, we need to know what whites learn about the behavior of blacks. In addition to parents and peers, schools and the mass media are the primary sources through which we learn about ethnic groups.[12] Although there is some evidence of improvement (Colle, 1967; Kane, 1970), the mass media and school textbooks have presented a distorted view of blacks and a distorted set of "facts," both of which contribute to anti-black prejudice.

The image of minorities is directly distorted in two major ways. First, minorities are at all times underrepresented in the media. This applies not only to blacks but also to all non-Northern-European Americans and to women as well (Johnson, Sears, and McConahay, 1971; Ehrlich, 1973, pp. 32-33). Second, when blacks are portrayed in textbooks, their African heritage is almost completely ignored, while the European heritage of most whites is covered in some detail (Kane, 1970). Although there is no direct evidence, this black invisibility in the present and black "non-past" may contribute to white prejudice in several ways. First, this media and textbook "black-out" keeps whites unaware of black culture, thus supporting what Jones (1972) terms "cultural racism": ". . . the individual and institutional expression of the superiority of one race's cultural heritage over that of another race" (p. 6). Second, invisibility in the past and present allows the development of assumed belief incongruence, which, as noted above, contributes to the rejection of out-groups. Third, invisibility gives whites psychological distance from blacks, and there is suggestive evidence from laboratory studies that psychological distance makes it easier for one person to aggress against another. Finally, lack of knowledge about blacks and their past makes them "strange," and there may be some psychological rejection of strangeness per se. (The latter three points are discussed in more depth by Johnson, *et al.* [1971].)

Part of the picture of blacks conveyed by the media is not so much direct distortion as presentation of "facts." For example, the high rate of TV and newspaper portrayal of black athletes and entertainers reflects the "fact"

[12] Although it seems surprising, actual contact with ethnic groups is not a major source of learning about such groups (see Sears and McConahay, 1973). Residential segregation sharply reduces the opportunity for interracial contact and most everyday interactions involve status-laden role contacts (e.g., the black janitor at work or a black waitress at the coffeeshop where you have lunch).

that blacks are overrepresented in these fields. And, the image on the six o'clock news of the black welfare mother or the black unemployed teenager is not a fabrication. Blacks are overrepresented on welfare roles (although in absolute numbers more whites receive welfare), and the unemployment rate of young black males far exceeds that for comparable whites. In sum, then, blacks are often portrayed in the media and school texts as entertainers, athletes, on welfare, out of a job, or involved in some protest or conflict situation.

How do these images promote and support prejudice? To seek an answer, we return to attribution theory and, in particular, to three of its basic propositions: (a) humans need to "explain" the causes of overt human behavior; (b) overt behavior is seen as caused by either internal dispositions (e.g., "He hit the other person because he has a violent nature") or external factors (e.g., "He hit the other person because that person was about to rob him"); (c) for an internal attribution to be made, the perceiver must feel that the perceived had the ability to make an alternative response (e.g., if in the above situation the person could have avoided being robbed without hitting, then we might infer some internal disposition as the cause of that behavior).

These three features of person-perception combine with a facet of American culture to cause whites to infer that blacks have a number of "bad" traits. Individualism and self-reliance are important values in American culture (Hsu, 1972), and a central part of our national ideology is that anything can be accomplished through individual effort. This aspect of our culture leads us to be predisposed toward individual attributions. If the system is open and external constraints don't determine our social position, then behavior must be due to either ability or motivation differences among individuals and groups. With respect to black Americans, then, they must be disposed, either by ability or motivation, toward athletics and entertainment (the idea of "rhythm"), they must be either stupid or lazy (or why do they not have jobs?), and, since the mid-1960s, they must be violent (or why do they protest and riot?). The athlete-entertainer image has been demonstrated in several studies (Karlins, Coffman, and Walters, 1969; Maykovitch, 1972), and the stereotype of blacks as violent will be discussed in the section on "perceived racial threat."

An analysis of changes over time in whites' beliefs regarding the intelligence and motivation of blacks clearly illustrates the attribution process. Schuman (1969) noted that over the past several decades whites have shown a marked decline in accepting the idea of the innate biological inferiority (particularly regarding intelligence) of blacks. Yet, blacks continue to be overrepresented at the bottom of the socioeconomic ladder and the media convey this image to whites. In seeking to "explain" this situation most whites do not invoke environmental factors (an external attribution) such as discrimination, poor health care, poor housing, and poor schools—even though social scientists have done much to demonstrate the existence and deleterious effects of such conditions (see Ashmore and McConahay, in press, Chapter 3). Rather, they say that blacks must not be motivated to get ahead. In other words, once the ability explanation for group differences was removed it was replaced by a second internal factor—i.e., blacks are lazy.

There is yet another way in which American culture predisposes us to make attributions that denigrate blacks. American political socialization plays down conflict (e.g., "Democrats and Republicans both really want the same thing"), stresses that voting is the only way to change social arrangements, and creates in the child generalized positive attachment to the country and its symbols (see Ashmore and McConahay, in press, Chapter 8). Thus, when individuals or groups openly challenge the status quo they are seen as extremists and ingrates. For the past two decades (and particularly since the mid-1960s), blacks have openly challenged "the way things are done here." White Americans—ill-equipped to cope with conflict and vaguely positive to the system—respond by denying the need for reform and rejecting those who call for change.

## NEW DIRECTIONS IN THE PSYCHOLOGY OF PREJUDICE

Until recently, most psychological research on race relations was concerned with assessing the validity of the various intrapersonal and interpersonal explanations of prejudice covered in the preceding pages. Although this work has greatly enhanced our understanding of psychological factors contributing to negative intergroup relations, there remain a number of unanswered questions. It is our belief that many of the ambiguities that exist result from two aspects of this research: (1) Prejudice as an attitude held by individuals has not been adequately considered in terms of the societal context in which individuals exist. (2) Prejudice has been treated as an isolated variable (generally being related to some supposed antecedent variable) rather than as an interacting and interconnected aspect of an individual's complete self-system (i.e., the organized, integrated set of personality, cognitive, ability, and self-perception factors that characterize the individual). In this section we will review a number of lines of research that we feel begin to redress these inadequacies of previous work.

As we noted near the outset of this chapter, black-white relations have been in a state of open competition since the mid-1960s. This clearly competitive relationship has posed a threat to almost all white Americans. The type and degree of threat perceived, however, is affected by a number of factors. In the first subsection below, three threat-related constructs—"perceived racial threat," "symbolic racism," and "tokenism"—are discussed. Each of these constructs is tied to the sociostructural context in two ways: the current competitive nature of black-white relations sets the stage for the perception of threat but the nature of the threat varies as a function of the individual's position in the socioeconomic system.

The second subsection contains an overview of three lines of research, which consider prejudice as an integral part of an individual's self-system rather than as an isolated variable. The first two are concerned with rather specific aspects of interaction: factors in interracial aggression and the effects of intergroup harm-doing. The final topic is Rokeach's (1973) schema for placing attitudes (including prejudice) in the context of an individual's total belief system (which includes self-concept, values, etc.). It must be noted that all of these conceptualizations are highly tentative. They are all of very recent origin, much of the directly supportive research is limited to one group of researchers (and thus lacks independent cross validation), and the research itself is far from conclusive.

## Reactions to the current competitive state of black-white relations

Most of the work discussed to this point has paid little attention to the precise identification of what feelings and beliefs accompany anti-black attitudes. Prejudice was most often operationally defined in terms of self-report scales. Most of these scales assumed a paternalistic state of black-white relations and the respondents indicated their prejudice by agreeing or disagreeing with this assumed state. For example, when Woodmansee and Cook (1967) factor-analyzed the responses of whites to "a large group of conventional Negro content items" (p. 240), they obtained factors that either explicitly (e.g., "Negro Inferiority," "Subtle Derogatory Beliefs") or implicitly (e.g., "Integration-Segregation Policy," "Acceptance [of Negroes] in Status-Superior Relationships") define anti-black prejudice in terms of acceptance or rejection of blacks as inferior—and, by implication, unfit to be near or supervise whites. Two new scales have been added to the Woodmansee and Cook instrument because recent changes in black-white relations have highlighted new content areas relevant to prejudice (Brigham, Woodmansee, and Cook, in press). Such changes have necessitated the development of new concepts for understanding the anti-black beliefs and attitudes of whites.

Traditional conceptualizations and measurements of anti-black prejudice tied it to the feeling of contempt and a set of beliefs about the moral, motivational, and intellectual inferiority of blacks. Over the past few decades, there has been a significant decline in the number of whites who endorse paternalistic stereotypes such as "Blacks have lower morals than whites," "Blacks keep untidy homes," and "Blacks have less native intelligence than whites" (Schwartz, 1967, particularly pp. 19-22; Harris, 1971). There has been a parallel decline in support for segregation based on the notion of black inferiority (Greeley and Sheatsley, 1971). This reduction in the acceptance of paternalistic sterotypes and formal segregation has not brought racial peace to America. On the contrary, many whites retain their anti-black attitudes, and there is intense resistance to black demands for a greater share of our nation's wealth.[13] Two new concepts have been advanced to account for such resistance: perceived racial threat (Ashmore and Butsch, 1972) and symbolic racism (Sears and Kinder, 1970; Sears and McConahay, 1973). Perceived racial threat is the feeling that blacks are a direct threat to one's personal security and is most prominent among the urban working class whose members are in rather direct competition with blacks for socioeconomic resources. Symbolic racism is felt most by middle-class suburbanites who see blacks as threatening values that the white sees as central to the continuance of the American way of life. The current state of black-white relations is threatening to yet a third group of Americans—upper-middle-class "liberals" who are unsure how they should behave in interracial settings and whose self-concept is threatened by the possibility of acting like a racist. This idea of self-concept threat and its implications for behavior will be discussed under the label "tokenism."

*Perceived Racial Threat.* As discussed above, the 1970s brought blacks into direct and open competition with whites for social, political, and economic resources. This state of competition has produced in some whites the belief that blacks are powerful and threatening, a belief that stands in sharp contrast to the childlike image of previous decades.[14] The concept of perceived racial threat is designed to capture the subjective meaning of this new image and the feelings it arouses. Perceived racial threat is a negative attitude just as is prejudice. In contrast with prejudice as it has been conceptually and operationally defined, however, perceived racial threat has a larger fear and a smaller contempt component and involves beliefs that blacks are trying to usurp the position of whites in this society rather than notions about black inferiority.

Results of several different studies provide preliminary evidence for the existence of the fear-threat syndrome we call perceived racial threat. While white acceptance of traditional anti-black stereotypes was decreasing during the 1960s, a new belief—blacks are violent—was added; in 1970, 36% of white

[13] As can be seen in Table 2, the social distance ranking of Negroes by whites has remained quite constant over the last five decades. Using the Bogardus social distance scale, Negroes were rated 24th (out of 28 national and ethnic groups) in 1926, 27th in 1946, 25th in 1956, and tied for 26th in 1966.

[14] Boskin (1970) points out that both the Brute (blacks as sexually powerful and subject to violent fits) and Sambo (blacks as childlike) images have been around since slave times. He argues that whites suppressed the Brute image in the past because they feared that it might come true. Our feeling, however, is that the predominance of one or the other image depends on the nature of intergroup interdependence—the Sambo image characterizes paternalistic or dominance relationships, while the Brute image occurs most often in times of intense intergroup competition.

adults agreed that blacks are more violent than whites (Harris, 1971).[15]

A recent survey of adults living in Sacramento, California, produced similar results (Maykovitch, 1972). Using the Katz and Braly (1933) adjective checklist, both college and noncollege respondents indicated that blacks were "musical." and noncollege adults felt that they were "lazy" (see above section on attribution theory and stereotype acquisition). Other adjectives agreed to by both groups—"aggressive" and "revengeful"—suggest the existence of perceived racial threat. Three prominent traditional stereotypes—"ignorant," "unreliable," "frivolous"—were not thought characteristic of blacks by either group. (The traditional paternalistic view of blacks was not completely absent: "pleasure loving" and "happy-go-lucky" were checked as characteristic of blacks by many of the noncollege adults.)

Two small-scale studies suggest that the fear-threat syndrome is a homogeneous construct. In an interview of a sample of urban policemen, Groves and Rossi (1970) included five items that get at this syndrome very nicely: "Negroes have tried to move too fast in gaining what they feel to be equality," "Negroes are draining away resources through welfare payments," "Negroes are taking over political power," "Negroes are moving into areas that, until recently, were occupied only by whites," "Negroes are socializing with whites." All five items were significantly intercorrelated, thus supporting the idea of a unitary, rather than situation-specific, fear-threat syndrome. This idea is further supported by two other studies—one employing middle-class high school students (Ashmore, Turner, Donato, and Nevenglosky, 1973) and the other involving almost 1000 students attending a college summer school session (Ashmore and Butsch, 1972). As part of a long attitude questionnaire, items were included to tap perceived racial threat in the areas of employment (e.g., blacks get preferential treatment for jobs), personal safety (e.g., blacks might riot in white neighborhoods), economic resources (e.g., too much of the national budget goes to blacks), housing (e.g., blacks drive down property values), as well as more general threat items (e.g., "Black Power means blacks taking from whites"). In both studies the perceived racial threat items were significantly correlated with each other.[16]

The studies above deal primarily with beliefs about blacks as threats. As present there is little direct evidence about the fear component of perceived

[15] Unfortunately, "violent" was not included in earlier polls so we can't conclusively demonstrate that this stereotype has increased in acceptance over the past decade. That it was included in later polls and received a high rate of endorsement suggests that black violence is a more salient concern among whites now than it was when Harris did his first race relations poll in 1963 (Brink and Harris, 1963).

[16] In the Ashmore et al. (1973) study, reversed items were included (e.g., "Blacks are no more of a threat to my personal safety than whites") and these did not correlate well with each other or with items positively keyed for perceived racial threat. Thus, the existing perceived racial threat items may contain an acquiescence response component or it might be that it is difficult to write reversals for this issue. Rokeach's (1960, p. 405) experience with the Dogmatism scale supports this latter possibility.

threat.[17] There is, however, some indirect evidence that perception of threat involves fear. In the Ashmore and Butsch (1972) and Ashmore, *et al.* (1973) studies there was a significant correlation between items not obviously involving fear (e.g., threats in employment and education) and items regarding threats to personal safety that presumably do involve fear. Also, whites expect more retaliation from a black than from another white in a situation where they have been led to hurt that person (Donnerstein, Donnerstein, Simon, and Ditrichs, 1972). This latter point is supported by another study in which white college students rated blacks as more "unforgiving" than whites while at the same time rating blacks as more "ambitious," "good," and "attractive" than whites (Perlman and Oskamp, 1971, p. 508).

Although a full nomological net is not available for the perceived racial threat variable, there are three types of evidence regarding its construct validity: (a) correlations with other variables, (b) differences between known-groups, and (c) prediction of behavior in experimental settings (Cronbach and Meehl, 1955). First, perceived racial threat correlates very highly (.75) with evaluative ratings of blacks. Furthermore, this correlation is higher, though not significantly so, than that between the F scale—which repeatedly has been found to correlate with traditional measures of anti-black prejudice—and evaluation of blacks (.48) (Ashmore, *et al.*, 1973). Although this provides evidence of convergent validity, there is little support for discriminant validity (Campbell and Fiske, 1959) since perceived racial threat and the F scale correlated significantly (.44).

Perceived racial threat is also correlated with other variables that reflect racial fears and threats. Urban policemen who scored high in perceived threat also tended to view ghetto residents as hostile; this perceived hostility was apparently more related to the policemen's perceived threat level than to actual hostile acts by ghetto residents (Groves and Rossi, 1970). Caprio (1972) found that outer-city ethnic whites were not only high in fear of black crime but were also unwilling to make minor repairs on their homes, thus suggesting a link between perceived threat and the social obsolescence of housing owned by threatened whites. And, finally, whites who agreed that the urban riots were "a way for black people to take over the cities" were more likely to consider buying guns to protect their homes against crime than those who disagreed with this assertion (Feagin, 1970).

Second, the perceived racial threat formulation predicts that whites who are in the most direct competition with blacks will be highest on the fear-threat syndrome. In a nationwide survey (Campbell, 1971), whites were asked questions tapping four different orientations regarding blacks: (a) feelings about interracial contact, (b) attitudes toward anti-discrimination laws, (c) amount of perceived anti-black discrimination, and (d) sympathy for protest

---

[17]As Ehrlich (1973, Chapter 4, especially pp. 95-97) points out, however, little attention has been paid to the affective component of anti-black prejudice as traditionally conceptualized.

by blacks. The fourth index comes closest to a measure of perceived racial threat since those who score high on it support attempts by blacks to protest and, presumably, to change the existing race relations pattern. And, it is only on this index that there is a difference between city-dwelling whites and those who live outside of cities. City-dwellers (who are probably most in competition with blacks for housing and other resources) were lower in sympathy for black protest. In a second and independent investigation, Sears and Kinder (1970) found that white suburbanites (who presumably are shielded economically, socially, and geographically from blacks) were not as high in personal fear of blacks as they were in symbolic racism, and that level of perceived racial threat was not as strong a predictor of voting against a black mayoral candidate as was symbolic racism.

The foregoing research suggests that perceived racial threat was high for at least some Americans during the late 1960s and early 1970s. This may remain true in the future or the federal government's policy of "benign neglect" together with the less provocative behavior of national black leaders (e.g., Black Panther leader Bobby Seale running for mayor of Oakland rather than urging the "Offing of Pigs") may make race relations a less salient concern of whites. Even if perceived threat does recede, we are left with the question of why and how it emerged. As noted above, intergroup attitudes tend to mirror the nature of intergroup interdependence. Since the 1960s brought blacks into open and direct contact with whites, we should expect the development of attitudes that "explain" this competition—i.e., they are pushing to displace me and my kind. Also, the urban riots, while not directly aimed at whites, convinced whites that black violence could be directed at them in the future. And, finally, the concentration of mass media on interracial conflict in the late 1960s (Johnson, Sears, and McConahay, 1971) served to feed the fear-producing, threatening image of blacks.

Still another question remains regarding perceived threat: How does it influence societal discrimination against blacks? Blalock (1967) has proposed a theory of discrimination based on threat that is quite congruent with the idea of perceived threat. He presents data suggesting a positive monotonic relationship between conditions producing threat and amount of discrimination. It is difficult to relate the theories, however, since Blalock relies almost exclusively on aggregate data and does not directly assess the presumed intervening psychological variable of threat perception. One point of seeming disagreement is Blalock's contention that economic threat and power (or political) threat, which are combined in perceived threat, are distinguishable and are related to potential threat (as indexed by "Percent Non-White") in different ways.

*Symbolic Racism.* While perceived threat may help to account for the resistance of outer-city and occupationally threatened whites to demands for black progress, additional variables must be provided to explain such resistance on the part of white suburban dwellers who are not in competition or abrasive contact with blacks. Sears and Kinder (1970) present preliminary evidence that "symbolic racism" may be a key variable.

Sears and Kinder interviewed a sample of middle-class whites living in suburban Los Angeles communities during the 1969 mayoral campaign between Sam Yorty (white, conservative) and Thomas Bradley (black, liberal). They sought to explain the racial attitudes of these suburban dwellers by analyzing a large number of belief statements and by relating stands on these statements to voting intentions. The people interviewed did not score high on traditional indices of anti-black prejudice.

> They do not believe in racial differences in intelligence, and there is virtually no support for segregated schools, segregated public accommodations, or job discrimination. Moreover, most of the sample recognizes the reality · problems that blacks face in contemporary American society. They perceive Negroes as being at a disadvantage in requesting services from government, in trying to get jobs, and in general getting what they deserve. And they feel that integration *can* work: they feel the races can live confortably together. (Sears and Kinder, 1971, p.63)

Furthermore, traditional prejudice indices were not significant predictors of voting for or against the black mayoral candidate.

Also, as we noted above, the sample was not particularly high in perceived racial threat. About one-third to one-half of the respondents expressed some concern that blacks could (although at the time they did not) threaten their neighborhoods, their personal safety, or their children's schools. Agreement with "potential racial threat" items did tend to be higher for those who favored the white mayoral candidate. However, the differences were not as impressive as for a third class of racial orientation items (those tapping symbolic racism), and the differences were largely erased by statistically controlling for symbolic racism while the reverse was not true.

Symbolic racism is a combination of the generalized feeling that the social, economic, and political status quo should be maintained with the belief that blacks are somehow responsible for threatening this status quo and, by implication, the whole American way of life—that is, blacks are seen as threatening values that are quite important to suburban whites. (It should be noted that this value-threat interpretation of symbolic racism is an extrapolation and extension of what Sears and Kinder say.) While traditional anti-black prejudice and perceived racial threat both center around specific issues and questions (e.g., Are blacks intellectually inferior? Are blacks out to get me and my family?), symbolic racism is centered around highly abstract, or "symbolic," issues. (See Edelman, [1971], for a discussion of "symbolic politics.") For example, a symbolic racism item on crime and violence is "Streets aren't safe these days without a policeman around," while perceived racial threat on the same issue is assessed by asking "How likely do you think it is that Negroes will bring violence to this neighborhood?" Other symbolic issues used by Sears and Kinder were welfare, governmental responsiveness to whites vs. blacks, economic gains of blacks, as well as the general statement "Negroes shouldn't push themselves where they are not wanted."[18] As noted above, the suburban whites were quite high in symbolic racism and symbolic racism was the most significant predictor of voting against a black mayoral candidate. Those high in symbolic racism tended to vote against the black candidate even when perceived racial threat and *nonracial liberalism-conservatism* were statistically controlled (Sears and Kinder, 1970, see particularly Table 8).

Where does symbolic racism come from? How does it develop? Sears and Kinder (1970) speculate that the rise of symbolic racism among white middle-class suburban-dwellers is due to three factors: (a) black invisibility and lack of equal-status black-white contact, (b) early socialization of anti-black and pro-status quo orientations, and (c) media coverage of interracial conflict over the past five to ten years. As we pointed out above, blacks and other minorities are underrepresented in all forms of mass and educational media. This invisibility, plus the fact of increasing residential segregation and an economic situation where blacks tend to occupy lower-status positions, means that middle-class whites have little first-hand personal interaction with blacks. Such isolation makes these whites susceptible to thinking of blacks in terms of abstract generalizations rather than as individual human beings. As noted above, socialization of whites makes blacks an object of anxiety and predisposes them to reject anyone who challenges the status quo. Finally, the militant black strategy of the 1960s has not only increased racial fears but has also placed blacks (along with student activists and criminals) clearly at the center of those who challenge the status quo. Taken together, then, symbolic racism has resulted from the social insulation of whites, which predisposes them to abstract views of blacks, together with a media-conveyed view of blacks as trying to destroy the "American way of life." The resistance to black progress has become centered around symbolic issues for middle-class whites because they feel a threat to the system as a whole rather than to their position as individuals.

*Tokenism: Protection of egalitarian self-concept, but bar to significant racial altruism.* Over the past decade, the terms "reverse discrimination" and "tokenism" have appeared often in the debate on black progress and white resistance. Blacks often charge that the changes offered by whites in hiring,

---

[18] As can be seen from the items used to assess both constructs, the operational definitions of perceived racial threat and symbolic racism are not unrelated. Although in part this reflects similarities in the concepts, future work should be directed at developing coperationalizations that more clearly assess the concepts without including items that tap generalized anti-black prejudice.

housing, etc. are only insignificant "tokens." Whites often retort that it is blacks who are getting special consideration, that today "reverse discrimination" favors blacks, not whites. A recent series of studies (Dutton, 1971, 1973; Dutton and Lake, 1973; Dutton and Lennox, 1974) suggests that both phenomena exist.

In his first two studies, Dutton demonstrated the existence of reverse discrimination. In the first, either a white or black couple entered a Toronto or Vancouver restaurant; the man wore a turtleneck sweater in violation of the restaurants' "coat-and-tie" policy. The white couple was seated 30% of the time, while the black couple was allowed to dine over twice as often (75%). One possible explanation is that middle-class whites who value egalitarianism, and don't have much interaction with blacks—true in the United States as well as Canada (see Johnson, Sears, and McConahay, 1971)—bend over backward for the black in an interracial encounter where their behavior might be seen as discriminatory. If this is true, then reverse discrimination should be highest for minority groups that are perceived as most oppressed. Dutton (1973) tested this hypothesis in a second study. A survey of middle-class whites in Vancouver revealed that both blacks and Indians were seen as greatly discriminated against, while Orientals were not. In both public and private settings, more money was donated to a charity if the solicitor was black or Indian than if he was Oriental.[19]

To more precisely test the notion that reverse discrimination results from attempts by middle-class (Particulary upper-middle-class, college-educated) whites not to appear prejudiced (to themselves and/or to others), a laboratory experiment was conducted (Dutton and Lake, 1973). Out of a pool of 500 college students, 80 were selected who scored low in anti-black prejudice and high in their ranking of equality. Half the subjects were led to believe that they might be prejudiced through false autonomic feedback to interracial slides (high threat of being prejudiced). The low-threat subjects received feedback indicating only minor response to such slides. After the feedback session, all subjects were panhandled by either a white or a black. The threat manipulation had no effect on money given to the white panhandler, but high-threat subjects gave significantly more money to the black panhandler than did those in the low-threat condition. In all three of these studies the reverse discrimination was of a trivial nature—it neither did much

[19] As Dutton and Lake (1973) point out, extant studies of the effect of race on altruism in the United States don't support this notion of "reverse discrimination." One study revealed no difference in aid to a white vs. black target (Wispe and Freshley, 1971), while two others (Bryan and Test, 1967; Gaertner and Bickman, 1971) found significantly more help-giving to a white than a black target. However, the size of the differential in the latter two studies was quite small, and, more importantly, both took place in or quite near central-city areas (Trenton, New Jersey, and Brooklyn, New York) where whites have opportunities for interracial contact and probably score rather high in perceived threat.

to advance interracial harmony nor cost the white much time or effort. It may be that middle-class whites demonstrate their egalitarian values through such "token" altruisms and that once having "proved" that they are nonracist they are less likely to make more significant contributions to minority group progress. To test this hypothesis, three groups of college students were run under the high-threat conditions of the previous experiment (Dutton and Lennox, 1974). The first group was panhandled by a white, the second by a black, and the third was not panhandled. The next day all subjects were asked to volunteer some time for an "interracial brotherhood campaign." Whites who had given money to the black panhandler volunteered less time than subjects in the other two conditions.

The foregoing research demonstrates that both "reverse discrimination" and "tokenism" exist. All of the research was done in Canada, but the results of the previously mentioned Ashmore and Butsch (1972) and Perlman and Oskamp (1971) studies suggest that middle-class American whites who want to see themselves as nonprejudiced are also susceptible. In the Ashmore and Butsch experiment subjects low in perceived threat (and presumably similar to Dutton's low-prejudice/high-egalitarian subjects) rated an aggressor more harshly if his victim was black as opposed to white. Perlman and Oskamp's subjects, also college students, rated black faces as more attractive, less lazy, and more positive than comparable white faces. Thus, it seems that bending over backward or reverse discrimination may occur for middle-class Canadian and American whites who do not want to appear racist. The Dutton and Lennox (1974) findings suggest, however, that such bending over backward may be restricted to trivial behaviors (hence "tokenism") and may actually impede significant white contributions to interracial harmony.

## Prejudice in the context of other self-system variables

The three topics covered in this section are united by the assumption that negative intergroup attitudes and their influence on behavior are best understood by considering them in relation to other individual-level variables. The first two topics deal specifically with interracial harm-doing: Donnerstein and his associates (1972) explicate the several interacting variables that predict when and how whites will aggress against blacks, and Katz et al. (1973) are concerned with how a multifactor approach can explain whites' responses to having committed an aggressive interracial act. The final subsection overviews a conceptual framework for attitudes in the context of an individual's total system of beliefs.

*White aggression and fear of retaliation.* Edward Donnerstein and his associates have studied the factors governing whites' punishing of blacks in a series of laboratory experiments. In the first (Donnerstein et al. 1972) they placed white college students in the role of teacher, using electric shock to punish incorrect responses by a learner (either a white or black). The learning task was preceded by two orthogonal manipulations, which both served to maximize or minimize the possibility of future counteraggression by the learner. The first induction was to either reveal or not reveal the subject's identity to the learner, thereby heightening the possibility of future counter-aggression in the nonanonymous conditions. The second induction involved instructions that called for or did not call for role-switching by the teacher and learner, thus creating the possibility of immediate counteraggression in the role-switching conditions. Two major dependent variables were employed—direct aggression (mean number of shocks) and indirect aggression (mean length of shocks). When the experimental conditions allowed for the possibility of counteraggression, the subjects delivered less direct aggression and more indirect aggression to black targets while no such differential was observed for white targets. Donnerstein interpreted this differential as due to fear of retaliation by black targets—an interpretation supported by the fact that subjects anticipated more direct aggression from black targets regardless of the punishment delivered.

Shortly after a campus disturbance in which black students damaged university property and roughed up some white students, a second experiment was conducted that demonstrated the effects of historical or context factors on punishing behavior. This experiment was a partial replication of the first—a white subject delivered shocks to either a white or black under either anony-mous or nonanonymous conditions. When compared with the predisturbance results, the second experiment yielded higher levels of direct aggression and reduced indirect aggression against black targets, but, again, there were no differences with regard to white targets. And the punishing behavior of whites was less dependent on the opportunity for counteraggression than in the first experiment.

In still another experiment (Donnerstein and Donnerstein, 1972), white subjects' rewarding behavior was assessed using this same general paradigm. Specifically, subjects were allowed to give varying amounts of money (one to eight pennies) for correct responses by the target as well as electric shocks for incorrect ones. In line with the first experiment, there was more direct rewarding of (the equivalent of less shocks under the assumption that low-level rewards are punishing when higher levels could be administered) but more indirect aggression toward a black target under conditions that allowed for retailiation. As in the previous studies, no comparable differential was shown for a white target. The Donnerstein research demonstrates the need to consider both overt and covert forms of interracial behavior. While fear of retailiation can reduce overt aggression (and increase overt rewarding), it seems to increase indirect aggression. The results of the experiment following a racial disturbance suggest that incidents of racial violence may serve to increase direct interracial aggression by whites rather than increase their fear of retaliation.

*Guilt, ambivalence, and interracial harm-doing.* While the Donnerstein studies were concerned with the situational and historial determinants of white aggression against blacks, research by Katz, Glass, and Cohen (1973) looked at what happens after the harm has been done. Two experiments were conducted to test the notion that ambivalent racial attitudes, and not simply anti-black prejudice, heighten the derogation of a black victim once a white has been induced to aggress against him. That is, harming another person produces "guilt," which is heightened by ambivalent feelings about the target, and derogation of the victim is one way to justify harm-doing and to reduce guilt. Both studies involved a shock-learning paradigm similar to that used by Donnerstein and his associates. In the first experiment subjects delivered either mild or strong shocks to either a black or white confederate. As predicted, there was a significant Shock x Race interaction with a large decrease in pre- to postexperimental evaluations of the black confederate in the high-shock condition. In the second experiment, the high-shock/black-confederate condition was replicated using four types of subjects: high in anti-black prejudice— low in sympathy for blacks; high in prejudice—high in sympathy; low in prejudice—low in sympathy; low in prejudice—high in sympathy.[20] Again, the guilt-ambivalent hypothesis was borne out. There was a significant Prejudice x Sympathy interaction with the high-prejudice/high-sympathy subjects (those presumably highest in ambivalence) showing a relatively large decrease in evaluation of the black confederate after delivering electric shocks to him.

Although these results do not rule out other interpretations,[21] they are compatible with the guilt-ambivalence hypothesis—i.e., a white harm-doer with ambivalent racial attitudes can reduce his guilt by derogating his victim. As Katz and his associates point out, however, the guilt-ambivalence interpretation does not preclude the possibility of other means of guilt reduction. In particular, altruistic behavior has been shown to follow guilt induction (e.g., Freedman, 1970) but an altruistic alternative was not allowed in either experiment. Future research could fruitfully assess the individual and situational factors that lead an ambivalent harm-doer to either derogation of his victim or to altruism.

[20]Prejudice was assessed by means of three subscales of the Multi-Racial Attitude Inventory (Woodmansee an;Cook, 1967), while sympathy was operationalized via the Sympathetic Identification with the Underdog scale (Schuman and Harding, 1964).

[21]The use of the word "guilt" in this study is particularly problematic. Although there is *suggestive* evidence that accidental harm-doing increases general altruism by increasing guilt (Freedman, 1970), the application of the concept in the present study seems quite tenuous. The harm-doing more likely causes "cognitive dissonance" (a term having less excess conceptual baggage than guilt) with derogation of the victim serving to reduce the dissonance.

*Prejudice in the context of the total "belief system."* Recently, Rokeach (1973, Chapter 8) has proposed a model that conceptualizes an individual's values and attitudes as being part of his "belief system." This system consists of hierarchically arranged types of cognitions. The highest type of cognitions concern self, followed by terminal values (i.e., cognitions about valued end-states such as "Freedom"), instrumental values (i.e., cognitions about valued types of behavior such as "Obedience"), attitude systems (e.g., a political ideology such as Conservatism), individual attitudes (e.g., anti-black prejudice), and so on, down to cognitions about inanimate objects. This hierarchical arrangement expresses Rokeach's belief that higher order elements are more stable but that if changes in such elements are achieved they should exert pressure for change on related lower order elements. Rokeach further hypothesizes that changes anywhere in the belief system occur *only* when an individual's perception of some inconsistency leads him to feel self-dissatisfaction—i.e., only when the perceived inconsistency has negative implications for self-perception. Although Rokeach's ideas have not been widely test, they seem to represent a vast improvement over previous work on cognitive consistency as a factor in prejudice acquistion and maintenance. They suggest a fairly coherent framework for placing prejudice in relation to other relevant cognitions and predicting the conditions under which change in prejudice should or should not occur.

Rokeach has conducted a number of studies demonstrating the utility of his schema for suggesting ways to alter social attitudes. Specifically, he has shown that making people aware of certain inconsistencies within their belief system can produce relatively long-term alteration of racial attitudes. The general procedure in these experiments requires subjects to rank-order 18 terminal values and indicate the degree to which they sympathize with the aims of civil rights demonstrations. Subjects are then confronted with inconsistencies or discrepancies in their value-attitude systems. Subjects frequently discover that they hold incompatible values (e.g., "freedom" is ranked high and "equality" rather low) or that they have engaged in behavior that is incompatible with their attitudes or values (e.g., expressing pro-civil rights sentiments and placing a relatively low value on equality). The dissonance produced by the value-discrepancy manipulation has led to highly significant changes in values and attitudes that are evident for many months. Rokeach found that experimental subjects were significantly more likely than controls to respond to a NAACP solicitation 15 to 17 months after the experimental session. Not only does the Rokeach schema allow one to design an effective procedure for changing racial attitudes (although independent replication is required before this conclusion can be accepted unequivocally), but it also may be a fruitful way of organizing and guiding research on how such prejudices develop and are maintained.

## SUMMARY AND SERMONIZING

We began this chapter by noting that psychological approaches to intergroup conflict stress internal dispositions, particularly prejudice. We then covered a large number of factors that have been offered to account for the development, maintenance, and expression of ethnic prejudice, particularly the anti-black prejudice of white Americans. Though we treated these explanations separately and as opposing ideas (e.g., symptom theories vs. the conformity explanation), this should not be construed to mean that we feel there is one correct theory of prejudice. On the contrary, prejudice is a multifaceted problem and many causal variables are needed to even begin to explain it. In evaluating each explanation we have tried to provide a rough estimate of each theory's explanatory power (essentially how much variance is accounted for—see Ashmore, 1970, pp. 246-247).

At the societal level, the nature of intergroup interdependence is critical in determining the direction and content of intergroup attitudes. Competition—whether open and direct or completely defused through the establishment of a caste system—generates hostile intergroup attitudes, which become normative. These normative intergroup attitudes are passed on via socialization and group pressures for conformity. Another interpersonal input to individual prejudice is the stereotyped images of and "facts" regarding the out-group: via attribution processes, these images and "facts" contribute to derogatory beliefs that bolster prejudice. Intrapersonal factors are also significant in fully understanding prejudice, although the attention devoted to such explanations by psychologists is out of proportion to the amount of variance they account for. While the idea of hostility displacement is little supported as a theory of prejudice development, there is considerable evidence that frustration, together with social norms, are important factors in predicting when and how prejudice will be acted out. The authoritarian personality, though far from being a complete theory of prejudice, does highlight the role of child-rearing practices in shaping personalities with varying susceptibility to prejudice.

The last section of the chapter was devoted to more tentative psychological conceptions of negative intergroup relations. We think that these ideas are important for a number of reasons. First, they point us not only to the present but also to the likely future of race relations. Both perceived racial threat and symbolic racism seek to explain important varieties of current racial attitudes. At the same time, by stressing historical and context factors in prejudice, they alert us to how these factors might change in the future, and what such changes might mean at the level of individual attitudes. For example, black-white relations today are much less openly antagonistic than they were in 1967, and the current federal administration seems to be faithfully following its program of "benign neglect." There is only a moderate level of overt competition but still an awareness that "it" (the riots) could happen again. This is likely to make race a less open, but still anxiety-arousing issue, which ought to increase the symbolic nature of black-white conflict. Second, the Dutton (1971, 1973, 1974) research and the Katz, *et al.* (1973) studies focus attention not just on the "bad guys" (the bigot or racist) but also on "us good guys" (the white liberals). How do our attitudes and values shape our behavior in interracial settings? Third, all of the "new directions" research is concerned with making explicit the multidimensional nature of racial attitudes and the multiple, interacting causes of individual-level prejudice. This multiple-factor approach is evident not only in the research covered but also in the area of prejudice measurement—e.g., the behavioral differential (Triandis, 1964) and the multifactor racial attitude inventory (Woodmansee and Cook, 1967)—and observational analyses of interracial behavior (Weitz, 1972).

We think that all of these trends are promising and bode well for the immediate future of the psychology of prejudice. However, the relative scarcity of recent research concerned with traditional explanations raises questions about their continued validity. While it would be useful to simply replicate previous research, it would be even more advisable to design studies relevant to several explanations (e.g., assess the parental attitudes that are relevant to socialization explanations and the child-rearing practices that are important in personality-based explanation) using different subject samples (e.g., inner-city or suburban whites). This would permit comparisons among the various explanations in terms of accounting for the variance in prejudice and would also allow us to know the generalizability of the various explanations. In addition, the application of causal models and related techniques (Borgatta, 1969, Parts I and II) to such data, might enable us to build more integrated explanations of prejudice rather than having the many isolated models of today. Attempts at theoretical and empirical integration would seem to be among the highest priorities for psychological approaches to intergroup relations.

## REFERENCES

Adorno, T.W., Frenkel-Brunswik, E., Levinson, D.J., and Sanford, R.N. *The authoritarian personality.* New York: Harper, 1950.

Allport, G.W. *The nature of prejudice.* New York: Doubleday, 1958.

Allport, G.W., and Kramer, B.M. Some roots of prejudice. *Journal of Psychology,* 1946, 22, 9-39.

Anderson, C.C. and Cote, A.D.J. Belief dissonance as a source of disaffection between ethnic groups. *Journal of Personality and Social Psychology,* 1966, 4, 447-453.

Aptheker, H. *A history of Negro slave revolts.* New York: International Publishers, 1969.

Ashmore, R.D. Prejudice: Causes and cures. In B.E. Collins, (Ed.) *Social psychology: Social influence, attitude change, group processes, and prejudice.* Reading, Mass.: Addison-Wesley, 1970.

Ashmore, R.D., and Butsch, R.J. Perceived threat and the perception of violence in biracial settings: Toward an experimental paradigm. Eastern Psychological Association, Boston, April 1972.

Ashmore, R.D., and McConahay, J.B. *Psychology and America's urban dilemmas.* New York: McGraw-Hill, in press.

Ashmore, R.D., Turner, F., Donato, D.A., and Nevenglosky, T. How white Americans view the concept of black power. Unpublished manuscript, 1973.

Berkowitz, L. Antisemitism and the displacement of aggression. *Journal of Abnormal and Social Psychology,* 1959, **59**, 182-187.

Berkowitz, L., and Green, J.A. The stimulus qualities of the scapegoat. *Journal of Abnormal and Social Psychology,* 1962, **64**, 293-301.

Bernard, J. The sociological study of conflict. In J. Bernard *et al.* (Eds.), *The nature of conflict.* Paris: UNESCO, 1957.

Bettelheim, B., and Janowitz, M. *Dynamics of Prejudice.* New York: Harper, 1950.

Bettelheim, B., and Janowitz, M. *Social change and prejudice.* New York: Free Press, 1964.

Billig, M.G. Normative communication in a minimal intergroup situation. *European Journal of Social Psychology,* 1973, in press.

Billig, M.G., and Tajfel, H. Social categorization and similarity in intergroup behavior. *European Journal of Social Psychology,* 1973, **3**, 27-52.

Bird, C., Monachesi, E.D., and Burdick, H. Infiltration and the attitudes of white and Negro parents and children. *Journal of Abnormal and Social Psychology,* 1952, **47**, 688-699.

Blalock, H.M., Jr. *Toward a theory of minority-group relations.* New York: Wiley, 1967.

Bogardus, E.S. Racial distance changes in the United States during the past thirty years. *Sociology and Social Research,* 1958, **43**, 127-135.

Bogardus, E.S. Comparing racial distance in Ethiopia, South Africa, and the United States, *Sociology and Social Research,* 1968, **52**, 149-156.

Borgatta, E.F. (Ed.). *Social methodology.* San Francisco: Jossey-Bass, 1969.

Boskin, J. Sambo. In G. Nash and R. Weiss (Eds.), *The great fear: Race in the mind of America.* New York: Holt, Rinehart and Winston, 1970.

Boulding, K.E. *Conflict and defense: A general theory.* New York: Harper, 1962.

Brigham, J.C., Woodmansee, J.J., and Cook, S.W. Dimensions of verbal racial attitudes: Interracial marriage and approaches to black progress. In R. D. Ashmore (Ed.), Black and white in the 1970's, *Journal of Social Issues,* in press.

Brink, W., and Harris, L. *The Negro revolution in America.* New York: Simon & Schuster, 1964.

Bryan, J.H., and Test, M.A. Models and helping: Naturalistic studies in aiding behavior. *Journal of Personality and Social Psychology,* 1967, **6**, 400-407.

Byrne, D., and McGraw, C. Interpersonal attraction toward Negroes. *Human Relations,* 1964, **17**, 201-213.

Byrne, D., and Nelson, D. Attraction as a linear function of proportion of positive reinforcements. *Journal of Personality and Social Psychology,* 1965, 1, 659-663.

Byrne, D., and Wong, T. Racial prejudice, interpersonal attraction, and assumed dissimilarity of attitudes. *Journal of Abnormal and Social Psychology,* 1962, 65, 246-253.

Campbell, A. *White attitudes toward black people.* Ann Arbor: Institute for Social Research, 1971.

Campbell, A.A. Factors associated with attitudes toward Jews. In T.M. Newcomb and E.L. Hartley (Eds.), *Readings in social psychology.* New York: Holt, 1947.

Campbell, D.T. Ethnocentric and other altruistic motives. In D. Levine (Ed.), *Nebraska symposium on motivation.* Lincoln: University of Nebraska Press, 1965.

Campbell, D.T., and Fiske, D.W. Convergent and discriminant validation by the multitrait-multimethod matrix. *Psychological Bulletin,* 1959, 56, 81-105.

Caprio, R.J. Place utility, social obsolescence, and qualitative housing change. *Proceedings of the Association of American Geographers,* 1972, 4, 14-19.

Christie, R. Authoritarianism re-examined. In R. Christie and M. Jahoda (Eds.), *Studies in the scope and method of "The authoritarian personality."* New York: Free Press, 1954.

Christie, R. and Jahoda, M. (Eds.). *Studies in the scope and method of "The authoritarian personality."* New York: Free Press, 1954.

Colle, R.D. Color on T.V. *The Reporter,* November 30, 1967, pp. 23-25.

Collins, B.E. *Social psychology: Social influence, attitude change, group processes, and prejudice.* Reading, Mass.: Addison-Wesley, 1970.

Cook, S.W., and Selltiz, C. A multiple-indicator approach to attitude measurement. *Psychological Bulletin,* 1964, 62, 36-55.

Coopersmith, S. *The antecedents of self-esteem.* San Francisco: Freeman, 1967.

Cowen, E.L., Landes, J., and Schaet, D.E. The effects of mild frustration on the expression of prejudiced attitudes. *Journal of Abnormal and Social Psychology,* 1958, 58, 33-38.

Cox, O.C. *Caste, class and race: A study in social dynamics.* New York: Doubleday, 1948.

Cronbach, L.J., and Meehl, P.E. Construct validity in psychological tests. *Psychological Bulletin,* 1955, 52, 281-302.

Deutsch, M., Katz, I., and Jensen, A.R. (Eds.). *Social class, race, and psychological development.* New York: Holt, Rinehart and Winston, 1968.

Deutscher, I. Words and deeds: Social science and social policy. *Social Problems,* 1966, 13, 235-254.

Dickens, S., and Hobart, C. Parental dominance and offspring ethnocentrism. *Journal of Social Psychology,* 1959, 49, 297-303.

Dienstbier, R.A. A modified belief theory of prejudice emphasizing the mutual causality of racial prejudice and anticipated belief differences. *Psychological Review,* 1972, 79, 146-160.

Dillehay, R.C. On the irrelevance of the classical negative evidence concerning the effect of attitudes on behavior. *American Psychologist,* 1973, 28, 887-891.

Doise, W., Csepeli, G., Dann, H.D., Gouge, C., Larsen, K., and Ostell, A. An experimental investigation into the formation of intergroup representations. *European Journal of Social Psychology,* 1972, **2**, 202-204. Doise,

Doise, W., and Sinclair, A. The categorization process in intergroup relations. *European Journal of Social Psychology,* 1973, **3**, 145-157.

Dollard, J. *Caste and class in a southern town.* New Haven: Yale University Press, 1937.

Donnerstein, E., and Donnerstein, M. White rewarding behavior as a function of the potential for black retalliation. *Journal of Personality and Social Psychology,* 1972, **24**, 327-334.

Donnerstein, E., Donnerstein, M., Simon, S., and Ditrichs, R. Variables in interracial aggression: Anonymity, expected retaliation, and a riot. *Journal of Personality and Social Psychology,* 1972, **22**, 236-245.

Dutton, D.G. Reaction of restaurateurs to blacks and whites violating restaurant dress requirements. *Canadian Journal of Behavioral Science,* 1971, **3**, 298-302.

Dutton, D.G. The relationship of amount of perceived discrimination toward a minority group on behavior of majority group members. *Canadian Journal of Behavioral Science,* 1973, **5**, 34-45.

Dutton, D.G., and Lake, R. Threat of own prejudice and reverse discrimination in interracial situations. *Journal of Personality and Social Psychology,* 1973, **28**, 94-100.

Dutton, D.G., and Lennox, V.L. The effect of prior "token" compliance on subsequent interracial behavior. *Journal of Personality and Social Psychology,* 1974, **29**, 65-71.

Eddy, E.M. Attitudes towards desegregation among Southern students on a Northern campus. *Journal of Social Psychology,* 1964, **62**, 285-301.

Edelman, M. *Politics as symbolic action.* Chicago: Markham, 1971.

Ehrlich, H.J. *The social psychology of prejudice.* New York: Wiley, 1973.

Epstein, R., and Komorita, S.S. The development of a scale of parental punitiveness towards aggression. *Child Development,* 1965a, **36**, 129-142.

Epstein, R., and Komorita, S.S. Parental discipline, stimulus characteristics of outgroups, and social distance in children. *Journal of Personality and Social Psychology,* 1965b, **2**, 416-420.

Epstein, R., and Komorita, S.S. Prejudice among Negro children as related to parental ethnocentrism and punitiveness. *Journal of Personality and Social Psychology,* 1966, **4**, 643-647.

Feagin, J.R. Home defense and the police: Black and white perspectives. *American Behavioral Scientist,* 1970, **13**, 717-814.

Feshbach, S., and Singer, R. The effects of personal and shared threats upon social prejudice. *Journal of Abnormal and Social Psychology,* 1957, **54**, 411-416.

Freedman, J.L. Guilt, equality, justice and reciprocation. In J. Macaulay and L. Berkowitz (Eds.), *Altruism and helping behavior.* New York: Academic Press, 1970.

Frenkel-Brunswik, E. A Study of prejudice in children. *Human Relations,* 1948, **1**, 295-306.

Frenkel-Brunswik, E., and Havel, J. Prejudice in the inverviews of children: Attitudes toward minority groups. *Journal of Genetic Psychology,* 1953, **82**, 91-136.

Gaertner, S.L., and Bickman, L. Effects of race on the elicitation of helping behavior: The wrong number technique. *Journal of Personality and Social Psychology,* 1971, **20**, 218-222.

Genthner, R.W., and Taylor, S.P. Physical aggression as a function of racial prejudice and the race of the target. *Journal of Personality and Social Psychology,* 1973, **27**, 207-210.

Goldstein, M., and Davis, E. Race and belief: A further analysis of the social determinants of behavioral intentions. *Journal of Personality and Social Psychology,* 1972, **22**, 346-355.

Goodman, M.E. *Race awareness in young children.* Second edition. New York: Crowell-Collier, 1964.

Gordon, A.I. Frustration and aggression among Jewish university students. *Jewish Sociological Studies,* 1943, **5**, 27-42.

Greeley, A.M., and Sheatsley, P.B. Attitudes toward racial integration. *Scientific American,* 1971, **225**, 13-19.

Grossack, M.M. Attitudes towards desegregation of southern white and Negro children. *Journal of Social Psychology,* 1957, **46**, 299-306.

Groves, W.E., and Rossi, P.H. Police perceptions of a hostile ghetto: Realism or projection. *American Behavioral Scientist,* 1970, **13**, 727-744.

Halsey, M. *Color blind.* New York: Simon & Schuster, 1946.

Harding, J.B., Proshansky, H., Kutner, B., and Chein, I. Prejudice and ethnic relations. In G. Lindzey and E. Aronson (Eds.), *The handbook of social psychology.* Second edition. Volume 5. Reading, Mass.: Addison-Wesley, 1969.

Harris, L. Racial stereotypes at heart of communication gap. *The Home News,* New Brunswick, N.J., October 5, 1971, Vol. 93, No. 209.

Harris, D.B., Gough, H.G., and Martin, W.E. Children's ethnic attitudes. II: Relationships to parental beliefs concerning child training. *Child Development,* 1950, **21**, 169-181.

Hastorf, A.H., Schneider, D.J., and Polefka, J. *Person perception.* Reading, Mass.: Addison-Wesley, 1970.

Hendrick, C., Bixenstein, V., and Hawkins, G. Race versus belief similarity as determinants of attraction. A search for a fair test. *Journal of Personality and Social Psychology,* 1971, **17**, 250-258.

Horowitz, E.L., and Horowitz, R.E. Development of social attitudes in children. *Sociometry,* 1938, **1**, 301-338.

Hovland, C.I., and Sears, R.R. Minor studies of aggression. VI. Correlation of lynchings with economic indices. *Journal of Psychology,* 1940, **9**, 301-310.

Hsu, F.L.K. American core value and national character. In F.L.K. Hsu (Ed.), *Psychological anthropology.* Cambridge, Mass.: Schenkman, 1972.

Hyman, H.H., and Sheatsley, P.B. "The authoritarian personality"—A methodological critique. In R. Christie and M. Jahoda (Eds.), *Studies in the scope and method of "The authoritarian personality."* New York: Free Press, 1954.

Insko, C.A., and Robinson, J.E. Belief similarity versus race as determinants of reactions to Negroes by Southern white adolescents: A further test of Rokeach's theory. *Journal of Personality and Social Psychology,* 1967, **7,** 216-221.

Johnson, P.B., Sears, D.O., and McConahay, J.B. Black invisibility, the press, and the Los Angeles riot. *American Journal of Sociology,* 1971, **76,** 698-721.

Jones, E., Kanouse, D., Kelley, H., Nisbett, R., Valins, S., and Weiner, B. *Attribution: Perceiving the causes of behavior.* Morristown, N.J.: General Learning Press, 1971.

Jones, J. *Prejudice and racism.* Reading, Mass.: Addison-Wesley, 1972.

Jordan, W.D. *White over black: American attitudes toward the Negro, 1550-1812.* Chapel Hill: University of North Carolina Press, 1968.

Kane, M.B. *Minorities in textbooks.* Chicago: Quadrangle, 1970.

Karlins, M., Coffman, T., and Walters, G. On the fading of social stereotypes: Studies in three generations of college students. *Journal of Personality and Social Psychology,* 1969, **13,** 1-16.

Kates, S.L., and Diab, L.N. Authoritarian ideology and attitudes on parent-child relationships. *Journal of Abnormal and Social Psychology,* 1955, **51,** 13-16.

Katz, D., and Braly, K.W. Racial stereotypes of 100 college students. *Journal of Abnormal and Social Psychology,* 1933, **28,** 280-290.

Katz, D., Sarnoff, I., and McClintock, C. Ego-defense and attitude change. *Human Relations,* 1956, **9,** 27-45.

Katz, I., Glass, D., and Cohen, S. Ambivalence, guilt, and the scapegoating of minority group victims. *Journal of Experimental Social Psychology,* 1973, **9,** 423-436.

Katz, P.A. Perception of racial cues in preschool children: A new look. *Developmental Psychology,* 1973, **8,** 295-299.

Katz, P.A., Sohn, M., and Zalk, S.R. Perceptual concomitants of racial attitudes in urban grade school children. *Developmental Psychology,* 1974 in press.

Kelly, J.G., Ferson, J.E., and Holtzman, W.H. The measurement of attitudes toward the Negro in the South. *Journal of Social Psychology,* 1958, **48,** 305-317.

Kirscht, J.P., and Dillehay, R.C. *Dimensions of authoritariansim: A review of research and theory.* Lexington: University of Kentucky Press, 1967.

Klineberg, O. Tensions affecting international understanding. *Social Science Research Council Bulletin, 62.* New York: Social Science Research Council, 1950.

Knowles, L.L., and Prewitt, K. (Eds.). *Institutional racism in America.* Englewood Cliffs, N.J.: Prentice-Hall, 1969.

Kutner, B. Patterns of mental functioning associated with prejudice in children. *Psychological Monographs,* 1958, **72,** 7.

Lesser, G.S. Extrapunitiveness and ethnic attitudes. *Journal of Abnormal and Social Psychology,* 1958, **56,** 281-282.

Lindzey, G. Differences between the high and low in prejudice and their implications for a theory of prejudice. *Journal of Personality,* 1950, **19,** 16-40.

Lyle, W.H., Jr., and Levitt, E.E. Punitiveness, authoritarianism, and parental discipline of grade school children. *Journal of Abnormal and Social Psychology*, 1955, **51**, 42-46.

Martin, J.G. *The tolerant personality.* Detroit: Wayne State University Press, 1964.

Maykovitch, M.K. Reciprocity in racial stereotypes: White, black and yellow. *American Journal of Sociology*, 1972, **77**, 876-897.

McCandless, B.R. *Children and adolescents: Behavior and development.* New York: Holt, Rinehart and Winston, 1961.

McClosky, H. Conservatism and personality. *American Political Science Review*, 1958, **52**, 27-45.

McCord, W., McCord, J., and Howard, A. Early familial experiences and bigotry. *American Sociological Review*, 1960, **25**, 717-722.

McLean, H.V. Psychodynamic factors in racial relations. *The Annals of the American Academy of Political and Social Science*, 1946, **244**, 159-166.

McWilliams, C. *Prejudice. Japanese-Americans: Symbol of racial intolerance.* Boston: Little, Brown, 1944.

Mezei, L. Perceived social pressure as an explanation of shifts in the relative influence of race and belief on prejudice across social interactions. *Journal of Personality and Social Psychology*, 1971, **19**, 69-81.

Miller, N.E., and Bugelski, R. Minor studies in aggression: The influence of frustrations imposed by the in-group on attitudes expressed toward out-groups. *Journal of Psychology*, 1948, **25**, 437-442.

Mintz, A. A re-examination of correlations between lynchings and economic indices. *Journal of Abnormal and Social Psychology*, 1946, **41**, 159-160.

Morse, C., and Allport, F.H. The causation of anti-Semitism: An investigation of seven hypotheses. *Journal of Psychology*, 1952, **34**, 197-233.

Mosher, D.L., and Scodel, A. A study of the relationship between ethnocentrism in children and the ethnocentrism and authoritarian rearing practices of their mothers. *Child Development*, 1960, **31**, 369-376.

Nash, G. Red, white, and black: The origins of racism in colonial America. In G. Nash and R. Weiss (Eds.), *The great fear: Race in the mind of America.* New York: Holt, Rinehart and Winston, 1970.

Pearlin, L.I. Shifting group attachments and attitudes towards Negroes. *Social Forces*, 1954, **33**, 47-50.

Perlman, D., and Oskamp, S. The effects of picture content and exposure frequency on evaluations of Negroes and whites. *Journal of Experimental Social Psychology*, 1971, **7**, 503-514.

Pettigrew, T.F. Personality and sociocultural factors in intergroup attitudes: A cross-national comparison. *Journal of Conflict Resolution*, 1958, **2**, 29-42.

Pettigrew, T.F. Regional differences in anti-Negro prejudice. *Journal of Abnormal and Social Psychology*, 1959, **59**, 28-36.

Pettigrew, T.F. *Racially separate or together?* New York: McGraw-Hill, 1971.

Pettigrew, T.F., and Cramer, M.R. The demography of desegregation. *Journal of Social Issues*, 1959, **15**, 61-71.

Pinderhughes, C.A. Racism: A paranoia with contrived reality and processed violence. Paper presented at the joint meeting of the American Psychiatric Association and the American Psychoanalytic Association, Washington, D.C., May 3, 1971.

Pompilo, P.T. The relationship between projection and prejudice; with a factor analysis of anti-Semitic and anti-Negro attitudes. Ph.D. dissertation, Catholic University, Washington, D.C., 1957.

Porter, J.D.R. *Black child, white child: The development of racial attitudes.* Cambridge, Mass.: Harvard University Press, 1971.

Quinn, O.W. The transmission of racial attitudes among white Southerners. *Social Forces,* 1954, **33**, 41-47.

Rabbie, J.M., and Horwitz, M. Arousal of ingroup-outgroup bias by a chance win of loss. *Journal of Personality and Social Psychology,* 1969, **13**, 269-277.

Rabbie, J.M., and Wilkins, G. Intergroup competition and its effects on intragroup and intergroup relationships. *European Journal of Social Psychology,* 1971, **1**, 215-234.

Radke-Yarrow, M., Trager, H., and Miller, J. The role of parents in the development of children's ethnic attitudes. *Child Development,* 1952, **23**, 13-53.

Rapaport, D. The structure of psychoanalytic theory: A systematizing attempt. In S. Koch (Ed.), *Psychology: A study of a science.* New York: McGraw-Hill, 1959.

Raper, A.F. *The tragedy of lynching.* Chapel Hill: University of North Carolina Press, 1933

Rhyne, E.H. Racial prejudice and personality scales: An alternative approach. *Social Forces,* 1962, **41**, 44-53.

Richert, K.C. Explorations into the specific behavioral determinants of authoritarians. *Psychological Reports,* 1963, **13**, 950.

Rokeach, M. (Ed.) *The open and closed mind.* New York: Basic Books, 1960.

Rokeach, M. *Beliefs, attitudes and values.* San Francisco: Jossey-Bass, 1968.

Rokeach, M. *The nature of human values.* New York: Free Press, 1973.

Rokeach, M., and Mezei, L. Race and shared belief as factors in social choice. *Science,* 1966, **151**, 167-172.

Rokeach, M., Smith, P.W., and Evans, R.I. Two kinds of prejudice or one? In M. Rokeach, (Ed.), *The open and closed mind.* New York: Basic Books, 1960.

Rose, A.M., and Rose, C.B. (Eds.). *Minority problems.* New York: Harper & Row, 1965.

Rosenberg, M. *Society and the adolescent self-image.* Princeton, N.J.: Princeton University Press, 1965.

Rosenblith, J.F. A replication of "some roots of prejudice." *Journal of Abnormal and Social Psychology,* 1949, **44**, 470-489.

Rubin, I.M. Increased self-acceptance: A means of reducing prejudice. *Journal of Personality and Social Psychology,* 1967, **5**, 233-238.

Schuman, H. Free will and determinism in public beliefs about race. *Trans-Action,* 1969, **7**, 44-48.

Schuman, H., and Harding, J. Prejudice and the norm of rationality. *Sociometry,* 1964, **27**, 353-371.

Schwartz, M.A. *Trends in white attitudes toward Negroes.* Chicago: National Opinion Research, 1967.

Sears, D.O., and Abeles, R.P. Attitudes and opinions. *Annual Review of Psychology,* 1969, **20**, 253-288.

Sears, D.O., and Kinder, D.R. Racial tensions and voting in Los Angeles. In W.Z. Hirsch (Ed.) *Los Angeles: Viability and prospects for metropolitan leadership.* New York: Praeger, 1971, 51-88.

Sears, D.O., and McConahay, J.B. *The politics of violence.* Boston: Houghton Mifflin, 1973.

Secord, P.F., and Backman, C.W. *Social psychology.* New York: McGraw-Hill, 1964.

Secord, P.F., Bevan, W., and Katz, B. The Negro stereotype and perceptual accentuation. *Journal of Abnormal and Social Psychology,* 1956, **53**, 78-83.

Seidenberg, R. The sexual basis of social psychology. *Psychoanalytic Review,* 1952, **39**, 90-95.

Sherif, M. Experimental study of intergroup relations. In J.H. Rohrer and M. Sherif (Eds.), *Social psychology at the crossroads.* New York: Harper & Row, 1951.

Shills, E.A. Authoritarianism: "Right" and "Left." In R. Christie and M. Jahoda (Eds.), *Studies in the scope and method of "The authoritarian personality."* New York: Free Press, 1954.

Simpson, G.E., and Yinger, J.M. *Racial and cultural minorities: An analysis of prejudice and discrimination.* Third edition. New York: Harper, 1965.

Smith, C.R., Williams, L., and Willis, R.H. Race, sex and belief as determinants of friendship acceptance. *Journal of Personality and Social Psychology,* 1967, **5**, 127-137.

Stagner, R., and Congdon, C.S. Another failure to demonstrate displacement of aggression. *Journal of Abnormal and Social Psychology,* 1955, **51**, 695-696.

Stein, D.D. The influence of belief systems on interpersonal preference: A validation study of Rokeach's theory of prejudice. *Psychological Monographs: General and Applied,* 1966, No. 616.

Stein, D.D., Hardyck, J.A., and Smith, M.B. Race and belief: An open and shut case. *Journal of Personality and Social Psychology,* 1965, **1**, 281-289.

Tabachnik, B.R. Some correlates of prejudice toward Negroes in elementary age children. *Journal of Genetic Psychology,* 1962, **100**, 193-203.

Tajfel, H. Cognitive aspects of prejudice. *Journal of Social Issues,* 1969, **25**, 79-97.

Tajfel, H. Experiments in intergroup discrimination. *Scientific American,* 1970, **223**, 96-102.

Tajfel, H., Flament, C., Billig, M., and Bundy, R. Social categorization and intergroup behavior. *European Journal of Social Psychology,* 1971, **1**, 149-178.

Tajfel, H., Sheikh, A.A., and Gardner, R.C. Content of stereotypes and the inference of similarity between members of stereotyped groups. *Acta Psychologica,* 1964, **22**, 191-201.

Tajfel, H., and Wilkes, A.L. Classification and quantitative judgment. *British Journal of Psychology,* 1963, **54**, 101-114.

Triandis, H.C. A note on Rokeach's theory of prejudice. *Journal of Abnormal and Social Psychology,* 1961, **62**, 184-186.

Triandis, H.C. Exploratory factor analyses of the behavioral component of social attitudes. *Journal of Abnormal and Social Psychology,* 1964, **68**, 420-430.

Triandis, H.C., and Davis, E. Race and belief as determinants of behavioral intentions. *Journal of Personality and Social Psychology,* 1965, **2**, 715-725.

van den Berghe, P. *Race and racism: A comparative perspective.* New York: Wiley, 1967.

Wadeson, R.W. Empathy: An antidote to individual racism. Paper presented at the joint meeting of the American Psychoanalytic Association and the American Psychiatric Association, Washington, D.C., May 3, 1971.

Weatherley, D. Anti-Semitism and the expression of fantasy aggression. *Journal of Abnormal and Social Psychology,* 1961, **62**, 454-457.

Weitz, S. Attitude, voice and behavior: A repressed affect model of interracial interaction. *Journal of Personality and Social Psychology,* 1972, **24**, 14-21.

Wicker, A.W. Attitudes versus actions: The relationship of verbal and overt behavioral responses to attitude objects. *Journal of Social Issues,* 1969, **25**, 41-78.

Willis, R.H., and Bulatao, R.A. Belief and ethnicity as determinants of friendship and marriage acceptance in the Philippines. Presented at the American Psychological Association Convention, Washington, D.C., 1967.

Wilson, W.C. Development of ethnic attitudes in adolescence. *Child Development,* 1963, **34**, 247-256.

Wispe, L.G., and Freshley, H.B. Race, sex and sympathetic helping behavior: The broken bag caper. *Journal of Personality and Social Psychology,* 1971, **17**, 59-65.

Woodmansee, J.J., and Cook, S.W. Dimensions of verbal racial attitudes: Their identification and measurement. *Journal of Personality and Social Psychology,* 1967, **7**, 240-250.

Zawadski, B. Limitations of the scapegoat theory of prejudice. *Journal of Abnormal and Social Psychology,* 1948, **43**, 127-141.

# 4

# *The Acquisition of Racial Attitudes in Children*

PHYLLIS A. KATZ

Folk wisdom tells us that the tree grows as the twig is bent. This notion seems particularly appropriate when considering the issue of how children acquire attitudes towards other groups. As Allport (1954) has suggested, early negative attitudes may be "caught, rather taught"—and once caught, may be most intransigent to change. The relative imperviousness of adult prejudice to the effects of conflicting evidence and experience strongly suggests that predispositions acquired at early developmental levels may form the irrational but potent foundation for racism.

Because there is general agreement that basic attitudes are learned in childhood, there has been a great deal of interest exhibited by social scientists in the ontogenesis of intergroup attitudes. Empirical investigations of children's attitude development through the mid-1960s have been comprehensively reviewed by Proshansky (1966). This chapter, therefore, will not attempt to duplicate that review. Instead, it will attempt to delineate the basic developmental trends obtained in earlier research, and to discuss the major theoretical viewpoints that have been offered to account for the origins of prejudice.

## HOW EARLY IS THE TWIG BENT?

The age at which children begin to acquire racial attitudes has been a question of continuing interest. Most of the evidence available suggests that many children of about three or four years of age make differential responses to skin color and other racial cues. The dawning of racial awareness follows a supposed period of color-blindness. It should be noted that this latter belief, though widely held, has no empirical support, since no studies have been reported with children younger than three.

There appears to be general agreement that ethnic attitudes begin to take shape during the nursery school years, although some questions exist concerning the generality of early stated preferences. According to many theorists (e.g., Goodman, 1952), the development of ethnic attitudes is integrally related to the establishment of a child's self-identity. It is typically assumed that the child must necessarily learn about which groups he does and does not belong to as part of the self-discovery process. At about the same time, positive and negative feelings come to be associated with various groups. In summarizing the empirical work in this area through 1965, Proshansky (1966) concludes that racial awareness: (a) appears at about three years of age in both black and white children; (b) increases rapidly for the next several years; and (c) is pretty well established by the time children enter first grade. Although there is some disagreement in the literature as to whether white or black children achieve racial awareness earlier, the preponderance of evidence seems to indicate that black children are more sensitive to racial cues.

In a classic study of young children's attitudes in a Northeastern urban community, Goodman (1952) studied 103 black and white children. One of the unique features of this frequently cited study is that the investigator made intensive observations of both the children and their families over the course of a full year. Consequently, she was able to study responses that might not have been evident to an observer who knew the children less well. According to Goodman, racial awareness was not only present at age three and four (although there was some variability along this dimension), but she maintains that 25% of the children at age four were already expressing strongly entrenched race-related values. White children *never* expressed a wish to be like a black child, whereas black children exhibited a great deal of denial and conflict about their evaluations of blackness. For some of the children, the words were there even though the feelings were still to come, as in the case of one little four-year-old who made the haunting comment: "The people that are white, they can go up. The people that are brown, they have to go down."

One of the interesting findings reported was the discrepancy that appeared to exist between what Goodman referred to as the children's "precocious raciality" and their parents' beliefs that their children were relatively unaware of race. Another extensive and more recent study of preschool children in the Northeast was conducted by Porter (1971). A sizable proportion of three-year-old children in this sample also exhibited preferences for white dolls. Although the preference for white dolls was clearly not as strong for black children as it appeared to be in the earlier cited investigation by Goodman, white children did reveal a marked increase in such responses between three and five years of age.

The presence of racial awareness in children as young as three suggests that its antecedents must have come at an earlier age—perhaps in nonverbal form. This view is in accord with some recent theorizing by John Williams (1972) who suggests that early racial awareness may, in fact, be reflecting primitive feelings about day and night. According to Williams, children exhibit fear of the dark, and this, he argues, may well generalize to dark-skinned people. Offered in support of this view is the finding that all cultures tested prefer light to dark colors. This viewpoint does not readily explain the attitudes of black children, however. Even if one were to assume that all children, irrespective of group, exhibit fear of the dark, the black child's positive associations to dark-skinned parents and other loving adults should more than offset this supposed generalization. Williams' view is a provocative though admittedly speculative one, requiring some empirical documentation.

In sum, the evidence on early racial awareness suggests that the twig may be bent at a very early age—perhaps much earlier than our current evidence suggests. The parameters underlying its development are not known at the present time.

## WHAT DOES RACIAL AWARENESS MEAN?

People are often quite surprised to learn that a three-year-old attends to differences in skin color. Undoubtedly, the very notion goes against our Rousseau-type beliefs of young children's innocence. Upon reflection, however, the results with regard to early awareness should not surprise us all that much. Children of three and four are obviously quite capable of making a number of considerably more subtle distinctions in the world around them, and many of them are quite sophisticated about the color dimension in nonanimate objects (e.g., Gaines, 1971). Thus, what may be unusual is not that children can and do perceptually distinguish brown and white skins, but that such distinctions have already taken on evaluative components.

In order to understand the ramifications of early racial awareness, it becomes necessary to attend to how it is actually measured in young children. By far, the most frequently employed task has been the use of doll choices. This preference task, originally employed by Clark and Clark in 1947, initially seems quite straightforward. The child is asked to choose the nice doll, the pretty one, etc., from pairs of Negro and Caucasian dolls. The seeming simplicity of the task may have accounted for its ready acceptance, and consequent historical significance in the 1954 *Brown* v. *Board of Education of Topeka, Kansas* Supreme Court decision, which barred segregation in the schools partially on the basis of the Clarks' results.

Closer examination, however, reveals a number of methodological problems associated with choice instruments of this type. In most studies, the dolls differ not only in skin color cues but in eye color and hair color as well—i.e., white dolls have blonde hair and blue eyes, whereas black dolls have brown hair and brown eyes. Thus, it is not clear what cues might be accounting for the earlier-obtained preference for white dolls. Kircher and Furby (1971), for example, found that both skin color and hair type could be significant determinants of young children's preferences for pictures. Moreover, a recent study that held hair and eye color constant (Katz and Zalk, 1974) found no preference for a doll's skin color.

Some additional problems with the use of this technique concern its psychometric properties. Reliability data has not yet been presented, despite its wide usage, and it is entirely conceivable that children of this age might give very different responses to the same questions a second time. Furthermore, no validity data for this task have been presented. Problems of reliability and validity are not, of course, unique to doll choice measures of racial attitudes, but are applicable to a wide range of measures. Investigators employing adults are somewhat more cognizant of these issues, whereas early investigators utilizing young children have not been. Studies of children have generally assumed that a one-to-one correspondence exists between responses to the index and other behavior, in the absence of supporting evidence. Interestingly, the few studies that have attempted to assess task performance and how nursery school children actually behave with regard to children of differing groups have not obtained positive findings. Stevenson and Stevenson (1960) have maintained, for example, that nursery school children do not exhibit same-race play preferences. The previously referred to study by Porter (1971) also noted that play patterns were unrelated to doll preferences, and Hraba and Grant (1970) found no relation between doll task performance and stated friendship choices. Thus, the possibility exists that the nursery school child, when confronted by a racial choice, may simply be responding in a way he feels an adult (who is usually white) expects him to. Because of these varied problems, it is difficult to know how best to interpret such a measure. Despite this, however, the technique has been used in numerous studies.

In the past three or four years there have been several studies that have contradicted the Clarks' earlier findings that black children exhibit strong preferences for white dolls (Hraba and Grant, 1970; Datcher, Savage, and Checkosky, 1973; Fox and Jordan, 1973; Katz and Zalk, 1974). It is tempting to attribute such changes in children's responses to societal changes that have occurred over the past few years. The importance of black people's developing pride in their blackness is certainly a factor. Moreover, the more positive exposure given to black people by the media (see Chapter 9 of this volume) should not be underestimated as a potentially significant parameter for changing attitudes of children. There are several problems with the societal change interpretation, however. For one thing, the results have not been completely unambiguous. A number of recent studies (e.g., Morland, 1966; Greenwald and Oppenheim, 1968; Asher and Allen, 1969) have, in fact, replicated the earlier findings regarding white doll preferences. The work of Williams and his colleagues, using a picture preference test rather than a doll preference, has consistently found that white figures are associated with positive adjectives and black figures associated with negative ones (Renninger and Williams, 1966; Williams and Roberson, 1967). This has been true for both black and white children at the preschool level. How, then, can one reconcile these seeming contradictions?

One possibility that follows from the methodological problems discussed above is that the doll measure is inadequate, and discrepant results may simply be reflecting its lack of reliability. Most investigators working with young children seem unwilling, however, to abandon the technique, and continue to attribute some conceptual meaning to childrens' preferences.

A second possible explanation is that there may be geographic variations in children's attitudes. Interestingly, most of the work reporting more positive attitudes towards black dolls and pictures has occurred in large urban centers (e.g., Hraba and Grant, 1970; Fox and Jordan, 1973), whereas the older attitudes appear to be more prevalent in the South and in smaller towns (e.g., Morland, 1966). It might thus be fruitful to conduct geographical comparisons utilizing the same instrument. Another interesting difference that emerges between studies showing no preference and those that do is that the former often use black testers. This may again tell us something about the young child's degree of sophistication in that he may well be giving what he gauges to be the socially desirable response.

Even if one assumes that measures of racial awareness are valid and reliable, a final problem arises with regard to the theoretical relation of such measures to subsequent attitude development. It is clear that all children ultimately exhibit some degree of racial awareness. It is equally clear, however, that not all children develop negative intergroup attitudes. What, then, is the relationship (if any) between these earlier expressed preferences and later feelings and behavior? Do children who exhibit early awareness develop different attitudes than those who manifest it later? Is intensity of awareness related to strength of later attitude? Unfortunately, there seems to be no evidence on these issues. We know that racial awareness may be a necessary condition for attitude development, but it is certainly not a sufficient one. A longitudinal study is very much needed to clarify these theoretical issues.

## MECHANISMS UNDERLYING RACIAL ATTITUDE DEVELOPMENT

A number of theoretical formulations have been posited regarding the acquisition of racial attitudes. Interestingly, most of these formulations have been generated by work with adults, and extrapolations to children have been made primarily on a theoretical, rather than an empirical, basis. Although all investigators in this area pay lip service to the belief that attitudes are complex and multiply determined, most theorists have, in fact, focused upon a single determinant. This section will delineate some of the major variables that have been discussed in relation to attitude acquisition.

## Direct instruction

In contrast to Allport's belief about prejudice being caught rather than taught, the song from *South Pacific* expresses the notion that, "you have to be carefully taught." This latter belief may be the most commonly accepted view, both by the general public and by a number of social scientists. Why are children prejudiced? Obviously, it is argued, their parents are. If parents are, they will consequently transmit such feelings to children.

Although the variable of parental instruction has considerable common sense appeal, actual evidence supporting this view is scanty and inconsistent. An early study by Harris, Gough, and Martin (1950), for example, suggests that there may be positive but relatively small correlations between elementary school children's racial attitudes and those of their parents. Mosher and Scodel (1960) obtained a relation between the social distance scores of 12-year-olds and ethnic attitudes of mothers. On the other hand, Radke-Yarrow, Trager, and Miller (1952) found that kindergarten and first-grade white children often displayed negative reactions to blacks even when their parents held more liberal attitudes. Other studies have also found no relationship with either young children (Bird, Monachesi, and Burdick, 1952; Frenkel-Brunswik and Havel, 1953; Pushkin, 1967) or adolescents (Byrne, 1965). With regard to this latter study, it may be argued that the impact of parental attitudes would not be expected to be as salient during adolescence since many additional factors—such as peer group feelings, school experiences, type and variety of interracial encounters—have influenced earlier attitudes. If this is the case, however, then the importance of parental attitudes may have been very much overemphasized. If negative parental training can indeed be counteracted so readily, the implications for modification research are considerable.

The developmental relationship between the attitudes of children and their parents appears to be a complex one that cannot readily be disentangled without longitudinal data. The expectation that direct instruction from parents is involved has not received much empirical support. Moreover, the mechanisms underlying attitude transmission have not been well delineated. Besides direct instruction, other variables to be considered in the parent-child relationship include observational learning and modeling (e.g., Liebert, Sobol, and Copemann, 1972). The specific timing of instruction may also be of significance. It might well be, for example, that certain early types of training leave an indelible impression, whereas later types of negative exposures are more readily changed.

Social scientists obviously have little control over the actual behavior of parents. Increased understanding of the factors involved in parental attitude transmission, however, might ultimately be utilized to select those children who might be most amenable to various attitude change techniques on the basis of their particular experiences.

## Reinforcement components

The mechanism of reinforcement has frequently been offered as an explanation of how children learn prejudice. Within this view, either peers or adults in the child's environment are seen as positively rewarding the expression of negative attitudes. The rather complex responses subsumed under the attitude construct would probably not typically be acquired under conditions of consistent reinforcement, since the communications themselves are often ambivalent (cf Katz, Glass, and Cohen) and thus may lead to inconsistent reinforcement. Thus, for example, if first-grader Jane (white) asks her mother if she can invite her friend Lotus (black) for lunch, the mother may say yes, but use a slightly different tone of voice than Jane is accustomed to. When Jane asks her mother whether she may go to Lotus' house the following week, the mother may well say no, while using many circumlocutions and rationalizations. The message, then, that often gets transmitted to the child is a confusing one with many overtones.

Nevertheless, despite the complexity of both the communication and the reinforcement contingencies, the possibility exists that certain basic components of racial attitudes can best be understood in reinforcement terms. The early learned affective aspects of attitudes may well fall into this category.

Williams has been the most active proponent of an operant learning viewpoint with regard to racial attitude acquisition. In a series of recent studies, Williams and his colleagues have focused on the issue of how preschool children acquire the evaluative color concepts underlying racial attitudes. One of the basic measurement techniques used by these investigators with young children is described in a study by Williams and Roberson (1967). It is based upon the rationale of the semantic differential indices, whose evaluative components correlate highly with scores on traditional attitude tests in adults. This technique, called the Color Meaning Test, consists of showing the child pictures of two objects or animals, alike in all respects but color (black or white); the child's task is to select which evaluative adjective (e.g., good, nice, sad, naughty, etc.) is to be applied to which animal. Findings obtained with preschool Caucasian children in North Carolina revealed that positive words clustered around the white animals and objects, whereas negative words clustered around the black ones. This parallels trends obtained with white college students in the South (Williams, 1964; Williams, Tucker and Dunham, 1971). In addition to the Color Meaning Test, a second measure called the Preschool Racial Attitude Measure (PRAM) is also utilized with young children. This latter technique is a more direct racial attitude scale, depicting Negro and Caucasian children and adults. As in the Color Meaning Test, the child is asked to complete a story with an adjective to be applied to either the black or the white person in the picture. Findings on this latter instrument revealed that most of the children tested associate positive adjectives with the white persons and negative ones with the black. In each of 13 studies cited in Williams, Best, Boswell, Mattson and Graves (in press 1974) conducted in a variety of geographical locations, preschool children were found to have a pro-Caucasian, anti-Negro bias.

In a theoretical discussion of these findings, Williams *et al.* argue that if the attitude acquistion process is one of gradually learning what the Caucasian-dominated society teaches, older and more intelligent children should show evidence of better learning. Since such a developmental relationship was not obtained, this "normative" theory of prejudice is rejected. Alternative explanations offered to account for attitude variability include parameters such as: (a) (as yet unspecified) parental behavior, or (b) earlier learned attitudes toward light and darkness, e.g., fear of the dark. This latter possibility was further delineated in another recent paper by Williams (1972) in which the possibility is suggested that darkness is intrinsically aversive to young humans, much as it is apparently to subhuman primates. This view would imply that children younger than those ordinarily tested should display white preferences, and that fear of the dark should correlate with such preferences. As noted in the earlier section of this chapter, evidence of this type is not yet available. An additional problem with this position has to do with the developmental sequence itself. Thus, according to this theory, the learning of color connotations should precede the development of racial attitudes. A study that assessed both on the same group of children (Williams and Roberson, 1967), however, found that racial attitudes with regard to people showed more bias than did attitudes toward the colors black and white.

The operant color connotation position espoused by Williams, then, may be summarized as follows. Very young children have innate preferences for lightness over darkness. Such preferences generalize to skin color cues (as well as to other things). The connotative aspects of the color name "white" tend to be associated with "goodness," whereas "black" is more frequently associated with symbols of "badness." Thus, both cultural expectations and linguistic symbolism serve to reinforce racial stereotypes.

The relationship between children's responses to racial cues and reinforcement has been studied in other types of experimental paradigms. Doke and Risley (1972), for example, attempted to assess the relative importance of race and sex as discriminative cues in the behavior of black preschool and grade-school children. They showed subjects pictures of a Caucasian boy and a Negro girl, and taught them to press a different button to each one. Other pictures of Negro girls and Caucasian boys were then presented, and generalization on the button-pressing was obtained. A transfer task was then introduced in which subjects were shown slides of Negro boys and Caucasian girls. The question raised was whether the earlier discrimination was learned on the basis of skin color or gender cues. It was found that younger children generalized along the sex dimension, whereas the older children (aged 9 to 12) generalized on the basis of race. The finding with young children corroborates the previously cited study by Katz and Zalk (1974) with regard to preschool children's doll preferences, in that gender cues were more salient than skin color.

Another approach relevant to the reinforcement aspects of children's racial attitudes is concerned with the differential reward values associated with individuals of different races. The experimental paradigm employed by Katz, Henchy, and Allen (1968) demonstrates this perspective: Children participated in a rote-memory learning task and received verbal approval from either a white or black male examiner. In this particular study, persons of the same race were found to be the most effective reinforcers (although it should be noted that some complicated interactions were obtained). With younger children, an examiner of another race may be more effective as a reinforcer (e.g., Katz, 1973a). Not only are adults of different races associated with differential social reinforcement, but recent evidence with young children suggests that peers are also associated with such patterns (Coates, Arnstein and Jordan, 1973).

Investigations pertinent to children's learning behavior with same- and other-raced adults have recently been reviewed by Sattler (1973), and this review suggests that a wide variety of parameters are associated with how effective a reinforcing person is to a child. It is interesting to note that such investigations are generally categorized under the rubric of "race of examiner effects," as if it were primarily the objective characteristics of the adult, rather than the child's learned patterns that account for observed behavior differences. It is the view of the present author that this misplaced emphasis has had the effect of confusing rather than clarifying the complex patterns of results obtained. Attention has not been paid, for example, to such questions as whether a relationship exists between a child's racial attitudes and the differential reinforcing value of adults. It is clear from the bewildering array of findings obtained with regard to "race of examiner effects" in children that considerably more theoretical delineation is required before unambiguous predictions can be generated. Greater reliance upon general theories of learning might be useful in this regard.

## Personality factors and child-rearing techniques

Perhaps the most widely known theoretical treatment of prejudice is the one that attributes negative intergroup attitudes to an authoritarian personality structure (Adorno, Frenkel-Brunswik, Levinson, and Sanford, 1950). This work represents one of social science's major attempts to understand the roots of prejudice. The theory assumes that prejudice in children is generated by harsh and rigid parents. The child is viewed as having to continually submit to arbitrary and often severe parental authority. Because of the parents' uncompromising natures, the resultant hostility of the child is never permitted direct expression. Accordingly, as a defense mechanism, the child identifies with the frustrating authority figures, tends to idealize them, and displaces his aggression toward out-group persons.

One of the major tenets of this theory is that prejudice serves a particular function for the individual and is integrally related to other aspects of the individual's personality. The authoritarian-personality type is viewed as a basically insecure individual who represses impulses, views life as threatening, and perceives social relationships in terms of power. Some behavioral consequences of this syndrome are: rigidity, a tendency toward stereotyped thinking, an avoidance of introspection, and excessive moralism. The authoritarian person idealizes "toughness," has contempt for "weakness," and perceives the world in sharply defined categories of black or white, right or wrong, good or bad. For the authoritarian personality, there is very little gray in the world.

The original formulations concerning the authoritarian personality were based upon an anonymous anti-Semitism scale administered to 100 college students. The eight women who scored highest and the eight who scored lowest were then given depth interviews and projective tests. It could be argued that such a far-reaching theory was initially formulated on relatively little evidence. Nevertheless, this approach has had considerable theoretical impact and heuristic value. It has also generated a lot of controversy with regard to the adequacy of research purporting to document its suppositions (cf. Christie, 1954). The adult research with regard to this position is discussed in more detail in Chapter 3 of this volume. This section, then, will only discuss evidence with children.

The most convincing study with regard to the relationship between authoritarian parents and ethnocentrism in children was the previously cited work conducted by Harris et al. (1950). Attitude questionnaires were given to 240 fourth-, fifth-, and sixth-grade children, and their parents, and positive correlations were obtained between the two sets of measures. More intensive investigation of the extreme groups demonstrated a strong relationship between maternal beliefs about child rearing and the degree of prejudice in children. The mothers of high-prejudiced subjects stressed the value of obedience, preferred quiet children to noisy ones, and discouraged sex-play in their children, often by the use of physical punishment. This pattern contrasted with the more permissive practices of the mothers of low-prejudiced children. Thus, the picture that emerges from this study is in accordance with the authoritarian personality theory. Several other studies have found similar results (e.g., Lyle and Levitt, 1955; Hart, 1957; Weatherley, 1963).

A continuing problem in evaluating this research has to do with the confounding of authoritarianism scores with other variables that may explain the above-cited trends equally well. As noted by several investigators (Hyman and Sheatsley, 1954; Proshansky, 1966), both intelligence and educational level are negatively related to authoritarian personality tendencies. Each of these, in turn, is related to socioeconomic level. This latter variable, in and of itself, could readily account for differences in parental beliefs about child-rearing practices. Thus, in the Harris *et al.* study, the high-prejudiced children may well have come from lower socioeconomic families where values might be expected to more closely approximate the "authoritarian" type. Without such essential controls, it is impossible to ascertain whether differences are to be attributed to parental personality or to sociocultural factors. Moreover, as other investigators (Epstein and Komorita, 1965; Proshansky, 1966) have noted, children of authoritarian parents may have acquired their attitudes via direct instruction rather than the particular disciplinary techniques they were exposed to.

In summary, research with regard to the authoritarian personality has provided some provocative work in this area, but it is difficult to interpret. It should be pointed out that even if this research were not surrounded by methodological ambiguity, it would still be a somewhat disheartening theory from the point of view of attitude change. If the authoritarian viewpoint is correct, it follows that authoritarian parents would have to change first in order for their children to become more tolerant.

Even if one does not subscribe wholeheartedly to the theory of the authoritarian personality, one may still postulate that particular types of parental behavior and/or personality factors serve to instill negative racial attitudes. A study by Tabachnick (1962) attempted to test the hypothesis initially set forth by Allport (1954) that racial prejudice in children was an expression of frustration. According to this theory, individuals (both children and adults) who are unhappy with themselves or maladjusted should exhibit a tendency to take out such dissatisfaction on others who are more socially vulnerable.

Tabachnick tested 300 white fifth-grade children, employing the direct questionnaire measure of attitudes towards Negroes previously used by Gough and his associates (1950). Satisfaction with self was assessed by means of "objective frustration" by classifying children as underachievers, overachievers, or normal. This classification was based upon the obtained discrepancy between the child's grades and his IQ scores. Those children classified as underachievers by means of this rating scale were considered to be the most frustrated group. Findings revealed small (but in some instances, statistically significant) correlations between prejudice scores and self-reports of satisfaction. Thus, children who scored higher on the prejudice scale tended also to report more dissatisfaction with themselves. The highest correlation reported, however, was -.27. In terms of predictability, then, approximately 9% of the variability in prejudice scores could be accounted for by knowing the childrens' ratings of self-satisfaction. No significant relationships were obtained between degree of achievement (the investigator's objective frustration measure) and racial attitudes. Thus, it appears that personality measures may be related to attitudes, but certainly not to the degree that some theorists have contended.

The study by Tabachnick is instructive because it demonstrates some of the pitfalls frequently encountered in attempts to assess theory in this area. The correlational format of the study is typical of such investigations, and it, of course, precludes saying anything about the particular nature of the relationship between personality and attitudinal variables. Even if the correlations were high (which they weren't), we would not know whether the self-dissatisfaction anteceded or succeeded the development of racial attitudes, or whether some additional but unmeasured variables accounted for the concurrent development of racial prejudice and unhappiness. An additional difficulty in interpreting such findings is the reliance upon a direct questionnaire measure of attitudes whose validity has not been established. It would appear that social scientists sometimes try to chase butterflies with meat axes.

An example of a somewhat better controlled study with children was conducted by Epstein and Komorita (1965). These investigators attempted to assess the effects of the child's perceptions of parental discipline and particular stimulus characteristics of an out-group upon social distance scores. Social distance responses were obtained in response to pictures that were systematically varied along two dimensions: social class (determined by the relative shabbiness of the clothes and surrounding environment) and race (white vs. Oriental). The target pictures were introduced to the sample (white middle-class children from the third to the eighth grades) as a fictitious group called Piraneans. The major finding of the study was a curvilinear relationship between perceived parental permissiveness and social distance scores made to out-groups.

This finding is an interesting one, which in some ways contradicts authoritarianism theory. The children who appeared to be least prejudiced were those who perceived their parents as being either very permissive or very punitive. Those who perceived their parents as exhibiting an intermediate degree of permissiveness (one is tempted to say middle America) expressed the greatest social distance towards out-groups. Most theoretical positions that stress childrearing and defense mechanism components of social attitudes would generate the prediction that children whose parents are least permissive should have stronger negative attitudes towards out-groups. Such parental rigidity is, indeed, supposed to provide the motivating force behind the projection and displacement towards out-groups involved in prejudice. The study clearly does not support this expectation.

In view of the pervasive quality of most personality variables, it would be quite surprising to find that they were not related to social attitudes in some way. Nevertheless, the insistence by some theorists (e.g., Bettelheim and Janowitz, 1950) that racial attitudes in children are to be understood primarily as an outgrowth of emotional maladjustment does not seem warranted on the basis of the data available. Personality factors seem to be only tangentially related to racial attitudes, or related in ways that go contrary to existing theory. Although it may be more comforting to think that highly prejudiced children must be emotionally disturbed in some way (and some undoubtedly are), the empirical evidence does not support this view unless one is willing to assume that prejudice and emotional disturbance are synonymous. Evidence that measures the two constructs separately suggests that they are not highly related to one another. Large numbers of children express racial prejudice but do not seem to be maladjusted in other areas.

## Cognitive aspects of racial attitudes

While the bulk of the evidence concerned with attitudinal antecedents has focused upon emotional determinants, some investigations of the cognitive correlates of attitudes have also been conducted and will be reviewed in this section. There are at least two ways in which cognitive components of attitudes have been conceptualized. One approach has been to view the cognitive aspects as the resultant expression of more primary and deep-rooted personality variables. A second position has approached cognitive aspects as developmental determinants of attitudes. The first approach has been the more common one.

Concern with the thought processes underlying attitudes is not a new one. Allport, in his most comprehensive and scholarly treatment of the topic (1954), suggests that the major problem in prejudice is, in fact, a thought problem. The prejudiced individual displays what Allport calls "overcategorization" in that he assumes that all people placed within a class behave in the same way and exhibit the same traits. Such overcategorization is relatively impervious to new information that may logically contradict this belief. Thus, according to Allport, prejudice is not easily reversible.

The approach that regards this type of thinking as the outgrowth of personality factors (e.g., authoritarian theory) tends to conceptualize it as disordered and the result of rigid, moralistic upbringing. According to this position, children raised in excessively strict homes acquire a tendency to "jump the gun." They categorize prematurely, overgeneralize, and resist changing categories once they are formed. Two studies are generally cited to support this position. The first one was conducted by Frenkel-Brunswik in 1948. In this investigation, high- and low-prejudice groups of children (determined by scores obtained on the California E scale) were asked to look at a series of pictures in which a cat was gradually transformed into a dog. The child's task was to label each picture. High-prejudice subjects were found to change their verbal responses more slowly from one category to another than did less prejudiced subjects, thus supporting the theoretical expectation. The possibility exists, however, that the problem exhibited by the high-prejudice subjects was perceptual rather than cognitive—i.e., they may not have perceived the discrepant cues as readily.

A second study, conducted by Kutner (1958), does not have this interpretive problem. Kutner employed 60 seven-year-old white children, dichotomized on the basis of racial attitude scores. They were given a series of conceptual tasks, which included exercises in syllogistic reasoning, critical thinking, and other types of problem solving. The major finding was that the high-prejudice youngsters were defective in reasoning ability when contrasted with their age mates. Furthermore, they were found to be more intolerant of ambiguity, thus providing some support for the position outlined above. Interestingly, some of the same children were observed again when they were 16 years of age, and some of the earlier obtained differences were still present (Kutner and Gordon, 1964). This latter study is one of the very few longitudinal follow-ups ever done in this area, and, as such, is laudable. Nevertheless, the differences between the groups might be explained more parsimoniously on the basis of obtained significant differences in intelligence test scores. It could be that high-prejudice children did not reason as well because they were less bright. Thus, there may well be differences in the cognitive styles of high- and low-prejudice children, but whether these can be attributed primarily to child-rearing practices or to other factors such as intelligence or socioeconomic status has yet to be determined.

As noted above, a second view is possible with regard to the role of cognitive factors that is more in accordance with cognitive-developmental theory. Within this approach, cognitive processes are considered significant in the acquisition of attitudes in their own right, and are not conceptualized as a mere outgrowth of emotional problems. The work of the major developmental theorists (e.g., Werner, Piaget) suggests some interesting parallels between the thought processes of the young child and those of the prejudiced person described by Allport. The person who assumes that because two people are alike in one respect (e.g., blackness), they must be alike in other attributes (e.g., intelligence) is exhibiting what Piaget has labeled "transductive reasoning." According to Piaget (1928, 1951), such generalizations from the particular to the particular are characteristic of the reasoning processes of three- and four-year-old children. In some respects, this type of reasoning also resembles what Werner (1948) calls syncretic thought—a type of process in which a stimulus configuration is considered as changed in its entirety when only a minor component changes. Such thinking is frequently observed in young children.

What this developmental position suggests, then, is that there is a time in the child's life when the seemingly distorted reasoning processes associated with prejudicial attitudes are quite normal. These thought processes are characteristic of early levels of maturation. In fact, racial awareness apparently begins its development in the context of both transductive reasoning and syncretic thought—i.e., in the early preschool years. Such developmental concordance may be more than coincidence. At the very least, it suggests that the processes of categorization in young children be investigated much more closely than has been done.

There is no good reason to believe that children's cognitions about people differ in kind from the maturational level exhibited in other areas of thought. If a child has difficulty, for example, in solving problems with neutral geometric stimuli that involve classification along two dimensions (e.g., Parker and Day, 1971), he should have equal difficulty categorizing a person simultaneously in terms of gender and race. If he cannot understand the relationship between subordinate and superordinate classes with regard to inanimate objects (e.g., as in Piaget's experimental bead tasks), we should not assume that he can easily place an individual who looks somewhat different in the same category as himself.

The importance of cognitive aspects in the acquisition of prejudice has recently been discussed by Tajfel (1973). He suggests that in interpreting ambiguous social stituations, individuals tend to utilize group characteristics because it is cognitively simpler to do so. Tajfel presents evidence that shows that when group classification appears to be correlated with another continouous dimension (e.g., a personality trait), there is a tendency to exaggerate group differences along that dimension and to minimize such differences within the groups. Although most of Tajfel's work has been conducted with adults, the previous discussion suggests that such tendencies might be even more pronounced in young children. More intensive study of the role of cognitive determinants of racial attitudes would undoubtedly lead to some interesting directions for future research with children.

## Perceptual factors

It is commonly agreed among most investigators that perceptual differentiation of groups may be the most basic prerequisite to the development of hostile intergroup attitudes. In view of this, it is somewhat surprising that so little empirical attention has been devoted to the perceptual processes that underlie and maintain racial attitudes.

Allport (1954) has discussed the potential role of fear of the strange for young children—a fear that is elicited by inanimate objects, unexpected occurrences, and perhaps people who look different as well. In accordance with the previously mentioned views of Piaget, Allport suggests that visible differences between people imply real differences to the child; he goes on to suggest that this may be the perceptual foundation upon which subsequent attitudes are based.

Allport's reasoning suggests that if interracial contact occurs at an early age, it should decrease strangeness and thus hinder the development of consequent negative attitudes. A recent study by Cantor (1972)–(based upon the Zajonc et al. (1971) "mere exposure" hypothesis)–suggests that familiarity with other-race faces may be positively related to children's attitudes. Historical and anecdotal evidence, however, suggests the opposite. White, upper-class Southern children were typically brought up by black women, and did not apparently become immunized against racial prejudice. Allport himself, in fact, recognizes some of the theoretical problems involved with the "strangeness" explanation in his discussion of the rather rapid habituation that children display towards strangers.

Despite the empirical ambiguity of the "strangeness" hypothesis, it is possible that a systematic exploration of other factors involved in the perceptual categorization of ethnic groups may well increase our understanding of the attitude acquisition process. As was the case with cognitive parameters, perceptual factors may be viewed either as an outcome or an antecedent of the socialization process. That perceptual outcomes differ as a function of attitudes has been demonstrated in adults. Highly prejudiced individuals apparently perceive persons of another race differently than do less prejudiced individuals (e.g., Engel, 1958; Pettigrew, Allport and Barnett, 1958; Reynolds and Toch, 1965; Iverson and Schwab, 1967), suggesting that particular perceptual styles may accompany the presence of prejudiced attitudes. Findings with adults, however, tell us nothing about a number of important issues, including the causal sequence of attitudinal and perceptual processes, the age at which the two intertwine, and the developmental course of their interaction.

For the past several years, the present author and her colleagues have conducted a series of interrelated studies with urban children aimed at gathering such information within a developmental context. The theoretical rationale underlying these studies assumes that the perceptual and linguistic parameters involved in group differentiation are of considerable importance in attitude acquistion. This view holds that perceptual differentiation is a function of (a) the observed stimulus characteristics associated with individuals (i.e., their distinguishing cues), and (b) the particular labels and evaluative statements applied by peers and adults to groups. With regard to this latter factor, theories of learning (e.g., Dollard and Miller, 1950) suggest that labels and perceptions influence each other in significant ways. The association of distinctive labels to different ethnic groups would be expected to facilitate discrimination between groups (this has been referred to as acquired distinctiveness of cues). In contrast, the continued use of the same name for all members within a group would be expected to reduce the capacity for differentiating among individual members. (This phenomenon is called acquired equivalence of cues.) Each of these processes has implications for subsequent attitude development because it may either facilitate or impede the learning of other responses (such as stereotypes) to groups.

The research to be described addressed itself to a number of issues, including: (a) the relationship of differentiation ability to maturational level, (b) the effects of labels on person-perception, (c) the types of visual cues children use in differentiating people at various developmental levels, and (d) the relationship between attitudes and person-perception.

The first study was conducted with 192 nursery school and kindergarten children (Katz, 1973a) and assessed the hypothesis that differences between members of another group are more difficult to discriminate than differences within one's own group. Black and white subjects at two preschool age levels were given a two-choice discrimination learning task that utilized drawings of faces varying in shade as discriminanda. They were asked to pretend that they were space explorers, and to select the "moon person" they were to bring back to earth. Children were randomly assigned to one of three groups in which they viewed either Negro, Caucasian, or green faces. Either the lighter or darker member of each pair was reinforced by a marble. The prediction was made that subjects would more readily learn to discriminate pairs of faces of their own race than those of another. The green-face condition was included as a control for the effects of possible unfamiliarity of other-race stimuli. If the presumed difficulty of learning to discriminate other-race stimuli was due simply to unfamiliarity, green faces and other-race faces should be equally difficult to discriminate. If, on the other hand, the predicted lack of discriminability was attributable to the continued use of the same label, then other-race and green faces should elicit differential learning patterns. This, in fact, was what was found. Children at both age levels took more trials to learn a discrimination based on shade cues with faces of another race than their own. This was not true when green faces were used, however, suggesting that the labeling process was the important factor. Black children generally showed superior performance on all learning tasks, and younger children of both races learned more quickly when tested by an examiner of another race. These latter two findings suggest that color cues have differential salience, based upon the age and racial group of the children. It would appear that by the age of three, children already reveal sophisticated differential perceptual patterns associated with racial cues.

As a follow-up to this study, the same children were subsequently administered a doll preference task (Katz and Zalk, 1974). In contrast to the type of stimuli typically used in doll choice tasks, which give Ss a choice between blonde, blue-eyed Caucasian dolls and dark-haired, brown-eyed Negro dolls, the present study utilized four dolls that differed only in skin color and gender cues. Male and female dolls with brown hair and brown eyes were used. As in the Clark and Clark (1947) procedure, children were asked to tell E (either a black or white female) which they thought was the good doll, the naughty doll, the one they liked best, etc. Results with regard to racial preferences were not in accord with those reported by most earlier investigators (e.g., Clark and Clark, 1947; Morland, 1966; Asher and Allen, 1969). The strong preference for white dolls previously obtained was not found in this study. Preferences were based more on gender cues than on racial ones, suggesting that racial cues may not be as salient as other types of person characteristics for young children.

In another study (Katz, Sohn, and Zalk, 1974), the developmental relationship between attitudes and perceptual factors was assessed in second-, fourth-, and sixth-grade youngsters from two racially integrated New York City public schools. Subjects were classified into high- or low-prejudice conditions on the basis of scores obtained on a multiple-choice projective instrument, consisting of slides depicting ambiguous interracial stituations. Subjects were asked to select, for example, which of several children was instigating an aggressive act, was winning a prize or trophy, was being scolded by a teacher, etc. In the perceptual task children were asked to judge the similiarity of pairs of faces that systematically varied along a number of dimensions, including color, shade, type of facial expression, type of hair, and shape of eyebrows. A factorial design was employed that varied grade level, race of child (black or white), race of examiner (black or white), prejudice level, and type of slide.

The clearest finding to emerge was that high-prejudice children viewed racial cues (i.e., color and shade) as more distinctive than did low-prejudice children. This occurred with all age and racial groups. In contrast, however, other types of cues (e.g., presence of eyeglasses, facial expression) elicited more similar judgments from high-prejudice children viewing other-race faces. These findings are in accordance with the theoretical expectations originally advanced, but the trends were more pronounced for white than for black children.

In the previous study, predictions about perception were made on the basis of labeling experiences that occurred many years before we saw the children. In the last study to be described in this section (Katz and Seavey, 1973) the theoretical rationale concerning language and person perception was tested directly by manipulating the labeling experiences children received. Eighty second- and sixth-grade children were randomly assigned to one of four label conditions in conjunction with two purple and two green faces (one each either smiling or frowning). One group was taught to associate a common name with each color pair—i.e., the two green faces had the same name, and the two purple faces another. A second group was taught to associate common labels on the basis of facial expression—i.e., the two smiling faces had the same name, and the two frowning ones another. A third group learned to associate a distinctive label with each of the four faces. Finally, the control group viewed the stimuli for the same number of trials, but without labels. Following the labeling training, the children were asked to judge the similarity of all possible pairs of the four faces. As was true for all the studies described in this section, the race of both the child and the examiner was varied.

As in the previously cited studies, results with regard to the white children were in accord with predictions. A significant interaction was found among race of subject, label condition, and type of stimulus-pair observed. For white children, labels that grouped stimuli on the basis of color cues augmented perceptual differentiation of color cues, whereas labels associated with facial expression enhanced the distinctiveness of expression differences.

The association of four different names for each of the four faces affected the perception of color and expression cues equally. Thus, the particular types of labels used modified the subsequent perception of facial cues for white children. In contrast, however, color cues were perceived as salient by black children even in the absence of labels, and labeling training did not significantly alter their subsequent perception.

Thus, in almost all of the studies conducted in this research program, predictions were confirmed for white children, but not for black children. The question may be raised, therefore, of why this disparity exists. There are several possible explanations. The first is that white society does not permit blacks to "forget" color, even if they wished to. In all studies, color cues, even "nonmeaningful" ones such as purple and green, appeared to have greater salience for black children. Despite this increased attention to color, however, black grade-school students judged shade variations within their own race as not being an important basis for perceptual distinctiveness. In view of earlier work (e.g., Freeman, Armor, Ross and Pettigrew, 1966) suggesting that a strong positive valence within the black community was placed upon being light-skinned, this latter trend may well be reflecting recent strides made by blacks in their struggle for equality and dignity. Recent black political ideology stresses the importance of blackness as a force for unity and pride. Thus, the ignoring of subtle color gradations by contemporary black children that may have been important to their parents in earlier years, suggests that things may indeed be changing for minority group self-perceptions. Although perceptual factors may well play an important role in the development of black children's attitudes towards themselves and other groups, alternative theoretical positions to the one described here may be required to delineate their development.

Since the most severe societal problems have been associated with white racism, however, it is interesting to note that the perceptual concomitants of white children's racial attitudes, although varied and complex, do tend to follow a somewhat predictable developmental course, which can be summarized as follows. Preschool children make distinctions on the basis of racial cues, although these may not be quite as salient as earlier work has implied when appropriate controls are included. An acquired equivalence of cues phenomenon that permits children to more readily distinguish faces of their own race than those of another race appears to be operative by four years of age. This relative discriminative difficulty may well be reflecting the fact that once individuals come to be categorized into a group, it is their defining characteristic (in this case, color) that becomes the most salient feature, whereas other cues are attended to less. Perception of facial cues can be very much influenced by the labeling process, as was indicated by the way white children responded to faces linguistically categorized by either color or expression. Moreover, attitudes of white grade-school children are related to their perceptions of people. Black and white faces alike in all respects but color were viewed as exceedingly different from one another by high-prejudice youngsters. Other individual differences between black faces was seen by high-prejudice children as a much less salient basis for differentiating two black faces than two white faces. Thus, contrary to the notion that children are "color-blind," these results suggest that for white children with negative racial attitudes, color, in fact, blinds.

It would appear then that for white children, perceptual mechanisms may well play an important role in the development and maintenance of prejudice. In the only study to date that has attempted to manipulate these patterns (Katz, 1973b) a reduction of negative attitudes was found to result, suggesting that such patterns are not irrevocable in children. As long as adult society magnifies the differences between racial groups, and deindividuates members of minority groups, however, it is laying a firm perceptual basis for the maintenance of prejudice.

## ATTITUDE ACQUISITION: TOWARDS A THEORETICAL SYNTHESIS

This chapter has attempted to review some of the more prominent theoretical positions that have been offered to account for how children acquire negative intergroup attitudes. The literature suggests a number of important trends. To summarize, relatively young children exhibit awareness of racial cues, although the salience of earlier obtained evaluations and racial preferences may have been attributable to both the particular measurement technique employed and other methodological problems. The most obvious determinant of prejudice would seem to be parental attitudes, although the evidence regarding the importance of direct instruction is not overpowering. Reinforcement may play a role, particularly with regard to learning the cultural and linguistic connotations of color cues, which generalize in turn to skin color. Personality variables and child-rearing techniques have received considerable theoretical and empirical attention as sources of racial prejudice, but the empirical findings are inconclusive and are fraught with methodological ambiguity. Moreover, facts such as these typically lie beyond the province of social science modification, and thus such theories generate little change research. Investigations pertinent to the cognitive and perceptual components of children's prejudice are more recent, but appear more promising in terms of the consistency of positive findings and their potential applicability to attitude change.

Clearly, the child is not split up neatly into the learning, personality, cognitive, and perceptual components our organization might imply; all of these areas are interrelated. Nevertheless, focus on some of these components may well have more pay-off than others. It is the contention of the present author that some of the directions taken in earlier research may well have led us into conceptual deadends. If most preschool children show pro-white bias, for example, it makes little sense to consider such bias the outgrowth of maladaptive personality structures. If the perceptual and cognitive roots of prejudice are present in all young children, the statistically abnormal individual may well be the one in whom negative attitudes are stifled. Considerably more theoretical and empirical attention to the normal developmental context in which attitude acquistion takes place appears to be needed. It is the view of the present investigator that particular emphasis be given to the perceptual, cognitive, and reinforcement parameters underlying the early development of attitudes, and the interrelationships that exist among these factors.

Almost all theorists in this area have used terms such as "complex," "multifaceted," and "multiply determined" to describe the ontogenesis of racial attitudes, but they have usually not applied these concepts in their own research efforts. We will, however, not develop a comprehensive understanding of how children acquire racial attitudes until more than lip service is paid to the multiplicity of concomitants. The last section of the chapter will attempt to theoretically integrate some of the diverse findings summarized above within a developmental context.

## Parallels between the acquisition of racial and other attitudes

It seems parsimonious to begin this discussion with the assumption that a child's percepts and concepts about people follow the same rules as their perceptions and cognitions about other kinds of stimuli. The rules governing the effects of reinforcement should not differ whether the content of the learning concerns proper table manners or who might be welcomed as a friend. Interestingly, however, psychologists have preferred to study the processes of concept formation, perception, and learning in children by observing their reactions to relatively neutral stimuli. Those interested in racial attitudes, on the other hand, have often investigated attitudes as if they existed apart from other ongoing processes in the child. Attitudes about others neither exist nor develop in a vacuum.

The most obvious parallel to racial attitude acquistion in young children is the constellation of responses involved in sex-role learning. There are both important similarities as well as differences between the two that will be considered below. One similarity is the age at which such learning is exhibited. There is evidence that by the age of three, children have the rudiments of both race and gender awareness. This suggests that in both cases, important events must have occurred prior to three years of age. Because of the absence of data on children younger than three, the following account is necessarily speculative, although it will draw upon evidence pertinent to acquistion of neutral concepts where relevant.

Evidence of person variability is available to the child as soon as he can use his senses. While it would not be expected that very young children would cognitively organize such variability, differential responding by infants to gender cues has been demonstrated both in the laboratory (e.g., Lewis, 1972) and anecdotally. Parents typically note, for example, that babies often "like" women (or men) more. Although the particular configuration of cues utilized by children is not yet understood, it does not seem too farfetched to assume that young children might exhibit a generalized pattern of responses to, say, individuals with high-pitched voices and certain types of sweet odors. As the child begins to express himself linguistically, his early words communicate the nature of these rudimentary concepts. A frequently used example in developmental psychology textbooks illustrates the "overgeneralization" inherent in these primitive concepts: The child may (sometimes to mommy's chagrin) call all adult males "daddy." Although this example is meant to demonstrate the child's conceptual error, it should be noted that insofar as the word "daddy" is not used to refer to women or children, the child is displaying (albeit with an incorrect label) a clear concept of male adults. Such developmentally early concepts may be based upon particular perceptual cues that are salient to the child, such as the size or type of dress of the individual. As language and communication skills develop, parents assist the child in honing in on the particular defining characteristics of a concept. Thus, for example, the child learns that the category "dogs" does not contain all small, furry animals, but only those that make a particular sound. Such continual correction, differentiation, and selective attention form the basis of much of a young child's interactions with his parents.

A point to keep in mind at this juncture is that concepts are defined by both positive and negative instances, both by logical necessity and pedagogical practice with young children. It is difficult to imagine a parent explaining the concept "dog" to a young child without some mention of a cat. Indeed, it may be for this reason that opposites are the most frequent and most rapid responses elicited by a word association task. Juxtaposition of what is and what is not a member of a particular category is included in the definition process itself. When the concept in question refers to groups of persons, the juxtaposition of positive and negative instances may embody the seeds of future conflict at a later stage of development. This is particularly true when concepts are dichotomous rather than continous in nature, like male-female or black-white.

There are certain concepts about people that all young children must learn during the course of development. The distinction between self and other may well be the earliest. Many global theories of child development (e.g., Freud and Piaget) have stressed the importance of this distinction. The child's concepts about himself, however, become more finely differentiated as he develops and learns about others. Concepts about others may be based upon a variety of cues, but early ones will invariably include those based upon gender, age, kinship, and race. Of these, gender may well be the earliest. Information about gender is continually given to the child, practically from birth, both directly and indirectly, although the specific defining characteristics may be left for the child to discover. Another important person concept is the distinction between children and adults. Although initially based upon size perceptions, this concept may later become elaborated on the basis of differential behavioral prerogatives. Concepts about racial groups probably enter at a somewhat later stage, and their introduction may well be more variable, particularly for nonminority youngsters. Categorization on the basis of religion and nationality are also variable, and would be expected to occur at an even later age because they are often not associated with highly visible types of cues.

In addition to the similarities, there are important distinctions between how the concepts about racial cues and other-person characteristics are learned. One important difference has to do with the differential availability of models. Unless the child's family lives in an integrated neighborhood, a child may not have any exposure to a racially different person until he or she enters school. Moreover, for many middle-class white children, the first introduction to a black person is often someone who is a domestic servant. Hopefully, television programs for young children may eventually counteract this situation by presenting more ethnic and racial variability, but the apocryphal story of the white three-year-old who sees a black infant for the first time and says, "Look mom, a baby maid!" may indeed tell us a great deal about the origins of racism. Thus, race concepts will inevitably enter the child's repertoire, but the timing of this will probably depend more upon chance experiential factors than upon direct and continual parental instruction.

Not only are racial concepts different with regard to timing and variability, they differ in two additional respects as well. The first has to do with the person who provides the negative instances of the concept and his or her relation to the child. As the child learns that he is male, or she is female, there is usually an opposite-sexed adult present who provides a continual and complex example of the "other." Similarly with the child-adult concept—a parent or caretaker is present to show how big people look and behave. It becomes difficult for the child to oversimplify the "other" too much because of this continual interaction. This is not the case with racial concepts, however. In this latter instance, unless the child grows up in an interracial family, his information about race generally comes exclusively from a person who is a member of the same group, and models of the "other" may not be readily available enough to dispel misconceptions. This suggests that the age for integration may have to be much earlier than the school years to have any substantial impact.

A second important difference between the acquisition of race concepts and other person concepts is that evaluative components may be more intrinsically involved in early learning with regard to race. Although most theorists suggest that racial awareness precedes evaluation by several years, evidence pertinent to preschool children does not support this. Few children who are aware of racial cues exhibit such awareness with neutrality. It may take a child quite a few years after he knows he is a child to ascertain that grown-up status is more valuable. Similarly, it may take a male child quite a while after he correctly labels himself a boy to have negative evaluations of girls. The fact that so few white children express the desire to be anything but white is indicative that differential status evaluations must get communicated to children at the outset.

## Attitude acquisition: A developmental sequence

Based upon the investigations and theoretical considerations reviewed in this chapter, the acquisition of racial attitudes in children does, indeed, appear to be a complex and multifaceted process. Goodman (1964) has suggested a three-stage theory of attitude development consisting of ethnic awareness (ages 3-4), ethnic orientation (4-7), and then attitudes. The present investigator is of the belief that this is an oversimplified view. There appear to be at least eight overlapping, but separable, steps in the developmental sequence of racial attitude acquisition, which span approximately ten years of the child's life. These include the following: (1) early observation of racial cues, (2) formation of rudimentary concepts, (3) conceptual differentiation, (4) recognition of the irrevocability of cues, (5) consolidation of group concepts, (6) perceptual elaboration, (7) cognitive elaboration, and (8) attitude crystallization. These steps are described in more detail below.

1. *Early observation of racial cues.* As noted earlier, a child's observation of cues associated with another race may be based upon chance environmental events. The specific effects of such observations, however, would be related to the developmental level of the child. Thus, in the first year of life, the presence of such cues may not be particularly salient, whereas later, he is maturationally capable of processing such cues and demonstrating that difference or novelty is being observed. Without opportunity for such stimulus input, however, the start of this process will be delayed. Little is known about the specific developmental timetable involved here other than that it generally occurs prior to the age of three.

2. *Formation of rudimentary concepts.* Once the child verbally expresses a differential response to an individual from another group, the chances are good that a label will be supplied by either surrounding adult or siblings—e.g., "Oh yes, that person has darker skin because he is a Negro." Evaluative components may also be communicated at this time. This may be accomplished either directly—e.g., "And I don't want you to play with him"—or indirectly, through generalization from either: (a) fear of the strange (Allport, 1954), (b) fear of the dark (Williams, 1972), or (c) already learned connotations to colors such as black and white (Williams, 1964; Stabler *et al.*, 1969).

This stage seems to occur in many, but not all, children prior to three years of age, and it is generally complete by age four.

3. *Conceptual differentiation.* Once a label is provided, the child will encounter additional opportunities to observe positive and negative examples of the concept and will receive feedback for his responses. Both group boundaries and defining characteristics are probably taught by the utilization of verbal feedback. Is this person a member of Group X? Adult responses may be primarily informational (e.g., "Yes, he is black even though his skin is light, because he has broad lips and very curly hair"), or may contain evaluative components as well (e.g., "Yes, he is black, and I would rather that you not be too friendly with him"). In terms of concept acquistion, such evaluative responses may actually facilitate learning by providing redundancy of cues.

4. *Recognition of the irrevocability of cues.* Kohlberg (1966) has noted that certain person-cues the child must learn about are subject to change over time, while others are not. Thus, he comes to realize that in spite of present size differentials, he will become both an older child and an adult. There is growing recognition that his status as a child is a temporary one. When he applies this same reasoning to gender differences, however, he must learn that his sex is (generally speaking) immutable. Clinical psychologists have repeatedly discussed the difficulties that young children have in believing this. Little girls believe that they will become boys, and little boys believe that they will bear children, etc. Early cognitions about racial characteristics may provide similar difficulties for the child. He must learn that racial cues, unlike size, do not change with age. This may well be a very complex concept for a young child, particularly because summer vacations and suntans provide him with continual evidence to the contrary. Since no evidence is available with regard to this factor, the age at which it typically occurs cannot be stated.

5. *Consolidation of group concepts.* It is not until the child can correctly label and identify both positive and negative instances, and can recognize the immutable nature of group membership, that he can be said to have an accurate concept of a group. When consolidation occurs, the perceptual and the cognitive components of attitudes are functionally interrelated. Where evaluative content was introduced earlier, this too becomes part of the concept. On the basis of the evidence, the consolidation process typically begins during the latter part of the preschool period—i.e., by about five years of age—and may extend over a considerable period of time.

6. *Perceptual elaboration.* Once the concepts of "us" and "them" are accurately established in terms of racial cues, subsequent perception of racial cues may be modified. Differences among groups may be accentuated, particularly for children exposed to heavy doses of evaluation, whereas intragroup differences, particularly of other-race people, become diminished. There is some evidence that this occurs in preschool children (Katz, 1973a) and that it shows further development throughout the grade-school age range (Katz,

Johnson and Parker, 1970; Katz, Sohn and Zalk, 1974). Additional evidence (Tajfel, 1969) with British grade-school children suggests that affective processes inherently favor members of one's in-group, even when this group is defined quite arbitrarily and transiently. The mechanisms underlying this perceptual elaboration facilitate the learning of other differential responses to out-group individuals.

7. *Cognitive elaboration.* There has been a great deal of vacillation in the literature as to whether a child's early responses to racial cues can properly be called "attitudes." Some investigators have argued that they are, insofar as evaluative components are included. It is the view of the present author that the term "concept attitude" is a more appropriate designation of a young child's responses, and that the term "attitude" be reserved for the more complex responses exhibited by older children and adults. The relationship between early concept attitudes and later attitudes is not well understood beyond the rather obvious point that the former may provide a foundation for the latter. The process by which concept attitudes or preferences become racial attitudes is what is meant by cognitive elaboration.

It is clear that a child's school experiences may be extremely important in the elaboration of racial attitudes. The particular experiences (or the lack of them) the child has with other-race children and adults, the attitudes expressed by his teachers and peers ... these will all be significant in determining future attitudes and feelings. Continuing research focus on the preschool years may well have obscured the importance of the early grade-school years as focal points in attitude transition. Moreover, evidence suggests that attitudes continue to develop and differentiate during the middle childhood years.

8. *Attitude crystallization.* This phase is comparable to the last stage postulated by Proshansky (1966), and probably occurs during the later grade-school years. A study of the development of racial stereotypes (Brigham, 1971) shows an increase in within-group agreement with age after the fourth grade. The effects of cultural conditioning are apparent at this level. It is as if the child has, in effect, come to terms with his attitudes. Consequently, he probably will not "rethink" them again unless he is placed in a situation that requires it—i.e., his social environment changes markedly. It is necessary to postulate such a stage because of the seeming intransigence of adult attitudes. Though diversity may be beautiful, the child's mind does not remain open indefinitely.

# REFERENCES

Adorno, T. W., Frenkel-Brunswik, E., Levinson, D.J., and Sanford, R.N. *The authoritarian personality.* New York: Harper, 1950.

Allport, G.W. *The nature of prejudice.* Reading, Mass.: Addison-Wesley, 1954.

Asher, S.R., and Allen, V.L. Racial preference and social comparison processes. *Journal of Social Issues,* 1969, **25,** 157-165.

Bettelheim, B., and Janowitz, M. Reactions to fascist propaganda: A pilot study. *Public Opinion Quarterly,* 1950, **14,** 53-60.

Bird, C., Monachesi, E.D., and Burdick, H. Infiltration and the attitudes of white and Negro parents and children. *Journal of Abnormal Social Psychology,* 1952, **47,** 688-699.

Brigham, J.C. Views of white and black school children concerning racial personality differences. Paper presented to the Midwestern Psychological Association, 1971.

Byrne, D. Parental antecedents of authoritarianism. *Journal of Personality and Social Psychology,* **1,** 369-373.

Cantor, G.N. Effects of familiarization on children's ratings of pictures of whites and blacks. *Child Development,* 1972, **43,** 1219-1229.

Christie, R. Authoritarianism re-examined. In R. Christie and M. Jahoda (Eds.), *Studies in the scope and method of "The authoritarian personality."* Glencoe, Ill.: Free Press, 1954.

Clark, K.B., and Clark, M.P. Racial identification and preference in Negro children. In T.M. Newcomb and E.L. Hartley (Eds.), *Readings in social psychology.* New York: Holt, 1947.

Coates, B., Arnstein, E., and Jordan, J. Racial preferences in the behavior of black and white children. Paper presented at The Society for Research in Child Development, Philadelphia, March 1973.

Datcher, E., Savage, J.E., and Checkosky, S.F. Investigation of school type, grade, sex and race of examiner on the racial preference and awareness of black and white children. Paper presented at the Society for Research in child Development, Philadelphia, April 1973.

Doke, L.A., and Risley, T.R. Some discriminative properties of race and sex for children from an all-Negro neighborhood. *Child Development,* 1972, **43,** 677-681.

Dollard, J., and Miller, N. *Personality and psychotherapy.* New York: McGraw-Hill, 1950.

Engel, E. Binocular fusion of dissimilar figures. *Journal of Psychology,* 1958, **46,** 53-57.

Epstein, R., and Komorita, S.S. Parental discipline, stimulus characteristics of outgroups, and social distance in children. *Journal of Personality and Social Psychology,* 1965, **2,** 416-420.

Fox, D.J., and Jordan, V.B. Racial preference and identification of black, American Chinese, and white children. *Genetic Psychology Monographs,* 1973, **88,** 229-286.

Freeman, H.F., Armor, D., Ross, M.J., and Pettigrew, T.F. Color gradation and attitudes among middle-income Negroes. *American Sociological Review,* 1966, **31,** 365-374.

Frenkel-Brunswik, E. A study of prejudice in children. *Human Relations*, 1948, **1**, 295-306.

Frenkel-Brunswik, E., and Havel, J. Prejudice in the interviews of children: Attitudes toward minority groups. *Journal of Genetic Psychology*, 1953, **82**, 91-136.

Gaines, R. Variables in color perception of young children. Paper presented at the Society for Research in Child Development, 1971.

Goodman, M. *Race awareness in young children*. Cambridge, Mass.: Addison-Wesley, 1952. (Second edition, New York: Crowell-Collier, 1964.)

Gough, H.G., Harris, D.B., Martin, D.B., and Edwards, M. Children's ethnic attitudes. I: Relationship to certain personality factors. *Child Development*, 1950, **21**, 83-91.

Greenwald, H.J., and Oppenheim, D.B. Reported magnitude of self-misidentification among Negro children—Artifact? *Journal of Personality and Social Psychology*, 1968, **8**, 49-52.

Harris, D., Gough, H., and Martin, W.E. Children's ethnic attitudes. II: Relationships to parental beliefs concerning child training. *Child Development*, 1950, **21**, 169-181.

Hart, I. Maternal child-rearing practices and authoritarian ideology. *Journal of Abnormal Social Psychology*, 1957, **55**, 232-237.

Hraba, J., and Grant, G. Black is beautiful: A reexamination of racial preference and identification. *Journal of Personality and Social Psychology*, 1970, **16**, 398-402.

Hyman, H., and Sheatsley, P.B. "The authoritarian personality"—A methodological critique. In R. Christie and M. Jahoda (Eds.), *Studies in the scope and method of "The authoritarian personality."* Glencoe, Ill.: Free Press, 1954.

Iverson, M.A., and Schwab, H.G. Ethnocentric dogmatism and binocular fusion of sexually and racially discrepant stimuli. *Journal of Personality and Social Psychology*, 1967, **7**, 73-81.

ᐧKatz, I., Glass, D.C., and Cohen, S. Ambivalence, guilt, and the scapegoating of minority group victims. *Journal of Experimental Social Psychology*, 1973, **9**, 423-436.

Katz, I., Henchy, T., and Allen, H. Effects of race of tester, approval-disapproval, and need on Negro children's learning. *Journal of Personality and Social Psychology*, 1968, **8**, 38-42.

Katz, P.A. Perception of racial cues in preschool children: A new look. *Developmental Psychology*, 1973a, **8**, 295-299.

Katz, P.A. Stimulus predifferentiation and modification of children's racial attitudes. *Child Development*, 1973b, **44**, 232-237.

Katz, P.A., Johnson, J., and Parker, D. Racial attitudes and perception in black and white urban school children. Paper presented at the American Psychological Association, September 1970.

Katz, P.A., and Seavey, C. Labels and children's perception of faces. *Child Development*, 1973, **44**, 770-775.

Katz, P.A., Sohn, M., and Zalk, S.R. Perceptual concomitants of racial attitudes in urban grade-school children . *Developmental Psychology*, 1974, in press.

Katz, P.A., and Zalk, S.R. Doll preferences: An index of racial attitudes? *Journal of Educational Psychology*, 1974, **66**, 663-668.

Kircher, M., and Furby, C. Racial preferences in young children. *Child Development*, 1971, **42**, 2076-2078.

Kohlberg, L. A cognitive-developmental analysis of children's sex-role concepts and attitudes. In E.E. Maccoby (Ed.), *The development of sex differences*. Stanford, Calif.: Stanford University Press, 1966.

Kutner, B. Patterns of mental functioning associated with prejudice in children. *Psychological Monographs*, 1958, **72**, No. 7.

Kutner, B., and Gordon, N. Cognitive functioning and prejudice: A nine-year follow-up study. *Sociometry*, 1964, **27**, 66-74.

Lewis, M. Parents and children: Sex-role development. *School Review*, 1972, **80**, 229-240.

Liebert, R.M., Sobol, M.P., and Copemann, C.D. Effects of vicarious consequences and race of model upon imitative performance by black children. *Developmental Psychology* 1972, **6**, 453-456.

Lyle, W.H., Jr., and Levitt, E.E. Punitiveness, authoritarianism, and parental discipline of grade school children. *Journal of Abnormal Social Psychology*, 1955, **51**, 42-46.

Morland, J.K. A comparison of race awareness in Northern and Southern children. *American Journal of Orthopsychiatry*, 1966, **36**, 22-31.

Mosher, D.L., and Scodel, A. A study of the relationship between ethnocentrism in children and the ethnocentrism and authoritarian rearing practices of their mothers. *Child Development*, 1960, **31**, 369-376.

Parker, R.K., and Day, M.C. The use of perceptual, functional and abstract attributes in multiple classification. *Developmental Psychology*, 1971, **5**, 312-319.

Pettigrew, T.F., Allport, G.W., and Barnett, E.O. Binocular resolution and perception of race in South Africa. *British Journal of Psychology*, 1958, **40**, 265-278.

Piaget, J. *Judgment and reasoning in the child*. New York: Harcourt, Brace, 1928.

Piaget, J. *The child's conception of the world*. New York: Humanities Press, 1951.

Porter, J. *Black child, white child: The development of racial attitudes*. Cambridge, Mass.: Harvard University Press, 1971.

Proshansky, H. The development of intergroup attitudes. In I.W. Hoffman and M.L. Hoffman (Eds.), *Review of child development research*. Volume 2. New York: Russell Sage Foundation, 1966.

Pushkin, I. A study of ethnic choice in the play of young children in three London districts. Unpublished Ph.D. thesis, University of London, 1967.

Radke-Yarrow, M., Trager, H., and Miller, J. The role of parents in the development of children's ethnic attitudes. *Child Development*, 1952, **23**, 13-53.

Renninger, C.A., and Williams, J.E. Black-white color connotations and race awareness in preschool children. *Perceptual and Motor Skills*, 1966, **22**, 771-785.

Reynolds, D., and Toch, H. Perceptual correlates of prejudice: A stereoscopic-constancy experiment. *Journal of Social Psychology*, 1965, **66**, 127-133.

Sattler, J.M. Racial experimenter effects. In K.S. Miller and R.M. Dreger (Eds.), *Comparative studies of blacks and whites in the United States*. New York: Seminar Press, 1973.

Secord, P.F., and Backman, C.W. *Social psychology*. New York: McGraw-Hill, 1964.

Stabler, J.R., Johnson, E.E., Berke, M.A., and Baker, R.B. the relationship between race and perception of racially related stimuli in preschool children. *Child Development*, 1969, **40**, 1233-1239.

Stevenson, H.W., and Stevenson, N.G. Social interaction in an interracial nursery school. *Genetic Psychology Monographs*, 1960, **61**, 37-75.

Tabachnick, B.R. Some correlates of prejudice toward Negroes in elementary age children. *Journal of Genetic Psychology*, 1962, **100**, 193-203.

Tajfel, H. Cognitive aspects of prejudice. *Journal of Social Issues,* 1969, **25**, 79-97.

Tajfel, H. The roots of prejudice: Cognitive aspects. In P. Watson (Ed.), *Psychology and race*. Chicago: Aldine, 1973.

Weatherley, D. Maternal response to childhood aggression and subsequent anti-Semitism. *Journal of Abnormal Social Psychology*, 1963, **66**, 183-185.

Werner, H. *Comparative psychology of mental development*. Chicago: Follett, 1948.

Williams, J.E. Connotations of color names among Negroes and Caucasians. *Journal of Perceptual and Motor Skills*, 1964, **18**, 721-731.

Williams, J.E. Racial attitudes in preschool children: Modification via operant conditioning, and a revised measurement procedure. Paper presented at the American Psychological Association, Honolulu, 1972.

Williams, J.E., Best, D.L., Boswell, D.A., Mattson, L.A., and Graves, D.J. Preschool racial attitude measure II. *Educational and Psychological Measurement*, 1974, in press.

Williams, J.E., and Roberson, J.K. A method for assessing racial attitudes in preschool children. *Educational and Psychological Measurement*, 1967, **27**, 671-689.

Williams, J.E., Tucker, R.D., and Dunham, F.Y. Changes in the connotations of color names among Negroes and Caucasians. *Journal of Personality and Social Psychology*, 1971, **19**, 222-228.

Zajonc, R.B., Swap, W.C., Harrison, A.A., and Roberts, P. Limiting conditions of the exposure effect: Satiation and relativity. *Journal of Personality and Social Psychology*, 1971, **18**, 384-391.

# Part III
## Review of Research:
## Attitude and Behavior Change

# 5

# *Laboratory Controlled Studies of Change of Racial Attitudes*

T.A. WEISSBACH

## INTRODUCTION

### Purpose

There are relatively few laboratory controlled investigations of race-related attitude and behavior change. And, if the studies of change in race-related attitudes under controlled conditions have been too few, laboratory controlled studies of changes in overt behavior are practically nonexistent. Yet, race and racism have been a central concern of social psychologists for 30 to 40 years. Why this neglect?

Brigham and Weissbach (1972) suggest that racial attitudes are poor attitude-change research risks. An essential condition for the experimental study of how attitudes change is attitude change. Race-related attitudes, because they are likely to be central rather than peripheral (Rokeach, 1968; Scott, 1968) are poor choices for the relatively weak manipulations employed in the usual laboratory experiment. And, since racial attitudes carry a strong connotation of "right" or "wrong," the probability of socially desirable responses would seem unusually high. Thus, the attitude-change theorist is unlikely to pick the domain of racial attitudes as a suitable vehicle.

Katz (1970) contends that the limitations of past research were a reflection of the social constraints placed upon black-white interactions. Studies focusing on behavior change were eschewed in favor of attitude-change studies because of the general belief that behavior change was dependent upon attitude change. Sumner's alleged aphorism that "stateways cannot change folkways" guided both the courts and the social scientists until fairly recently (e.g., Clark, 1965; Hyman, 1969).

The purpose of this chapter is twofold. First, what has been done will be reviewed, hopefully without stretching too far the definition of "laboratory controlled" or "change." Because studies of change in children are dealt with elsewhere in the book (cf. Chapter 7), the studies reviewed will be restricted to those that used adult subjects. Second, an attempt will be made to suggest some untapped possibilities for further research.

157

## Some methodological and ethical considerations

Aronson and Carlsmith (1968) remind us that the social psychological experiment has both advantages and disadvantages. The disadvantages include difficulty in design, consumption of large amounts of time for a meager return (perhaps a single datum), elaborate deception, apparent lack of *external* (i.e., applicability to nonexperimental settings) validity (Campbell, 1957), difficulty of replication, and an impact that often produces statistically reliable but psychologically insignificant results. Yet, despite these problems, we have not yet designed other techniques that provide the necessary control to allow us to make causal inferences (see McGuire, 1973).

The products of the social psychology laboratory have also forced us to examine the ethics of research on socially sensitive topics. As our power to affect change increases, the responsibility for determining the direction of change also grows. Although the recent report of the Ad hoc Committee on Ethical Standards in Psychological Research (1973) stresses the need for a careful view of proposed research by colleagues, the scope of the review may be too narrow. Is it possible that we are not sensitive enough to the influence of our own values on the attitude and behavior changes we advocate for others (see, for example, Sherwood and Nataupsky, (1968)? And, have we been sufficiently diligent in assessing the long-term effects of change studies, not only upon the specific attitude or behavior but upon the relationships of the subject with important people in his life? Perhaps our disbelief in our ability to make significant changes in socially important realms of behavior has made us a little careless.

## Scope

The body of the paper will consider a possible precondition for change—belief similarity—first. This will be followed by reviews of: (a) contact studies, (b) techniques intended to bring about cognitive and/or personality changes, (c) techniques to reduce aggression or hostility toward out-groups, and (d) propaganda and education. The final section will attempt to state briefly some principles of change derived from the reviews of the content areas listed above.

## Belief similarity: A precondition for change?

This body of work can be traced to Rokeach's statement that "insofar as psychological processes are involved, belief is more important than ethnic or racial membership as a determinant of social discrimination" (Rokeach, Smith, and Evans, 1960, p. 135). It is important to consider this because it relates directly to a very basic assumption about interracial relationships. The assumption is that people are really alike—they want the same things, have the same values, share most beliefs, and so on. It is the problem of the social scientist to arrange conditions (for example, the desegregation of schools) that make it possible to realize these similarities. The realization will then lead to friendly relationships characterized by reduction of prejudice and discrimination. Since 1960, this assumption has been intensively investigated in the laboratory. As might be expected, the findings are equivocal.

A series of laboratory studies (e.g., Stein, Hardyck, and Smith, 1965; Triandis and Davis, 1965; Stein, 1966; Smith, Williams, and Willis, 1967) using paper-and-pencil labels of stimulus persons report that belief appears to account for more of the variance than race in determining interpersonal choice when: (a) social distance is large (i.e., intimacy is not great), and (b) social norms appear to *pre*scribe an interracial choice and/or there are no explicit social pressures *pro*scribing interracial choice. Race similarity appears to be a stronger determinant than belief similarity when: (a) social distance is small (in which case there are usually strong social taboos *pro*scribing interracial choice), and (b) belief similarity is either not salient or beliefs are not made known at all.

The studies cited above lead to the conclusion that if belief similarity is not the most important determinant of interpersonal choice between people of different races it is at least a major determinant and, in some cases, is more important than race similarity. Thus, if people of different races could be shown that they are really alike (i.e., hold similar beliefs), we could break down a good deal of social discrimination. Such a conclusion would be misleading, for it is based on findings that may not be generalizable to real-life situations. The relation between paper-and-pencil tests of behavioral intentions and actual behavior is often either nil or negative. As Krech, Crutchfield, and Ballachey (1962) point out, "the 'Negro' on an attitude scale may be a quite different subject . . . from the Negro in a face-to-face situation" (p. 160).

In laboratory studies comparing the relative contributions of race similarity and belief similarity to interpersonal choice, subjects are asked to respond to paper-and-pencil "Negroes," and these subjects probably respond, at least in part, to the situation. The situation in which the experiments have taken place is the traditional one—a classroom or laboratory at a school or university. The stimuli are presented by university researchers. There is some likelihood that egalitarian responses, interpersonal choices in terms of belief similarity rather than race similarity, are not generalizable beyond the situation in which they were elicited.

Dienstbier (1972) has criticized both the race prejudice and the belief prejudice advocates for oversimplifying the nature of the causal relationships that exist between race membership, belief similarity, and prejudice. He argues that the work that supports the "belief similarity causes racial prejudice" position suffers conceptual and experimental deficiencies. Among the prob-

lems of the research are: confounding of social desirability with racial prejudice (demand characteristics), assumptions of equality of paper-and-pencil
blacks and whites by subjects (assumptions they probably would not make in
"real life"), no checks on suspicions of subjects about purpose of the experiments, results dependent on the choice of dependent variables, and so on.
Hendrick *et al.* (1971) are criticized for using belief issues that may be
insensitive to race differences (e.g., the Vietnam war) rather than such issues
as ambition, morality, cleanliness, etc. Dienstbier (1972) argues that "it is not
possible to consider *realistic and racially relevant* belief manipulations to be
independent of the race manipulations; these two types of variables are . . .
interactive" (p. 152).

Recent work by Wilson (1970) also gives us some reasons to doubt the
absolute efficacy of the belief similarity approach. Not only do whites appear
to assume belief differences exist with "the Negro" in the absence of information to the contrary, but whites may in fact have different beliefs than blacks
in crucial race-relevant domains. Wilson (1970) compared the rankings of 50
relatively prejudiced whites, 50 relatively unprejudiced whites, and 100 blacks
on 14 possible goals of social action. Subjects also estimated the rankings of
the other race. All three groups preferred political, legal, and economic rights
to integration of schools or neighborhoods, and all three groups preferred
self-help rather than hand-out programs for blacks. While the estimates of
black people's rankings of both prejudiced and unprejudiced whites correlated
fairly well with actual blacks' ratings ($r = .62$ and $.82$, respectively), blacks'
estimates of white rankings correlated well only with the prejudiced whites
group ($r = .80$).

The greatest disagreement was reflected in the rankings for the goal
"Firmer law enforcement to maintain civil order and to prevent riots and
other violence" (Wilson, 1970, p. 120) Whites ranked this goal second, while
blacks ranked it thirteenth. Whites saw blacks as ranking this goal last; blacks
saw whites ranking it first. According to Wilson, " . . . this profound degree
of both perceived and actual disagreement does not harken well for the future
course of race relations" (p. 121).

Dienstbier (1972) demonstrates that while the anticipation of belief
differences may dispose a person to be prejudiced, it is also true that
information to the contrary will not necessarily alleviate prejudice. In fact,
prejudice appears to cause the assumption of belief differences as well as the
reverse.

Is belief similarity the necessary precondition for harmonious race relations? Apparently not, although the discovery of belief similarity might
convince some people that a group is not so bad. On the other hand, if a
person creates belief dissimilarity to justify discrimination and prejudice, it
would seem unlikely that education about belief similarities would be either
acceptable or effective. In our subsequent examination of attitude change
studies, the reader will see that belief similarity is sometimes used in conjunction with other techniques to effect change.

## STUDIES OF CHANGE

### Contact studies

Amir (1969) in his review of the contact hypothesis refers to the commonly held belief

> that contact between people—the mere fact of interacting—is likely to change their beliefs and feelings toward each other. Such a view would maintain that men are basically good and seek understanding and mutual appreciation. If only one had the opportunity to communicate with the others and to appreciate their way of life, understanding and consequently a reduction of prejudice would follow. (pp. 319- 320)

Amir goes on to point out that both anecdotal and experimental evidence for the efficacy of contact in reducing prejudice is equivocal and inconsistent. He cites Cook (1962) who reminds us that the proper question is not whether or not intergroup contact reduces prejudice but under what circumstances and with which kind of people intergroup contact will result in reduced prejudice. The bulk of the studies in this area are field studies with varying degrees of control. These will be discussed elsewhere in the text (Chapter 8). Only a very few studies meet the criterion of "laboratory controlled" experiments.

In a fairly typical early study, Mann (1959) assigned 78 students in a graduate education class at Teachers College, New York City, to small discussion groups, all of which contained both blacks and whites, some from the North and some from the South. They met for three weeks, at least four times per week. The participants were administered the Berkeley E scale (ethnocentrism) and sociometric measures at the beginning and at the end of the meetings. The use of race as a basis for friendship choice and prejudice as measured by the E scale were both significantly reduced at the end of the sessions.

The results of Mann's (1959) study are subject to various interpretations. An actual reduction in prejudice may have occurred (lower E scale scores). However, it is also possible that the pretest sensitized the subjects to the purpose of the experiment and that the subsequent reduction in prejudice reflects acquiescence to the demand characteristics of the experiment. A control group would be necessary to assess this sensitization effect. The change in friendship choices could have been similarly affected by the demands of the situation. Even if the changes in friendship choices were genuine, whether or not such choices would be generalized beyond the specific members of the group and beyond the classroom setting is questionable. Cook (1963) cites Minard's (1952) description of interracial contacts among black and white miners as a particularly striking example of how approval may not be generalized. Within the mine, whites and blacks worked together on a friendly basis in racially mixed teams. However, racially segregated shower and changing rooms facilitated the transition to an almost entirely separate existence outside the mine. Thus, contact in one situation, even if it results in positive feelings, may not stimulate contact in other situations nor lead to a general reduction in intergroup hostility.

Allport (1954) suggested that "pursuit of common goals," or cooperation as opposed to competition, would facilitate the reduction of intergroup hostility in the contact situation. Sherif (1966) goes even further and states that if initially hostile groups are brought together without the benefit of mutually attractive superordinate goals, they will use the opportunity only to further group conflicts. Intergroup cooperation was likely when the goal could be reached only through mutual assistance.

Intergroup cooperation to achieve common goals may lead to increased attraction when the attempt to reach the goal is successful but not when there is failure. Burnstein and McRae (1962) hypothesized that shared threat of failure in interracial task-oriented work groups would result in a reduction of prejudice. The hypothesis was confirmed; blacks in work groups that succeeded were evaluated more positively by whites than blacks in work groups that failed. However, the number of messages passed to the black member of the work group, which could be considered an indirect measure of attraction or esteem, did not differ in the failure and success conditions. Rather, significantly fewer messages were passed by high- than low-prejudiced subjects. Thus, while reported attraction was affected by threat of failure, increased communication did not result. The finding of relatively greater attraction under the failure condition is contradicted by Ashmore (1970), who reported that in interracial dyadic work groups that failed to achieve their goals anti-black prejudice increased.

These inconsistent findings provided, in part, the impetus for two studies by Weigel, Blanchard, Adelman, and Cook (1973). In addition to manipulating success-failure in a group task, they also varied the level of participation in the group's decisions and the race of the group's participants. In their first experiment attraction for group members varied only as a function of level of participation, while in the second study attraction was greater in the success as opposed to the failure condition. In neither experiment did race have an effect upon ratings of interpersonal attraction. Because of differences in the way success-failure and participation were operationalized in the two studies, Weigel et al. (1973) suggest that the results in the two studies reflect a common antecedent—satisfaction or dissatisfaction with the group experience. They go on to suggest that weak success-failure manipulations often work because the experimenter has removed other sources of possible satisfaction from the experimental situation.

Weigel et al. (1973) conclude that their findings concerning the effects of success-failure upon attraction to blacks are consistent both with Burnstein and McRae (1962) and with Ashmore (1970). They suggest that the Burnstein and McRae findings of greater cohesion under threat of failure may be explained by the relatively harsh induction of threat. This induction may have led to defensive and protective intermember attraction and the projection of negative feeling onto the experimenter. That this reaction was stronger for prejudiced than for nonprejudiced subjects may be explained by a theory advanced by Katz (1970). He argues that prejudiced persons often have guilt feelings that the objects of their prejudice really are treated unfairly. This ambivalence, Katz argues, leads to amplification of reactions to members of the disliked group. Friendly reactions are more friendly and hostile reactions are more hostile. Thus, when even minimal feelings of attraction are aroused, such as might have occurred under threat of failure and mild humiliation, positive feelings toward group members who belong to the disliked group are amplified.

When Amir (1969) reviewed the status of the contact hypothesis, he specified six conditions that end to reduce prejudice. Five of the conditions were created in a study by Cook (1970): (a) equal status contact between blacks and whites, (b) a favorable social climate for intergroup contact, (c) intimate rather than casual contact, (d) pleasant and rewarding contact, and (e) the members in both groups engage in an activity with a mutual superordinate goal. Subjects for the study, which took place over a period of about eight years, were recruited from two predominantly white universities in a large, border, Southern city. All subjects were white women.

Subjects were recruited via newspaper advertisements and handbills offering part-time employment at the Educational Testing Institute (located at University A) taking paper-and-pencil tests. Respondents were given a 12-hour series of tests, which included a number of measures of racial prejudice. At the time of testing, the potential subjects were told about test-retest reliability and that they would have an opportunity some weeks later to work again, thus preparing them for the postexperimental measures.

Potential subjects with strong anti-Negro attitudes and availability for part-time work two hours daily for four weeks were then contacted by a faculty member at University B. He invited the potential subject to apply for work on a project. The subject was told that the purpose of the project was to evaluate a management task being considered as a training device for isolated units such as exist at early-warning radar outposts. Potential subjects who agreed to be interviewed and agreed to work for the 20 days were told that payment depended upon completion of the full month of work.

Subjects were trained to play a management game that required intragroup cooperation for its success. The game was rigged so that the group always won in the end and earned a bonus. The team consisted of the white female subject and two female confederates—one white and one black. Both confederates were college students and approximately the same age as the subjects.

Although the game is important because it provided the superordinate goal (winning and earning the bonus), the equal status contact (the subject and the confederates rotated jobs), and a basis for fairly close contact (two hours per day for 20 days), it provided only part of the manipulation. During each two-hour session, planned breaks occurred that provided the opportunity for discussions that could include race-related topics (support for positive intergroup contact) and personal topics that provided the black confederate the opportunity to establish herself as an individual and to weaken racial stereotypes held by the subject.

Following the completion of the management game, the subjects interviewed other possible participants (black and white) in order to provide an opportunity to generalize the positive experience with black confederates beyond the task situation. In addition, subjects were recalled by the Educational Testing Institute at University A between one and four months later to participate in another 12 hours of testing, which included repetition of the racial attitude measures.

This summary of procedure greatly oversimplifies the actual manipulations, which are detailed by Cook (1970, 1971). However, there is little doubt that these procedures represent the most intensive laboratory study of interracial contact extant. It differs from the typical laboratory study in a number of ways. Measurement of the dependent variable—change in racial attitude—is clearly separated from the experimental procedure itself both in physical distance and time. The more typical pre-post study that occupies but a very brief time in the subject's life is extended as much as six to eight months between initial and final contact. The independent variable is extremely complex—equal status interracial contact. Because the subvariables were not independently manipulated, any effects that were produced cannot be easily related to specific aspects of the procedure. Finally, the study is aimed at the intensive investigation of an event (unintended interracial contact) rather than the testing of a theory.

The results are both encouraging and disappointing. Compared to a control group of women who took only the pre- and postmeasures, the experimental group had a significantly greater favorable attitude change (toward a more positive attitude of blacks) on direct measures of racial attitude. Seventeen of 22 experimental subjects changed as much as .82 standard deviations in the favorable direction; only 5 out of 42 control subjects had changes as large as .82 standard deviations. Among the subjects who showed substantial change, acceptance of blacks as measured by self-descriptive statements was clearly greater in situations ranging between great social distance (Negroes on the city council) to fairly intimate social distance (Negroes as dinner guests, and sharing restrooms, beauty parlors, and dressing rooms with Negroes).

On indirect measures, the experimental and control groups did not reliably differ. Behavior toward blacks in the game was inconsistent with the subjects' initial attitudes, but was consistent with the experimental demands. Actions during the first few hours of unintended contact were generally courteous and civil. This was less true of those subjects who had earlier indicated that they would quit if assigned a black co-worker and was more true of those who had indicated that they would continue working and act in a friendly manner. Apparently, both racial attitudes and situational influences affected behavior, although the situational influences appeared to be more powerful; none quit the study.

Of the 42 experimental subjects, 38 reported favorable views of their black colleague after their association. Apparently many of these highly prejudiced subjects could learn to like individual blacks without a significant reduction in prejudice toward blacks in general.

Although Cook's work is monumental compared to most laboratory controlled studies of racial attitude or behavior change, it still leaves a number of questions partly or completely unanswered. For example, while 40% of the experimental subjects showed "substantial" racial attitude change, 60% showed little or no change. What accounts for the difference between these subjects? Cook's (1971) analysis indicates that amount of change was not related to initial racial attitude nor to personality measures explored thus far. If contact is a powerful technique for changing attitudes, why only 40% success? The manipulations were certainly powerful (especially compared to the usual laboratory study). Perhaps an unexplored aspect of racial attitude change is the degree to which subjects have learned to ignore exceptions to the rule. Perhaps for a majority of Southern girls at that time, learning about Negroes included learning that no matter how many intelligent, attractive, similar, industrious blacks one meets, the race as a whole is still to be rejected. Or, perhaps one good experience, no matter how good, simply cannot undo 18-20 years of other influences.

Although some of the experimental subjects indicated their willingness to behave in new ways to blacks outside the experimental context, no follow-up of their behavior was made. Their intensions and their attitudes may have changed, but would that negate the effect of the situational influences of their everyday lives? Would a sorority girl return to her sisters and argue that having black members might be acceptable? Would she go home and relate her new views to her parents? Or, as in the study, would she generally remain silent or acquiesce when racial bias was advocated?

While Cook's study is promising, the results should not be overgeneralized. Cook (1971) is careful to note that the procedures indicate that the management of desegregation could be facilitated by administrative practices that would lead to more harmonious racial relations and favorable changes in racial attitude. However, the operational parallels are not known nor is it known how successful they might be. Nevertheless, the approach holds real promise.

## Techniques intended to bring about cognitive and/or personality changes.

The studies to be reviewed in this section would fall roughly into what Ashmore (1970) (and Chapter 3 of this volume) calls a symptom-theory approach to reducing prejudice. This approach is characterized by attempts to reduce the intrapersonal conflicts that are supposed to underlie prejudice. The person who exhibits a well-integrated personality should be less likely to need prejudice as a crutch. Processes intended to achieve conflict reduction vary, but include psychotherapy, self-insight training, catharsis, humor, complexity training, role playing, and others. Not all of these have been subjected to carefully controlled laboratory experimentation.

*Therapy.* Psychotherapy, particularly group psychotherapy, has shown some promise of reducing prejudice if the studies are viewed uncritically. Haimowitz and Haimowitz (1950) achieved a significant reduction in prejudice, as measured by the Bogardus Social Distance Scale, after 35 hours of Rogerian (client-centered) group therapy. Subjects were M.A. level employees of the Veterans Administration. Follow-up two years later of 19 of the original 24 subjects indicated that the reduction in hostility was largely retained. Haimowitz and Haimowitz report that change was obtained for subjects who were mildly hostile originally, but not for extremely hostile subjects.

Unfortunately, the premeasure may have sensitized the group to the desire of the experimenters to achieve a reduction in prejudice. However, if that was the case, it only worked for mildly hostile subjects. The groups were ethnically mixed so that the effect of the therapy is confounded with the effect of the contact. Although the investigators report that subjects were initially consistently friendly or hostile to all racial, religious, and occupational groups on the Bogardus Scale, they do not report whether changes were different for the specific ethnic groups with which subjects came in contact as opposed to groups they did not contact, or if the changes were the same across all the ethnic groups. As the study is reported, it is difficult to choose among competing explanations for change.

Pearl (1954, 1955) reported on a study of hospitalized neurotics whose racial attitudes (California E scale) and personality integration (California F scale) were measured before and after psychotherapy of different kinds. Subjects received either individual therapy (type unspecified), intensive group psychotherapy (with an option of a supplementary weekly half-hour individual session), or brief group psychotherapy. A control group of sorts, recovering tuberculosis patients, were also given the scales but were not exposed to psychotherapy.

The data indicate a significant reduction in E scale scores in the Intensive Group condition, a nonsignificant reduction in the Brief Group condition, and nonsignificant increases in the Individual and Control conditions. The Intensive Group change in E scores differed significantly from the

Individual and Control groups; no other group differences were significant. F scale scores did not change significantly in any of the conditions, nor did F scale changes correlate with E scale changes. Hours of therapy also did not relate to E scale changes.

Apparently, something in the intensive group psychotherapy experience was effective in reducing E scale scores, but not in achieving changes in the personality dispositions that were conceived of as underlying ethnocentric attitudes. Pearl questions both the permanence and the practical significance of the changes achieved.

Rubin (1967a, 1967b) examined the relationship of changes in self-acceptance after participation in a two-week, "live-in," sensitivity training workshop. As in the Haimowitz and Haimowitz (1950) study, interracial contact and therapy are confounded. "There were 8 Negroes in the population, and the trainers made certain that each of the five training groups . . . had at least one Negro . . ." (Rubin, 1967a, p. 234) This study also parallels the Haimowitzs' study in subject selection—highly educated professionals.

Rubin found an initial negative correlation between self-acceptance and prejudice. He predicted that an increase in self-acceptance brought about through sensitivity training should have the concomitant effect of reducing prejudice. Self-acceptance did increase, prejudice decrease, and the changes in both were found to be related. That is, as acceptance of self increases, acceptance of others also increases. It is important to note that subjects in Rubin's study did not decrease the proportion of self-critical statements after training. Thus, while they continued to describe themselves in the same way, they accepted themselves (and apparently others) more.

*Insight.* The therapeutic approach is characterized by increased acceptance of self—a better attitude toward self. Another approach to attitude has been to concentrate on function rather than affect. The functionalists argue that attitudes are formed, maintained, and changed in the service of the individuals' motives. "The most basic assumption is that the key factors in attitude change are not the situational forces or the amount and types of information to which the individual is exposed but the relation of these factors to the individual's motive pattern" (Katz and Stotland, 1959, p. 456).

Katz, Sarnoff, and McClintock (1956) state that an attitude could serve

> one or more of three major motivational determinants: 1. reality-testing and the search for meaning: the need to acquire consistent knowledge about the external world, 2. reward and punishment, including the need to gain social acceptance and to avoid social disapproval, and 3. ego-defense: the need to defend against innter conflict. (p. 27)

Affects towards an object may in fact depend upon the extent to which that object is perceived as useful or rewarding in obtaining valued goals—one of the functions described above. A relevant study by Carlson (1956) demonstrated that attitudes could be changed by altering perceptions of values. The attitudes were towards the issue of changing the perceived instrumentality of allowing Negroes to move into white neighborhoods. An experimental communication was used which aimed at obtaining four important goals: (a) American prestige in other countries, (b) protection of property values, (c) equal opportunity for personal development, and (d) being experienced, broadminded, and worldly-wise. This communication resulted in a changed attitude toward housing segregation for subjects with an initially moderate view toward the issue, but not for extremely prejudiced and nonprejudiced subjects. This is an example of how attitudes that serve to support important goals or values may change if such a change does not require giving up those values.

However, a greater number of investigators have been concerned with the ego-defensive function of attitudes than with the value or reward function. Katz, Sarnoff, and McClintock (1956) reasoned that anti-Negro bias that serves an ego-defensive function should be amenable to change via self-insight procedures designed to uncover the underlying personality dynamics of racial prejudice. They also reasoned that if prejudice is a product of ego-defensive reactions rather than misinformation, then new information about Negroes shoold have little effect on attitudes.

In order to bring about self-insight in the subjects, the experimenters asked them to read an essay that described the dynamics of prejudice with respect to the development of anti-minority attitudes. This was followed by an illustrative case study. The information presentation concentrated on developing a new frame of reference—cultural relativity—in which to view Negroes and went on to describe black-white differences in terms of that framework.

They found no immediate postexperimental differences in prejudice between the self-insight and information conditions, but six weeks later (presumably after personality reorganization had a chance to occur) the self-insight group measured significantly lower on the measures of prejudice than the information group. A predicted superiority of the self-insight procedure for middle-range ego-defensives was not confirmed. Nor did the low ego-defensive subjects change most in response to information, as originally predicted. Thus, while predicted changes in attitude occurred, they are not totally consistent with the theory. If personality reorganization took place, what aspects of personality were changed cannot be easily deduced from the results.

Later work by Stotland, Katz, and Patchen (1959) essentially confirmed the earlier findings that self-insight reduces prejudice. Stotland *et al.* combined self-activity (subject interprets materials pertaining to psychodynamics of prejudice), relevance of the self-activity (content similar to attitude to be changed), and arousal of self-consistency (an appeal to the importance of consistency for effective functioning) to produce an increase in self-insight and a reduction in prejudice. As in the Katz *et al.* (1956) study, changes in racial attitude occurred only after some time had passed (four weeks after treatment). Again, in this study, the predicted relationship between level of ego-defense and attitude change was not confirmed. While high ego-defenders did resist the self-insight manipulations, low- as well as middle-range ego-defenders changed significantly.

Attitude change was restricted to those subjects who received insight into the workings of defense mechanisms from a case study of a prejudiced person. Other case studies concerning family relationships were not effective. Personality reorganization should be effective despite the nature of the case study, but this was not the case. Further, the self-consistency induction was important in achieving maximum attitude change. It appears as if some subjects, rather than achieving a personality reorganization, simply reorganized their attitudes to achieve consistency with self-image.

Regardless, the "self-insight" technique has been effective with a limited population—college students. Whether it would also be effective with other populations is not clear. The delay in achieving change should encourage other researchers to perform assessments at some time other than immediately following treatment. However, repeated measurement may sensitize the subjects to the experimenter's expectations for change. Combined with the university setting, change could be due, in part, to situational influences and sensitization as much as to the experimental manipulation itself. This problem could be remedied by using more elaborate research designs (Solomon, 1949).

*Inconsistency.* The problem of consistency, alluded to in the discussion of Stotland *et al.* (1959) has been investigated by Rokeach (1971). He has investigated the effects on cognitive states of exposing states of inconsistency that exist within a person's value-attitude system. The inconsistency to which Rokeach refers exists whenever a person's behavior in any given situation leads him to be dissatisfied with himself because his behavior is inconsistent with his values. The experimental procedure has concentrated upon highlighting inconsistencies between ratings of two values (freedom and equality) and between ratings of these values and attitudes toward civil rights issues. Subjects are shown a table that indicates the relative importance of 18 terminal values for 298 Michigan State University students. The table shows that "Freedom" is ranked first, "Equality" eleventh. The experimenter interprets this "discrepancy" for the subjects as follows: "Michigan State University students, in general, are much more interested in their own freedom than they are in freedom for other people" (p. 454). His subjects are then given time to compare their responses with those in the table.

After subjects have indicated whether or not they are sympathetic to or have participated in civil rights demonstrations, they are shown a second table. This second table shows that students who rank equality high are more likely to participate in or sympathize with civil rights demonstrations. The implication, drawn for the subjects by the experimenter, is that people who are against civil rights value their own freedom but not the freedom of others.

Rokeach has found relatively long-lasting value and attitude changes as a result of his fairly simple experimental procedures. Further, he has found changes in behavior toward civil rights organizations and toward registration in ethnic relations courses among college students. Experimental subjects were more likely than controls (who had not received information about inconsistencies within their value-attitudes system) to respond favorably to a NAACP solicitation for memberships 15-17 months after the experimental treatment and to register for courses in ethnic relations 21 months after the treatment.

The experimental treatment combined not only an appeal to consistency, in my opinion, but an appeal to reexamine just what support of certain values means. Further, the treatment seems to indicate that subjects who value freedom for themselves but not others (downgrade equality) are hypocrites and unworthy of the experimenter's respect. The communication appears to imply that subjects who do not reinterpret the meaning of the values, which in turn would lead to changes in ratings, will be refused the respect of an important reference person—the experimenter. Rokeach interprets the process differently. He argues that the experimental procedure arouses self-dissatisfaction, which in turn is responsible for significant changes in value rankings and for group differences in civil rights related behaviors. As evidence that this is the process responsible for change, rather than demand characteristics and/or evaluation apprehension, he cites the positive correlation between self-dissatisfaction ratings and value changes. However, it is possible that the response to the self-dissatisfaction measure itself reflects evaluation apprehension and demand characteristics. If the subject understands the experimenter's message (MSU students are hypocrites, and hypocrites do not support civil rights), then he might indeed indicate dissatisfaction with himself as a way of telling the experimenter that he has received the message and is adequately apprehensive about his lack of consistency. At this point, the choice between interpretations may be less important than the startling results: behavior differences between groups receiving the treatment and control groups up to 21 months after the experiment.

Rokeach and McLellan (1972) extend Rokeach's (1971) work in an important way. They point out that it may not always be convenient to inform subjects individually that their own values, attitudes, and behaviors are inconsistent. Can information about others without comparable information about oneself have a long-term impact on values, attitudes, and behaviors? The answer seems to be a qualified yes.

Rokeach and McLellan (1972) compared the effects of the procedures described in Rokeach (1971) with a procedure that did not confront subjects with information about their own values. Subjects saw the two tables— described above for Rokeach (1971)—but did not rank the values for themselves nor compare their rankings with the tables. Upon posttest measurement of the value rankings, no differences in results were found between the two procedures. Both procedures resulted in significant positive changes in the rankings of the values freedom and equality. In addition, these two procedures were significantly more effective than a control group in affecting willingness to support a campus civil rights group four months after the experiment.

Rokeach and McLellan (1972) discuss the possible practical and "ominous" implications of such a value-change procedure, should it be used by the mass media. However, certain distinctions must be drawn between a captive audience of introductory psychology students and the mass media audience. If nothing else, the mass media audience can refuse to read, to watch, or to listen to appeals that might upset his sense of self-satisfaction. The reader can easily find many other points of dissimilarity between the two situations. Problems of this nature will be discussed in more detail in the section on propaganda and education.

Rokeach and Cochrane (1972) ask whether face-to-face confrontation with the experimenter (as might occur in therapy) would either enhance or detract from the value-change procedure. Would sharing embarrassing facts about oneself with a significant other arouse a defensive, ego-protecting reaction, or would such a therapy-like situation produce greater willingness to receive and act upon unpleasant feedback?

The investigators found support for neither possible hypothesis. Instead, they report no difference in the anonymous and confrontation conditions. Both produce lasting value changes. Confrontation by a significant other neither enchanced nor detracted from the amount or quality of change in any meaningful way.

Taken together, the investigations by Rokeach suggest a powerful and relatively simple tool for use with college students. Whether or not such a procedure would be equally effective with others (or even with college students not at large, fairly liberal universities, or not in psychology classes) is not known.

*Cognitive Training.* The studies reviewed above in this section have concentrated mainly on rearranging existing concepts (values, attitudes, and beliefs) as a result of new information in such a way as to make prejudice less likely. Gardiner (1972) has explored ways to change existing concepts through complexity training. He argues that prejudice is a likely outcome of simple cognitive structures. A simple cognitive structure is one that is poorly differentiated and poorly integrated. Persons who are cognitively simple appear to make extreme judgments, anchor their judgments upon external influences, exhibit a high degree of conformity, and show low resistance to frustration, rapid change, or environmental complexity. On the other hand, the more cognitively complex individual can use conflict and stress because he is able to conceptualize events in alternative ways. Attitude alone is an inadequate measure of prejudice in this formulation because the cognitively simple person is so amenable to external pressures to change. For these persons, an attitude measure can only reflect a state of affairs dependent on external anchoring, not on lasting dispositions to action.

If such a formulation is correct, training leading to increased complexity should result in decreased prejudice. Gardiner reports that because of earlier work (Abelson, 1968), which indicated that cognitive ability may not be generalizable across domains, the complexity training in his study uses stimulus materials in the domain of race relations.

Three groups of white high school subjects were given either no complexity training (control), uniconceptual training (IC), or multiconceptual training (2C). Uniconceptual training involved giving subjects a number of conceptual dimensions to help them form a single concept of a stimulus person. In addition, subjects were encouraged to add other dimensions that would aid in the formation of the concept. Multiconceptual training was identical except that two concepts rather than one were formed. The basic hypothesis was that multiconceptual training would be more effective than uniconceptual training, which would be superior to the control group, in achieving conceptual complexity in the area of race relations and in reducing racial prejudice.

While the results do not unequivocally support the hypothesis, both complexity training procedures were effective in reducing prejudice. However, the multiconceptual training group did not uniformly outperform the uniconceptual training group. Gardiner points out that the multiconceptual training procedure may have overwhelmed very cognitively simple subjects, thus producing less change because of stress. He argues that complexity training should start at a point consistent with a person's current level of complexity and proceed to more complex levels.

One further result bears mentioning. No immediate postexperimental treatment effect was observed, but the significant effects were achieved after a one-week period. This finding, as Gardiner points out, is analogous to the findings of Katz et al. (1956) and Stotland et al. (1959). The importance of allowing the treatment to take effect seems to be crucial in these studies as well as in those by Rokeach and his associates (Rokeach, 1971; Rokeach and Cochrane, 1972; Rokeach and McLelland, 1972).

## Techniques to reduce aggression or hostility toward out-groups

Two approaches will be reviewed here. The first concerns reducing aggression and hostility through catharsis, the second—inhibition of aggressive behavior in various ways. Allport (1945) has argued that if aggressive or hostile feelings against a minority group are a function of a general level of aggression within an individual, then a reduction in that level of aggression might lead to reduced prejudice. The term catharsis is used to describe this release of psychic tension. However, none of the reported studies attempt a reduction in overall feelings of aggression or aggressive motivation. Rather, aggression toward specific groups is the target. For example, Allport described the release of tension experienced by a group of policemen who discussed their prejudices openly. However, this was not an experimental study and alternate explanations are available.

Singer (1968) investigated the effect of humor upon aggressive feelings towards segregationists and white supremacists in black subjects. Aggressive feelings were aroused by a communication that detailed some of the horrors of segregationist thinking and action with respect to blacks. There were two humor conditions: (a) hostile anti-white humor, and (b) a neutral humor presentation. In a third condition, subjects listened to a documentary. The experimenters were black, and the humor and documentary tapes were excerpted from presentations by well-known blacks.

Results indicated that the arousal communication evoked strong aggressive feelings as well as considerable anxiety. Because the study was conducted between the months of April and September of 1963, a time of considerably increasing racial tension, it is important to note the increase in aggressive motivation, anxiety, and involvement in subjects tested later in the study as compared to those tested earlier in the summer. Both hostile and neutral humor reduced aggressive motivation and tension for aroused subjects, although hostile humor was especially effective for aroused subjects in late summer. A negative correlation between humor appreciation and reduction in aggression and motivation for late-summer subjects supports the catharsis interpretation. For early-summer subjects, the relationship was insignificant. Singer suggests that aggression reduction for these subjects may have been a result of diversion provided by the humor, which generated responses temporarily incompatible with aggression and tension. He also suggests that the hostile aspect of the humor may not have been crucial. Rather, the humor may have aroused feelings of mastery over intolerable circumstances. Singer concludes that "under appropriate conditions gratifying fantasy can have profound cathartic effects . . ."(1968, p. 13).

A series of studies (Donnerstein and Donnerstein, 1972; Donnerstein, Donnerstein, Simon, and Ditrichs, 1972; Donnerstein and Donnerstein, 1972) has investigated the effects of several variables upon the expression of interracial aggression. The focus of the studies has been the examination of conditions that stimulate or inhibit the delivery of direct and indirect aggression by members of one race to members of another race. They begin with the notion that fear of black retaliation may be inhibiting white aggression toward blacks.

In all three studies, direct aggression is measured by the intensity of electric shock delivered by the subject to a victim of his own or another race. Indirect aggression is measured by duration of shock. Several interesting findings are reported.

First, when there is a clear potential for black retaliation, less direct but more indirect aggression against blacks by whites was discovered than when retaliation was precluded. However, following a campus racial disturbance, subjects were more directly hostile to blacks even though retaliation might have been considered more likely. Apparently, the increase in hostility was sufficient to disinhibit fear and elicit greater aggression (Donnerstein and Donnerstein, Simon, and Ditrichs, 1972). A second finding (Donnerstein and Donnerstein, 1972) was that, under threat of retaliation, increased rewards were given to blacks by whites, but indirect aggression also increased. The potential for in-group censure has also been found to affect levels of aggression (Donnerstein and Donnerstein, 1973). In-group censure referred to the possibility that the experimenter would review a videotape of the subject delivering reward or punishment to the target. It was found that potential censure had no effect on direct aggression toward whites, but substantially reduced direct aggression toward blacks. For indirect aggression, the results were practically reversed. Black targets received significantly more indirect aggression under the potential censure than the noncensure condition, while for whites the results were in the opposite direction.

Donnerstein and Donnerstein (1973) suggest that their results provide support for the motions of response substitution (Dollard, Doob, Miller, Mowrer, and Sears, 1939; Berkowitz, 1962). Where direct aggression is inhibited, indirect aggressive responses are likely to be displayed. They suggest that such inhibition of direct aggression, unaccompanied by a general reduction in hostility and aggressive drive, may not have the desired effect of reducing aggressive behavior toward blacks. They propose that Feshbach's (1964) suggestion to change the meaning of stimuli that elicit aggression might reduce both forms of aggression.

Jones (1972) reports Kovel's (1970) suggestion that active and passive racial aggression reflect two different types of racism—dominative and adversive; these categories are considered in more detail in Chapter 6. The dominative racist acts out his bigoted beliefs while the aversive racist tries his best to ignore the existence of blacks and to express his racism in more subtle ways. The Donnersteins' work suggests that the quality of expression of racism may depend upon opportunity rather than preference. The important point is to find ways of reducing opportunities for either dominative or aversive racism to be expressed. Whether the best approach is to inhibit opportunity, threaten retaliation, or reduce the impetus for aggression is an open question.

## Propaganda and education

The potential effect of propaganda upon prejudice is blunted by the potential for evading or distorting the message (Cooper and Jahoda, 1947, cited in Ashmore, 1970). A person can read or listen to propaganda, but miss the point. Or, he can judge the message invalid for one reason or another. Third, a person may misperceive in such a way that he changes the frame of reference so that the meaning of the message is made to conform to his preconceptions. Finally, the message may be poorly designed (too complicated, for example) and thus miss its target.

Studies of the effects of motion pictures (e.g., Goldberg, 1956), of oral arguments (Knower, 1936), or of various sorts of discussion sessions (Greenberg, Pierson, and Sherman, 1957) have been inconclusive. Although changes are occasionally achieved, they are as likely due to experimental artifacts (the experimenter delivers the argument or teaches the class, or the experimenter administers pre- and postmeasures) as to the experimental treatment. None of the studies have done much to clarify how propaganda or education might change attitudes if they in fact do so.

A rather intensive, if unsystematic, propaganda attempt to substitute black power ideology connotations of blackness for the negative connotations that previously existed has been prominent for about ten years. Lessing and Zagorin (1972a, 1972b) have attempted to relate the effects of this effort to the racial attitudes of both blacks and whites. Generally, they found that both blacks and whites who endorse the black power ideology exhibit more favorable racial attitudes toward blacks. Both blacks and whites, regardless of black power orientation, rated black person more potent and active than Negro person, colored person, or white person—giving support for the success of the black power ideology. The difficult problem with this study is drawing any conclusion about causality of either racial attitudes or acceptance of black power ideology. Nor is it clear, as the authors point out, whether improved attitudes toward blacks and/or endorsement of black power ideology will affect overt behavior. Nevertheless, the suggestion remains that here is a propaganda campaign that has had some effect on the racial attitudes of whites and blacks and on the self-concepts of blacks. The behavioral correlates have not yet been experimentally explored.

A recently reported study by Crawford (1974) illustrates some of the difficulties that the potential educator or propagandist must face. Strictly speaking, his study is fieldwork rather than laboratory-controlled experimental work, but it could at least be called quasiexperimental. Following black ghetto riots and open housing demonstrations that were accompanied by stone-throwing white counter demonstrators, a Catholic bishop in a Midwestern city ordered his parish priests to deliver sermons opposing racial hatred and injustice. The sermons were part of a multifaceted program to oppose racism.

Crawford surveyed attitudes toward racial integration and reactions to attempts to change such attitudes among Catholic parishioners prior to and after the sermons concerning racial hatred and injustice were delivered.

The bishop provided rather explicit guidelines for the sermons that were to be delivered by his parish priests. However, observers who judged the sermons' intensity (basically, each sermon's effectiveness as a prointegration message) found wide variations in content and effectiveness. Even though the bishop's intensions were clear, the message was often not delivered at all or, at best, was delivered in a half-hearted and very guarded fashion. Sermon intensity was highly positively correlated with levels of education, income, occupational status, and prointegration attitude of parishioners, and negatively correlated with level of authoritarian aggression. This means that those most likely to oppose integration heard the weakest sermons favoring integration. The findings suggest, according to Crawford, that parish priests were more influenced by their perceptions of parish norms than by the bishop's dictum.

In light of the fact that sermons appeared to be tailored to what the parishioners already believed, Crawford's finding that the sermons had no impact on racial attitudes is not surprising. What seems to be most important is that propaganda or education may never reach those who need it most. The parish priests may have believed that their parishioners would not tolerate stronger appeals to racial justice than were delivered, and the priests may or may not be correct. Attitude change theorists differ in their expectations about the results of highly discrepant messages (messages whose contents advocate a position very distant from the listener's) on attitudes. Some argue that the greater the discrepancy, the greater the change. Other claim that if a persuasive message is too discrepant from the receiver's position, a boomerang effect will occur. The receiver will become defensive and retrench, taking a position even more extreme than before (and in the direction opposite to the persuasive message).

The general picture this section presents is that education and propaganda cannot be shown to have any serious effect upon racial attitudes. Should we then put Rokeach and McLellan's (1972) fears to rest? Could their techniques, used by the mass media, be more successful than any others? It is difficult to say, but the evidence seems to suggest that it is too easy to avoid delivering the message or hearing it.

On the other hand, it seems much too pessimistic to say that education and/or propaganda do not affect values, beliefs, and attitudes. Perhaps the experimental psychologist simply defines education too narrowly (lectures, sermons, movies) and, in addition, is too impatient to assess the effects of educational efforts. Perhaps, as a number of studies reviewed here suggest, attitude and behavior changes take time to manifest themselves. The laboratory approach may be inadequate in this case to measure the effectiveness of such programs. Still another possibility is that education is a necessary contributor to change, but insufficient by itself to affect change. It is much too early to reject education as a tool for eradicating racism.

## PRINCIPLES OF CHANGE

Belief similarity appears to be a correlate of low prejudice. However, it has not been demonstrated experimentally that increasing belief similarity, by itself will result in decreased prejudice. Further, it appears as if important belief differences exist between blacks and whites in such important domains as civil rights priorities. The finding that interracial belief differences are assumed in the absence of evidence to the contrary leads to further pessimism. Since the discovery of belief similarities would apparently rest upon education and propaganda (not very encouraging) or upon interracial contact, the outlook cannot be too optimistic. Finally, situational and predispositional influences also affect perceived belief similarity. It would seem that while belief similarity is important, it may be a more likely outcome than cause of reduced racial prejudice.

Studies of interracial contact hold more promise. When interracial contact can be arranged, and when the conditions of contact are supportive, then reduction in prejudice for at least some subjects seems to follow. The supportive conditions, set out by Amir (1969) and in Chapter 6, that tend to reduce prejudice are: equal status, favorable social climate, intimacy, pleasant and rewarding outcome, and superordinate goals. The relative contributions of the various components in reducing prejudice are not known, nor in most cases do we know whether or not attitude changes that have been achieved affect discriminatory behaviors.

Changes in cognitive organization and structure, increases in self-insight or self-respect, and training in cognitive complexity have all been moderately successful in reducing prejudice for well-educated persons. Those methods that do not involve therapy or that might be adapted in educational settings may hold real promise for bringing about attitude change. There is no reason why the case study method of achieving insight into the personality dynamics could not be adapted to educational settings or even to the various entertainment media. And, one would suppose that increased cognitive complexity should in any case be a by-product of a sound educational program. More carefully constructed propaganda and education might make the current dismal picture considerably brighter.

Reduction of aggression toward specific groups through catharsis or through inhibition has also been shown to be an effectivy means of reducing prejudice. It is also possible that campaigns to reduce the general availability of aggressive cues (e.g., guns) and aggressive models (e.g., TV violence), if successful, might also reduce prejudice caused by aggressive feelings.

As a note, many areas of research have not yet been exploited with respect to their potential for alleviating racial tension. For example, only one role-playing study with adults exists to my knowledge (Culbertson, 1957). Yet, recent work with children would indicate that role playing might prove an effective means of achieving change (Weiner and Wright, 1973). In their study, a third-grade class was randomly divided into Orange and Green people. The two groups alternated status positions. On one day Orange was "superior," Green "inferior," on another day, the status positions were reversed. The experience of suffering discrimination apparently resulted in a decrease in prejudice and an increased willingness to interact with black children when compared to a control group. The technique of role playing is often used as a therapeutic tool and as an educational device. It can provide opportunities for modeling new behaviors or for viewing old (and perhaps threatening) behaviors in a new and nonthreatening way. Role playing is apparently a popular tool of human relations experts who must attempt to alleviate interracial tensions, but its effectiveness has not yet been systematically studied.

Recent work on conditioning of attitudes indicates that conditioning may be most effective with adults who are more readily formed or changed during the earlier years as opposed to the later years of development, and the belief that attitudes are most easily acquired by conditioning when the person is unaware he is being conditioned. On the other hand, O'Donnell and Brown state that their procedure may work best with attitudes that are primarily cognitive rather than affective. With respect to racial attitudes, this might mean that certain kinds of racial attitudes (those based upon "rational" beliefs) could be changed by classical conditioning even in adulthood, but that racial attitudes that are primarily affective ("I just hate 'em!") might require different and earlier intervention procedures.

Four trends in the studies reviewed make the potential application of further studies increasingly promising. First, more attention is being paid to behavior. The lack of a consistent relationship between attitudes and behavior (Wicker, 1969) makes it particularly important to test for behavioral effects if change procedures are to have practical consequences. Second, long-term follow-ups are more common. Two factors may be responsible for this trend. Many procedures take time to work, and transitory changes are no longer considered satisfactory evidence of the utility of a procedure. Third, attitude measurement has become more subtle and more divorced from the experimental treatments themselves. This raises the hope that effects of treatment are just that rather than artifacts. Finally, stimuli are more complex, reflecting the complexity of the forces that mediate behavior in the real world. Laboratory experimenters have managed to increase realism (and therefore generalizability) with little or no sacrifice of the controls that make the laboratory experiment a powerful tool.

# REFERENCES

Abelson, R.P. When the polls go wrong and why. *Trans-Action*, 1968, **5**, 20-27.

Ad hoc Committee on Ethical Standards in Psychological Research. *Ethical principles in the conduct of research with human participants.* Washington, D.C.: American Psychological Association, 1973.

Allport, G.W. Catharsis and the reduction of prejudice. *Journal of Social Issues*, 1945, **1**, 3-10.

Allport, G.W. *The nature of prejudice.* Reading, Mass.: Addison-Wesley, 1954.

Amir, Y. Contact hypothesis in ethnic relations. *Psychological Bulletin*, 1969, **71**, 319-342.

Aronson, E., and Carlsmith, J.M. Experimentation in social psychology. In G. Lindzey and E. Aronson (Eds.), *The handbook of social psychology.* Second edition. Reading, Mass.: Addison-Wesley, 1968.

Ashmore, R.D. Solving the problem of prejudice. In B.E. Collins, (Ed.) *Social psychology: Social influence, attitude change, group processes, and prejudice* (Ed.). Reading, Mass.: Addison-Wesley, 1970.

Berkowitz, L. *Aggression: A social psychological analysis.* New York: McGraw-Hill, 1962.

Brigham, J.C., and Weissbach, T.A. (Eds.) *Racial attitudes in America.* New York: Harper & Row, 1972.

Burnstein, E., and McRae, A.V. Some effects of shared threat and prejudice in racially mixed groups. *Journal of Abnormal and Social Psychology*, 1962, **64**, 257-263.

Campbell, D.T. Factors relevant to the validity of experiments in social settings. *Psychological Bulletin*, 1957, **54**, 297-312.

Carlson, E.R. Attitude change through modification of attitude structure. *Journal of Abnormal and Social Psychology*, 1956, **52**, 256-261.

Clark, K.B. *Dark ghetto.* New York: Harper & Row, 1965.

Cook, S.W. The systematic analysis of socially significant events: A strategy for social research. *Journal of Social Issues*, 1962, **18**(2), 66-84.

Cook, S.W. Desegregation: A psychological analysis. In W.W. Charters, Jr., and N.L. Gage (Eds.), *Readings in the social psychology of education.* Boston: Allyn & Bacon, 1963.

Cook, S.W. Motives in a conceptual analysis of attitude-related behavior. In W.J. Arnold and D. Levine (Eds.), *Nebraska symposium on motivation, 1969.* Lincoln: University of Nebraska Press, 1970.

Cook, S.W. The effect of unintended interracial contact upon racial interaction and attitude change. Final Report, August 1971, University of Colorado. Contract OEC-4-7-051320-0273, Department of Health, Education and Welfare.

Cooper, E., and Jahoda, M. The evasion of propaganda: How prejudiced people respond to anti-prejudiced propaganda. *Journal of Psychology*, 1947, **23**, 15-25.

Crawford, T.J. Sermons on racial tolerance and the parish neighborhood context. *Journal of Applied Social Psychology*, 1974, **4**, 1-23.

Culbertson, F.M. Modification of an emotionally-held attitude through role playing. *Journal of Abnormal and Social Psychology*, 1957, **54**, 230-233.

Dienstbier, R.A. A modified belief theory of prejudice emphasizing the mutual causality of racial prejudice and anticipated belief differences. *Psychological Review*, 1972, **79**, 146-160.

Dollard, J., Doob, L.W., Miller, N.E., Mowrer, O.H., and Sears, R.R. *Frustration and aggression*. New Haven: Yale University Press, 1939.

Donnerstein, E., and Donnerstein, M. White rewarding behavior as a function of the potential for black retaliation. *Journal of Personality and Social Psychology*, 1972, **24**, 327-333.

Donnerstein, E., and Donnerstein, M. Variables in interracial aggression: Potential ingroup censure. *Journal of Personality and Social Psychology*, 1973, **27**, 143-150.

Donnerstein, E., Donnerstein, M., Simon, S., and Ditrichs, R. Variables in interracial aggression: Anonymity, expected retaliation, and a riot. *Journal of Personality and Social Psychology*, 1972, **22**, 236-245.

Feshbach, S. The function of aggression and the regulation of aggressive drive. *Psychological Review*, 1964, **71**, 257-272.

Gardiner, G.S. Complexity training and prejudice reduction. *Journal of Applied Social Psychology*, 1972, **2**, 326-342.

Goldberg, A.L. The effects of two types of sound motion pictures on the attitudes of adults toward minorities. *Journal of Educational Sociology*, 1956, **29**, 386-391.

Greenberg, H., Pierson, J., and Sherman, S. The effects of single-session education techniques on prejudice attitudes. *Journal of Educational Sociology*, 1957, **31**, 82-86.

Greenwald, A.G. When does role playing produce attitude change? Toward an answer. *Journal of Personality and Social Psychology*, 1970, **16**, 214-219.

Haimowitz, M.L., and Haimowitz, N.R. Reducing ethnic hostility through psychotherapy. *Journal of Social Psychology*, 1950, **31**, 231-241.

Hendrick, C., Bixenstein, V.E., and Hawkins, G. Race versus belief similarity as determinants of attraction: A search for a fair test. *Journal of Personality and Social Psychology*, 1971, **17**, 250-258.

Hyman, H.H. Social psychology and race relations. In I. Katz and P. Gurin (Eds.), *Race and the social sciences*. New York: Basic Books, 1969.

Jones, J.M. *Prejudice and racism*. Reading, Mass.: Addison-Wesley, 1972.

Katz, D., Sarnoff, I., and McClintock, C. Ego-defense and attitude change. *Human Relations*, 1956, **9**, 27-45.

Katz, D., and Stotland, F. A preliminary statement to a theory of attitude structure and change. In S. Koch (Ed.), *Psychology: A study of a science*. Volume 3. New York: McGraw-Hill, 1959.

Katz, I. Experimental studies of Negro-white relationships. In L. Berkowitz (Ed.), *Advances in experimental social psychology*. Volume 5. New York: Academic Press, 1970.

Kiesler, C.A., Collins, B.E., and Miller, N. *Attitude change: A critical analysis of theoretical approaches*. New York: Wiley, 1969.

Knower, F.H. Experimental studies of changes in attitude. II. A study of the effect of printed argument on changes in attitude. *Journal of Abnormal and Social Psychology*, 1936, **30**, 522-532.

Kovel, J. *White racism: A psychohistory.* New York: Pantheon, 1970.

Krech, D., Crutchfield, R.S., and Ballachey, E.L. *Individual in society.* New York: McGraw-Hill, 1962.

Lessing, E.E., and Zagorin, S.W. Black power ideology and college students attitudes toward their own and other racial groups. *Journal of Personality and Social Psychology*, 1972a, **21**, 61-73.

Lessing, E.E., and Zagorin, S.W. Black power ideology and college students' attitudes toward their own and other racial groups: A correction. *Journal of Personality and Social Psychology*, 1972b, **22**, 414-416.

Mann, J.H. The effects of inter-racial contact on sociometric choices and perceptions. *Journal of Social Psychology*, 1959, **50**, 143-152.

McGuire, W.J. The yin and yang of progress in psychology: Seven koan. *Journal of Personality and Social Psychology*, 1973, **26**, 446-456.

Minard, R.D. Race relationships in the Pocahontas coal field. *Journal of Social Issues*, 1952, 8(1), 29-44.

O'Donnell, J.M., and Brown, M.J.K. The classical conditioning of attitudes: A comparative study of ages 8 to 18. *Journal of Personality and Social Psychology*, 1973, **26**, 379-385.

Pearl, D. Ethnocentrism and the self concept. *Journal of Social Psychology*, 1954, **40**, 137-147.

Pearl, D. Psychotherapy and ethnocentrism. *Journal of Abnormal and Social Psychology*, 1955, **50**, 227-230.

Rokeach, M. A theory of organization and change within value-attitude systems. *Journal of Social Issues*, 1968, **24**, 13-33.

Rokeach, M. Long-range experimental modification of values, attitudes, and behavior. *American Psychologist*, 1971, **26**, 453-459.

Rokeach, M., and Cochrane, R. Self-confrontation and confrontation with others as determinants of long-term value change. *Journal of Applied Social Psychology*, 1972, **2**, 283-292.

Rokeach, M., and McLellan, D.D. Feedback of information about the values and attitudes of self and others as determinants of long-term cognitive and behavioral change. *Journal of Applied Social Psychology*, 1972, **2**, 236-251.

Rokeach, M., Smith, P.W., and Evans, R.I. Two kinds of prejudice or one? In M. Rokeach (Ed.), *The open and closed mind.* New York: Basic Books, 1960.

Rubin, I.M. Increased self-acceptance: A means of reducing prejudice. *Journal of Personality and and Social Psychology*, 1967a, **5**, 233-238.

Rubin, I.M. The reduction of prejudice through laboratory training. *Journal of Applied Behavioral Science*, 1967b, **3**, 29-50.

Scott, W.A. Attitude measurement. In G. Lindzey and E. Aronson (Eds.), *The handbook of social psychology.* Second edition, Volume 2. Reading, Mass.: Addison-Wesley, 1968.

Sherif, M. *In common predicament: Social psychology of intergroup conflict and cooperation.* Boston: Houghton Mifflin, 1966.

Sherwood, J.J., and Nataupsky, M. Predicting the conclusions of Negro-white intelligence research from biographical characteristics of the investigation. *Journal of Personality and Social Psychology*, 1968, **8**, 53-58.

Singer, D.L. Aggression arousal, hostile humor, catharsis. *Journal of Personality and Social Psychology Monograph Supplement.* 1968, **8**, No. 1, Part 2.

Smith, C.R., Williams, L., and Willis, R.H. Race, sex, and belief as determinants of friendship acceptance. *Journal of Personality and Social Psychology,* 1967, **5**, 127-137.

Solomon, R.L. Extension of control group design. *Psychological Bulletin,* 1949, **46**, 137-150.

Stein, D.D. The influence of belief systems on interpersonal preference: A validation study of Rokeach's theory of prejudice. *Psychological Monographs,* 1966, No. 616.

Stein, D.D., Hardyck, J.A., and Smith, M.B. Race and belief: An open and shut case. *Journal of Personality and Social Psychology,* 1965, **1**, 281-289.

Stotland, E., Katz, D., and Patchen, M. The reduction of prejudice through the arousal of self-insight. *Journal of Personality,* 1959, **27**, 507-531.

Triandis, H.C. Exploratory factor analysis of the behavioral component of social attitudes. *Journal of Abnormal and Social Psychology,* 1964, **68**, 420-430.

Triandis, H.C., and Davis, E.E. Race and belief as determinants of behavioral intentions. *Journal of Personality and Social Psychology,* 1965, **2**, 715-725.

Weigel, R.H., Blanchard, F.A., Adelman, L., and Cook, S.W. Interpersonal attraction in cooperating interracial groups: Effects of group success, participation in decision making, and race. Unpublished manuscript, University of Colorado, 1973.

Weiner, M.J., and Wright, F.E. Effects of undergoing arbitrary discrimination upon subsequent attitudes toward a minority group. *Journal of Applied Social Psychology,* 1973, 3, 94-102.

Wicker, A.W. Attitudes versus actions: The relationship of verbal and overt behavioral responses to attitude objects. *Journal of Social Issues,* 1969, **25**, 41-78.

Wilson, W. Rank order of discrimination and its relevance to civil rights priorities. *Journal of Personality and Social Psychology,* 1970, **15**, 188-124.

# 6

# *Nonreactive Measures in Racial Attitude Research: A Focus on "Liberals"*

SAMUEL L. GAERTNER

The problem of how progress toward the elimination of racism shall be assessed is complicated by the fact that traditional instruments used to gauge racial attitudes are, at best, moderately effective.

Critiques of questionnaire and interview methodologies as well as those of traditional laboratory paradigms have usually focused on the subject's awareness that *he* is the target of empirical inquiry. Unfortunately, the subject's awareness of "being experimented upon" is believed to arouse motives that may be incompatible with the investigator's objectives. While the investigator is concerned with eliciting behavior that reflects his subjects' "true" attitudes or the impact of specified independent variables, subjects may be concerned with issues that are of more immediate personal importance to them. For example, a subject may distort, deemphasize, or elaborate upon his responses in a manner that he believes would favorably influence the investigator's evaluation of him as a person. This contaminating factor is especially pertinent when the research is concerned with controversial issues such as racial attitudes. Rosenberg (1965) furthermore suggests that "evaluation apprehension" may systematically affect the results of an experiment when its saliency differs across experimental conditions.

In addition, Martin Orne (1962) hypothesized that subjects may wish to be regarded as good, valuable subjects and therefore they may actively seek cues from the experimenter or from the experimental situation that tip them off as to the experimenter's purposes and expectations. The responses of "good" subjects, then, would be guided by what they believe is expected or demanded of them. Recalcitrant subjects similarly would discover the means to their ends.

The thrust of these arguments is that subjects may *react* strongly to the experimental intervention and thereby sacrifice the naturalness, spontaneity, and even the integrity of their behavior. Research methods that impose these threats to the investigator's objectives are known as "reactive" methods (Campbell, 1957). Cook and Selltiz (1964) suggest a number of strategies researchers may use to reduce the effects of reactivity. Nevertheless, the most effective tack deals directly with the source of the problem: the subject's

183

awareness that he is being experimented upon. Webb, Campbell, Schwartz, and Sechrest (1966) propose several methods that minimize the obtrusiveness of the inquiry. They suggest, for example, the more extensive use of archival data and observation and experimentation in natural settings, during which subjects are unaware of their research participation. Bickman and Henchy (1972) offer the reader an interesting collection of studies conducted in natural settings, which have minimized reactivity without a substantial reduction of experimental rigor.

Although less reactive methods may be necessary for the accurate assessment of racial attitudes, they may not be sufficient. This chapter will consider the possibility that some people retain and value an unprejudiced self-image while their negative feelings toward blacks and other minorities are frequently disassociated from their self-concept. Encounters with blacks in everyday life or with questionnaire administrators challenge this prejudice-free image. Then racially "appropriate" behavior is purposely offered to preserve their self-concept until the costs for maintaining the egalitarian image becomes prohibitive (e.g., until contact with blacks is soon to become too intimate). In a sense, most interactions with blacks inject these people into a reactive experiment that arouses evaluator apprehension. In these instances, however, they are concerned with their self-evaluation rather than an experimenter's evaluation of their behavior.

The analysis of racial and ethnic attitudes focuses on the individual's beliefs, feelings, or behavioral intentions towards the target group. It is often assumed that these rather intangible components of racial attitudes in some way affect overt behavior, or vice versa. Empirical evidence, however, suggests that attitudes alone, assessed by questionnaire and interview procedures, are usually poor predictors of overt behavior (Wicker, 1969).

Since attitudes are always inferred from some form of behavior, this inconsistency across various measures poses obvious problems for the researcher attempting to assess racial attitudes. A researcher might consequently begin to speculate as to which indicator measures the "true" attitude or to question the usefulness of a component model of attitudes. Most explanations for the apparent inconsistency between thought and deed rely heavily upon the validity of questionnaire measures and assume that factors within the immediate behavioral situation (e.g., group norms, reinforcement contingencies, etc.) influenced the overt response. Such confidence in questionnaire measures of racism, however, appears overzealous.

Campbell's approach (1963) to the problem of "inconsistency" between word and deed is to seriously doubt whether inconsistency between two measures has ever been demonstrated in the first place. Rather, Campbell suspects that the apparent inconsistency may be due to the fact that on one of the measures it might be very difficult for a person to appear racist while on the other measure it might be equally difficult for him to appear egalitarian; in other words, the two measures are maximally sensitive at opposite ends of the attitudinal continuum. For example, on a questionnaire, given the degree of evaluator apprehension and reactivity usually present, it may be very difficult for a person to respond in a bigoted fashion; perhaps only the extreme bigot would answer in such a manner, while everyone else would provide more socially acceptable responses and would be regarded, perhaps incorrectly, as egalitarian. In the overt behavioral situation, however, it may be very difficult for a person to respond in an egalitarian fashion because of the high cost of engaging in the act itself; only the extreme egalitarian would behave as an egalitarian, everyone else being classified as a bigot. Campbell's analysis suggests that it would not be inconsistent for a person to respond as an egalitarian on the questionnaire and as a bigot in the behavioral situation. However, to respond as a bigot on the questionnaire (or in situations in which it is difficult to respond as a bigot) while responding as an egalitarian in the overt behavioral situation (or when it is easier to respond as a bigot) would be inconsistent.

Generally, as long as the assessments differ widely in their areas of sensitivity, consistency should be observable only among the extreme egalitarians and the extreme bigots. Those with less extreme attitudinal positions should appear more inconsistent across a variety of measures. If several measures representing different degrees of difficulty in appearing bigoted were incorporated in a behavioral situation inventory, a reasonably accurate assessment of individual racism might be possible. Naturally, a questionnaire methodology would be most convenient. To rely primarily on currently available questionnaires, however, for the valid assessment of racial attitudes would be a tenuous enterprise at best.

The insightful analysis of individual racism by Kovel (1970)—developed further by Jones (1972)—is especially pertinent to the assessment of racial attitudes. At the individual level, Kovel distinguishes between the "dominative" racist and the "aversive" racist. Jones points out that the difference between these types is not one of degree but of kind. The dominative racist is

> the type who acts out of bigoted beliefs—he represents the open flame of race hatred—he openly seeks to keep the black man down, and he is willing to use force to further his ends. (Kovel, 1970, p. 54)

The aversive racist is

> the type who believes in white race superiority and is more or less aware of it but does nothing about it. An intrapsychic battle goes on between these sentiments and a conscience which seeks to repudiate them, or at least to prevent the person from acting wrongly upon them. (Kovel, 1970, p. 54)

Thus, the aversive racist tries to avoid contact with blacks; when contact is unavoidable, his manner is polite, correct, but cold. Within the aversive type are found persons who, upon threat of intimate racial contact, regress to the more primitive dominative form. Other aversive racists are "impelled by a strong social conscience, consider themselves liberals and, despite their sense of aversion (which may not even be admitted inwardly) do their best within the given structure of society to ameliorate the conditions of the Negro" (Kovel, 1970, p. 55). These efforts at reform, however, involve impersonal, remote solutions, which preclude contacting blacks intimately. Regardless of the effectiveness of these remote solutions, they nevertheless serve to cool the conscience of the aversive racist; he is doing his fair share for equality. Aversion is the predominant underlying affective response to blacks of the aversive racist. Yet his social conscience, his fair-minded self-image, and his relative unawareness of this aversion produces what superficially appears to be a favorable racial attitude. Thus, the aversive racist's attitude is highly complex.

Analogously, Katz (1970) and Katz, Glass, and Cohen (1973) characterize the racial attitudes of most whites as neither all favorable nor all negative but as "ambivalent." As an example of possible ambivalence, Katz refers to the Brink and Harris (1964) survey, which indicated that 71% of white Americans acknowledged that blacks were treated unfairly in jobs, housing, and educational opportunities, yet questions about amelioration of these inequities elicited strong resistance.

Borrowing from the dynamics of Freudian theory and the empirical work of Gergen and Jones (1963), Katz reasoned that if whites are ambivalent toward blacks, then an amplification of both positive and negative responses toward blacks should be possible in such an individual. Response amplification is observed when, in an attempt to resolve a conflict fostered by ambivalence, the energy of one impulse is withdrawn and added to the opposite impulse. Thus, the reactions to blacks of most whites would be marked by an exaggerated, or amplified, positivity or negativity depending upon the specific situation. Should the behavior of a black person have favorable or unfavorable consequences for the ambivalent white observer, the black person would be evaluated as extremely good or extremely bad relative to the less extreme evaluation of a white person whose behavior had similar positive or negative consequences for the observer.

In the study by Katz, Glass, and Cohen (1973), the authors reasoned that having an ambivalent racial attitude may tend to increase one's susceptibility to feelings of guilt over actions that adversely affect the attitude target, resulting in extreme behavior whose function is the reduction of guilt. In an experimental arousal of guilt, subjects were required to administer painful electric shocks to a black learner (actually an accomplice of the experimenter) as punishment for each error. It was assumed that the harm-doer's need to reduce this moral discomfort would increase with the magnitude of guilt aroused. Since harm-doers were not provided with the subsequent opportunity to compensate their victims, the preferred mode of guilt reduction was predicted to be denigration of the victim. Denigration is generally believed to function to justify the harmful act by lowering the worth of the victim (Davis and Jones, 1960; Davidson, 1964; Glass, 1964; Friedman, 1970; Walster, Berscheid, and Walster, 1970).

The investigators hypothesized that subjects scoring high both in prejudice—as indicated by subscales of Woodmansee and Cook's inventory (1967)—and in sympathy toward blacks—using Schuman and Harding's "sympathy with the racial underdog" scale (1964)—would experience the most guilt arousal due to their ambivalence. Such subjects would thus have a greater tendency to denigrate the victim following harm-doing than subjects scoring high on prejudice and low on sympathy, low on prejudice and high on sympathy, or low on both scales. The results regarding victim denigration dramatically supported the hypothesis. Thus, according to Katz *et al.* (1973), ambivalence resulted in an amplification of responses regarding guilt arousal and guilt reduction.

Given the Katz *et al.* (1973) questionnaire method for assessing ambivalence, which requires subjects to disclose to themselves and to the experimenter that they have some less-than-favorable feelings toward blacks, speculation arises about the similarities between Kovel's aversive racist and Katz's ambivalent white. If aversive racists have a strong social conscience, consider themselves liberal, are relatively unaware of their aversion to blacks, and favor programs to ameliorate the consequences of racism, it seems unlikely that most currently available questionnaires accurately assess this form of individual racism. Potentially, however, the most effective paper-and-pencil instrument for detecting the aversive type may be the Schuman and Harding (1964) Irrational Pro Scale; although on most instruments, the aversive type may bend over backwards to convince himself and the administrator that he is indeed extremely unprejudiced. Therefore, it would be unlikely for the aversive racist to denigrate a black victim and, furthermore, to admit such feelings to an experimenter to whom moments before he expressed favorable regard for the prospective victim. The low-prejudice/low-sympathy subjects have racial attitudes that similarly reflect a type of ambivalence that perhaps is characteristic of the aversive racist, yet they do not denigrate the black victim. In terms of Campbell's analysis, it would be difficult for the possible aversive racist to respond in a bigoted fashion on these reactive, obtrusive measures. Since aversive racists do not consciously seek to act against blacks and do not harbor negative racial feelings on their shirt sleeves, measures of aversive racism should be appropriately subtle and indirect. Therefore, the assessment of questionnaire validity by means of contrasting the responses of groups suspected of having different racial attitudes (e.g., Ku Klux Klan members vs. New York State Liberal Party members) would only be partially effective because aversive racists would go undetected.

As did Myrdal's earlier conclusions regarding the "American dilemma," Kovel's concept of the aversive racist and Katz's ambivalence hypothesis characterize the attitudes of many white Americans toward blacks as laden with conflict. The aversive racist struggles with his negative feelings toward blacks and with a conscience that seeks to repudiate or disassociate such feelings from his self-image. Similarly, Katz's ambivalent person is depicted as struggling with coexisting positive and negative feelings toward blacks. In a sense, both types are ambivalent toward blacks. With some speculation, however, the distinction between aversive and ambivalent types could be sharpened.

Apparently, the ambivalent type—defined as high-prejudice/high-sympathy—is not as morally disturbed by his personal recognition of his negative feelings toward blacks as is the aversive racist. In fact, the ambivalent type's antagonism is readily admitted on questionnaire measures that are reasonably subtle, in the sense that the respondent feels free to express his antagonism without appearing stupid, irrational, or completely bigoted. Actually, the ambivalent type probably despises irrationality and therefore can readily point out evidence in support of his negative feelings. Furthermore, he probably does not view himself as bigoted and his favorable beliefs and feelings personally support his apparent objectivity. The ambivalent type would deny that "blackness" in itself is despised—"if only they would learn to live more decently."

The aversive racist's social conscience, however, precludes self-disclosure to some degree and certainly precludes public confession of anti-black feelings. Given his value system, the costs would be too great for him to think and behave in a manner obviously tinged with bigotry. In the same way that Rokeach (1960) argued that the F scale was insensitive to authoritarianism for political left-wingers, we might speculate as to whether most questionnaire measures are similarly insensitive to racism of the left-wing. When attempting to characterize the unfavorable racial or ethnic attitudes of people across the political spectrum, it may be useful to conceptualize Katz's ambivalent type as characteristic of ideological conservatives and middle-of-the-roaders, while Kovel's aversive type may characterize the attitudes of ideological liberals. That is, although many people across the political spectrum are probably nonracist, when racism exists, it will be manifested differently, in a qualitative sense, across the political spectrum.

Paper-and-pencil measures have traditionally indicated that the magnitude of unfavorable racial and ethnic attitudes increases as the respondent's political ideology varies from liberalism to conservatism (Adorno et al., 1950; McClosky, 1958). That conservatives tend to endorse anti-black questionnaire items rejected by liberals suggests perhaps that conservatives more readily recognize and reveal feelings of racial antagonism—an important distinction between ambivalent and aversive types.

The existence of the aversive and ambivalent types impose special problems on researchers interested in assessing racial attitudes. Aversive types tend not to admit racial antagonism inwardly or otherwise; therefore, traditional questionnaire assessment of their racial attitudes would usually be ineffective. Furthermore, the negative racial attitudes of the aversive type would not necessarily be revealed in nonreactive behavioral situations either. As long as there is no strong threat of intimate racial contact, the aversive types would not actively discriminate in situations in which their "wrong-doing" would be obvious to them. In these low-cost, nonintimate situations, the aversive racist might bend over backwards to demonstrate his egalitarianism, amplifying his positive behaviors toward blacks. Dutton (1973) has labeled a similar phenomenon "reverse discrimination."

Ambivalent types, although generally willing to express disaffection for blacks on questionnaire measures, may respond either favorably or unfavorably toward blacks on questionnaires and in overt behavioral situations. The nature of their response is dependent upon the available response alternatives and the immediate situational context.

Assuming for the moment that dominative, ambivalent, aversive, and nonracist accurately characterizes the range of interracial attitudes, the problem of the accurate assessment of progress toward the elimination of racism again arises. Surely, questionnaire methodologies should not be abandoned, given their potential effectiveness in detecting dominative and ambivalent types. Aversive types, however, would escape detection by most currently available questionnaire measures though their scores would probably fall among those indicating *extremely* favorable attitudes toward the target group. Although the aversive type may represent a relatively small proportion of the population now, time, legal intervention, and attitude change programs may convert dominative or ambivalent persons to express racial antagonism via the aversive form rather than converting them to the desired nonracist level. Questionnaires and some behavioral measures would then attest incorrectly to the reduction of racial tension. Therefore, it is especially important at this time to develop instruments that are sensitive to aversive racism.

The remainder of this discussion will present some empirical evidence that may be interpreted as supporting the inclusion of the *aversive type* in a taxonomy of racial attitudes. The process of reviewing the evidence supportive of the concept of aversive racism will simultaneously present some methodological suggestions for the assessment of this form of individual racism. Progress toward the elimination of individual racism could be assessed in part by the periodic administration of questionnaires and other instruments that are sensitive to the dominative and ambivalent forms, while other instruments may be necessary for the aversive type.

1. *Although the aversive racist perceives himself as prejudice-free, when possible he attempts to avoid contact with blacks or other target groups. If contact is unavoidable, however, his manner is polite, correct, but cold.*

The aversive racist's self-image has been characterized as egalitarian and unprejudiced. Nevertheless, because of his feelings of aversion, which may not be admitted inwardly, the aversive racist tries to avoid contact with blacks; when contact is unavoidable, his manner is polite, correct, but cold. Shirley Weitz (1972) obtained results from a sample of relatively unprejudiced students at Harvard University that are consistent with the above characterization of the aversive racist. In Weitz's study each subject was told that he would be working with another subject, described as a black or white garage attendant or law student, who (supposedly) was waiting in an adjoining room. Under the guise of facilitating the selection of tasks that would be compatible for each subject pair, the experimenter asked the subject to indicate his impression of his partner on a questionnaire after reading a detailed biographical sketch of this person. The item on this questionnaire, "How friendly would you feel toward this person in a year's time," constituted the primary indicator of the subject's verbal attitude toward his black or white partner. Verbal attitudes toward the black partner ranged from moderately favorable to extremely favorable.

In addition to the verbal indicator, overt behavioral measures of subjects' attitudes toward their partners prior to the interaction was obtained from subjects' performance on a series of tasks. The primary behavioral measure was the subject's voice tone recorded without his awareness while he was reading instructions over an intercom to the other participant. Judges, blind to the subject's experimental condition, rated the tape recordings of the subject's voice on the dimensions of warm-cold, admiring-condescending, etc. There was a positive relationship between the verbal measure of friendliness and the warmth of the subject's voice tone when the other participant was described as white. When the other participant was black, however, a negative relationship was obtained between these measures. Those subjects with the most favorable verbal attitudes toward their black partner had the least friendly (i.e., cold and condescending) voice tone, while those with moderately favorable verbal attitudes had the most favorable voice tone. Furthermore, when the partner was black the subject's responses on other behavioral indicators correlated negatively with the verbal measure of friendliness but correlated positively with the voice tone ratings. That is, relative to the subjects who expressed only moderately favorable attitudes toward the black partner, the subjects with the most extreme favorable attitudes (but with the coldest voice tone) selected joint tasks that required relatively *remote* forms of interaction. These subjects also claimed to have fewer hours available for retesting sessions with their partner during the coming week. The fact that the subjects with the most extreme favorable verbal attitudes towards their black partners seemed to attempt avoidance of close or further contact with him and maintained cold voice tones over the intercom is consistent with the characterization of the aversive racist.

Weitz employed a "repressed affect" model to interpret these findings.

She writes, "It appears that these subjects [those with the most extreme favorable attitudes toward their black partner] were repressing negative or conflicted affect toward blacks by overreacting in the positive direction on the verbal measure (the "doth protest too much" syndrome)" (Weitz, 1972, p. 17). Actually, it is unclear whether subjects presented a "true" assessment of their attitude toward their black partner on the questionnaire measure or whether their ratings merely reflected the reactivity—i.e., demand characteristics and evaluator apprehension prevalent during the questionnaire assessment. Nevertheless, the general pattern of the findings and the author's interpretation are compatible with the concept of aversive racism. Also, these findings suggest the fruitfulness of paralinguistic and proxemic measures for the assessment of racial attitudes.

2. *The aversive racist perceives himself as politically liberal and as the type of person who does not discriminate against blacks or other groups. In situations with normative prescriptions for appropriate behavior the aversive type tends to behave in accord with his prejudice-free self-concept. However, he may discriminate in situations that lack normative prescriptions because "wrong-doing" here would not be obvious.*

Gaertner (1973a) reported a field study that examined the likelihood of black or white persons eliciting altruistic acts from white liberals and conservatives. In this study registered members of the Liberal and Conservative Parties of New York State, residing in Brooklyn, N.Y., constituted the samples of liberals and conservatives.

Utilizing a method devised earlier by Gaertner and Bickman (1971), 231 liberals and 216 conservatives selected for Study I received an apparent wrong-number telephone call, which quickly developed into a request for their assistance. Each wrong number call was made by either a black or white, male or female caller. Pilot studies indicated that the race and sex of the caller was clearly discernible on the basis of the caller's voice and speech characteristics.

Using grammatically identical messages, the black and white callers contacted subjects between 6:30 p.m. and 9:30 p.m. When the call was answered by anyone who was judged to be over 18 years of age, the callers repeated the following dialogue:

*Caller:* Hello ... Ralph's Garage. This is George (or Mrs. Williams) ... listen I'm stuck out here on the parkway ... and I'm wondering if you'd be able to come out here and take a look at my car?

*Subject's Expected Response:* This isn't Ralph's Garage ... you have the wrong number.

*Caller:* This isn't Ralph's Garage!? Listen I'm terribly sorry to have disturbed you but listen ... I'm stuck out here on the highway ... and that was the last dime I had! I have bills in my pocket, but no more change to make another phone call.... Now I'm really stuck out here. What am I going to do now?

*Subject:* . . . . . (subject might volunteer to call the garage).

*Caller:* Listen . . . do you think you could do me the favor of calling the garage and letting them know where I am. . . ? I'll give you the number . . . they know me over there.

*Prod A:* Oh brother . . . listen I'm stuck out here . . . couldn't you PLEASE help me out by simply calling the garage for me? (Pleadingly)

*Prod B:* Listen. . . . If YOU were in my situation . . . wouldn't you want someone to help you?

If after Prod B the subject refused to help, he was relieved of any concern he may have had for the stranded motorist when the caller reported: "Oh, one second . . . here comes a police car . . . I think he will be able to give me a hand."

If the subject agreed to help, the victim gave him a telephone number to call. If the subject refused to help after Prod B, or hung up after the caller stated ". . .and that was the last dime . . ." a "No Help" response was recorded. However, if the subject hung up prior to the word "dime," a "Premature Hang-Up" response was scored and was treated separately from the Help-No Help categories. In the case of a Premature Hang-Up, it was believed that the subject did not have ample opportunity to learn that *his* help was needed.

The results, excluding consideration of premature hang-ups, indicated that conservatives discriminated against the black victim to a greater extent than liberals did. In what seemed to be the most appropriate analysis (i.e., liberals and conservatives matched for age), liberals helped the black and white victims 76% and 85% of the time, respectively (a nonsignificant difference). Conservatives, however, helped the black victims only 65% of the time, while white victims were assisted 92% of the time ($p < .001$).

In spite of the nature of the victim's dilemma, the data failed to support a prediction that female victims would elicit more help than male victims. Furthermore, the race of the victim effect was almost equivalent for male and female victims. However, male subjects generally helped more frequently than females.

Thus, the present study found that in a situation in which help was solicited, conservatives discriminated against blacks to a greater extent than liberals did, supporting the traditional findings regarding political ideology and anti-black attitudes. However, the data supported these traditional findings only when subjects obtained sufficient information to recognize that their personal assistance was required. Actually, a number of subjects hung up prematurely, prior to the delivery of the full appeal for help. As compared to conservatives, liberals hung up prematurely more frequently on the black than on the white victims. The liberals discriminated against the black male in particular; the black and white male victims received premature hang-ups from liberals 27.5% and 9.5% of the time, respectively. Conservatives, however, hung up prematurely only 8.3% and 4.7% of the time on the black and white male victims, respectively. Thus, the usual claim that liberals harbor less anti-black sentiment than conservatives was not wholly supported since liberals, rather than conservatives, hung up prematurely more frequently on black than on white callers.

Consistent with the concept of aversive racism, Gaertner (1973a) suggested that the anti-black attitudes of liberals differ qualitatively rather than quantitatively from the racial attitudes of conservatives. It was suggested that conservatives may have a different sense of justice, a different sense of sympathy, a different sense of social responsibility toward "others" of their own kind than liberals. The liberal's value system, however, may require him to help another person regardless of his personal feelings toward the victim. The American Civil Liberties Union, for example, defended the legal rights of George Lincoln Rockwell and George Wallace. Apparently, the liberal tends to ignore the personal characteristics of those requiring assistance and is guided more strictly by the general principle involved. That is, for the liberal, "freedom of speech" means freedom of speech for all. Liberals thus apply such principles in a more egalitarian manner than conservatives. Therefore, in the telephone situation, when it was recognized that help was needed, a normative prescription—i.e., the social responsibility norm—that one ought to help others in need of assistance prevailed. In this situation, liberals did not discriminate against the black victim.

The anti-black attitudes of liberals, which are here hypothesized to resemble those of the aversive racist, may be revealed more readily in nonreactive situations in which there are few, if any, clearly definable principles or norms to guide behavior. In these situations the liberal need not be concerned with the egalitarian application of a general principle. In these types of situations "wrong-doing" would not be obvious since concepts of "right and wrong" are not applicable. Therefore, liberals in such situations may behave according to their deep-seated inclinations.

The question of the morality of hanging up on a person reaching the wrong number after informing him of his error has no prescribed answer. Thus, liberals who hung up prematurely on the black victim did not behave inappropriately in the sense that they violated normative prescriptions. Consistent with the style of the aversive racist, liberals avoided further contact with blacks when further contact was not prescribed. White callers, however, did not elicit a desire to terminate the encounter so readily. Why, however, did conservatives hang up prematurely less frequently than liberals and why did they fail to discriminate against the black motorist in this regard? Since the liberal may apply normative directions universally (i.e., when such directions are clearly salient), he may be compelled, to a greater degree than the conservative, to erect devices that function to reduce the impact of situational demands for involvement lest the satisfaction of his own needs be frustrated.

Compared to the conservative, who may apply normative prescriptions based on the personal characteristics of the other person(s), the liberal may require stronger demand stimuli (e.g., more serious emergencies) before normative directives become salient. This may account for the fact that white victims fared somewhat better with conservatives than with liberals. Also, as an adaptive strategy, the liberal may seek early disengagement from and he may be especially sensitive to situations which *may later* demand his personal involvement. Disengagement from these situations prior to learning for sure that his personal involvement is necessary, protects the liberal from clearly recognizing that he has violated normative prescriptions. That low-authoritarians have been shown to have a higher tolerance for ambiguity than high-authoritarians (Harvey and Rutherford, 1958; Steiner and Johnson, 1963) supports the hypothesis that the liberal can more readily disengage himself from a situation at a time when the exact nature of that situation is still ambiguous. The conservative, on the other hand, may refrain from hanging up prematurely and discriminating against blacks in this regard because he is compelled to gain more information about the situation and thereby reduce its ambiguity.

One limitation in this analysis of premature hang up responses concerns the possibility that those liberals hanging up prematurely actually might not have helped, even if they had fully comprehended the nature of the stranded motorist's dilemma. That is, maintaining a Premature Hang-Up category may have eliminated the unhelpful, bigoted liberals.

Clearly, it would be desirable to randomly assign subjects suspected of being aversive racists to situations of varying normative structure. As long as there was no great threat of intimate racial contact, discrimination against blacks should occur only in those situations with relatively low normative structure. For example, blacks and whites might be sent to local meetings of liberal organizations to seek directions to: (a) nearby places that actually exist; and (b) places that in reality don't exist (e.g., the Monroe Memorial). In the first situation, it would be expected that the race of the solicitor would not affect the respondent's behavior because it would be "wrong" to mis-inform a stranger. However, when a stranger requests directions to a place that is unfamiliar to the aversive racist, the normative structure of the situation collapses once the bystander has confessed his unfamiliarity with the specified location. Once this confession is delivered, the bystander is free to terminate the encounter without violating normative prescriptions. Although it is not prescribed, this bystander may choose, instead, to help the stranger indirectly by providing him with suggestions as to where he may obtain the information desired. The bystander could, for example, intercept another passerby and solicit information in behalf of the stranger or suggest that he consult the local druggist. In this situation aversive racists would be expected to be less helpful to black than to white strangers in the sense that they would (a) terminate the encounter more readily and (b) offer fewer suggestions for obtaining the desired information.

The premature hang-up response was also revealing in a subsequent study that sought to gauge the magnitude of anti-Semitism within the black and white Gentile communities of New York City (Gaertner, 1973b). Based upon the actions and statements of some members of the black community, many have come to believe that anti-Semitism among blacks is something more than a more reflection of anti-white feelings held by a minority of the black population. Incidents with anti-Semitic overtones in New York City regarding a 1968 confrontation between members of the black community and the predominantly-Jewish United Federation of Teachers brought the situation into focus nationally. In 1969 Rabbi Jay Kaufman, Executive Vice President of B'nai B'rith stated, in reference to anti-Semitism among blacks, "I am one of those who believe it has become significantly widespread and that considerable forces contributing to its extension face feeble deterrence" (Kaufman, 1969, p. 43).

In phase I of this study, black and white female interviewers telephoned black and white households, respectively, to elicit information pertinent to the household's socioeconomic status in the context of a survey about women's role in society. Eight months later, during phase II, white male callers contacted 205 white households and 225 black households called during phase I, including those who would not cooperate during phase I. The callers identified themselves as either, "Tom Scott on the way home from the mens' club" (non-Jewish victim) or "Israel Goldstein on the way home from the Jewish Center" (Jewish victim). Once again subjects were asked to call the garage in behalf of the stranded motorist.

Among the black sample, the Jewish and non-Jewish victims were helped 68% and 70% of the time, respectively. Incidentally, these findings are identical to those found three and one-half years earlier when black subjects were contacted by white victims (Gaertner and Bickman, 1971). Although anti-Semitism was not generally apparent within the black sample, an analysis of this sample in terms of their willingness to be interviewed during phase I reveals some possible anti-Semitism among blacks. Among the 40% of the black sample who refused to be interviewed, 74.6% helped the non-Jewish victim while only 53.9% helped the Jewish victim.

In the white sample, the Jewish and non-Jewish victims were helped 74% and 73.5% of the time, respectively. However, within this white sample there was an interaction between the subject's level of education and the help offered Jewish and non-Jewish motorists. Those white subjects with formal education beyond high school (33% of the interviewed white sample also contacted in phase II fell into this category) discriminated against the Jewish victim to a greater extent than those whose formal education terminated with high school ($p < .02$). Although these findings regarding education and discrimination contradict those usually obtained, they are consistent with the findings of Stember (1961) and are partially consistent with Williams' finding

(1964) that middle- and upper-class whites are more anti-Semitic than lower-class whites but that lower-class whites are more anti-black than middle- and upper-class whites. In the present study similar but insignificant trends were obtained with respect to the occupational categories "blue collar" and "white collar."

In terms of premature hang-up responses, black subjects did not discriminate against the Jewish victim, while white subjects did. Black subjects hung up prematurely on the Jewish and non-Jewish motorists 8.3% and 5.8% of the time, respectively. White subjects, on the other hand, hung up prematurely 15.5% of the time on the Jewish victim but only 3.9% of the time on the non-Jewish victim ($p < .01$). Thus, it may be that anti-Semitic attitudes among the black and white populations in New York City differ qualitatively, with ambivalent and aversive forms present in white groups, but only dominative and ambivalent forms in black groups. If the magnitude of anti-Semitism among blacks and whites were roughly equivalent, questionnaire measures would thus be expected to indicate greater anti-Semitism among blacks than among whites. The results of the phase I interview support this contention. In phase I, the subjects were asked to respond to the following item: "Some people do have negative feelings toward the Jews. Do you think that this is at all deserved? For example, do you think that Jewish landlords or storekeepers are better, worse, or no different than other white landlords or storekeepers?" In response to this item 12.2% (18 out of 148) of the blacks and 7.6% (10 out of 132) of the whites claimed that Jews were worse. Incidentally, responses to this item were not predictive of helping behavior in phase II.

3. *The aversive racist may be inclined to misinterpret situations in a manner that precludes the necessity for interacting with blacks or other target groups. This misperception then enables the aversive type to avoid contact with members of these groups while permitting him to believe that he did not act inappropriately.*

In a second phase of the liberal-conservative wrong number study (Gaertner, 1973a) additional samples of Liberal and Conservative Party members were engaged in a telephoned interview. Subjects were asked whether they believed they would call the garage if they received an *actual* wrong number call from each of the four motorist victims—a black male, a black female, a white male, and a white female. Liberals and Conservatives claimed that they would help the victims 97% of the time without regard for race. Furthermore, no differences were found between Liberals and Conservatives regarding their indicated degree of personal helpfulness.

In his discussion of the findings Gaertner (1973a) suspected that most subjects truly believed that they would, if called upon, help each of the victims without regard for his race. Although an "evaluator apprehension" explanation is tempting, it seems unlikely that even Conservatives, hypothesized here to have ambivalent racial attitudes, perceive themselves as anti-black to the extent that they would deny assistance to a black person when the cost for helping was so trivial.

Why, then, did Conservative Party members discriminate in the actual wrong number situation and why was the overall level of helping considerably lower than would be expected on the basis of all the subject's personal claims? Respondents in the interview situation may have been incapable of anticipating the fear, disgust, or annoyance possibly aroused during the actual wrong number call. For the same reasons that subjects were *more* helpful when they were "feeling good" (Isen and Levin, 1972), subjects in the wrong number situation may have been *less* helpful in the presence of "unpleasant" emotional arousal.

An alternative explanation, however, is that in the interview study the wrong number situation was defined for the subjects as one in which their assistance was really needed. In the actual wrong number situation, subjects were responsible for defining the situation themselves; they may therefore have been more likely to interpret the situation as a prank or to reach some other interpretation suggesting that their help was unnecessary. The by-stander's attitude toward the victim, then, may have affected the degree to which the bystander perceived that help was needed, particularly for aversive types. That is, the victim's race may not directly affect the bystander's willingness to help, but his interpretation of whether or not help is needed. For the aversive type, this strategy would facilitate the avoidance of contact with blacks while at the same time permitting him to believe that he did not act inappropriately with respect to a black person—a most important consideration for the aversive racist. Based on the misperception explanation, it would be predicted that attitudes toward the victim would play increasingly important roles in mediating bystander intervention as factors in the situation more easily permit "no help needed" interpretations. Previous research to be discussed below, seems to offer some initial support for this hypothesis. Although other explanations for these findings may have merit, the "no help needed" hypothesis fits the data as well.

Piliavin, Rodin, and Piliavin (1969) reported that, in a New York City subway, white and black victims carrying a cane and falling, apparently unconscious, were assisted as frequently by bystanders of the same race as by those of a different race. When the victims were portrayed as drunk, however, a trend for same-race helping was uncovered. Perhaps bystanders confronting the drunk victim had greater freedom to conclude either that help was not needed or that help was unwarranted. In the Drunk condition, the cause of the victim's unconsciousness was obvious (i.e., he smelled of alcohol and carried a bottle wrapped in a brown paper bag); furthermore, he could be expected to regain sobriety with the passage of time. With the cane victim, however, unconsciousness may have been believed to be more serious (e.g., a heart attack) and the bystander's freedom to conclude that help was unnecessary greatly restricted thereby. Bystanders may also have perceived the drunk victim as more personally responsible for his dilemma than the cane victim, and thus may have found it easier to believe that help was unwarranted for the drunk victim.

Wispe' and Freshley (1971) engaged black and white passersby in a helping-behavior situation in which a black or white woman, leaving a supermarket, dropped her packages in the path of the oncoming pedestrians. The responses of the passersby were categorized as: (a) "ignores," in which the subject ignored the victim and walked by; (b) "reacted but without help," in which the subject hesitated and showed surprise but failed to help; (c) "perfunctory help," in which the subject helped the victim with a few of her groceries, and then hurried on; and (d) "positive help," in which the subject helped the victim with all of her groceries, offered to get a new grocery bag, etc.

With regard to interracial helping, Wispe' and Freshley report that there was a suggestion of a racial interaction between helpers and victims, but for white female helpers only. The results were complicated: white females helped the white victim more often than they helped the black victim (category d), but they also ignored the white victim more often (category a).

A reanalysis of the Wispe' and Freshley data that forms a single "no help" category by combining category a ("ignores") with category b ("reacts without help"), but that maintains the integrity of the "perfunctory help" and "positive help" categories produces interesting results in terms of the "no help needed" hypothesis. A race of victim effect is revealed for both male and female white subjects that is marginally significant statistically. The results of this analysis indicate that white passersby did not discriminate between black and white victims in terms of "no help" responses. However, of those white subjects providing at least some assistance, 63% gave "positive help" (complete help) to the white victim while only 30% offered this degree of assistance to the black victims. On the other hand, 70% of the white bystanders offered "perfunctory help" to the black victim while only 30% offered this small amount of assistance to the white victim. Evidently, white subjects dealing with white victims are more apt to provide complete help than perfunctory help. When dealing with black victims, however, they are more likely to provide perfunctory help than complete help. Although the magnitude of this effect was only marginally significant ($p < .10$), these results are consistent with the hypothesis that, in ambiguous emergency situations, ambivalent or aversive attitudes toward the victim may predispose the bystander to more readily accept "no help needed" or "less help needed" interpretations of the situation.

Based on the *post hoc* analysis of the previous findings, the "no help needed" hypothesis seems tenable. A predictive test of this hypothesis was undertaken by Gaertner (in press). The paradigm, developed by Latane and Darley (1969), permitting subjects to witness an emergency either alone or together with others was combined with a manipulation of the victim's race. An initial test of the manner in which racial attitudes affect overt helping behavior for subjects scoring at the extremes of a prejudice scale that correlates +.83 with three subscales from Woodmansee and Cook's inventory (1967) was thus arranged.

In the Alone condition, the only input for the subject is the reality of the emergency (pilot testing of the emergency has affirmed its compellingness). The lack of additional input regarding the nature of the emergency creates a situation in which it is relatively difficult to misinterpret its severity. The face-to-face Together condition, however, provides two possibly conflicting inputs: the compellingness of the emergency and the suggestion that help is unnecessary, provided by the passivity and calmness of other (confederate) bystanders. There is, thus, a greater probability that in the Together condition subjects will reach a "no help needed" conclusion. Obviously, the passivity of others may suggest other interpretations to the bystander (e.g., others recognize that help is needed but are unmotivated to help). These other possibilities were investigated in the postexperimental interview phase of this initial study and will be further studied in subsequent research.

If attitudes directly mediate behavior in that the bystander recognizes that help is needed yet intentionally withholds his assistance because of the victim's race, then black victims should be helped less frequently than white victims in the Alone condition and possibly in the Together condition. However, if attitudes toward the victim indirectly mediate behavior by differentially affecting the bystander's definition of the situation, then: (a) black victims should be helped as frequently as white victims in the Alone condition, where it is difficult to misinterpret the severity of the emergency, and (b) black victims should be helped less frequently than white victims in the Together condition, where it is relatively easier to reach a "no help needed" definition.

Subjects were engaged in what was described as an Extra-Sensory Perception study with either one additional person (Alone condition) or four additional persons (Together condition). All other participants were actually confederates of the experimenter, posing as naive subjects. In both conditions the victim was either a black or white female and all other confederates and the subjects were females.

The experimenter explained to the participants that, in the course of the ESP task, all subjects would have the opportunity to receive ESP messages in the "receiving room" down the corridor. All participants remaining in the "sending room" would simultaneously attempt to transmit 15 messages telepathically to the receiver. Afterwards, the receiver would report his judgment as to which one of five symbols was sent on that particular trial via a one-way intercom system. The subject was always the first receiver.

The receiving room was somewhat in disarray. In one corner was a stack of heavy chairs piled almost to the ceiling. Other chairs were overturned on table tops. In the middle of the room a vacuum cleaner was clearly evident. Upon entering the receiving room, the experimenter exclaimed as though surprised, "I wish the janitorial staff would do this at a more convenient time." Following the subject's 15 trials as a receiver, she returned to the sending room, whereupon the second participant (the future victim) left for the receiving area. At this point, the experimenter, who was believed to be waiting in the hall, outside of the sending room, substituted a prerecorded audio tape for the victim's guesses. After 7 ESP trials, the receiver interrupted the procedure by claiming that the stack of chairs in the corner looked as though it was about to fall, and that she had better adjust them. After about five seconds, the receiver screamed, "They're falling on me . . . (Scream . . Scream . .)." A loud crash sounded, followed by a thud and then silence.

Absolutely no differences between high- and low-prejudiced subjects were observed on either the helping measures or on postexperimental questionnaire items dealing with the perceived seriousness of the emergency. Therefore, the further analyses combined the data of the high- and low-prejudice groups.

In the Alone condition 100% of the subjects helped both the black and the white victims. However, in the Together condition, the white victim was helped 90% of the time, while the black victim was helped only 30% of the time.

In the postexperimental interview subjects were asked to indicate on a seven-point scale how seriously they had believed the receiver to be injured. These results, however, did not support the prediction that subjects would perceive that the black victim was hurt less seriously than the white victim.

Subjects in the Together condition, asked to indicate their impression of the extent to which the other bystanders thought the receiver was injured, judged that the other bystanders thought that the black victim was injured less seriously than the white victim. Perhaps, if subjects were more inclined to accept a "no help needed" interpretation of the situation for black than for white victims, they were also more likely to interpret the passivity of others in a manner that supported their own inclination.

In general, the results tend to support the viability of the hypothesis that attitudes towards the victim can mediate helping behavior by differentially affecting the bystander's definition of the situation. Alternative explanations, however, must be considered. That black victims were helped as frequently as white victims in the Alone condition, but less frequently in the Together condition, suggests that whites may be more inclined to diffuse responsibility for black victims than for white victims. It should be noted that diffusion of responsibility can occur only when the bystander has defined the situation as one in which help is needed and when he believes that other bystanders similarly recognize the necessity for help. He must also perceive that others are willing and able to intervene.

A second alternative explanation for the Alone-Together racial interaction effect involves the idea of social pressure. In the presence of passive bystanders, a person may be more influenced to conform to the norm of nonintervention for black victims than for white victims. This conformity explanation suggests that the bystander recognizes that help is needed but feels restrained from helping by his concern for being viewed as a deviant. Although the postexperimental inquiry regarding the perceived seriousness of the emergency may be interpreted several ways, it seems to speak more favorably of the "no help needed" hypothesis. Additional research is planned to directly test the alternative explanations.

4. *The aversive racist's positive actions toward blacks are not based on a truly dedicated effort to implement egalitarian values but rather to reaffirm a prejudice-free self-concept. This then, could lead to "tokenism."*

Earlier, aversive racists were described as having a strong social conscience and an image of themselves as being liberal, unprejudiced, and favorably disposed towards programs designed to ameliorate the inequities of a racist society. However, their personal commitment to improving the quality of life among blacks and other minorities rarely exceeds impersonal, remote, low-cost action. These efforts at reform, however, may serve primarily to reaffirm their liberal, unprejudiced self-image. If this reaffirmation is gained so easily through trivial action, more extensive forms of commitment may be precluded. Donald Dutton's research, particularly a study by Dutton and Lennox (1974), deals directly with this issue. The reader is cautioned, however, against generalizing too readily from Dutton's findings with a Canadian sample to the behavior of whites in the United States or elsewhere, since Canada: (a) has a relatively low density black population, and (b) is relatively free of black-white tensions. Nevertheless, Canadians residing in Vancouver agree that blacks and Indians are discriminated against to a considerable degree in the Vancouver area as well as in North America in general, while whites and Orientals are not perceived to be targets of prejudice (Dutton, 1973).

Dutton's research on this issue began with a field experiment (1971) to examine the effects of the race of a male customer on the tendency of restaurateurs in Vancouver and Toronto to enforce restaurant dress regulations. The primary findings indicated that, when blacks without tie entered the restaurant, they were admitted 75% of the time while whites were admitted only 30% of the time. While the race of the customer was shown to affect the administration of restaurant policy, the apparently flexible policy favored blacks. When blacks were preceded by a white dress-violator 45 minutes earlier, however, their admittance rate dropped to 40%.

Dutton explained the restaurateurs' "reverse discrimination" as an attempt to avoid the accusation that they were refusing service on the basis of race rather than dress. "Rather than run the risk of being labeled as racist (perhaps in front of other customers) the restaurateur relents and provides service for the dress regulation violator who is black" (Dutton, 1971, p. 301). Support for this interpretation was offered by the finding that, in the condition in which blacks were preceded by whites, their chances of being admitted dropped from 75% to 40%. That is, having established himself as the enforcer of dress regulations for white customers, the restaurateur could now enforce these regulations for black customers without fear that this act would be misinterpreted by other patrons (or by the restaurateur himself).

A second study (Dutton, 1973) tested and confirmed the "reverse discrimination" hypothesis in a different context. Contrary to the findings of Bryan and Test (1967), Dutton reported that in Vancouver black and Indian solicitors for an established charitable organization received greater donations, in terms of percentage of persons donating and average amounts donated, than did white and Oriental solicitors. That these results were obtained in both public and private settings suggests that subjects may not have been concerned singularly with the attributions by others but may have been operating to avoid cues from their own behavior that suggested to themselves that they might be prejudiced. Because alternative explanations can account for the "reverse discrimination" phenomenon (e.g., blacks and Indians may have been perceived as more threatening solicitors than whites and Orientals and thus were treated more generously to get rid of them), Dutton later shifted his research to a laboratory paradigm to gain greater control over extraneous factors.

According to Dutton (1973), "reverse discrimination" is an attempt by would-be egalitarians to reaffirm their unprejudiced self-image. Therefore, "reverse discrimination" would occur more readily when a person's egalitarian self-concept has been threatened. In a laboratory setting Dutton and Lake (1973) attempted to manipulate the degree of threat to a would-be-egalitarian's unprejudiced self-concept prior to a staged interaction with a black or white panhandler in a different setting.

Subjects in this study (University of British Columbia undergraduate male and females) were selected on the basis of earlier pretesting, which revealed that they were "would-be egalitarians." Specifically, during pretesting these subjects: (a) ranked equality as an important terminal value (Rokeach, 1960); (b) rated themselves as very low on prejudice; and (c) rated themselves as less prejudiced than the average Canadian college student.

In the laboratory setting, these subjects were led to believe that they were participating in a study of "voluntary control of autonomic behavior" during which the threat to their unprejudiced self-image was effected by providing them with false physiological feedback (heart rate and GSR) regarding their deep-seated emotional reactions to pictures of interracial interactions. To further impress the subjects with the authenticity of the physiological feedback equipment and of their emotional reactivity to the pictorial stimuli, they initially viewed a number of pictures that were highly arousing but were not of an interracial nature. During the presentation of these truly highly arousing scenes (e.g., homicide victims, scenes of sexual intercourse, and scenes of riot police beating students), the experimenter provided the subject with appropriate high arousal feedback. In addition to these high-arousal scenes, subjects also viewed emotionally neutral pictures (e.g., bottles, books, etc.) during which the false feedback indicated that the subject was suitably unaroused.

During the presentation of the critical interracial scenes, subjects in the High-Threat condition were given high arousal feedback while Low-Threat subjects were given feedback indicating that they were unaroused. Subjects had been told that many psychologists feel that autonomic responses are the truest measure of the underlying reactions that we have to social groups and situations, and that high arousal indicates negative attitudes toward the groups or situations depicted. In light of this explanation, it was believed that the unprejudiced self-image of the High-Threat subjects would be effectively threatened. Postexperimental inquiries following the panhandling incident supported this assumption.

After collecting a $2.00 payment (in quarters) for participating in the study, the subjects left the building to return to the main part of the campus. On the path leading back to the main campus, each subject was greated by a black or white panhandler who said, "Can you spare some change for some food?" Based on Dutton's earlier findings, it was predicted that subjects whose unprejudiced self-image had been highly threatened would contribute more generously to the black panhandler than subjects receiving the low-threat manipulation. Because the threat manipulation was not expected to affect general altruism, it was predicted that the threat manipulation would not affect the contributions to white panhandlers.

Clearly supporting the investigators' predictions, the results indicated that the average contribution to the black panhandler was almost 48 cents from the High-Threat group while he received an average of only 17 cents from the subjects whose unprejudiced self-image had *not* been threatened. The white panhandler received average contributions of 29 cents and 28 cents from the High- and Low-Threat groups, respectively.

Somewhat surprising, however, is the absence of a "reversed discrimination" effect among the Low-Threat subjects. In fact, contrary to Dutton's previous findings (1971, 1973), the Low-Threat subjects contributed an average of 28 cents to the white panhandler but only contributed an average of 17 cents to the black panhandler. Perhaps the Low-Threat manipulation was extremely successful in convincing these subjects that they were indeed unprejudiced. Upon the subsequent solicitation by the black panhandler, these subjects felt no overwhelming need to prove to themselves, through their generosity, that they were unprejudiced. Instead, these subjects now could donate freely an amount that seemed truly appropriate. In a sense, they could behave as freely and spontaneously toward blacks as did the restaurateurs who tended to refuse admittance to black dress-violators after they had refused admittance to white dress-violators 45 minutes earlier. In fact, there was a trend among these Low-Threat subjects to donate less generously to the black than to the white panhandler. Perhaps they were merely testing their reaffirmed self-image by purposely being especially frugal with the black panhandler.

Up to this point in the discussion, Dutton's research has indicated that threatening the would-be egalitarian's unprejudiced self-image results in dramatically favorable behavior toward blacks—"reverse discrimination." Apparently, the amplification of such trivial positive responses as contributing generously to a black panhandler may have been an effort by the would-be egalitarian to reaffirm his prejudice-free self-image. That is, the major factor motivating the would-be egalitarian's behavior toward blacks may not have been a truly dedicated effort to implement the values he espouses, but an effort, directed inwardly, to reaffirm his self-image.

If, indeed, the intent underlying the would-be egalitarian's behavior toward blacks is inwardly directed, it might be expected that favorable behavior towards blacks in trivial situations would serve to preclude more extensive forms of commitment to their espoused values. After reaffirming his egalitarian self-concept in situations that require no long-term, high-cost commitment or in which there is no reduction in the socioemotional distance between himself and blacks, the would-be egalitarian is liberated to the extent that he can passively accept sociopolitical policy (i.e., institutional racism), which severely restricts the quality of life among blacks and other minorities. Paradoxically, he views himself as part of the solution rather than as part of the problem.

Dutton and Lennox (1974) addressed this issue of "tokenism" among would-be egalitarians empirically. The initial procedures of this study were basically identical to the earlier Dutton and Lake study (1973) but only the high threat induction via false physiological feedback was used. Immediately following the threat manipulation, these subjects were either approached by a black or white male panhandler or not solicited at all on the path leading back to the main campus. A fourth group of subjects, which served as a control, did not participate in the initial phases of the study.

Two days later, all students in the classes that constituted the subject pool were informed by their instructor that on behalf of a "Brotherhood Society" on campus, he was going to distribute forms requesting students to donate time to a "Brotherhood Week" campaign. These commitment forms listed eight possible activities for which the student could volunteer. Previously, 50 other college students rated each of these activities on the degree of effort required. The extent to which the subjects in each condition committed themselves to the activities relating to "Brotherhood Week" served as the critical measure in this study.

Replicating the earlier findings, the results indicated that subjects whose unprejudiced self-concept was threatened by the false feedback procedure contributed more frequently and more generously to the black than to the white panhandler. In terms of the extent to which these would-be egalitarians subsequently committed themselves to the "Brotherhood Week" activities, however, the results supported the "tokenism" hypothesis. The group that was neither threatened nor solicited committed itself less to the "Brotherhood Week" activities than any of the groups that received the threat induction. This finding may indicate that the base rate among would-be egalitarians for self-commitment to such activities is not especially high unless their self-image is threatened; this interpretation is highly tenuous in the absence of information about the commitments made by subjects who did not consider themselves to be egalitarians. Among the threatened groups, those subjects approached by a black, and thereby provided with the opportunity to reaffirm their unprejudiced self-image, committed themselves less to "Brotherhood Week" activities than those approached by a white. Finally, as expected, no difference was found among the threatened groups between those subjects approached by a white panhandler and those subjects who were not solicited at all.

Apparently, the opportunity for would-be egalitarians to act favorably toward blacks in a trivial situation does preclude a more extensive commitment to act in a manner consonant with their espoused values. This finding may be interpreted as consistent with the aversive racist hypothesis.

5. *The aversive racist's attitude toward blacks or other groups is ambivalent; however, he attempts to dissociate his negative beliefs and feelings from his self-concept. These negative components, however, may be revealed in situations in which responding is immediate and impulsive rather than carefully deliberated.*

Since conflict is hypothesized to characterize the attitudes of both the ambivalent and aversive types, their behavior in situations that require spontaneous responding may reveal this conflict in identical fashions. For example, Gaertner and McLaughlin (1974) obtained identical patterns of response in a word recognition task among high- and low-prejudice subjects, which may exemplify the conflict underlying both types.

Intrigued by a procedure used previously by Meyer and Schvaneveldt (1971), Gaertner and McLaughlin adapted the stimuli to the area of intergroup relations. The procedure engaged subjects in a reaction time experiment during which they were to judge whether or not two strings of letters presented simultaneously, one above the other, were both words. If both strings of letters were words (e.g., blacks: lazy), the subject was instructed to press the "yes" button; if both strings of letters were not words (e.g., blacks: kupod), he was to press the "no" button. In order to motivate the subjects to respond as quickly and as accurately as possible, the amount of money won in this study was dependent on both their speed and accuracy.

The research of Meyer and Schvaneveldt (1971) has demonstrated that when the two strings of letters are both words and are highly associated with one another (e.g., bread: butter), the time taken by subjects to press the "yes" button is reliably faster than if both strings of letters are words but relatively unassociated with one another (e.g., doctor: butter). The Gaertner and McLaughlin (1974) study selected extremely high and low scorers on a prejudice-toward-blacks inventory that correlated highly with Woodmansee and Cook's (1967). The study was designed to examine the degree of association between word pairs relevant to the traits stereotypically ascribed to blacks.

Among the critical word pairs used in this study were, for example— blacks: stupid; blacks: lazy; whites: stupid; whites: lazy; blacks: clean; blacks: smart; whites: clean; whites: smart; etc. Each pair was presented twice so as to vary the order of presentation within each word pair. An equal number of trials requiring a "no" response was also included to provide the structure necessary for the task. The words "blacks," "whites," and others, therefore, were paired frequently with nonsense syllables. Note that subjects were never asked to endorse or reject the appropriateness of the specific word pair but only to indicate whether or not both strings of letters were words. In a sense, the procedure is nonreactive and void of demand characteristics in that subjects cannot purposely delay their responses by 200 msec.

The results, presented in Fig. 1, indicated that no meaningful differences emerged between the high- and low-prejudiced subjects. Their patterns of response were identical and suggestive of attitudinal conflict. Both high- and low-prejudiced subjects responded as quickly to blacks: negative word pairs (e.g., blacks: lazy) as they did to whites: negative word pairs. However, they responded significantly slower to blacks: positive word pairs (e.g., blacks: clean) than they did to the whites: positive word pairs.

That subjects responded as quickly to the blacks: negative as to whites: negative word pairs decreases the tenability of a simple familiarity interpretation. Surely these subjects were more familiar with the ascription of the traits

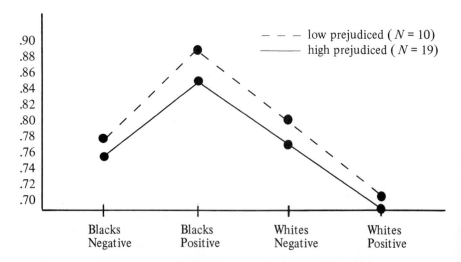

**Fig. 1.**    Average median latencies for critical word-pair groups.

"lazy" and "stupid" to blacks than to whites. To clarify this issue, Gaertner and McLaughlin (1974) replicated the procedure of this study substituting the word "Negroes" for "blacks." The possibility that the negative traits may have been more strongly associated with the word "Negroes" than with "blacks" during the subjects' formative years was thus tested. Nevertheless, the results of this replication were identical to those of the first study.

The findings suggest that the attitudes toward blacks among college students are subtly laden with conflict. Perhaps these students do not ascribe negative characteristics differentially to blacks and to whites, but do ascribe positive traits differentially. That is, these high- and low-prejudiced subjects (hypothesized here to resemble the ambivalent and aversive types, respectively) may not believe that blacks are more lazy or more stupid than whites; rather, they may believe that blacks just aren't as smart or as ambitious as whites. The tone of this pattern of trait attribution, therefore, seems extremely subtle and perhaps diagnostic of underlying conflict.

The tone of this pattern of trait attribution (if indeed the word-pair recognition procedure truly reflects trait attribution) seems consistent with the style of the aversive racist in that negative beliefs about the target group are not immediately apparent given that only positive traits are differentially ascribed. The more traditional procedures in stereotyping research that utilize adjective check lists, however, might simply characterize the aversive racist's beliefs about blacks as not very negative but indeed as rather positive, given his inclination to refrain from responding in a manner obviously tinged with bigotry. The obtained pattern of trait attribution is similarly consistent with the style of the ambivalent type because this pattern reflects conflict within the belief component of the attitude—i.e., blacks aren't more stupid than whites, they just aren't as smart as whites. The fact that there were no differences between the high- and low-prejudice scoring subjects (hypothesized here to represent the ambivalent and aversive types, respectively) is not too disturbing because conceptually the major difference between these two types, perhaps, is the degree to which they are morally disturbed by their personal recognition of their negative beliefs and feelings toward the target group(s).

## CONCLUSION

Taken together, the studies discussed above seem to support the inclusion of the aversive type in a taxonomy of racial and ethnic attitudes. The aversive racist has been depicted as struggling with his negative feelings toward blacks or other target groups and his conscience, which attempts to repudiate or disassociate such feelings from his self-image. The aversive racist generally regards himself as unprejudiced, liberal, and in favor of programs to solve the problems of blacks fostered by institutional racism. Actual encounters with blacks or with questionnaire administrators, however, represent a challenge to this prejudice-free self-concept. To reaffirm this self-image, the aversive racist responds favorably toward blacks until the costs for maintaining the egalitarian image become prohibitive. Favorable responses toward blacks or other groups, however, are not based on a truly dedicated effort to implement his egalitarian values but rather on an effort, directed inwardly, to reaffirm his self-image. Usually, this reaffirmation can be effected with trivial gestures (i.e., tokenism), which serve to preclude the necessity for more extensive, costly action.

Neither questionnaires nor nonreactive field experiments necessarily would reveal the aversive racist's true attitudes. As long as the interaction situation contains norms or directives for "appropriate" behavior and this "appropriate" response requires relatively low personal costs, the aversive racist would not intentionally act unfavorably toward blacks or other minorities. In fact, in some of these low-cost situations he may actually respond more favorably toward blacks than to whites. In situations with relatively low normative structure, however, "wrong-doing" would not be obvious and the aversive racist may then discriminate against the target group(s). Furthermore, the aversive racist may be predisposed to interpret situations in a fashion that precludes the necessity for intimate contact with the targe group(s). When contact is unavoidable, however, his manner is polite, correct, but cold.

Admittedly, the support offered for the concept of aversive racism often relied on *post hoc* analyses, findings that were of marginal statistical significance, or studies that may be open to alternative explanations. Therefore, this description of aversive racism should be viewed as tentative. Hopefully, however, this analysis will generate additional thinking and research that would explore more directly the usefulness of the concept of aversiveness for describing intergroup attitudes.

## REFERENCES

Adorno, T.W., Frenkel-Brunswik, E., Levinson, D., and Sanford, R.N. *The authoritarian personality.* New York: Harper, 1950.

Bickman, L., and Henchy, T. *Beyond the laboratory: Field research in social psychology.* New York: McGraw-Hill, 1972.

Brink, W., and Harris, L. *The Negro Revolution in America.* New York: Simon & Schuster, 1964.

Bryan, J.H., and Test, M.A. Models and helping: Naturalistic studies in aiding behavior. *Journal of Personality and Social Psychology,* 1967, **6**, 400-407.

Campbell, D.T. Factors relevant to the validity of experiments in social settings. *Psychological Bulletin,* 1957, **54**, 297-312.

Campbell, D.T. Social attitudes and other acquired behavioral dispositions. In S. Koch (Ed.), *Psychology: A study of a science.* New York: McGraw-Hill, 1963.

Cook, S.W., and Selltiz, C. A multiple-indicator approach to attitude measurement. *Psychological Bulletin,* 1964, **62**, 36-55.

Darley, J.M., and Latane, B. Bystander intervention in emergencies: Diffusion of responsibility. *Journal os Personality and Social Psychology,* 1968, **8**, 377-383.

Davidson, J. Cognitive familiarity and dissonance reduction. In L. Festinger (Ed.), *Conflict, decision, and dissonance.* Stanford, Calif.: Stanford University Press, 1964.

Davis, K.E., and Jones, E.E. Changes in interpersonal perception as a means of reducing congitive dissonance. *Journal of Abnormal and Social Psychology,* 1960, **61**, 402-410.

Dutton, D.G. Reactions of restaurateurs to blacks and whites violating restaurant dress requirements. *Canadian Journal of Behavioral Science,* 1971, **3**, 298-302.

Dutton, D.G. Reverse discrimination: The relationship of amount of perceived discrimination toward a minority group on the behaviour of majority group members. *Canadian Journal of Behavioral Science,* 1973, **5**, 34-45.

Dutton, D.G., and Lake, R.A. Threat of own prejudice and reverse discrimination in interracial situations. *Journal of Personality and Social Psychology,* 1973, **28**, 94-100.

Dutton, D.G., and Lennox, V.L. Effect of prior "token" compliance on subsequent interracial behavior. *Journal of Personality and Social Psychology,* 1974, **29**, 65-71.

Free, L., and Cantril, H. *The political beliefs of Americans: A study of public opinion.* New Brunswick: Rutgers University Press, 1967.

Friedman, J.L. Guilt, equity, justice and reciprocation. In J. Macaulay and L. Berkowitz (Eds.), *Altruism and helping behavior.* New York: Academic Press, 1970.

Gaertner, S.L. Helping behavior and racial discrimination among Liberals and Conservatives. *Journal of Personality and Social Psychology,* 1973(a), **25**, 335-341.

Gaertner, S.L. Helping behavior and anti-Semitism among the black and white communities. Paper presented to the Annual Convention of the Eastern Psychological Association, Washington, D.C., 1973(b).

Gaertner, S.L. The role of racial attitudes on helping behavior. *Journal of Social Psychology,* in press.

Gaertner, S.L., and Bickman, L. Effects of race on the elicitation of helping behavior: The wrong number technique. *Journal of Personality and Social Psychology,* 1971, **20**, 218-222.

Gaertner, S.L., and McLaughlin, J.P. An indirect measure of racial stereotyping: Word-pair recognition reaction time. Unpublished manuscript, University of Delaware, 1974.

Gergen, K.J., and Jones, E.E. Mental illness, predictability and affective consequences as stimulus factors in person perception. *Journal of Abnormal and Social Psychology,* 1963, **67**, 95-104.

Glass, D.C. Changes in liking as a means of reducing cognitive discrepancies between self-esteem and aggression. *Journal of Personality,* 1964, **32**, 531-549.

Harvey, O.J., and Rutherford, J. Gradual and absolute approaches to attitude change. *Sociometry,* 1958, **21**, 61-68.

Isen, A.M., and Levin, P.F. The effect of feeling good on helping: Cookies and kindness. *Journal of Personality and Social Psychology,* 1972, **21**, 384-388.

Jones, J.M. *Prejudice and racism.* Reading, Mass.: Addison-Wesley, 1972.

Katz, I. Experimental studies of Negro-white relationships. In L. Berkowitz (Ed.), *Advances in experimental social psychology.* Volume 5. New York: Academic Press, 1970.

Katz, I., Glass, D.C., and Cohen, S. Ambivalence, guilt, and the scapegoating of minority group victims. *Journal of Experimental Social Psychology,* 1973, **9**, 423-436.

Kaufman, J. Thou shalt surely rebuke thy neighbor. In N. Hentoff (Ed.), *Black anti-Semitism and Jewish racism.* New York: Baron, 1969.

Kovel, J. *White racism: A Psychohistory.* New York: Pantheon, 1970.

Latane, B., and Darley, J.M. Bystander "apathy." *American Scientist,* 1969, **57**, 244-268.

Latane, B., and Rodin, J. A lady in distress: Inhibiting effects of strangers on bystander intervention. *Journal of Experimental Social Psychology,* 1969, **5**, 189-202.

Marx, G.T. *Protest and prejudice.* New York: Harper & Row, 1967.

McClosky, H. Conservatism and personality. *American Political Science Review,* 1958, **52**, 27-45.

Meyer, D.E., and Schvaneveldt, R.W. Facilitation in recognizing pairs of words: Evidence of a dependence between retrieval operations. *Journal of Experimental Psychology,* 1971, **90**, 227-234.

Orne, M.T. On the social psychology of the psychological experiment: With particular reference to demand characteristics and their implications. *American Psychologist,* 1962, **17**, 776-783.

Piliavin, I.M., Rodin, J., and Piliavin, J.A. Good samaritanism: An undergroud phenomenon? *Journal of Personality and Social Psychology,* 1969, **13**, 289-299.

Rokeach, M. (Ed.) *The open and closed mind.* New York: Basic Books, 1960.

Rosenberg, Milton, J. When dissonance fails: On eliminating evaluator apprehension from attitude measurement. *Journal of Personality and Social Psychology,* 1965, **1**, 28-42.

Schuman, H., and Harding, J. Prejudice and the norm of rationality. *Sociometry,* 1964, **27**, 353-371.

Steiner, I., and Johnson, H. Authoritarianism and "tolerance of trait inconsistency." *Journal of Abnormal and Social Psychology,* 1963, **67**, 388-391.

Stember, C.H. *Education and attitude change.* New York: Institute of Human Relations Press, 1961.

Sutcliffe, J.P. A general method of analysis of frequency data for multiple classification designs. *Psychological Bulletin,* 1957, **54**, 134-137.

Walster, E., Berscheid, E., and Walster, G.W. The exploited: Justice or justification? In J. Macaulay and L. Berkowitz (Eds.), *Altruism and helping behavior.* New York: Academic Press, 1970.

Webb, E.J., Campbell, D.T., Schwartz, D.S., and Sechrest, L. *Unobtrusive measures: Nonreactive research in the social sciences.* Chicago: Rand McNally, 1966.

Weitz, S. Attitude, voice and behavior: A repressed affect model of interracial interaction. *Journal of Personality and Social Psychology,* 1972, **24**, 14-21.

Wicker, A.W. Attitudes vs. action: The relationship of verbal and overt behavioral responses to attitude objects. *Journal of Social Issues,* 1969, **25**, 41-78.

Williams, R.M., Jr. *Strangers next door.* New York: Harper & Row, 1964.

Wispé, L., and Freshley, H. Race, sex, and sympathetic helping behavior: The broken bag caper. *Journal of Personality and Social Psychology,* 1971, **17**, 59-65.

Woodmansee, J.J., and Cook, S.W. Dimensions of verbal racial attitudes: Their identification and measurement. *Journal of Personality and Social Psychology,* 1967, **7**, 240-250.

# 7

# *Attitude Change in Children: Can the Twig Be Straightened?*

PHYLLIS A. KATZ

In a sensible and rational world, the diagnosis of problems and their treatment would be clearly related to one another. Scientists would construct theories that delineate the causes of events and would receive substantial support for testing out those theories, particularly when the societal consequences are far-reaching. Under such circumstances, the eradication of predictable negative events could be logically accomplished by directing sustained efforts at eliminating the causal variables.

The real world is seldom sensible or rational, however. Despite the verbalizations of high-sounding ideals by Presidential commissions to "reduce the racism that cripples all children" (White House Conference on Children, as reported in *The New York Times,* December 19, 1970), there has been remarkably little recent follow-through in terms of current research resources and contemporary effort. Thus, we are nowhere near the point at which our theories might lead to appropriate treatment techniques.

Earlier investigators have evidenced considerable interest in how children acquire racial attitudes, as attested to by numerous studies over the past 30 years. Some of this work is reviewed in Chapters 3 and 4 of this volume. Paradoxically, however, this work has had little actual impact upon the pragmatic issue of how prejudice, once developed, might be effectively reduced in children. There appear to be several reasons for this knowledge gap.

The first and most obvious problem with existing research is the sheer paucity of studies that have attempted to change children's ethnic attitudes. In a very comprehensive review of children's racial attitude studies through 1966, Proshansky (1966) cites 56 modification studies. Of these, only eight were conducted with children, and six of those were with high school students. Although a few promising approaches employing young children have been published since this 1966 review, and will be discussed in this chapter, it is clear that relatively little experimental modification research has been done with children over the past 30 years.

A second difficulty with many earlier investigations is their relative lack of theoretical orientation. Although numerous theoretical positions have been advanced to elucidate prejudice in adults, research on the development of children's racial attitudes has been largely descriptive and atheoretical (Harding *et al.*, 1969). Furthermore, the most influential theories of attitude acquisition to date have stressed such global and deep-seated variables as child-rearing practices (Adorno, *et al.*, 1950), personality organization (e.g., Bettelheim and Janowitz, 1950), personality organization (e.g., Bettelheim and Janowitz, 1950), and social structure (e.g., Myrdal, 1944; Clark, 1955). Clearly, factors of this type are not amenable to experimental modification by social scientists. The continuing emphasis upon them may indeed account for the relative lack of change studies with children.

Clearly, the magnitude of contemporary racial problems makes the efforts of social scientists seem rather puny by contrast. Nevertheless, the evidence available with children gives more reason for optimism than for pessimism. The purpose of the present chapter is to reveiw this evidence, much of it collected within the past ten years.


## WHAT DO WE CHANGE? MEASUREMENT OF ATTITUDES IN CHILDREN

Intrinsic to any concept of change is the issue of what is to be changed and how we are to measure it. Consequently, this first section will review some of the indices that have been employed to assess racial attitudes in children.

In reviewing the earlier literature, it is apparent that many investigations employing children have not adequately taken into account the multifaceted and complex nature of either the attitude construct or the child. Consequently, a single, sometimes crude attitude index has often been employed in studies, with little regard for psychometric considerations such as reliability or validity. Although recent studies are more sensitive to such methodological issues, earlier work, comprising the bulk of research in the area, has been far from exemplary in its research design aspects. The need for increased methodological sophistication may be of even greater importance today than it was 20 years ago, since contemporary children undoubtedly are more aware of racial issues. In this regard, our knowledge regarding the impact of television coverage of civil rights struggles upon young children's attitudes is far from comprehensive. Although some recent investigators contend that the content of children's attitudes has exhibited little change over the past 20 years (Campbell, 1971), it still seems fair to assume that contemporary children are more racially sophisticated, and thus more difficult to assess.

A considerable variety of assessment techniques has been employed to measure racial attitudes in children. For children at the preschool age range, the most frequently employed measure of attitudes has been a doll preference task, originally used by Clark and Clark (1947), which involves offering the child a choice of a black or white doll to associate with negative or positive attributes (e.g., goodness, niceness, etc.). A somewhat more complex doll task involving stories was used by Porter (1971), although the scoring appears to be difficult. Pictures have also been used to elicit preferences. A recent good instrument using pictures has been designed by John Williams (Williams, 1973) and is called the Preschool Racial Attitude Measure (PRAM). In this latter technique, the child is shown a series of pictures containing two children or adults and is asked to select the figure that best completes a story, e.g., "Here are two girls. One of them is happy and smiles almost all the time. Which one is the happy girl?" Adequate group reliability is reported for this instrument. Several investigations have attempted to gather behavioral data on young children's interracial interactions, although they are very few in number (Stevenson and Stevenson, 1960; McCandless and Hoyt, 1961; Harrison, Messe, and Stollak, 1971).

With elementary school children, the range of attitude indices has been much broader and diverse. Measures used have included the following:

### Direct questionnaire techniques

This has been the most frequently utilized method. The child is typically asked questions regarding his attitudes toward various groups, or is presented with statements to agree or disagree with (e.g., from Gough *et al.* [1950]: "Negroes: I do not like them"). Many of these have been based upon the California E and F Scales (e.g., Frenkel-Brunswik, 1948; Gough, *et al.*, 1950; Kates and Diab, 1955; Kutner, 1958). On the surface, it might well appear that this is the most straightforward technique for assessing children's attitudes. Moreover, studies reporting reliability data suggest that such scales have an acceptable degree of internal consistency. Some major problems, however, are associated with this method. The first is that despite relatively good reliabilities, earlier questionnaires frequently contain crude items that may be both offensive and no longer relevant to today's children. Subjects in Kutner and Gordon's study (1964), for example, were asked to agree or disagree with statements like, "Most Negroes would become overbearing and disagreeable if not kept in their place." It is hard to imagine many school administrators, at least in urban centers, permitting the use of such a questionnaire in their school. An additional problem with the use of this method is that children are very much aware of what the "correct" answer is. The socially desirable response is quite obvious. This was demonstrated in a study conducted by Katz, Johnson, and Parker (1970), which found a marked developmental decline in prejudice from the second to the sixth grade on a questionnaire. In contrast, however, prejudice scores obtained on a projective instrument where socially desirable responses were less obvious remained relatively constant across the same age range.

## Picture preferences

This technique is an older and more complex version of the doll preference technique. Horowitz and Horowitz (1938), for example, gave children a choice of 16 photographs (six white boys and girls, six black boys and girls, three Filipino boys, and an owl). Children were asked to select all those they's want to play with, all those who lived in a dirty house, etc. Similar techniques have been used by Radke and Sutherland (1949) and Morland (1966). The previously described PRAM test (Renninger and Williams, 1966; Williams and Roberson, 1967) is primarily intended for preschool children, but has recently been used with young elementary school children as well. Another picture attitude test used with children from kindergarten through high school was recently described by Cullen, Hannah, and Katzenmeyer (1971).

## Projective techniques

Variations on the Thematic Apperception Test have been employed, utilizing biracial pictures, and asking children to tell an open-ended story about them (e.g., Human Relations Test, used by College Study Group, Wayne University, [1948]). A movie story game was used by Evans and Chein (1948), in which children were asked to manipulate black and white dolls on a stage, and to provide dialogue.

A less open-ended projective technique, similar in some ways to the picture preference techniques referred to above (the Katz-Zalk Projective Test), has been used in several studies (Katz, Johnson, and Parker, 1970; Katz, 1973b) and has since been revised. It is intended for children in the elementary school grades, and consists of ambiguous interracial slides of common school situations, plus buffer items of same-race slides with same- or cross-sexed groups of children. The subjects are asked to select which of several children will win a trophy, do better on a spelling test, be reprimanded by the teacher, etc. Its group reliability is adequate. Although similar in some ways to the picture preference test previously described, it differs in that actual photographs of children are used in dramatic situations, race is never mentioned, and the subject is not asked for direct descriptions about the depicted children (like which is the "good" one).

## Social distance scales

This technique is one of the earliest measures of racial attitudes used. In earlier versions with children (e.g., Gough *et al.*, 1950; Radke, Sutherland, and Rosenberg, 1950; Yarrow, Campbell, and Yarrow, 1958), a particular minority is mentioned and subjects are asked to indicate the degree of social intimacy desired, usually on a Guttman-type scale that may range from statements like, "I would like to live in the same country" to "I would like to invite home."

More recent techniques have varied the social distance construct in several ways. Instead of utilizing a group label, the present author (Katz, 1973b) has employed pictures of male and female children of various groups, including their own, thus particularizing the task and providing a comparison group for general degree of friendliness desired with a strange child. A very interesting variation has been used by Koslin, Amarel, and Ames (1969), which is both nonverbal and more disguised. The test booklet is designed so that pages contain fixed target figures (drawings of black and white children and adults) and movable gummed paper figures (drawings of black and white children and adults plus a stick drawing of a self-figure). Subjects are asked to remove the gummed figure and place it as close to the target person as they wish. Social distance on this instrument, then, is defined as the actual linear distance between two such figures. A similar idea was carried even further by Yando, Zigler, and Gates (1971), who measured the actual distance a child preferred in playing with an examiner of another race. This latter technique can only be employed, however, on an individual basis, whereas the others can be utilized in group situations.

## Disguised measures: Learning, memory, and perceptual indices

A diverse number of original indirect measures have been employed to assess attitudes. One such technique was the Aussage test used by Horowitz and Horowitz (1938). Ten pictures were briefly exposed to children in grades one through ten, and questions were asked to assess both memory and faulty perception. One scene, for example, takes place in a library and depicts four white boys, three sitting at a table, and one standing up reading. The subject was asked questions like: "What was the Negro child doing?" Another interesting method was used by Frenkel-Brunswik and Jones (cited in Campbell, 1950) to tap a child's stereotypes without mentioning any groups by name. The child would be asked questions like, "Some people are mean. What people?" In this way, the child was permitted to verbalize what he thought without being forced into making a choice. Other nonobvious methods such as completion and perceptual tasks have been used by Stevenson and Stewart (1958), Vaughan (1963), and Goodman (1964). Several interesting disguised techniques have been used by Stabler and his colleagues. In one study, Stabler, Johnson, Berke, and Baker (1969) attempted to see whether children had preferences for the colors black or white by asking them whether a number of objects with both positive and negative valences were hidden in a black or white box. A closely related technique was to play tape recordings of negative and positive self-statements. Children were asked which box (again, black or white) the various statements emanated from. In a recent study (Stabler and Johnson, 1972), a technique is described in which children are presented with sticks and large black and white boxes in a playground. They are told that they can hit the boxes with the sticks, and film records are made of which box is hit and demolished first.

Many of these unobtrusive techniques are quite ingenious. In counteracting some of the problems involved in direct measures, however, they give rise to others. Reliability figures are usually never mentioned in discussions about them. Moreover, since the child's response is so unstructured, it is difficult to see how reliability could even be assessed in some instances. An additional problem, common to the open-ended projective technique, is that the child's response may have nothing to do with the attitude one is interested in tapping.

### Behavioral measures

Few studies with elementary school children have attempted to use behavioral indices. Earlier studies have occasionally attempted to gather sociometric information, which, although verbal in nature, does try to get a specific group interactions. For example, a sociometric choice measure used by Koslin et al., (1972) asked children to write the names of three classmates they play with most often at school and those they would like to invite to a birthday party. A scale used by Cullen, Hannah, and Katzenmeyer (1971) elicited friendship choices in various areas—i.e., academic, social, and athletic.

Several desegregation studies have looked at, for example, seating patterns in the school lunchroom (Zimbardo, 1953, cited in Zimbardo and Ebbeson, 1969), but these have tended to be at the high school and college level. In a study currently in progress by the author and her colleagues an attempt is being made to ascertain whether a relationship exists between behavioral indices and other measures of attitudes. Indices used include which examiner (a same or cross-raced one) is selected to play a game, which one is imitated more, how close they choose to sit to a cross-raced adult, and how much and what kind of verbal interaction is elicited.

It is clear that there is no lack of ideas on how to measure racial attitudes in children. The variety of techniques employed is very great. It is equally clear, particularly from studies conducted prior to 1965, that earlier investigators have not been cognizant of a number of critical issues in attitude conceptualization and measurement that have become prominent in recent years (e.g., Scott, 1968). Thus, although it is widely accepted that racial attitudes are composed of multiple components, a typical practice with children is to use only a single measure, thus precluding the opportunity to assess how correlated the measures are.

In a recent exception to this trend, the present author and her colleagues (Katz, Sohn, and Zalk, 1974) obtained multiple attitude measures on urban grade-school children. These included: (a) the Katz-Zalk multiple-choice projective technique previously described, (b) a social distance measure using pictures of children, (c) a General Intolerance questionnaire adapted from Gough *et al.*, (1950) and (d) a Dogmatism Scale adapted from Rokeach (1960). In contrast to work with adults, which shows substantial intercorrelations among different verbal measures, the findings with children showed little overlap in responses to the various instruments. A factor analysis revealed a number of separate factors, most of which had primary loadings on individual tests. These low intercorrelations obtained with children may turn out to be a significant issue for modification research, raising the question of what responses are to be changed.

A related issue concerns the nature of the relationship that exists between expressed verbal attitudes and overt behavior. This question has been of continuing concern to investigators of adult attitudes who have attempted to delineate the conditions that affect the extent of this attitude-behavior discrepancy (cf. Wicker [1969] and Chapter Three in this volume for a fuller discussion of this issue). Only in the last few years has any data about this relation in children been forthcoming (Hraba and Grant, 1970; Katz and Zalk, 1974). This relative lack of information may be due in part to the widely held belief that children are less cognitively complex than adults—a belief that leads to the expectation that children's expressed attitudes will be more consistent with their behavior. Recent evidence indicates that this conceptualization of children's attitudes is far too oversimplified. Even in nursery school children, interracial friendship choices and racial preferences on a doll task do not relate highly to each other (Hraba and Grant, 1970; Porter, 1971), suggesting that a one-to-one correspondence between a score on an attitude test and other relevant behavior cannot be assumed with children in the absence of other information. The need for obtaining behavioral criteria to validate attitude measures is not only a psychometric issue. It has important ramifications for modification studies as well. If a disparity exists, what is to be changed: attitudes, behavior, or both?

In addition to these issues, several other psychometric considerations have been ignored in earlier research with children. It is, for example, extremely unusual to find any reliability information about children's tests in published reports. Of the almost 200 references cited in Proshansky's (1966) review, only two report internal consistency data for tests used. Indirect measures such as those used by Horowitz and Horowitz (1938) are sometimes cited as exemplary by attitude theorists (e.g., Campbell, 1950), yet no information regarding the adequacy of these measures has ever been given in terms of reliability and validity. Generally speaking, direct questionnaire techniques pose fewer measurement problems in terms of reliability (Gough *et al.* [1950] report a split-half reliability of .80, for example). Nevertheless, as previously noted, the content of the items may pose other types of problems for researchers.

A final problem area with regard to the measurement of children's attitudes concerns the characteristics of the testing situation itself and, more specifically, with the adult who administers it. Despite considerable evidence attesting to the importance of racial "experimenter effects" on a wide variety of children's behavior (e.g., Katz, Henchy, and Allen, 1968; Bucky and Banta, 1972; Sattler, 1973), most grade-school assessment efforts have not systematically varied this factor, and often even fail to describe the racial characteristics of the testers.

Fortunately, some of these issues are now being addressed by current investigators in the area and contemporary research is becoming increasingly sophisticated. Concern about the validity of attitude indices remains a relevant and continuing one, however. Moreover, in view of the relatively low intercorrelations among measures, multiple indices should be obtained wherever possible. Each of the techniques described contain both advantages and disadvantages. The lack of comparative data makes it difficult to suggest which may be the "best." What the foregoing discussion does suggest, however, is that earlier modification results may have to be interpreted with caution because of measurement problems.

## ATTITUDE MODIFICATION STUDIES WITH CHILDREN

Although there have been many attempts to modify prejudiced attitudes of adults in a variety of contexts, there have been comparatively few studies conducted with children. This is particularly surprising in view of the differential findings that have emerged from adult and child populations. Specifically, research on modifying prejudice in adults, utilizing a broad variety of techniques, has not yielded many studies that have produced consistent or lasting attitude changes. When attitudes are deep-rooted, the task of changing them is apparently a formidable one. In contrast, the studies using children have obtained somewhat more encouraging results. This section will review some of the techniques that have been employed with children.

### The frontal-assault approach

A long-held assumption by educators (and others) has been that increased education will provide a panacea for decreasing prejudice. There is no well-delineated theory specifying the ways in which information might affect children's attitudes (see Chapter 4 for a review of available theories). Nevertheless, educators typically proceed with the assumption that negative attitudes are primarily the result of ignorance, which can be counteracted by the appropriate knowledge and information. This, in fact, is the basis upon which most traditional elementary school courses in civics and history are formulated and taught in the schools. Generally, such courses stress democratic ideology and attempt to impart limited information about minority group history and culture.

One finding that can be interpreted as support for this view is the negative relation often obtained between scores on prejudice questionnaires and amount of education (Proshansky, 1966). Of course, there are many other interpretations of this correlation other than the causal one usually postulated. Given the social desirability factors present in most questionnaires, it would be surprising if well-educated individuals were not sophisticated enough to respond to such questionnaires by placing themselves in a favorable light. Whether greater degrees of education actually result in more positive intergroup attitudes is another question, however.

Evidence attempting to link particular kinds of educational experiences with measured attitude change is very scanty, and most of it has been done with college students. The few studies employing younger groups have obtained negative findings. McNeill (1960) tested white high school seniors before and after information about blacks was given and actually found an increase in prejudice. Kagan (1952) found that information about Jews generally did not decrease anti-Semitism. Such a decrease occurred only when knowledge was combined with direct discussions about anti-Semitism. Such a decrease occurred only when knowledge was combined with direct discussions about anti-Semitism, and generally was more effective after class than during it. Hayes and Conklin (1953) found that academic instruction about prejudice had very little effect upon the attitudes of eighth-grade students. Role playing, on the other hand, did elicit significant changes. Kraus (1960) and Elrod (1968) employed movies in a course with high school students which were generally ineffective. Thus, it would appear that, at least within the age ranges utilized, there is no evidence that education about prejudice without emotional involvement actually influences attitudes. This generalization seems to be true for college populations as well (e.g., Murphy and Likert, 1938; Greenberg, Pierson, and Sherman, 1957; Mann, 1960; Eddy, 1964).

Recently, several investigators have attempted to assess the effects of special kinds of curricula upon the attitudes of younger children, particularly those concerned with black history and culture. Such investigations, usually initiated by the school system, often lack the necessary control groups and/or measures to adequately ascertain the effect of the curriculum.

One such project was conducted in Gary, Indiana, by Georgoff and Jones (1967). The focus of the study was upon fourth graders, and the experimental groups (19 classes in all) studied "Negro heritage and contributions to America" for a semester. Seven control classes did not study this unit. Despite the fact that the project was done in cooperation with the city, direct attitude tests were not permitted in the schools since they were deemed "unadvisable" by school officials. Instead, the dependent measures included: (a) a sociometric test asking children to list three others with whom they preferred to sit, play, or study, (b) a self-concept measure, and (c) an assessment of facts about Negro heritage. The findings were clear only with regard to the knowledge test. Not surprisingly, children who studied the Negro history unit learned more about it than children not so exposed. Attitude change, as measured by the sociometric instrument, was minimal.

A more comprehensive evaluation effort was undertaken in Salt Lake City with six-grade youngsters (Leslie, Leslie, and Penfield, 1972). The experimental group (all white, middle-class, and Mormon) had three months of curriculum changes, which included units about Africa, famous black personalities, and problems of blacks. A variety of materials were used including films, records, books, and special guest lecturers. Children in this group were also given additional opportunities to interact with younger black children in a tutorial and advisory capacity. Two control groups were utilized—one studying the "traditional" social studies curriculum (i.e., the Middle Ages, the Industrial Revolution, etc.), and the other a more contemporary, relevant unit on student political activity. In contrast to most modification studies, multiple attitude measures (both direct and indirect) were administered to the children before and after the introduction of the information. Unfortunately, however, the statistical analyses presented in the article were flawed, since subjects who showed no change were dropped from the analysis. This extraordinary procedure is not justified in any way in the paper and clearly makes the results difficult to interpret. In view of this, the finding that all groups decreased in prejudice on the posttests is not surprising. The authors report, additionally, that this drop was not related to treatment group. Thus, the control group children improved as much as those exposed to the special curriculum. There is no way of assessing from the publication whether the numbers of subjects dropped for "failure to change" were equivalent in all groups.

Perhaps the best study available on the relationship of curriculum innovations to racial attitudes was that done by Litcher and Johnson (1969) with second-grade white Midwestern children. The particular sample had very little exposure to black children or adults. The curriculum innovation instituted in the experimental group (two classrooms) was the use of a multiethnic reader, which contained interracial stories. The control group children used readers in which the characters were all white. Teachers participating in the study were asked not to initiate or encourage discussion with regard to racial or ethnic differences so that no special attention was drawn to the material in the classroom. A pre-post design was employed in which the children were given a battery of attitude tests, including a doll preference task, the "Show Me" and Categories Tests used by Horowitz and Horowitz (1938), and Blake and Dennis' Direct Comparison Test. In this latter instrument, subjects were asked to indicate whether a particular trait (e.g., honesty, cleanliness, etc.) was more characteristic of whites, blacks, or both. The correlations between the tests were relatively low, in accordance with other recent findings previously described (Katz, Sohn, and Zalk, 1974), suggesting that different measures of prejudice may not be tapping the same dimension. Results indicated, however, that the experimental group had significantly more favorable attitudes on each of the four instruments than did the control group after using the multiethnic reader.

This last study appears to be the only one obtaining clear, unequivocally strong results with regard to curriculum innovation and racial attitudes. In view of the lack of discussion about race to the children, however, it might be argued that the experimental condition was primarily a perceptual experience rather than a cognitive one.

The relative absence of clear-cut findings in this area may appear somewhat puzzling to the reader since strong common sense notions exist that increased knowledge about other groups should elicit more positive attitudes. The actual experimental evidence, however, is not convincing.

One possible reason is that many of the studies attempting to link increase of information to attitudes abound in methodological problems. Measures lack reliability, children are not randomly assigned to conditions, and there is often confounding of control and experimental groups. It is interesting to note that the only study demonstrating strong positive change was conducted with young white children who did not have experience with blacks. In such a situation, then, knowledge may be a much more important component.

Another possibility, admittedly speculative, is that curriculum may have an effect on later attitudes that is not discernible immediately after the treatment. Some evidence with adults on the attitudinal effects of various therapeutic effects (e.g., Stotland, Katz, and Patchen, 1959) suggests that a germination period may have to occur before effects are observable. It is, thus, possible that increased information may make a child less susceptible to racist appeals at a future point in his life. Although this notion is frankly hypothetical, the possibility of an "inoculation" type of effect should not be overlooked and should be empirically tested in future research.

It does not follow from the literature that schools should not attempt to teach about minority culture and history. Such knowledge is important in its own right, and might redress the long-standing bias in our traditional textbooks. Moreover, the effects upon minority group children may well be considerable. What the studies do suggest, however, is that the immediate attitudinal effects of curriculum innovations upon white children appear to be weak.

## The contact approach

As noted in the previous section, a commonly held (but perhaps errone-ous) view is that increasing a child's information and knowledge will reduce his prejudices. Another widely held prescription for prejudice reduction is the belief that increasing the amount of interaction among children of differing groups will lead to greater tolerance and acceptance of each other. As with the previously described educational approach, an examination of the evidence suggest that this expectation may be an oversimplified one. Although there have been no well-delineated theories that describe the mechanisms relating contact to attitudes, the basic and widely held assumption, recently elaborated by Pettigrew (1969), is that increased contact enables groups to learn that they are more alike than they assumed, while preventing value differences from occurring because of mutual isolation. The negative effects of such isolation and segregation have been underscored again by Kenneth Clark. In a recent essay (*The New York Times,* 1974), he has stated that racial segrega-tion in the schools inflicts "irreparable damage" by dehumanizing and stigma-tizing minority group children and imposing "ethical anxieties, conflicts and guilt" upon white children.

Based in part on the above beliefs, desegregation has been the most widely used intervention technique with children over the past decade. It should be noted, however, that researchers typically have little control over the conditions under which desegregation occurs. Nevertheless, assessments of its effects have been numerous, focusing more frequently upon the educa-tional achievements of the children than upon their racial attitudes.

A detailed review of the effects of desegregation on attitudes (with both children and adults) is contained in Chapter 8 of this volume and the legal aspects are covered in Chapter 11. This section, therefore, will not duplicate these efforts, but will summarize some major trends obtained with children and will describe recent directions in attitudinal research on contact.

A review of attitude change studies resulting from school desegregation by Carithers (1970) illustrates the generally contradictory findings obtained. A number of investigations report more positive attitudes following desegregation (e.g., Coleman Report, 1966; Jansen and Gallagher, 1966; US Commission on Civil Rights, 1967), many report no change (e.g., Roth, 1969; Trubowitz, 1969), whereas some obtain more negative attitudes after desegregation (e.g., Webster, 1961; Beecher, 1970, cited in Weinberg, 1970).

It is difficult to ascertain why desegregation attempts are sometimes successful and boomerang at other times. Methodological problems abound in many of the studies. Control groups are frequently not comparable, measures are poor, etc. In addition, the conditions of contact—the major independent variable—have frequently not been adequately described. Placing black and white children in the same classroom does not ensure positive interaction. The distinction between desegregation and integration (Pettigrew, 1969) may be useful to consider to this regard. Integration refers to a situation in which positive interaction between children is actively encouraged and reinforced by the school staff and the community, a condition that would be expected to foster more positive attitudes than merely placing children together in the same room. Frequently, such a distinction is not made in published studies. The US Commission on Civil Rights recently reported (1973) that the prevailing mood of the community toward integration efforts is a very significant factor. In addition to adult reinforcement, other factors that have been related to successful attitude change through the contact approach include equal status between groups and pursuit of common goals (Allport, 1954). The importance of this latter variable was demonstrated in a now classic study by Sherif (1958) at a summer camp. Intergroup conflict (the groups were not racially different) was reduced when the boys were confronted by a common problem requiring cooperation for its solution. In a school situation, setting up conditions like this may require more active efforts on the part of teachers and administrators than are usually found. It is necessary to keep such background factors in mind when considering the results of school desegregation upon children's attitudes, since interaction does not occur in a vacuum.

Some interesting recent research in this area has focused more closely on the integration variable in both its quantitative and qualitative aspects. In contrast to earlier work, which viewed integration as an all-or-none variable, several recent studies have investigated the relationship between attitudes and the racial composition of the classroom. Koslin, Amarel, and Ames (1969) studied classrooms in which the number of children of each race varied from 25% to 75%. The target age group was 254 third-grade youngsters. Measures used included: (a) sociometric choices, (b) a classroom preference test, consisting of classroom sketches of varying racial composition, and (c) the People Test—a nonverbal social distance index described in more detail in the earlier section on measurement. Results revealed a relatively high level of racial polarization on all measures, but less so in balanced classrooms. "Balance" in this context was defined in terms of the relationship between the racial composition of the class and that of the school as a whole. Thus, if the class mirrored the school, it was deemed "balanced." In their discussion of these findings, the investigators cautiously point out that the relationship between classroom balance and attitudes is not necessarily a causal one; and they discuss the possibility that administration and faculty attitudes may have influenced both grouping policies and student attitudes. Nevertheless, the use of the classroom may be a more appropriate unit for study than the school since there frequently is so much variability.

In a later, more extensive study (Koslin, Koslin, Pargament, and Waxman, 1972), conducted with 3200 children in the third through sixth grades, utilizing classrooms where the proportion of blacks ranged from 5% to 50%, it was found that increased opportunity to interact with others of a different race produced more similar social distance structures between blacks and whites. Moreover, it was found that when the proportion of minority students was less than 15%, black boys expressed feelings of isolation. Although the emphasis throughout this chapter has clearly been upon negative interracial attitudes of white children, this latter finding is an important reminder of the fact that many factors must be considered in making school decisions of this type. More detailed discussions of the effect of contact on young black children can be found in a book by Powell (1973). Williams (1968) has also addressed himself to the feelings of somewhat older black students in desegregated environments, and documented their apprehension regarding acceptance by white peers and fairness of white teachers.

An interesting recent study by DeVries and Edwards (1973) investigated the effects of the type of interaction in integrated settings. They attempted to restructure seventh-grade classes with the aim of creating more positive intergroup relationships. The major manipulation involved the use of four-member study teams. Additionally, type of reward was varied so that it was administered on either an individual or group basis. It was found that the use of teams elicited more cross-race choices on a sociometric measure than the more traditional classroom approach. In some instances, however, the choices were not always reciprocal—black students were sometimes friendlier to whites than the reverse. This investigation appears to be a start in the right direction, however, in that considerably more attention needs to be devoted to the specific classroom structures associated with intergroup contact.

It is clear that desegregation of the schools is not the panacea for eliminating racism in children that some people had hoped it would be. Increased contact alone is often insufficient to induce favorable and prolonged attitude change. Whether it does or not appears to depend upon many factors—some related to the school and community, some a function of the children and their existing attitudes, and others primarily related to the particular kinds of interactions. Better controlled research is required to adequately assess and disentangle these variables.

As was the case with regard to curriculum innovation, however, the case for desegregation does not rest solely on whether it produces more positive racial attitudes in children. There are moral and legal reasons for desegregation aside from its hoped-for effects upon children's attitudes and educational accomplishments. Occasionally, the social scientist's concern with quantifiable dependent measures may cause him to lose sight of these latter realms. Thus, although some of the data with regard to the relationship between contact and children's attitudes may be inconclusive, this suggests the need for additional attitude intervention techniques, not the diminution of desegregation efforts. Desegregation may be a necessary but not sufficient condition.

## Recent experimental approaches

Although integration has often been regarded as the most promising and most frequently employed technique for inducing positive racial attitudes in children, studies that have explored other, more experimentally oriented procedures have obtained more consistently positive results. This section will review this work, some of it generated by the theoretical positions elaborated in Chapter 4 on attitude acquisition.

*Perceptual approaches.* There have been four modification studies undertaken with children that have emphasized the perceptual components of attitudes, and each of these has taken a very different approach.

The first investigation conducted by Hohn (1973) utilized a training procedure that attempted to "facilitate the perceptual ability involved in discriminating differences between people." Subjects were white kindergarten children. The two treatment groups were drawn from an experimental university laboratory school in the Midwest, whereas the control subjects came from a public elementary school. One training condition was based upon Piagetian theory and utilized tasks designed to reduce "cognitive egocentrism"—a variable presumed to be related to prejudice. The training in this condition consisted of teaching children logical operations such as conservation of number, reversibility, multiple relations, superordinate classification, and perspective. Some of the perspective tasks included asking children to draw objects as if they were sitting on the other side of the table. The second training condition was based on Flavell's role-taking studies (Flavell *et al.*, 1968) and emphasized empathic skills. In this group, children played "Let's pretend" games in which they were asked to pretend that they were "poor," "dirty," "the President," "the teacher," etc. Each of these groups met twice a week for six weeks. The control group met for the same amount of time, during which they discussed the "social environment." A pre-post design was utilized and attitude measures included: (a) a picture preference measure, (b) a doll choice task, and (c) a person choice task in which S selected whether to plays a game with a black or white adult. The picture preference test was similar in format to the Williams and Roberson (1967) technique discussed earlier (i.e., the child was asked to complete a story by choosing whether the white or black child in the picture was associated with a positive or negative adjective). Results were positive in that the two experimental groups showed a significant decline in white bias on the picture preference posttest, whereas the control group showed more pro-white bias on the posttest. Additionally, slightly more black doll and adult preferences were made on the posttest by the experimental subjects than by the controls. These findings are interpreted by the author as indicating that both treatments facilitated a more logical approach and sharpened perceptual awareness—both of which are assumed to underlie racial preference. One difficulty in accepting such an interpretation, however, is that the experimental treatments were confounded with type of subject. Children in the laboratory school, the only ones exposed to the training, may well have been more sophisticated and hence more readily "sensitized" by the pretest measures to change on the posttests. Although the reader is given to understand that no differences in intelligence existed between the two school settings, other types of differences between the samples may be involved here. Nevertheless, if one is willing to minimize this methodological shortcoming, the results are encouraging.

A more direct test of role playing with somewhat older children was conducted recently by Weiner and Wright (1973), utilizing an ingenious technique previously described in the popular press to elicit change. They had classroom teachers temporarily assign white children to either "orange" or "green" people groups, and arbitrarily gave negative or positive generalizations about each group. The immediate behavioral effect was a polarization of the class. In addition, they found that playing the "underdog" for a day elicited a more positive social distance response several weeks later with regard to going on a picnic with a group of black children. Unfortunately, the possibility of reactivity to the posttest as a result of the manipulation was not controlled for so that it is difficult to disentangle the effects of the experience from the children's desire to please their teacher on the test. The interesting experimental procedure employed, however, should be replicated with more stringent controls since it seems to be a promising method for enabling children to more readily adopt the perspective of victimized groups. It would appear from both this study and the previously described one by Hohn (1973) that increased practice in empathy and attempting to perceive things from the perspective of others may be helpful in modifying negative attitudes.

A second viewpoint, utilized by Cantor (1972), is based upon the "mere exposure" hypothesis put forth originally by Zajonc (1968) to account for adult data relating frequency of stimulus exposure to attitudes. Essentially, this view suggests that, within certain limits (cf. Zajonc, Swap, Harrison, and Roberts, 1971), repeated exposure to an unfamiliar stimulus may enhance one's attitude towards that stimulus. Zajonc's work has been with college students, utilizing responses to unfamiliar and ambiguous stimuli such as abstract paintings and Chinese ideographs. Cantor attempted to assess the effect of stimulus familiarization upon children's racial attitudes, utilizing pictures of other children as stimuli. He employed 80 white children, aged nine to 11. The stimuli were photographs of six white boys and six black boys. Children were first asked to rate the pictures in terms of how they would feel about bringing each boy home to spend time with their family. A rather ingenious five-point rating was devised, which ranged from a face with a large frown to one with a large smile. The subject was asked to place an X on the face that was most indicative of his feelings. Following the ratings, a familiarization procedure was introduced in which photographs of three of the white boys and three black boys were each exhibited ten times for ten seconds duration. Following the familiarization phase, subjects were asked to rate the 12 stimuli again. A number of significant findings were obtained. Interestingly, the children rated the black faces more favorably than the white ones. A significant interaction of race of picture by familiarity indicated that the familiarity treatment was most effective in eliciting more positive ratings towards black children. Finally, a race of picture by sex of subject interaction was obtained, in which the male subjects rated the pictures of black boys more positively than did the female subjects. This latter interaction may be partially attributable to the fact that female pictures were not used as stimuli, and that cross-sex friendships in grade school may have different connotations for children. The finding most germane to this discussion, however, is the more positive affective response white children of both sexes gave to familiar as opposed to nonfamiliar blacks.

The present author (Katz, 1973a) conducted the last study to be described in this section, attempting to link attitude change to perceptual processes. This investigation was based upon the supposition that other-race stimuli acquire more perceptual equivalence for children as they develop than do same-race stimuli. Empirical support for the expectation that faces of another race appear more similar has been obtained with both preschool (Katz, 1973b) and grade-school (Katz, Johnson, and Parker, 1970) children. According to this view, such acquired equivalence should facilitate the generalization of both affective responses and evaluative statements to all members of the out-group. If this is the case, then it follows that techniques that increased perceptual differentiation of out-group members should also decrease negative attitudes.

The study to be described attempted to assess the validity of this hypothesis. It was conducted with 96 white and black urban children who had previously demonstrated negative racial attitudes on: (a) a social distance index, employing photographs as stimuli, and (b) a multiple-choice projective instrument, described earlier, depicting ambiguous interracial situations. Subjects were randomly assigned to one of three treatments, which consisted of: (a) learning to associate different names to other-race pictures, (b) making perceptual judgments of "same" or "different" to pairs of other-race faces, or (c) observing the faces without the labels. This latter condition was considered to be a control group in the present context, although it should be noted that in some respects it corresponds to the "familiarity" procedure employed by Cantor (1972) and described above. The stimuli utilized were photographs of an adult female light-skinned black model, which systematically varied type of make-up, type of wig, presence or absence of glasses, and facial expression (smile or frown). The same face was used throughout in order to control for facial features. White children viewed photographs with black make-up, whereas black children viewed those with white make-up. The attitude tests were readministered several days after participation in the perceptual phase by the same white or black examiner. The results corroborated the major hypothesis of the study. Subjects who were assigned to the labeling and differentiation conditions had lower (i.e., less prejudiced) posttest scores on both attitude indices than did children in the control group. In addition to this main effect, several interactions were obtained with the race of examiner variable, which indicated that more change occurred with a cross-raced examiner for some treatments. This latter finding reflects the complexity of a child's responses to measures of racial attitudes. The overall findings of both measures, however, supports the view that modifying the perceptual concomitants of attitudes can result in attitude change. When children are trained to individuate members of another race, it apparently becomes more difficult for them to maintain negative attitudes towards that group.

The theoretical orientations underlying the studies discussed in this section appear to be quite different, with Kohn, and Weiner and Wright emphasizing the important of role-taking, Cantor stressing exposure effects, and the present author focusing upon the importance of perceptual differentiation. Although these theoretical differences need to be analyzed and delineated in future empirical work, it is interesting to note that each attempt to manipulate the child's perception of other-race stimuli did, in fact, result in attitude modification. This suggests that perceptual processes may be an important avenue for eliciting more positive racial attitudes.


## Reinforcement approaches

A good deal of recent research has been generated by the position that young children's negative racial attitudes result from the differential connotations and rewards associated with the colors black and white. This view has been elaborated in greatest detail by Williams (1972, 1973). He and his colleagues have amassed considerable evidence demonstrating that both adults (Williams, 1964, 1966) and children (McMurty and Williams, 1972; Renninger and Williams, 1966; Williams and Rousseau, 1971) associate positive evaluative adjectives to whiteness and negative ones to blackness. It follows from this view that changes in these associations should lead to modified attitudes. Such association changes have most frequently been accomplished through the use of direct reinforcement with young children.

The first study attempting to change pro-white bias by reinforcement techniques was conducted by Williams and Edwards (1969). Eighty-four white five-year-old children were used. The experimental procedure utilized pictures from the color meaning test, described earlier. The target pictures contain black and white animals or toys. No person pictures are utilized in this index. The child is asked to choose, for example, which is the dirty teddy bear, which is the pretty airplane, etc. As noted above, children exhibit a strong initial tendency to associate positive adjectives to white objects, and negative adjectives to black ones. In this study, Williams and Edwards utilized four experimental conditions. One group was negatively reinforced (i.e., had to give up pennies) for making negative evaluative responses towards black-colored stimuli; another group was positively reinforced for making positive judgments towards black stimuli; a third group was appropriately reinforced for both negative and positive responses; finally, a control group received no reinforcement. The PRAM test, utilizing pictures of people, was subsequently administered to all the children in order to assess the generalizability of the reinforcement procedures. No differences were obtained among the three reinforcement groups. All of them, however, obtained lower scores on the PRAM test than did the control. Thus, the results substantiate that changing young children's associations to the colors black and white by means of reinforcement procedures can modify their evaluative responses to people.

Although two recent studies (Shanahan, 1972; Collins, 1972) failed to obtain significant attitude change with this technique, most of the other studies employing reinforcement with young children have obtained positive findings (Edwards and Williams, 1970; McAdoo, 1970; McMurty and Williams, 1972; Yancey, 1972). In addition to direct attitude manipulations, similar reinforcement procedures have also been used to encourage interracial contact in young children (Hauserman, Walen, and Behling, 1973).

Spencer and Horowitz (1973) recently attempted a somewhat different reinforcement procedure than that used in the earlier cited studies. These investigators employed 48 black and white nursery school children and dispensed reinforcement with a mechanized puppet apparatus. The particular puppet used was the same race as the child. In addition, these investigators enlisted the assistance of parents as reinforcers at home. In a rather unique procedure, they provided parents with a game modeled after Stabler's technique with black and white boxes. Parents were instructed to reward children for associating positive objects with the black box. They found, however, that this particular procedure did not modify attitudes on the PRAM test any more than did the laboratory sessions conducted with the experimenter. The overall findings with regard to attitude change, however, were positive.

It would thus appear that reinforcement procedures can successfully be used with young children to modify pro-white, anti-black attitudes, and that such changes are generalizable to attitudes about people. The oldest group that these techniques have been used with, however, was first graders, and this study was one that did not obtain statistically significant results (Shanahan, 1972). Therefore, the question of how applicable such procedures are to older children remains an open one. Nevertheless, the consistency of the findings with young children is most encouraging.

## Use of the media

Everyone would undoubtedly agree that the mass media, and particularly television, is a most powerful tool for molding and changing attitudes.

Chapter 9 in this volume reviews in detail the literature with regard to television's treatment of minority groups. The role of the media in maintaining racism in the past has been well documented. Pierce (1973), for example, states that:

> All the characteristics of racism in our society can be seen on TV. The black, with statistical predictability even in the make-believe world, is more likely to be server than served. He is more likely to defer to whites and to require white guidance, instruction and sponsorship. If he presents something important it can be legitimized only by white approval. (p. 74)

On the more general effects of television, the same author states that television, as the dominant communicator in our society:

> ... influences and directs all other types of communications to blacks and about blacks. Thus, what blacks or whites think of themselves and how they behave toward each other in interracial processes has much to do with how the communicator influences others which controls the way they are permitted to live and the way they are allowed to think. (p. 73)

In view of this potency, one might expect, therefore, that there would be many studies dealing with the effects of the mass media attempting to reverse prejudiced attitudes. Surprisingly, this is not the case. Of the 400 sources listed in Weiss' chapter on mass media and attitude change in *The Handbook of Social Psychology* (1969), only four refer to prejudice and these are with adults. As noted above, the evidence suggests that until fairly recently, the mass media may well have done more to perpetuate prejudice than to fight it (Colle, 1968). Nevertheless, the new willingness of the media to present both pro-tolerance messages and attractive minority group role models has not yet elicited much social science research.

Psychological investigations of the effects of television upon children have been primarily concerned with the possible consequences of viewing aggressive formats (e.g., Comstock and Rubinstein, 1971; Liebert and Baron, 1972; Friedrich and Stein, 1973), and considerable governmental and foundation support has been devoted to this issue. Another area of concern to social scientists has been the effect of educational programs such as Sesame Street upon children's cognitive gains (e.g., Bogatz and Ball, 1971). There has been practically no research conducted on the effects of television on intergroup attitudes. This is particularly surprising to anyone who has watched programs such as Sesame Street or The Electric Company. The messages being communicated by these programs are clearly multiple ones, and they are obviously not limited to the cognitive sphere. The many attractive black models that children are exposed to, the very natural quality of the interracial groups of children, the introduction of Spanish to non-Spanish speaking children—events such as these may well be as important to a young child as the creative and whimsical teaching of alphabet letters.

As the parent of a nursery school child, the present author cannot help but be impressed by the effects of such programming. Anything more than anecdotal evidence, however, is difficult to find. The only bit of data supporting these beliefs is contained in the longitudinal evaluation of Sesame Street conducted by Bogatz and Ball (1971). A comparison was made between a group of preschool children that had viewed the programs for 18 months and one that had been exposed to it for only 12 months. Those who viewed the program for the longer period—a sample of 31 children—were more likely to have positive attitudes towards the race of others than the other group of 29 children. Attitudes were measured through the use of six pictures, and the subjects' task was to associate either a smiling or a frowning face with each picture. Little information is given about the measure in the report, and it is clear that such attitudes were far from the central focus of the evaluation. The authors suggest that this finding should be followed up in subsequent research but, to date, this has not been done. The need for more research in this vitally important area cannot be emphasized too strongly.

## CONCLUSIONS AND FUTURE DIRECTIONS

This chapter has reviewed research relevant to both the assessment and modification of children's intergroup attitudes. With regard to assessment, attitude measures employed with children have been quite diverse, and each technique is associated with particular advantages and disadvantages. Direct questionnaires tend to be the most reliable method, but also the least sophisticated. Some questions on older ones, in fact, would now be regarded as offensive. Some recent picture preference techniques are available that have reported adequate internal consistency, but the choices would probably be relatively obvious to children older than seven or eight years of age. Social distance indices remain a commonly used procedure, and some interesting new revisions are now available. Projective techniques are less obvious to children, but reliability has not been established, particularly on unstructured ones.

In addition to the specific problems associated with each of the various assessment procedures, there are some problems common to all. The first problem concerns the lack of validity data on any of the instruments. Very little work has been done on intergroup behavior in children, and the ability of any measure to predict such behavior has never been demonstrated. Clearly, this is an area requiring additional empirical work. A second problem has to do with the relative lack of overlap among the various techniques, each purporting to measure the same thing. Although verbal measures of attitudes are fairly well correlated in adults, the few studies that have employed multiple measures with children have obtained surprisingly low intercorrelations, suggesting that prejudice may not be a unidimensional construct for children. Each of these problems (i.e., low or no relation to behavior or other verbal indices) has implications for modification research, since they make both the goal of change and interpretation of obtained change a difficult matter. At the very least, these issues suggest that the contemporary researcher employ multiple measures in modification research with children. On a less technical level, it suggests that new conceptualizations may be required to further delineate the attitude construct in children.

If one is willing to assume some validity of children's racial attitude measures, however, the data available with regard to attitude modification in children are quite promising. Though there are relatively few studies, the literature suggests that changing children's intergroup attitudes may be a less formidable task than changing adult attitudes. Some approaches have been more consistently successful than others. Educators have placed great reliance upon the informational and increased contact approaches to attitude change. The evidence suggests, however, that curriculum changes have not been particularly successful, at least on a short-term basis. Similarly, the desegregation literature suggests that increased racial contact by itself is not invariably successful in effecting positive attitude change. The conditions under which this result occurs remain to be specified with precision, although some of the concomitants of success may include a cooperative rather than competitive atmosphere, positive rewards for contact from significant adults, and the structuring of groups in ways that increase the amount of positive contact.

In terms of consistency, it would appear that some of the experimentally oriented approaches have been more successful in eliciting positive attitude change. All of the studies that focused on the perceptual parameters of attitudes obtained positive results, even though their theoretical rationales differed. Thus, increasing a child's familiarity with other-race faces or his ability to differentiate them or his capacity to perceive things from the other's perspective—all of these are related to positive attitude change. Most of the studies reviewed that manipulated the reinforcement contingencies associated with color preferences also obtained significant attitude change. Teaching positive associations to the color black had some generalizability to attitudes towards people, particularly for very young children. Each of the laboratory techniques described in this chapter could be revised for utilization with larger groups of children in the school system. To date, however, applications of the principles learned in the laboratory to the schools have not been made. There is an obvious need for applied research of this kind.

In terms of evaluating particular techniques that have been employed, it would appear that the laboratory-oriented approaches have had a higher success rate than the contact and educational approaches. Yet, in terms of potential impact, there is little question that the schools and the mass media are the vastly more powerful agents of social change. Social scientists may be of considerable assistance here by communicating to these institutions what the necessary ingredients are for successful change to occur.

A general need, however, exists for greater commitment, particularly on the part of the schools. At this particular moment in history, many school adminstrators shy away, ostrich-like, from any mention of race, much in the same way as they do with regard to sex education. Admittedly, controversy is not something that administrators deliberately seek out. Nevertheless, until schools are willing to come to terms with their responsibility in this area, the chances for developing effective attitude change programs seem minimal. Also needed, however, is a greater commitment on the part of both funding sources and social scientists to come up with the necessary information.

In short, we need more studies, more theory, more attention to procedural and technical details, more comparisons of various techniques, more interplay between applied and basic research, and much more utilization of societal resources to eliminate "the racism that cripples all children." Evidence to date suggests no good reasons as to why the twig we bend so successfully can't be straightened.

## REFERENCES

Adorno, T.W., Frenkel-Brunswik, E., Levinson, D.J., and Sanford, R.N. *The authoritarian personality.* New York: Harper, 1950.

Allport, G. *The nature of prejudice.* Reading, Mass.: Addison-Wesley, 1954.

Amir, Y. Contact hypothesis in ethnic relations. *Psychological Bulletin,* 1969, **71**, 319-342.

Beecher, R.H. A study of social distance among adolescents of ethnic minorities. Reported in M. Weinberg, *Desegregation research: An appraisal.* Phi Delta Kappa, Bloomington, Indiana, 1970.

Bettelheim, B., and Janowitz, M. *Dynamics of prejudice.* New York: Warper, 1950.

Bogatz, G.A., and Ball, S. The second year of Sesame Street: A continuing evaluation. Educational Testing Service, November 1971.

Bucky, S.F., and Banta, T.J. Racial factors in test performance. *Developmental Psychology,* 1972, **6**, 7-13.

Campbell, A. *White attitudes toward black people.* Ann Arbor: Institute for Social Research, 1971.

Campbell, D. The indirect assessment of social attitudes. *Psychological Bulletin,* 1950, **47**, 15-38.

Cantor, G.N. Effects of familiarization on children's ratings of pictures of whites and blacks. *Child Development,* 1972, **43**, 1219-1229.

Carithers, M.W. School desegregation and racial cleavage, 1954-1970: A review of the literature. *Journal of Social Issues,* 1970, **26**, 25-47.

Clark, K.B. Desegregation: An appraisal of the evidence. *Journal of Social Issues,* 1953, **9**.

Clark, K.B. *Prejudice and your child.* Boston: Beacon, 1955.

Clark, K.B. 20 years after 'Brown'—the unresolved dilemma. *The New York Times,* May 17, 1974.

Clark, K.B., and Clark, M.P. Racial identification and preference in Negro children. In T.M. Newcomb and E.L. Hartley (Eds.), *Readings in social psychology.* New York: Holt, 1947.

Coleman, J.S., Campbell, E.Q., Hobson, C.J., McPartland, J., Mood, A.M., Weinfeid, F.D., and York, R.L. *Equality of educational opportunity.* Washington, D.C.: US Government Printing Office, 1966.

Colle, R. Negro image in the mass media: A case study in social change. *Journalism Quarterly,* 1968, **45**, 55-60.

College Study Group. Human Relations Test. Wayne University, 1948.

Collins, J. The effect of differential frequency of color adjective pairings on the subsequent rating of color meaning and racial attitude in preschool children. Unpublished Master's thesis, East Tennessee State University, 1972.

Comstock, G.A., and Rubinstein, E.A. (Eds.). *Television and social behavior.* Volume 3. Television and adolescent aggressiveness. Washington, D.C.: US Government Printing Office, 1971.

Cullen, R.J., Hannah, J.W., and Katzenmeyer, C.G. Development of picture attitude scale to assess attitudes of inner-city students, K-12, toward black and white persons at different socioeconomic levels. Paper presented at the American Educational Research Association Convention, 1971.

Dentler, R.A., and Elkins, C. Intergroup attitudes, academic performance, and racial composition. In R.A. Dentler, B. Mackler and M.E. Warshauer (Eds.), *Urban education.* New York: Praeger, 1967.

DeVries, D.L., and Edwards, K.J. Student teams: Integrating desegregated classrooms. Paper presented at the Annual Convention of the American Psychological Association, Montreal, August 1973.

Eddy, E.M. Attitudes towards desegregation among Southern students on a Northern campus. *Journal of Social Psychology,* 1964, **62**, 285-301.

Edwards, C.D., and Williams, J.E. Generalization between evaluative words associated with racial figures in preschool children. *Journal of Experimental Research in Personality,* 1970, **4**, 144-155.

Elrod, W. The effect of persuasive communication on interracial attitudes. *Comtemporary Education,* 1968, **39**, 148-151.

Evans, M.C., and Chein, I. The movie story game: A projective test of interracial attitudes for use with Negro and white children. Paper presented at the American Psychological Association meeting, Boston, 1948.

Flavell, J.H., Botkin, P., Fry, C., Wright, J., and Jarvis, P. *The development of role-taking and communications skills in children.* New York: Wiley, 1968.

Frenkel-Brunswik, E. A study of prejudice in children. *Human Relations,* 1948, **1**, 295-306.

Friedrich, L.K., and Stein, A.H. Aggressive and prosocial television programs and the natural behavior of preschool children. *Monographs of the Society for Research in Child Development,* 1973, **38**, No. 4.

Georgoff, J., and Jones, I. The curriculum as a factor in racial understanding. Summary report on the Gary, Indiana, Curriculum Research Project, November, 1967.

Goodman, M. *Race awareness in young children.* Second edition. New York: Crowell-Collier, 1964.

Gough, H.G., Harris, D.B., Martin, D.B., and Edwards, M. Children's ethnic attitudes. I: Relationship to certain personality factors. *Child Development,* 1950, **21**, 83-91.

Greenberg, H., Pierson, J., and Sherman, S. The effects of single-session education techniques on prejudice attitudes. *Journal of Educational Sociology,* 1957, **31**, 82-86.

Harding, J., Proshansky, H., Kutner, B., and Chein, I. Prejudice and ethnic relations. In G. Lindzey and E. Aronson (Eds.), *The handbook of social psychology.* Second edition Volume V Reading, Mass.: Addison-Wesley, 1969.

Harrison, M.G., Messe, L.A., and Stollak, G.E. The effects of racial composition and group size on interaction patterns in preschool children. Proceedings of the 79th Annual Convention of the American Psychological Association, 325-326, 1971.

Hauserman, N., Walen, S.R., and Behling, M. Reinforced racial integration in the first grade: A study in generalization. *Journal of Applied Behavior Analysis,* 1973, **6**, 193-200.

Hayes, M.L., and Conklin, M.E. Intergroup attitudes and experimental change. *Journal of Experimental Education,* 1953, **22**, 19-36.

Hohn, R.L. Perceptual training and its effect on racial preferences of kindergarten children. *Psychological Reports,* 1973, **32**, 435-441.

Horowitz, E.L., and Horowitz, R.E. Development of social attitudes in children. *Sociometry,* 1938, **1**, 301-338.

Hraba, J., and Grant, G. Black is beautiful: A reexamination of racial preference and identification. *Journal of Personality and Social Psychology,* 1970, **16**, 398-402.

Jansen, V.G., and Gallagher, J.J. The social choices of students in racially integrated classes for the culturally disadvantaged talented. *Exceptional Children,* 1966, **33**, 221-226.

Kagan, H.E. *Changing the attitude of Christian toward Jew: A psychological approach through religion.* New York: Columbia University Press, 1952.

Kates, S.L., and Diab, L.N. Authoritarian ideology and attitudes on parent-child relationships. *Journal of Abnormal Social Psychology,* 1955, **51**, 13-16.

Katz, I., Henchy, T., and Allen, H. Effects of race of tester, approval, disapproval, and need on Negro childrens learning. *Journal of Personlity and Social Psychology,* 1968, **8**, 38-42.

Katz, P.A. Perception of racial cues in preschool children: A new look. *Developmental Psychology,* 1973a, **8**, 295-299.

Katz, P.A. Stimulus predifferentiation and modification of children's racial attitudes. *Child Development,* 1973b, **44**, 232-237.

Katz, P.A., Johnson, J., and Parker, D. Racial attitudes and perception in black and white urban school children. Presented at the American

Psychological Association, September 1970.

Katz, P.A., Sohn, M., and Zalk, S.R. Perceptual concomitants of racial attitudes in urban grade-school children. *Developmental Psychology*, 1974, in press.

Katz, P.A., and Zalk, S.R. Doll preferences: An index of racial attitudes? *Journal of Educational Psychology*, 1974, in press.

Koslin, S., Amarel, M., and Ames, N. A distance measure of racial attitudes in primary grade children: An exploratory study. *Psychology in the Schools*, 1969, 6, 382-385.

Koslin, S., Koslin, B., Pargament, R., and Waxman, H. Classroom racial balance and students' interracial attitudes. *Journal of Sociology of Education*, 1972.

Kraus, S. Modifying prejudice: Attitude change as a function of the race of the communicator. *Audiovisual Communication Review*, 1960, 10, 12-22.

Kutner, B. Patterns of mental functioning associated with prejudice in children. *Psychological Monographs*, 1958, 72, No. 7.

Kutner, B., and Gordon, N. Cognitive functioning and prejudice: A nine-year follow-up study. *Sociometry*, 1964, 27, 66-74.

Leslie, L.L., Leslie, J.W., and Penfield, D.A. The effects of a student centered special curriculum upon the racial attitudes of sixth graders. *Journal of Experimental Education*, 1972, 41, 63-67.

Liebert, R.N., and Baron, R.A. Some immediate effects of televised violence on children's behavior. *Developmental Psychology*, 1972, 6, 469-475.

Litcher, J.H., and Johnson, D.W. Changes in attitudes toward Negroes of white elementary school students after use of multiethnic readers. *Journal of Educational Psychology*, 1969, 60, 148-152.

Mann, J.H. The differential nature of prejudice reduction. *Journal of Social Psychology*, 1960, 52, 339-343.

McAdoo, J.L. An exploratory study of racial attitude change in black preschool children using differential treatments. Ph.D. dissertation, University of Michigan, 1970.

McCandless, B.R., and Hoyt, J.M. Sex, ethnicity, and play preferences of preschool children. *Journal of Abnormal Social Psychology*, 1961, 62, 683-685.

McDowell, S. The willingness of Negro youths to associate with whites. Reported in M. Weinberg, *Desegregation research: An appraisal.* Phi Delta Kappa, Bloomington, Indiana, 1970.

McMurty, C.A., and Williams, J.E. The evaluation dimension of the affective meaning system of the preschool child. *Developmental Psychology*, 1972, 6, 238-246.

McNeill, J.D. Changes in ethnic reaction tendencies during high school. *Journal of Educational Research*, 1960, 53, 199-200.

Morland, J.K. A comparison of race awareness in Northern and Southern children. *American Journal of Orthopsychiatry*, 1966, 36, 22-31.

Murphy, G., and Likert, R. *Public opinion and the individual.* New York: Harper, 1938.

Mussen, P. Some personality and social factors related to changes in children's attitudes toward Negroes. *Journal of Abnormal and Social Psychology,* 1950, **45**, 423-441.

Myrdal, G. *An American dilemma: The Negro problem and modern democracy.* New York: Harper, 1944.

Pettigrew, T.F. Racially separate or together? *Journal of Social Issues,* 1969, **25**, 43-70.

Pierce, C. Race, deprivation and drug abuse in the U.S.A. *Proceedings of the Anglo-American Conference on Drug Abuse,* London: Royal Society of Medicine, 1973.

Porter, J. *Black child, white child: The development of racial attitudes.* Cambridge, Mass.: Harvard University Press, 1971.

Powell, G. *Black Monday's children.* New York: Appleton-Century-Crofts, 1973.

Proshansky, H. The development of intergroup attitudes. In I.W. Hoffman and M.L. Hoffman (Eds.), *Review of child development research.* Volume 2. New York: Russel Sage Foundation, 1966.

Radke, M., and Sutherland, J. Children's concepts and attitudes about minority and majority American groups. *Journal of Educational Psychology,* 1949, **40**, 449-468.

Radke, M., Sutherland, J., and Rosenberg, P. Racial attitudes of children. *Sociometry,* 1950, **13**, 154-171.

Renninger, C.A., and Williams, J.E. Black-white color connotations and race awareness in preschool children. *Perceptual and Motor Skills,* 1966, **22**, 771-785.

Rokeach, M. (Ed.) *The open and closed mind.* New York: Basic Books, 1960.

Roth, R.W. The effects of integral curriculum on Negro and white fifth grade students. Ph.D. dissertation, University of Michigan, 1969.

Sattler, J.M. Racial experimenter effects. In K.S. Miller and R.M. Dreger (Eds.), *Comparative studies of blacks and whites in the United States.* New York: Seminar Press, 1973.

Scott, W.A. Attitude measurement. In G. Lindzey and E. Aronson (Eds.), *The handbook of social psychology.* Second edition. Volume II . Reading, Mass. Addison-Wesley, 1968.

Shanahan, J.K. The effects of modifying black-white concept attitudes of black and white first grade subjects upon two measures of racial attitudes. *Dissertation Abstracts International,* 1972, **33**, 2181.

Sherif, M. Superordinate goals in the reduction of intergroup conflicts. *American Journal of Sociology,* 1958, **63**, 349-356.

Spencer, M.B., and Horowitz, F.D. Effects of systematic social and token reinforcement on the modification of racial and color concept attitudes in black and white preschool children. *Developmental Psychology,* 1973, **9**, 246-254.

Stabler, J., and Johnson, E. Children's perception of black and white boxes as a reflection of how they regard their own and others racial membership. Paper presented at the American Psychological Association meeting, Honolulu, August 1972.

Stabler, J.R., Johnson, E.E., Berke, M.A., and Baker, R.B. The relationship between race and perception of racially related stimuli in preschool children. *Child Development,* 1969, **40**, 1233-1239.

Stevenson, H.W., and Stevenson, N.G. Social interaction in an interracial nursery school. *Genetic Psychology Monographs,* 1960, **61**, 37-75.

Stevenson, H.W., and Stewart, E.C. A developmental study of racial awareness in young children. *Child Development,* 1958, **29**, 399-409.

Stotland, E., Katz, D., and Patchen, M. The reduction of prejudice through the arousal of self-insight. *Journal of Personality,* 1959, 27, 507-531.

Trubowitz, J. *Changing the racial attitudes of children.* New York: Praeger, 1969.

United States Commission on Civil Rights. *Racial isolation in the public schools.* Washington, D.C.: US Government Printing Office, 1967.

United States Commission on Civil Rights. *School desegregation in ten communities, a report.* June 1973.

Vaughan, G.M. Concept formations and ethnic awareness. *Journal of Genetic Psychology,* 1963, **103**, 93, 103.

Webster, S. The influence of interracial contact on social acceptance in a newly integrated school. *Journal of Educational Psychology,* 1961, **52**, 292-296.

Weinberg, M. *Desegregation research: An appraisal.* Bloomington, Indiana: Phi Delta Kappa, 1970.

Weiner, M.J., and Wright, F.E. Effects of undergoing arbitrary discrimination upon subsequent attitudes toward a minority group. *Journal of Applied Social Psychology,* 1973, **3**, 94-102.

Weiss, W. Effects of the mass media of communication. In G. Lindzey and E. Aronson (Eds.), *The handbook of social psychology.* Second edition. Volume V, Reading Mass.: Addison-Wesley, 1969.

White House Conference on Children. Report in *The New York Times,* December 19, 1970.

Wicker, A. Attitudes vs. actions: The relationship of verbal and overt behavioral responses to attitude objects. *Journal of Social Issues,* 1969, **25**, 41-78.

Williams, J.E. Connotations of color names among Negroes and Caucasians. *Journal of Perceptual and Motor Skills,* 1964, **18**, 721-731.

Williams, J.E. Connotations of color name and racial concepts. *Journal of Personality and Social Psychology,* 1966, **3**, 531-540.

Williams, J.E. Racial attitudes in preschool children: Modification via operant conditioning, and revised measurement procedure. Paper presented at the meeting of the American Psychological Association, Honolulu, September 1972.

Williams, J.E. Personal communication, 1973.

Williams, J.E., and Edwards, C.D. An exploratory study of the modification of color and racial concept attitudes in preschool children. *Child Development,* 1969, **40**, 737-750.

Williams, J., and Roberson, J.K. A method for assessing racial attitudes in preschool children. *Educational and Psychological Measurement,* 1967, **27**, 671-689.

Williams, J.E., and Rousseau, C.A. Evaluation and identification responses of Negro preschoolers to the colors black and white. *Perceptual and Motor Skills,* 1971, **33,** 587-599.

Williams, R.L. Cognitive and affective components of Southern Negro student's attitude toward academic integration. *Journal of Social Psychology,* 1968, **76,** 101-111.

Yancey, A.V. A study of racial attitudes in white first grade children. Unpublished paper, Pennsylvania State University, 1972.

Yando, R., Zegler, E., and Gates, M. The influence of Negro and white teachers rated as effective or noneffective on the performance of Negro and white lower-class children. *Developmental Psychology,* 1971, **5,** 290-299.

Yarrow, M.R., Campbell, J.D., and Yarrow, L.J. Acquisition of new norms: A study of racial desegregation. *Journal of Social Issues,* 1958, **14,** 8-28.

Zajonc, R.B. Attitudinal effects of mere exposure. *Journal of Personality and Social Psychology Monograph Supplement,* 1968, **9,** (2, Part 2).

Zajonc, R.B., Swap, W.C., Harrison, A.A., and Roberts, P. Limiting conditions of the exposure effect: Satiation and relativity. *Journal of Personality and Social Psychology,* 1971, **18,** 384-391.

Zimbardo, P., and Ebbeson, E.B. *Influencing attitudes and changing behavior.* Reading, Mass.: Addison-Wesley, 1969.

# Part IV
# Change in the Real World

# 8

# *The Role of Intergroup Contact in Change of Prejudice and Ethnic Relations*[1]

YEHUDA AMIR[2]

"Racially separate or together?" (Pettigrew, 1969) is the major concern of this article. This question has recently been raised and evaluated by many people and groups: political ideologists, philosophers, and national policy makers on the one hand, and social scientists on the other. All of them are in search of ways to reduce intergroup tension and ethnic prejudice and to improve relationships among national, cultural, and ethnic groups. The issue is of major social importance since the numerous inter- and intraethnic conflicts have drained much of the physical and mental resources of the involved groups, and additionally influence political stability and morale.

Can ethnic interaction and contact affect people in positive ways? Popular notions, various social ideologies, and diverse good will programs all offer an affirmative answer to this question, founded on the belief that the sheer interaction between people changes their beliefs and feelings toward each other. The change will at first comprise the interacting members only, but will later generalize to the entire ethnic group. Thus, if only one had the opportunity to communicate with others and to appreciate their way of life, understanding and consequently a reduction of prejudice would follow.

This view is exemplified in the objectives of various international exchange programs: student and professional exchanges, organized tours, visits to foreign countries, international conferences, the Olympic games; all of these are often thought to be effective in promoting international understanding because of the opportunities for contact that they afford. The basic premise is

[1] This paper is partly based on a previous article by the author (Amir, 1969).

[2] I would like to thank Aaron Bizman and Miriam Rivner who have worked with me on studies in this field for a number of years, and to Rachel Ben-Ari who prepared much of the material presented here. Their assistance, questions, speculations, and ideas can be found throughout this chapter. The same holds for many of the graduate students who prepared their dissertations on related topics under my supervision. Special appreciation is extended to S. Sharan and E. Greenfield who contributed many critical and useful remarks while reading drafts of this chapter. Finally, many thanks to the Department of Psychology at the University of Wisconsin, Madison, where this was written while I was on a sabbatical leave. The time and help they were able to provide enabled me to complete this chapter.

that personal contact can overcome difficulties where other efforts have failed. The same belief underlies some major national policy decisions such as integration in schools, housing projects, work situations, and the military.

On the other hand, there is evidence that intergroup contact does not necessarily reduce intergroup tension or prejudice. At times, it may even increase tension and cause violent outbreaks and racial riots. Bloom (1971) states that "there is probably more casual interracial contact in South Africa than in most multi-racial states, yet it would be a feat of irresponsibility to argue that race attitudes and behavior in South Africa are benign" (p. 163). Historical documentation of anti-Semitism in Europe, the attitude toward blacks in the South of the United States, or analysis of the communities in which ethnic riots broke out in the US in the 1960s offer additional examples. In these instances, contact does not seem to have fostered friendly relations and mutual understanding.

The purpose of the present chapter is threefold: (a) to summarize and evaluate studies of intergroup contact and its effect on ethnic attitudes and relations; (b) to evaluate the state of research in this area both with regard to theoretical and to methodological considerations; and (c) to generalize from these studies to our understanding of ethnic contact as a vehicle for changing intergroup relations and attitudes.

## GENERAL CONSIDERATIONS

Several reviews of the literature and theoretical considerations on the "contact" hypothesis have already been published. (Williams, 1947; Arnold Rose, 1948; Saenger, 1953; Allport, 1954; International Sociological Association, 1957; Cook, 1962, 1970; Amir, 1969; Harding, Proshansky, Kutner, and Chein, 1969; Pettigrew, 1969; Ashmore, 1970; Brigham and Weissbach, 1972; Simpson and Yinger, 1972; Watson, 1973). In addition, a number of summaries can be found on the effects of school desegregation on blacks, including the effects of ethnic contact on attitudes (Katz, 1964, 1968; Berkowitz, 1967; St. John and Smith, 1967; Weinberg, 1967, 1970; St. John, 1969; Carithers, 1970).

Most studies conducted in this area in the 1950s and early '60s found some reduction in some aspect of the prejudice toward the minority group as a result of a contact situation between two ethnic groups. Nevertheless, many investigators remarked that indiscriminate generalizations might be misleading and warned against drawing hasty conclusions. Results from later studies validated these evaluations. Later studies reported more frequently that intergroup contact had either no effect or even had a negative effect on ethnic attitudes and relationships.

This issue is important because social scientists as well as policy makers may generalize from the results of contact studies to the advisability of using ethnic contact as a major tool for social change. Pettigrew (1969), though aware that not all ethnic contact will be successful, feels that our aim should be "true integration" and not mere desegregation. He strongly argues that integration should be the major policy in our efforts to reduce intergroup conflict and hostility, such as that which exists between whites and blacks in the United States.

A number of recent investigators, however, have questioned whether the conditions necessary for achieving such "true integration" can actually be met (Eisenman and Pettigrew, 1969; Massey, 1972), whether this state could actually solve our racial problems (Bronfenbrenner, 1967; Zimbardo and Ebbeson, 1969; Jordan, 1973), and whether minority group members desire such a state (Teele and Mayo, 1969; Berreman, 1972).

The fact that many social scientists and policy makers accept interethnic contact as the main way of resolving conflict between ethnic groups is somewhat surprising. As Drake and Cayton (1962) observe: "Almost mystical faith in 'getting to know one another' as a solvent of racial tensions is very widespread" (p. 281). After all, there is enough evidence today to show that people prefer interaction with others who are similar to themselves (Newcomb, 1961; Byrne, 1969). Billig and Tajfel (1973) have lately shown that mere random "labeling" of a group makes a difference in preference and choice of individuals. Ethnic groups are definitely different from each other in one way or another. Even if we accept the notion that these differences are to a large extent assumed and not real (Rokeach, 1960), people will still prefer others who appear similar to themselves and will tend not to interact with those whom they perceive, even mistakenly, as different from themselves. One should also remember that intergroup contact may be needed primarily when intergroup conflict or tension is present (otherwise, why bother). In these cases, overall differences between the groups whether in status, belief, or perception actually do exist. Why then, should these groups want to interact across ethnic lines?

It is possible that we are not differentiating clearly between two separate aspects of the problem—the social-ideological and the scientific. The former issue pertains to the way we want to live or prefer society to be—namely, ethnically separate or together. The second orientation raises different and specific questions such as: (a) are people more likely to interact with their own group? (b) what needs can be satisfied by interactions with other groups? (c) under what conditions will intergroup contact occur? and (d) what will be the result of such contact?

The social-ideological aspects are contingent upon personal beliefs and social value systems, whereas answers to the other types of questions depend upon the scientific evidence that can be obtained. It is possible that one's personal beliefs would support ethnic togetherness—i.e., integration—though scientific findings may point in different directions. This does not mean that one has to relinquish one's ideas and social goals; it simply indicates the difficulties in achieving them. It also suggests that different ways or techniques should be explored to reach the same goals.

The research literature on ethnic contact indicates that not all social scientists have made a clear-cut differentiation between the ideological and scientific aspects. Some have assumed on the basis of their beliefs that ethnic integration was the primary or only way to resolve the intergroup conflicts of our time and then attempted to produce somewhat ambiguous evidence to try to prove their point. It is reasonable to assume that many social scientists are liberal and progressive in their social beliefs and therefore would like to see a world in which ethnic differences, prejudice, and discrimination are eliminated. However, it appears necessary to keep our social beliefs from influencing our scientific evaluations.

One thing that most social scientists in this field agree upon is that "contact" per se is an ambiguous and therefore an inadequate term, and that unqualified ethnic contact is not sufficient to produce positive changes. Sherif and Sherif (1953), for example, argued that "in any discussion on the effects of contact on intergroup attitudes, we must specify: What kind of contact? Contact in *what capacity*?" (p. 221). Cook and Selltiz (1955) have similarly noted the wide variability of contact situations that have been utilized in research. Instead of asking whether intergroup contact reduces prejudice, we should, according to Cook (1962), be asking "In what types of contact situations, with what kinds of representatives of the disliked group, will interaction and attitude change of specified types occur—and how will this vary for subjects of differing characteristics?" (p. 76).

Several investigators have attempted to specify what the relevant characteristics of specific content situations might be. Cook suggests that there are seven components that require analysis. These include: (a) degree of proximity between races, (b) direction and strength of the norms of one's own group toward interracial association, (c) expectations regarding interracial association believed to characterize authority figures, (d) relative status of groups, (e) interdependence requirements of the interacting individuals, (f) acquaintance potential, and (g) implications for social acceptance. Allport (1954) suggests an even more comprehensive list of 30 variables, including categories of contact such as quantitative aspects, status aspects, role aspects, the social atmosphere surrounding the contact, the personality of the individuals experiencing the contact, and areas of contact. In view of the complexity of the problem, we should not be surprised to find that many of these variables have not been extensively investigated. On the other hand, research has already advanced far enough to indicate what some of the most relevant factors might be.

Table I represents an attempt to schematize the various factors that have been studied. The table does not present a theoretical or conceptual framework, but rather a minimal list of relevant variables. Part 1 of the table enumerates the dependent variables, whereas Parts 2 and 3 specify the independent ones. The first column in Part 1 defines the specify the independent ones. The first column in Part 1 defines the specific group in the intergroup situation that is the primary focus of investigation—i.e., the minority or the majority group. Clearly, results of the same contact situation could be different for these two groups. The next two columns delineate the particular dimensions (i.e., cognitive, emotional, behavioral) of the attitude or behavior being studied. Once again, different results could be obtained for the different dimensions involved. The fourth column differentiates as to whether change is observed in the direction of the attitude or behavior, in their intensity, in the importance attributed to ethnic issues, or other yet unexplored aspects. The next column delineates the group toward which change is anticipated—i.e., own group (self-acceptance) or other group (prejudice). Then comes the specific content area involved—i.e., change with respect to social acceptance, work relations, business communications, legal equality, etc. The last column raises the question of generality: Is there a change in relation to the specific contact situation and interacting group(s) only or are there also generalizations to other ethnic groups and/or situations.

Part 2 of the table deals with the initial characteristics of the individuals and groups involved in the contact situation. Individuals may differ with respect to attitudes towards their own group, towards the other group, towards themselves as individuals, and towards the contact situation itself (Column 1). Differences in each of these aspects may affect the contact outcomes. The second column is similar to the previous one, only here the norm of the group and its effect upon the interacting individual is the focus of attention. The third and fourth columns take into account various personal characteristics, such as personality type, status variables, age, and sex, both on the individual and group levels. The fifth column specifies a number of special group characteristics, such as the ratio between the interacting groups, their respective goals, and other group distinctions. These five columns refer to one's own group. However, the same differentiations could also be made for the other group (last column).

Part 3 enumerates different situational variables, all of which have been studied and seem to affect the results of the ethnic contact. The first and second columns specify these situations and some of their characteristics. The succeeding review of the literature will largely follow the categorization presented here. The third column differentiates between ethnic contact, which can or cannot be avoided, and the fourth column distinguishes between enjoyable and nonenjoyable situations. This last factor may be considered as both a dependent and an independent variable: it is dependent on the contact situation, but in turn it affects the results of contact.

There are two major difficulties in trying to analyze the studies conducted on ethnic contact and to arrive at some generalizations. First, the variables involved in many studies are not or cannot be specified. Sometimes it is clear that a number of variables are included, but they cannot be

**Table 1.** Mapping of social-psychological factors in the study of change in prejudice and ethnic relations as a result of intergroup contact

| | Which Group | On which dimension | Of which function | In respect to | Toward which group | In what content area | With generalization on |
|---|---|---|---|---|---|---|---|
| **PART 1:** CHANGE OF | minority (low status) | cognitive | attitude | direction | own | different content areas (i.e., social, work, business, etc.) | same group and situation only |
| | majority (high status) | emotional | behavior | intensity | other | | groups outside contact experience |
| | no status difference | behavioral | (achievement, i.e., scholastic, job advancement) | salience (importance) of ethnic problem | | | situations outside contact experience |

Own Group  Other Group

| | In attitudes of the | | Of personal characteristic of the | | of group characteristics | | |
|---|---|---|---|---|---|---|---|
| | Individual | Group | Individual | Group | | | Other Group |
| | toward other group | (same as individual) | personality, i.e., authoritarianism | (same as individual) | ratio between ethnic groups | | (same as own group) |
| **PART 2:** WITH INITIAL | toward own group | (same as individual) | socio-economic status | | group goals, expectations, | | |
| | | | IQ | | | | |
| CHARACTER-ISTICS | toward self | | age | | | | |
| | | | sex | | | | |

250

| | toward contact | In situations of status differences between groups | At occasions of | When intergroup contact | And contact is |
|---|---|---|---|---|---|
| | other relevant status characteristics — educational or professional level | | work | | |
| | specific group distinctions, i.e., volunteers, enemy | competition vs. cooperation | school | | |
| | | intensity of contact (superficial vs. personal involvement) | recreation | can be avoided | rewarding, enjoyable |
| | | extent (amount) of contact | social | | |
| | | | housing | | neutral |
| | | institutional support (i.e., society, leaders, family, teachers) | religious | cannot be avoided | |
| PART 3: AS A RESULT OF CONTACT | | | military | | not rewarding |
| | | | training | | |

differentiated from each other. Another difficulty stems from the type of research conducted in this area. As most of the studies are field investigations, analyses of interactions between variables are almost nonexistent.

The effect of contact on intergroup relations is discussed under several subheadings. This particular organization of the subject follows to some extent the suggestions advanced earlier (Allport, 1954; Cook, 1962). Since opportunities for contact may be regarded as prerequisite for intergroup contact, a preliminary section on the opportunities for contact opens the discussion. Following this, topics related to the contact situation are discussed. These include the status of the interacting groups, cooperative and competitive factors, intimate versus casual contact, and the degree of institutional support. After this review, there is a discussion of the characteristics of the interacting individual, which includes considerations of the role of personality factors and initial attitudes. Specific techniques utilizing contact for ethnic change are then reviewed and summarized. The chapter closes with sections on research considerations and practical applications.

## OPPORTUNITIES FOR CONTACT

Cook (1962) formulated the phrase "acquaintance potential," which "refers to the opportunity provided by the situation for the participants to get to know and understand one another." (p. 75) Some contact situations provide little opportunity for attitude change. On the other hand, contacts of the same proximity and frequency in a different social setting or with different individuals may produce more psychologically meaningful communications and thereby facilitate attitudinal or behavioral changes.

The importance of this acquaintance potential has been observed in studies of various student exchange programs. Cook (1962), for example, in his study on the attitudes of foreign students in the United States, evaluated the differences between university settings in terms of the extent to which they provided opportunities for intergroup contact. He concluded that foreign students in small college communities had *more* personalized and frequent interactions with Americans than students in large communities. Situational differences in opportunity for contact appear to be important. The absence of such opportunities may account for negative findings obtained in some student exchange programs (e.g., National Education Association, 1932; Schild, 1962), whereas full involvement may produce favorable attitude change (Kelman, 1962). The importance of the opportunity for intergroup contact was also revealed in various housing projects (Deutsch and Collins, 1951; Wilner, Walkley, and Cook, 1952). In these studies, it was possible for white subjects who made contact with blacks to revise their initial attitudes and prejudices as a result of their contact. Such contact should, according to Ehrlich (1973), "increase the veridicality of intergroup imagery." If contact occurs under circumstances in which the perception of group similarities is limited, however, the possibility that stereotypes will be corrected through observation is reduced.

Barriers to intergroup contact, then, may arise from the situation itself. They may also be caused by a number of other factors, including tendencies to associate primarily with members of one's group, perception of out-group members as "invaders" (Wolf, 1957; 1960), and actual differences between groups in language, religion, and perceived status.

An example of in-group preference barriers was obtained by Weingrod (1965) in his Israeli study of differing ethnic groups. He found that they tended to establish minimal social contact with each other, despite living in proximity to each other, and noted that this was because immigrants' primary bonds were to people "like themselves." When questioned regarding their social relations with neighboring villagers, Iraqi settlers responded that they rarely saw the Moroccans, Tunisians, and Hungarians who lived *near* them, but that they tended to visit other Iraqi settlers who lived miles away.

The importance of how out-group members are perceived was raised by Wolf (1957) in regard to integrated housing projects. She found that although white attitudes toward living together with blacks showed a long-term trend in the direction of greater acceptance, this shift was not reflected in home-occupancy patterns. Her explanation of this phenomenon refers to the racial invasion-succession sequence, which is an example of a self-fulfilling prophecy. She found that middle-class home owners in the area, almost without exception, came to define the area as one destined to become predominantly Negro. It was hence assessed as "undesirable" either because whites did not wish to be a minority or because they felt that the neighborhood would lose its middle-class character. These factors may also account for the findings of Stinchcombe, McDill, and Walker (1969), which showed that as the percentage of black children in a school increase, so does the number of white children leaving the school.

The role of language and religious barriers in restricting opportunities for contact between different national or racial groups has been demonstrated in a number of studies. Brislin (1968), studying different ethnic groups in Guam, found that almost all people knowing only one language indicated few sociometric out-group choices, while among those knowing more than one language 50% had a few, while the other 50% had many out-group choices. Masuoka (1936) showed similarly that in Hawaii the knowledge of several languages allows a greater opportunity for interaction with people from other races. The Indian class structure exemplifies the importance of religious barriers. Anant (1972, 1973) has shown that more than 20 years after the official abolition of untouchability and guaranteed equality of status to all the citizens, the Hindus' attitudes towards physical contact with untouchables and interaction with them in the area of food and dining still show a considerable amount of resistance to interaction. It was found that the caste Hindus resolved the cognitive imbalance created by conflicting caste and legal rules by differentiating between those areas of interaction that are public and relatively peripheral and those that are relatively more personal, intimate, and central. Such differentiation between formal and informal contact was also demonstrated in American children by Rosenthal, Miller, and Teryenyi (1967).

One factor that may prove to be very important in ethnic contact situations, but has been almsot completely ignored, is the attitude of the interacting or the potentially interacting individuals toward ethnic contact. This attitude may be quite different from the general attitude towards the other group, although some correlation between these two attitudes probably does exist. A negative attitude towards the other groups initially restricts the probability of having contact with this group. Moreover, even if contact is established, there is a good chance of a consequent increase in the negative attitude. Thus, for people having strong negative attitudes toward another group, intergroup contact may not be desirable. The distinction between general attitude and attitude towards contact may be important, however, since the latter one may be easier to change. Then, when this attitude is positive (or at least not negative) and a more positive attitude toward contact is rewarded, a change in the attitude towards the other group may eventually be achieved. One way of affecting the attitude toward ethnic contact would be to increase the attractiveness of the contact situation (cf. the exchange theory proposed by Homans [1958]). In a school situation, for example, one could set up special facilities or laboratories in the integrated school. Such procedures or manipulations could facilitate positive attitudes towards the ethnic contact situation. Further research with regard to this variable is indicated.

The most extensive and complex treatment of the "opportunity" variable is found in the Cornell studies on contact by Williams (1964). These studies investigated, among other things, the relationships among opportunities for intergroup contact, actual intergroup interaction, and prejudices. With regard to opportunity for interaction, the following variables were studied: biographical determinants (e.g., sex, age, education, economic status), place of possible interaction (e.g., work, neighborhood, or organization), and personality variables (e.g., initial attitudes, sociability, authoritarianism). Thus, for example, it was found that (a) males are more likely than females to be exposed to intergroup contact, and (b) work situations provide the best opportunities for intergroup contact. With respect to personality variables, individuals who participate most in intergroup contact are the more sociable and relatively nonauthoritarian ones.

A number of studies have investigated characteristics of minority group members in relation to their desires for intergroup contact. Hartnett (1970) found that black students entering integrated colleges were more independent, more liberal, and more concerned with social injustice. In addition, they received higher scores on a scholastic aptitude test and higher educational aspirations than did students entering traditionally black colleges. In a study of black adults, Noel (1966) found that those who positively identify with their ethnic group are more favorably disposed toward integration and intergroup contact than blacks who express negative feelings toward their own ethnic group. In contrast, however, Rabushka (1969) found for both Chinese and Malay students in Malaya that those who express more ethnocentric attitudes are less willing to interact across ethnic lines. Similarly, in a study on Arab students in the United States, Ibrahim (1970) found that students who were less involved in affairs of the Organization of Arab Students tended to interact more with Americans. Thus, results with regard to group identity and contact in minority group members appear to be contradictory.

In sum, the above discussion suggests that if a positive change in ethnic relations is desired, opportunities for intergroup contact should be provided. Though it is quite clear that such contact does not necessarily produce positive results, without it changes cannot even be hoped for. Unfortunately, the more prejudiced a person is and the more vulnerable his personality makeup is, the less likely he is to have interethnic contacts. Therefore, techniques and procedures should be devised to make intergroup contact situations more attractive in order to overcome the resistance of those who are most prejudiced and therefore most in need of change. Furthermore, it is suggested that studying and manipulating attitudes towards the contact situation may be fruitful in terms of producing positive changes in ethnic relations.

## CHARACTERISTICS OF THE INTERACTING GROUPS

### Relative status of groups

Some of the concepts advanced by Allport (1954) and Allport and Kramer (1946) can serve as guiding principles in the entire subject of contact in attitude research. Allport (1954) pointed out that if contact is to serve as a factor in reducing prejudice it must be based on "equal status contact between majority and minority groups in the pursuit of common goals" (p. 281). If such contact is also supported by social institutions (such as the law, the community, etc.), its effect on attitude change may be pronounced.

The concept of "equal status" has been refined by Kramer (1950), who suggests differentiation between equality within and outside the specific contact situation. The relative status of group members within the contact situation may be the more important factor for attitude change. If this is the case, then more success in improving intergroup relations may be achievable, since it is easier to assign members of minority and majority groups to equal status positions *within* a given situation than to bring together individuals who are of equal socioeconomic and educational status outside of the contact situation. This view is supported in studies by Brophy (1945), Mannheimer and Williams (1949), and Amir, Bizman, and Rivner (1973).

Equal status between the interacting groups has generally been accepted by psychologists involved in this area as a prerequisite for positive change. It has been argued that although equal status does not necessarily produce better ethnic relations, positive change cannot be anticipated at all in its absence. Research findings are not always in accordance with these beliefs about equal status, however. A number of studies have obtained positive attitude change when status has been equal (e.g., Allport and Kramer, 1946; Man, 1959; Sayler, 1969) and negative change with unequal groups (e.g., Watson, 1950; Sapir, 1951). The direction of such changes may be a function of initial attitudes, as was demonstrated in a study of German adolescents whose attitudes became more positive after contact with French students, and more negative after contact with Italians (Wolf, 1961). The direction of change may not necessarily be reciprocal, as was shown in a study of American and Greek groups by Triandis and Vassiliou (1967). Moreover, positive changes in inter-group relations have been found in many studies (some to be discussed below) where real equal status did not exist, either within or outside the interaction. Thus, the concept of equal status seems to require reconsideration as to (a) its importance in inducing attitude change, and (b) its presumed role as a necessary prerequisite. If the latter factor is not as significant as previously believed, it may have valuable practical applications, because in real-life situations it is generally very difficult to establish equal status contact between dissimilar groups.

Social scientists have not yet suggested alternatives for the equal status assumptions, although one potentially positive characteristic of the contact situation, suggested by Cook (1970), is when the attributes of the members of the low-status or minority group contradict the prevailing stereotyped beliefs about them. This condition may be sufficient to produce positive changes even when the equal status condition is not met. Some recent findings by Amir, et al.[3] on effects of interpersonal contact between Jewish Israelis and Arabs from occupied territories support this supposition. A reduction in hostile attitudes occurred, even though the contact situation can hardly be defined as one of equal status between the groups. One possible explanation for this positive finding could be the discrepancy between very negative attributes expected of the opposite group and the actual characteristics exhibited in the contact situation itself. The degree of discrepancy between previously held stereotypes and present evaluations may be linearly related to the degree of attitude change obtained or they may be related in more complex ways (e.g., as suggested by Sherif and Sherif [1967]).

A large number of studies have been conducted that focus upon the

---

[3] Amir, Y., Bizman, A., and Rivner, M. Love thy enemy? A study on the effects of interpersonal contact between hostile groups. In preparation.

status of the interacting groups. These are reviewed below, according to the setting where contact occurs.

*Military Settings.* Data reported by Mannheimer and Williams (1949) from World War II indicated that white soldiers markedly changed their attitudes toward black soldiers after the two ethnic groups had been together in combat situations. When asked how they would feel if their company had included blacks as well as white platoons, 62% of the white soldiers who were in completely segregated units answered that they would dislike this very much, whereas only 7% of the white soldiers who had black platoons in their company gave the same answer. The question of whether it was a good idea to have both white and black platoons in combat companies was answered affirmatively by 18% of the soldiers in segregated units and by 64% of those who had black platoons in their company. Further evidence suggested that whether attitude change took place was not determined by *general* social characteristics (such as socioeconomic or educational level, status or role) but rather by factors that were *relevant* to the specific contact situation (i.e., the behavior of the black in his unit and his courage in combat). In this situation, the blacks were volunteers (a highly select group), whereas the white soldiers were drafted into the units. Thus, the discrepancy notion advanced above could also explain the results. As a special group, the blacks may well have produced a discrepancy for white soldiers between their previously held stereotypes and the presently evaluated characteristics of these soldiers, leading to a change in attitudes. Positive findings have also been reported in army studies by Roberts (1953) and among sailors at sea by Brophy (1945). This latter investigator found a marked reduction in anti-black prejudice among white seamen who had sailed one or more times with black sailors: 33% of those who had never sailed with blacks were rated as unprejudiced on an attitude scale. This proportion increased to 46% for those who had shipped once with blacks, 62% for those who had shipped twice, and 82% for those who had shipped five or more times. Special favorable conditions for a reduction in prejudice that could have affected these latter results were the highly intimate relations between the sailors, and a strict anti-segregation policy of the CIO union to which the sailors belonged. It is possible, however, that some kind of voluntary selection took place—i.e., that those who did not like to work with blacks left these union ships after one or two trips with them.

In a summary of findings regarding ethnic integration in the United States armed forces, Stillman (1969) noted that the armed forces advanced further than other groups in their integration policies and practices. He concluded, however, that although integration was successfully achieved in the military setting, races were still often segregated outside of it—i.e., in housing of army personnel and schooling for their children.

A study conducted in a different country (Amir, Bizman, and Rivner, 1973), however, obtained mostly negative findings. Fifty-one field platoons

numbering 1,411 soldiers, of the Israeli army, were studied in this investigation. At the beginning of basic training, soldiers of European ethnic origin
(higher-status group) revealed a significant preference for friends from their
own group, whereas soldiers of Middle-Eastern descent (lower-status group)
showed no ethnic preference. No overall significant change was found as a
result of contact. In certain specific situations, however, soldiers of European
origin did choose more Middle-Eastern friends after training. This occurred
with units of paratroopers comprised only of volunteers, and was similar to
the situation in the Mannheimer and Williams (1949) study. Thus, even in the
military, where equal status for everyone is stressed, ethnic preference does
not easily change. When special situational factors prevail that are conducive
to positive change, however, change can occur even in the absence of completely equal status.

Apparently, people do adapt themselves fairly well to changes in ethnic
relations if they are required to do so by social practice, by law, or by any
other authority. As Stillman (1969) points out, however, they can live part of
their daily life in integrated situations and simultaneously continue to function in different segregated settings. This phenomenon has been demonstrated
in other studies as well (e.g., Minard, 1952), and has bearing on the generality
or specificity of the change.

*School and Camp Settings.* Research on ethnic contact in school settings
has been the most extensively studied area of contact situations. As in the
military, integration in the schools is an area where equal status is generally
granted, but the social status of the interacting ethnic groups is, in most cases,
far from equal. In a summary of the results of studies on school desegregation, Carithers (1970) states:

> There is no general agreement about the effects of interracial contacts
> on attitude change. Some studies have found heightened tolerance;
> some heightened resistance; some no change. There seems to be,
> however, a general agreement that racial contact *per se* will not bring
> about increased tolerance or acceptance. (p. 41)

The reason for these contradictory results stems from the fact that
diverse and even unrelated independent variables (situations, subjects, geographic places, types of schools, and communities) have been studied in
different investigations. Furthermore, the theoretical sophistication and the
analyses in many of the contact studies in this area are quite shallow.
Carithers' criticism is to the point when she notes that most attitudinal
research on the effects of school desegregation has been too simplistic and
atheoretical, and has not paid sufficient attention to group interaction processes. Furthermore, in many of the studies it is very difficult to ascertain
which factors contributed to the results.

Research in the area has focused upon two major variables: attitude change of the majority group and self-concept change of the minority children. For each of these variables, positive as well as negative results are reported. We shall first review the attitude studies.

There have been many positive attitude change results, reported for all age levels, as a result of contact in school settings (e.g., Mann, 1959; Jansen and Gallagher, 1966; Koslin, Amarel, and Ames, 1969; Meltzer, 1970; Sisenwein, 1970; Holz, 1971; Miller, 1971; Aboud, Taylor, and Doumani, 1973). Similar results were reported following intergroup experience in summer camps (Bjerstedt, 1962; Yarrow, Campbell, and Yarrow, 1958a; Garti, 1973) and with YMCA groups (Williams, 1948). Some of these studies have obtained positive change in friendship choices (e.g., Jansen and Gallagher, 1966), in attitude scales (e.g., Mann, 1959), in increased behavioral similarity of the interacting groups (e.g., Koslin et al., 1969), and in perceptual and cognitive processes (e.g., Aboud et al., 1973). The latter two areas are quite interesting and merit some discussion. They suggest that emphasis on the salience of ethnic cues may be attenuated, which in turn may facilitate reduction of prejudice and promotion of better intergroup relations. Aboud, Taylor, and Doumani (1973) studied the effect of interethnic contact on the use of role and ethnic stereotypes in person perception. The subjects were French Canadians who studied in either French- (control group) or English-speaking (experimental group) schools. The authors emphasize the positive aspects of the contact situation, including equal status and extensive and multidimensional cross-cultural contact for the experimental group. Results showed that the group experiencing ethnic contact used fewer ethnic cues in person perception than the control group. Comparable results were reported by Holz (1971). Meltzer (1970) found that length of intergroup contact is related to the cognitions of the other group. He showed that initially unfamiliar people are perceived in a less fully developed, less differentiated and integrated fashion, and that increasing contact leads to more mature levels of interpersonal understanding and cognition. Miller (1973) found that members of the interacting groups may become more similar to each other in some respects as a result of the ethnic contact. His study of cooperative behavior of Indian and white children showed that their patterns of competitive behavior became more similar as a result of school integration. Aellen and Lambert (1969) found indications of some fusion of the two cultures among Canadian boys with mixed French-English parentage. The values subjects received from their parents showed the influence of both ethnic backgrounds. This may be one way that contact molds our cultures.

Nevertheless, many studies have reported no changes as a result of contact (Horowitz, 1936; Kupferer, 1954; Webster, 1961; Smith, 1969; Spiro and Lotan, 1970; Wade and Wilson, 1971; Amir, Rivner, Bizman, and

Sharan[4]). Several have obtained change in certain areas, but not others. Trubowitz (1969), in an evaluation of a special integration program for urban fourth and fifth graders, found positive change only when black and white children from similar socioeconomic backgrounds interacted. In a study of 300 English grade-school children, Durojaiye (1969) found positive change in the leadership area, but not in friendship choices. A similar differentiation between leadership and friendship choices was also obtained by Berkun and Meeland (1958). In addition to no change and mixed results, a few studies have reported more prejudice after contact than before. Webster (1961), for example, found that white subjects become less accepting of black high school students after six months of school integration. These varied results raise the question of which factors are required for successful attitude change to occur.

One factor that has been discussed in this regard is the optimal age level for contact to occur. From general studies on prejudice, we know that the ethnic attitudes develop relatively early in life (Horowitz, 1936). Therefore, a common sense answer to the question of age would be: the earlier the better, possibly even before negative ethnic attitudes are established. The little research available on this subject seems to support this common sense notion. Dwyer (1958) reported that in an interracial setting the lower the age, the more accommodating were the subjects. The US Commission on Civil Rights (1967) reported that both black and white students were more likely to favor desegregated classes if they were in desegregated classes, and that the effect was stronger for those who had entered desegregated classrooms early in their school careers. Brown and Johnson (1971), in a study of British children's contact with immigrants, found that six-year-old British children who had more interactions with immigrants were less prejudiced against them. These differences, significant for the six-year-old children, were found to a lesser extent at age four, but not at age three. The authors conclude that

> children with no close contacts with immigrants tend to rely on stereotypes derived from hearsay, or from atypical situations. Such stereotyping, and its associated prejudices, is diminished by close contact with immigrants, since there is then an opportunity to form evaluative judgments which are truly representative of the racial group. (p. 311).

This is evidence that ethnic differentiations are already made as early as age three. Thus, intergroup contact may sometimes be too late even at that age to change ethnic behavior. Although a study by Stevenson and Stevenson (1960) did not find that the social interaction of three-year-olds in an

---

[4] Amir, Y., Rivner, M., Bizman, A., and Sharan, S. Ethnic integration in the schools. In preparation.

intergroup setting is significantly influenced by race, a number of investigators found otherwise. Goodman (1952) studied children between the ages of 2.9 and 4.0 in biracial nursery schools and found that the black children displayed a systematic out-group identification. Feitelson, Weintraub, and Michaeli (1972) investigated how heterogeneous and homogeneous ethnic grouping influences social interactions. The subjects were 96 three-year-old Israeli children from two different ethnic origins in kindergartens specifically designed for research purposes. Results indicate that the minority (low-class) ethnic group in the heterogeneous setting remained very dependent on adults and showed less interactions as compared with either similar children in a homogeneous (segregated) setting or with children from the higher-status ethnic group. Furthermore, in the heterogeneous (ethnic contact) setting each of the two groups continued to interact *within* their own ethnic group. The researchers attribute the difficulties of the lower ethnic group in the contact situation to a lack of shared life experiences. By providing shared experiences, teachers were sometimes able to overcome these obstacles and achieve mutual play.

All of the above studies concentrated on possible changes in attitudes. Another major area of research interest has centered around the self-concept of children from the low-status group. Most studies have reported a more negative self-concept associated with integration. Clark and Clark (1952), for example, found that black children in a racially isolated school have a more positive concept of their own group and consequently a more substantial sense of self than those in a biracial situation. Similar results are reported by Berlin (1963), Coles (1963), Haggstrom (1963), Anderson (1966), Barber (1968), and Benson (1969). The Coleman report (1966) also noted a lower academic self-concept for black children in integrated schools despite the fact that they showed higher achievement than black children attending segregated schools. This more negative self-concept may include lower acceptance of self and others, more distrust, and stronger anti-social feelings.

Armstrong and Gregor (1964) discuss the negative influences of intergroup contact on the black student's personality development. They argue that: "One would expect Negro children insulated in an all-Negro environment during critical initial phases of socialization outside the family to have a more substantial conception of themselves and less intrapsychic tension" (pp. 70-71). Biracial school experience may shape certain defensive patterns in Negro personality development. Pugh (1972) presents convincing life experiences to illuminate this point. Havighurst and Neugarten (1967) agree but point out that segregated students "may be purchasing comfort now at the price of later discomfort, when they find themselves at a disadvantage in competing in interracial situations" (p. 373).

There are, however, two sides to the issue. Proshansky and Newton (1968) basically accept the above negative considerations but challenge the view that the intergroup contact in school necessarily lowers black self-identity. They feel that there are many possible influences that may degrade the black's self-image, aside from the contact itself. These influences include factors such as the attitudes of the white and the black teachers, differences in attitudes between the black student and the teacher, the teachers' expectations, the relationship between the ethnic groups in the school, etc. Moreover, some studies have obtained positive results. Lammers (1970) found that Indians studying in integrated schools were higher on self-acceptance than Indians in segregated schools. Chesler and Phyllip (1967), Walker (1969) and Williams and Byars (1970), found similar results for black populations. Abramson (1971) found that black students attending integrated schools had higher levels of aspiration as compared to students from segregated schools.

In an extensive study of blacks in the Northern United States Crain and Weisman (1972) showed that for Northern black students, integrated schools were more advantageous then segregated ones. The former tended to reduce anxiety, inhibition, and anger and increase the black's sense of security, feeling of internal control, and happiness. The authors claim tha even if black students in integrated schools are exposed to prejudice and mistreatment, these phenomena are even stronger and more evident in segregated neighborhoods. On the other hand, in the South the black student is unprepared for integration and therefore cannot benefit from it. Expectations learned in the South are unfulfilled by the integration experience, thus leaving the individual disoriented. An important factor stressed by Crain and Weisman that affects personality characteristics of blacks is the *consistency* of one's experience with integration. The most positive outcomes were reported for blacks who had attended both integrated elementary and integrated high schools. The next best situation was for both schools to be segregated. Studying in both types of school at one level or another comprised the worst situation.

Other studies found either inconsistencies or a lack of influence of interethnic contact on personality variables. James (1971) studied segregated and desegregated groups of black students and found that no differences on measures of self-concept were found between these groups after a year of contact. Similar results were reported by Scott (1969).

A study that throws some light on the contradictory results in this area was reported by Meketon (1969). She compared black students from three different, but comparable schools: a de facto segregated school, a peacefully integrated one, and a school in which conflict and overt hostility accompanied integration. Students in the peacefully integrated school were lower on measures of self-esteem than students in the segregated school and, contrary to prediction, were also lower than students in the "anxiety-arousing" integrated school. Thus, it is evident that intergroup contact in the school can have different influences on the self-esteem of the minority/low-status group as a result of different circumstances. Meketon explains these results in the light of the high level of morale and group support for the black students among the black parents and within the black community and their effectiveness upon motivation and self-esteem of the children.

*Residential Contact.* Studies have shown that residential ethnic contact, especially in public housing projects, produces some positive effects on the ethnic attitudes and relations of the residents involved (e.g., Deutsch and Collins, 1951; Jahoda and West, 1951; Wilner, Walkley, and Cook, 1952). In public housing projects one may assume a high degree of equal status contact. Wilner, Walkley, and Cook (1952) showed that white women who held blacks in high esteem were likely to interact more and perceive the social climate as favorable for interracial associations. Meer and Freedman (1966) found a favorable change in attitude toward interracial housing as a result of equal status contact. Caucasians who had Japanese neighbors were more likely to have Japanese house guests, to engage in mutual assistance, and were less anti-Japanese than those Caucasians who did not have Japanese neighbors (Irish, 1952). Anti-white prejudice among blacks diminished through intimate interracial contacts between persons equal in status in an integrated housing project (Works, 1961).

Studies on interracial housing in Israel demonstrated how specific circumstances are apt to influence the results of the contact. In a study carried out in new housing projects[5] better ethnic relations were found in neighborhoods with a relatively high economic status than in poorer neighborhoods. Shuval (1962) studied the relationships between neighbors in immigrant villages and new settlements and found that satisfaction with the neighborhood was related to the status attributed to the ethnic groups of neighbors. Contact with neighbors from the higher status group contributed to satisfaction whereas neighbors from lower status groups elicited dissatisfaction. Soen and Tishler (1968) report different findings regarding the relationship between contact and attitudes in another Israeli immigrant town. They found that most people in the community were relatively indifferent to the ethnic background of their neighbors, possibly because of status similarities between the groups. Secondly, the more heterogeneous the neighborhood, the more receptive were its inhabitants toward members of other ethnic groups.

One must be cautious in drawing final conclusions on the effect of neighborhood contact on ethnic relations, since several negative findings have also been reported. Herman (1968), for example, compared racial attitudes of sixth-grade white and black children living in segregated and integrated neighborhoods. He found no differences among blacks living in these two types of neighborhood in their attitudes toward whites. However, white children from integrated neighborhoods showed less tolerence toward other racial groups than did whites from segregated areas. In another study, no differences in attitude toward blacks between whites from segregated and integrated neighborhoods were found (Morris, 1970).

[5] L. Guttman, personal communication.

Noel (1971) suggests that since the United States is still mainly a racially segregated society, little equal status interracial contact actually occurs in housing and communities. The results of Bradburn, Sudman, Gockel, and Noel (1971) underscore the extremely small amount of interracial interaction that takes place in integrated neighborhoods.

An additional variable that should be considered in future research is the potential threat that each group elicits. If one or both of the interacting groups are perceived as threatening, the chance of a positive change will be reduced.

*Occupational Contact.* Occupational contact may also have a decisive effect on the attitude of people toward a minority group, depending on the differential occupational status of the members of the two ethnic groups. MacKenzie (1948) found that "acquaintance with Negroes of relatively high occupational status is an important factor in determining favorable attitudes of white persons toward Negroes" (p. 439). In this study, only 5% of war veterans who had made contact with unskilled blacks expressed favorable attitudes toward blacks. On the other hand, of those who had worked with blacks on a skilled level equal to their own, or had made personal acquaintance with skilled or professional blacks elsewhere, 64% gave favorable responses. Fifty-five percent of college students who had worked in the war industry with blacks occupying equal or higher level jobs expressed favorable attitudes toward blacks, as compared to only 13% of those who had not worked with blacks. White employers who had known professional blacks, such as physicians or teachers, were more favorably inclined toward blacks than those who had not met professional blacks.

Gundlach (1950) investigated the attitude change of whites toward their black co-workers when the blacks were no longer in inferior jobs, and found significant positive shifts in attitude. A study of white department store employees (Harding and Hogrefe, 1952) found that equal status work contact increased their willingness to work with Negroes but produced no change in their willingness to enter into other types of relationships. Both Palmore (1955) and Reed (1947) describe the process involved in introducing black workers into previously all-white organizations. In both studies the change initially produced some hostile feelings among white workers. However, management firmly maintained an employment policy of ethnic nondiscrimination and gradual acceptance occurred. In these studies a phenomenon characteristic of many ethnic contact situations is apparent—i.e., that people once introduced to interethnic contact generally accommodate to it and begin to accept it as a way of life. Whether they like it or not and whether they consequently change their ethnic attitudes and behavior is a different matter, however. Moreover, when changes does occur, it may be restricted to the contact situation itself.

The issue of how the minority group perceives the work situation has also been addressed in several studies. Katz, Goldston, and Benjamin (1958) and Katz and Benjamin (1960) created experimental work situations involving both white and black participants of equal status. They found that whites were more active and productive than blacks and directed their communications more to their own group, whereas blacks tended to address themselves more to whites than to other blacks. These investigators conclude that even when blacks are given objective evidence of equal mental ability they still tend to feel inadequate and may be less productive in interracial settings. Similar results were recently reported by Cohen (1972).

*Religious Settings.* All studies in church settings have reported positive changes. Leacock, Deutsch, and Fishman (1959) found that as a result of actual church contact, the feeling of the clergy toward blacks became more positive. Parker (1968) reported on highly positive ethnic relations in an integrated church in Chicago. Four factors seemed to be related to this process: the adoption of integration patterns in the area where the church is located, freedom of association in the church, the fairly high status of the membership, and positive leadership on the part of this church's ministers. Finally, a study by Irving (1973) of 390 clergymen from five denominations found that white and black ministers with more experience in both integrated educational institutions and churches reported more favorable attitudes towards the other race than those with less experience of this type.

*Contact with High-Status Representatives of a Minority Group.* Friendly contact between members of a majority (or high-status) group and high-status individuals of a minority (low-status) group tends to reduce prejudice toward the entire minority group. Some of the previously cited studies had this as one of their conditions: the army study (Mannheimer and Williams, 1949) with black volunteers, the residential study (Irish, 1952) with a highly selected group of Japanese-American newcomers, and the study by Smith (1943), which employed contact with prominent black families, leaders, and artists. All obtained positive findings. Unfortunately, there is no evidence as to what influence contact may have for the minority group members.

There are several other studies relevant to the attitudinal effects of the status of minorities. Morris (1970), studying segregated and integrated neighborhoods observed that white respondents who perceived the social class of blacks they knew as being higher than or equivalent to their own had more favorable attitudes than those who perceived black status as being lower than their own.

James (1955) found that white English pupils changed their attitudes favorably toward Africans in general after having an African teacher. Beard (1970) reported similar results. Contact with black university teachers coupled with lectures on problems of black children was more effective in bringing about a favorable ethnic change among white students than comparable contact with white teachers. Charley (1970), on the other hand, found no such change for elementary school children in a community where preference for white persons was very strong.

Exposure to high-status blacks may have been a major factor in a study by Holmes (1968) involving future white secondary teachers in two different types of experience with blacks. One group participated in a program that consisted of listening to black speakers, participating in discussions, and watching movies about blacks in urban societies. The other group visited homes, offices, school classrooms, and business establishments owned or populated predominantly by blacks. Both programs were effective in changing ethnic attitudes towards the blacks, relative to a control group. However the field contact was even more effective than the campus experience, emphasizing the importance of direct interpersonal contact in changing ethnic attitudes.

Mothers and children participating in a busing program that involved relatively high social status black children reported more interethnic friendships than other mothers and children (Jonsson, 1966). Nevo (1971) studied regular high school students from Jerusalem studying together with specially selected, talented students from low-status ethnic groups in Israel, and found no ethnic preferences. However, Young (1932), in one of the earliest studies on the effects of contact on attitude change, studied graduate students who had taken a course in American race relations, and "put [them] through a term's work consisting largely of unusual contacts with Negroes who were in startling contrast with popular racial stereotypes" (p. 16). They visited a black hospital and watched a skillful operation performed by a black doctor, they were entertained by a wealthy and cultured black couple, and they visited the charming home of an excellent black pianist. The results were characterized by considerable variability. Some students showed less prejudiced attitudes after the course than before it, whereas others acquired more prejudice.

The reason for these latter inconclusive results may be in part because the visiting students never became a real "part" of the black group they visited. They observed the blacks and evaluated their way of life as outsiders and not as fellow members of the same group. In relation to this, Sherif and Sherif (1953) observed that contact is likely to produce favorable attitude changes between members of socially distant groups only when the contact involves their

> joint participation as members in an in-group whose norms favor such participants ... In situations in which in-group members meet with members of an out-group held at considerable distance on a very limited scale, such as a tea party, there is little likelihood of change in attitudes of in-group members." (pp. 221-222)

There is, however, another possible explanation, which would emphasize the gap between the new experiences and the established ethnic attitudes. Following some of the notions advanced by Sherif and Sherif (1967), it would seem reasonable that if the gap between the new experience and the established attitude is too wide, the former may fall in the "latitude of rejection" and thereby not be influential. This may have been the case in this study.

*Summary of Studies Related to Status.* Most researchers would agree that in cases where no hindering conditions are present, equal status contact is likely to produce positive attitude changes. However, there is some doubt that equal status of the interacting groups is a completely essential requirement for change. What may be important is the gap between what is expected from the other group and what is actually perceived and experienced in the contact situation. Findings strongly suggest that people tend to adjust to ethnic interaction and accept it. Therefore, one may expect to find that people will accept one social situation in an integrated setting and reject another one in the same setting. Thus, generalization of attitude to diverse situations as a result of interethnic contact is not the rule but the exception. In real-life situations, ethnic contact is generally not in conditions of equal status. In these cases contact can generate negative effects on attitudes as well as on the self-concept of the minority or low-status group member. Equal status contact may also affect (a) change in the salience of or the importance attributed to one's own ethnic group, and (b) the "averaging" of different social attitudes or behavior in the interacting groups, thereby creating a new unified group. Finally, positive ethnic changes are more easily achieved when contact occurs with high-status individuals of the minority (or low-status) group.

## Cooperative and competitive factors

Contact situations may differ in the degree to which they involve cooperative and competitive factors such as common or conflicting goals, shared concerns and activities, mutual interdependence or competition in the achievement of objectives and needs. Many theorists (Williams, 1947; Allport, 1954; Ashmore, 1970) regard cooperative and competitive factors as extremely important considerations in intergroup contact, and some (e.g., Schild, 1962) have concluded that the most effective way of inducing lasting attitude changes among participants is through "participation" involving joint interaction, mutual interests, common goals, and active give-and-take contact situations. The role of cooperation has also been stressed in studies on intergroup contact among students in foreign countries (Selltiz and Cook, 1962).

Sherif was of the opinion that in many contact situations it was not sufficient to bring the antagonistic groups into contact but, rather, that they be given superordinate goals to make them cooperative across group lines. This was based on his finding (Sherif, 1967) that group conflicts were aggravated by contact even when the activities were satisfying. Only in situations with superordinate goals of high appeal did previously antagonistic groups cooperate across group lines. Such intergroup cooperation followed the realization that goals could not be attained with the resources of one group alone.

The principle of superordinate goals was involved in a study by Burnstein and McRae (1962), who sought to test the relationship between shared threat and the expression of prejudice. Subjects were placed in task-oriented, cooperative work groups under conditions of threat and nonthreat to the group. A black confederate was a member of each group. Under conditions of shared threat, the white members expressed less prejudice toward the black member. Thus, maintenance of group integrity may have served as the superordinate goal that caused white members to evaluate their black colleague more positively. Similarly, Sherif (1967) found that when intergroup hostility increased, solidarity and cooperativeness *within* each group also increased.

Ashmore (1970) reported that white subjects who were cooperatively interdependent with a black person had a more positive attitude toward him than did subjects who worked in the presence of a black person but without being interdependent with him. A strong emphasis on interracial, cooperative activity in desegregated schools elicits more favorable attitudes toward blacks and toward intergroup contact (Katz, 1955; Singer, 1964; Costin, 1966). The Katz study suggests, in addition, that when group competition factors were present, interracial hostility increased.

Witte (1972) compared two different grading systems in a college setting—one based on individual achievements, the other on the average score of one's group. Assigning of group grades in the experimental group was intended to encourage the development of peer tutoring activity and to elicit peer group support for academic cooperation and achievement. Results showed that intergroup interaction increased in the experimental group and there was a much higher rate of interracial acceptance.

The absence of mutual concern or common goals was a factor in studies by Dodd (1935) and Ram and Murphy (1952). Dodd (1935) examined attitude changes between ethnic groups in the Middle East. He reported that social distances are not determined by geographic proximity nor by abundance of contacts as much as by definite acts of a benevolent or malevolent sort between groups. Groups that lived side by side and had many commercial and other relations together were not nearly as close as groups who had fewer contacts but were felt to be benefactors.

Ram and Murphy (1952) showed that the contact between hostile groups in India did not reduce hatred or modify the attitudes of these groups. Nor did the type of experience with the other groups have any bearing on the attitude of these groups. Nor did the type of experience with the other groups have any bearing on the attitude. "Hindu refugees who suffered directly at Moslem hands seem to harbor no more hostility to Moslems than those who made good their escape without suffering any such personal misfortune" (p. 14). Murphy (1953) suggested that to be a good Hindu or Moslem implies accepting as true all the negative qualities and practices attributed by one's own group to the adversary. Therefore, new information concerning the adversary, such as that obtained through intergroup contact, will not alter—for better of worse—the initial attitude.

Common fate and shared intergroup situations do not neccessarily produce positive ethnic change in stress situations. Wertzer's (1971) study of black and white women who lived together during the last three months of their pregnancy in an interracial residence for unmarried mothers-to-be reported an increase in white negative attitudes toward blacks after contact.

A major problem with the common (and/or superordinate) approach is that such goals can be produced by means of experimental manipulations, but are rarely found in real-life situations. On the other hand, it is easier to find, plan, or invent real-life situations in which each ethnic group has *different* goals, which can be achieved only through intergroup contact.

An example of the above is provided by a current situation in the Middle East. Tens of thousands of Arabs from territories occupied by Israel during the 1967 war work daily in Israel side by side with Jewish employees. These groups can certainly be regarded as hostile to each other. Superordinate or even common goals are nonexistent. However, each group can achieve its own goals only by working interdependently, and they are aware of this. The Arabs working in Israel receive higher wages and dramatically improve their economic and social status. The Israelis realize that Arab labor greatly helps their economy and also raises their personal status because the low-level positions previously filled by Israelis are now held primarily by Arabs. Naturally, the question can be raised as to whether these conditions facilitate intergroup understanding. No answer to this is yet available, but a study by Amir *et al.* (see note 3) suggests an affirmative answer. If this proves true, new avenues for positive intergroup contact will be opened even for hostile groups, for it is much easier to create contact situations in which different groups achieve *different* important goals for themselves than situations involving the satisfaction of common or superordinate goals.

Common and superordinate goals are generally absent where the contact situation itself is in contradiction to the objectives and the immediate needs of one or more of the interacting groups. When the contact between the groups is to the disadvantage of one of them (i.e., economic disadvantage, lowered prestige or status level, etc.) or when goals are competitive and can be achieved only by undermining the other group, hostility and intergroup hatred ensues. The phenomena are evident in many studies on intergroup relations (e.g., Doise and Sinclair, 1973). Lawrence (1968) noted: "It is a sociological truism that inter-minority tensions are likely to be highest between those groups who are in closest competition with one another" (p. 103).

Sherif (1967) reported an experiment with groups of 12-year-olds where the basis of common or superordinate goals was absent and aspects of competition present. He found that the contact situations were utilized as occasions to exchange invectives, and degenerated beyond the point of reciprocal attribution of blame for existing tension. Kramer (cited in Allport, 1954, pp. 269-270) studied residential contact in Chicago in five zones in which the proximity of blacks and whites varied greatly. He showed that the closer the black and whites lived, the more frequent were spontaneous expressions of hostility. This was not due to negative stereotypes (these were weaker the nearer the white people lived to the blacks), but rather to fears that white children might associate more with blacks and that such intermixing might result in lowered status for whites.

A similar study was reported by Winder (1952), who was concerned with the effects of biracial contact on attitudes of white residents toward black "invaders." He found that

> attitude toward biracial contact became more hostile with increasing residential contact. The middle status residents were accepting in the unthreatened area, hostile in the threatened area and superficially accommodating in the invaded areas. The lower-status residents were more hostile in the invaded area. (p. 331)

Similar results were reported by Star (1967) in Chicago and by Orbell and Sherrill (1969) in Ohio.

In analyzing these residential studies we should keep in mind that the black population was not "invited" into the area; they were perceived as "invaders." The white population in these areas regarded the "invasion" as a threat to their status. The further away the white people lived from the invaded areas, the more remote the threat and therefore the less the fear and hostility expressed in their attitude toward the invading group. In Winder's (1952) study it is interesting to note the difference in the expressed attitudes of middle- and low-status residents. Whereas those of middle status were "superficially accommodating," those of lower status were most hostile toward the invaders. Perhaps the low-status whites competed more strongly with the blacks for the limited low-income housing facilities in the area, while the middle-status whites used better facilities, which blacks could not afford. Moreover, the actual contact between middle-status whites and blacks may have been more limited, because of the status differences, so that the whites' fear of intermixing and of consequent lowering of their status may not have been very strong. Some of the results in Burnstein and McRae's (1962) study parallel these findings.

Bradburn et al. (1971) found that blacks who faced hostile neighborhood reaction when they moved into neighborhoods were less happy with their neighborhoods and more willing to move out than blacks who either did not face such white hostility or who moved into a segregated black neighborhood. However, no differences in the general satisfactions of living in integrated or segregated neighborhoods could be detected among whites. Similarly, Grossman (1967) found no differences in the ethnic attitudes of white residents in ethnically changing areas as compared to those of residents in stable areas. The interpretation offered by Grossman for these results is interesting. He suggests that although residents of the changing area felt threatened by the new in-migration, they were willing to accept the in-migration that had already occurred, which was perceived in a somewhat positive light. Thus the effects of "threat" and of "contact" with Negro-Americans produced two equal and opposing forces for attitude change in these individuals. Somewhat similar to the above is St. John's (1966) interpre-tation of her finding of no relationship between degree of segregation and aspirations of black students. She suggests that two forces may work at cross-purposes for the black integrated child: "On the one hand, a more favorable social milieu may tend to raise the aspirations and achievement of Negro children. But on the other hand, they may be placed in an unfavorable competitive position that more than offsets such advantage" (p. 294). The effects of such competition upon white children can be seen in Lombardi's (1963) results where white students who failed in school after desegregation occurred became more negative toward blacks, possibly using them as scape-goats for their own failure and frustration.

The threat-producing "invasion" phenomenon may also be present in contact situations between natives of a country and immigrants. Kawwa (1968), for example, investigated the effects of interaction between local pupils and immigrants (Cypriots and black people) in England. The results indicated that children in mixed neighborhoods showed more negative atti-tudes than children who lived in an area where few, if any, immigrants lived.

Guggenheim and Hoem (1967) conducted a study on the effects of cross-cultural contact between Lapp and Norwegian children in northern Norway, comparing groups of Lapps with different degrees of contact with Norwegians. They found positive inter- and intragroup attitudes in all groups studied and no differences in self-esteem, but felt that more intensive contact might pose a threat to Lapp values and thus produce negative attitudes. Slann (1973) compared attitudes of two Israeli groups residing in Jerusaleum toward Jerusalemite Arabs. One group consisted of residents of European origin; the other had come to Israel from Arab countries. The latter group expressed consistently more negative attitudes toward Arabs, suggesting that those who had confronted an Arab minority as equals or superiors had a more liberal attitude than those who had themselves been a minority under Arab rule. Thus the "threat" may sometimes be a function of perception of own group status.

Paradoxically, equal status contact, which allegedly is a minimal require-ment for positive ethnic change, may itself be the basis for intergroup threat and produce negative changes. This occurs when an ethnic group of low social standing moves upwards and interacts with individuals of the out-group of higher social status. On this topic, Mack (1965) noted: "The rapid change in the status of the Negro will be accompanied by an increase in interracial conflict" (p. 40). He listed three necessary conditions for conflict: intergroup contact, intergroup competition, and visibility. Apparently, these three are present in a number of our intergroup situatjions. Katz and Cohen (1962) evaluated an experimental attempt to modify the behavior of blacks toward white teammates that backfired. The investigators felt that the training induction had threatened the whites' performance in two ways: first, the similarity between their own and their black partner's performance may have wounded their pride; second, the rising influence of the partner may have been experienced as a deprivation of power.

An interesting observation was made by the Deputy Mayor of Jerusalem[6] regarding relations between Israelis and Arabs in Jerusalem. He felt that as long as the conflict between Arabs and Israelis continues, no major municipal and social problem will arise and the different groups may live in relative peace together. The reason is that Arabs do not demand various rights they may have because they feel that this could be interpreted as "cooperating with the enemy." However, once peace is achieved, Arabs will undoubtedly demand their full and equal rights as citizens, which in turn may arouse resentment and even opposition among Israelis. Subsequent intergroup conflict may then ensue.

To sum up, it is evident that cooperative and competitive factors may be significant and decisive in situations of intergroup contact: cooperative factors and rewarding contact situations, especially if superordinate goals can be established, help to promote intergroup relations. To obtain a positive change, it may be sufficient for each group to achieve *different* goals through the intergroup contact. Competitive factors, including situations involving frustration, conflict, threat, or simply discontent hinder the improvement of intergroup relations. Also, a common fate for people from different groups may increase tension if the contact situation is frustrating or just not satisfying. Finally, equality of group status may in some cases produce frustration and conflict if one group feels threatened by it.

### Intimate versus casual contact

Intimate contact with members of another ethnic group is considered by many social-psychologists as one of the most potent agents for ethnic change. Ashmore (1970) feels that

> Intergroup friendships are often what brings about the reduction of prejudice . . . These friendships operate in two ways to reduce intergroup prejudice (1) Attraction to an individual member of a minority

---

[6]M. Benbenisty, personal communication.

group generalizes to other members and to the group as a whole . . . (2) Intergroup friendship causes a redeployment of motivation with respect to the intergroup attitude. The prejudiced person wants to hang onto his prejudice; but becoming friendly with a member of an out-group makes him more amenable to information that favors tolerance. (pp. 320-321).

Jordan (1973), summarizing the studies that he and his coworkers (Erb, 1970; Dell Orto, 1971; Jordan, 1971; Frechette, 1971; Williams, 1971; Radcliffe, 1973) conducted in this area, stated that "the degree of object-subject intimacy influences attitude favorableness more than any other variable." Many other studies support the importance of the intimacy factor (e.g., Brophy, 1945; Mannheimer and Williams, 1949; Stouffer *et al.*, 1949; Irish, 1952; Gray and Thompson, 1953; Neprash, 1953; James, 1955; Campbell, 1958; Kelly, Ferson, and Holtzman, 1958; Yarrow *et al.*, 1958a; Works, 1961; Segal, 1965; Hofman and Zak, 1969).

According to Jordan (1971), "Amount of contact *per se* leads to greater intensity of attitudes but does not produce favorableness of attitudes unless accompanied by enjoyment of the contact as well as perceived voluntariness of the contact" (p. 23). Thus, casual contact between ethnic groups in itself is not sufficient to change attitudes, nor does high frequency of contact necessarily foster positive ethnic relations. High frequency of contact may even increase prejudice. Anti-Semitism flourished in countries with large Jewish communities where contact between Jews and non-Jews was relatively frequent. The same is true in relation to anti-black feelings in the South, where the black population is more dense than in other parts of the United States. Pinkney (1963) doubts the assumption that prejudice by members of the dominant group toward minorities is correlated with the ratio of a minority in the population of a community. He presents data from four American cities to demonstrate that other factors aid in determining whether or not favorable attitudes will prevail. Smith (1969) found that the larger the proportion of Jews in the community, the stronger the negative stereotypes against them among white gentiles. Similar findings with regard to anti-Semitism are presented by Harlan (1942) and Saenger (1953).

Evidence that superficial intergroup contact does not necessarily produce changes in intergroup relations in everyday life is also found in public schools in the United States. Williams and Ryan (1954) reported that in many newly desegregated schools, relations between white and black students within the schools are matter-of-fact and sometimes even friendly, but the two groups go their separate ways outside of school. Similarly, Dwyer (1958), Lombardi (1963), St. John (1963), and Cole, Steinberg, and Burkheimer (1968) pointed out that contact between the ethnic groups in desegregated schools was quite superficial and therefore ineffective. On the other hand, the two major governmental studies on this topic (Coleman *et al.*, 1966; US Commission on

Civil Rights, 1967) reported some positive results—namely, that both whites and blacks who had experienced desegregated schooling favored desegregation more than others, that the longer such experience the more favorable the attitude, and that having a black friend was related to more positive attitudes towards blacks.

Another area where the intimacy factor may be involved is work situations. No changes in the overall attitudes of majority group members towards members of the minority group have been reported in most of the research in this area as a result of contact. Some investigators report no changes in attitude as a result of contact. Others find changes confined to work, 1948; Gundlach, 1950). Thus, white customers may treat black personnel in business interactions as equals, but still maintain their overall anti-black attitude (Saenger and Gilbert, 1950). Irish (1952) found that whether one worked or did not work with Japanese-Americans made no difference in one's attitude towards them, and people who had business associations with Japanese-Americans had only a slightly, but not significantly, more favorable attitude towards them than did those who had no such contact. Only a slight relationship was found between work experience and attitudes towards blacks among white housewives in a segregated biracial housing project (Deutsch and Collins, 1951).

Why does intergroup contact in work situations produce only limited attitude changes? One possible explanation may be that work situations involve superficial interethnic contact; even when the relationship becomes more personal, it is generally confined to the work situation only.

Casual intergroup relationships were probably prevalent in David's (1971) study involving American groups living in five Far-Eastern countries. The results did not indicate any particular preference among these American groups for the ethnic group of the country in which they lived.

Selltiz and Cook (1962) studying the effects of an orientation program on attitudes of foreign students toward Americans found no change. As in the previous study, lack of intimate relations between students and hosts could have contributed to the negative results.

On the other hand, several other studies suggest that frequency of contact and proximity in living quarters may be related to reduction in prejudice. Greater conceptual clarity of this problem can be obtained by reference to Cook's (1962) important distinction between the characteristics of the contact situation itself and the characteristics of the interaction that transpires within the situation. Proximity seems to produce more frequent intergroup contact. Frequency of contact can in some cases produce intimate relationships and advance better intergroup relations, but in other instances it may strengthen prejudice and ethnic hostility.

Wilner et al. (1952), for example, found a clear-cut relationship between the relative proximity in living quarters between a white and black family and the amount of attitude change: the closer a white and black family lived to each other, the more frequent the contact between them and the larger the favorable shift in attitude of the white residents towards the blacks. Basu and Ames (1970) found that Indian students' attitudes towards Americans were positively related to amount of contact with Americans. In a different cross-cultural setting Brislin (1968; 1971) and Stouffer et al. (1949) found similar results.

An interesting study in this area, reported by Chadwick-Jones (1962), investigated attitudes of English people towards a minority group of Italian workers. Attitudes were found to be related to proximity in a curvilinear fashion. People who lived relatively far from the Italian group and who had only slight contact with them were indifferent or expressed unclear attitudes towards the Italian group; those who were living near the center of town and saw the Italians in groups in restaurants or in movie houses expressed disapproval regarding their behavior and clothing; those who had experienced frequent face-to-face contact expressed positive attitudes and also differentiated more between individual members of the minority group.

Changed perceptions were also obtained in a study by Prontho and Melikan (1955) who found that Lebanese students attributed to Americans new characteristics after interactions. These new characteristics related more directly to personality (e.g., sociable or jolly) than to national ·stereotypes (e.g., democratic or industrial). Similar results were reported by Graham (1951).

One area where more intimate contact might be expected is in residential settings. In this regard, Merton, West, and Jahoda (cited in Jahoda and West, 1951) found that previous experience of living in an unsegregated project is associated with a more favorable attitude towards biracial housing. A positive relation emerged between length of a person's residence and the number of his friends among the tenants of the other race. Moreover, the stronger the informal contact between the races, the less the prejudice between them. Results from the Deutsch and Collins study (1951) are similar, and showed that segregation was favored by only 40% of the tenants in integrated projects as contrasted with 70% of the tenants in segregated projects. Much greater intimacy between black and white housewives was found in the integrated projects, and the stereotyping of blacks by whites was less common where contact between the races was more intimate. Also, those who had closer contact with members of the other ethnic group felt that the differences between the races are smaller.

But even in more intimate contact situations, any change of attitude may be relatively limited. Thus, Wilner et al. (1952) reported that occupants of both the building-integrated and building-segregated housing projects desired for the future only that type of occupancy pattern that they had experienced. Another study (Meer and Freedman, 1966) found that attitudes with regard to interracial living changed favorably as a result of intergroup contact on an equal status basis, but no such changes occurred in other aspects of the ethnic attitude. What may have occurred in these cases is that people adjusted to and began to accept the situation in which they were involved without necessarily changing their belief and attitude system towards the other group.

Elaborating on this problem, Cook (1963) stated that

> while individuals rather quickly come to accept and even approve of association with members of another social group in situations of the type where they have experienced such association, this approval is not likely to be generalized to other situations unless the individuals have quite close personal relationships with members of the other group. (pp. 41-42)

Cook quotes Minard's (1952) description of a mining community in West Virginia as a particularly dramatic example of the extent to which behavior may be limited to a specific situation. White and black miners worked amicably together in mixed teams, sometimes having a black supervising white workers. Yet the workers separated at the mine shaft and led their above-ground lives in complete segregation.

The problem of generalization is also exemplified in the following two studies. Chen, Shapiro and Hausdorff (1970) investigated the effect of intergroup contact between Israelis and foreign students at an Israeli university. The amount of contact with Israelis was not related to the foreign students' attitude towards the country and its ideological aspects. Generalization was found only when contact with Israelis was extensive and positive. Kawwa (1968) also obtained no generalization of attitude from the individual to the group.

To summarize, the evidence suggests that intergroup contact may produce different forms of relationships. At one end are the casual and superficial relations; at the other end, the ego-involving and intimate relations. Proximity and frequency of contact as well as other factors may exert decisive influence in determining both the amount and nature of intergroup contact. Casual intergroup contact typically has little or no effect on basic attitude change. When such contact is frequent, it may even reinforce negative attitudes, especially when it occurs between nonequal status groups. Intimate contact, on the other hand, tends to produce favorable changes, though they may be restricted to the contact situation. It is also possible that intimate relationships involve enjoyment and satisfaction from the contact situation, which in turn may be the main antecedent for change. When the intimate relations are established, the in-group member no longer perceives the member of the out-group in terms of stereotypes but begins to consider him as an individual and thereby discovers many areas of similarity.

## The role of institutional support

The effectiveness of interracial contact is greatly increased if the contact is sanctioned by institutional support. The support may come from the law, a custom, a spokesman for the community, or simply from a social atmosphere and a general public agreement. In some cases, governmental policy may be the influential factor (Israel Government, Ministry of Education, 1970; Anant, 1972; Ogunlade, 1972). However, in many intergroup situations neither the social atmosphere nor institutions favor intergroup mixing for a variety of reasons. When such a state occurs, it may strongly hinder the development of successful intergroup contact and ethnic integration.

Why is institutional support for ethnic interaction and reducing of prejudice so important? Partly, at least, because it produces social desirability and consequently people will be more willing to act in the required direction. Once positive intergroup behavior has taken place, attitude change may follow. Aronson (1972) explains this process by invoking a principle of inevitability:

> If I know that you and I will inevitably be in close contact, and I don't like you, I will experience dissonance. In order to reduce dissonance, I will try to convince myself that you are not as bad as I had previously thought. I will set about looking for your positive characteristics, and will try to ignore, or minimize the importance of, your negative characteristics. Accordingly, the mere fact that I know that I must at some point be in *close contact* with you will force me to change my prejudiced attitudes about you, *all other things being equal.* (p. 194)

Since Aronson considers inevitability so important, he feels that institutional support for ethnic integration should be uncompromising. Pettigrew's work supports this evaluation. He found that "violence has generally resulted in localities where at least some of the authorities give prior hints that they would gladly return to segregation if disturbances occurred; peaceful integration has generally followed firm and forceful leadership" (1961, p. 105).

Institutional support probably did produce favorable attitude changes recorded in a number of studies (Horowitz, 1936; Brophy, 1945; Minard, 1952; Wilner et al., 1952; James, 1955; Parker, 1968; Trubowitz, 1969). Yarrow et al. (1958b), in summary of their findings on contact, state: "The development of new norms is facilitated if what is 'appropriate' and 'expected' in the situation is clarified immediately by the persons in authority roles. The definition of the situation is established effectively by leader model, by leader direction, by manipulation of physical environment" (p. 60). A number of investigators have substantiated this (Whitmore, 1957; Campbell, 1958; Sartain, 1966) by finding a relationship between the attitudes of authority figures (e.g., parents, friends, or peers) and the child's attitude with regard to minority groups.

The importance of the social norm as manifested by an "authority" was brought out clearly in the previously cited study by Deutsch and Collins (1951). In the segregated housing projects, white people expressed the view that they would not mix with blacks because "it just isn't done" or "they'd think you're crazy." In many cases, it was clear that the white residents had actually no objection to mixing with the blacks, but would not dare to do so publicly. In the integrated project, on the other hand, people felt quite differently. Both the social atmosphere and the official policy of the housing authority were in favor of social integration. As expected, there was marked reduction in prejudice and in stereotyped opinions among the residents of the integrated project. Similarly, Wilner, Walkley, and Cook (1952) reported that white housewives in nonsegregated housing developments who perceived the norms as favoring interracial contact were less anti-black than housewives who felt that the norms called for avoidance of interracial contact. Proximity seems to be related to this: white women who lived closer to blacks had more opportunities to observe other white women associating with blacks, thereby accepting that interracial activity was socially approved.

On the other hand, Eisenman (1965) argued that real-life situations are typically more complicated than was the case in the Deutsch and Collins housing study. In some instances, contact leads to an increase in prejodice rather than a reduction. Eisenman cited evidence from different studies to show that other situational and personality variables are related to the maintenance of prejudice. The role of such factors are considered in the following section.

## CHARACTERISTICS OF INTERACTING INDIVIDUALS

### Personality factors

It can hardly be expected that contact will be so effective as to change the attitudes of all the members of the interacting groups. There are always factors that resist or counteract the influence of the contact. Certain personalities, too, will not be affected positively by interracial contact. Apparently, the personality of the interacting individual can play a major role in determining the outcome of the contact situation, but studies on this topic are suprisingly rare.

Mussen (1950) studied the effect of contact on attitudes of white boys after a four-week stay of white and Negro boys in an unsegregated summer camp. The group as a whole did not change its attitude towards blacks. About 25% of the white boys showed more prejudice after the camp experience, and about the same percentage became less prejudiced. There was no question of unequal status because there was no racial discrimination in the camp and everyone enjoyed the same privileges and was treated equally. Nevertheless, positive changes equaled negative ones. The boys who became less prejudiced were those who enjoyed their stay at the camp more and who made better adjustments at the camp. The boys who became more prejudiced, on the other hand, exhibited more aggression and greater need to defy authority in their test-responses. This suggests that personality factors may be related to the direction of attitude change obtained.

Garti (1973), on the other hand, found no relationship between authoritarian personality structure and change in ethnic attitude in a study conducted in a summer camp in Israel. Thus, it seems that although personality may have an influence on the outcomes of contact, research is still too scarce to enable us to draw any clear conclusions on this topic.

## Intensity of initial attitude

Mussen's (1950) study presented an interesting phenomenon. Although he found no relationship between contact and attitude change, contact was clearly related to the intensity of the initial attitude. This phenomenon has also been found in several other studies. Hogrefe, Evans, and Chein (1947) found that white children who attended an interracial play center once a week for several months did not differ from a control group in attitudes towards blacks as measured by a social distance scale. However, a projective test showed a larger proportion of play-center children either very favorable to racial segregation in play situations or strongly opposed to it. Taylor (cited in Cook, 1963, p. 46) reported that white residents who were relatively favorable towards blacks at the time the first black family was about to move into their block became even more favorable after the blacks had been living there a few weeks, while those who were initially unfavorable became still more unfavorable. Similarly, Lombardi (1963) failed to find any overall changes in attitudes of white children in a newly desegregated school. However, children of less educated mothers changed in a positive direction. Jordan (1971) also found that the amount of contact did not produce changes in the direction of attitudes, but rather in their intensity.

Two studies demonstrated the importance of the initial attitude in contact situations, though not with ethnic groups. Festinger and Kelley (1951) studied contact in a housing project where residents expressed a high degree of hostility towards each other. Results indicated that people who were favorable towards contact became less hostile whereas those who were in the program but unfavorable towards it became even more hostile in their attitudes. Guttman and Foa (1951) investigated the attitude of the Israel, population towards government employees and found that although there was no overall change in the direction of attitudes, their intensity increased with the amount of contact: the more contact, the more extreme the attitude. Shift in attitude towards the extreme as a result of specific contact situations was also reported by Deutsch and Collins (1951) and by Wilner *et al.* (1952).

The intensity of the initial attitude was also investigated in the Cornell studies (Williams, 1964), which tried to relate degrees of ethnic attitudes both to contact opportunities and to attitude change. Summarizing findings on these topics, Williams commented:

> It seems safe, if not surprising, to conclude that when ethnic contacts do occur, it will be the less prejudiced persons, on the average, who are most likely to develop those close associations and friendships that will, on the whole, contribute to further reduction of stereo-typing, categorical hostility, and feelings of social distance. (p. 201)

The direction of change was different for the more prejudiced individuals.

In summary, two generalizations may be drawn: (1) Contact between ethnic groups may intensify the initial attitude of an individual: (2) The intensity of an individual's initial attitude may exert decisive influence on the outcome of the ethnic contact.

## SPECIFIC TECHNIQUES UTILIZING CONTACT FOR ETHNIC CHANGE

Within the last five years, a relatively large number of studies have been conducted in an attempt to discover or evaluate specific techniques designed to promote better ethnic relations and understanding by means of intergroup contact. Apparently, the present general appraisal is that ethnic intergroup contact per se will not achieve the desired results, hence the effort to reappraise the old and discover new methods. Some of these experiments will be reviewed in this section.

A number of studies utilizing specific techniques have already been mentioned. Some involved contact between whites and high-status blacks (Young, 1932; Smith, 1943; James, 1955). Many other techniques have also been tried. Katz and Cohen (1962), for example, employed a special program of assertiveness and authority training on blacks in biracial teams. Witte (1972) utilized group-reward techniques. The pattern of results in these studies is remininiscent of those obtained in areas of intergroup contact. Some studies showed positive results (Smith, 1943; James, 1955; Witte, 1972), others found no major effects (Young, 1932), and some were partly positive and partly negative (Katz and Cohen, 1962). The same trend of qualified results can be found in more recent studies as well.

Williams, Cormier, Sapp, and Andrews (1971) appraised the effects of four treatment conditions (contingent teacher reinforcement, teacher rein-forcement, role modeling, group process) on biracial sociometric measures and behavioral interaction with junior high school students in Tennessee. A positive before-after change was obtained on both the sociometric and the behavioral measures; however, differences between groups, including the no-treatment control group, were not significant.

Lilly (1970) studied different methods for improving social acceptance of children of low sociometric status and low academic achievement. The results indicated that gains in social acceptance could be achieved by low-status children by means of the investigated methods, but such gains were not lasting.

Roth's (1969) study concentrated on the effects of a curriculum that presented information about black contributions to society. Results showed that black students exposed to such a curriculum improved their self-concept more than black students not exposed to it, but whites exposed to this curriculum did not significantly improve their attitudes towards blacks unless they were also in integrated classes. This suggests that in order to induce positive changes, a *number* of positive factors may be needed in the contact situation.

Many situations with adults have made use of techniques variously referred to as sensitivity training, encounter, or T-groups. The basic assumptions underlying the use of sensitivity training for reduction of intergroup tensions and prejudice is as follows: participants first examine and observe their own feelings; they then listen to and (hopefully) understand the out-group member's point of view after being allowed to express some of their hostilities, including those toward out-group members. Insight into one's own motives, acceptance of one's own self, and sensitivity to the needs of others, then, are believed to be the antecedents of a positive change in intergroup attitude and behavior. Thus, the purpose of the sensitivity group is to help bridge intergroup barriers and to reduce feelings of mutual hostility.

Evidence is lacking as to whether this process actually occurs in sensitivity training, although studies in this area do tend to obtain positive findings. Most studies showed more acceptance of the self, of out-group members, and of the out-group as a whole as a result of intergroup sensitivity training (I. Rubin, 1967; I.M. Rubin, 1967; Carkhuff and Banks, 1970; Dodson, 1971; Beasely, 1972; Elenewsky, 1972; Steele and Nash, 1972). One study (Diller, 1971) found more acceptance of self and of out-group members, but no change on direct measures of prejudice, whereas another (Gamez, 1970) conducted with Mexican-American and Anglo-American college students found no changes as a result of such training.

A number of studies have used sensitivity training in an international frame-work. Doob and Foltz (1973), for example, assembled Irish Catholic and Protestant citizens of Belfast in order to help them learn more about their own behavior and understand their political opponents' situation. These authors discuss the difficulties involved in setting up such an enterprise. In another study Doob (1971) convened influential people from Ethiopia, Kenya, and Somalia for sensitivity training and discussions on the resolution of the conflict between their nations. Most of the original participants were interviewed a year later. Doob concluded that the training was worthwhile and that it made some contribution in the disputes of the above-mentioned nations. Lakin, Lomranz, and Lieberman (1969) investigated the effects of sensitivity training of groups of Jews and Arabs in Israel. Participants expressed favorable attitudes and evaluations towards the training. The authors, however, felt that the participants were too involved in their national conflict to enable them to accept, or even to understand, the point of view of the out-group members; therefore, the actual achievements in conflict reduction were small.

Another line of research has employed an instruction period in which members of one group are familiarized with the norms, expectations, or behavior patterns of the other group. This technique was derived from Triandis' notion of the "subjective culture"—i.e., each group's characteristic way of perceiving the social environment. One study (Davis and Triandis, 1971) found that subjective cultural measures (perception, evaluation, and attitudes towards members of other groups, as well as basic value and belief systems) predicted success in intergroup activities. This suggests that such measures might fruitfully be used for selection or training purposes in intergroup relations. They might also be used to decide which groups to involve in intergroup contact. In general, the more the gap between the subjective cultures of two groups can be reduced, the greater the probability that interactions between them will lead to successful results. Triandis and Malpass (1971) have proposed a variety of training methods to increase the probability that each group will "understand" the other one better.

Similar techniques have been used in an international context. Collett (1971) tested the hypothesis that Arabs would be more favorably inclined to Englishmen who behaved nonverbally, in a manner common in Arab society. Two groups of Englishmen were involved—one that had received training in nonverbal behavior and another one that had been studying unstructured material related to the Arab world. Results indicated that Arabs significantly preferred members of the other ethnic group who had received nonverbal training. Chemers, Fiedler, Lekhyananda, and Stolurow (1966) studied ROTC cadets who received either geographic information about Arab culture or culture assimilator training (Fiedler, Mitchell, Triandis, 1971). The latter kind of training involved verbal discrimination of culturally relevant cues and generalization within culturally relevant concepts. When the cadets were required to perform different cooperative tasks in small groups that included Arabs, the culture assimilator trained cadets achieved higher levels of performance and rapport with the Arabs than their geographically trained counterparts. It should be mentioned that these differences were achieved after only three hours of training.

In sum, studies reviewed in this section suggest that practical techniques can be devised to promote better intergroup relations and understanding. Techniques like sensitivity training and others often appear quite elaborate and too expensive to be used on a large scale or for an entire population, yet they could quite easily be introduced in structured settings such as schools, the military, or in work organizations. In considering cost factors, one should also take into account the price society pays for not introducing such techniques. A high-priced technique that could change intergroup tensions may prove to be the least expensive. It thus appears worthwhile to develop and test additional techniques for ethnic change via intergroup contact. Selection of such techniques should preferably be made on the basis of theories of ethnic attitude formation or change.

## OTHER VARIABLES

There are a number of variables not discussed heretofore that deserve mention though they have received scant attention from investigators. The optimal proportions of the interacting groups is one such factor. The Coleman report (1966) suggests a 60:40 ratio of whites and blacks as the optimum proportions for producing attitude change. Pettigrew and Pajonas (1964) suggested an optimum level of 20% to 45% blacks in integrated schools. However, little evidence can be provided on this topic and therefore such suggestions are to be regarded as very tentative. Gottlieb and Tenhouten (1965) showed that in three high schools the different ratio of blacks (99%, 50%, 5%) strongly affected both the extracurricular activities and the prestige ratings of activities for black students. In the high-percentage black school, activities and in-group memberships were the most important factors for social achievement and leadership; in the balanced school, the important factors were athletics and party going; and in the low-percentage black group, being a good student was most important (incidentally, in all schools activities were *within* the ethnic group).

Different results were reported by Zirkel and Moses (1971), who selected black, Puerto-Rican, and white students from fifth and sixth grades of three schools in which a different ethnic group constituted the majority. Results indicated that the self-concept of these children was significantly affected by their ethnic group membership, but not by the majority-minority status of the group.

The same external situation may affect boys and girls quite differently. Thus, Carithers (1970) states that interracial associations in desegregated schools are more threatening to black girls than to black boys and, consequently, girls have a much more difficult time in an integrated school setting. Martinez Monfort (1971) found similar results.

Aronson's (1972) principle of inevitability has important practical application, because it means that one need not be too concerned about compelling people to interact across ethnic lines. Once they know that they have to live with it, they will tend to accept it. Erskine (1967) presents data from a 1963 *Newsweek* report showing that whites who had social contact with blacks felt more strongly about giving more rights and opportunities to blacks than whites without such contact. Though it is not clear from such data if the contact produces the attitudes or vice versa, it indicates that once a person has had contact with out-group members, he is more willing to accept both the out-group member and the intergroup situation.

Another variable that is implied though not specified in many of the contacts studied deals with the enjoyment derived from the contact situation. One could easily categorize most of the studies on status, on cooperative vs. competitive situation, and on intimate vs. casual contact according to the satisfaction or dissastifaction they give to the interacting individual. It stands to reason that contact with higher status individuals on a cooperative or intimate basis is satisfying and enjoyable. The opposite may be true for contact with low-status persons or in a competitive situation. In the first instance, ethnic change will tend to be positive, in the latter it may be negative. Enjoyment of contact was specifically studied by Jordan (1971, 1973) and his co-workers (Erb, 1970; Dell Orto, 1971; Williams, 1971; Radcliffe, 1973). In all these studies, enjoyment of intergroup contact was positively related to ethnic attitude. Garti (1973) found that children who enjoyed their stay in a summer camp changed their ethnic attitudes towards another ethnic group more than children who did not enjoy the camp. Trubowitz (1969) also found a positive relationship between satisfaction with the ethnic contact and attitude change.

The outcome—i.e., success or failure—of the contact situation is probably related to the enjoyment aspect. If the interacting groups or members are successful in accomplishing their goals, the contact will probably be regarded as enjoyable, whereas if they fail to achieve their goals, the contact will be perceived as less enjoyable. Although outcome seems to be an important and probably quite powerful phenomenon, there are almost no studies that investigated this aspect directly in interethnic contact situations. One exception is a study by Fromkin, Klimoski and Flanagan (1972), which investigated preferences of success and failure groups towards newcomers. It was found that success groups preferences were made largely on the basis of the newcomers' competency and not on the basis of race, whereas the nonsuccess group preferences were determined by both task competency and the race of the newcomers.

Thus far in this section we have dealt exclusively with independent variables. Let us turn now to an examination of a dependent variable. Earlier, the point was made that intergroup contact may affect the intensity of the initial attitude in addition to its direction. Another potentially important variable is the salience of the intergroup problem or the importance attributed to it. It is possible, for example, that an in-group member may not change the direction or intensity of his attitude towards an out-group, but may ascribe less (or more) importance to the ethnic issue as a result of the contact situation. Results from studies that reported reduction in some aspect of prejudice but no change in other aspects might be explained in terms of change in salience of the ethnic issue in the eyes of the participants. Where ethnic issues became less important, differentiation according to ethnic lines may become less pronounced (e.g., as in the Aboud *et al.* [1973] study), which consequently leads to changes in attitudes. Thus, change in the importance attributed to the ethnic issue may be an important dependent variable in ethnic contact situation. However, direct research evidence is still not sufficient to reach firm conclusions about this topic.

## SUMMARY OF RESEARCH FINDINGS ON ETHNIC INTERGROUP CONTACT

A few general remarks and some critical comments and words of caution regarding the drawing of generalizations from these studies are relevant. There appear to be two major periods of research publications. One was around the first half of the 1950s. The second period started in the late 1960s and is continuing into the 1970s. The first period emphasized the change of attitudes of the majority or high-status group member (i.e., the white subject in the white-black contact studies in the US) toward a minority or low-status group. During the second period, greater emphasis is on the minority group member (typically blacks) and the effects of contact on his self-concept or self-acceptance.

Another difference between the two periods lies in the research situation used. Many investigators during the first period sought and expected a reduction of prejudice. The social situation studied was thus selected with this aim in mind (e.g., public housing projects in which authorities encourage ethnic contact or summer camps where equal status is strictly enforced). Therefore, even if many studies appear to prove that contact between ethnic groups reduces prejudice, it does not necessarily follow that these results are typical for other social situations. The type of contact previously studied is, unfortunately, rare, and even when it occurs it generally produces only casual interactions rather than intimate relationships. In the second period the social situations seem to be more typical of "average" everyday life (such as the large variety of school integration situations), and studies are conducted with more diverse ethnic and national groups. As a consequence of these differences, there is also a difference in results obtained. The majority of studies conducted during the first period report positive results in terms of change in ethnic attitude and relations. In the second period a much larger percentage of studies report either no-difference findings, qualified results, or unfavorable changes.

It seems that contemporary researchers view the possibilities of change in ethnic attitude and relationships by means of intergroup contact more realistically than did previous ones. A change in the present attitude of the scientific community toward ethnic contact can be seen in the introductory statements of almost all recent studies in this field. Most writers agree with and even stress the point that contact per se cannot be considered an an unqualified tool or a general panacea for changing prejudice or promoting better intergroup relations: only in specific situations or under special conditions will intergroup contact achieve this end. Even when individuals were given optimal conditions for the improvement of ethnic relations, only minor changes might occur, as was shown in Cook's (1970) study.

A factor to be considered particularly in some of the earlier studies is that respondents may have been indirectly influenced by and tended to comply with the expectations of researchers who sought to demonstrate positive attitude change (Rosenthal, 1966). Similarly, studies in which prestigious persons such as teachers have led subjects through a series of experiences with blacks have the problem that the research subjects simply cooperated by providing their leader with the changes they knew he was looking for. It should also be recalled that studies involving previous contact and current attitudes suffer from the danger of contamination between the two—that is, current attitude may have influenced one's recall of earlier experience. More recent studies attempt to overcome these pitfalls. The fact that current researchers tend not to "look for" positive results may also add to the reliability of the results.

In summary, when evaluating research on this topic, one should remember Cook's (1963) warning: "Almost all studies have been carried out in situations where whites and Negroes were already in contact at the time of investigation; initial attitudes had to be recalled by the respondents or inferred by the investigators on the basis of indirect evidence" (p. 47). In a number of studies, a relationship was found between the contacts with an ethnic group and a positive attitude change towards this group. But which came first, the contact or the favorable attitude? The same question has also been raised by Williams (1964). He was of the opinion that the answer should be: "First one, then the other. Both sequences are plausible; indeed, both are known to occur" (p. 202).

To the best of this author's knowledge, the only study that tackled this problem empirically was conducted by Eshel and Peres (1973). Their findings are based on a stratified sample of 800 Israeli males from low-status ethnic subgroups originating from Asian-African countries. They hypothesized that the flow of events in the process of social integration starts from independent variables such as family background, amount of acculturation into Israeli society, socioeconomic status, and opportunites for interactions with the higher status groups. This in turn facilitates ethnic contact and interactions that can be regarded as the intervening variables in this paradigm. Finally, the dependent variables are the attitudinal ones—i.e., change in prejudice, social distance, and political separatism. Thus, social conditions facilitate intergroup contact, which in turn promotes favorable attitudes, and not the other way around. In their study they found strong support for the above hypothesis, while alternative models were refuted.

Finally, there is the question of the generality of the findings. Can one generalize from one situation to another, from group to group, and from contact results within one culture to conclusions about a different culture? Can contact between different ethnic subgroups of one national group be regarded as the same as contact in an international setting? Many of the studies in this area concentrate on interactions between whites and blacks in the United States, and these represent high-status majority versus low-status minority groups. Can we generalize from such studies on contact between majority and minority groups that do not differ in status, such as American gentiles and Jews? And are results from studies on the latter groups comparable to contact of French people in Germany or Americans in England? And how about contact between ethnic groups that are numerically the same in the population but different in their status, such as the Israeli Western and Middle-Eastern subgroups? Are differences in number or status more important?

The literature on ethnic contact has not addressed such questions. Sociologists have dealt with general aspects of these problems, but not necessarily with regard to ethnic contacts. In the absence of theory, it is very difficult to give conclusive answers to such questions. However, certain assumptions can be made. No doubt, generalizations from any study involving specific characteristics to other situations or groups would not be justified. But insofar as some overall principles do emerge from varied research in settings, these principles may be generally valid regardless of the specific groups or situations considered. One should also keep in mind that the generalizations suggested here are not based on one culture (i.e., black-white relationships in the US) but stem from research on a large variety of ethnic groups and nations. In attempting to make generalizations, the first consideration should be whether the general characteristics of one contact situation are similar to the characteristics of the other situation. If they are, generalizations might be more valid.

Keeping the above cautions in mind, the following are the main principles that seem to emerge from the studies on contact between ethnic groups:

1. Making individuals interact across ethnic lines seems to be a major difficulty, because evidence suggests that when given a choice people prefer to interact within rather than between ethnic groups.

2. People who are more in need of ethnic interactions—i.e., more prejudiced persons—avoid them more strongly than the less prejudiced individuals. Moreover, once contact is established, the former tend to change their attitude in a more negative direction and the latter in a more positive direction.

3. Once a person is interacting in an intergroup situation, he tends, sooner or later, to accept the situation as well as the members of the other group.

4. There is evidence to support the view that once contact is established between members of ethnic groups, it tends to produce changes in attitude between these groups.

5. The direction of the change depends largely on the conditions under which contact has taken place; "favorable" conditions tend to reduce prejudice, "unfavorable" ones may increase prejudice and intergroup tension.

6. The change that may occur is not necessarily in the *direction* of the attitude. The change may be in the *intensity* of the attitude, in the *importance* attributed to ethnic aspect, or in other, as yet unexplored dimensions.

7. In most cases, where an attitude change is produced as a result of the contact situation, change is limited to a certain specific area or aspect of the attitude (such as to work situation), and does not generalize readily to other aspects.

8. Although many of the investigations on the effects of contact on the reduction of prejudice report "favorable" findings, this outcome might be attributed to the selection of favorable experimental situations. It is doubtful whether intergroup contact in real life takes place generally under favorable conditions and whether, therefore, in most cases contact actually reduces prejudice.

9. Some of the favorable conditions that tend to reduce prejudice are: (a) equal status contact between the members of the various ethnic groups; (b) positive perceptions of the other group as a result of the contact (even under unequal status conditions); (c) contact between members of a majority group and *higher* status members of a minority group; (d) contact situation requiring intergroup cooperation; (e) contact situation involving interdependent activities, superordinate goals, or separate aims that can be achieved only by intergroup cooperation; (f) contact of an intimate rather than a casual nature; (g) an "authority" and/or social climate being in favor of and promoting the intergroup contact; and (h) contact that is pleasant or rewarding.

10. Some of the unfavorable conditions that tend to strengthen prejudice are: (a) the contact situation producing competition between the groups; (b) unpleasant, involuntary, tension-laden contact; (c) lowering of prestige or status of one group as a result of the contact situation; (d) the groups or some of its members being in a state of frustration; (e) the groups in contact having moral or ethnic standards that are objectionable to each other; and (f) members of a minority or low-status group being lower in status or in relevant characteristics than the members of the majority or high-status group (except for 9b above). In this latter instance we may expect a negative change in attitude in the high-status group toward the low-status group and in the latter's self-concept.

## SCIENTIFIC AND RESEARCH CONSIDERATIONS

Despite a substantial amount of research on ethnic contact, our theoretical understanding of what contact involves as a potential agent of change and what are the underlying processes is still very limited. Although a sound general theory on this topic is still lacking, various explanations are available. The most frequent one assumes a simple disruption of ethnic stereotype as a result of interpersonal contact; others stress an unlearning process, especially linked to unlearning of assumed dissimilarity or incongruence of beliefs (Rokeach, Smith, and Evans, 1960; Byrne, 1969); still others relate the change process to role interpretation (Secord and Backman, 1974). Many of these explanations make use, in one way or another, of Festinger's (1957) theory of cognitive dissonance, others stress group interdependence (Sherif, 1967; Ashmore, 1970). However, very little has been done to study these explanations and theories independently in order to test their validity.

The lack of basic theory is also exemplified in the little interaction between studies in ethnic contact and general theories of attitude formation and change, or theories in other psychological fields such as perception, attraction, and motivation. Little has been done in trying to apply them to or to test their validity in ethnic contact situations. There is also a need to refine some of the concepts used in this field. For example, studies attribute different meanings to the term "equal status," which include (a) general equal status of the interacting groups, (b) equal status within the contact situation, or (c) equal status attributed to the groups by an outside agent. Whether these are the same phenomenon is questionable. The term "intimate contact" also needs refinement. What does intimacy involve? What exactly is meant by it? Many studies fail to adequately delineate concepts.

Thus, the area of intergroup contact urgently needs a more theoretical orientation, which would facilitate a better understanding of the basic phenomena. This would also help to produce more integrated and systematic research rather than the specific, piecemeal studies from which generalizations cannot easily be drawn.

One theory of prejudice that has stimulated a great deal of research in the last 15 years is Rokeach's view of belief dissimilarity. According to this theory, contact facilitates change by providing people the opportunity to test whether the beliefs prevalent in other ethnic groups are as dissimilar as they had assumed. The basic notion is that an individual learns through intergroup contact that he was wrong in assuming that beliefs and attitudes of the other group are different from his own. As a result of discovering similarities in beliefs between himself and members of the other group, an individual could consequently change his negative attitude towards the other group. The empirical status of this view remains unclear, and the relevant research is reviewed in detail in several places (e.g., Rokeach, Smith, and Evans, 1960; Stein, Hardyck, and Smith, 1965; Triandis and Davis, 1965; Dienstbier, 1972) including Chapter 3 of this volume.

Even if one accepts the major tenets of this position, however, a basic question remains of whether *everyday* contact (and not the manipulations with students in the psychology laboratory) provides the opportunity for the rejections of assumed dissimilarities of beliefs between ethnic groups. Thibaut and Kelley (1959) suggest that strangeness and dissimilarity tend to facilitate formation of negative first impressions which, in turn, may affect ensuing communication and interaction. Furthermore, ethnic relations occur in most cases between groups that are different in socioeconomic status, religion, cultural origin, or any other characteristic that may be correlated with differences in attitude and belief systems. In these cases contact may reinforce prejudice, because it provides the individual with the opportunity to observe directly that some of the "assumed" dissimilarities are real ones. Evidence for this is easily provided by many intergroup contact situations in everyday life, in school desegregation, housing, or not-equal-status work situations in many countries. Even when dissimilarities between the groups are only assumed and not real, having them interact and accept each other constitutes a major problem. Mehrabian and Ksionzky (1971) have shown that increasing discrepancy in status or attitudes led to lower judgments of compatability and liking. The fact that this is especially true for subjects who were sensitive to rejection may produce an additional difficulty, as these subjects may be the more prejudiced ones. Smith (1969) remarked that in everyday reality a person generally does not receive information regarding other people's beliefs and values, and therefore one's preferences are inevitably influenced by race, religion, or status.

These comments are not intended to detract from Rokeach's contribution. His hypothesis opens new avenues to our understanding of prejudice and intergroup conflicts, and suggests practical techniques to combat them. However, its application to ethnic contact outside the psychological laboratory should be made with care.

Many problems in investigations of ethnic contact (some of which have already been mentioned) have to do with the type and method of research utilized. Most of these studies have used field settings, with a very loose definition of variables and with little experimental control. There are only a small number of experimental studies and almost all of these were conducted in the laboratory with university (probably psychology) students. This state of affairs has some serious effects on the quality and validity of the research as well as on the possibility to generalize from its findings. With field studies, the lack of control limits generalizability. On the other hand, experimental laboratory studies may have low validity, since in many instances the manipulations may be meaningless or even trivial for the subjects. In addition, university students are a very special group for the study of prejudice because of their specific age, their liberal outlook, their experimental sophistication, and the unique equal intergroup status that university contact provides. Therefore, findings from such studies are of doubtful generality.

In general, the methodological sophistication of most investigations in this area is far from satisfactory. Many studies use inadequate data-gathering procedures; there is often a lack of appropriate control groups; only-after designs may unjustifiably assume initial similarity of groups; utilization of "change" scores in a before-after design often ignore some of the statistical problems involved, etc. There are some notable exceptions in the existing research literature. Jordan (1971, 1973), for instance, tried to overcome some of the above problems by utilizing Guttman's facet analysis and replicating some of his research on a number of different samples. McGuire's (1969) suggestion to employ the field-experiment type of research should be utilized more frequently. This approach requires the use of socially meaningful groups functioning in real-life settings, but the investigator has control over the involved variables and can manipulate some of them. Although this type of research is time consuming, rather expensive, and complicated to design, it may ultimately contribute more to scientific knowledge than the scores of the fragmented studies presently being conducted.

In sum, if research is to provide us in the future with a broader understanding of ethnic contact and its effects on change of intergroup attitudes and behavior, more emphasis should be place on basic theoretical aspects and on the development and utilization of more sophisticated and appropriate research methods.

## PRACTICAL APPLICATION AND POLICY ORIENTATION

In addition to scientific considerations, there are a number of practical applications of ethnic contact research. In light of the evidence, one need not elaborate on the conclusion that mere interethnic contact cannot be regarded as a major remedy for social prejudice and tensions. The question can be raised, therefore, of why so much emphasis is put upon programs involving contact by policy makers even when such policy goes contrary to the preferences of the groups involved. Several possible explanations suggest themselves.[7] The first is that policy makers generally do not know (or do not want to know) what social scientists have already found, and therefore still cling to belief in the omnipotence of ethnic contact and social integration. A second explanation is that it is politically important to the policy makers to suggest "something" constructive, and thus they offer ethnic contact or integration, which is the only available or known tool, despite its limitations.

Another approach, which seems most valid to this writer, involves

---

[7] Mr. E. Peled, General Director of the Israel: Department of Education and Culture, suggested helpful ideas on this subject.

clearly differentiating between social-ideological aspects and scientific considerations. Ethnic contact should not necessarily be conceived of as a tool for better intergroup relations, though it is hoped that this will also be achieved. The main emphasis should be on intergroup contact as a way of life; the earlier this process takes place, and the more people get used to living together, the better. Furthermore, there seems to be a strong conviction, already backed by research evidence, that equal opportunities for all ethnic groups, especially for the disadvantaged, can only be achieved in intergroup settings. If these settings (i.e., schools, work, housing) are racially separate, the disadvantaged groups will get less, even if strict equality is the policy. Thus, for the sake of long-range social and ethnic tranquility, intergroup contact and functioning is a necessity, even though each group may prefer within-group interaction and actually continue to behave accordingly.

If interethnic contact is a social necessity, one should make the most of it from the point of view of improving ethnic relations. Unfortunately, policy makers seem to fail here. Their tendency is to be content with the formal aspects of intergroup contact—i.e., contact per se—and disregard the conditions under which contact may prove to be beneficial or damaging to the interacting groups. Let us take the problem of school integration in Israel as an example.

A major goal of school integration in Israel is to provide opportunities for intergroup contact among children and youth. Schools and classes in Israel are populated, to a large extent, by children from the same socioeconomic class and ethnic background due to residential patterns. This situation calls for a change because of the relationship between the social class and ethnic background of the different subgroups: the lower socioeconomic classes are composed mainly of immigrants from African and Asian countries, while the higher socioeconomic classes are composed of groups originating from Europe and America. A national plan for educational reorganization is presently underway to create an educational structure in which children from different ethnic groups and diverse social classes study together, particularly from the seventh grade and up. A number of problems are associated with such a plan. The first concerns its implementation. Since 50% of the children come from ethnically homogeneous communities (Ben-Or, 1973), interethnic control in schools may not be easy to achieve without extensive busing. (Comparable problems also exist in the US—e.g., US Commission on Civil Rights, 1967; US Department of Health, Education and Welfare, 1968.) A second problem concerns the possibility of positive attitude change on the part of the high-status children. Since children from Middle-Eastern communities do tend to be lower in socioeconomic level and scholastic achievement, it is possible that attitudes may change in a negative direction. The situation with respect to the lower status student is not a simple one either. Although he may profit academically, if conditions for contact are not optimal, the social situation could be damaging to his self-esteem, and could increase intergroup hostility.

Such outcomes have, in fact, been obtained.[8]

The above considerations raise serious doubts as to whether increasing ethnic contact in school is the ultimate tool in improving the attitudes and the ethnic relations between the children. It is rather difficult to forecast whether thic contact, if it occurs at all, will cause a change in attitude, and whether such change will be in a desirable or undesirable direction. At any rate, we should not be surprised if no general or consistent change in the ethnic attitude of the children can be detected as a result of the intergroup contact.

Similar considerations apply to other areas of ethnic contact, such as the military. Although the belief is prevalent that the army serves as an instrument for furthering understanding and closing the gap between ethnic groups, it is doubtful whether intergroup contact in the army situation really changes and improves ethnic relations. Findings from published (Amir *et al.*, 1973) and from two unpublished studies seem to support this evaluation.

What then should our answer be to the original question of this article: Racially separate or together? If is difficult to give a clear-cut answer. The major difficulty does not lie in our ability to give a valid research-based reply to our question. The dilemma lies in the interdependence between scientific and social-ideological issues, and the contradiction that exists between our knowledge and our values.

My suggested answer to the above question of "racially separate or together" would be that both should be considered or, more specifically—a qualified togetherness. A frequently stated fundamental goal of contemporary Western society is equal opportunity for all. Until this is established, racial desegregation is essential because evidence clearly indicates that services and opportunities within segregated groups of unequal status will always be unequal. Desegregation has on the other hand, increased the availability of adequate services and facilities for low-status groups. Thus, unless "togetherness" is fostered, the principle of equal opportunities will turn out to be mere lip service. Such togetherness implies some degree of intergroup contact. But the question can be raised of whether such contact necessitates the deeper, more involved interactions that are sometimes referred to as "true integration" or, ultimately, the "melting" of ethnic subgroups. Social scientists have lately cast serious doubt on the validity of the melting-pot theory in ethnic relations (Novak, 1972; Laumann, 1973), since little evidence exists that the unique characteristics of ethnic groups tend to melt away, at least in stable, already established societies. Furthermore, social psychological evidence suggests that people often avoid interethnic contact if possible and prefer associating with members of their own groups. No doubt true ethnic integration has the major advantage of reducing ethnic conflicts, but can this be achieved realistically?

[8] These findings are based on studies presently underway at Bar-Ilan University.

If equal opportunities are to be given to all groups, ethnic contact, intergroup communications, and relationships have to become a way of life. Whether one likes this or not, it will have to be adjusted to and accepted, and the earlier in life, the better. However, social planning can make the difference of whether one will like it, just accept it, or even fight against it. We have tried to point out some of the principles that should be taken into consideration in such planning. In many instances it may prove preferable or practical to have the groups together in certain respects, but let them function "side by side" (as Bradburn *et al.* [1971] phrased it) in other situations. In different instances social intervention may produce a more integrated society. One thing, however, should not be done: bringing ethnic groups together without considering and evaluating the pros and cons of achieving positive results. Furthermore, as knowledge in this area is not always sufficient to enable *a priori* evaluations and prognosis, any planned ethnic interaction should be accompanied by research, or at least by an ongoing evaluation as to its development and possible outcomes. If one wishes to achieve positive results in the area of intergroup relations, it would be wise to consider carefully if prevailing conditions are suitable to bring about such a change. Experimentation prior to policy making may eliminate illusions in this sensitive area and would enable the policy makers to choose those programs that have the best chances of producing the hoped for results.

Finally, as ethnic contact cannot always be achieved in real life—and even when achieved, does not always produce positive results—we should not put *all* our eggs into this basket. Though only limited avenues are open today in our knowledge of how to improve ethnic relations, additional options should be sought. Some of these alternatives could be based on our knowledge of psychology or sociology, but solutions should also be looked for in economics, education, or any other discipline involved in social change and planning.

## REFERENCES

Aboud, F.E., Taylor, D.M., and Doumani, R.G. The effect of contact on the use of role and ethnic stereotypes in person perception. *Journal of Social Psychology*, 1973, **89**, 309-310.

Abramson, E.E. Levels of aspiration of Negro 9th grade males in integrated and segregated schools. *Psychological Reports*, 1971, **29**, 258.

Aellen, C., and Lambert, W.E. Ethnic identification and personality adjustments of Canadian adolescents of mixed English-French parentage. *Canadian Journal of Behavioral Science*, 1969, **1**, 69-86.

Allport, G.W. *The nature of prejudice*. Reading, Mass.: Addison-Wesley, 1954.

Allport, G.W., and Kramer, B.M. Some roots of prejudice. *Journal of Psychology*, 1946, **22**, 9-39.

Amir, Y. Contact hypothesis in ethnic relations. *Psychological Bulletin,* 1969, **71**, 319-342.

Amir, Y., Bizman, A., and Rivner, M. Effects of interethnic contact on friendship choices in the military. *Journal of Cross-Cultural Psychology,* 1973, **4**, 361-373.

Anant, S.S. *The changing concept of caste in India.* Delhi: Vikas, 1972.

Anant, S.S. Caste Hindu attributes toward Marijans: A follow-up after four years. Paper presented at the 81st American Psychological Association Convention, Montreal, 1973.

Anderson, L.V. The effects of desegregation on the achievement and personality patterns of Negro children. (Doctoral dissertation, George Peabody College for Teachers) Ann Arbor, Mich.: University Microfilms, 1966, No. 66-11, 237.

Armstrong, C.P., and Gregor, A.J. Integrated schools and Negro character development: Some consideration of the possible effects. *Psychiatry,* 1964, **27**, 69-72.

Aronson, E. *The social animal.* San-Francisco: Freeman, 1972.

Ashmore, R.D. Solving the problem of prejudice. In B.E. Collins (Ed.), *Social psychology.* Social influence, attitude change, group processes, and prejudice. Reading, Mass.: Addison-Wesley, 1970.

Barber, R.W. The effects of open enrollment on anti-Negro and anti-white prejudices among junior high school students in Rochester, N.Y. (Doctoral dissertation, The University of Rochester) Ann Arbor, Mich.: University Microfilms, 1968, No. 68-15, 871.

Basu, A.K., and Ames, R.G. Cross-cultural contact and attitude formation. *Sociology and Social Research,* 1970, **55**, 5-16.

Beard, E. The ethnic identity of the classroom instructor as a factor in changing anti-Negro attitudes of white college students (Doctoral dissertation, University of Maryland) Ann Arbor, Mich.: University Microfilms, 1970, No. 70-15, 389.

Beasely, L.M. A beginning attempt to eradicate racist attitudes. *Social Casework,* 1972, **53**, 9-13.

Ben-Or, T. *Integration in the Hebrew school system in the state of Israel* (Hebrew). Jerusalem: Ministry of Education and Culture, 1973.

Benson, F. A comparison of social and academic acceptance among core city students and non-core city students in October and May of a school year. *Child Study Center Bulletin,* State University College, Buffalo, New York, 1969, **5**(4-5), 84-87.

Berkowitz, M.I. *Studies of school desegregation and achievement: A summary.* Pittsburgh, Pa.: Commission on Human Relations, 1967.

Berkun, M., and Meeland, T. Sociometric effects of race and of combat performance. *Sociometry,* 1958, **21**, 145-149.

Berlin, I.N. Desegregation creates problems too. *Saturday Review,* June 15, 1963, pp. 66-67.

Berreman, G.D. Race, caste and other invidious distinctions in social stratification. *Race,* 1972, **13**, 385-414.

Billig, M., and Tajfel, H. Social categorization and similarity in intergroup behavior. *European Journal of Social Psychology,* 1973, **3**, 27-52.

Bjerstedt, A. Informational and non-informational determinants of nationality stereotypes. *Journal of Social Issues,* 1962, **18**, 24-29.

Bloom, L. *The social psychology of race relations.* London: Allen and Unwin, 1971.

Bradburn, N.M., Sudman, S., Gockel, G.L., and Noel, J.R. *Side by side.* Chicago: Quadrangle, 1971.

Brigham, J.C., and Weissbach, T.A. (Eds.). *Racial attitudes in America.* New York: Harper & Row, 1972.

Brislin, R.W. Contact as a variable in intergroup interaction. *Journal of Social Psychology,* 1968, **76**, 149-154.

Brislin, R.W. Interaction among members of nine ethnic groups and belief-similarity hypothesis. *Journal of Social Psychology,* 1971, **85**, 171-179.

Bronfenbrenner, U. The psychological costs of quality and equality in education. *Child Development,* 1967, **38**, 909-925.

Brophy, I.N. The luxury of anti-Negro prejudice. *Public Opinion Quarterly,* 1945, **9**, 456-466.

Brown, G., and Johnson, S.P. The attribution of behavioral connotations to shaded and white figures by Caucasian children. *British Journal of Social and Clinical Psychology,* 1971, **10**, 306-312.

Burnstein, E., and McRae, A.V. Some effects of shared threat and prejudice in racially mixed groups. *Journal of Abnormal and Social Psychology,* 1962, **64**, 257-263.

Byrne, D. Attitudes and attraction. In L. Berkowitz (Ed.), *Advances in experimental social psychology.* Volume 4. New York: Academic Press, 1969.

Campbell, E.Q. Some social psychological correlates of direction in attitude changes. *Social Forces,* 1958, **36** 335-340.

Carithers, M.W. School desegregation and racial cleavage, 1954-1970: A review of the literature. *Journal of Social Issues,* 1970, **26**, 25-47.

Carkhuff, R.R., and Banks, G. Training as a preferred mode of facilitating relations between races and generations. *Journal of Counseling Psychology,* 1970, **17**, 413-418.

Chadwick-Jones, J.K. Intergroup attitudes: A stage in attitude formation. *British Journal of Sociology,* 1962, **13**, 57-63.

Charley, B.H. The effectiveness of Negro teachers for changing developing racial attitude in young children. (Doctoral dissertation, University of Nevada) Ann Arbor, Mich.: University Microfilms, 1970, No. 70-12, 976.

Chemers, M.M., Fiedler, F.E., Lekhyananda, D., and Stolurow, L.M. Some effects of cultural training on leadership in heterocultural task groups. *International Journal of Psychology,* 1966, **1**, 301-314.

Chen, M., Shapiro, R., and Hausdorff, H. Acquaintance with Israelis and attitude change among foreign students in an Israeli University (Hebrew). *Megamot,* 1970, **17**, 158-165.

Chesler, M.A., and Phyllip, S. *Characteristics of Negro students attending previously all white schools in the Deep South.* Ann Arbor: Institute for Social Research, University of Michigan, 1967.

Clark, K.B., and Clark, M.P. Racial identification and preference in Negro children. In T.M. Newcomb, and E.L. Hartley (Eds.), *Readings in social psychology.* Revised edition. New York: Holt, 1952.

Cohen, E.G. Interracial interaction disability. *Human Relations,* 1972, **25,** 9-24.

Cole, S., Steinberg, J., and Burkheimer, G.J. Prejudice and conservatism in a recently integrated Southern college. *Psychological Reports,* 1968, **23,** 149-150.

Coleman, J.S., Campbell, E.Q., Hobson, C.J., McPartland, J., Mood, A.M., Weinfeld, F.D., and York, R.L. *Equality of educational opportunity.* Washington, D.C.: US Government Printing Office, 1966.

Coles, R. *The desegregation of Southern schools: A psychiatric study.* New York: Anti-Defamation League of B'nai B'rith, 1963.

Collett, P. Training Englishmen in the non-verbal behavior of Arabs: An experiment on intercultural communication. *International Journal of Psychology,* 1971, **6,** 209-215.

Cook, S.W. The systematic analysis of socially significant events: A strategy for social research. *Journal of Social Issues,* 1962, **18,** 66-84.

Cook, S.W. Desegregation: A psychological analysis. In W.W. Charters, Jr., and N.L. Gage (Eds.), *Readings in the social psychology of education.* Boston: Allyn & Bacon, 1963.

Cook, S.W. Motives in a conceptual analysis of attitude-related behavior. In W.J. Arnold and D. Levine (Eds.), *Nebraska symposium on motivation, 1969.* Lincoln: University of Nebraska Press, 1970.

Cook, S.W., and Selltiz, C. Some factors which influence the attitudinal outcomes of personal contact. *International Social Science Bulletin,* 1955, **7,** 51-58.

Costin, F. Behavioral and attitudinal changes resulting from an intergroup youth project. *Journal of Intergroup Relations,* 1966, **5,** 53-64.

Crain, R.L., and Weisman, C.S. *Discrimination, personality and achievement.* New York: Seminar Press, 1972.

David, K.H. Effect of intercultural contact and international stance on attitude change toward host nationals. *Psychologia: An International Journal of Psychology in the Orient,* 1971, **14,** 153-157.

Davis, E.E., and Triandis, H.C. An experimental study of black-white negotiations. *Journal of Applied Social Psychology,* 1971, **1,** 240-262.

Dell Orto, A.E. A Guttman facet analysis of the racial attitudes of rehabilitation counselor trainees. (Doctoral dissertation, Michigan State University) Ann Arbor, Mich.: University Microfilms, 1971, No. 71-2053.

Deutsch, M., and Collins, M.E. *Interracial housing: A psychological evaluation of a social experiment.* Minneapolis: University of Minnesota Press, 1951.

Dienstbier, R.A. A modified belief theory of prejudice emphasizing the mutual causality of racial prejudice and anticipated belief differences. *Psychological Review,* 1972, **79,** 146-160.

Diller, J.V. The encounter group as a means of reducing prejudice. (Doctoral dissertation, University of Colorado) Ann Arbor, Mich.: University Microfilms, 1971, No. 71-25, 816.

Dodd, S.C. A social distance test in the Near East. *American Journal of Sociology.* 1935, **41**, 194-204.

Dodson, J.P. Participation in a biracial encounter group: Its relation to acceptance of self and others, racial attitudes and interpersonal orientations. (Doctoral dissertation, Purdue University) Ann Arbor, Mich.: University Microfilms, 1971, No. 71-9386.

Doise, W., and Sinclair, A. The categorization process in intergroup relations. *European Journal of Social Psychology,* 1973, **3**, 145-157.

Doob, L.W. The impact of the Fereda workshop on the conflicts in the horn of Africa. *International Journal of Group Tensions,* 1971, **1**, 91-101.

Doob, L.W., and Foltz, W.J. The Belfast workshop. *Journal of Conflict Resolution,* 1973, **17**, 488-512.

Drake, St. C., and Cayton, H.R. *Black metropolis.* Revised edition. New York: Harper & Row, 1962.

Durojaiye, M.O.A. Patterns of friendship and leadership choices in a mixed ethnic junior school—a sociometric analysis. *British Journal of Educational Psychology,* 1969, **39**, 88-89.

Dwyer, R.J. A report on patterns of interaction in desegregated schools. *Journal of Educational Sociology,* 1958, **31**, 253-256.

Ehrlich, H.J. *The social psychology of prejudice.* New York: Wiley, 1973.

Eisenman, R. Reducing prejudice by Negro-white contacts. *Journal of Negro Education,* 1965, **34**, 461-462.

Eisenman, R., and Pettigrew, T.F. Comments and rejoinders on: "Racially separate or together?" *Journal of Social Issues,* 1969, **25**, 199-206.

Elenewski, I.T.M. The effects of a racial confrontation group on self-reported interpersonal attitudes and on intrapersonal behavior. (Doctoral dissertation, University of Miami) Ann Arbor, Mich.: University Microfilms, 1972, No. 72-22, 926.

Erb, D.L. Racial attitudes and empathy: A Guttman facet theory examination of their relationships and determinants. (Doctoral dissertation, Michigan State University) Ann Arbor, Mich.: University Microfilms, 1970, No. 70-9529.

Erskine, H. The polls: Negro housing. *Public Opinion Quarterly,* 1967, **31**, 482-498.

Eshel, S., and Peres, Y. *The intergration of a minority group: A causal model.* Tel-Aviv: Tel-Aviv University, 1973.

Feitelson, D., Weintraub, S., and Michaeli, O. Social interactions in heterogeneous preschools in Israel. *Child Development,* 1972, **43**, 1249-1259.

Festinger, L., and Kelley, H.H. Changing attitudes through social contact. Ann Arbor: Institute for Social Research, University of Michigan, 1951.

Festinger, L. *A theory of cognitive dissonance,* Evanston: Row, Peterson, 1957.

Fiedler, F.E., Mitchell, T., and Triandis, H.C. The culture assimilator: An approach to cross-cultural training. *Journal of Applied Psychology,* 1971, **55**, 95-102.

Frechette, E.J. Attitudes of French and English speaking Canadians toward West Indian immigrants: A Guttman facet analysis. (Doctoral dissertation, Michigan State University) Ann Arbor, Mich.: University Micro-films, 1971, No. 71-18, 203.

Fromkin, H.L., Klimoski, R.J., and Flanagan, M.F. Race and competence as determinants of acceptance of newcomers in success and failure work groups. *Organizational Behavior and Human Performance*, 1972, **7**, 25-42.

Gamez, G. T-groups as a tool for developing trust and cooperation between Mexican-American and Anglo-American college students. (Doctoral dissertation, University of Texas at Austin) Ann Arbor, Mich.: University Microfilms, 1970, No. 70-18, 234.

Garti, H. Interpersonal contact and changing of ethnic attitudes. Unpublished M.A. thesis, Bar-Ilan University, 1973.

Goodman, M.E. *Race awareness in young children.* Cambridge, Mass.: Addison-Wesley, 1952.

Gottlieb, D., and Tenhouten, W.D. Racial composition and the social systems of three high schools. *Journal of Marriage and the Family*, 1965, **27**, 204-217.

Graham, M.D. An experiment in international attitudes research. *International Social Science Bulletin*, 1951, **3**, 529-539.

Gray, J.S., and Thompson, A.H. The ethnic prejudices of white and Negro college students. *Journal of Abnormal and Social Psychology*, 1953, **48**, 311-313.

Green, J.A., and Gerard, H.B. School desegregation and ethnic attitudes. In H.L. Fromkin and J.J. Sherwood (Eds.), *Integrating the organization.* New York: Free Press, in press.

Grossman, J.S. Psychological determinants of reaction to neighborhood racial change. (Doctoral dissertation, Western Reserve University) Ann Arbor, Mich.: University Microfilms, 1967, No. 67-4640.

Guggenheim, F., and Hoem, A. Cross-cultural and intra-cultural attitudes of Lapp and Norwegian children. *Journal of Social Psychology*, 1967, **73**, 23-36.

Gundlach, R.H. Effect of on-the-job experience with Negroes upon social attitudes of white workers in union shops. *American Psychologist*, 1950, **5**, 300.

Guttman, L., and Foa, U.G. Social contact and an intergroup attitude. *Public Opinion Quarterly*, 1951, **15**, 43-53.

Haggstrom, W.C. Self-esteem and other characteristics of residentially desegregated Negroes. (Doctoral dissertation, University of Michigan) Ann Arbor, Mich.: University Microfilms, 1963, No. 63-359.

Harding, J., and Hogrefe, R. Attitudes of white department store employees toward Negro co-workers. *Journal of Social Issues*, 1952, 8, 18-28.

Harding, J., Proshansky, H., Kutner, B., and Chein, I. Prejudice and ethnic relations. In G. Lindzey and E. Aronson (Eds.), *The handbook of social psychology* Second Edition, Volume 5. Reading, Mass.: Addison-Wesley, 1969.

Harlan, H.H. Some factors affecting attitude toward Jews. *American Sociological Review*, 1942, **7**, 816-827.

Hartnett, R.T. Differences in selected attitudes and college orientations between black students attending traditionally Negro and traditionally white institutions. *Sociology of Education,* 1970, **43**, 419-436.

Havighurst, R.J., and Neugarten, B.L. *Society and Education.* Third Edition. Boston: Allyn & Bacon, 1967.

Herman, B.E. The effect of neighborhood upon the attitudes of Negro and white sixth grade children toward different racial groups. (Doctoral dissertation, University of Connecticut) Ann Arbor, Mich.: University Microfilms, 1968, No. 68-1355.

Hofman, J.E., and Zak, I. Interpersonal contact and attitude change in a cross-cultural situation. *Journal of Social Psychology,* 1969, **78**, 165-171.

Hogrefe, R., Evans, M.C., and Chein, I. The effects on intergroup attitudes of participation in an inter-racial play center. *American Psychologist,* 1947, **2**, 324.

Holmes, F.E. The effect of a community field study on the tolerant-prejudice attitude of prospective secondary teachers toward Negroes. (Doctoral dissertation, University of Denver) Ann Arbor, Mich.: University Microfilms, 1968, No. 68-6117.

Holz, R.F. Racial identification of verbal communication: Stereotyping and school integration. *Communication Research Center Report,* 1971, No. 52.

Homans, G. Social behavior as exchange. *American Journal of Sociology,* 1958, **63**, 597-606.

Horowitz, E.L. The development of attitude toward the Negro. *Archives of Psychology,* 1936, No. 194.

Ibrahim, S.E.M. Interaction, perception and attitudes of Arab students toward Americans, *Sociology and Social Research,* 1970, **55**, 29-46.

International Sociological Association. *The nature of conflict.* Paris: UNESCO, 1957.

Irish, D.P. Reactions of Caucasian residents to Japanese-American neighbors. *Journal of Social Issues,* 1952, **8**, 10-17.

Irvine, S. Racial attitudes of American ministers. Paper presented at the 81st convention of the American Psychological Association, Montreal, 1973.

Israel Government, Ministry of Education. Recommendations of the committee on the structure of elementary and high school education (Hebrew). *Knesset Transcripts,* 1970, **52**(36), 3037-3039.

Jahoda, M., and West, P.S. Race relations in public housing. *Journal of Social Issues,* 1951, **7**(1, 2), 132-139.

James, D.H. The effect of desegregation on the self-concept of Negro high school students. (Doctoral dissertation, University of Southern Mississippi) Ann Arbor, Mich.: University Microfilms, 1971, No. 71-5391.

James, H.E.O. Personal contact in school and change in intergroup attitudes. *International Social Science Bulletin,* 1955, **7**, 66-70.

Jansen, V.G., and Gallagher, J.J. The social choices of students in racially integrated classes for the culturally disadvantaged talented. *Exceptional Children,* 1966, **33**, 221-226.

Jonsson, M. Teacher and pupil attitudes toward busing integration and related issues in Berkeley elementary schools. Berkeley: Berkeley Unified School District, October 1966, p. 19.

Jordon, J.E. Attitude-behavior research on physical-mental-social disability and racial-ethnic differences. *Psychological Aspects of Disability,* 1971, **18**, 5-26.

Jordon, J.E. Caste-ethnicity-race-tribalism (CERT): Object specificity, situation specificity, object generalizability, cultural specifity, and cross-cultural invariance. Symposium presented at the 81st convention of the American Psychological Association, Montreal, 1973.

Katz, I. *Conflict and harmony in an adolescent interracial group.* New York: New York University Press, 1955.

Katz, I. Review of evidence relating to effects of desegregation on the intellectual performance of Negroes. *American Psychologist,* 1964, **19**, 381-399.

Katz, I. Factors influencing Negro performance in the desegregated school. In M. Deutsch, I. Katz, and A.R. Jensen (Eds.), *Social class, race and psychological development.* New York: Holt, Rinehart and Winston, 1968.

Katz, I., and Benjamin, L. Effects of white authoritarianism in biracial groups. *Journal of Abnormal and Social Psychology,* 1960, **61**, 448-456.

Katz, I., and Cohen, M. The effects of training Negroes upon cooperative problem solving in biracial teams. *Journal of Abnormal and Social Psychology,* 1962, **64**, 319-325.

Katz, I., Goldston, J., and Benjamin, L. Behavior and productivity in biracial work groups. *Human Relations,* 1958, **11**, 123-141.

Kawwa, T. A survey of ethnic attitudes of some British secondary school pupils. *British Journal of Social and Clnical Psychology,* 1968, **7**, 161-168.

Kelly, J.G., Ferson, J.E., and Holtzman, W.H. The measurement of attitudes toward the Negro in the South. *Journal of Social Psychology,* 1958, **48**, 305-317.

Kelman, H.C. Changing attitudes through international activities. *Journal of Social Issues,* 1962, **18**, 68-87.

Koslin, S.C., Amarel, M., and Ames, N. A distance measure of racial attitudes in primary grade children: An exploratory study. *Psychology in the Schools,* 1969, **6**, 382-385.

Kramer, B.M. Residential contact as a determinant of attitudes towards Negroes. Unpublished doctoral dissertation, Harvard University, 1950.

Kupferer, H.J. An evaluation of the integration potential of a physical education program. *Journal of Educational Sociology,* 1954, **28**, 89-96.

Lakin, M., Lomranz, J., Lieberman, M.A. *Arab and Jew in Israel.* Washington, D.C.: NTL-Institute for Applied Behavioral Science, 1969.

Lammers, D.M. Self-concepts of American Indian adolescents having segregated and desegregated elementary backgrounds. (Doctoral dissertation, Syracuse University) Ann Arbor, Mich.: University Microfilms, 1970, No. 70-14, 723.

Laumann, E.O. *Bonds of pluralism.* New York: Wiley, 1973.

Lawrence, C.R. Problems in intergroup relations: A. Negro Americans and other minority groups. In C. Senior and W.S. Bernard (Eds.), *Toward cultural democracy*. New York: Associated Educational Services, 1968.

Leacock, E., Deutsch, M., and Fishman, J.A. The Bridgeview study: A preliminary report. *Journal of Social Issues*, 1959, **15**, 30-37.

Lilly, M.S. An exploratory study of methods for improving social acceptance of children of low sociometric status and low academic achievement. (Doctoral dissertation, George Peabody College for Teachers) Ann Arbor, Mich.: University Microfilms, 1970, No. 70-7616.

Lombardi, D.N. Factors affecting changes in attitudes towards Negroes among high school students. *Journal of Negro Education*, 1963, **32**, 129-136.

Mack, R.W. The changing ethnic fabric of the metropolis. In A. Kerber and B. Bommarito (Eds.), *The schools and the urban crisis*. New York: Holt, Rinehart and Winston, 1965.

MacKenzie, B.K. The importance of contact in determining attitudes towards Negroes. *Journal of Abnormal and Social Psychology*, 1948, **43**, 417-441.

Mann, J.H. The effects of inter-racial contact on sociometric choices and perceptions. *Journal of Social Psychology*, 1959, **50**, 143-152.

Manheimer, D., and Williams, R.M., Jr. A note on Negro troops in combat. In S.A. Stouffer, E.A. Suchman, L.C. DeVinney, S.A. Star, and R.M. Williams, Jr. (Eds.), *The American soldier*. Volume 1. Princeton: Princeton University Press, 1949.

Martinez-Monfort, A. Racial attitudes of high school students attending desegregated schools in a Southern metropolitan area. (Doctoral dissertation, Louisiana State University) Ann Arbor, Mich.: University Microfilms, 1971, No. 71-3424.

Massey, R.F. Meta-subjectivity: A model for interracial understanding. *International Journal of Group Tensions*, 1972, **2**, 71-85.

Masuoka, J. RAce preference in Hawaii. *American Journal of Sociology*, 1936, **41**, 635-641.

McGuire, W.J. Theory-oriented research in natural settings: The best of both worlds in social psychology. In M. Sherif and C.W. Sherif (Eds.), *Interdisciplinary relationships in the social sciences*. Chicago: Aldine, 1969.

Meer, B., and Freedman, E. The impact of Negro neighbors on white home owners. *Social Forces*, 1966, **45**, 11-19.

Mehrabian, A., and Ksionzky, S. Anticipated compatibility as a function of attitude or status similarity. *Journal of Personality*, 1971, **39**, 225-241.

Meketon, B.F. The effects of integration upon the Negro child's responses to various tasks and upon his level of self-esteem. (Doctoral dissertation, University of Kentucky) Ann Arbor, Mich.: University Microfilms, 1969, No. 69-20, 406.

Meltzer, B. The influence of the duration of interracial classroom contact on the development of interpersonal cognitive skills. (Doctoral dissertation, Clark University) Ann Arbor, Mich.: University Microfilms, 1970, No. 70-11, 183.

Miller, A.G. Integration and acculturation of cooperative behavior among

Blackfoot Indian and non-Indian Canadian children. *Journal of Crosscultural Psychology*, 1973, **4**, 374-380.

Miller, J.K. Bratenahl: A case study of planned integration. (Doctoral dissertation, University of Michigan) Ann Arbor, Mich.: University Microfilms, 1971, No. 71-15, 240.

Minard, R.D. Race relationships in the Pocahontas coal field. *Journal of Social Issues*, 1952, **8**, 29-44.

Morris, D.C. White racial orientations toward Negroes in an urban context. (Doctoral dissertation, Ohio State University) Ann Arbor, Mich.: University Microfilms, 1970, No. 70-14, 078.

Murphy, G. *In the minds of men*. New York: Basic Books, 1953.

Mussen, P.H. Some personality and social factors related to changes in children's attitudes toward Negores. *Journal of Abnormal and Social Psychology*, 1950, **45**, 423-441.

National Education Association, Department of Superintendence. *Tenth Yearbook*. Washington, D.C.: National Education Association, 1932.

Neprash, J.A. Minority group contacts and social distance. *Phylon*, 1953, **14**, 207-212.

Nevo, D. Social acceptance of underprivileged students in homogeneous and heterogeneous school settings (Hebrew). Unpublished M.A. thesis, Tel-Aviv University, 1971.

Newcomb, T.M. *The acquaintance process*. New York: Holt, Rinehart and Winston, 1961.

Noel, J.R. White anti-black prejudice in the United States. *International Journal of Group Tensions*, 1971, **1**, 59-76.

Noel, R.L. Minority group identification and social integration. Paper presented at the annual meeting the American Sociological Association, 1966.

Novak, M. *The rise of the unmeltable ethnics*. New York: Macmillan, 1972.

Ogunlade, J.O. Ethnic identification and preference of some school children in wester Nigeria. *Sociology and Social Research*, 1972, **56**, 195-201.

Orbell, J.M., and Sherrill, K.S. Racial attitudes and the metropolitan context: A structural analysis. *Public Opinion Quarterly*, 1969, **33**, 46-54.

Palmore, E.B. The introduction of Negroes into white departments. *Human Organization*, 1955, **14**, 27-28.

Parker, J.H. The interaction of Negroes and whites in an integrated church setting. *Social Forces*, 1968, **46**, 359-366.

Pettigrew, T.F. Social psychology and desegregation research. *American Psychologist*, 1961, **16**, 105-112.

Pettigrew, T.F. Racially separate or together? *Journal of Social Issues*, 1969, **25**, 43-69.

Pettigrew, T.F., and Pajonas, P.J. Social psychological considerations of racially-balanced schools. Unpublished working paper prepared for the New York State Commissioner of Education, 1964.

Pinkney, A. The quantitative factor in prejudice. *Sociology and Social Research*, 1963, **47**, 161-168.

Prontho, E.T., and Melikan, L.H. Studies in stereotypes: V. Familiarity and the kernel of truth hypothesis. *Journal of Social Psychology,* 1955, **41,** 3-10.

Proshansky, H., and Newton, P. The nature and meaning of Negro self-identity. In M. Deutsch, I. Katz, and A.R. Jensen (Eds.), *Social class, race and psychological development.* New York: Holt, Rinehart and Winston, 1968.

Pugh, R.W. *Psychology and the black experience.* Monterey, Calif.: Brooks/Cole, 1972.

Rabushka, A. Integration in a multi-racial institution: Ethnic attitudes among Chinese and Malay students at the University of Malaya. *Race,* 1969, **11,** 53-63.

Radcliffe, A. A Guttman facet analysis of the racial attitudes of black and white adults toward the opposite race. (Doctoral dissertation, Michigan State University) Ann Arbor, Mich.: University Microfilms, 1973, No. 73-5472.

Ram, P. and Murphy, G. Recent investigations of Hindu-Moslem relations in India. *Human Organization,* 1952, **11,** 13-16.

Reed, B.A. Accommodation between Negro and white employees in a West Coast aircraft industry, 1942-1944. *Social Forces,* 1947, **26,** 76-84.

Roberts, H.W. The impact of military service upon the racial attitudes of Negro servicemen in World War II. *Social Problems,* 1953, **1,** 65-69.

Rokeach, M. (Ed.) *The open and closed mind.* New York: Basic Books, 1960.

Rokeach, M., Smith, P.W., and Evans, R.I. Two kinds of prejudice or one? In M. Rokeach (Ed.), *The open and closed mind.* New York: Basic Books, 1960.

Rose, Alvin. Race relations in a Chicago industry. (Unpublished study, University of Chicago, 1946.) In Arnold Rose, *Studies in reduction of prejudice.* Chicago: American Council on Race Relations, 1948.

Rose, Arnold. *Studies in reduction of prejudice.* Chicago: American Council on Race Relations, 1948.

Rosenthal, B.G., Miller, D., and Teryenyi, F. The measurement of social interaction among Negro and white children in a housing community. *Journal of Social Psychology,* 1967, **71,** 27-37.

Rosenthal, R. *Experimenter effects in behavioral research.* New York: Appleton-Century-Crofts, 1966.

Roth, R.W. The effects of integral curriculum on Negro and white fifth grade students. (Doctoral dissertation, University of Michigan) Ann Arbor, Mich.: University Microfilms, 1969, No. 69-18, 095.

Rubin, I. The reduction of prejudice through laboratory training. *Journal of Applied Behavioral Science,* 1967, **3,** 29-50.

Rubin, I.M. Increased self-acceptance: A means of reducing prejudice. *Journal of Personality and Social Psychology,* 1967, **5,** 233-238.

Saenger, G. *The social psychology of prejudice.* New York: Harper, 1953.

Saenger, G., and Gilbert, E. Customer reactions to the integration of Negro sales personnel. *International Journal of Opinion and Attitude Research,* 1950, **4,** 57-76.

St. John, N.H. De facto segregation and interracial associations in high school.

*Sociology of Education*, 1963, **37**, 326-344.

St. John, N.H. The effect of segregation on the aspirations of Negro youth. *Harvard Educational Review*, 1966, **36**, 284-294.

St. John, N.H. *Minority group performance under various conditions of school ethnic and economic integration: A review of research*. New York: Yeshiva University, 1969.

St. John, N.H., and Smith, N. *Annotated bibliography on school racial mix and the self-concept, aspirations, academic achievement and interracial attitudes and behavior of Negro children*. Cambridge, Mass.: Publications Office, Center for Research and Development on Educational Differences, Harvard University, 1967.

Sapir, R. A shelter. *Megamot*, 1951, **3**, 8-36.

Sartain, J.A. Attitudes of parents and children toward desegregation. (Doctoral dissertation, Vanderbilt University) Ann Arbor, Mich.: University Microfilms, 1966, No. 66-10, 999.

Sayler, R. An exploration of race prejudice in college students and interracial contact. (Doctoral dissertation, University of Washington) Ann Arbor, Mich.: University Microfilms, 1969, No. 69-20, 269.

Schild, E.O. The foreign student, as stranger, learning the norms of the host culture. *Journal of Social Issues*, 1962, **18**, 41-54.

Scott, L.J. An analysis of the self-concept of seventh grade students in segregated-desegregated public schools of Oklahoma City. (Doctoral dissertation, University of Oklahoma) Ann Arbor, Mich.: University Microfilms, 1969, No. 69-18, 465.

Secord, P.F., and Backman, C.W. *Social psychology*. Second edition. New York: McGraw-Hill, 1974.

Segal, B.E. Contact, compliance and distance among Jewish and non-Jewish undergraduates. *Social Problems*, 1965, **13**, 66-74.

Selltiz, C., and Cook, S.W. Factors influencing attitudes of foreign students toward the host country. *Journal of Social Issues*, 1962, **18**, 7-23.

Sherif, M. *Group conflict and cooperation*. London: Routledge & Kegan Paul, 1967.

Sherif, M., and Sherif, C.W. *Groups in harmony and tension: An integration of studies in intergroup relations*. New York: Harper, 1953.

Sherif, M., and Sherif, C.W. Attitude as the individual's own categories: The social judgment-involvement approach to attitude and attitude change. In W. Sherif and M. Sherif (Eds.), *Attitude, ego-involvement and change*. New York: Wiley, 1967.

Shuval, J.T. The micro-neighborhood: An approach to ecological patterns of ethnic groups. *Social Problems*, 1962, **9**, 272-280.

Simpson, G.E., and Yinger, J.M. *Racial and cultural minorities: An analysis of prejudice and discrimination*. Fourth edition. New York: Harper & Row, 1972.

Singer, D. The impact of interracial classroom exposure on the social attitudes of fifth grade children. Unpublished study, 1964. Cited by J. Harding, H. Proshansky, B. Kutner, and I. Chein, Prejudice and ethnic relations. In G. Lindzey and E. Aronson (Eds.), *The handbook of social psy-*

*chology*. Second edition, Volume 5. Reading, Mass.: Addison-Wesley, 1969.

Sisenwein, M. A comparison of the self-concept of Negro and white children in an integrated school. (Doctoral dissertation, Columbia University) Ann Arbor, Mich.: University Microfilms, 1970, No. 70-19, 699.

Slann, M. Jewish ethnicity and the integration of an Arab minority in Israel: A study of the Jerusalem incorporation. *Human Relations*, 1973, **26**, 359-370.

Smith, M.B. The schools and prejudice: Findings. In C.Y. Glock and E. Siegelman (Eds), *Prejudice U.S.A.* New York: Praeger, 1969.

Smith, F.T. An experiment in modifying attitudes toward the Negro. *Teachers College, Columbia University Contributions to Education*, 1943, No. 887.

Soen, D., and Tishler, I. *Urban renewal: Social surveys.* Tel-Aviv: Institute for Planning and Development, 1968.

Spiro, S., and Lotan, H. Social aspects of a project of planned education mobility (Hebrew). Tel-Aviv University, School of Social Work, 1970.

Star, S.A. An approach to the measure of interracial tension. In W. Burgess and J. Bogue (Eds.), *Urban sociology*. Chicago: The University of Chicago Press, 1967.

Steele, R.E., and Nash, K.B. Sensitivity training and the black community. *American Journal of Orthopsychiatry*, 1972, **42**, 424-430.

Stein, D.D., Hardyck, J.A., and Smith, M.B. Race and belief: An open and shut case. *Journal of Personality and Social Psychology*, 1965, **1**, 281-289.

Stevenson, H.W., and Stevenson, N.G. Social interaction in an interracial nursery school. *Genetic Psychology Monographs*, 1960, **61**, 37-75.

Stillman, R. Negroes in the armed forces. *Phylon*, 1969, **30**, 139-159.

Stinchcombe, A.L., McDill, M.S., and Walker, D. Is there a racial tipping point in changing schools? *Journal of Social Issues*, 1969, **25**, 127-136.

Stouffer, S.A., Lumsdaine, A.A., Lumsdaine, M.H., Williams, R.M., Jr., Smith, M.B., Janis, I.L., Star, S.A., and Cottrell, L.S., Jr. *The American soldier.* Volume 2. Princeton: Princeton University Press, 1949.

Teele, J.E., and Mayo, C. School racial integration: Tumult and shame. *Jouranl of Social Issues*, 1969, **25**, 137-156.

Thibaut, J.W., and Kelley, H.H. *The social psychology of groups*. New York: Wiley, 1959.

Triandis, H.C., and Davis, E.E. Race and belief as determinants of behavioral intentions. *Journal of Personality and Social Psychology*, 1965, **2**, 715-725.

Triandis, H.C., and Malpass, R.S. Studies of black and white interaction in job settings. *Journal of Applied Social Psychology*, 1971, **1**, 101-117.

Triandis, H.C., and Vassilious, V. Frequency of contact and stereotyping. *Journal of Personality and Social Psychology*, 1967, **7**, 316-328.

Trubowitz, J. *Changing the racial attitudes of children.* New York: Praeger, 1969.

United States Commission on Civil Rights. *Racial isolation in the public schools.* Washington, D.C.: US Government Printing Office, 1967.

United States Department of Health, Education and Welfare, Office for Civil Rights. *Directory of pulic elementary and secondary schools in selected districts.* Washington, D.C.: Department of Health, Education and Welfare, Fall 1968.

Wade, K., and Wilson, W. Relatively low prejudice in a racially isolated group. *Psychological Reports,* 1971, **28**, 871-877.

Walker, K.D. Effects of social and cultural isolation upon the self-concepts of Negro children. (Doctoral dissertation, University of Miami) Ann Arbor, Mich.: University Microfilms, 1969, No. 69-6518.

Watson, J. Some social and psychological situations related to change in attitude. *Human Relations,* 1950, **3**, 15-56.

Watson, P. (Ed.). *Psychology and race.* Baltimore: Penguin, 1973.

Webster, S.W. The influence of interracial contact on social acceptance in a newly integrated school. *Journal of Educational Psychology,* 1961, **52**, 292-296.

Weinberg, M. *School integration: A comprehensive classified bibliography of 3100 references.* Chicago: Integrated Education Associates, 1967.

Weinberg, M. *Desegregation research: An appraisal.* Second edition. Bloomington, Ind.: Phi Delta Kappa, 1970.

Weingrod, A. *Israel; Group relations in a new society.* New York: Praeger, 1965.

Wertzer, F. The effect of a shared stress situation on racial attitudes. (Doctoral dissertation, Columbia University) Ann Arbor, Mich.: University Microfilms, 1971, No. 71-20, 033.

Whitmore, P.G., Jr. A study of school desegregation: Attitude change and scale validation. (Doctoral dissertation, University of Tennessee) Ann Arbor, Mich.: University Microfilms, 1957, no. 57-1419.

Williams, D.H. The effects of an interracial project upon the attitudes of Negro and white girls within the Y.W.C.A. (Unpublished Masters thesis, Columbia University, 1944) In Arnold Rose, *Studies in reduction of prejudice.* Chicago: American Council on Race Relations, 1948.

Williams, R.L., and Byars, H. The effect of academic integration on the self-esteem of Southern Negro students. *Journal of Social Psychology,* 1970, **80**, 183-188.

Williams, R.L., Cormier, W.H., Sapp, G.L., and Andrews, H.B. The utility of behavior management techniques in changing interracial behavior. *Journal of Psychology,* 1971, **77**, 127-138.

Williams, R.M., Jr. *The reduction of intergroup tensions.* New York: Social Science Research Council, 1947, Bulletin 57.

Williams, R.M. Jr.Williams, R.M., Jr. *Strangers next door.* Englewood Cliffs, N.J.: Prentice-Hall, 1964.

Williams, R.M., Jr., and Ryan, M.W. (Eds.). *Schools in a transition: Community experiences in desegregation.* Chapel Hill: University of North Carolina Press, 1954.

Wilner, D.M., Walkley, R.P., and Cook, S.W. Residential proximity and intergroup relations in public housing projects. *Journal of Social Issues,* 1952, **8**, 45-69.

Winder, A.E. White attitudes toward Negro-white interaction in an area of changing racial composition. *American Psychologist,* 1952, **7**, 330-331.

Witte, P.H. The effects of group reward structure on interracial acceptance peer tutoring and academic performance. (Doctoral dissertation, Washington University) Ann Arbor, Mich.: University Microfilms, 1972, No. 72-9373.

Wolf, E.P. the invasion-succession sequence as a self-fulfilling prophecy. *Journal of Social Issues,* 1957, **13**, 7-20.

Wolf, E.P. Racial transition in a middle-class area. *Journal of Intergroup Relations,* 1960, **1**, 75-81.

Wolf, H.E. Judgments formules sur les Francais et les eleves allemands. [Judgments of French and Italians by German students] *Revue de Psychologie des Peuples,* 1961, **16**, 287-305.

Works, E. The prejudice-interaction hypothesis from the point of view of the Negro minority group. *American Journal of Sociology,* 1961, **67**, 47-52.

Yarrow, M.R., Campbell, J.D., and Yarrow, L.J. Acquisition of new norms: A study of racial desegregation. *Journal of Social Issues,* 1958a, **14**, 8-28.

Yarrow, M.R., Campbell, J.D., and Yarrow, L.J. Interpersonal change: Process and theory. *Journal of Social Issues,* 1958b, **14**, 60-62.

Young, D. *American minority peoples: A study in racial and cultural conflicts in the United States.* New York: Harper, 1932.

Zimbardo, P., and Ebbesen, E.B. *Influencing attitudes and changing behavior.* Reading, Mass.: Addison-Wesley, 1969.

Zirkel, P., and Moses, E.G. Self-concept and ethnic group membership among public school students. *American Educational Research Journal,* 1971, **8**, 253-265.

# 9

# *Racial Issues in Mass Media Institutions*

BRADLEY S. GREENBERG and SHERRIE L. MAZINGO

Basically, this chapter attempts to provide an encompsing perspective of just what kind of role minorities have played in the growth and development of the major mass media—both the mass media owned and controlled by whites and those more recent media developments within the social structure of the minorities. Five basic questions are examined: (1) What is and has been the nature of minority employment within the majority media (2) Are new patterns of media development evolving within the social system of the minorities? (3) What key regulatory and legislative efforts have been introduced to aid minority assimilation within the majority mass media institutions? (4) How have the majority mass media presented and portrayed minority groups? (5) What manifest social effects have been demonstrated as a result of recent changes in available mass media content?

It would be comforting if we could say that we have been definitive in our answers to these questions, but that has been impossible. Minority roles in the economic development of their own media, the great demand of the majority media to further encompass minority groups in editorial, creative, business and other positions, and ongoing unavailable research all suggest that large gaps exist. Nevertheless, this chapter appears to be the first comprehensive attempt to synthesize such information. As such, it is designed to serve as a baseline for further parallel efforts.

Some gaps have been deliberate. There has been no attempt to examine certain media institutions—e.g., instructional television, communication technology in general, computer information systems, or satellite communication—because of some self-imposed parameters. Included was an attempt to survey the major print and broadcast institutions; therefore, newspapers, magazines, radio, television, and film have been examined. Two major media institutions that would have qualified for examination had sufficient data been available would have been the book industry and the record industry.

The thrust of the chapter will begin with the economics of the mass media, as they reflect on minority groups in this country and will end with the early returns of research designed to tap the effects of mass media content about minorities.

## MINORITY ECONOMICS IN THE MASS MEDIA

Immediately after two major and intertwined historial events in 1968, American media institutions responded with intense efforts to channel minorities into their structure. The events were the assassination of Dr. Martin Luther King, Jr., and the report of the National Advisory Commission on Divil Disorders (1968). The creation of this Commission was triggered by the epidemic riots that began with Watts in 1965 and engulfed the nation for the next six years.

In its report, the Commission accused the media of widening "the black-white schism" by not communicating to its predominantly white audience "a feeling for the difficulties and frustrations" of being black in America. It urged immediate promotion, recruitment, and training of blacks in the media.

These events—the riots, the assassination, and the report—also gave rise to changes in black economic development in media ownership.

What will be examined here is the status of those early and later media efforts in the areas of employment and ownership, and recent legislation affecting those areas. Finally, we will turn to efforts by the media aimed at extracting dollars from a rapidly expanding minorities market.

### Minority employment in majority media

In 1972 a committee of the American Society of Newspaper Editors (1972) reported some grim news concerning the minority hiring practices of the fourth estate:

> Members of the standard minority groups (Negroes, Mexican-Americans, Puerto Ricans, Cubans and those of Oriental descent) do not as yet constitute 1 percent of the professional news force. The . . . Committee was able to locate only 253-minority group professionals on daily newspapers . . . the total professional figure nationally may reasonably be estimated at approximately 300—or three-fourths of 1 percent of the total writer-photographer-editor employment (of 40,000). . . . (p. 624)

Newspapers were not alone among the media in lagging on minority employment. Information synthesized from several sources[1] reveals that in 1972

---

[1] Percentages based on information from the Equal Employment Opportunity Commission (EEOC), the Federal Communications Commission (FCC), The Newspaper Guild, Editorial Research Reports, and the Congressional Black Caucus.

white-controlled media hiring practices for blacks in *professional* [2] positions was about:

   . . . 1.5% on newspapers,
   . . . 2.5% on magazines,
   . . . 6% in broadcasting,[3]
   . . . 2.6% in the motion picture industry.

For other racial minorities (Spanish-surnamed Americans, American Indians, and Orientals) the total comparable percentages were approximately: [4]

   . . . 0.13% on newspapers,
   . . . 2.4% on magazines,
   . . . 2.7% in broadcasting,[5]
   . . . 3.7% in the motion picture industry.[6]

Table 1 lists the totals and percentages for employment in all job categories.

## The Top 50 Television Markets

In an analysis of minority employment, former FCC Commissioner Nicholas Johnson (Johnson, 1973) ranked network affiliates in the top 50 markets by comparing minority employment to minority population in the areas served by the television stations. The minority population was based on the Standard Metropolitan Statistical Areas (SMSA) of the Census Bureau. A station with a resultant factor of 1,000 would have employed exactly the same percentage of minorities as existed in its area population.

The top station in the ranking was WTEV—an ABC affiliate in Providence, Rhode Island—with a factor of 2.451. WTEV employed 8.33% minorities in an area with a minority population of 3.4%.

The bottom-rated stations in Johnson's survey were WKZO—a CBS

•

---

[2] According to the EEOC, the job category "professional" includes accountants, auditors, artists, editors, librarians. Another classification, which is not listed above, is officials and managers. This includes executives, middle management, department managers and superintendents, purchasing agents and buyers. In this category, the EEOC figures taken separately are based on 639 newspapers, 118 magazines, 518 radio and television stations, and 254 motion picture firms. The black percentages for this category are newspapers—1.5; periodicals—0.5; radio and television stations—2.8; and motion picture firms—1.6.

[3] This also includes the three major television networks—ABC, CBS, and NBC.

[4] For all other minority groups combined, in the officials and managers categories, the EEOC percentages are newspapers—1.2; periodicals—0.9; radio and television stations—1.5; and motion picture firms—2.4.

[5] See note 3.

[6] According to the Equal Employment Opportunity Commission, American Indians held no "professional" jobs in the motion picture industry, of all such units with more than 100 employees, required to file reports with the commission. In the category of officials and managers, American Indians held .6 percent of these positions.

**Table 1.** Minority Employment in Selected Media*

| Totals | Newspapers | Magazines | Broadcasting | Films |
|---|---|---|---|---|
| Employees | 240,000 | 37,000 | 130,650 | 36,000 |
| Blacks | 12,000 | 3,200 | 8,700 | 2,500 |
| Spanish-speaking Surname | 4,500 | 1,000 | 4,000 | 2,200 |
| Orientals | 657 | 300 | 690 | 570 |
| American Indians | 416 | 20 | 530 | 170 |
| Pct. Black | .05 | .08 | .06 | .06 |
| Pct. Spanish-speaking | .01 | .02 | .03 | .06 |
| Pct. Oriental | .002 | .008 | .005 | .015 |
| Pct. American Indians | .001 | .0005 | .004 | .004 |

*Based on information from EEOC, 1972 minority group employment statistics, and the FCC. The EEOC figures are based on 639 newspapers, 118 magazines, 518 radio and television stations, and 254 motion picture firms.

affiliate serving the Kalamazoo-Grand Rapids (Michigan) area—and KMSP—an ABC affiliate in the Minneapolis-St. Paul (Minnesota) area. Each had a factor rating of 0.0. Neither station allegedly employed any minorities in areas with a minority population of 6.1 and 3.7%, respectively.

In his report, Johnson noted:

> While this method of ranking does tend to favor stations in a region with a lower minority population, we would point out that a number of such stations, in markets like Salt Lake City (Utah) and Minneapolis-St. Paul, nevertheless found themselves at the very bottom. . . (p. 84)

Johnson continued: "It is rather appalling to note that some 82 percent of the stations . . . have total employment factors of less than 1.000 and more than 35 percent . . . have factors of less than 0.500. Certainly the latter group deserves a more serious inquiry" (p. 84).

Nevertheless, with this measure, it would be possible for a station to attain a relatively high position in the rankings and still have most of its minorities in low-paying, menial positions.

"Discrimination in filling the higher paying, more influential positions may be every bit as significant to the minority group member discriminated against," said Johnson (p. 88).

This finding prompted Johnson to rerank stations based only on the percentage of minorities they employed as officials, managers, professionals, technicians, sales workers, and skilled craftsmen.

In this listing, KABC—an ABC affiliate in Los Angeles, California—was at the top, with minorities holding 45 of its 162 high-paying positions.

A number of stations made the bottom of the list for employing no minorities in high paying positions. They were: WKZO; KMSP; WHTN (ABC), Charleston-Huntington, West Virginia; KUTV (NBC), Salt Lake City, Utah; WRGB (NBC), Albany-Schenectady, New York, and WSPA (CBS), Greenville-Ashville, North Carolina.

## Public Television Stations

In 1973 the Office of Communication, United Church of Christ, released a study of 125 of the 223 public television stations. The stations reported that 9.4% (650) of all full- and part-time employees were minority group members, an increase of 1% from the previous year. About 500 were full-time (Jennings, Kerr, and Parker, 1973).

The majority of all full-time public television station employees (75%) are in the top three job categories as officials and managers, professionals, and technicians. Seven percent (281) of these positions were held by minorities in 1972.

The licensees reported a total of 6,910 employees (5,430 full-time) in 1972, an increase of 392 from the previous year.

According to the report, blacks held the largest proportion of the minority group positions, 426 in all, while Spanish-surname Americans, Orientals, and American Indians accounted for 205 of the positions.

The report noted that 44 of the stations employed no minority group members on a full-time basis in 1972, and 52 of the stations employed no minority group members in any of the top three job categories.

Another finding in the report was that of 644 members of boards of directors, 7% were members of minority groups.

As corroborative evidence, the National Association of Educational Broadcasters (1972) noted in its 1972 report of 156 public television stations that minority groups represented 9.6% of full- and part-time employees. It reported 494 minorities in full-time positions and 172 in part-time positions.

The minority group employment figures show a decline in public broadcasting between 1970-1972. Both reports generally show a total minority employment percentage of about 9.5% in 1972, 8% in 1971, and a peak of 12% in 1970.

Neither report presents a comprehensive employment picture for the 223 stations, since only a broadcast licensee with five or more full-time employees is required to file an employment report. Because so many of the public radio licensees employ less than five persons, employment data from public radio stations were unobtainable.

A comparison of minority employment in commercial and public television appears in Table 2.

**Table 2.** Minority Employment in Commercial and Public Television*

|  | Commercial TV | Public TV |
|---|---|---|
| Full-time positions held by minorities | 10% | 9% |
| Part-time positions held by minorities | 19% | 10% |
| Total of all full- and part-time positions combined | 11% | 9% |
| Stations employing no minorities on a full-time basis | 22.5% | 35.2% |
| Stations employing no minorities as officials and managers, professionals and technicians | 35% | 42% |

*Based on a sample of 609 commercial television stations and 125 public television stations, taken by the Office of Communication, United Church of Christ, New York, November 1972 and January 1973 (Jennings, 1972; Jennings, Kerr, and Parker, 1973).

### Economic growth of minority media

With a broadened economic base—aided by federally assisted programs, private firms, and foundations—and the increased earning power of blacks themselves, it appears that for the first time blacks are able to consider media ownership on an extensive basis.

*Newspapers*

Black-owned and black-content newspapers have existed since 1827 when *Freedom's Journal* was published in New York City by John Russwurm and Samuel Cornish (Costello, 1972).

By January 31, 1973, there were an estimated 216 black newspapers with a total circulation of nearly 4.1 million. Four of the papers were dailies: *The Atlanta Daily World,* the *Chicago Daily Defender,* the *Columbus Times,* and the *New York Daily Challenge.* Most of the remaining black newspapers were weeklies (Editor and Publisher International Yearbook, 1973).

This compares to 1,761 white dailies (total circulation, 62.5 million) and 8,862 weeklies.

The black publications had a total work force of about 2,500, of whom 10% were white.

More than half the newspapers—120—reported a circulation of 10,000 or more. Each of 11 newspapers claimed a circulation in excess of 50,000. The largest circulation—600,000—was claimed by the Muslim newspaper, *Muhammed Speaks,* based in Chicago.

It has been generally though that circulation of the black press would increase based on two factors: the increased size of the black population and a concomitant economic growth in this population.

That this is already happening may be attested to by the circulation figures cited above and a trend toward black newspaper chains. According to the 1973 Editor and Publisher Yearbook, seven black newspaper chains were in existence. The newest of these is the 7-paper San Francisco Metro Group, which began October 1, 1972, and has a circulation of about 89,000.

Other major chains included the Los Angeles-based Central News-Wave chain (eight newspapers), with a circulation of more than 240,000; the six Sengstacke papers, with a combined circulation of more than 151,000; and the Afro-American chain, with a circulation of about 79,000.

At the 1972 convention of the National Newspaper Publishers Association, black publishers reported a 70% increase in circulation since 1970 and a 23% increase in advertising since 1971 (Costello, 1972).

For the Spanish-surname population in the United States, 17 newspapers were owned by Spanish-surname Americans, with a total circulation of 295,530, according to the 1973 Editor and Publisher International Yearbook. No employment figures were given.

About 100 American Indian-owned newspapers exist, according to Richard LaCourse, news director of the American Indian Press Association. Two are national newspapers—*Akwesasne Notes,* published in Rooseveltown, New York, by the Iroquois Nation, and *Wassaja,* published in San Francisco, California, by the American Indian Historical Society. Total circulation and employment figures were not available.

*Magazines*

On July 17, 1972, *Newsweek* commented: "there are black magazines for virtually every taste from the academic (*Black Scholar*) to the athletic (*Black Sports*)."

Since the end of World War II, black magazines have indeed proliferated. One well-known journalism-educator has estimated that about 60 such publications existed as of 1972, including 50 specialized journals and nearly a dozen general magazines.[7]

There are about 9,000 total magazines, nationally.

The five largest-circulated black periodicals as of mid-1973 were *Tuesday* (a supplement distributed primarily to about 25 white newspapers)—2,000,000 circulation; *Ebony*—over 1,000,000; *Jet*—560,000; *Essence*—150,000; and *Black Enterprise*—about 125,000.

Three companies prevail in general magazine circulation: Tuesday Publications, Johnson Publishing Co., and Good Publishing Co. Johnson publishes *Ebony, Jet, Tan,* and *Black World* (formerly *Negro Digest*). Products of the Good Publishing Co. are *Sepia, Jive, Bronze Thrills, Hep,* and *Soul Concessions.*

Black magazines, like black newspapers, are increasing as well. Between 1972 and 1973, at least three new publications entered the black magazine field: *Encore, Relevant,* and *Foxtrapper.*

No central sources were located for determining magazine ownership by Spanish-surname Americans. The American Indian Press Association reports that there are nine general interest magazines owned by American Indians and 18 Indian-owned printing firms.

*Television Stations*

Of the nearly 1,000 television stations in the country, blacks currently own two of them. Both are UHF stations—one in Detroit and the other in Washington, D.C. The licenses for the more prevalent VHF stations are all held by whites (Black Enterprise).

Indications of television stations owned by Spanish-surname Americans could not be located, and no television stations are owned by American Indians.

*Radio Stations*

While about 360 of the 7,000 AM and FM radio stations program to the black community, blacks own about 30 of them. One researcher estimated

[7] Roland Wolseley, in *Editorial Research Reports*, August 1972, p. 638.

that 75% of black-owned and/or operated radio stations feature a soul music format (Meyer, 1971).

There are 253 stations programming to the Spanish-surname population in the United States, but no indications of ownership could be found. Of 55 radio stations devoting time to American Indian programming, only one is owned by American Indians.

## Cable Television

A major black business magazine has projected that several large cities will have a penetration level of 20% to 35% of the houses in cable television areas. In some metropolitan areas, the saturation level may be 100%.[8]

There is a strong movement by blacks to enter the cable television field, both in employment ranks and, especially, in ownership ranks.

In a message to a 1971 workshop on "Minority Business Opportunities in Cable TV," former FCC Commissioner Nicholas Johnson stated:

> You may have lost out on radio. You may have lost out on over-the-air television. And few of you can really claim effective organs of print communication. Now comes cable television, perhaps the biggest communication bonanza of them all, and in my estimation the last hope for a significant minority involvement in our communications revolution. . . . You must begin to get involved at once.[9]

Of the more than 4,500 cable franchises, blacks own only a handful of them. Their franchises have been limited to predominantly black communities and in urban areas with a sizable black population.

Other ethnic minorities appear to own no cable systems.

While the precise number of cable franchises wholly or partly owned by blacks is not known at this time, at least 11 such operations do exist (Ledbetter and Lomax, 1973).

## The Film Industry[10]

A black official in the film industry recently commented:

> If blacks want a piece of the movie business, they are going to have to get into the business side of things and stop trying simply to be

---

[8] *Black Enterprise*, August 1973, p. 37.

[9] Meeting held in Washington, D.C., June 24-27, 1971.

[10] All information for this section is from *Black Enterprise*, September 1973, pp. 47-53.

stars. They must become producers, distributors, and finally, begin to open up some of those boarded-up movie houses that sit empty in black communities. . . .

Black production companies are not new. All-black movies were around in the 1920s, '30s, and '40s, produced by such black companies as Colored Players Film and Nicheaux Picture.

In 1972-73 more than 40 full-length motion pictures featuring blacks in major roles were produced, compared to ten such films precisely a decade before that. About 72 black films were produced between 1967 and 1973.

Of the more than 20,000 movie theaters in the country, only a few are owned by blacks, according to Joseph E. Porter, an attorney for International Pictures.

## Changes in regulatory control and legislation

In what clearly has to be regarded as one of the most important cases affecting the FCC, the US Circuit Court of Appeals in 1968 ruled that public groups have a right to intervene in station licensing procedures.

In a decision handed down by Judge Warren Burger, now Chief Justice of the US Supreme Court, the circuit court determined that responsible community organizations such as "civic associations, professional societies, unions, churches and educational institutions or associations" have the right to contest the license renewal of a station that ignores its public responsibilities.

The decision was the result of a 1964 action by the Office of Communication, United Church of Christ. The Office petitioned the FCC to deny license renewals to two Jackson, Mississippi, television stations on grounds of consistent discrimination against black viewers. At that time, black viewers constituted 45% of the stations' audience (Prowitt, 1971).

The FCC ordered the stations to cease discrimination but refused to hold a hearing. That ruling was overturned in the court's landmark decision.

The decision augered the onslaught of license renewal protests that deluged FCC commissioners and staff for months, but at the same time opened channels for license renewal reform.

In June 1969, the Federal Communications Commission adopted rules prohibiting discrimination in employment. Among other requirements, licensees must file annual reports indicating the number of minority employees in several job categories.

FCC records showed that 104 complaints were filed (about 90 from minority groups) between June 30, 1971, and May 5, 1972.

In addition, complaints of discrimination may also be filed with the Equal Employment Opportunity Commission. If a station has 15 or more employees, the complaint is handled by the EEOc; if less than 25 employees-

–the FCC will inquire or investigate. Complaints regarding the print media are referred to the EEOC. The EEOC also requires employers of 100 or more persons to file minority employment reports. Complaints against public television and radio stations may be filed with the Department of Health, Education and Welfare, since most of the funding for those operations is channeled through that agency.

Under the FCC rules, stations are charged with developing "positive recruitment, training, job design and other measures in order to insure genuine equality of opportunity to participate fully in all organizational units, occupations and levels of responsibility in the station" (Prowitt, p. 12)

Practices that each station should follow in recruitment, selection, training, placement, promotion, pay, working conditions, demotion, layoff, and termination are also specified.

The Commission urged that broadcasters "consider the adoption of special training programs for qualifiable minority group members, [and] cooperative action with other organizations to improve employment opportunities and community conditions that affect employability . . . " (Prowitt, p. 12)

In 1970, after the US Circuit Court of Appeals decision, the FCC announced that it would eliminate the competitive hearing process held on license challenges. This emulated a move in 1969 by Sen. John Pastore, Democrat from Rhode Island, to prevent new applicants from seeking radio and television licenses unless the FCC had previously revoked the existing license.

Black Efforts for Soul in Television (BEST), an organization formed to aid minority interests in the media, successfully challenged the FCC action before the US Court of Appeals in Washington, D.C. The Court in its ruling of June 1971 stated: "As new interest groups and hitherto silent minorities emerge in our society, they should be given some stake and chance to broadcast on our radio and TV frequencies. . . ," (Costello, p. 624) It remains possible for new groups to challenge existing license holders.

## Minorities as an advertising market

To many media advertisers, the road to the ghetto seems to be paved with gold. Ethnic broadcasting is big business. Advertising revenues–and rates –are skyrocketing; national sponsors are budgeting more money for black-oriented and foreign language stations than any time previously.

An increased concern for ethnic minorities has been posited by some for the rise, but most observers agree that the primary–and perhaps only–impetus is money.

The black consumer market, based on a population of approximately 23 million, will spend about $45 billion in 1973-74 for goods and services. In the top 78 radio and television markets, this represents one of every three consumers (Glenn, 1973).

The 11 million Spanish-surname Americans in the US will spend $20 billion during that period.

A common list of sponsors for ethnic broadcast stations includes food and beverage companies, automobile manufacturers, airlines, and drug companies, among others.

A decade ago, for many black-oriented media, advertising would have been concentrated on hair pomades and straighteners, skin whiteners, make-up, soul food, and similar items geared exclusively to blacks.

In a content analysis of advertising in *Ebony* close to a decade ago, more advertisements were devoted to "Negro cosmetics and hair products" and "money-making opportunities" than any other categories (Berkman, 1963).

Certainly the increase in earning power and other financial opportunities made available to minorities have contributed to the new emphasis by national advertisers.

To paraphrase one radio executive: "Today the media of ethnic minorities are viable. Ten years ago, they weren't."

Supporting this is the fact that several of the independent (nonnetwork affiliated) radio and television stations are either including for the first time or expanding ethnic formats.

Market analyses by advertisers and media researchers show that the buying power of ethnic minorities has risen sharply in the last dozen years, concomitant with the urbanization and economic growth of many minority groups. Since 1939, the cash income of blacks, for example, has risen from $10.3 billion to $16 billion (1957), to $20 billion (1960) (Bauer and Cunningham, 1970), to the present $45 billion black consumer market in 1973.

Several market observers are attributing a significant portion of the increase in media revenues this year to expanded ethnic advertising.

In the latest figures for 1972, television revenues were slightly more than $3 billion, a nearly 16% increase from the previous year. Pretax earnings were $552 million, a 42% jump. Billings in 1973 were 13% above 1972.

In radio, a survey by the National Association of Broadcasters indicated the average radio outlet had an 11.4% gain in revenues and a 25.2% gain in pretax profits. According to the 1973 Broadcasting Yearbook, total revenues were $1.2 billion for radio stations and networks.

This prosperous picture of the ethnic minorities market has implications for increased minority ownership in the media. By fate, design, or both, the minority groups are beginning to stem the one-way flow of dollars—previously from their respective communities to media owners and advertisers. Now, it seems assured, a significant share of these dollars will flow back to their original source—minority groups who are becoming active in media ownership.

# THE INCIDENCE AND PORTRAYAL OF BLACKS IN THE MASS MEDIA

Thus far, the question of racism in the media has been examined in terms of the economic access of minorities to the media—both job opportunities and job levels—and in terms of recent legistlative changes that may alter job options. That same legislation is capable of increasing minorities access to the media for programming purposes and to create their own messages for public dissemination. This potential opportunity for minorities has been designed to offset what minorities themselves have described as unequal or biased presentations by the majority media. The question here, then, is whether and in what ways the majority media, through the messages they have disseminated, have depicted, ignored, or ridiculed racial minorities in their news and entertainment content. To make the question more causally oriented, any potential media effects on attitudes or behavior of an audience must be a function of the content to which those audiences are exposed.

This section is confined to an examination of black portrayals in the mass media. Our screening of the literature yields no comprehensive efforts to deal with Indians, Chicanos, or any other minority group. Some who have attempted such efforts with those minorities have been frustrated by the empty sets obtained. The number of Chicanos featured in television advertisements or television programs is virtually nil. No systematic studies of Indians were located, and one must rely on the continuing western image of the Bad Indian as the most prevalent one available. But numerous studies have focused on the mass media images of blacks and it is these that will be synthesized here.

This overview begins with the paradigm suggested by Clark (1969). He has argued forcefully that minority groups develop through four phases of mass media transition, particularly in entertainment media. There is non-recognition—or the invisible man (let alone woman)—where for all purposes the minority does not exist in the media. There is ridicule, when it becomes fashionable to lampoon specific groups—e.g., lazy blacks, drunk Irish, stupid Polish, miserly Jew. There is then a regulatory stage. This is not external regulation imposed on the media, but rather the use of the minorities in regulatory roles within media programming. These are the cops and robbers roles. Clark believes that blacks are now being treated primarily in this fashion by televison—as assistants to police chiefs, as rookie cops, as private eyes, and as the nemeses of these good guys. A fourth level of development will be respect.

Motion pictures provided the earliest media opportunities to see black people, and the films were almost uniformly negative or anti-black in their themes. Reddick's (1944) survey of 100 such films identified 75% of them as anti-Negro and another 13% as neutral. There has obviously been a progression from the Steppin-Fetchit/Ethel Waters portrayals through Sidney Poitier to the love scenes between Jim Brown and Racqual Welch. Mapp (1972) has documented the increasing frequency of blacks in American films, and his critical study, through 1970, touches on the beginning of the black film—those designed primarily for black audiences, rather than black overflow to what are basically white films with black actors and actresses. Full documentation of the major changes of the last half-decade is not available, but it remains apparent that no black actress has yet achieved the stature or fame—for the majority society—of half a dozen black actors. Current concerns have been expressed by the NAACP, among others, that the old stereotyped movie black has been replaced by another stereotype—the pusher, fast with women of both races, in flashy cars and clothes. Movies such as "Sounder" remain rare events.

It is in the media areas of the press and broadcasting that more comprehensive and analytical studies have been made.

Shuey (1953) examined pictures of blacks in advertising and non-advertising content for the period 1949-50 in six general circulation magazines (e.g., *Life, Time, Saturday Evening Post*). She found blacks in 0.5% of all ads and in 2.5% of the nonadvertising material. Nearly 80% of all the blacks in ads were maids, cooks, or servants—for whites. Most of the whites were "idle," enjoying lunch, sitting in cars, eating, drinking. In nonadvertising content, somewhat different occupations were identified for blacks—entertainers, athletes, and primitives—so the greater frequency in editorial matter was in the direction of a continuing stereotype. These proportions did not correspond to the distribution of blacks in occupations according to census data.

Colle (1968) described the early presentation (in the 1930s and 1940s) of blacks in any media as a distinctly negative stereotype, and then said that post-War presentations in the late '40s and '50s could be assessed as non-representations—the "invisible" black. The Shuey (1953) study supports the invisibility notion, but the Colle estimate of when it occurred must be extended well into the 1960s. Kassarjian (1969) compared 12 general circulation magazines in 1964-65 with the same magazines in 1969, but still found blacks in less than 2% of all ads in 1969, although the total number tripled. Given a baseline of virtually zero, any increase seems large proportionally, but not numerically. This kind of change is better documented by Stempel (1971), who compared the presentation of blacks in ads and news pictures in *Life, Look, Newsweek, Time,* and *U.S. News* for both 1960 and 1970. Blacks appeared in .6% of the 1960 ads and in 5% of all news pictures; by 1970, these percentages had increased to 3% of the ads and 13% of all news pictures. The advertising emphasis was still trivial.

In newspapers, the advertising situation was even more dismal. Boyenton (1965) found 14 ads with blacks in some 20,000 ads in a sample of issues of *The New York Times,* two ads in 380 pages of the *Chicago Tribune,* and two ads in some 2,000 ads in the *New York Times Magazine,* all during 1963 and 1964. From these analyses, it is apparent that more concern was being shown by editors than by advertisers, but the total concern was marginal.

The Shuey (1953) study was replicated by Cox in 1967 and 1968 for advertisements only (Cox, 1969-70). Faces of blacks in ads had increased from less than 1% to barely more than 2%. Cox was elated, however, in finding that the vast majority of blacks were also now being portrayed in occupations that fell in the above-skilled-labor category and that "idle" blacks had increased from 1% to 14%. However, Colfax and Sternberg (1972) had a less favorable interpretation of those changes when they did a second replication in 1970. By then, 7% of all ads had blacks, although only 4% of all people depicted in ads were blacks. But Colfax and Sternberg emphasized that the qualitative presentation of these blacks was still highly questionable. They pointed out that: (a) 40% of all ads with blacks in 1970 showed blacks on the covers of record albums being advertised; (b) more than half of all blacks on nonrecord ads were "token" blacks, appearing with from 5-1,000 white people at the same time; (c) one-third of those ads had only black children in them—where a white was counselor, teacher, or master in some other fashion; and (d) another 10% of the ads showed blacks as "losers," receiving welfare, charity, and similar largesse.

It is emphases such as this that led the National Advisory Commission on Civil Disorders (1968) to conclude that:

> If what the white American reads in the newspapers or sees on television conditions his expectations of what is ordinary and normal in the larger society, he will neither understand nor accept the black American. By failing to portray the Negro as a matter of routine and in the context of the total society, the news media have, we believe, contributed to the black-white schism in this country.

And the Commission was not cognizant of the differentiation we have documented between the greater concern of the news media and the lesser concern of the advertisers.

The content of fictional print material has not been documented to any extent, nor does one find evidence about the treatment of blacks in the news columns of American newspapers outside of rather limited and localized content analyses. Although we wish to turn more directly to what television has done with blacks, perhaps the reader can tolerate one further print example for its novelty at least. Blacks in *Playboy* cartoons were examined from 1956 through part of 1969 (Greenberg and Kahn, 1970). This liberal magazine has long been at the center—if not centerfold—of civil rights issues, the encouragement of black writers, and the mocking of bigotry. It is also this country's chief humor magazine. How did it treat blacks in its cartoons? In the decade from 1956 through 1966, less than 1% of all cartoons contained a black character in a non-African setting. This was 12 cartoons in 84 issues! There were an equal number of cartoons in aboriginal settings. In 1967, cartoons with blacks numbered 1.4%, in 1968—2.7%, and by mid-1969 the number had increased to 3.5%. Blacks were not included in the humor in *Playboy*; they had not been assimiliated into that content area. Characteristics of the cartoon characters were also examined. Black women were half as frequent, proportionately, as their white counterparts; cartoons with blacks averaged eight people in them and cartoons without blacks averaged five, reinvoking the tokenism concept of Colfax and Sternberg (1972); cartoons with no blacks were far more likely to be in middle-class settings; the basis for the humor in nearly half the black cartoons was race-related; and if a black had a major role in the cartoon, it was less likely to be in a cartoon that focused its humor on sex. Perhaps on the positive side, there was a linear growth pattern over the years in the frequency of blacks showing distinctively black choices in their dress or appearance—e.g., Afros, dashikis.

Whatever awakening to black America occurred in the print media, it did not manifest itself until the late 1960s, and even then at a barely observable level.

Shifting finally to the depiction of blacks in television, the present authors updated a series of studies done by Dominick and Greenberg (1970). In the original studies, a week of prime-time and daytime television was viewed for 1967, 1968, and 1969 on three networks. All ads and programs were analyzed for black presentations from 1:00-4:00 p.m. and 7:30-11:00 p.m. for 7 consecutive days and nights. In the update of these data, a composite week of prime-time television was watched.* The first studies were based on 73.5 hours of night-time programming each year, the current (1973) study on 24.5 hours.

In the earliest TV study identified, Plotkin (1964) found a black face on television once every 2.5 hours during 1962. Let us briefly recall those glorious days of yesteryear. In 1951, blacks on television were "Amos 'n' Andy," and this series was in syndication until the mid-1960s. In addition, one could see several Beulahs or Jack Benny's Rochester. Occasional singers and dancers appeared, but not regularly until Nat Cole's 1957 program, which failed its first year for lack of sponsor support.

The black breakthrough came with Bill Cosby's role in the "I Spy" series. This was 1965. In the late 1960s, some two dozen black actors and actresses acquired major or minor roles in continuing series. Blacks were very visible, at least as "second bananas." But it was the novelty that was apparent, and not necessarily the frequency. Lemon (1968) found that in 1967 barely 2% of all commercials used any blacks, Orientals, Puerto Ricans, or Indians. These same groups could be seen in about one-fourth of all variety shows, but less than one-fifth of the dramatic offerings.

The original studies by Dominick and Greenberg were done to provide a

---

*The authors wish to acknowledge the valuable aid of Mrs. Jan Shubert in this coding project.

Table 3. Characteristics of Blacks in TV Ads During Prime Time

|  | 1967 | 1968 | 1969 | 1973 |
|---|---|---|---|---|
| Ads with blacks | 4% | 6% | 10% | 14% |
|  | (777) | (940) | (1176) | (366) |
| Ads with blacks by network: |  |  |  |  |
| CBS | 4% | 6% | 11% | 12% |
| NBC | 5% | 7% | 10% | 15% |
| ABC | 4% | 6% | 10% | 17% |
| Median number of characters: |  |  |  |  |
| Ads without blacks | 1.6 | 1.7 | 1.9 | 1.8 |
| Ads with blacks | 10.0 | 7.0 | 6.0 | 6.4 |
| Type of ad: |  |  |  |  |
| Product | 3% | 6% | 8% | 13% |
| Promotion | 6% | 4% | 20% | 15% |
| PSA | 24% | 18% | 21% | 29% |
| Number of blacks: | 55 | 71 | 168 | 318* |
| Role |  |  |  |  |
| Major | 13% | 7% | 28% | 18% |
| Minor | 40% | 48% | 42% | 17% |
| Background | 47% | 45% | 30% | 65% |
| % Female | 27 | 44 | 41 | 36 |
| % Holding product | 16 | 34 | 23 | 27 |
| % Speaking | 9 | 23 | 27 | 19 |

*The raw figure for 1973 was 106. Projecting to the same number of hours as coded in the prior years yields this estimate.

more systematic assessment of what kinds of changes were occurring, if any. Table 3 provides both an historical and current assessment of the quality and quantity of blacks in commercial television advertising. The major trends appear to be:

1. A continuing and significant linear trend in the frequency with which at least one black face is seen in commercials. The shift is best characterized as moving from one black face every two hours in 1967, to two every hour in 1973.

2. The most likely advertising vehicle in which a black is likely to be seen is the public service announcement; however, blacks were identified in 13% of all product ads.

3. The total number of blacks in ads has increased geometrically from 1967 through 1973. For the 1973 week, an estimated 318 blacks could be seen in one week of evening commercials, compared to 55 six years earlier. The blacks constituted a fraction less than 7% of all the people in commercials.

4. As the number of blacks has increased, there has been a significant increase in the use of blacks in background or walk-on roles rather than major roles.

5. There continues to be a sharp distinction between ads with and without blacks in terms of the composition of the group in the ads. Ads without blacks typically have two people in them; those with blacks have more than six people. Blacks are less visible in ads in which they appear; during the 1973 study week, 96 ads without blacks had but a single person in them; only one ad had a lone black. One-third of the ads that contained a black person had from 15-100 other people in the ad.

6. The Afro is now an accepted television symbol of blacks. Two-thirds of all blacks in commercials had Afro-style hair.

Certainly, then, there are far more blacks in ads, numerically and proportionately. Their presentation remains highly selective in terms of context. However, television's use of blacks far surpasses that of any other identified mass medium. Independent validation of these findings comes from Roberts (1971), who identified 10% blacks in a week of prime time commericals in 1970.

Turning to dramatic offerings, our 1973 analysis provided data from 34 shows aired during the study period. Fifteen of these shows, or 44%, had blacks; 11% of all the people were black—49 blacks in all. However, 15 of them were on one ABC variety program. Table 4 excludes three variety shows and one public affairs program in its summary of the black presentations on 30 situation comedy and action-adventure shows. On these shows, 9% of all people were black. Major findings in Table 4 are:

1. About half of all shows now and during the last five years have had at least one black character; Roberts' (1971) independent study reports the same figure.

2. ABC dominates in its trend toward using black actors and actresses; it also has begun to emerge as the leader in advertising with blacks.

3. The number of blacks being used has continued a sharp upturn; the proportion in major roles may be stabilizing at about one-fifth.

4. Giving and taking orders by blacks during any given program has been equalized; half do and half don't.

5. Very few story lines contain any racial references in shows with blacks.

6. Now, more than ever, blacks are seen with both other blacks and whites in these shows; tokenism in drama has disappeared or is less visible.

7. The best guess is that blacks still appear more often and with greater emphasis on nondramatic shows—i.e., variety shows.

Clearly, the record for television has been a promising one since 1967—and probably somewhat earlier than that—in terms of its use of blacks in both advertising and programming. That medium's record is far more inclusive than any we have been able to identify for a print institution.

**Table 4.** Blacks in TV Shows

|  | 1967 | 1968 | 1969 | 1973 |
|---|---|---|---|---|
| Dramas with black characters | 34% | 52% | 52% | 43% |
| (total shows) | (59) | (64) | (58) | (30) |
| By network: |  |  |  |  |
| CBS | 45% | 43% | 39% | 24% |
| NBC | 43% | 47% | 55% | 40% |
| ABC | 20% | 67% | 60% | 88% |
| Number of blacks | 40 | 74 | 70 | 99* |
| Role: |  |  |  |  |
| Major | 63% | 45% | 20% | 18% |
| Minor | 30% | 46% | 31% | 30% |
| Background | 7% | 7% | 49% | 52% |
| Orders: |  |  |  |  |
| Gave | 25% | 28% | 30% | 48% |
| Took | 43% | 39% | 53% | 51% |
| Racial References | 40 | 16 | 13 | 9 |
| Seen: |  |  |  |  |
| Only with whites | 70 | 35 | 39 | 27 |
| With blacks and whites | 30 | 46 | 50 | 72 |
| Other | 0 | 19 | 11 | 1 |

*The raw figure for 1973 was 33. This is a projection to the same number of hours as coded in prior years.

One further comparison point is possible in this analysis of television content. Other Western countries have developed media systems and parallel charges of minority discrimination are being vocalized. One such country is

England. In 1971, Greenberg (1971) studied a week of prime-time British television. The same methodology was used as in the studies cited above. What was sought were any instances of nonwhite presentations, inclusive of Indians, West Indians, Africans, Pakistani, Orientals, and American Negroes. The population of those groups in England is 2.5% of the total population. All programs on the two BBC channels and the independent channel were analyzed; advertising exists only on the independent channel.

Thirty-four dramas were analyzed, excluding feature films that were included in the American studies. In those British TV shows, eight contained 35 nonwhites compared with 648 whites in all the programs. More than half the whites spoke, but only one-quarter of the nonwhites. US programs on British television yielded nearly half of the nonwhites seen. There was but one nonwhite in a major role on any British-produced program. In terms of commercials on the channel, 2.5% of all ads contained a nonwhite, forming .8% of all the people in ads. The nonwhite is virtually nonexistent on British-produced programs in England, either in dramatic programs or in commercials.

In this section, we have tried to map the nature of black presentations in several mass media. Early, uniformly negative stereotypes in films gave way to a specific absence from most media and led to what is a now increasing incidence of blacks in all media. The question is no longer, are there any blacks in the media. The answer is yes—more in some media than others, with television apparently setting the standard to which other media might refer, at least in terms of sheer frequency. The remaining content analytic question is to more fully determine the nature of the kinds of presentations being made. The question of what effects the current presentation of blacks may be having is the issue in the final section of this chapter.

## SOCIAL EFFECTS OF THE MASS MEDIA BY RACE

In this concluding section, we shall attempt to map the interface between what is available in terms of general media content and media content about blacks, with the usage made of this content by black and white viewers. This section will proceed through these issues: (a) comparative mass media use of black and whites, (2) significant media attitudes of the two races, and (c) the use of media content as a means of minority socialization, including the effects of exposure to blacks on television.

### Comparative media usage

Two results predominate. First, race as a predictor of mass media use is confounded with income; the patterns of low-income blacks and whites is more similar than dissimilar, and both tend to be discrepant from middle-class whites. Second, the major medium of the poor is television; it occupies a significant time portion of the lives of poor people in general, and blacks even more so (Greenberg and Dervin, 1970).

Among nine- and ten-year-old children, the blacks watched weekday and evening television slightly more than six hourse each day, regardless of their income level; low-income whites watched six hourse, middle-class—five hours, and high-income—slightly less than four hours each day. The low-income kids were more likely to watch television before going to school in the morning, during their lunch hour, after school, and in the late evening.

As to other media, all racial-income groups spent about an hour each day listening to the radio, but the white children were more frequent listeners of radio newscasts. Black children listened more often to records (about 80 minutes) and were more likely to be moviegoers (about two per month). Both these latter media activities permitted the black viewer to be selective in choice of media content, seeking available culturally appropriate stimuli.

White children reported reading a newspaper three or four time a week and blacks less than three times a week (Greenberg and Dominick, 1970).

Among teen-agers, weekend viewing for blacks exceeds six hours a day, with low-income whites at five, and middle-income whites at four. Radio listening among whites averaged two and one-half hours per day, compared with two for the black teen-agers. Black teen-agers average a full half hour more per day listening to records than did whites of any income group, but were significantly less frequent users of the newspaper (Greenberg and Dominick, 1969).

Parallel differences exist among adult samples. The most frequent television viewers are black, low-income adults, averaging close to six hours per weekday, followed by white, low-income adults who watch just under five hours a day. General population viewing is now about two and one-half hours. Low-income adults read the newspaper less frequently and read fewer sections of the newspaper; low-income blacks do not differ much from low-income whites in newspaper reading.

For the other media, there are consistent income group differences—i.e., more radio listening, more magazine reading, and more movie-going among the higher income groups, but there are no racial differences within the poor for these media behaviors. However, as with younger people, blacks spent more time listening to records than whites (Greenberg and Dervin, 1970).

Although these studies indicate lesser media usage among the poor and blacks for news information, trend studies indicate the gap is closing. McCombs (1968) examined Negro use of television and newspapers for political information from the Presidential campaigns of 1952 through 1964. In 1952, fully 63% of the Negroes were low users of either medium for political information; by 1964, only 41% remained in the low-use category. There was increased usage of both media, but far more of television than papers.

## Media attitudes

Here, there is research evidence that examines three aspects of media attitudes between races and between social groups. The three aspects encompass the relative credibility of the mass media as sources of information or enlightenment, the perceived reality of television in terms of its entertainment presentations, and the set of reasons that audience members use to explain their media orientations (Greenberg and Dervin, 1970).

In one of the classic media research traditions, many of the studies already referenced ask variants of this question: "If you got conflicting reports from television and your newspaper (or radio), which would you most likely believe?" The poor or low-income respondents give a resounding and virtually unanimous "TV" as their answer, no matter how or by whom the question is phrased.

Television comes out on top as the most reliable, the most important, the most preferred for world news, and the most believable medium. It does its job the best, and it is the last one that blacks would forego. Although a majority of all Americans respond with television to such questions, that majority for low-income segments exceeds three-fourths of that subpopulation. And, as would be predicted from the media use trends described above, low-income blacks are even more favorable to television than low-income whites. Only when the media referent is "local news," do the trends differ. There, low-income people cite radio and television about equally; low-income blacks report that other people would be their primary source in about 22% of the instances, compared to 7% among low-income whites citing that source of information.

This devotion to and faith in television among all blacks spills over into their perceptions of how true-to-life television is. "TV tells it like it is" would be a capsule descriptor of the perceived reality of television among low-income segments of the population. Several studies have used a series of similar items to index this reality. Sample items include: "My favorite TV show tells about life the way it really is." "The people in my favorite TV show are like people I meet in real life." Results show a consistent trend across age levels from childhood through adolescence to adulthood. The poor, in general, see TV as more realistic than the general population. Poor blacks see TV as more real than poor whites. Among a black adult urban sample, for instance, more than a majority of the respondents said that statements like those exemplified were "true" (Dervin and Greenberg, 1972).

Further, the relationship is not modified when key control variables have been introduced. For example, the consistently greater perception of television reality persists when controlling for sex, the credibility of television, newspaper reading, church attendance, or source of control over television program choices.

In the final section we shall return to this reality issue as it pertains to the perceived reality of television blacks in particular.

The third issue here deals with the functions of television for minorities. Perhaps it would be more conceptually correct to describe it as the perceived gratifications derived by those who use the medium.

In cited studies of pre-teens and teen-agers (Greenberg and Dominick, 1969, 1970), items were developed to tap potential uses of television. Here, we will summarize those that showed substantial racial and/or income differences. Black youngsters, whether pre-teen or teen, use television as a "school of life" to learn about the world that exists outside the classroom. Low-income youngsters, and the black ones in particular, were most prone to state that they watched television because. .

"I can learn from the mistakes of others."

"I can learn a lot from it."

"It teaches me things I don't learn in school."

"I get to see what people are like."

"I watch TV so I can learn how I'm supposed to act."

These describe a particular motivation in black youngsters' approach to television—a set of expectations that may lead to selective interpretation of the visual experiences available.

A second major function for black youngsters—more so than for their white counterparts—is the seeking of certain kinds of emotional stimulation; the more disadvantaged seek excitement and thrill from TV more often. The same pattern of progressive dependence has been identified; blacks most dependent, low-income white next, and middle-income whites least dependent on TV for those kinds of stimulation.

The evidence in this section lends credence to the overall dependence of low-income people and blacks to the medium of television. It is the main source of news, of information, of entertainment. It is trusted, believed, and not to be parted with. It consumes enormous portions of their daily lives. Justification for this devotion is expressed in terms of how real television is, how much can be learned from it, and how it brings excitement.

## Socialization effects of specific mass media content

The distinction between the socialization effects that will be examined here and what might be termed socialization effects from the last section stems from the degree of content specificity involved. Above, we talked of socialization as a function of overall attitudes toward a medium, of overall expectations from a given medium. But what it is in the medium that produces specific functions or beliefs was indeterminate. Here, we shall review studies that focus on specific media content or on specific socialization experiences, and trace the passage of media content into the verbal and/or physical behaviors of minority users. Two kinds of studies contribute to our understanding. One focuses on what blacks may be learning in specific areas of socialization from general television exposure; the other looks more closely at the reactions of white and black viewers to black presentations in television.

Although it is difficult to abstract the theoretical viewpoints of different investigators into a common framework, it does appear that much of the media socialization research has been guided by a "surrogate" rationale. The argument generally proceeds that if an individual does not have desired inputs or "information" available from normal sources, then media information is likely to be acquired, accepted, and followed. Or, alternatively, if the individual is deprived of the needed source of stimulation, the media will be utilized as a substitute provider. Either way, the receiver is conceived of as lacking something in his behavioral environment that is available through media content.

Gerson (1966) described a socialization agent as one that teaches the individual to be adequate in performing certain roles; for some roles, local social structures may not have needed information, and the mass media can fill the gap. He examined the use of the mass media by Negro and white adolescents as an agent of premarital cross-sex socialization. As he posited, black teen-agers were much higher users of the mass media for both reinforcing existing dating practices and for acquiring new ones—i.e., getting ideas or advice about dating. The acquisition tendency was even greater than the reinforcing one. Controlling for other factors, Gerson identified those subgroups for whom the media were particularly important socializers. Negro boys were especially likely to use the media for dating information, as were Negro nondaters and Negroes least or not at all integrated into their own peer culture. So, the Negroes most likely to use the media for this socialization information were those with interpersonal problems. The question of whether the information they accepted aggravated or relieved their problems remains an open one.

Surlin and Dominick (1970-71) hypothesized that program preferences and actual choices of black and white teen-agers would reflect vacuums in their social milieu. Given data that demonstrate a less stable family life among the blacks, they posited that blacks would tend to seek media substitutes for this instability. Their data demonstrated a marked tendency for the blacks to prefer and watch more programs that featured a family as a central unit. Given that the bulk of television variety shows contain nothing culturally significant for blacks, they expected low preferences for such shows; data supported their expectation. In their discussion, they posit that low-income blacks use TV as a learning device, that blacks acquire the behavior perceived as appropriate for family members in the predominantly white, middle-class world. What was done with the information about family life from this "third parent" also remains unknown.

Now, let us examine evidence that isolates blacks on television as a focal point. Greenberg and Hanneman (1970) examined television behaviors of blacks and whites (e.g., watching shows with blacks), and then examined the role of the racial attitudes of the whites. From parallel samples of adults, it was determined that blacks were more regular viewers of shows with black performers than were whites, and they watched nonblack shows with the same frequency as whites.

The white sample judged TV newscasts as fairer to minorities than did the black sample. The blacks said television was more realistic; the degree of perceived reality was a function of the amount of TV viewing done, among both blacks and whites. For the whites, a measure was constructed to tap their attitudes toward militant blacks—e.g., Black Panthers, Rap Brown. The more negative whites said that there were more blacks on television to be seen, that television was fairer to minorities, and that there was a tendency for them to watch more shows without blacks. No difference existed between the more and less negative whites in terms of watching shows with blacks. It seems that the whites who were more negative to militant blacks derived reinforcing impressions from what they viewed.

Finally, Greenberg (1972) studied children's reactions to television blacks, using samples of black urban children and white children from urban, suburban, and rural settings. The study premise was that large numbers of white children, given their early and persistent exposure to television, and their limited exposure to real-life blacks if they lived in suburban or rural areas, might be obtaining their earliest attitudinal impressions about blacks from TV. Although viewing differences were expected and obtained (e.g., black children watched more shows with blacks), the function of identification was of major interest and importance. The children were asked to name up to three persons on television they would most like to be like; 75% of the blacks cited at least one black character and so did 43% of the white children (nine- and ten-year olds).

This same-race identification increased with the numbers of black shows watched. Prior studies of race-identification (Clark and Clark, 1947, 1950; Morland, 1958) all found that about one-third of their black children identified with a white model; in this study it was 25%—a not very different figure. However, these same previous studies found no white children identifying with a black model; here, with each child making an average of two choices, nearly half of the white children identified strongly with a black TV performer.

White children were being socialized in other ways. Significantly more of them said that TV was their principal source of information as to how the other race talked and dressed—more so than blacks who were using TV to find out about whites.

For the perceived reality of television, the black kids said television was more realistic—but in a measure of the reality of TV blacks in particular there were no racial differences among the children. Both groups were at the scale's midpoint in terms of how realistic TV blacks were. It was for rural white children that television was a more important socializing agency; nearly two-thirds of them said that television was their principal source of information as to how blacks talked, looked, and dressed—nearly double that of suburban children, who also exceeded the urban whites in their TV dependency for such impressions.

A measure of racial attitudes also differentiated the white children by area of residence. Most negative attitudes toward blacks already existed among the urban whites, and the least negative among the rural ones.

Finally, this study cross-tabulated the frequency of watching blacks on television, for white children, with the frequency of their direct personal contact with blacks in, for example, school and their neighborhoods. In summary, these analyses found that TV exposure to blacks for white children contributed to identification with black TV characters and black-featured shows; personal exposure did not. Television exposure contributed to the belief that TV blacks are real-to-life; personal contacts did not. No differences were found in racial attitudes toward real or TV blacks as a function of mediated vs. personal contact.

In the final two sections of this chapter, we have tried to map the portrait of black presentations in the mass media, and then determine the effects such portraiture may be having. Admittedly the fit is an imperfect one, and some of the imperfections suggest questions for continuing research in this area.

In terms of the symbolic aspects of mass media content, the quantitative studies have done little to caputre major themes, stereotypes, or emphases of programming that features blacks. Do the messages of "Room 222" or "Sanford and Son" have some consistency? Are they the same messages or different? How? What do nonblack shows, like "All in the Family" or "Hee-Haw," contribute to the racial issue? The entertainment aspects of the mass media were never intended to be true-to-life portrayals; the media whites are perhaps no more realistic than the nonwhites, at least in terms of marital patterns, occupations, problems, and the nature of interpersonal exchanges. Therefore, making some qualitative judgments as to the presence or absence of racism increases in difficulty. The portrayal of minorities in the news media has been examined principally in terms of the presence or absence of black faces. The grossness of this approach is self-evident. The cultural indicators of blacks in the media have barely been subjected to critical examination.

To the extent that there has been little thoroughness in the content analytic approaches, there is even less evidence that can be mustered as to what difference this content makes to black and white alike, or differently.

Perhaps what is needed is a two- or three-pronged research approach. For one, a continuous, systematic assessment of mass media content is necessary in order to begin to look for possible effects of real-world media presentations. Content patterns are in flux in terms of emphasis, location, and scope. The nature of the fluctuations, through trend analysis, is a needed element for the potential researcher of this phenomenon. The cultural indicators of minorities, which are presented through the mass media to non-minority members, may create false or correct impressions, but the mapping remains a requisite piece of datum.

A second research approach must encompass the real-world behaviors of readers and viewers. Documentation is minimal as to the level and nature of exposure to minorities in the mass media for different subgroups; what do people see, read, and hear. Further, this input must be examined in the context of other potential socializing agents if we are to fully trace the development or acquisition of interracial attitudes.

Third, the noticeable lack of experimental work in this area, founded in some sound theoretical base, is surprising, given the social and central nature of the issues involved. Even the extensive corpus of research done on Sesame Street and Electric Company was concerned almost exclusively with cognitive changes and attitudes toward learning, and not with the potential influence of black and white performers on black or white children's conception of race. Experimental projects, in which children are exposed to specific kinds of program content and in which the program content has been experimentally created, would provide some more secure basis for our understanding of the situation we have tried to describe.

## EPILOGUE

An optimist reading this paper might say, "Things are getting better." His partner, the pessimist, should respond, "They couldn't have been any worse." The media institutions have discriminated, perhaps more from insensitivity than intent. We have not tried to assess motivation here. Perhaps a brief concluding section should tie together some separate components of what we have observed in assembling this information.

It seems that whatever discriminatory patterns may have existed within a segment of any media institution permeated that entire system. If one compares employment data with pictorial news data, or if one compares economic data with advertising content, then the institutional medium lagging in one data category was laggardly in the others as well. Newspapers had the most generally deficient record in all areas examined here, matched closely by the magazine field. Broadcasting media, on the other hand—save for ownership criteria—have consistently been more generous in their treatment of minorities in content, in employment practices, in advertising, and elsewhere. If this is a valid observation, tentative as it may be, then the search for reasons suggests one proposition: those media in which the government has had more direct access or quasi-control (e.g., the awarding of channels, the stipulation for public service activities) are media that appear to have been more responsive to minority needs or minority pressures. Pressures, actual or perceived, to be more inclusive of minorities have had some positive impact. Pressure certainly was a supplement to whatever self-provoked humanitarian motives may have existed. This is not an argument for more specific legislation within the print industries, but it does suggest that where such controls exist, the response is likely to be more expansive.

Where do the media go from here? How much minority emphasis is enough? Although it is difficult to answer such questions by stipulating objective criteria, one might attempt to generalize somewhat from the principles used by FCC Commissioner Johnson in evaluating minority employment practices by television stations.

Perhaps two baseline standards are necessary. With regard to such things as jobs, appearances in ads, characterizations in comic strips or television roles, news pictures, the real-world distribution of minorities provides an appropriate reference point. A different referent would be pertinent for the kind of role presentation offered to minorities in fictional media areas; it would be the census of fictional people in the media—i.e., the distribution of fictional jobs, roles, or what have you. If 40% of major roles on television are "heavies" or "cops" or "cowboys," then it is reasonable to expect that 10% of those "heavies" be blacks, 2% be Spanish-Americans, and so forth. This kind of notion would then subsume some qualitative considerations as well as quantitative ones. We run the risk of offending both sides on the issue. Some minority groups could reasonably claim that they have too long been overcast in certain roles and want no further share in them; the media might claim not enough talented people to hire.

One might question whether the distribution of role types is in itself subject to review, given the perceived reality of TV for most Americans. But this is a question of a different order. For the moment, such views will be shunted in the attempt to arrive at a compromise, but not a compromising measure or operationalization of "fair" representation. We are suggesting for consideration that minorities be included in media content to the extent that they exist in the society, but that the nature of their roles be compared against the distribution of roles in the medium. This does not then serve to impede dramatic license, as we understand it, nor to force the entertainment media to subject themselves to real-world comparisons in their dramatic, farcical, or variety offerings.

As usual, a synthesis of research evidence provides more questions than answers. In particular, this research suffers from the lack of integrated study paradigms. We shall not offer one, but we do urge some systematic consideration of the research possibilities suggested, and those that might easily be added.

# REFERENCES

American Society of Newspaper Editors, Report of the committee on minority employment and education in journalism, Easton, Pennsylvania, April 1972.

Bauer, R., and Cunningham, S. The Negro market. *Journal of Advertising,* April 1970, **20**, 3-13.

Berkman, D. Advertising in Ebony and Life: Negro aspirations vs. reality. *Journalism Quarterly,* 1963, **40**, 53-64.

Boyenton, W., The Negro turns to advertising. *Journalism Quarterly,* 1965, **42**, 227-235.

Clark, C. Television and social controls: Some observations on the portrayal of ethnic minorities. *Television Quarterly,* Spring 1969, **8**, 19.

Clark, K., and Clark, M.P. Racial identification and preference in Negro children. T.M. Newcomb and E.L. Hartley (Eds.), In *Readings in social psychology.* New York: Holt, Rinehart and Winston, 1947.

Clark, K., and Clark, M.P. Emotional factors in racial identification and preferences in Negro children. *Journal of Negro Education,* 1950, **19**, 341-350.

Colfax, D., and Sternberg, S. The perpetuation of racial stereotypes: Blacks in mass circulation magazine advertisements. *Public Opinion Quarterly,* Spring 1972, **36**, 8-18.

Colle, R. Negro image in the mass media: A case study in social change. *Journalism Quarterly,* 1968, **45**, 55-60.

Costello, M. Blacks in the news media. *Editorial Research Reports,* August 16, **2**, 623-644.

Cox, K. Changes in stereotyping of Negroes and whites in magazine advertisement. *Public Opinion Quarterly,* Winter 1969-70, **33**, 603-606.

Dervin, B., and Greenberg, B. The communication environment of the urban poor. In *Current perspectives in mass communication research.* F.G. Kline and P. Tichenor (Eds.), Beverly Hills, Calif.: Sage, 1972.

Dominick, J., and Greenberg, B. Three seasons of blacks on television. *Journal of Advertising Research,* 1970, **10**, 21-37.

*Editor and publisher international yearbook.* New York: Editor and Publisher, 1973.

Gerson, W. Mass media socialization behavior: Negro-white differences. *Social Forces,* 1966, **45**, 40-50.

Glenn, A. Minorities market—broadcasters make an effective pitch. *Barron's,* September 3, 1973, **3**, 8.

Greenberg, B. Non-whites on British television. British Broadcasting Corporation, Report VR/72/56, 1971.

Greenberg, B. Children's reactions to TV blacks. *Journalism Quarterly,* 1972, **49**, 5-14.

Greenberg, B., and Dervin, B. Mass communication among the urban poor. *Public Opinion Quarterly,* Summer 1970, **34**, 224-235.

Greenberg, B., and Dominick, J. Racial and social class differences in teenagers' use of television. *Journal of Broadcasting,* Fall 1969, **13**, 331-344.

Greenberg, B., and Dominick, J. Television behavior among disadvantaged children. In *Use of the mass media by the urban poor.* B. Greenberg and B. Dervin (Eds.), New York: Praeger, 1970.

Greenberg, B., and Hanneman, G. Racial attitudes and the impact of TV blacks. *Educational Broadcasting Review,* 1970, **4**, 27-34.

Greenberg, B., and Kahn, S. Blacks in *Playboy* cartoons. *Journalism Quarterly,* 1970, **47**, 557-560.

Jennings, R. Television station employment practices: The status of minorities and women. New York: Office of Communication, United Church of Christ, November 1972.

Jennings, R., Kerr, M., and Parker, T. Public television station employment practices and the composition of boards of directors: The status of women and minorities. New York: Office of Communication, United Church of Christ, January 1973.

Johnson, N. Broadcasting in America: The performance of network affiliates in the top 50 markets. Washington, D.C.: Office of Information, FCC, July 1973.

Kassarjian, H. The Negro and American advertising, 1946-65. *Journal of Marketing Research,* 1969, **6**, 29-39.

Ledbetter, T., and Lomax, L. Blacks move into cable TV on nationwide scale. *Black Enterprise,* September 1973, 54-60.

Lemon, R. Black is the color of TV's newest stars. *Saturday Evening Post,* November 30, 1968, pp. 42-44.

Mapp, E. *Blacks in American films: Today and yesterday.* Metuchen, N.J.: Scarecrow Press, 1972.

McCombs, M. Negro use of television and newspapers for political information, 1952-1964. *Journal of Broadcasting,* Summer 1968, **12**, 261-266.

Meyer, A. Black voices and format regulations: A study in black-oriented radio. Mimeographed manuscript, Department of Communication-Research, Stanford University, February 1971.

Morland, J.K. Racial recognition by nursery school children in Lynchburg, Virginia. *Social Forces,* 1958, **37**, 399-410.

National Advisory Commission on Civil Disorders. *Report of the National Advisory Commission on Civil Disorders.* New York: Bantam, 1968.

National Association of Educational Broadcasters, Minority employment practices of public television stations. Washington, D.C.: Office of Minority Affairs, October, 1972.

Plotkin, L. *The frequency of appearance of Negroes on television.* New York: The Committee on Integration, New York Society for Ethical Culture, 1964.

Prowitt, M. Guide to citizen action in radio and television. New York: Office of Communication, United Church of Christ, 1971.

Reddick, C.D. Educational programs for the improvement of race relations. *Journal of Negro Education,* Summer 1944, **13**, 369.

Roberts, C. The protrayal of blacks on network television. *Journal of Broadcasting,* 1971, **15**, 45-53.

Shuey, A. Stereotyping of Negroes and whites: An analysis of magazine pictures. *Public Opinion Quarterly,* Summer 1953, **17**, 281-287.

Stempel, G. Visibility of Blacks in news and news-picture magazines. *Journalism Quarterly*, 1971, **48**, 337-339.

Surlin, S., and Dominick, J. Television's Function as a "Third Parent" for Black and White Teen-agers. *Journal of Broadcasting*, Winter 1970-71, **15**, 55-64.

West, H. A question of control, ownership and role. *The Washington Post*, B1, January 29, 1973, pp. 5-6.

# 10

# *Achieving Racial Equality: An Analysis of Resistance to Social Reform*

MYRON ROTHBART

This chapter will examine some of the factors that affect resistance to social reforms designed to bring about racial equality. The first section will examine some of the survey data reflecting white Americans' attitudes and opinions toward racial discrimination, racial equality, and integration. The second section will focus on whites' reactions to specific social reforms, and an attempt will be made to analyze the dimensions that influence public acceptance of various reform proposals. The chapter will conclude with a brief discussion of some specific reforms that show promise of being effective in reducing racial inequality, yet appear capable of achieving popular support from the white majority.

In writing a chapter such as this, one is clearly torn between two paths of inquiry. One path—familiar at least in principle to the vast majority of academicians—requires a cautious, deliberate pace, along with careful and exhaustive scrutiny of all relevant information that one encounters. When taking this path, the investigative traveler becomes much more anxious about making the mistake of publicizing a spurious causal relationship (a Type I error in psychology parlance) than he does about failing to recognize a true causal relationship (a Type II error). The greater anxiety that this traveler associates with Type I rather than Type II errors causes him to be conservative and tentative in his public utterances; this conservatism is in turn associated with good scientific inquiry, but tends to ignore the social costs associated with making Type II errors.

The second path, familiar to most of us in our daily lives, allows a fairly brisk pace—at the expense of missing much of the interesting scenery—and frequently requires that observations be made cursorily. This traveler becomes much more anxious about failing to recognize a true causal relationship than

---

[1] I am indebted to my colleagues in the psychology department at the University of Oregon for their thoughtful reactions to this chapter. In particular, Sheldon Cohen, Robyn Dawes, Ray Hyman, Steven Keele, Michael Posner, and Mary Rothbart contributed substantially to this chapter through their criticisms and suggestions. While the quality of this effort has been demonstrably improved by their comments, I alone accept responsibility for errors of fact, logic, or interpretation.

about incorrectly publicizing a false relationship (greater fear of a Type II error), causing him to be bold, and occasionally rash, in his public statements. This boldness is often necessitated by the demands of everyday life, but tends to minimize the costs associated with making Type I errors.

Although I feel much greater safety in taking the first path, the ideas contained in this chapter were in most instances arrived at by the second route. In approaching the problems associated with white resistance to efforts to bring about racial equality, I believe that it may be of greater benefit to the reader to present and incautiously discuss a few potentially useful ideas than to comprehensively review all relevant literature and conclude with some temperate and restrained comments. Given the magnitude of racial inequality in America and the enormity of human suffering thereby generated, I have taken the view that to be cautious is of lesser virtue than to be venturesome.

One final preface to this chapter is in order. Since our task is to understand the sources of white resistance to social reforms that are designed to bring about racial equality, the data to be examined has been collected almost entirely from white respondents. This chapter will not specifically examine the data on black attitudes and opinions, even though in many instances interesting similarities and differences from white attitudes emerge from the survey data.

## WHITE ATTITUDES TOWARD RACIAL EQUALITY

Over the past quarter century, a large body of public opinion data has been collected on whites' attitudes toward blacks and toward reform proposals to eliminate racial inequality. Among the more prominent studies are the National Opinion Research Center's (NORC) research on integrationist attitudes (Hyman and Sheatsley, 1956, 1964; Sheatsley, 1966; Greeley and Sheatsley, 1971, 1972), the surveys of white and black attitudes commissioned by *Newsweek* (Brink and Harris, 1964, 1966), and the research sponsored in part by the National Advisory Commission on Civil Disorders to investigate white and black attitudes in 15 major US cities (Campbell, 1971). An additional and highly valuable information source has been provided by Hazel Erskine, who brought together virtually all of the diverse public opinion surveys prior to 1968 that pertain to race relations. These have appeared in eight separate installments in the journal *Public Opinion Quarterly* between 1967 and 1969.

On the basis of these public opinion polls, it would be possible to variously characterize whites' attitudes toward blacks as "increasingly egalitarian," as "racist," or as "inconsistent." Depending on the data one wishes to cite, it would be possible to find evidence consistent with each of the above characterizations. This unfortunate state of affairs has led some to despair that "it is devilishly difficult to make sense out of the wealth of [public opinion] data," (Brigham and Weissbach, 1972, p. 3).

It will be the thesis of this paper that in fact there is greater consistency to this body of data than is immediately apparent, that each of the above characterizations is in itself inadequate, that several dimensions may underlie a subject's evaluative response to a particular reform proposal (only one of which may involve liking or disliking of blacks), and that an exposition of these underlying dimensions may enhance our ability to understand the public's reaction to proposed social reforms.

## Evidence for "increasingly egalitarian" attitudes

The main body of evidence in favor of this view comes from research conducted by the National Opinion Research Center at the University of Chicago over the 28-year period between 1942 and 1970 (Hyman and Sheatsley, 1956, 1964; Sheatsley, 1966; Greeley and Sheatsley, 1971, 1972). They have asked a variety of questions pertaining to integration and more recently have developed a seven-item Guttman scale designed to measure pro-integrationist attitudes. They have noted consistent and dramatic increases in integrationist attitudes over the past 28 years. Table 1 presents responses to three questions for which data is available for all (or almost all) of the time periods sampled[2] Items 1 and 2 were used in the pro-integrationist scale and refer to integration of public transportation and public schools, respectively. Item 3, although not used in this scale, was present in the earlier surveys and represents an interesting change in opinion about the relative intelligence of whites and blacks. Basically, there are substantial shifts in opinion about black-white relations from the early 1940s to the present. Both Northerners and Southerners show large, consistent shifts in favor of integrating public facilities. On the topic of segregation in public transportation, for example, only 4% of white Southerners favored integration of transportation facilities in 1942, whereas 67% favored it in 1970 (white Northerners shifted from 57% to 95%). With respect to school integration, only 2% of white Southerners favored it in 1942, while 45% favored it in 1970 (white Northerners shifted from 40% to 83%). In 1942, only 21% of white Southerners believed that blacks could be as intelligent as whites, whereas 59% believed this to be true in 1963 (white Northerners shifted from 50% to 84%).

There are three important points that should be noted in this data. First, the changes over time are consistent and show no reversals. This is particularly important when assessing the 1970 data that was collected after the period of extreme racial disturbance in the middle and late 1960s.

---

[2] It is not possible to follow every item used in the NORC surveys over all the time periods, since items that come to elicit almost total agreement or disagreement are retired from the survey.

**Table 1.** Percentage of Respondents Answering Favorable toward Integration to Selected Items in the NORC Surveys (adapted from Hyman and Sheatsley, 1964; Greeley and Sheatsley, 1971)

| Item | 1942 | | 1956 | | 1963 | | 1970* | |
|---|---|---|---|---|---|---|---|---|
| | North | South | North | South | North | South | North | South |
| 1. Generally speaking, do you think there should be separate sections for Negroes in street-cars and buses? | 57 | 4 | 73 | 26 | 88 | 51 | 95 | 67 |
| 2. Do you think white students and Negro students should go to the same schools or to separate schools? | 40 | 2 | 61 | 14 | 75 | 30 | 83 | 45 |
| 3. In general, do you think that Negroes are as intelligent as white people—that is, can they learn things just as well if they are given the same education and training? | 50 | 21 | 84 | 57 | 84 | 59 | — | — |

*Numerical values in these columns estimated from bar graphs.

Although the conventional wisdom at that time predicted a strong "white backlash," there is precious little evidence of it in the NORC surveys. Second, both Northerners and Southerners show strong increases in favorable sentiment to integration. And third, strong regional differences in attitudes toward integration remain as of the 1970 survey.[3] Before pursuing the issue further, it should be noted that the results of the NORC survey are highly consistent with those of other large-scale surveys (e.g., Harris poll cited in Erskine, 1967a; Campbell, 1971).

It would be useful at this point to examine the public's response to all seven items on the Guttman scale used in the NORC survey for the available years, 1963 and 1970. Table 2 presents national responses to those items, with the items ranked from the most to least frequently endorsed. It is apparent from this table that all items except number 7 show greater integrationist response in 1970 than in 1963 and that the least frequently endorsed items relate to matters involving more intimate and/or long-term contact: items relating to integrated neighborhoods, dinner guests, and marriage show less integrationist endorsement than the other items that emphasize equal access to transportation, public facilities, and schools. Differences in attitudes about integration at the societal and at the personal level appear fairly consistently in studies on racial attitudes (e.g., Triandis and Davis, 1965).

Since the NORC surveys do not explicitly ask respondents what should be done to achieve equality for blacks, it would be useful to cite a Harris survey conducted for *Newsweek* in October 1963 (cited in Erskine, 1967a). A nationwide sample of whites was asked: "Should the law guarantee Negroes equal rights to white people in job opportunities? Voting? Getting good housing? Using buses and trains? Using restaurants and lunch counters? Giving their children integrated schooling?" Ninety-five percent felt the laws should guarantee voting rights, 91%—the use of buses and trains, 85%—getting good housing, 80%—job opportunities, 79%—using restaurants and lunch counters, and 75% felt laws should guarantee integrated schooling.

On the basis of the above findings, it could be concluded that (a) integrationist attitudes have shown dramatic increases in the past three decades, and (b) integrationist principles are supported by a large majority of white Americans.

Critics of opinion polls on race relations have argued that responses to

---

[3] An unpublished NORC survey indicates a large increase in support for integrated schools between the 1970 pool and a 1972 survey (Greeley and Sheatsley, 1972). They report that Item 2 in Table 1 (school integration) showed an increase in *national* support from 74% to 86%, with large gains in the South, but they do not present separate figures for the Southern sample. The thesis of the paper is that regional differences in attitudes toward integration are diminishing with the South becoming integrationist at a faster rate than the North.

**Table 2.** Guttman Scale of Pro-Integration Sentiments
(taken from Sheatsley, 1966*, Greeley and Sheatsley, 1971)

| Item | Percent Giving Pro-Integration Response (December 1963) | (1970) |
|---|---|---|
| 1. "Do you think Negroes should have as good a chance as white people to get any kind of job, or do you think white people should have the first chance at any kind of job?" ("As good a chance.") | 82 | — |
| 2. "Generally speaking, do you think there should be separate sections for Negroes in street cars and buses?" ("No.") | 77 | 88 |
| 3. "Do you think Negroes should have the right to use the same parks, restaurants and hotels as white people?" ("Yes.") | 71 | 81 |
| 4. "Do you think white students and Negro students should go to the same schools, or to separate schools?" ("Same schools.") | 63 | 75 |
| 5. "How strongly would you object if a member of your family wanted to bring a Negro friend home to dinner?" ("Not at all.") | 49 | 62 |
| 6. "White people have a right to keep Negroes out of their neighborhoods if they want to, and Negroes should respect that right." ("Disagree slightly" or "Disagree strongly.") | 44 | 50 |
| 7. "Do you think there should be laws against marriages between Negroes and whites?" ("No.") | 36 | 48 |
| 8. "Negroes shouldn't push themselves where they're not wanted." ("Disagree slightly" or "Disagree strongly.") | 27 | 15 |

*Reprinted by permission of *Daedalus,* Journal of the American Academy of Sciences, Boston, Massachusetts. Winter, 1966, *The Negro American.*

questions posed by, say, the NORC and Harris surveys are tapping what people feel they ought to say rather than what they truly feel. While this may be true to some degree, it is also true, as Campbell (1971) and Greeley and Sheatsley (1971) argue, that the mere fact that subjects feel that segregationist attitudes are less socially acceptable today indicates a somewhat more favorable racial atmosphere. Even this guarded conclusion may be unduly pessimistic, however, since several recent experiments on interracial helping suggest a lack of racial bias.

If we assume that the tendency to help another person in distress represents a behavioral measure of affective orientation (attitude), then the findings from research on interracial helping prove interesting. Since the helping research is reviewed elsewhere in this book (cf. Chapter 6), there is no need to duplicate such a review here. Suffice it to say that several noteworthy attempts to assess interracial helping showed little or no tendency for whites to offer more help to white than black victims. Research by Piliavin, Rodin, and Piliavin (1969) showed that whites were no more likely to aid a white than a black victim in a subway car; Gaertner and Bickman (1971) found only slight differences in whites' tendency to aid whites rather than blacks who made an over-the-phone request for aid. The latter study becomes a bit difficult to interpret, however, because of a confounding between race and class.

One study that varied race and class independently was conducted by Cohen (1973). Cohen (1973) "lost" 276 wallets in a white neighborhood, some of which contained a photograph of a black male and some a photograph of a white male; in addition half of the wallets in each condition contained information suggesting that the wallet's owner was middle class and half indicated thw owner was lower class. There were no significant differences in the return rates for white and black wallets (54% vs. 64%, respectively), and no differences as a function of social class.

These helping studies present a reasonably consistent picture. Although one could argue that different subject populations or different helping paradigms could be used that would reveal significant anti-black discrimination, the present findings suggest that in situations involving *low personal sacrifice or cost*, there does not appear to be a significant degree of anti-black discrimination shown by whites. This generalization will be examined in greater detail later, but first it will be necessary to examine some of the less sanguine findings concerning race relations.

## Evidence for "racist" attitudes

This section will examine evidence concerning whites' perceptions of the (a) magnitude of discrimination shown against blacks, (b) black protests and the speed of integration, and (c) causes of blacks' inferior socioeconomic status. Since the data on these topics (particularly the first one) are complex, I have attempted to present the existing data first with only minimal interpretation. Following the presentation of data in the four areas, I shall offer more detailed interpretations of the implications of these results.

## Beliefs about the magnitude of discrimination

Survey questions that attempt to reveal whites' perceptions of the magnitude of discrimination shown against blacks have yielded widely varying results. Depending on the specificity or generality of the question, and even minimal differences in wording, one may find whites to be largely sympathetic or almost totally unaware of discrimination.

In response to a rather terse question posed by a Harris poll—"Are Negroes discriminated against?"—61% of a nationwide sample of whites responded affirmatively (Brink and Harris, 1966, p. 125). Interestingly enough, the only large regional differences emerged in comparing the South with the rest of the country: 39% of white Southerners answered affirmatively, white 47% indicated that blacks were not discriminated against. It would have been interesting to ask people *where* blacks are discriminated against, because in many cases it appears that blacks must be mistreated somewhere else. A national Gallup poll conducted in May 1968 found 73% of whites saying that blacks were treated the same as whites in *their* community (cited in Erskine, 1968b); only 30% of white Californians and 34% of Minnesotans felt that blacks were denied job opportunities or fair treatment in their home state (cited in Erskine, 1968a).

Research conducted by the Institute for Social Research (ISR) at the University of Michigan also asked people how much discrimination occurred in their own city, but divided questions into several categories: housing discrimination, job discrimination, police harassment, and the perceived cause of economic inferiority. Table 3 presents these findings based on surveys conducted in 15 major US cities (Campbell, 1971). Summarized briefly, whites perceived the largest discrimination against blacks in the area of housing (38% of whites describe "many" blacks subject to housing discrimination), followed by job discrimination (22% of whites indicate "many" blacks suffer job discrimination), with the least discrimination perceived at the hands of the police (only 9% of whites believe that blacks "definitely" are subject to more police harassment than whites). It is difficult to compare the data in Table 3 with previously cited findings, since the response alternatives provided for the first two items in the ISR survey ask subjects to make magnitude estimations, whereas most other survey questions simply allow a yes or no response. If we make the somewhat arbitrary assumption that the respondents who have answered "yes" to a question about the existence of discrimination did so because they thought that "many" blacks suffer from discrimination, then the ISR data is consistent with the other findings.

It should be noted that Item 4 in Table 3, which attempts to assess

**Table 3. White Perception of Discrimination Against Negroes (taken from Campbell, 1971)**

| | Many | Some | Only a Few | None | Don't Know | TOTAL |
|---|---|---|---|---|---|---|
| 1. "Do you think that in (CITY) many, some, or only a few Negroes miss out on good housing because white owners don't rent or sell to them?" | 38% | 30 | 22 | 4 | 6 | 100% |
| 2. "Do you think that in (CITY) many, some, or only a few Negroes miss out on jobs and promotions because of racial discrimination?" | 22% | 34 | 26 | 12 | 6 | 100% |

| | Definitely | Probably | Probably not so | Definitely not so | Don't Know | TOTAL |
|---|---|---|---|---|---|---|
| 3. "It is sometimes said that the things we have just been talking about, such as unnecessary roughness and disrespect by the police, happen more to Negroes in (CITY) than to white people. Do you think this is definitely so, probably so, probably not so, or definitely not so?" | 9% | 29 | 30 | 26 | 6 | 100% |

| | Mainly due to discrimination | Mainly due to Negroes themselves | A mixture of both | Don't Know | TOTAL |
|---|---|---|---|---|---|
| 4. "On the average, Negroes in (CITY) have worse jobs, education, and housing than white people. Do you think this is due mainly to Negroes being discriminated against, or mainly due to something about Negroes themselves?" | 19% | 56 | 19 | 6 | 100% |

whites' beliefs about the relative importance of racial discrimination in contributing to inferior living conditions, reveals that only 38% of whites attribute inferior conditions either in whole or in part to racial discrimination. This finding, although suggestive that whites do not place a great amount of weight on discrimination as a determinant of economic status, will be discussed more fully in a later section.

The complexity of tapping white attitudes about discrimination becomes apparent from the following example. A NORC survey conducted in June 1942 asked, "In general, do you feel that right now Negroes have just as good a chance as white people to get defense jobs or not?" Thirty-nine percent indicated that Negroes did *not* have as good a chance. However, this figure jumps to 70% with this slightly reworded question (asked in October 1942), "In general, do you feel that right now Negroes have an equal chance to get *good* [italics mine] war jobs, or do you think white people have the best chance?" (questions taken from Erskine, 1968a). In other words, not only does the response vary depending on whether the question asks about "discrimination" or "*job* discrimination," it also depends on whether the question specifies "jobs" or "*good* jobs." But even in this question there is considerable ambiguity, because it is not clear whether blacks are perceived as having a poorer chance for "good jobs" because they are less well trained than whites or because they are victims of arbitrary discrimination. One question that did attempt to clarify the question of unequal training yielded provocative results. A NORC survey in October 1947 asked, "In general, if a Negro and a white person *with the same training* [italics mine] were trying to get some good job around here, which one do you think would be likely to get it?" (cited in Erskine, 1968a). Ninety-one percent of the respondents indicated the job would probably go to the white. Although it was not possible for the author to locate a similarly worded question for cross-validation, these results are clearly at variance with the more optimistic view that whites hold of discrimination against blacks.

One further difficulty in interpreting discrimination items concerns whites' beliefs about whether job discrimination *ought* to exist. A 1946 NORC survey found only 47% of whites endorsing the proposition that " . . . Negroes should have as good a chance as white people to get any kind of job . . .," but fortunately this number climbed to 82% by 1963 (cited in Erskine, 1968a). Part of the problem in interpreting this data comes from the subtlety in meaning that is attached to the word "should." When a question asks whether blacks "should have as good a chance as white people to get any kind of job," a respondent could interpret that to mean either (a) that blacks have the moral right to be treated the same as whites, or (b) that blacks, because of lesser job skills, will be able to compete less successfully than whites for jobs. If respondents interpret "should" as a moral imperative rather than a logical necessity, then the results of the opinion polls were truly appalling. However, it may well be that a substantial portion of the population does not use the word "should" in the same way that a social scientist thinks the word ought to be used. The 1942 NORC survey mentioned earlier may be instructive on this point. In response to the question on "good war jobs," the people who thought that whites had the best chance for the jobs were substantially more likely to believe that was the way "it ought to be" than people who felt that Negroes had an equal chance for good jobs. While this kind of correlational data is not unambiguously interpreted, it may be that the correlation between "what is" and "what ought to be" is reasonably high for a substantial proportion of the population. In other words, a significant number of people may be interpreting "should" questions not as statements of moral propriety, but rather as the "logical consequence" of imperfect conditions.

Clearly, the data on whites' perceptions of discrimination do not allow any simple interpretation. One of the possible reasons why slight changes in wording will often vastly alter the response is that asking people about "discrimination" or "fair treatment" is inherently complex and ambiguous. Is it "fair" to turn down a black who does not have a high school diploma for a job as a sales clerk? It is clearly unfair if we take the view that the black's failure to complete high school is ultimately attributable to America's historic role in the economic oppression of black people. It is clearly fair if we take the view that at least a high school diploma is a prerequisite for the job.

The result of this lengthy discussion is a complex pattern of results that will be interpreted later in this chapter: a clear majority endorses the view that blacks are "discriminated against," yet an equally clear majority avows that blacks are given equal treatment in their own community. The ISR data suggest that only a minority of whites see "many" blacks as the victims of job or housing discrimination, yet an earlier NORC study indicated that 91% of whites felt that a black who was as well trained as a white would be turned down for a job.

## Attitudes toward black protest and the pace of integration

Probably the clearest opinion poll results relate to whites' disapproval of black protests and the speed of integration.

*Black Protests.* Erskine reports that approximately six dozen questions have been asked in the past 30 years by various polling organizations regarding approval or disapproval of black protests ranging from peaceful marches to looting in riot-torn areas. All of the data cited under the above heading will be taken from her article (Erskine, 1967b).

In 1963 Gallup found that of the 69% of his sample who had heard about the civil rights rally in Washington (March on Washington), 63% disapproved of the rally. In 1963 NORC categorized its sample according to the degree of favorability toward integration, and found that even people who approved of integration disapproved of "actions Negroes had taken to obtain civil rights." Thirty-three percent of whites highly in favor of integration opposed Negro actions, 62% moderately in favor of integration opposed Negro actions, 73% moderately opposed to integration also opposed Negro actions, and 89% of those highly opposed to integration opposed Negro actions. While whites consistently oppose demonstrations, some demonstrations are clearly more unacceptable than others: a 1963 Harris poll for *Newsweek* found that for a nationwide sample of whites, 91% disapproved of lying down in front of trucks at construction sites to protest hiring discrimination, 67% disapproved of sit-ins at lunch counters, 56% disapproved of going to jail to protest discrimination, and 55% disapproved the boycott of products whose manufacturers do not hire enough Negroes. Thus, objection to even peaceful forms of protest are strong and consistent; polls taken after 1963 showed virtually identical results. In addition, most people feel that both nonviolent and violent protests have hurt the Negro cause (the latter much more so than the former).[4]

*Pace of Integration.* Although the responses of whites to the speed of racial integration or racial equality is not as consistently negative as toward black protests, the findings generally suggest that whites feel that the pace of integration has been too fast. Opinion polls collected by Erskine (1968c) provide the source of data under this heading. A Gallup poll conducted in November 1963 asked whether "the Kennedy administration is pushing racial integration too fast, or not fast enough?" Forty-six percent responded "too fast," 12%–"not fast enough," and 31%–"about right." As was the case with many other polls, strong regional (North-South) differences were manifest. A later Gallup poll asking the same question about the Johnson administration in April of 1968 found 42% saying "too fast," 20%–"not fast enough," and 24%–"about right." Again, although there is considerable regional variation, there is not a public clamoring for greater racial integration.

### Beliefs about the causes of racial inequality

Probably one of the most interesting—and also most revealing—findings from the opinion polls centers around whites' perceptions of the causes of racial inequality. Referring back to Table 3, whites were asked if the Negro's inferior socioeconomic status was "due mainly to Negroes being discriminated against, or mainly due to something about Negroes themselves." Nineteen percent of the respondents attributed the inferior status of blacks to

---

[4] It should be noted, however, that there is almost complete disagreement between blacks and whites on the question of how the protests have influenced the black cause; blacks consistently see the protests as effective and whites do not.

discrimination, 56%—"due to Negroes themselves," and 19%—"a mixture of both." A slightly different question was asked in a 1968 Gallup poll, yet it yielded similar results: "Who do you think is more to blame for the present conditions in which Negroes find themselves—white people, or Negroes themselves?" (Erskine, 1968d). For a national sample of whites, 23% blamed white people and 56% blamed Negroes, with only minor regional differences in evidence.

Research reported by Feagin (1972) attempted to determine somewhat more precisely how people viewed the causes of poverty. Feagin presented respondents with 11 possible "explanations" for poverty and asked them to indicate how important (or unimportant) each item was as a "reason" for poverty. The eleven items included individualistic items (such as "lack of effort by the poor themselves"), structural items (such as "failure of society to provide good schools for many Americans"), and fatalistic items (such as "just bad luck"). Individualistic explanations were clearly seen as the most important reasons for poverty, with structural and fatalistic factors relegated to secondary importance. A further analysis of the data, which included breakdowns by socioreligious groupings, race, geographic region, age, family income, and education, revealed only two groups that regarded structural factors to be more important than individualistic factors—blacks and Jews. For all other groups, it appears that the perceived causal locus for poverty is the poor themselves, or, as Feagin indicates in his title, "we still believe that God helps those who help themselves."

In an article that examines the implications of the previously cited ISR data, Schuman (1969) suggests that white Americans may have relinquished their beliefs about biological racism, but in exchange they appear to have substituted a kind of "sociological racism" in which one's inferior socioeconomic status is attributed not to inferior talent but to inferior motivation, drive, values, and ambition. To quote Schuman:

> Thus from one standpoint—certainly the black standpoint—the phrase "white racism" appears wholly appropriate. Most white Americans may not be racists in the more technical sense, but nothing said above suggests that they are willing to accept past or present responsibility for the prejudice and discrimination, and general inequality in the spread of opportunities. In espousing free will, white Americans deny the reality of the problems faced by black Americans and thus place the whole burden of black disadvantage on black Americans themselves. The distinctions concerning the definition of racism made here are, from such a standpoint, distinctions that do not make much of a difference." (1969, p. 48).

## Evidence for "inconsistent" or "ambivalent" attitudes

Thus far we have considered two sources of evidence concerning whites' attitudes toward blacks. One source indicates that whites' attitudes are increasingly egalitarian and integrationist, while the other source indicates that whites, in some instances at least, minimize the extent of discrimination experienced by blacks, are unsympathetic both to ameliorative protests and to the speed of integration, and in fact blame blacks for their own disadvantaged position. This apparent discrepancy has led some to conclude that whites' attitudes are either inconsistent or ambivalent. Katz (1970) has argued that white attitudes may be ambivalent and still reflect the "American dilemma" observed by Gunnar Myrdal 30 years ago. White feelings of both sympathy and disdain for blacks suggest ambivalence rather than a simple favorable or unfavorable orientation toward blacks. Katz has argued that the behavioral consequence of ambivalent attitudes would be that of response amplification—that is, an individual with ambivalent feelings toward a stimulus person would show a greater positive response or a greater negative response (depending on the behavior of the stimulus person) than he would toward someone from whom he did not have ambivalent feelings. A recent study in which white subjects administered shocks to black and white victims provided some support for the ambivalence-amplification idea (Katz, Glass, and Cohen, 1973). Black victims were denigrated more than white victims following the administration of shock, indicating that at least for negative experiences with blacks, whites' reactions appeared to be amplified. Analyses of white attitudes and behavior toward blacks in terms of the ambivalence amplification hypothesis appears to be fruitful, if for no other reason than it views the determinants of whites' reactions as more complex than a simple favorable or unfavorable attitude.

## INTERPRETING WHITES' ATTITUDES AND OPINIONS ABOUT BLACKS

Gordon Allport, in his historical overview of social psychology, observed that many 19th (and 20th) century theorists were prone toward "simple and sovereign" theories of social behavior, and that "both social scientists and reformers sought unitary solutions of social riddles" (Allport, 1954). The bias toward analyzing complex social phenomena in terms of a single underlying dimension is indeed powerful, and may lead to unnecessary confusion in trying to understand apparently discrepant survey research findings. Since most attitude and opinion questions are phrased in a way that allow people to respond along a single dimension (such as favor-oppose, like-dislike, etc.), it is frequently assumed that there is an isomorphic mapping to the underlying psychological determinants of that response; that is, it is assumed that a unitary psychological variable (such as favorability toward blacks) determines the single, unitary response (such as endorsement of school integration). Unfortunately, many of the judgments that people are asked to make about busing, guaranteed incomes, or the causes of racial inequality are in fact rather complex and quite probably are determined by more than one underlying dimension. To assume that complex judgments are in fact very simple decisions may generate an erroneously pessimistic (or optimistic) view of the possibilities for social reform. The remainder of this section of the chapter will be devoted to discussing the multidimensional approach to interpreting attitude surveys in the context of the previously presented survey data.

## WHAT IS THE OBJECT OF JUDGMENT?

Although at first blush it appears that whites, in response to the variety of questions cited earlier, are making judgments about blacks in actuality they are making decisions that may relate only partially—if at all—to their attitudes toward blacks. For example, in response to the question about the desirability of various kinds of black protests, we found that many of the people who favored integration object to black protests. The fact is that Americans have typically objected to even minimally disruptive protests including those of the suffragettes at the turn of the century, the labor strikes during the 1930s, the civil rights marches during the 1960s, and most recently the Vietnam War protests. Most survey data on the Vietnam War protests, for example, indicate that even at that point when the vast majority of Americans had turned against the war there was still considerable opposition to public protests against the war. As disappointing as it may be to those of us who view public protest as a legitimate means to petition the government, it nonetheless appears that even peaceful protests designed to achieve basic civil rights are regarded as undesirable. The point is that it is not so much *black* protest that is resented, it is that most forms of protest are considered undesirable, with the more extreme forms being most strongly rejected. To state the problem in another way, the difficulty in interpreting responses to multidimensional stimuli is that we often do not know which dimension (or dimensions) subjects are responding to; we do not have the appropriate control questions to know whether respondents object to *blacks* protesting or whether they object to any protests against the established order (cf. Schuman, 1972).

When we examine whites' attitudes toward the causes of racial inequality, we face the same problem. While it is true, as Schuman (1969) has suggested, that whites appear to have shifted their attributions about the causes of racial inequality from biological to motivational determinants, the present author disputes Schuman's belief that this is just a slightly modified form of "white racism." Beliefs about rugged individualism, free will, and a just world in which good is rewarded and evil punished is in no way limited to whites' attitudes toward blacks. Lerner's experimental work provides convincing evidence for a rather powerful belief in this principle, quite apart from any racial overtones (Lerner, 1965, 1971; Lerner and Simmons, 1966).

Lerner has argued that people have a strong need to believe in a predictable world—that is, a world in which one can expect to be rewarded for good behavior and punished for bad behavior. The converse of this also appears to be true: when we observe individuals being rewarded, we assume that they are worthy; when we observe individuals being punished, we assume that they are unworthy. Lerner (1965) created an experimental setting in which a subject observed two people working on a joint task. The experimenter *randomly* selected one of the two workers to be financially rewarded, even though both had done equally well on the task. Following this, the subject was asked to rate both workers on a variety of evaluative dimensions; even though subjects realized that the decision to reward was random, they rated the rewarded worker as significantly more desirable and attractive. In a comparable set of studies in which arbitrarily selected individuals received punishment (in the form of electric shocks), subjects again confirmed the "just world" predictions and viewed the hapless victims as less desirable on a set of personality characteristics (Lerner and Simmons, 1966; Lerner, 1971).

Thus, it does not come as a great surprise when Feagin (1972) observes that people tend to regard the "victims" of an inferior economic class as the cause of their own problems. The important point here is that again race does not appear to be the critical factor as much as people's implicit ideology about success and failure. It should be noted additionally that Feagin's research, unlike the previously cited opinion polls, did not specifically ask about the condition of blacks but asked about "reasons . . . to explain why there are poor people in this country."

The tendency to blame blacks for their own problems thus seems consistent with the belief in a "just world" and probably does not differ very much from whites' beliefs about any other economically disadvantaged group. Again it appears that asking whites about causes of racial inequality presents them with a multidimensional stimuli that may tap their attitudes toward blacks or may tap their attitudes about the causes of success and failure in America.

## INTERPRETING THE DATA ON
## PERCEIVED DISCRIMINATION AGAINST BLACKS

We have already examined the confusing data on whites' perception of discrimination shown against blacks. A Harris poll (Brink and Harris, 1966) indicated that 61% of white Americans felt blacks were treated unfairly. However, they must have been treated unfairly "somewhere else" because when people were asked if there was much discrimination in *their* city or community or in *their* labor union or plant or by *their* police, they tended to perceive blacks as receiving the same treatment as whites (Erskine, 1967a, 1967b, 1968d). To add to this confusion, it appears that whites can be forced to perceive the massive difficulties of blacks when hit with the right question. For example, the overwhelming agreement that a job decision would go to a white rather than an equally well-trained black (Erskine, 1968a), and the observation by Brink and Harris (1964) that whites were "outraged at the thought of being treated like a Negro" suggests that at *some level* whites are aware of the magnitude of discrimination suffered by blacks. The major discrepancy in these findings is that little discrimination is perceived at the local level (state, community, city, town, labor union) while other questions indicate, in varying degrees, that blacks are indeed treated unfairly.

There may be at least two interpretations of this discrepancy. One interpretation, to be discussed later in this chapter, has been described by the author as the "liberal distance function" (Rothbart, 1973). This explanation posits that the perceived magnitude of social injustice increases as a function of the distance between the observer and the locus of injustice. Although the "liberal distance function" may be involved in this discrepancy, a somewhat more plausible interpretation is based on the differential experiences of blacks and whites.

It is perhaps a truism that the effects of racial inequality in America frequently serve to minimize the visibility of discrimination. Because of extreme segregation in employment, housing, and education in the North and South, most whites can go through their entire day seeing few, if any, blacks. Given the infrequent contact between whites and blacks, and given that *mis*treatment of blacks by its very nature will occur in ways that are not highly visible to whites, it is not surprising that whites underestimate discrimination shown toward blacks. Mistreatment of blacks by police, for example, is more likely to occur in a black ghetto than a white suburb, and the injustice of a qualified black who is turned down for a job (or an apartment) is known only to the black and the perpetrator of the injustice. Since most instances of injustice occur neither publicly nor overtly, chances are fairly good that whites will have few "available instances" of mistreatment (to use Tversky and Kahneman's [1973] term). In those instances where mistreatment of blacks is publicly portrayed to whites—as in the march at Selma, Alabama—whites' response has been sympathetic (Erskine, 1967b). Thus, when whites are asked how blacks are treated in their community, they will assume the experience of blacks to be comparable to their own experiences; as Campbell (1971) has suggested, whites view the condition of blacks from the vantage of their own experiences.

There is nothing pleasant or satisfying about racial injustice and inequality, and it seems reasonable that most whites will not actively seek out information suggesting that conditions are worse than they appear to be. It is interesting that Campbell (1971) found that educational level was one of the few variables that played a major role in attitudes toward racial equality, and it is possible that one contributing factor to this was the increasing exposure to racial problems in high school and college curricula. The fact that whites tend to see rather little injustice in their own community, yet perceive unfair treatment at a more general level, suggests that whites may be intellectually aware of discrimination, but that this awareness is not buttressed by numerous first-hand observations—a combination of circumstances that may yield less passionate commitment to the cause of racial equality than one might hope. Although it would be erroneous to describe white Americans as deeply committed to the cause of racial equality, it would be equally erroneous to assume that Americans are indifferent to this goal.

It was the goal of this chapter to explore some of the factors that influence whites' resistance to reforms designed to bring about racial equality and, by implication, to examine some specific proposals that show promise for being viable, effective reforms. In order to achieve this goal, it is necessary to consider three interrelated questions. First, do white Americans want to achieve racial equality? Second, how strongly motivated are whites in their desire to achieve equality? And third, what kinds of reform proposals would be acceptable to the majority of white Americans?

Thus far we have examined evidence that bears on at least two of these questions. In response to the first question, the NORC and ISR surveys clearly indicate that the vast majority of white Americans support goals associated with racial integration and racial equality. Even the period of extreme racial disturbance in the late 1960s did not alter whites' increasingly egalitarian views. The answer to the second question—concerning whites' motivation to achieve equality—is less sanguine. Data drawn from surveys investigating the perceived magnitude of discrimination and the desired speed of integration all indicate a notable lack of urgency or passion in whites' avowed desire to achieve racial equality. Thus, although whites' motivation cannot be said to be zero, it is also clear that their motivation is not intense.

We have not yet explored, in any complete way, the answer to the third question concerning the types of reforms that would be acceptable to whites. However, the answer to the second question suggests that whites may be unwilling to support social reforms that exact a high degree of personal sacrifice or cost. A second source of data that may bear on the third question concerns whites' perception that poor people are responsible for their inferior circumstances. It is likely that acceptable social reforms will have to be consistent, in some degree, with ideological beliefs about "just rewards" for industry and effort. The following section will examine these problems more fully.

## PROPOSALS TO REDUCE RACIAL INEQUALITY:
## SOME SURVEY DATA

Any attempt to assess the public's response to a particular reform proposal through the use of interviews or questionnaire methods is subject to considerable error. Even attempts to predict the public's acceptance of relatively clear and simple plans—such as fluoridation programs—have led to notable failures (cf. Sapolsky, 1969). It would therefore be inappropriate to expect a close correspondence between survey research findings and voter behavior in this area, although it may be possible to identify some important variables through an examination of survey research.

One of the difficulties in predicting public acceptance of a reform plan again revolves around the multidimensionality of the stimulus. Consider, for example, the issue of open housing legislation. We have already observed that whites favor integration and, in a previously cited Harris poll, that 85% of whites indicated that the "laws should guarantee Negroes equal rights to white people in getting good housing." Yet with a fair degree of consistency, whites have voted down open housing referenda. An excellent analysis of this problem has been suggested by Levine (1971), who attempted to reconcile publicly expressed integrationist attitudes with the reality of segregated neighborhoods and defeated open housing referenda. By examining a variety of opinion data related to housing for blacks collected over the last 30 years, Levine divided the questions into four different content categories indicating attitudes toward: (a) enforcement of residential segregation, (b) the principle of residential integration, (c) open housing laws, and (d) living near Negroes. As suggested by the NORC surveys, opposition to enforced segregation (Category 1) has been consistently growing since pre-War years, from 13% in 1939 to 64% in 1968. On the other hand, attitudes toward integration in principle (Category 2 items; e.g., "Is integrated housing desirable?") indicate support by only about 40% of the sample. Data on open housing laws (Category 3) indicate, if anything, declining support for open housing laws with the most recent 1967 poll indicating only about one-third supporting such laws. Data from Categories 2 and 3 are actually consistent, then, with public referenda on open housing legislation. However, there is an interesting change in the picture when examining items relating to personal willingness to live near blacks (Category 4). The most recent surveys indicate that at least 50% of whites indicate no objection to Negroes moving next door, and about 65% indicate that they would not move if Negroes moved next door. Thus far, the results from Category 4 are more integrationist than from Categories 2 and 3. However, when whites are asked if they would move if many Negroes moved in, the number *declining* to move drops to about 30%.

It appears, then, that whites oppose housing segregation and would not move if some blacks moved next door, but they object to "legislated" integration (open housing laws) and would probably move if *many* blacks moved next door. Thus it appears that at least two dimensions are of importance in determining whites' response to housing reforms: (a) whether the move toward housing integration is perceived to be "forced" or not, and (b) the number of blacks that they could expect to move into the neighborhood. Depending on how the reform was described to the public, and what details were available about the numbers of blacks and whites, and presumably about expected changes in these ratios over time, whites' opinions could be either favorable or unfavorable. It does not seem unreasonable, given the history of white neighborhoods that have "tipped" to black, that whites might feel some concern about the eventual ratio of black to white that may ultimately evolve. In other words, the decision to move may be based in large part on the expectation that they (the whites) may become a minority in their neighborhood. As Levine (1971) states:

> It seems reasonably clear that while integration is acceptable to whites and may even be desirable, members of the majority race in this country are unwilling to live as a minority. Perhaps this is to be decried morally—who knows—but that's the way it is. And if integration is desirable (and I think it is) . . . then it should be possible to change the mechanism [that leads to tipping] so it will work for integration instead of against it. (p. 577)

Again it appears that decisions about reform proposals are complex and, depending on a multitude of factors—which may or may not be made clear in a survey question—the public's response may be favorable or unfavorable. The following analyses will attempt to clarify some of these factors that people may be responding to when assessing the desirability of social reforms.


## PERCEIVED COSTS: ECONOMIC AND SOCIAL

In one of his typically penetrating analyses, Art Buchwald once speculated on how people would behave if there were a day set aside each year in which people spoke only the truth. Thus, a top executive from a large corporation who was appearing before a wage and price control board to request price increases would justify the increase not on the grounds of increasing costs, but on the grounds of personal greed. A politician would run for office not on his ability to provide moral leadership for the nation, but on the basis of his self-avowed lust for power. It would not be too great a leap from Buchwald's analysis to suggest that when white parents are asked if they wish their child to be bused to an inner-city school, their public response may be a defense of the neighborhood school concept, but on Buchwald's day of truth they might say, "Given a choice between my child getting an inferior education, and someone else's child getting an inferior education, I will choose the latter."

By any rule of logic, the perceived costs or benefits of a proposed reform must play an important role in people's acceptance or rejection of that reform, yet there is a very strong norm not to justify one's preferences by naked self-interest. Since it is more acceptable to defend a lofty moral principle than one's immediate self-interest, it is not uncommon for people to translate the latter into the former: retaining one's slaves becomes the constitutional issue of states' rights, and taking land from American Indians for personal gain becomes Manifest Destiny. If we ignore the reasons that people give for their opposition to a program and simply concentrate on their acceptance or rejection of a policy, the evidence for the importance of cost becomes clear.

Feagin (1972), in his research on the perceived causes of poverty, also assessed people's reactions to welfare programs and anti-poverty proposals. Sixty-four percent of his sample indicated approval of a guaranteed job program for "every American who wants to work ..." However, when a follow-up question asked if they would favor such a program "even if it means that your own taxes would be increased a good bit?" only 35% supported the proposal. Self-interest clearly is influencing other results as well: 84% of blacks supported a guaranteed job program, while 61% of whites expressed support; 57% of blacks supported a guaranteed income program, as contrasted to 26% of whites; 39% of respondents earning under $4000 per year favored a guaranteed income of $3000, while 23% of those earning over $10,000 per year favored this plan; and, finally, a plan to have a $10,000 per year income for every family was received somewhat less enthusiastically by those earning over $10,000 per year than by those earning less than $10,000 per year (7% vs. 16% support, respectively).

Self-interest need not necessarily be economic in nature. This author has suggested elsewhere that favorable attitudes toward social reform will increase as a function of the distance between the observer and the locus of reform (Rothbart, 1973). Two attitude surveys corroborated this hypothesis. In the first survey, attitudes toward a proposed prison live-out program (whereby prisoners would work in the community part of the time) were sampled from groups living at three different distances from the prison. For the group living immediately adjacent to the prison, only 15% of those sampled supported the live-out program, whereas support increased to 75% for those living five miles from the prison. Control questions indicated that the differences among the groups were not an artifact of differences in general "liberalness." The second survey sampled reactions to a proposed low-income, publicly financed housing project to be built in Eugene, Oregon. Groups living at three different distances from the project were sampled, and again it was observed that those adjacent to the project were least favorable (55% opposed), while those living furthest (one and one-half miles away) were more favorable (30% opposed). A control question indicated that 84% of each group agreed that there was a need for such a housing project in Eugene. Thus, all groups appeared to be equally liberal on the question of the need for low-income housing in the community, as long as the project was not located next door. Since the negative consequences that could accrue from the implementation of these reforms would be experienced in proportion to one's proximity to the project, it is not surprising to find opposition decreasing with distance.

## COSTS ASSOCIATED WITH INTEGRATION REFORMS

There are few events as disheartening as that of a demonstration by whites against some project or policy that portends to improve the living conditions of blacks. Demonstrated opposition to school integration in Little Rock, Arkansas, Dearborn, Michigan, or the Canarsie district of New York City, and to integrated housing in Cicero, Illinois, or the Forest Hills section of New York City, indicates that opposition to specific reforms is not limited to "redneck" Southerners or "white ethnics." It is difficult to analyze this resistance in a dispassionate way, yet it is exactly this kind of resistance that requires the most careful scrutiny.

Since our society distributes its wealth in a way that disproportionately favors whites, it is clear that any attempt to equalize the economic status of blacks will result in some sacrifice by whites. Since whites are going to have to absorb the costs of achieving racial equality, the question that must be asked is what *magnitude* of costs and what *types* of costs will whites be willing to absorb, and, conversely, what kinds of costs will be unacceptable.

Rather than analyze in detail various education, housing, and income reforms that have been proposed (and resisted), the author has chosen to deal with the problem in a general way. Not all school integration plans are the same, and not all housing projects are the same. Some school busing programs designed to achieve racial balance, for example, have distributed blacks who were formerly concentrated in all-black schools to several (presumably better) white schools; some plans have bused white children to inner-city (presumably worse) formerly all-black schools. Some housing projects concentrate large numbers of blacks in a previously all-white neighborhood through high-rise projects, and others attempt to distribute the ratio of blacks to whites more evenly throughout a formerly all-white community (cf. Hammer, 1973). It would therefore be erroneous to assume that all school integration programs or housing projects are equally unacceptable to whites. But it does appear that there are some costs that whites will be extremely resistant to accept.

First, any plan that would cause their children to receive a significantly poorer education than they would otherwise receive will be tenaciously resisted. Erroneously or not, most white and black parents regard a good education as a prerequisite for upward mobility. If white parents are then asked to accept a plan that will result in a large decrease in the quality of education that their child will receive (and clearly not all school integration plans make such a demand), it is not surprising that those parents will show resistance. Clearly the task is to improve the quality of education for blacks without significantly decreasing the quality of education for whites. If the choice given to white parents is to achieve racial integration of the schools at the cost of vastly reducing the quality of schooling for their children, their choice will be depressingly clear. It should be noted here that a recent NORC poll showed overwhelming acceptance of racial integration in both the North and South, but almost total resistance to school busing (Greeley and Sheatsley, 1972). Six percent of white residents in the South and 15% of white residents in the North favored busing of Negro and white school children from one school district to another. Breakdown of the sample by age, educational level, religion, and ethnic (not racial) background showed slight variations in response, but no classification showed more than 24% support among whites for busing—although about 53% of the blacks favored busing. This pattern of results suggested to the authors that there is considerable doubt in white minds about the effectiveness of busing as a means of improving the quality of education for blacks. Even though both whites and blacks have doubts about the long-range efficacy of busing, clearly blacks have more to gain from busing than whites.[5]

Second, any plan that would cause whites to live as a minority will be strongly resisted. Although this argument appears ludicrous since whites are in fact the overwhelming majority group in America, the extreme instability of residential housing patterns and racial balance in the schools leaves whites with the expectation that the influx of even a few black families means the neighborhood is "changing" and will become virtually all black in a short period of time. Hammer (1973) reports of one elementary school in Kansas City, Missouri, whose racial composition changed from 25% to 65% black in a single year. As long as whites perceive the racial balance in their neighborhood as unstable, they may expect other white families to leave, may themselves plan to leave, and thus by their own expectations confirm the reality of a white exodus.

The important point to be made in this analysis is that the tendency to resist residential integration is not necessarily tied to racist attitudes or fear of blacks (although those feelings may be involved), but to (a) the perception

[5] A very recent Gallup poll conducted on August 3-6, 1973, is somewhat contradictory on the level of support for busing shown by blacks, but also somewhat enlightening on the issue of busing as a means to achieve racial integration (AP release, Eugene Register Guard, September 12, 1973). Although details of the poll were unavailable for inclusion in this chapter, the results again favor support of school integration: only 19% of whites opposed school integration. However, only 4% of whites and 9% of blacks thought that busing was the best way to achieve integration. The most popular choice for integrating schools was to change school boundaries to allow children from diverse ethnic and economic groups to attend the same school.

that the racial balance of the neighborhood will shift in an uncontrollable way from predominantly white to predominantly black, and (b) the aversion on the parts of whites, as Levine (1971) has suggested, to live as a racial minority. If we view the problem of residential segregation as one of white people's racist attitudes, it is not apparent to this author how the problem can be solved. If the problem is viewed as maintaining a predictable racial balance in a neighborhood, then there may be some specific measures that could ensure stability (Levine, 1971; Hammer, 1973).

The third and last principle concerns the magnitude of economic costs that whites will be willing to endure to elevate the economic condition of blacks. Put most simply, it is unreasonable to expect whites to endorse social reforms that will cause them to lose their jobs or to suffer a precipitous drop in income. Although this "principle" appears trivial in the extreme, it also appears to have been ignored in a significant number of instances. For example, many labor unions who have been notorious in excluding blacks from their membership, have tenaciously resisted efforts by the federal government to accept blacks into their unions. Although this resistance is appalling, it is nonetheless expected given the economic pressures facing many of these unions. Since unemployment has been high in many of the targeted industries (such as construction), accepting new members in a surplus labor market will decrease the prospects of employment for those already in the union. It should be clear to the reader that I am not advocating the exclusion of blacks from labor unions. What I am saying is that when social reforms are structured as a zero-sum game in which a black's gain is a white's loss, it is unrealistic to expect whites to be enthusiastic about such reform. It would be more sensible to consider reforms that reduce the direct competition between whites and blacks for jobs and thus eliminate the extrinsic motives that whites have been given for excluding blacks from the labor market. This implies that a program of full employment, or its equivalent, may be an important precondition for bringing significant numbers of blacks into jobs that have been traditionally held by whites (Tobin, 1965). Since there exists a depressing abundance of psychological factors that may foster resistance to egalitarian reforms, there is little need to buttress this resistance by making it in whites' direct economic self-interest to exclude blacks from the labor market.

## THE DISTRIBUTION OF SOCIAL COSTS FOR REFORMS: DIFFUSED OR CONCENTRATED?

It has been stated as axiomatic that the full economic and social integration of blacks into American life will cause a relative diminution of the privileges and affluence of white Americans. It will, then, be impossible to propose reforms that do not incur some cost for whites. But it is possible to propose reforms that distribute the costs of reform in such a way that the magnitude of cost for any individual is not burdensome. For example, pressure to place blacks in unskilled and semi-skilled jobs, as already suggested, often places blue-collar whites in direct competition with blacks for jobs. Thus, the cost of blacks' entry into the labor market is borne largely by blue-collar workers who become resentful of the competition from blacks. This resentment, although understandable, is unfortunate because it really should be directed at middle- and upper-income whites who are not equitably sharing the costs of promoting racial equality.

In fact, most programs designed to achieve integration, such as low-income housing projects and school busing plans, have had the property of concentrating the costs in a geographically restricted area rather than in distributing the costs more representatively among the white population. To the degree that the economic and social costs of reform are concentrated in a particular geographic region or economic group, one would logically expect that group or region to show the greatest resistance to reform. It is possible to envisage reform programs that diffuse the costs of reform in an equitable way—for example, through a guaranteed income and/or job program that would be financed through federal income taxes. Such a program need not put the cost of achieving social equality on those whites who are least able to absorb it.

## FEAR AS A DETERMINANT OF RESISTANCE TO CHANGE

Probably the most popular single interpretation of whites' resistance to racial integration of schools or neighborhoods is that of fear, although it is not always obvious what kind of fear is being referred to. There may be, as has been suggested, the fear of a radical change in the social composition of one's neighborhood, or the fear of criminal assaults, race riots, a drop in the quality of schooling for white children, lowered property values, or fear of losing one's job in competition with blacks. Probably the greatest emphasis is placed on the fear of violence as the dominant concern over racial integration, although the opinion polls present a confusing, if sometimes interesting, pattern of results. A Harris poll taken in August of 1967 found 51% of whites in big cities responding affirmatively to the question, "Does the fear of racial violence make you personally feel more uneasy on the streets?"—38% indicated "less worried," "same," or "don't feel uneasy" (Erskine, 1967b). A poll taken a year later showed, interestingly enough, that blacks were more uneasy than whites about the prospect of racial violence—65% vs. 51% (Erskine, 1967b). This last finding is quite consistent with other results indicating that blacks suffer more from urban crime and rioting than do whites. It is hard to know how much of whites' feelings of uneasiness "on the streets" is due to a response bias, since a breakdown by community size in a January 1967 poll found that people in rural areas were virtually as fearful as those living in large cities! There is, however, little dispute that black ghettos are high crime areas and also little dispute that blacks suffer from personal and violent crime more than whites (Hacker, 1973). When whites face the prospect of ghetto residents moving in next door they are often fearful and, to the extent that crime rates are higher in black than in white areas, this fear is realistically founded.

It is clearly beyond the scope of this chapter (and the competence of the author) to propose any solutions to the problem of urban crime. The problem of crime, for both whites and blacks, is paramount and cannot be easily dismissed as a potent factor in race relations. However, the case can be made that whites overestimate the magnitude of the relationship between race and criminal behavior due to a variety of cognitive and affective psychological factors. For example, let us suppose that a white person who lived in an urban area comes into contact with blacks and whites in about equal proportions. Let us further suppose, for convenience, that out of 100 encounters with other whites, 99 of those encounters were nonmemorable while on the one other occasion he was mugged; let us also suppose that out of 100 encounters with blacks, 97 encounters were nonmemorable and on the three other occasions with blacks he was mugged. Although there is regrettably little research on how people actually make inferences from these experiences, my guess would be that the white will conclude that he is three times as likely to be mugged by a black than a white and would therefore act in a way to avoid *most* blacks.[6] If he were to compute, however, the probability of *not* being mugged by a black *vs.* a white, he would find the probabilities to be virtually the same (.99 vs. .97), yet his behavior would not be based on instances of nonoccurrence. If the supposition is correct that nonmemorable encounters are discounted while memorable experiences (in this case, highly negative) remain highly salient, then whites will greatly overestimate the number of blacks who are capable of criminal activities; since race then would be perceived as a highly valid cue for criminal behavior, whites might become quite fearful of attempts at residential integration. A recent study by Leon, Oden, and Anderson (1973) provides some support for the belief that an individual's judgments of a group is highly influenced by the characteristics of its most extreme members.

At the outset of this chapter it was stated that we would not deal with the attitudes of blacks or the question of the kinds of reforms that would be most beneficial to blacks, but would restrict our inquiry to the sources of white resistance; I should like, however, to deviate momentarily from that constraint. Although whites are fearful of an increase in neighborhood crime

---

[6] Probably the most relevant research here is that conducted by Chapman (1967) on "illusory correlation." They discuss various factors that may cause people to falsely overestimate the cooccurrence of two events.

that may result from residential integration, the consequence of continuing residential segregation will be to leave blacks as one of the most criminally victimized groups in America. Since crime rates are highest in black ghettos, it is logical for blacks to want to move into safer areas (often white), thus pitting the security of whites against the security of blacks. Although it is difficult to be optimistic about the problem of urban crime, it may be possible to produce residential integration in a way that will permit whites and blacks to remain more secure from crime than they are at present. High-density high-rise apartment buildings may be well-nigh impossible to defend against crime, whereas lower density projects may be quite defensible. To the degree that a *stable* integrated neighborhood evolves, residents will learn who does and who does not belong there, and may be able to spot suspicious individuals. Again, stability in a neighborhood may be promotive of less crime, whereas neighborhoods in flux may make criminal activity appear less risky. While the problem of crime by necessity must be approached at different levels (e.g., reducing crime created by drug use, finding jobs that offer some hope of advancement, etc.), some proposals for residential integration may be more useful than others to hold down personal crime; it is suggested here that at least two factors may be the density and the stability of the neighborhoods.

## PERCEIVED BENEFITS AS A DETERMINANT
## OF RESPONSE TO SOCIAL REFORM

So far we have considered various ways in which the perceived costs of social reform may bring about resistance from whites. But reforms also can vary in the degree to which they offer potential benefits to whites. A housing project for blacks cannot benefit a white worker, but a comprehensive form of federal medical insurance, while giving a disproportionate amount of help to the poor, will also benefit whites. Job training programs for the poor and special education programs for the disadvantaged do not help low- and middle-income whites, but a guaranteed job program would protect most people from the insecurity of unemployment, even though such a program would currently be of greatest aid to minority groups. To a large degree, many of the war on poverty programs to date have been targeted to provide services to disadvantaged minorities. Whatever wisdom and merit these various programs may have contained, they may have left many working-class whites with the (erroneous) impression that blacks now have more opportunities available to them than whites. A poll conducted by *Newsweek* in 1969 asked whites, "Do Negroes today have a better chance or worse chance than people like yourself to get well-paying jobs? To get a good education for their children? To get good housing at a reasonable cost? To get financial help from the government when they're out of work?" For the first three questions, about 40% of the whites believed that blacks enjoyed better opportunities than themselves, about 33% believed that whites and blacks have the same opportunities, and about 22% felt that blacks had worse opportunities. The last question, concerning financial help from the government, showed 65% believing blacks had superior opportunities, 22% believing equal opportunities existed for blacks and whites, and 4% believing that blacks had poorer chances than whites (Harris poll appearing in October 6, 1969, issue of *Newsweek*). Unfortunately, more in-depth interviewing would have been helpful in this poll since is is not clear what white respondents are thinking about when they view blacks as having greater opportunities than themselves.

Whatever the reasons for these responses, it may be that these whites resented federal programs that they believed were created for the sole benefit of racial minorities. Even though this impression of the war on poverty programs is inaccurate, it may be that reform programs that are targeted toward specific groups in a visible way may inadvertently create resentment toward those groups. If this is true, it would imply that social reforms that have either widespread benefits (such as a federal health insurance program) or that do not provide benefits in a way that stigmatizes its recipient (such as a guaranteed income program) would be least likely to arouse resentment.

## IDEOLOGY AS A DETERMINANT OF RESPONSE TO SOCIAL REFORM

In 1729, Jonathan Swift published *A Modest Proposal,* a satirical essay proposing to solve simultaneously the problems of overpopulation and poverty among Ireland's poorest classes. Swift proposed a simple plan whereby the Irish poor would bear children, nurse them until one year of age, and then sell them as food to the wealthy of Britain. Swift forthrightly analyzes the implications of his proposal and in considerable detail discusses the effects of his plan on the well-being of both rich and poor. He concludes his essay by avowing the purity of his intentions, and argues that the implementation of his proposal would lead to "... advancing our trade, providing for infants, relieving the poor, and giving some pleasure to the rich." When reading Swift's proposal, one is impressed by its elegant structure and by its compelling logic; in fact, the only real flaw in his proposal is that it is morally repulsive— although it was not so regarded by many of Swift's contemporaries.

Reform proposals, in order to gain any widespread degree of acceptance, must not only be perceived as effective, but must meet a criterion of ideological compatibility as well. Swift's modest proposal may satisfy the first criterion but clearly falls short of the second. Thurman Arnold, in his book *The Folklore of Capitalism,* analyzes resistance to many of the reforms proposed during the Depression of the 1930s (Arnold, 1937). He cites the Civilian Conservation Corps (CCC) as one of the most successful, and one of the most relentlessly attacked, New Deal experiments. Even though the CCC managed to put the unemployed to work on socially useful jobs—and thus simultaneously to reduce unemployment, provide money to workers, and achieve valuable conservation goals—it was doomed because *at the time* the belief that the federal government ought to deliberately create jobs was not ideologically consistent with most people's view of the government's role in a free enterprise economy. Although recent public opinion data no longer shows a guaranteed job program to be in disfavor, during the 1930s the CCC suffered the fate of Swift's effective but ideologically unacceptable proposal.

Public reactions to reform proposals designed to bring about racial equality have clearly been influenced by ideological factors. We have already discussed the influence of the Protestant Ethic in people's naive analyses about the causes of poverty. Feagin's (1972) data on attitudes toward reform proposals indicate the traditional ambivalence about welfare: on the one hand, people feel that it is necessary to keep the poor from starving, but on the other hand, welfare recipients are getting something for nothing and should be out working. Since welfare programs provide money to nonworking families, these programs attack the Protestant Ethic directly by severing the relationship between income and effort.

Feagin's data also shows interesting differences in the acceptability of various reform plans. Sixty-four percent of his sample favored guaranteed jobs (higher approval among blacks than whites), 30% favored a guaranteed income with a $3,000 base, and 13% favored an equal income of $10,000 for each family. Although it is probably an error to place much faith in the absolute percentages as an indication of popular support for these reforms (since minimal information about those plans were given to the respondents), the important data is the differing levels of support among the three plans.

The guaranteed job program does not negate the possibility of a person's rewards being proportionate to his efforts, but merely establishes the opportunity for this relationship to obtain. The guaranteed income program is probably perceived (erroneously) as largely incompatible with the Protestant Ethic, while the equal income plan of $10,000 is likely perceived as a total negation of the Protestant Ethic. Incidentally, this degree of popular support for a guaranteed job program is supported by other polls as well: a 1967 Harris poll showed 66% of whites and 91% of blacks endorsing the idea that "government work projects [giving] jobs to all the unemployed" might "help resolve the race problem in America" (cited in Erskine, 1968a).

Thus reform proposals vary in the degree to which they are compatible with the Protestant Ethic; depending on its nature, a particular reform program may benefit or suffer, depending on its degree of perceived compatibility with contemporary values.

For example, the guaranteed income plan, as proposed by Milton Friedman and James Tobin (e.g., Tobin, 1965), has the properties of (a) providing a guaranteed base of support for a family of given size (say $4,000 for a family of four), and (b) allowing the family to keep a large portion of the income they make above the base level. The size of the portion that they will keep decreases as total family income increases, but the main point is that there is a continual incentive to increase family income. In other words, unlike the welfare system that punishes people for working at low-paying jobs by cutting off welfare support, the guaranteed income plan—in the best tradition of the Protestant Ethic—retains the incentive for working by allowing the family to keep the base income when supplemented by additional monies.

It is believed by many that George McGovern, in his bid for the Presidency in 1972, lost considerable popular support when he cursorily proposed a plan to distribute a base income of $1,000 to every person in America. If this assessment is correct—and I suspect that it is—McGovern's error came not in his proposal for a guaranteed income but in his *exposition* of the guaranteed income plan. He unfortunately chose to stress that aspect of the guaranteed income plan that was least compatible with the Protestant Ethic rather than trumpet those aspects of the plan that are highly compatible with this Ethic. The guaranteed income plan, by the simple yardstick of compatibility with the Protestant Ethic, is superior to existing welfare programs that reinforce dependency and punish people for industrious behavior.

## SOME OBSERVATIONS ON SOCIAL REFORMS
## TO REDUCE RACIAL INEQUALITY

It was not the original intention of the author to advocate specific plans to reduce racial inequality, but it is difficult to conclude this rather lengthy analysis of resistance to social reform without having some strong feelings about the relative merits of some plans over others. Believing, as William Blake does, that "unfulfilled desire leads to pestilence," I should like to offer a few concluding observations about the virtues of some specific reform plans.

It is my judgment that reforms designed to guarantee jobs and a base income to America's poor show the greatest promise for reducing racial inequality. Two justifications are offered for this belief. The first justification I will offer only briefly since it is well beyond the scope of this chapter. Very simply, these proposals appear to be the simplest and most direct means to bring about an elevation of black people's economic status. Given the astronomical unemployment figures for unskilled young black males, and the high proportion of black families living below the federally defined poverty level, I would argue, as Jencks has in his book *Inequality* (1972), that public policy should focus on direct attempts to bring about economic equality through the manipulation and control of our economic institutions. For an excellent analysis of the role of the guaranteed income plan in reducing racial inequality the reader is referred to Tobin (1965).

The second justification for the two reform proposals is in fact quit germane to the preceding "multidimensional" analysis of whites' reactions to reform proposals. One of the central theses of this chapter has been that reform proposals designed to reduce racial inequality differ on several dimensions of potential importance. Specifically, it has been suggested that both the *magnitude* and *distribution* of costs of reforms are important, as well as the perceived potential benefit to whites and the reform's ideological compatibility with contemporary beliefs about work and economic renumeration (Protestant Ethic).

The guaranteed job proposal has been favorably received in public opinion surveys and, although high in cost, probably scores quite favorably in all other dimensions. Even though Feagin's (1972) research indicated that endorsement dropped precipitously when the proposal was qualified by the provision that "it means that your own taxes would be increased a good bit," this finding is difficult to evaluate since we do not know how people would actually respond to a concrete proposal. How much is "a good bit?" How would the tax burden for such a reform be distributed? These unanswered questions make it difficult to predict people's responses to a specific proposal, but the fact that there is public endorsement *in principle* for such a major reform is heartening.

The guaranteed income plan presents a less clear picture, probably because of the number of complex elements inherent in these proposals. Endorsement for such a plan has not reached majority proportions, but its popularity appears to be gaining. Feagin (1972) notes that support for the guaranteed income plan increased from 30% to 38% between 1969 and 1972. Unfortunately, the mere fact that this reform is labeled a "guaranteed income" quite probably constitutes a source of negative bias on the ideology dimension. On matters of ideology, slogans and phrases often carry considerable weight, and it is regretable that other designations of the plan—such as the "negative income tax"—did not carry forth. Since the plan does promulgate the work ethic through its incentive scheme, it appears likely that a fuller public exposition of this plan, in particular a comparison with existing welfare programs, may lead to fairly widespread public acceptance.

## CONCLUDING SUMMARY

Public opinion data on whites' attitudes toward racial equality and related reform proposals do not fit a simple unidimensional interpretation. Although it would be convenient to have a "simple and sovereign" explanation—to use Allport's phrase—for a problem as emotionally trying as racial attitudes, labels connoting a single affective orientation (such as "racist," "egalitarian," "sympathetic," or "selfish") are inadequate to account for the complexity of the results.

It would be helpful if future research on attitudes toward racial inequality and social reform were directed toward uncovering the dimensions that influence people's responses to reform proposals. Since such data is not currently in evidence, an attempt was made in the present chapter to take a "best guess" as to what these dimensions may be.

It would make the task of the social psychologist a good bit easier if, on the basis of a subject's strong endorsement of the principle of racial equality, we could predict that this respondent would also favor (a) black protests aimed at achieving equality, (b) a faster pace of integration, (c) school busing to achieve racial balance, and (d) a strong environmental bias in perceiving the causes of (and solutions to) poverty. Unfortunately, it is possible to be very sympathetic toward blacks without sharing a socialist's perspective about the causes of poverty; it is possible to believe in integrated schools without sharing the belief that busing is the best means to achieve school integration; and it is even possible to be sympathetic toward blacks and yet feel uncomfortable about organized social protests. An examination of the attitude data suggested at least four dimensions that appeared to be only imperfectly correlated with one another: (a) attitudes toward equal opportunities and equal treatment of blacks, (b) perceived magnitude of discrimination experienced by blacks, (c) attitudes toward organized protests and the pace of social reform, and (d) beliefs about the causes of socioeconomic inequality. It was argued that the patterns of whites' attitudes on these dimensions suggested considerable sympathy toward the goals of racial equality, tempered by a notable lack of urgency about achieving such goals (possibly because of the lack of visibility of many forms of discrimination), and a continuing belief in the individualist notion that the victims of poverty are themselves the causes of their own misfortune.

The survey data on whites' attitudes toward reform proposals was similarly analyzed, and at least four dimensions of reform proposals were identified: (a) the *magnitude* of the reform costs, (b) the *distribution* of those costs (diffuse vs. concentrated), (c) the *potential benefit* to whites (e.g., whether the locus of reform was specific to racial minorities), and (d) the *ideological compatibility* of the reform with individualist beliefs (the Protestant Ethic).

There are many possible reasons why whites resist efforts to bring about racial equality. Some of these reasons may be rooted in fear of change, fear of the unknown, and racist attitudes, but it is also clear that for many of the reform proposals there are realistic reasons for whites to resist change. To the degree that gains for blacks are tied rather directly to substantial losses for whites, resistance to egalitarian reforms will continue. To the degree that reforms can bring about gains for blacks without threatening whites with the loss of jobs or inferior schools for their children, resistance will be considerably reduced. The guaranteed job and guaranteed income programs were cited as reforms that hold considerable promise for increasing the opportunities and economic status for blacks in a way that substantially reduces the interdependence between black gains and white losses.

Since the achievement of racial equality in America will require notable changes in the attitudes, habits, and relative luxury of white Americans, it is essential to concentrate on reforms that will reduce the direct competition between blacks and whites for basic material resources. It may then be possible to concentrate on the psychological sources of resistance to change that may prove to be less tenacious than imagined once the extrinsic incentives to resist equality are reduced.

## REFERENCES

Allport, G.W. The historical background of modern social psychology. In G. Lindzey (Ed.), *The Handbook of social psychology*. Volume I. Reading, Mass.: Addison-Wesley, 1954.

Arnold, T.W. *The folklore of capitalism*. New Haven: Yale University Press, 1937.

Brigham, J.C., and Weissbach, T.A. The current racial climate in the United States. In J.C. Brigham and T.A. Weissbach (Eds.), *Racial Attitudes in America*. New York: Harper & Row, 1972.

Brink, W., and Harris, L. *The Negro revolution in America*. New York: Simon & Schuster, 1964.

Brink, W., and Harris, L. *Black and white*. New York: Simon & Schuster, 1966.

Campbell, A. *White attitudes toward black people*. Ann Arbor: Institute for Social Research, 1971.

Chapman, L.J. Illusory correlation in observational report. *Journal of Verbal Learning and Verbal Behavior*, 1967, **6**, 151-155.

Cohen, S.A. The effects of racial similarity-dissimilarity and social class similarity-dissimilarity on the elicitation of helping behavior. Unpublished doctoral dissertation, New York University, 1973.

Erskine, H. The polls: Negro housing. *Public Opinion Quarterly*, 1967(a), **31**, 655-677.

Erskine, H. The polls: Demonstrations and race riots. *Public Opinion Quarterly*, 1967(b), **31**, 655-677.

Erskine, H. The polls: Negro unemployment. *Public Opinion Quarterly*, 1968(a), **32**, 132-153.

Erskine, H. The polls: World Opinion of U.S. racial problems. *Public Opinion Quarterly*, 1968(b), **32**, 299-312.

Erskine, H. The polls: Speed of racial integration. *Public Opinion Quarterly*, 1968(c), **32**, 513-524.

Erskine, H. The polls: Recent opinion on racial problems. *Public Opinion Quarterly*, 1968(d), **32**, 696-703.

Erskine, H. The polls: Negro philosophies of life. *Public Opinion Quarterly*, 1969(a), **33**, 147-158.

Erskine, H. The polls: Negro finances. *Public Opinion Quarterly*, 1969(b), **33**, 272-282.

Feagin, J.R. God helps those who help themselves. *Psychology Today*, 1972, **6**, 101-129.

Gaertner, S., and Bickman, L. Effects of race on the elicitation of helping behavior: The wrong number technique. *Journal of Personality and Social Psychology,* 1971, **20**, 218-222.

Greeley, A.M., and Sheatsley, P.B. Attitudes toward racial integration. *Scientific American,* 1971, **225**, 13-19.

Greeley, A.M., and Sheatsley, P.B. Attitudes toward racial integration: The South "catches up." Unpublished manuscript, National Opinion Research Center Library, 1972.

Hacker, A. Getting used to mugging. *The New York Review of Books,* April 19, 1973, pp. 9-14.

Hammer, C. Racially changing neighborhoods. *The New Republic,* 1973, **169**, 19-21.

Hyman, H.H., and Sheatsley, P.B. Attitudes toward desegregation. *Scientific American,* 1956, **195**, 35-39.

Hyman, H.H., and Sheatsley, P.B. Attitudes toward desegregation. *Scientific American,* 1964, **211**, 16-23.

Jencks, C. *Inequality.* New York: Basic Books, 1972.

Katz, I. Experimental studies of Negro-white relationships. In L. Berkowitz (Ed.), *Advances in experimental social psychology.* Volume 5. New York: Academic Press, 1970.

Katz, I., Glass, D.C., and Cohen, S. Ambivalence, guilt, and the scapegoating of minority group victims. *Journal of Experimental Social Psychology,* 1973, **9**, 423-436.

Leon, M., Oden, G.C., and Anderson, N.H. Functional measurement of attitudes. *Journal of Personality and Social Psychology,* 1973, **27**, 301-310.

Lerner, M.J. Evaluation of performance as a function of performer's reward and attractiveness. *Journal of Personality and Social Psychology,* 1965, **1**, 355-360.

Lerner, M.J. Observer's evaluation of a victim: Justice, guilt, and veridical perception. *Journal of Personality and Social Psychology,* 1971, **20**, 127-135.

Lerner, M.H., and Simmons, C.H. Observer's reaction to the "innocent victim": Compassion or rejection? *Journal of Personality and Social Psychology,* 1966, **4**, 203-210.

Levine, R.A. The silent majority: Neither simple nor simple-minded. *Public Opinion Quarterly,* 1971, **35**, 571-577.

Piliavin, I.M., Rodin, J., and Piliavin, J.A. Good samaritanism: An underground phenomenon? *Journal of Personality and Social Psychology,* 1969, **13**, 289-299.

Rothbart, M. Perceiving social injustice: Some observations on the relationship between liberal attitudes and proximity to social problems. *Journal of Applied Social Psychology,* 1973, **3**, 291-302.

Sapolsky, H.M. The fluoridation controversy: An alternative explanation. *Public Opinion Quarterly,* 1969, **33**, 240-248.

Schuman, H. Sociological racism. *Trans-Action,* 1969, **7**, 44-48.

Sheatsley, P.B. White attitudes toward the Negro, *Daedalus,* 1966, **95**, 217-238.

Tobin, J. On improving the economic status of the Negro. *Daedalus*, 1965, **94**, 878-898.

Triandis, H., and Davis, E. Race and belief as determinants of behavioral intentions. *Journal of Personality and Social Psychology*, 1965, **2**, 715-725.

Tversky, A., and Kahneman, D. Availability: A heuristic for judging frequency and probability. *Cognitive Psychology*, **5**, 207-232.

# 11

# *Federal Legal Remedies for Racial Discrimination*

## ERIC HIRSCHHORN

The purpose of this chapter is to survey the existing federal laws relating to racial discrimination, including the rights they guarantee and the available means of enforcing those rights. In the belief that no consideration of the current state of the law in this area can be complete without some knowledge of its development, the principal discussion is prefaced by an historical overview.

## HISTORICAL DEVELOPMENT

Although the Declaration of Independence recited the "self-evident" principle that "all men are created equal," slavery and the slave trade were established institutions at the time the United States came into being. The view of the black race in England, which "was naturally impressed upon the colonies [it] founded on this side of the Atlantic,"[1] was that they were

> beings of an inferior order, and, altogether unfit to associate with the white race, either in social or political relations; and so far inferior, that they had no rights which the white man was bound to respect; and that the negro might justly and lawfully be reduced to slavery for [the white man's] benefit. He was bought and sold, and treated as an ordinary article of merchandise and traffic, whenever a profit could be made by it. This opinion was at that time fixed and universal in the civilized portion of the white race. It was regarded as an axiom in morals as well as in politics, which no one thought of disputing, or supposed to be open to dispute; and men in every grade and position in society daily and habitually acted upon it in their private pursuits, as well as in matters of public concern, without doubting for a moment the correctness of this opinion.[2]

[1] Scott v. Sandford, 60 U.S. (19 How.) 394, 408 (1857).
[2] *Id.* at 407.

The framers of our Constitution recognized the institution of slavery in three distinct places in that document. The apportionment of membership in the House of Representatives and of direct taxes was to be on the basis of the whole number of free persons plus three-fifths of "all other Persons,"[3] Congress was forbidden to prohibit the importation of "such Persons as any of the States now existing shall think proper to admit" until 1808,[4] and any slave escaping into a free state was not thereby to become free, "but shall be delivered up on Claim of the Party to whom [his] Service or Labour may be due."[5]

That there was by this time a minority view in opposition to slavery is demonstrated by the fact that the importation of slaves was protected for only 20 years and only in the original 13 states. Also, the Northwest Ordinance of 1787,[6] a compact wherein all of the states[7] ceded to the United States their territorial claims north and west of the Ohio River, provided that slavery should not exist in that area.[8] Subsequent to the adoption of the Constitution, the 1st Congress enacted the Ordinance (with minor technical changes) into federal law.[9]

The question of extension of slavery into new states carved out of the Louisiana Territory, which was acquired in 1803 and not covered by the Northwest Ordinance, came to a head in 1820, when it was proposed to admit Missouri as a slave state. The Compromise of 1820[10] demonstrated the growth of anti-slavery feeling in the 30 years following the adoption of the Constitution. Missouri was to be admitted as a slave state, but Maine, carved from territory previously a part of Massachusetts, was to be admitted as a free state in order to balance out the increased pro-slavery representation in Congress from Missouri, and slavery was to be prohibited in that part of the Louisiana Territory (except for Missouri) lying north of 36°30' North Latitude.[11]

Despite the Compromise of 1820, the pressure to limit slavery continued

---

[3] U.S. Const., art. I, § 2, cl. 3.

[4] U.S. Const., art. I, § 9, cl. 1.

[5] U.S. Const., art. IV, § 2, cl. 3.

[6] 1 Stat. 51 n.

[7] This was accomplished by enacting the Ordinance as a law of the United States (under the Articles of Confederation). Apparently because there existed some doubt as to the power of the Congress *qua* Congress to enact the Ordinance, it contained a recitation that it was a compact (1) among all of the states and (2) between the states and the people of the Northwest Territory.

[8] 1 Stat. 52 n., art. VI.

[9] 1 Stat. 51, c. 8 (1789).

[10] 3 Stat. 544, c. 19; 3 Stat. 545, c. 22.

[11] 3 Stat. 548, c. 22, § 8. This is the line constituting most of the southern border of the State of Missouri.

to mount. The delicate balance came unstuck with the Supreme Court's decision in the *Dred Scott Case*.[12] Scott was a slave who was owned by a citizen of Missouri, but who lived with his master for two years in the State of Illinois, where slavery was prohibited under the Northwest Ordinance and under state law, and then for two years in a portion of the Louisiana Territory in which slavery was prohibited under the Compromise of 1820.[13] Subsequent to his return to Missouri, he brought suit in the federal courts to secure his freedom, claiming that either his stay in Illinois or his stay in the Louisiana Territory had freed him from the bonds of slavery.

Chief Justice Roger Taney, writing for the Supreme Court majority, ruled that Scott was not a citizen and was therefore not entitled to sue in the federal courts. Although his ground alone was sufficient to dispose of the case, Taney went on to state the prohibition on slavery in a part of the Louisiana Territory contained in the Compromise of 1820 was unconstitutional and that Congress did not have the power to prohibit slavery in territory of the United States other than that covered by the Northwest Ordinance.[14]

By this ruling, the Court ended any pretense or suggestion (e.g., the counting of slaves as three-fifths of a person each) that slaves were human beings under the American legal system as it then existed. In the words of W.E.B. Dubois,

> Slaves were not considered men ... They could own nothing; they could make no contracts; they could hold no property, nor traffic in property; they could not hire out; they could not legally marry nor constitute families; they could not control their children; they could not appeal from their master; they could be punished at will.[15]

The further effect of this decision was that slavery would have to be permitted in any new state admitted to the Union if it so desired, and less than four years later, the struggle moved to the battlefield.

The Reconstruction period saw a rush of legislative activity with regard to slavery and racial discrimination, the heart of which was the addition of three amendments to the Constitution.[16] The Thirteenth Amendment, ratified at the end of 1865, prohibited slavery within the United States "or any place

---

[12] Scott v. Sandford, *supra*.

[13] 3 Stat. 548, c. 22, § 8.

[14] The Court further ruled that the question of whether Scott had been freed by virtue of his stay in Illinois was governed by Missouri law and that he had not become free while in Illinois.

[15] W. E. B. Dubois, Black Reconstruction in America 10 (1964).

[16] U.S. Const., amends. XIII, XIV, and XV. The full text of these amendments is set out in Appendix I, *infra*.

subject to their jurisdiction,"[17] and gave Congress the power to enforce the prohibition "by appropriate legislation."[18] The Fourteenth Amendment was ratified in 1868. Section 1 provided that

> [a]ll persons born or naturalized in the United States, and subject to the jurisdiction thereof, are citizens of the United States and of the State wherein they reside. No State shall make or enforce any law which shall abridge the privileges or immunities of citizens of the United States; nor shall any State deprive any person of life, liberty, or property, without due process of law; nor deny to any person within its jurisdiction the equal protection of the laws.

The Fifteenth Amendment, ratified in 1870, prohibited the United States and the individual states from denying the right to vote "on account of race, color, or previous condition of servitude."[19] Congress was empowered to enforce the Fourteenth and Fifteenth Amendments by appropriate legislation.[20]

It is important to note that the Thirteenth Amendment's bar to slavery was of a general nature, applicable to government and private citizen alike, while the guarantees of section 1 of the Fourteenth Amendment and the prohibition of the Fifteenth were directed to only the federal, state, and local governments and those acting "under color"[21] of their authority or laws. The

[17] U.S. Const., amend. XIII, § 1.

[18] U.S. Const., amend. XIII, § 2. This enforcement power is a broad as that granted in the "necessary and proper" clause of the original Constitution. Katzenbach v. Morgan, 384 U.S. 641 (1966); U.S. Const., art. I, § 8, cl. 18.

[19] U.S. Const., amend. XV, § 1.

[20] U.S. Const., amend. XIV, § 5; amend. XV, § 1.

[21] An act is "under color of state law" if it involves the use of "power, possessed by virtue of state law and made possible only because the [actor] is clothed with the authority of law," U.S. v. Classic, 313 U.S. 299, 326 (1941). Whether state law itself permits or prohibits the act is irrelevant, Screws v. U.S., 325 U.S. 91 (1945), as is the fact that an officer of the state acted in excess of his official duties, Ex parte Virginia, 100 U.S. 339 (1880), and acts done "under 'pretense' of law" are included within the definition, Screws v. U.S., supra, at 111. "State action" is the same as "under color of state law," id. at 110, and the term "state" includes local governments as well, Monroe v. Pape, 365 U.S. 167 (1961).

While there is a general rule that the receipt of funds or a license from the state does not clothe an otherwise private entity with the authority of the state does not clothe an otherwise private entity with the authority of the state, Don v. Okmulgee Memorial Hospital, 443 F. 2d 234 (10 Cir., 1971), Ouzts v. Maryland National Insurance Co., 470 F. 2d 790 (9 Cir., 1972), recent cases have held a restaurant holding a state liquor license, Bennett v. Dyer's Chop House, 350 F.Supp. 153 (N.D. Ohio, 1972), and a monopoly utility company, Ihrke v. Northern States Power Co., 459 F. 2d 566 (8 Cir.), ordered dismissed as moot, 409 U.S. 815 (1972), to be acting under color of state law. But see, Moose Lodge v. Irvis, 407 U.S. 163 (1972). See also, notes 162, 168, and 169, infra, and accompanying text.

significance of this distinction arises when the power of Congress and the federal courts to enforce the amendments is considered. The Federal Government is one of limited powers; that is, it can do only what the Constitution expressly or impliedly permits (as distinguished from the power of the individual states, which may do anything that the Constitution or federal laws do not expressly or impliedly prohibit). Thus, for example, the constitutional provision prohibiting "any state" from denying equal protection of the laws reaches actions taken by officials and others acting under color of state law, but not the acts of private individuals with no governmental connection, and the power of Congress to enforce such a provision does not include the power to enact legislation directed at purely private conduct.

In addition to these three constitutional amendments, Congress enacted a number of civil rights statutes, most notably those of 1866,[22] 1870,[23] 1871,[24] and 1875.[25] The Civil Rights Act of 1866,[26] passed over President Andrew Johnson's veto, provided that all citizens of the United States

> shall have the same right, in every State and Territory in the United States, to make and enforce contracts, to sue, be parties, and give evidence, to inherit, purchase, lease, sell, hold and convey real and personal property, and to the full and equal benefit of all laws and proceedings for the security of person and property, as is enjoyed by white citizens, and shall be subject to like punishment, pains, and penalties, and to none other, any law, statute, ordinance, regulation, or custom, to the contrary notwithstanding.[27]

The Enforcement Act of 1870[28] afforded citizens of the United States the right to vote at all elections regardless of race, color, or previous condition of servitude and required voting authorities to give them that right. The act also made it criminal to obstruct a citizen attempting to perform the necessary prerequisites for voting, or to prevent from voting a person guaranteed that right under the Fifteenth Amendment. The act contained a provision directed at the Ku Klux Klan, which made it a crime to "go in disguise" to threaten or intimidate anyone for exercising his rights under the Constitution or federal laws, a provision similar to the above-quoted portion of the 1866 act, but eliminating the language relating to real and personal

---

[22] 14 Stat. 27, c. 31.
[23] 16 Stat. 140, c. 114.
[24] 17 Stat. 13, c. 22.
[25] 18 Stat. 335, c. 114.
[26] 14 Stat. 27, c. 31.
[27] 14 Stat. 27, c. 31, § 1.
[28] 16 Stat. 140, c. 114.

property, and a provision reenacting the entire 1866 act. The reason for this last provision was apparently a fear that the 1866 act might go beyond the power of Congress to enforce the prohibition on slavery contained in the Thirteenth Amendment. By reenacting it after the ratification of the Fourteenth Amendment which, although it only applied to state action, contained far broader substantive guarantees, Congress created the possibility that the act would be upheld under its Fourteenth Amendment enforcement powers even if it failed to pass muster as an exercise of its Thirteenth Amendment enforcement powers. The failure of this ploy is discussed below.[29]

The Civil Rights Act of 1871[30] authorized anyone deprived, under color of state law, of his rights, privileges, or immunities under the Constitution of federal laws to sue for money damages and for injunctive relief, and provided for civil and criminal liability for a lengthy list of acts including conspiracies[31] to obstruct the enforcement of federal law, to intimidate parties, witnesses, or jurors involved in judicial proceedings, to deprive any person of his constitutional rights, or to obstruct any state's securing equal protection of the laws or due process of law within its borders.

The Civil Rights Act of 1875[32] marked the high water mark of Reconstruction and was the last federal civil rights law to be enacted *until 1957*. In language quite similar to that which would later be contained in title II of the Civil Rights Act of 1964,[33] it provided that

> all persons within the jurisdiction of the United States shall be entitled to the full and equal enjoyment of the accommodations, advantages, facilities, and privileges of inns, public conveyances on land or water, theaters, and other places of public amusement; subject only to the conditions and limitations established by law, and applicable alike to citizens of every race and color, regardless of any previous condition of servitude,[34]

and authorized civil and criminal remedies against anyone violating these rights. In addition, it prohibited disqualification from grand or petit jury

---

[29] Civil Rights Cases, 109 U.S. 3 (1883), *infra*.

[30] 17 Stat. 13, c. 22.

[31] A conspiracy is a combination or confederacy between two or more persons formed for the purpose of committing, by their joint efforts, some unlawful or criminal act, or some act which is innocent in itself, but becomes unlawful when done by the concerted action of the conspirators, or for the purpose of using criminal or unlawful means to the commission of an act not in itself unlawful. Black, Law Dictionary 382 (4 ed. rev., 1968).

[32] 18 Stat. 335, c. 114.

[33] 78 Stat. 243, § 201(a).

[34] 18 Stat. 336, c. 114, § 1.

service in the state or federal courts on account of race, color, or previous condition of servitude.

Regrettably, these far-reaching enactments fared poorly in the courts and in later Congresses. The provisions of the 1870 act that made it a crime to prevent a qualified individual from voting or from satisfying the prerequisites for voting[35] were held unconstitutional in 1875 on the ground that the Fifteenth Amendment only prohibited voting discrimination when it was based upon race, color, or previous condition of servitude, while the statute forbade *any* discrimination against a "qualified" individual and thus theoretically included prohibitions that Congress was not empowered to enact.[36] The prohibition on race discrimination in juries[37] was held to be within Congress' power to enforce equal protection of the laws,[38] but only applicable where state law (as opposed to custom or the unauthorized acts of state or local officials) required such discrimination.[39]

The greatest judicial blow came in 1883, when the Supreme Court struck down the public accommodations provisions[40] of the Civil Rights Act of 1875.[41] The opinion began by considering whether the statute could be sustained under the power of Congress to enforce the Fourteenth Amendment. Since the substantive portion of the Amendment contained only a prohibition against state action, which includes "customs having the force of law" but not customs generally,[42] the Court held that the statute's attempt to reach private conduct was not authorized under the Fourteenth Amendment. Proceeding to consider whether the enactment could be supported by the Thirteenth Amendment, the opinion stated that in addition to abolishing slavery, the Amendment "clothes Congress with power to pass all laws necessary and proper for abolishing all badges and incidents of slavery in the United States"[43] and permits legislation to that end which affects private as well as governmental action. However, reasoned the Court, the "badges and incidents of slavery" relative to which Congress could legislate included infringements of "fundamental rights,"[44] and since the public accommodations legislation concerned not fundamental rights but only "social

---

[35]  16 Stat. 140, c. 114, §§ 3, 4.

[36]  U.S. v. Reese, 92 U.S. 215 (1876).

[37]  18 Stat. 336, c. 114, § 4.

[38]  Strauder v. West Virginia, 100 U.S. 303 (1880).

[39]  Virginia v. Rives, 100 U.S. 313 (1880).

[40]  18 Stat. 336, c. 114, §§ 1, 2.

[41]  Civil Rights Cases, *supra*.

[42]  *Id.* at 16.

[43]  *Id.* at 20.

[44]  *Id.* at 22.

rights,"[45] it was not authorized by the Thirteenth Amendment. The Court spoke briefly to the question of whether the statute was constitutional as a regulation of interstate commerce, but held that it was not, as it clearly reached some commerce that was solely intrastate in nature. Justice John Marshall Harlan, in a solitary dissent,[46] argued that the public accommodations law was constitutional under either the Thirteenth or the Fourteenth Amendment. The former, he pleaded, not only abolished slavery, but created civil freedom for those of the black race, and Congress was empowered to enforce that freedom by any appropriate means. He also suggested that the Fourteenth Amendment's grant of citizenship to blacks included a grant of full civil rights, a grant that Congress could enforce under the terms of that Amendment.

The final judicial nail in the coffin of Reconstruction era civil rights legislation came in 1896, when the Supreme Court—again over the solitary dissent of Justice Harlan—held that the Fourteenth Amendment guarantee of equal protection permitted the states to segregate the black and white races, so long as they were provided facilities of equal quality.[47]

Congress, too, failed to rise to the occasion. The decision declaring two of the voting discrimination provisions of the Civil Rights Act of 1870 unconstitutional could have been corrected by amending the provisions to make them apply only to discrimination on the ground of race, color, or previous condition of servitude, but Congress did not act. In addition, most of the remaining voting provisions of the 1870 act and the voting and court obstruction provisions of the the 1871 act were repealed in the course of general recodifications of the laws in 1894[48] and 1909.[49]

The separate but equal doctrine approved in *Plessy v. Ferguson*[50] (in 1896) remained the law for over half a century. During that time, neither Congress nor the Supreme Court took a single significant step toward the achievement of racial justice under law in the United States. Finally, in 1954, growing pressure from black Americans and their many white allies, coupled with the obvious failure of the *Plessy* doctrine in securing equal—or even adequate—facilities for blacks, led the Supreme Court to discard the principle, at least in the field of public education. In *Brown v. Board of Education*.[51] the Court ruled that even if the tangible aspects of educational facilities were equal, segregation on the basis of race is inherently unequal and therefore violative of the equal protection clause of the Fourteenth Amendment. This

---

[45] *Id.*

[46] *Id.* at 26.

[47] Plessy v. Ferguson, 163 U.S. 537 (1896).

[48] 28 Stat. 36, c. 25.

[49] 35 Stat. 1153, c. 321, § 341.

[50] *Supra.*

[51] 347 U.S. 483 (1954).

principle, while truly an historic landmark, was at first limited only to instances wherein state or local law *required* segregation. Also, when the Court considered the question of how and when integration should be effected, it called for "all deliberate speed" rather than immediate action.[52] Nearly two more decades passed before the principle was clearly extended not just to places where segregation had been required by law, but also to places where the actions of local school authorities had created or continued segregated systems[53] and before "all deliberate speed" was changed to "at once."[54]

Congress awoke from its long sleep three years after the Supreme Court. The Civil Rights Act of 1957[55] prohibited intimidation of prospective voters and empowered the Attorney General to seek injunctive relief against such intimidation. It also created the Civil Rights Commission which, although given no enforcement powers, was authorized to study and investigate denials of voting rights, denials of equal protection of the laws, and federal policies relating to equal protection where discrimination on the basis of color, race, religion, or national origin was involved. Finally, the act created an additional Assistant Attorney General to head up the newly formed Civil Rights Division of the Justice Department.*

The Civil Rights Act of 1960[56] broadened the power of the Federal Government in the field of voting. It provided that where a federal court finds the existence of a pattern or practice of deprivation of voting rights due to race or color, it may appoint federal referees to register persons otherwise eligible who have been denied the right to vote due to their race or color.

Undoubtedly the most significant legislative breakthrough in the area of racial discrimination was the Civil Rights Act of 1964,[57] which included sweeping provisions designed to combat discrimination in the areas of voting, public accommodations, governmental facilities, public education, federally assisted programs, and employment. The act was passed early in the administration of Lyndon Johnson—the first Southern-born president in a century— and is considered by some a memorial to the assassinated John F. Kennedy. It limited the nature of literacy tests for voting, limited the types of errors in the tests for which an individual could be disqualified from voting, and created a presumption that anyone who has completed the sixth grade in a public school (or accredited private school) in the United States in which the

---

*References to the interpretation by the courts of the Civil Rights Act of 1957 and subsequent enactments appear in the following part of this chapter. It is sufficient for purposes of this part to note that all of the provisions of these laws that the Supreme Court has considered have been held to be constitutional and that there is little or no reason to expect different results as to the remainder, when and if considered by the Court.

[52] Brown v. Board of Education, 349 U.S. 294, 301 (1955).

[53] Keyes v. School District No. 1, Denver, Colo., 413 U.S. 189 (1973).

[54] Alexander v. Holmes County Board of Education, 396 U.S. 19, 20 (1969).

[55] 71 Stat. 634.

[56] 74 Stat. 86.

[57] 78 Stat. 241.

classes are carried on in English is literate for purposes of voting eligibility.[58] It barred discrimination in places of public accommodation on the basis of race, color, religion, or national origin; though its language was very much like that of the 1875 act,[59] it avoided the constitutional infirmities of that statute by limiting its coverage to places "affecting commerce"[60] and places wherein discrimination is required by state or local law, regulation, or "custom or usage required or enforced" by government officials.[61] Private clubs were expressly exempted. Discrimination victims (and, where a pattern or practice of resistance was present, the Attorney General) were entitled to sue for injunctive relief against segregation in establishments covered by the act. The act also empowered the Attorney General to sue to desegregate facilities owned and/or operated by state or local governments, including publicly run schools and colleges.

Title VI of the 1964 act prohibited discrimination on the basis of race, color, or national origin in "any program or activity receiving Federal financial assistance." Each federal department or agency extending financial assistance by grant, loan, or contract (with certain exceptions in cases of guarantees or insurance) was required to promulgate rules and regulations to effect the law's prohibitions and was empowered to cut off federal funding to any grantee failing to comply with them.

Title VII of the 1964 Civil Rights Act prohibited covered employers, employment agencies, and labor unions from discriminating in hiring or any other aspect of employment or job training on the basis of race, color, religion, sex, or national origin. The most noteworthy of its numerous exceptions,[62] one permitting discrimination where it involved "a bona fide occupational qualification reasonably necessary to the normal operation of the business enterprise," did not extend to discrimination on the ground of race or color. Title VII created the Equal Employment Opportunity Commission (EEOC) to administer the law and investigate alleged violations, but limited its role in actual enforcement to referral of complaints to the Attorney General; aggrieved individuals were authorized to sue on their own behalf, but only after threading their way through a maze of "informal" administrative conciliation proceedings that could easily consume a year's time. The court

---

[58] While this presumption may not be warranted in individual cases, or even as a general statement, Congress felt that the evils it prevented outweighed the evils it might permit, and Congress has the authority to make such a judgment in the exercise of its power to enforce the Fifteenth Amendment. South Carolina v. Katzenbach, 383 U.S. 301 (1966).

[59] Text accompanying note 27, *supra*.

[60] Interstate and foreign commerce is subject to plenary congressional control. U.S. Const., art. I, § 8, cl. 3.

[61] By including a "state action" nexus, this aspect of the statute clearly comes within the power of Congress to enforce the Fourteenth Amendment. U.S. Const., amend. XIV, § 5; see note 21, *supra*.

[62] See p.    , *infra*.

hearing a title VII suit was empowered to enjoin discriminatory practices and to "order such affirmative action as may be appropriate, which may include reinstatement or hiring of employees, with or without back pay."

Following the Democratic Party sweep in the presidential and congressional elections of 1964, the 89th Congress enacted the Voting Rights Act of 1965.[63] This act reflected the change in segregationist tactics from outright intimidation of prospective voters to the use of highly subjective literacy tests and other devices to prevent blacks from registering in significant numbers in the Southern states. It permitted federal courts, on complaint of the Attorney General, to order the appointment of federal registrars to determine whether prospective voters met the legitimate state qualifications, to suspend the use of literacy tests in any area where they were found to have been used to prevent voting because of race or color, and to require states to submit to the courts any changes in their voting laws or procedures if they had been found to have denied the franchise on the basis of race or color. In addition, literacy tests and other devices such as requirements of "good moral character" were suspended automatically in states or counties in which less than 50% of those eligible were registered or in which less than 50% of those eligible voted in the 1964 presidential election, and covered states were forbidden to alter their voting laws or procedures without submitting them to either the Attorney General or the federal district court in the District of Columbia. The Attorney General was permitted to use federal voting registrars in appropriate areas without going to court, so long as he had received at least 20 complaints and felt it necessary to enforce the guarantees of the Fifteenth Amendment; in such areas, he could also have observers at the elections themselves.

The 1965 act also contained limitations on the use of the poll tax in state and local elections[64] and, in a challenge to a type of discrimination found in such Northern cities as New York, provided that the right to vote could not be denied on the basis of English literacy requirements to anyone who has completed the sixth grade in a school in the United States (including Puerto Rico) in which the predominant classroom language was not English.

Title VIII of the Civil Rights Act of 1968[65] provided that "[i]t is the policy of the United States to provide, within constitutional limitations, for fair housing throughout the United States" and made it unlawful to discriminate in housing, including financing and brokerage services, because of race, color, religion, or national origin. Exceptions were allowed for one-family homes, boardinghouses with four or fewer families and a resident owner, religious organizations, and private clubs. Investigation and conciliation of complaints were vested in the Department of Housing and Urban Develop-

---

[63] 79 Stat. 437.

[64] The Twenty-fourth Amendment, ratified in 1964, had barred them in federal elections.

[65] 82 Stat. 81, title VIII.

ment, with aggrieved parties and (in pattern or practice cases) the Attorney General authorized to sue in the courts for relief.

The Equal Employment Opportunity Act of 1972[66] expanded the coverage of title VII of the Civil Rights Act of 1964 to include employers and unions with between 15 and 25 members or employees, state and local governments, and educational institutions. It also permitted the EEOC to issue administrative "cease and desist" orders in pattern or practice cases and provided for the eventual transfer of the Attorney General's powers in employment discrimination cases to the EEOC. Further, it contained a requirement that federal employment be freed from discrimination due to race, color, religion, sex, or national origin.[67] The administrative enforcement of the last requirement was to be vested in the Civil Service Commission, with employees entitled to bring suit in the federal courts if not satisfied with the administrative disposition of grievances. Available remedies were to include hiring and reinstatement, with or without back pay.

American law—like the society it reflects—began its existence firmly committed not only to racial discrimination but to the enslavement of the black race. Having traced their parallel development through the Antebellum and Reconstruction periods, the dormant years from about 1875 to the early 1950s, and the period of reawakening that has transpired since then, we now proceed to an examination of existing remedies for racial discrimination contained in federal law.

## EXISTING FEDERAL REMEDIES

The panoply of existing federal statutes relating to racial discrimination includes laws that cover a great variety of conduct, are available to a great variety of individuals, and provide for a great variety of relief and sanctions. Many overlap and some are quite complex. While it is the purpose of this part of the chapter to consider them in a fairly detailed fashion, the discussion herein should not be used instead of the advice of a lawyer. The facts of every case are different, and a fact that appears irrelevant or insignificant to a lay person may be crucial to his or her individual case. There are also numerous state and local laws and agencies relating to racial discrimination, and their availability and scope must be ascertained. In addition, the law in this area is constantly changing, and developments subsequent to the publication of this book may alter the legal principles and interpretations it sets forth.

---

[66] 86 Stat. 103.

[67] This had previously been the subject of Executive Order 11478, 34 Fed. Reg. 12985 (1969), as amended, Exec. Order No. 11590, 36 Fed. Reg. 1831 (1971); 42 U.S.C. § 2000e n.

This does not mean that someone who believes that he or she has been the victim of racial discrimination must go out and hire a private lawyer. For one thing, there are many organizations that provide free legal services in discrimination cases. A list of major national organizations of this sort appears as Appendix II to this chapter; these organizations, in addition to having legal resources of their own, may be able to refer a victim of discrimination to a local organization or lawyer who will handle the case without fee or charge a fee only if money damages or attorney's fees are awarded. Some of the laws discussed in this part are administered by government agencies that are authorized to sue on behalf of a victim. Also, several of these laws authorize a court to appoint a lawyer for someone who has tried unsuccessfully to find one on his own.

Federal statutes relating to racial discrimination include civil and criminal laws of a general nature, laws relating to such specific areas of discrimination as public accommodations, public facilities, public education, federally assisted programs, employment, voting, and housing, and laws relating to the general responsibilities of the Civil Rights Commission and the Community Relations Service. This part will consider them in that order.*

*All statutes discussed in this part will be referred to by their title and section in the United States Code (U.S.C.). Those with popular names will also be referred to by those names. All references to the U.S. Code are to the 1970 edition unless otherwise noted.

## General civil rights statutes

Section 1981 of title 42 of the U.S. Code, which is derived from part of the Civil Rights Act of 1866,[68] provides as follows:

> All persons within the jurisdiction of the United States shall have the same right in every State and Territory to make and enforce contracts, to sue, be parties, give evidence, and to the full and equal benefit of all laws and proceedings for the security of persons and property as is enjoyed by white citizens, and shall be subject to like punishment, pains, penalties, taxes, licenses, and exactions of every kind, and to no other.[69]

Although section 1981 has been on the statute books in one form or another since 1866, it received almost no use until quite recently. Because its constitutional underpinning is the Thirteenth Amendment, it can and does reach private as well as governmental discrimination[70] and is probably

[68] 14 Stat. 27, c. 31, § 1.

[69] 42 U.S.C. § 1981.

[70] Cf., Griffin v. Breckenridge, 403 U.S. 88, 104 (1971).

independent of the exceptions and time-consuming conciliation procedures found in more recently enacted civil rights statutes.[71] One reason for its lack of usage was the fact that until the passage of the Civil Rights Act of 1957,[72] section 1981 suits against private persons could be maintained only in the state courts—not noted for their hospitality to civil rights suits.

The courts have permitted this law to be used to attack racial discrimination in employment,[73] union membership,[74] facilities open to the general public,[75] professional licensing,[76] and admission to private schools.[77] Injunctive relief is definitely available, but the courts have divided on the question of whether money damages may be awarded generally;[78] damages are definitely available where state action is involved with the discriminatory practice.[79] It has been held in at least one instance that damages for emotional harm may not be awarded under this provision.[80] Lawsuits under section 1981 may be brought in the federal courts[81] and, in the opinion of this writer, in the state courts as well.[82]

Section 1983 of title 42 is the civil rights law under which the great majority of modern racial discrimination lawsuits have been brought:

[71] Brody v. Bristol-Meyers, Inc., 459 F. 2d 621 (8 Cir., 1972); Sanders v. Dobbs Houses, Inc., 431 F. 2d 1097 (5 Cir., 1970), cert. den., 401 U.S. 948 (1971); cf., Tillman v. Wheaton-Haven Recreation Assn., Inc., 410 U.S. 431 (1973). It has been suggested in one instance that although administrative proceedings required as prerequisites for suit under the newer statutes are not applicable to § 1981 as a matter of law, a court faced with a § 1981 suit should consider adjourning judicial proceedings while the aid of the Equal Employment Opportunity Commission or other appropriate government agency in securing consiliation is sought. Young v. International Telephone & Telegraph Corp., 438 F. 2d 757 (3 Cir., 1971).

[72] 71 Stat. 634.

[73] Sanders v. Dobbs Houses, Inc., supra; Waters v. Wisconsin Steel Works of International Harvester Co., 427 F. 2d 476 (7 Cir.), cert. den., 400 U.S. 911 (1970).

[74] James v. Ogilvie, 310 F. Supp. 661 (N.D. Ill., 1970).

[75] Valle v. Stengel, 176 F. 2d 697 (3 Cir., 1949); Scott v. Young., 307 F.Supp. 1005 (E.D.Va., 1969), aff'd, 421 F. 2d 143 (4 Cir.), cert. den., 398 U.S. 929 (1970).

[76] Jordan v. Hutcheson, 323 F. 2d 597 (4 Cir., 1963).

[77] Gonzales v. Fairfax-Brewster School, Inc., 363 F. Supp. 1200 (E.D. Va. 1973).

[78] Compare, Sanders v. Dobbs Houses, Inc., supraa, and Mizell v. North Broward Hospital District, 427 F. 2d 468 (5 Cir., 1970), with Hirych v. State, 376 Mich. 384. 136 N.W. 2d 910 (1965).

[79] 42 U.S.C. § 1983, infra.

[80] Howard v. Lockheed-Georgia Co., —F. Supp. ———, 42 USLW 2532 (N.D. Ga. 3/19/74)

[81] 28 U.S.C. § 1343(3), infra.

[82] See, Testa v. Katt, 330 U.S. 386 (1947); cf., Long v. District of Columbia, 469 F. 2d. 927 (D.C. Cir., 1972); Judo, Inc. v. Peet, 68 Misc. 2d 281, 326 N.Y.S. 2d 441(Civ. Ct. N.Y.C., 1971)(both permitting suits under 42 U.S.C. § 1983 to be maintained in state courts).

> Every person who, under color of any statute, ordiance, regulation, custom, or usage, of any State or Territory, subjects, or causes to be subjected, any citizen of the United States or other person within the jurisdiction thereof to the deprivation of any rights, privileges, or immunities secured by the Constitution and laws, shall be liable to the party injured in an action at law, suit in equity, or other proper proceeding for redress.[83]

Under this statute, a lawsuit for injunctive relief or money damages or both may be brought against any individual who violates a constitutional right if that individual is acting under color of state law.[84] Neither the right involved nor the reason for its violation need be related to race to support a suit under this provision,[85] and the defendant need not have had an improper motive[86] or an intent to discriminate[87] to support a decision in favor of a victim of discrimination.

Money damages may be granted under section 1983.[88] While punitive damages[89] and counsel fees[90] have been awarded in some instances, this is relatively infrequent. Prosecutors, judges, and legislators have generally been held immune from damage awards under section 1983,[91] unless acting wholly without jurisdiction,[92] but injunctive relief against such persons has been held permissible.[93]

Two significant limiting aspects of this law are that it does not cover the actions of federal officials or those acting purely under color of federal law[94] and that, although individual public officials may be sued, the governments of which they are functionaries may not.[95]

[83] 42 U.S.C. § 1983.

[84] Adickes v. S. H. Kress & Co., 398 U.S. 144 (1970).

[85] City of Greenwood v. Peacock, 384 U.S. 808 (1966).

[86] Hawkins v. Town of Shaw, 461 F. 2d 1171 (5 Cir., 1972).

[87] Jenkins v. Averett, 424 F. 2d 1228 (4 Cir., 1970).

[88] Basista v. Weir, 340 F. 2d 74 (3 Cir., 1965).

[89] Lee v. Southern Home Sites Corp., 429 F.2d 290 (5 Cir., 1970). While money (or actual) damages are awarded to recompense the victim, the purpose of punitive damages is to punish the wrongdoer.

[90] Monroe v. Board of Commissioners, 453 F. 2d 259 (6 Cir.), *cert. den.*, 406 U.S. 945 (1972).

[91] Pierson v. Ray, 386 U.S. 547 (1967).

[92] Rhodes v. Houston, 202 F. Supp. 624 (D. Neb.), *aff'd*, 309 F. 2d 959 (8 Cir., 1962), *cert. den.* 372 U.S. 909 (1963).

[93] Birnbaum v. Trussell, 347 F. 2d 86 (2 Cir., 1965).

[94] Norton v. McShane, 332 F. 2d 855 (5 Cir., 1964), *cert. den.* 380 U.S. 981 (1965); *cf.*, Bivens v. Six Unknown Agents, 403 U.S. 388 (1971), *on remand*, 456 F. 2d 1339 (2 Cir., 1972).

[95] Moor v. County of Alameda, 411 U.S. 693 (1973)

Suit may be brought in federal court under section 1983 in any instance of a violation of constitutional rights[96] or in case of a violation of a federal law providing for "equal rights of citizens"[97] or "the protection of civil rights, including the right to vote,"[98] and in the state courts for violation of any constitutional right or any right under a federal law (i.e., the law need not be one for the protection of equal rights or civil rights), unless jurisdiction over it is specifically limited to the federal courts by some other law.[99]

A final point with regard to this section is that the availability of administrative or judicial remedies under state law in no way requires that they be used (or exhausted) prior to the institution of a lawsuit under it.[100]

Because of its breadth in covering all violations of constitutional rights, is relative lack of exceptions, and its freedom from any requirement of going through administrative or state proceedings as a prerequisite to bringing a federal court suit, section 1983 is likely to remain the most popular statute for attacks on racial discrimination, either along or as an additional basis for relief in suits brought under such specific laws as those covering public accommodations and education.

Another law, derived from the Civil Rights Act of 1871,[101] provides for relief in the form of money damages[102] against anyone who conspires to deter a party or witness from attending and testifying in a federal court, or to injure anyone for so doing; to influence a juror; to obstruct state or local justice in order to deprive any citizen of equal protection of the laws or to punish him for attempting to enforce the equal protection rights of any person; to deprive any person of equal protection of the laws or equal privileges and immunities, or to hinder state or local authorities in providing these guarantees; or to prevent any citizen qualified to vote from advocating the election of a qualified person to federal office or to punish anyone for so doing. Relief is also provided, regardless of whether a conspiracy is involved, against any persons who "go in disguise upon the highway, or on the premises of another" to deprive anyone of equal protection or equal privileges and immunities, or to hinder the state or local authorities in providing for these

---

[96] 28 U.S.C. § 1343(3), *infra*; Lynch v. Household Finance Co., 405 U.S. 538 (1972).

[97] 28 U.S.C. § 1343(3), *infra*.

[98] 28 U.S.C. § 1343(4), *infra*.

[99] Long v. District of Columbia, *supra*; Judo, Inc. v. Peet, *supra*.

[100] Carter v. Stanton, 405 U.S. 676 (1972); King v. Smith, 392 U.S. 309 (1968); Monroe v. Pape, 365 U.S. 167 (1961).

[101] 17 Stat. 13, c. 22, § 2; 42 U.S.C. § 1985(2), (3).

[102] Though the language of the statute suggests that it is limited to money damages, injunctive relief has been granted in some instances. See, e.g., Brewer v. Hoxie School District No. 46, 238 F. 2d 91 (5 Cir., 1956); Mizell v. North Broward Hospital District, *supra*.

guarantees.[103] Damages are available for any of the acts enumerated above if the victim is injured or is deprived of "any right or privilege of a citizen of the United States."

This statute has been held to extend to private action and to be constitutionally supported in so doing by the Thirteenth Amendment and the commerce clause[104] of the Constitution.[105] In contradistinction to section 1983, discrimination is actionable under this section only if it is purposeful,[106] it denies *equal* rights,[107] and it is premised upon racial or some other "class-based" animus.[108] The plaintiff must show actual damages in order to recover,[109] but punitive damages may be awarded in an appropriate instance.[110]

Closely related to section 1985 is section 1986, which makes liable for money damages any person with knowledge of a violation or potential violation of section 1985 and able to prevent or aid in preventing it who fails to do so.[111]

In addition to the substantive provisions discussed above, the Judicial Code[112] contains five procedural statutes of a general nature that are particularly relevant to racial discrimination.[113]

Section 1343 is the basic civil rights jurisdictional statute. That is, it authorizes the federal courts to hear cases arising under the various civil rights laws. The reason why a separate jurisdictional provision is needed for civil rights suits is that the federal courts are tribunals of limited jurisdiction and can hear only cases specifically provided for by law. The provision in the Judicial Code that gives the federal courts jurisdiction over cases arising under federal law generally[114] requires an "amount in controversy" of over $10,000; if less than this is at issue, the parties are expected to take the case to state court. Since Congress has felt it important to provide a federal forum

---

[103] This provision is popularly known as the "Ku Klux Klan Act."

[104] U.S. Const., art, I, § 8, cl. 3.

[105] Griffin v. Breckenridge, *supra*.

[106] Snowden v. Hughes, 321 U.S. 1 (1944); Joyce v. Ferrazzi, 323 F. 2d 931 (1 Cir., 1963).

[107] Griffin v. Breckenridge, *supraa*.

[108] *Id.* at 102; Farkas v. Texas Instrument, Inc., 375 F. 2d 629(5 Cir.), *cert. den.*, 389 U.S. 977 (1967)(national origin).

[109] Providence Journal Co. v. McCoy, 94 F. Supp. 186 (D.R.I., 1950), *aff'd*, 190 F. 2d 760 (1 Cir.), *cert. den.*, 342 U.S. 894 (1951).

[110] Tracy v. Robbins, 40 F.R.D. 108 (D.S.C., 1966), *app. dismissed*, 373 F. 2d 13 (4 Cir., 1967).

[111] 42 U.S.C. § 1986.

[112] Title 28, U.S.C.

[113] 28 U.S.C. §§ 1343, 1344, 1357, 1443, and 1446.

[114] 28 U.S.C. § 1331.

for the enforcement of federally guaranteed civil rights, section 1343 grants the federal courts jurisdiction in most civil rights cases regardless of whether any money is involved.

Subsections (1) and (2) of the section specifically grant federal court jurisdiction in civil rights conspiracy cases under sections 1985 and 1986 of title 42.[115] Subsection (3) grants jurisdiction in suits

> to redress the deprivation, under color of any State law, statute, ordinance, regulation, custom or usage, of any right, privilege or immunity secured by the Constitution of the United States or by any Act of Congress providing for equal rights of citizens or of all persons within the jurisdiction of the United States,[116]

and subsection (4) in suits "under any Act of Congress providing for the protection of civil rights, including the right to vote."[117] The last provision was added by the Civil Rights Act of 1957,[118] while the other three date from the Reconstruction era.

Until recently, section 1343 had two significant limitations. For one thing, the courts had held that subsection (3) applied in cases alleging deprivation of constitutional rights only when they were "personal" in nature, and that, if they involved only property rights, they could not be brought in federal court unless the $10,000 jurisdictional requirement for federal cases generally[119] was satisfied.[120] Although this distinction did not apply to cases where racial discrimination was directly at issue, because that involved constitutional rights, it was held in at least one instance to prevent a welfare mother from suing to secure her rights because welfare benefits were "property" and less than $10,000 was involved.[121] In 1972, however, the Supreme Court concluded that the attempt to create two classes of constitutional rights was both improper and unworkable,[122] and it is now clear that any deprivation of constitutional rights may be redressed in the federal courts.[123]

---

[115] *Supra.*

[116] 28 U.S.C. § 1343(3).

[117] 28 U.S.C. § 1343(4).

[118] 71 Stat. 637, § 121.

[119] 28 U.S.C. § 1331.

[120] See, e.g., Eisen v. Eastman, 421 F. 2d 560 (2 Cir., 1969), *cert.. den.* 400 U.S. 841 (1970), *overruled in* Lynch v. Household Finance Co., *supra*, at 542.

[121] McCall v. Shapiro, 416 F. 2d 246 (2 Cir., 1969).

[122] Lynch v. Household Finance Co., *supra.*

[123] A recently created exception to this principle provides that a state prisoner claiming that he is being held unconstitutionally may not sue in federal court under §

The second shortcoming was that although subsection (3) permitted federal suits for violation of federal laws providing for equal rights, it did so only if the violation was "under color of any State law, statute, ordinance, regulation, custom or usage,"[124] thus requiring an individual whose right of contract[125] or right to own property[126] was violated by a private person to seek relief in the state courts. By and large, especially in the South, these tribunals were inhospitable to actions of this kind, and this defect in section 1343 was a major reasons why sections 1981 and 1982[127] were dead letters for so long. The 1957 Civil Rights Act added subsection (4), and private violations of civil rights laws (including sections 1981 and 1982) may now be redressed in the federal courts.

Section 1357 gives the federal courts jurisdiction over a civil suit

> commenced by any person to recover damages for any injury to his person or property on account of any act done by him, under any Act of Congress ... to enforce the right of citizens of the United States to vote in any State.[128]

This section is necessary because section 1343(3) permits damage suits only if the denial of rights is under color of state law, and although section 1343(4) permits suits to be brought under the voting rights laws, they provide only for injunctive relief.[129] This section permits, for example, an individual working on a voter registration drive to sue in the federal courts, for money damages, a private individual who attacks him because of that activity.

Section 1344 of the Judicial Code[130] also relates to voting rights. It authorizes a candidate for any state or local office (other than the state legislature) to bring suit in the federal courts to secure or recover his office if "the sole question touching the title to the office arises out of the denial of the right to vote, to any citizen offering to vote, on account of race, color, or previous condition of servitude." This provision is designed to cover instances wherein individuals denied their voting rights are too frightened to sue, but the candidate who anticipated enjoying their support (who presumably had to have some measure of temerity even to run) is willing to seek judicial

---

1343(3), but must follow the federal habeas corpus procedure, 28 U.S.C. §§ 2241-54, which requires exhaustion of available state judicial remedies before the federal case is brought. Preiser v. Rodriguez, 411 U.S. 475 (1973).

[124] 28 U.S.C. § 1343(3).

[125] 42 U.S.C. § 1981, *supra.*

[126] 42 U.S. C. § 1982, *infra.*

[127] 42 U.S.C. §§ 1981, *supra,* and 1982, *infra.*

[128] 28 U.S.C. § 1357.

[129] 42 U.S.C. §§ 1971-1973bb-4.

[130] 28 U.S.C. § 1344.

relief.[131] Few cases have been brought under this provision, and the enactment of comprehensive voting rights schemes such as those of 1957, 1965, and 1970 has probably limited the need for it even further.

Under subsection (1) of section 1443 of the Judicial Code,[132] a defendant in a civil or ciminal action in a state court may remove the case (i.e., have it transferred) to federal court if he "is denied or cannot enforce in the courts of [the] State a right under any law providing for the equal civil rights of citizens of the United States, or of all persons within the jurisdiction thereof."[133] Subsection (2) allows removal where the action has been instituted for "any act under color of authority derived from any law providing for equal rights, or for refusing to do any act on the ground that it would be inconsistent with such law,"[134] but that provision has been held to be available only to federal officials and to those acting under their direction or under a mandate of federal law.[135]

Although section 1433 was enacted as part of the Civil Rights Act of 1866,[136] it is applicable to any subsequent civil rights laws that are comparable to the 1866 act and relate to racial discrimination[137] (though it is available to whites as well as blacks[138]). By a vote of five to four in the *Peacock* case,[139] the Supreme Court gave an extremely narrow construction to subsection (1), holding that the phrase "is denied" means a denial in the state court itself and does not include instances where, for example, the original arrest was made in an attempt to deny the defendant's rights. The Court further held that the denial of rights in the state court must be plain from a state law,[140] such as will clearly appear "without any detailed analysis of the likely behavior of any particular state court,"[141] and that a mere violation of state law by some officer of the state is insufficient.[142] In the words of the Court,

---

[131] In fact, only a candidate may bring a suit under § 1344. Hubbard v. Anderson, 465 F. 2d 1169 (5 Cir., 1972), *cert. den.* 410 U.S. 910 (1973).

[132] 28 U.S.C. § 1443.

[133] 28 U.S.C. § 1443(1).

[134] 28 U.S.C. § 1443(2).

[135] City of Greenwood v. Peacock, 384 U.S. 808 (1966).

[136] 14 Stat. 27, c. 31, § 3.

[137] Georgia v. Rachel, 384 U.S. 780 (1966).

[138] Kentucky v. Powers, 201 U.S. 1 (1906).

[139] City of Greenwood v. Peacock, *supra.*

[140] This includes statutory interpretations by the state courts as well as the language of the statutes themselves. Kentucky v. Powers, *supra.*

[141] City of Greenwood v. Peacock, *supra*, 805.

[142] See also, Strauder v. West Virginia, 100 U.S. 303 (1880); Virginia v. Rives, 100 U.S. 313 (1880).

the vindication of the defendant's federal rights is left to the state courts except in the rare situations where it can be clearly predicted by reason of the operation of a pervasive and explicit state or federal law that those rights will inevitably be denied by the very act of bringing the defendant to trial in the state court.[143]

Although the closeness of the vote in *Peacock* permits some hope that it will someday be overruled, the present composition of the Supreme Court and the oft-repeated calls of Chief Justice Warren Burger for a decrease of the cases permitted to be brought to the federal courts indicate that such a day will not soon arrive.

Nevertheless, there are still some types of cases that are removable, and the procedure for removal is as follows:[144] In a civil case, the removal petition must be filed in the federal district court within 30 days after the receipt of the first pleading or the summons, whichever comes first,[145] while in a criminal case, removal may be sought at any time prior to trial. In any case, removal must be sought before judgment is rendered in the trial court,[146] is not available once the case reaches an appellate court,[147] and is not available when the matter is only before an administrative body.[148] The removal petition must state the factual basis for removal and, if in a civil case, must be accompanied by a bond to cover the court costs if removal is ultimately denied.

The individual seeking removal must give notice of his petition to the clerk of the state court at the same time that he files it in the federal court. This divests the state court of jurisdiction, and it may take no further action until and unless the federal court denies the petition; if the defendant is in

[143] City of Greenwood v. Peacock, *supra*, 828. The reference to federal law represents the concession by the courts that where an applicable federal enactment protects the conduct involved and prohibits intimidation for engaging in it (Georgia v. Rachel, *supra* [attempt to secure service at a facility subject ot the public accommodations provisions of the Civil Rights Act of 1964]; Whatley v. City of Vidalia, 399 F. 2d 521 [5 Cir., 1968] [exercise of rights under the Voting Rights Act of 1965]), or where the state tribunal is illegally constituted by virtue of a federal civil rights law (Thompson v. Brown, 434 F.2d 1092 [5 Cir., 1970] [new procedure for suit of white losing candidates to overturn election result had not been approved by federal authorities and was therefore illegal under the provisions of the Voting Rights Act of 1965]), removal will be permitted even in the absence of a state law discriminating on the basis of race or color.

[144] 28 U.S.C. § 1446.

[145] If the case is not originally a removable one, but becomes so after pleadings are amended, the removal petition must be filed within 30 days after receipt of the amended pleading.

[146] The Justices v. Murray, 76 U.S. (9 Wall.) 274 (1870).

[147] Lowe v. Williams, 94 U.S. 650 (1877).

[148] California Packing Co. v. International Longshoremen's and Warehousemen's Union, 253 F. Supp. 597 (D. Hawaii, 1966).

the state's custody, the federal court issues a writ of habeas corpus and federal authorities take custody of the individual until the petition is decided. Even if removal is ultimately denied, any action taken by the state court while the petition is pending before the federal court is void (i.e., the state cannot act and then, if removal is denied, have its action rendered effective by the return of the case to its jurisdiction.[149] While denials of removal petitions in most types of cases are not appealable, an amendment to the Judicial Code[150] contained in the Civil Rights Act of 1964[151] made an exception in civil rights removal cases,[152] which may now be appealed to the U.S. Court of Appeals for the area and then to the Supreme Court.

The federal Criminal Code[153] contains four criminal statutes relating specifically to racial discrimination.[154] Criminal prosecutions may be the brought by private citizens, but only by the Department of Justice and its local U.S. Attorneys. A private individual with a complaint under one of these criminal laws should take it to the local U.S. Attorney or to the local office of the Federal Bureau of Investigation.

Section 241 of the Criminal Code[155] covers conspiracies[156] against the civil rights of citizens and provides for both fine and imprisonment[157]

> [i]f two or more persons conspire to injure, oppress, threaten, or intimidate any citizen in the free exercise or enjoyment of any right or privilege secured to him by the Constitution or laws of the United States, or because of his having so exercised the same; or

> If two or more persons go in disguise upon the highway, or on the premises of another, with intent to prevent or hinder his free exercise or enjoyment of any right or privilege so secured.

This provision is derived from the Civil Rights Act of 1870,[158] and is

---

[149] South Carolina v. Moore, 447 F. 2d 1067 (4 Cir., 1971).

[150] 28 U.S.C. § 1447(d).

[151] 78 Stat. 266, § 901.

[152] Other types of cases in which removal is available are those subject to the original jurisdiction of federal district courts, 28 U.S.C. § 1441, those in which a federal officer is a defendant, 28 U.S.C. § 1442, and those which affect property in which the United States has an interest, 28 U.S.C. § 1444.

[153] Title 18, U.S.C.

[154] 18 U.S.C. §§ 241, 242, 243, and 245.

[155] 18 U.S.C. § 241.

[156] See, note 31, *supra*.

[157] Two years' imprisonment, or a $10,000 fine, or both; if death results, imprisonment for life.

[158] 16 Stat. 141, c. 114, § 6.

the criminal analogue of the civil conspiracy section discussed previously.[159] It is available not just for violations of equal protection of the laws and due process of law, but for all violations of constitutional rights.[160] Since equal protection, due process, and some other constitutional rights are only "secured" (by the Constitution) against state action, section 241 covers violations of those rights only where state action is involved;[161] however, state action has been found to exist in a broad variety of situations, including an instance wherein the accused were private individuals who had given local authorities false information designed to secure the arrest of blacks.[162] The victims need not be black to bring the conduct within the statute,[163] nor need the conduct have been racially motivated.[164] To support a conviction, two or more persons must have been involved, and the defendant must have had a specific intent to interfere with the right in question,[165] but no overt act in furtherance of the conspiracy need be shown if the case is brought under the first paragraph of the section[166] and no conspiracy at all need be proven if it is brought under the second paragraph.

Section 242 of the Criminal Code[167] makes criminal the deprivation of federal rights by an individual. Its full text provides that

> [w]hoever, under color of any law, statute, ordinance, regulation, or custom, willfully subjects any inhabitant of any State, Territory, or District to the deprivation of any rights, privileges, or immunities secured or protected by the Constitution or laws of the United States, or to different punishments, pains, or penalties, on account of such inhabitant being an alien, or by reason of his color, or race, than are prescribed for the punishment of citizens, shall be fined not more than $1,000 or imprisoned not more than one year, or both; and if death results shall be subject to imprisonment for any term of years or for life.

While the conduct complained of must be under color of law to come within the proscription of the statute, this requirement has been held satisfied

---

[159] 42 U.S.C. § 1985(3), *supra.*

[160] U.S. v. Guest, 383 U.S. 745 (1966)(right to travel under the commerce clause).

[161] U.S. v. Price, 383 U.S. 787 (1966).

[162] U.S. v. Guest, *supra*; see also, notes 21, *supra*, 168 and 169, *infra*, and accompanying text.

[163] Felix v. U.S., 186 F. 685 (C.C.E.D.La., 1911).

[164] See, e.g., U.S. v. Saylor, 322 U.S. 385 (1944)(vote fraud); Motes v. U.S., 178 U.S. 458 (1900)(attack on informer who provided information on violations of federal law).

[165] U.S. v. Guest, *supra.*

[166] Williams v. U.S., 179 F.2d 644 (5 Cir., 1950), *aff'd*, 341 U.S. 70 (1951).

[167] 18 U.S.C. § 242.

as to a private citizen when he participated in joint activity with the state or its agents[168] and as to a private detective when he had taken an oath as a special police officer and had received from the local police a "special police officer's card."[169]

The requirement that the conduct be willful has been interpreted by the Supreme Court in a novel and extremely narrow fashion. Ordinarily, conduct is considered to be willful if the actor is conscious of his action and its likely or probably consequences *in fact,* and his lack of knowledge of its *legal* consequences not available as an excuse. Under this formulation, a sheriff who kills a prisoner awaiting trial and thereby deprives him of due process of law would be guilty of violating section 242 if it were proven that his action in beating the prisoner was not accidental or in any way justified; it would not be necessary to prove that the sheriff knew that his act deprived the victim of the Fourteenth Amendment's guarantee of due process of law. However, when the Supreme Court considered the case of a sheriff who did commit the acts hypothesized above,[171] it ruled that the requirement of willfulness in this provision meant not only intent to commit the act, but also intent to deprive the victim of a specific right either expressed in the Constitution or laws or announced in some court decision prior to the incident in question.[171] The Court's reasoning, which was of scant consolation to the brutally murdered victim, was that otherwise, a defendant might be held criminally liable for an act which neither he nor anyone else knew was violative of federal rights at the time it was committed. While this interpretation may or may not limit convictions under section 242 to defendants who are constitutional lawyers, it undoubtedly makes them more difficult to secure.

While section 245 of the Criminal Code[172] includes a long list of prohibited acts involving "federally protected activities," no prosecution may be brought under it "except upon the certification in writing of the Attorney General or the Deputy Attorney General that in his judgment a prosecution by the United States is in the public interest and necessary to secure substantial justice."

Section 245(b)(1) makes it a crime, whether or not under color of law, to willfully interfere with, by force or threat of force, persons involved in such federal activities as voting, running for office, serving as an election official or poll watcher, participating in any activity "provided or administered

[168] U.S. v. Price, *supra*; see also, notes 21, 162, *supra*, 169, *infra*, and accompanying text.

[169] Williams v. U.S., 341 U.S. 97 (1951); see also, notes 21, 162, and 168, *supra*, and accompanying text.

[170] Screws v. U.S., 325 U.S. 91 (1945).

[171] "[I]n defiance of announced rules of law." *Id.* at 104.

[172] 18 U.S.C. § 245.

by the United States" or receiving federal financial assistance, holding federal employment, or serving as a grand or petit juror in a federal court. This provision, which does not contain any requirement of racial or similar motivation, relies solely upon the power of Congress to protect rights that flow directly and positively to the people from the Federal Government.[173]

Subsection (b)(2) prohibits willful interference by force or threat of force with individuals because of their race, color, religion, or national origin and[174] because they are attending a public school or college, participating in any activity "provided or administered by any State or subdivision thereof," seeking or holding employment, serving as a grand or petit juror in a state court, traveling in or using any interstate commerce facility or common carrier, using any hotel providing transient lodging, any restaurant "principally engaged in selling food or beverages for consumption on the premises," or any movie house or other place of public entertainment. Subsection (b)(4) outlaws such interference with anyone because he is participating (or affording anyone else the opportunity to participate) without discrimination on the basis of race, color, religion, or national origin in any of the activities listed above, and subsection (b)(5) outlaws it with any citizen because he is lawfully aiding or encouraging others to participate "or participating lawfully in speech or peaceful assembly opposing any denial of the opportunity to so participate."[175] These three provisions require some showing of motivation on the basis of race, color, religion, or national origin relative to the discrimination. Paragraph (2), for example, applies to attacks because the victim is black (or a member of some other minority group) and has participated in one of the enumerated activities that are not direct and positive federal activities. Paragraph (4) covers cases in which any person, white or black, is attacked because he has been participating in a nondiscriminatory program of either type, or affording someone else the opportunity to participate in such a program (e.g., a white restaurant owner who does not discriminate), or to intimidate other persons from participating in such a program (e.g., black or white civil rights worker attached to discourage black citizens generally from eating at restaurant that does not discriminate). Paragraph (5) covers instances wherein a citizen is attacked because he has been (or to deter him or others from) assisting or encouraging others to participate in nondiscriminatory activities or participating in speeches or demonstrations against those who deny the opportunity to participate in such activities.

---

[173] See, e.g., Ex parte Yarbrough, 110 U.S. 651 (1884)(voting in federal elections); U.S. v. Guest, *supra* (interstate commerce).

[174] Both criteria must be satisfied.

[175] Violators of § 245 are subject to a $1000 fine, one year in prison, or both; if bodily injury results, a $10,000 fine, ten years in prison, or both; and if death results, life imprisonment.

Section 245 was enacted as part of the Civil Rights Act of 1968[176] in an effort to plug the yawning gaps in sections 241 and 242, which had been pointed out by the Supreme Court.[177] In the *Guest* case,[178] for example, the Court held that section 241 did not reach purely private conduct that violated equal protection of the laws, but stated that Congress could so legislate, at least in instances wherein the discrimination was motivated by racial or similarly arbitrary grounds.[179] The difficulty with section 242, it will be recalled, was that the statutory proscription on violation of "any right or privilege secured ... by the Constitution or laws of the United States" was found by the Court to be too vague to afford adequate notice of the conduct prohibited, and the willfulness requirement was therefore construed to require knowledge of the legal right being violated as well as of the factual nature of the actor's conduct.[180]

The fourth federal criminal statute relating to racial discrimination is section 243 of the Criminal Code,[181] which provides for a $5000 fine for any person excluding an individual from jury service due to race, color, or previous condition of servitude. Section 243 applies to state as well as federal courts,[182] to grand as well as petit juries, and to cases in which the defendant is white as well as those in which he is black.[183] In civil cases brought by prisoners seeking reversal of their convictions because of race discrimination in jury selection, it has been held that although the mere absence of blacks on a jury is not unconstitutional,[184] evidence that no blacks (or few) have served on juries in the area over a period of time will lead to a reversal of the conviction in question unless the state comes forward with some sound explanation of the reason for that absence.[185] Presumably, a similar standard applies with respect to criminal prosecutions under section 243.

[176] 82 Stat. 73, § 101.

[177] See, e.g., Screws v. U.S., *supra*; U.S. v. Guest, *supra*.

[178] U.S. v. Guest, *supra*.

[179] The Guest case also held that § 241 could *and* did reach private conduct violative of rights directly secured to the people by the Constitution and federal laws (e.g., right to travel). The portion of Guest dealing with equal protection and due process held that the word "secured" in § 241 only covered state interference with those rights, but stated that Congress could if it wished pass a law preventing private interference with those rights as well. See also, S. Rep. No. 721, 90th Cong., 2d Sess. (1968), in 1968 U.S. Code Cong. and Adm. News 1837.

[180] Screws v. U.S., *supra*; see also, text accompanying notes 170 and 171, *supra*.

[181] 18 U.S.C. § 243.

[182] *Ex parte* Virginia, 100 U.S. 339 (1880).

[183] *Cf.*, Peters v. Kiff, 407 U.S. 493 (1972)(white defendant complaining of exclusion of blacks from jury).

[184] U.S. *ex rel.* Jackson v. Brady, 47 F. Supp. 362 (D. Md., 1942), *aff'd*, 133 F.2d 475 (4 Cir.) *cert. den.*, 319 U.S. 746 (1943).

[185] U.S. *ex rel.* Goldsby v. Harpole, 263 F.2d 71 (5 Cir.), *cert. den.* 361 U.S. 838 (1959).

## Public accommodations

Enacted as part of the Civil Rights Act of 1964,[186] the public accommodations law[187] provides that

> [a]ll persons shall be entitled to the full and equal enjoyment of the goods, services, facilities, privileges, advantages, and accommodations of any place of public accommodation, as defined in this section, without discrimination or segregation on the ground of race, color, religion, or national origin.[188]

Defined as a place of public accommodation, if its "operations affect commerce, or if discrimination or segregation by it is supported by State action," is any inn, hotel, or like establishment providing transient lodging,[189] any place "principally engaged in selling food for consumption on the premises," any movie house, sports arena, or other "place of exhibition or entertainment," and any other establishment that is physically within a covered establishment or that has physically within it a covered establishment and holds itself out as serving patrons of the covered establishment.[190] All inns, hotels, and lodging establishments are presumed to affect interstate commerce, as are restaurants serving interstate travelers or a substantial portion of whose merchandise has "moved in commerce," and entertainment places presenting films, teams, and like entertainment that has moved in commerce.[191] Private clubs are exempt from the operation of the title if they are "not in fact open to the public" and not available to customers of a covered establishment.[192] In addition to the various definitions and requirements of involvement with interstate commerce noted above, the law forbids discrimination on the basis of race, color, religion, or national origin at *any* establishment whose discrimination is required by state or local law.[193]

The constitutional basis of the prohibitions relating to establishments involved in commerce is the commerce clause,[194] while the basis of the prohibition relating to state-required discrimination is the Fourteenth Amend-

---

[186] 78 Stat. 243, title II.

[187] 42 U.S.C. §§ 2000a–2000a-6.

[188] 42 U.S.C. § 2000a(a).

[189] Except one having 5 or fewer rooms for hire and occupied by the owner as his residence.

[190] 42 U.S.C. § 2000a(b).

[191] 42 U.S.C. § 2000a(c).

[192] 42 U.S.C. § 2000a(e).

[193] 42 U.S.C. § 2000a-1.

[194] Heart of Atlanta Motel, Inc. v. U.S., 379 U.S. 294 (1964)(restaurant serving food which had moved in commerce).

ment. Private conduct is clearly—and constitutionally[195]—covered. Judicial constructions of the definitions have included within the act a restaurant that served food ready for consumption on the premises, even though much of it was in fact taken out and eaten elsewhere,[196] a golf course who pro shop sold goods that had moved in interstate commerce and were for entertainment purposes,[197] and a recreation area offering swimming, boating, miniature golf, and dancing, on the creative theory that the customers, who had traveled in interstate commerce to get there, provided the entertainment for one another.[198] Beer has been ruled not to be food within the restaurant definition, and bars have been held not covered unless they principally serve food[199] or provide entertainment.[200] The private club exemption has been strictly construed,[201] with the courts considering such factors as selectivity in membership,[202] self-government,[203] and member-ownership[204] when ruling on an exemption claim.

The public accommodations title provides for two avenues of judicial redress—one an action brought by the aggrieved individual,[205] the other an action brought by the Attorney General.[206] An aggrieved individual may bring a suit for injunctive relief in federal district court[207] and may have counsel appointed for him by the judge and bring his action without paying filing fees if the judge deems these measures appropriate. However, where the state or locality in which the alleged discrimination occurred has its own law prohibiting the practice in question and an agency empowered to enforce it,[208] no federal lawsuit may be instituted until 30 days after the local agency has been given notice of the charges; further, once the waiting period

[195] Offner v. Shell's City, Inc., 376 F.2d 574 (5 Cir., 1967).

[196] Newman v. Piggie Park Enterprises, Inc., 390 U.S. 400 (1968).

[197] U.S. v. Central Carolina Bank & Trust Co., 431 F.2d 972 (4 Cir., 1970).

[198] Daniel v. Paul, 395 U.S. 298 (1969).

[199] Cuevas v. Sdrales, 344 F.2d 1019 (10 Cir., 1965), *cert. den.*, 382 U.S. 1044 (1966).

[200] U.S. v. Vizenia, 342 F. Supp. 553 (W.D. La., 1972)(juke box and pool table held sufficient to make bar a place of entertainment).

[201] See, e.g., Tillman v. Wheaton-Haven Recreation Assn., Inc., 410 U.S. 431 (1973).

[202] Nesmith v. Young Men's Christian Assn. of Raleigh, N.C., 397 F.2d 96 (4 Cir., 1968).

[203] Daniel v. Paul, *supra.*

[204] *Id.*

[205] 42 U.S.C. § 2000a-3.

[206] 42 U.S.C. § 2000a-5.

[207] This suit may be brought as a class action if it satisfies the general rules for such treatment. Lance v. Plummer, 353 F.2d 585 (5 Cir., 1965), *cert. den.*, 384 U.S. 929 (1966); see, Rule 23, Fed R. Civ. P.

[208] The law and the mode of enforcement may be civil or criminal in nature.

has elapsed and the federal suit has been brought, the federal court may hold off action in the suit until the local proceedings have been completed. Even where there are no appropriate state or local laws, and therefore no 30 day waiting period, the federal court may refer the case to the Community Relations Service[209] "for as long as the court believes there is a reasonable possibility of obtaining voluntary compliance," but not more than a total of 120 days. Proceedings before the Community Relations Service are private, and no evidence given there may be made public.[210]

The Attorney General may, if the court deems it appropriate, intervene in a suit brought by a private individual. In addition, he may bring suit on his own initiative in any instance in which he has "reasonable cause" to believe that there exists "a pattern or practice of resistance to the full enjoyment of any of the rights secured" by the public accommodations title. A suit instituted by the Attorney General is not subject to any waiting period or referral to local agencies or the Community Relations Service; in addition, the Attorney General may obtain a special three-judge federal court,[211] from which a direct appeal may be taken to the Supreme Court. In either type of suit, the court may grant injunctive relief,[212] which may include all steps necessary to eliminate the continuing effects of past discriminatory practices,[213] such as requiring the posting in the facility of notices that it does not discriminate on the basis of race, color, religion, or national origin.[214] While money damages may not be granted in an action for violation of the public accommodations law,[215] the Supreme Court has ruled that a successful citizen-plaintiff, who is in effect acting not only on his own behalf, but as a private attorney general on behalf of the public, should recover attorney's fees unless special circumstances would render such an award unjust.[216] The significance of this seemingly technical ruling should not be underrated, for it is far easier for a victim of discrimination to obtain the legal assistance he needs to redress a wrong done him if a lawyer knows that there is a reasonable likelihood that he will be paid for his efforts.

While the injunctive relief provided for in the public accommodations title is the exclusive relief for violations of its guarantees,[217] other remedies may be pursued where the conduct complained of also violates rights set forth

---

[209] See, 42 U.S.C. §§ 2000g--2000g-3, and discussion *infra*.

[210] 42 U.S.C. § 2000g-2.

[211] See, 28 U.S.C. § 2284.

[212] U.S. v. Johnson, 390 U.S. 563 (1968).

[213] U.S. v. Medical Society of South Carolina, 298 F. Supp. 145 (D.S.C., 1969).

[214] U.S. v. Boyd, 327 F. Supp. 998 (S.D.Ga., 1971).

[215] Newman v. Piggie Park Enterprises, Inc., *supra*.

[216] *Id.*

[217] U.S. v. Johnson, *supra*.

in other statutes or in the Constitution.[218] For example, a refusal to serve a black in a restaurant covered by this title because state law prohibits integrated service would probably be actionable under section 1983 of title 42,[219] and damages would be available in such an instance.[220]

### Facilities owned or operated by state or local governments

An individual denied or discriminated against in the use of a facility owned or operated by a state may seek injunctive relief, money damages, or both under section 1983 of title 42.[221] In enacting the Civil Rights of 1964, however, Congress recognized that aggrieved individuals might lack the means or the temerity to bring such an action, and title III[222] authorized the Attorney General to bring suit against discrimination on the basis of race, color, religion, or national origin in a public facility owned, operated, or managed by a state or locality (other than a school or college, which is covered in title IV of the 1964 act[223]).

In order to institute such an action, the Attorney General must receive a written complaint[224] from an individual that he is being deprived of or threatened with loss of equal protection of the laws on account of his race, color, religion, or national origin, by being denied utilization of a public facility. In addition, the Attorney General may not sue unless he believes that the complaint has merit, that the complainant is unable to bring suit on his own (either because he cannot afford it or because he might be endangered because of it), and "that the institution of an action will materially further the orderly progress of desegregation in public facilities."[225]

The authorization for the Attorney General to sue is intended to be supplementary, rather than alternative, and the law expressly provides that nothing in the public facilities title affects the right of any individual to sue on his own behalf against discrimination in public facilities.[226]

---

[218] 42 U.S.C. § 2000a-6; Adickes v. S.H. Kress & Co., 398 U.S. 144 (1970).

[219] *Supra.*

[220] Adickes v. S.H. Kress & Co., *supra.*

[221] *Supra.*

[222] 42 U.S.C. §§ 2000b – –2000b-3.

[223] 42 U.S.C. §§ 2000c – –2000c-9, discussed *infra.*

[224] A false statement in such a complaint is subject to criminal prosecurtion under § 1001 of title 18, U.S.C., which prohibits the making of such statements in proceedings before federal agencies. 42 U.S.C. § 2000b-3.

[225] 42 U.S.C. § 2000b.

[226] 42 U.S.C. § 2000b-2.

## Public education

Most of the significant lawsuits attacking segregation and racial discrimination in public education have been brought under section 1983 of title 42[227] on the ground that they violate the right to equal protection of the laws guaranteed in the Fourteenth Amendment.[228] However, as in the case of public facilities, Congress has recognized that private persons may be for some reason unable to sue on their own behalf and has authorized the Attorney General to sue in certain instances.[229] In addition, provision has been made for technical and financial assistance for school districts involved in desegregation or other activities designed to aid in integration.[230]

The authorization for suit by the Attorney General, enacted as part of title IV of the Civil Rights Act of 1964,[231] requires his receiving a written complaint[232] either (a) signed by a parent[233] whose child is allegedly being denied equal protection of the laws by a school board or (b) signed by an individual or a parent[234] and alleging that the individual is being denied admission to or continuance at a public college because of his race, color, sex, religion, or national origin. The Attorney General must believe that the complaint is meritorious, that the signer is unable (because of expense or danger) to maintain a lawsuit on his own behalf, and that "the institution of an action will materially further the orderly achievement of desegregation in public education." In addition, before suit is instituted, the school board or college authority involved must be afforded notice of the complaint[235] and given a reasonable time to adjust the conditions complained of.

The authorizing language contains a recitation that nothing in it empowers a court to require transportation between schools or school districts to achieve racial balance or otherwise enlarges the power of the courts to insure complaince with constitutional standards. However, in interpreting this clause, the courts have held that it does not restrict in any way their existing

---

[227] *Supra.*

[228] E.g., Brown v. Board of Education, 347 U.S. 483 (1954); Alexander v. Holmes County Board of Education, 396 U.S. 19 (1969).

[229] 42 U.S.C. §§ 2000c–2000c-9.

[230] 20 U.S.C. §§ 1601-19, 1651-56; 42 U.S.C. § 2000d-5.

[231] 42 U.S.C. §§ 2000c-6, 2000c-7.

[232] A flase statement in such a complaint is subject to criminal prosecution under § 1001 of title 18, U.S.C., which prohibits the making of such statements in proceedings before federal agencies. 42 U.S.C. § 2000c-6.

[233] The word "parent" includes any individual acting *in loco parentis.*

[234] *Id.*

[235] The Attorney General is not required to divulge the identity of the complainant. U.S. v. Greenwood Municipal Separate School District, 406 F.2d 1086 (5 Cir.), *cert. den.,* 402 U.S. 943 (1971).

authority to enforce equal protection of the laws or any other constitutional guarantee,[236] and that all that it means is that the title is not intended to allow a court to require integration where there is no constitutional violation.[237]

The courts have interpreted the Fourteenth Amendment's guarantee that "[n]o State shall ... deny to any person within its jurisdiction the equal protection of the laws" to require integration only in instances wherein segregation in the schools arises as the result of action taken by state or local governments (i.e., *de jure*).[238] and not to reach instances where segregation in the schools has resulted from such private actions as residential segregation (*de facto*).[239] However, the Supreme Court has been affording an increasingly broad interpretation to the meaning of *de jure*.[240] In a recent case wherein the Denver, Colorado, school authorities were shown to have drawn district lines and constructed new schools in one area of the city with an intent to keep white and black students separate, the Court held that

> a finding of intentionally segregative school board actions in a meaningful portion of a school system, as in this case, creates a presumption that other segregated schooling within the system is not adventitious. It establishes, in other words, a prima facie case of unlawful segregative design on the part of school authorities, and shifts to those authorities the burden of proving that other segregated schools within the system are not also the result of intentionally segregative actions.[241]

The Court went on to state that in discharging the burden of proving that segregated schools are not the result of intentionally segregative acts, the school authorities must "adduce proof sufficient to support a finding that segregative intent was not among the factors that motivated their actions."[242]

Once *de jure* segregation is found to exist, school authorities have "the affirmative duty to take whatever steps might be necessary to convert to a unitary system in which racial discrimination would be eliminated root and branch"[243] and to eliminate from their schools "all vestiges of state-imposed

---

[236] Swann v. Charlotte-Mecklenburg Board of Education, 402 U.S. 1 (1971).

[237] U.S. v. School District No. 151, 404 F.2d 1125 (7 Cir., 1968), *cert. den.*, 402 U.S. 943 (1971).

[238] Swann v. Charlotte-Mecklenburg Board of Education, *supra.*

[239] Spencer v. Kugler, 326 F. Supp. 1235 (D. N.J., 1971), *aff'd*, 404 U.S. 1027 (1972).

[240] Keyes v. School District No. 1, Denver, Colo., 413 U.S. 189 (1973).

[241] *Id.* at 208.

[242] *Id.* at 210.

[243] Green v. County School Board, 391 U.S. 430, 438 (1968).

segregation."[244] This in turn means the desegregation of all six facets of a school system: student body, faculty, staff, transportation, extracurricular activities, and facilities,[245] and the requirement of immediate desegregation[246] will not yield to the practical difficulties of bringing it about.[247]

In addition to demanding immediate integration within public school systems, the courts have struck down attempts to avoid integration by circumventing the public school system altogether and funneling direct or indirect state[248] or federal[249] assistance to segregated private schools; also, a recent congressional attempt to stay federal court orders requiring the transportation of students "for the purposes of achieving a balance among students with respect to race, sex, religion or socioeconomic status" until all appeals therefrom were exhausted was held by Supreme Court Justice Lewis Powell not to apply to instances of *de jure* segregation.[250] Since *de jure* segregation is the only kind with which the courts have been involved, the effect of the Powell ruling was to nullify the provision altogether.

A further boost to the progress of school desegregation was afforded by a provision of the Education Amendments of 1972[251] which allowed for attorney's fees in school desegregation cases. Like the provision of the public accommodations title from which it was taken, this law has been held to require the granting of counsel fees to a successful plaintiff except in special cases.[252]

The provision for technical assistance and some training grants for local school personnel was enacted as part of the Civil Rights Act of 1964 and allows such assistance and grants for desegregation involving the assignment of pupils without regard to race, color, religion, sex, or national origin, but not for "the assignment of students to public schools in order to overcome racial imbalance."[253] While this definition means that no funds or technical assistance will be given for a pupil assignment plan designed to overcome

[244] Swann v. Charlotte-Mecklenburg Board of Education, *supra*, at 15.

[245] Scott v. Winston-Salem/Forsyth County Board of Education, 317 F. Supp. 453 (M.D.N.C., 1970), *aff'd in part, vacated in part on other grounds*, 444 F.2d. 99 (4 Cir.), *stay den.*, 404 U.S. 1221, *cert. den.*, 404 U.S. 912 (1971).

[246] Alexander v. Holmes County Board of Education, *supra*.

[247] Scott v. Winston-Salem/Forsyth County Board of Education, *supra*.

[248] Poindexter v. Louisiana Financial Assistance Commission, 275 F. Supp. 833 (E.D.La.; 1967), *aff'd*, 389 U.S. 571 (1968)(state program of tuition grants to private school students which was intended to maintain a system of segregated schools).

[249] Green v. Connally, 330 F. Supp. 1150 (D.D.C.), *aff'd*, 404 U.S. 997 (1971)(federal tax exemptions for segregated private schools).

[250] Drummond v. Acree, 409 U.S. 1228 (Powell, Circuit Justice, 1972).

[251] 86 State. 369, § 718; 20 U.S.C. § 1617 (Supp. II, 1972).

[252] Northcross v. Board of Education, 93 S.Ct. 2201 (1973).

[253] 42 U.S.C. §§ 2000c, 2000c-2–2000c-5.

racial imbalance,[254] it in no way makes such a plan illegal.[255]

Congress in 1972 enacted an Emergency School Aid program[256] authorizing $1 billion a year for fiscal years 1973 and 1974[257]

(1) to meet the special needs incident to the elimination of minority group segregation and discrimination among students and faculty in elementary and secondary schools;

(2) to encourage the voluntary elimination, reduction, or prevention of minority group isolation in elementary and secondary schools with substantial proportions of minority group students; and

(3) to aid school children in overcoming the educational disadvantages of minority group isolation.[258]

By "minority group" is meant "persons who are Negro, American Indian, Spanish-surnamed American, Portuguese, Oriental, Alaskan natives, and Hawaiian natives,"[259] and also "persons who are from environments in which a dominant language is other than English and who, as a result of language barriers and cultural differences, do not have an equal educational opportunity."[260] "Isolation" is present if the minority group enrollment exceeds half of the student body in a school.[261]

Grants are available under the program to local school agencies desegregating under order of a court or a state agency or under a plan approved by the Department of Health, Education and Welfare, agencies voluntarily adopting plans "for the complete elimination of minority group isolation in all the minority group isolated schools" in the locality, to eliminate or reduce minority group isolation, or to prevent minority group isolation reasonably likely to occur, and agencies voluntarily admitting nonresident children otherwise ineligible for admission into its schools to help eliminate minority group isolation in its area or in another area.[262] Local school districts that

---

[254] U.S. v. Jefferson County Board of Education, 372 F. 2d 836, *reaff'd*, 380 F. 2d 385 (5 Cir., 1966)(en banc), *cert. den.*, 389 U.S. 840 (1967).

[255] Olson v. Board of Education, 250 F. Supp. 1000 (E.D.N.Y.), *app. dismissed*, 367 F. 2d 585 (2 Cir., 1966).

[256] 20 U.S.C. §§ 1601-19 (Supp. II, 1972).

[257] Fiscal year 1973 runs from July 1, 1972, through June 30, 1973, and fiscal 1974 runs from July 1, 1973, through June 30, 1974.

[258] 20 U.S.C. § 1601 (Supp. II, 1972).

[259] 20 U.S.C. § 1619(9)(Supp. II, 1972).

[260] *Id.*

[261] 20 U.S.C. § 1619(10)(Supp. II, 1972).

[262] 20 U.S.C. § 1605 (Supp. II, 1972).

act to create or further segregation on or after the date of enactment of the program[263] are ineligible for aid under it.[264]

Emergency School Aid funds may be spent on such programs as special remedial services, professional staff, teacher aides, inservice teacher training, counselling for children, development of new curricula, instruction in minority language and culture, career education, community activities, administrative services, and facility remodeling.[265] Grants may also be made for bilingual education,[266] educational parks having a cluster of schools with a favorable mixture of white and minority students,[267] cross-district programs within a Standard Metropolitan Statistical Area,[268] and even educational television activities that employ minority individuals "in responsible positions in development, production and administrative staffs."[269]

A related provision of the Education Amendments of 1972[270] prohibits the use of any federal funds for the transportation of students or teachers in order (1) to overcome racial imbalance (i.e., *de facto* segregation) or (2) to carry out any desegregation without the express written voluntary consent of local school officials. Also, even if local officials do consent, funds may not be used for transportation when the time or distance involved would risk the health of students, impinge on the educational process, or transfer students to a new school that is substantially inferior in quality to their present one, and federal officials are forbidden to coerce or encourage local officials to use their own funds for purposes for which federal funds cannot be employed.[271]

Whether this relatively recent attempt to achieve racial integration by use of the carrot of federal funds in lieu of the stick of federal court orders will succeed remains to be seen, but the early indications appear to be that many districts, hungry for funds, will make concessions to the Department of Health, Education and Welfare that might not come as easily in court, if only for the reason that in the former case the local district stands to lose (or cause delay in) something it desperately needs to remain afloat.

---

[263] June 23, 1972.

[264] 20 U.S.C. § 1605 (Supp. II, 1972). Waivers of this prohibition may be granted in extraordinary circumstances.

[265] 20 U.S.C. § 1606 (Supp. II, 1972).

[266] 20 U.S.C. § 2607(c) (Supp. II, 1972): At least $40 million of the $1 billion authorized for each fiscal year is earmarked for this purpose. See also, 20 U.S.C. § § 880b–880b-5, as amended, 20 U.S.C. § 880b-3a (Supp. II, 1972).

[267] 20 U.S.C. § 1608 (Supp. II, 1972).

[268] *Id.*

[269] 20 U.S.C. § 1610 (Supp. II, 1972).

[270] 86 Stat. 371, § 802; 20 U.S.C. § 1652 (Supp. II, 1972).

[271] *Id.*

## Federally assisted programs

The law regarding discrimination in federally assisted programs[272] provides that

> [n]o person in the United States shall, on the ground of race, color or national origin, be excluded from participation in, be denied the benefits of, or be subjected to discrimination under any program or activity receiving Federal financial assistance.[273]

Every federal department or agency that awards financial assistance by means of a grant loan, or contract (except contracts of insurance or guarantee) must issue rules and regulations to effectuate this requirement,[274] and is empowered to obtain compliance by termination of federal aid altogether or "by any other means authorized by law."[275] No action is to be taken against a respondent until it has been informed of the allegation of noncompliance and compliance by voluntary means has been found unattainable; if a termination action is decided upon, it may not be put into effect until 30 days after a report on the case is filed with the committees of the House and Senate having jurisdiction over the program or activity in question.[276] Although each federal agency is given independent responsibility for the enforcement of this title, the Department of Justice coordinates enforcement activities[277] and all agency actions are subject to judicial review.[278]

The activities that have been held subject to this title include federally aided hospitals,[279] housing,[280] and welfare programs.[281] In addition, the courts have permitted individuals who are the beneficiaries of the programs

---

[272] Civil Rights Act of 1964, 78 Stat. 252, title VI; 42 U.S.C. §§ 2000d–2000d-6.

[273] 42 U.S.C. § 2000d. Religious discrimination is prohibited by article VI of the Constitution, which provides that "no religious Test shall ever be required as a Qualification to any Office or public Trust under the United States." Kator, "Third Generation Equal Employment Opportunity," Civil Service Jrnl. 1, 2 (July-Sept. 1972).

[274] 42 U.S.C. § 2000d-1; see, e.g., 49 C.F.R. §§ 21.1-21.23 (1972)(Dept. of Transportation); 7 C.F.R. §§ 15.1-15.143 (1973)(Dept. of Agriculture); 13 C.F.R. §§ 112.1-112.15 (1973)(Small Business Admin.).

[275] 42 U.S.C. § 2000d-1.

[276] Id.

[277] Exec. Order No. 11764, 39 Fed. Reg.) 2575 (1974)

[278] 42 U.S.C. § 2000d-2.

[279] Marable v. Alabama Mental Health Board, 297 F. Supp. 291 (M.D. Ala., 1968).

[280] Gautreaux v. Chicago Housing Authority, 265 F. Supp. 582 (N.D. Ill., 1967), aff'd, 436 F. 2d 306 (7 Cir., 1970), cert. den., 402 U.S. 922 (1971).

[281] Gardner v. Alabama, 385 F. 2d 804 (5 Cir., 1967), cert. den., 389 U.S. 1046 (1968).

involved to bring suit,[282] individually or on a class basis.[283]

The employment practices of grantees are specifically exempted from the application of title VI, "except where a primary objective of the Federal financial assistance is to provide employment."[284] However, the courts have ruled that this prohibition in no way limits their power to require faculty integration in segregated schools,[285] nor does it limit the power of the Federal Government generally to require nondiscrimination in employment by federal grantees where there is some basis for the power other than title VI.[286] It was on this basis that President Lyndon Johnson was able, in 1965, to issue Executive Order 11246,[287] parts II and III of which prohibited discrimination in employment by federal contractors and grantees' construction contractors on the basis of race, creed, color, or national origin. E.O. 11246 has been held to be legal and having the force of statutory law on the theory that the executive branch has an inherent or implied power to determine the terms and conditions under which the United States will contract.[288]

As presently in force, E.O. 11246 requires firms contracting with the Federal Government to agree in their contracts that

> (1) The contractor will not discriminate against any employee or applicant for employment because of race, color, religion, sex, or national origin. The contractor will take affirmative action to ensure that applicants are employed, and that employees are treated during employment, without regard to their race, color, religion, sex or national origin. Such action shall include, but not be limited to the following: employment, upgrading, demotion, or transfer; recruitment or recruitment advertising; layoff or termination; rates of pay or other forms of compensation; and selection for training, including

---

[282] Bossier Parish School Board v. Lemon, 370 F. 2d 847 (5 Cir.), *cert. den.*, 388 U.S. 911 (1967).

[283] *Id.* Cypress v. Newport News General and Nonsectarian Hospital Ass., 375 F. 2d 648 (4 Cir., 1967); *cf.*, Rule 23, Fed. R. Civ. P.

[284] 42 U.S.C. § 2000d-3. An example of this would be a manpower training program.

[285] U.S. v. Jefferson County Board of Education, *supra.*

[286] U.S. by Clark v. Frazer, 297 F. Supp. 319 (M.D. Ala., 1968).

[287] 30 Fed. Reg. 12319 (1965), as amended, Exec. Order No. 11375, 32 Fed. Reg. 14303 (1967)(added discrimination on the basis of religion and sex to prohibited list); Exec. Order No. 11478, 34 Fed. Reg. 12985 (1967); 42 U.S.C. § 2000e n.

[288] U.S. by Clark v. Local 189, United Papermakers and Paperworkers, 282 F. Supp. 39 (E.D.La., 1968), *aff'd*, 416 F. 2d 980 (5 Cir., 1969), *cert. den.*, 397 U.S. 919 (1970); Savannah Printing Specialties and Paper Products Local Union 604 v. Union Camp Corp., 350 F. Supp. 632 (S.D. Ga., 1972).

apprenticeship. The contractor agrees to post in conspicuous places, available to employees and applicants for employment, notices to be provided by the [federal] contracting officer setting forth the provisions of this nondiscriminatin clause.

(2) The contractor will, in all solicitations or advertisements for employees placed by or on behalf of the contractor, state that all qualified applicants will receive consideration for employment without regard to race, color, religion, sex or national origin.[289]

Clauses must also be included requiring notice to and nondiscrimination statements by labor unions representing employees of the contractor, the furnishing of appropriate information and the availability of the contractor's records to the Department of Labor, and the inclusion of identical clauses in all subcontracts and purchase orders entered into by the contractor.[290]

Sanctions for violation of E.O. 11246 or the nondiscrimination provisions of a contract subject to it include the cancellation of the contract in whole or part, exclusion of the contractor from future federal contracts, publication of the name of the contractor, and recommendation to the Department of Justice or the Equal Employment Opportunity Commission that appropriate civil and/or criminal proceedings be instituted.[291] Sanctions relating to termination of existing contracts or prohibition from future contracts may be conditioned upon the establishment and fulfillment of compliance programs.[292]

Part III of E.O. 11246[293] covers situations where a federal grantee enters into a construction contract with a firm that is not itself a federal grantee. It requires that the grantee, as a condition for approval of its grant, "undertake and agree to incorporate, or cause to be incorporated, into all construction contracts paid for in whole or in part with funds obtained from ..., or borrowed on the credit of the Federal Government," the provisions required for contracts between the Federal Government and its grantees under Part II of E.O. 11246.[294] Sanctions against a grantee who fails to comply include the cancellation of the federal grant, cancellation of the contract

---

[289] § 202, Exec. Order No. 11246, 30 Fed. Reg. 12319 (1965), as amended, Exec. Order No. 11375, 32 Fed. Reg. 14303 (1967); 42 U.S.C. § 2000e n.

[290] §§ 202, 203(c), 204(d), Exec. Order No. 11246, 30 Fed Reg. 12319 (1965), as amended, Exec. Order No. 11375, 32 Fed. Reg. 14303 (1967); 42 U.S.C. § 2000e n.

[291] § 209(a), Exec. Order No. 11246, 30 Fed. Reg. 12319 (1965); 42 U.S.C. § 2000e n.

[292] Id.

[293] Part III, Exec. Order No. 11246, 30 Fed. Reg. 12319 (1965); 42 U.S.C. § 2000e n.

[294] § 301, Exec. Order No. 11246, 30 Fed. Reg. 12319 (1965); 42 U.S.C. § 2000e n.

between the grantee and its construction contractor, and reference of the matter to the Justice Department for appropriate legal proceedings.[295]

The Office of Federal Contract Compliance (OFCC) established within the Department of Labor to implement E.O. 11246 has instituted compliance checks prior to the award of federal contracts[296] and its requiring specific affirmative action by construction contractors (the "Philadelphia Plan") has been sustained in the courts.[297] On the whole, though, the OFCC's performance in the area of the construction industry has been disappointing. The Nixon administration has depended heavily upon the support of the construction unions, and one of its leading lights, Peter Brennan, was named Secretary of Labor shortly after the 1972 election. Given the fact that the OFCC exercises jurisdiction over contracts involving 225,000 contractors who employ one-third of the total work force in the United States,[298] its potential leverage is enormous, but given the present political situation, it seems likely that efforts in the immediate future will have to come primarily through action by private citizens under titles VI[299] and VII[300] of the 1964 Civil Rights Act.

## Employment

The basic law governing discrimination in employment is title VII of the Civil Rights Act of 1964,[301] most recently amended by the Equal Employment Opportunity Act of 1972.[302] Title VII applies to employers, employment agencies, and labor organizations, with an "employer" defined as anyone engaged in an industry affecting commerce[303] and having 15 or more

---

[295] § 303(b), Exec. Order No. 11246, 30 Fed. Reg. 12319 (1965); 42 U.S.C. § 2000e n.

[296] 41 C.F.R. § 60-1.29 (1972).

[297] Contractors Assn. of Eastern Pennsylvania v. Secretary of Labor, 442 F. 2d 159 (3 Cir.), cert. den., 404 U.S. 854 (1971).

[298] U.S. Department of Labor, Fact Sheet on Office of Federal Contract Compliance (OFCC)(1972).

[299] 78 Stat. 252, title VI; 42 U.S.C. §§ 2000d–2000d-3; Bossier Parish School Board v. Lemon, supra; Cypress v. Newport News General and Nonsectarian Hospital Assn., supra.

[300] 78 Stat. 253, title VII, as amended, 42 U.S.C. §§ 2000e–2000e-17 (1970; Supp. II, 1972), infra.

[301] Id.

[302] 86 Stat. 103.

[303] I.e., affecting commerce between states or between the United States and foreign countries. Much commerce which is primarily intrastate in nature affects interstate and foreign commerce and is therefore subject to federal regulation generally and to this statute in particular. U.S. Const., art. I, § 8, cl. 3; U.S. v. Darby, 312 U.S. 100 (1941).

employees for each working day in each of 20 or more calendar weeks in the current or preceding calendar year.[304] Excluded altogether from the definition are civil service positions in the District of Columbia Government, any "bona fide private membership club" that is tax exempt,[305] employment of aliens outside the United States, or with respect to religious preferences in hiring by religious organizations and their educational institutions.[306] The United States Government is exempted from the general provisions of title VII,[307] but has its own special coverage within the title.[308]

A labor organization is covered if it is engaged in an industry affecting commerce. Almost all labor organizations that either have 15 or more members or procure employees for a covered employer are covered under title VII.[309] An employment agency is defined as anyone regularly procuring employees for a covered employer, regardless of whether the agency receives any compensation for its services.[310]

It is an "unlawful employment practice" for an employer

(1) to fail or refuse to hire or to discharge any individual, or otherwise to discriminate against any individual with respect to his compensation, terms, conditions, or privileges of employment, because of such individual's race, color, religion, sex, or national origin; or

(2) to limit, segregate, or classify his employees or applicants for employment in any way which would deprive or tend to deprive any individual of employment opportunities or otherwise adversely affect his status as an employee, because of such individual's race, color, religion, sex, or national origin.[311]

Unlawful employment pracitces for employment agencies and labor organizations are similarly defined,[312] with the latter also being forbidden to try to get an employer to discriminate.[313] Discrimination in apprenticeship and training programs is also prohibited.[314] Discrimination on the basis of

[304] 42 U.S.C. § 2000e(b)(Supp. II, 1972).

[305] Under 26 U.S.C. § 501(c).

[306] 42 U.S.C. §§ 2000e(b), 2000e-1 (Supp. II, 1972).

[307] 42 U.S.C. § 2000e(b)(Supp. II, 1972).

[308] 42 U.S.C. § 2000e-16(Supp. II, 1972).

[309] 42 U.S.C. §§ 2000e(d), 2000d(e)(1970; Supp. II, 1972).

[310] 42 U.S.C. § 2000e(c)(Supp. II, 1972).

[311] 42 U.S.C. § 2000e-2(a)(1970; Supp. II, 1972).

[312] 42 U.S.C. §§ 2000e-2(b), 200e-2(c) (1970; Supp. II, 1972).

[313] 42 U.S.C. § 2000e-a(c)(3).

[314] 42 U.S.C. § 2000e-2(d).

religion, sex, or national origin (but not on the basis of race or color) is permitted where it is "a bona fide occupational qualification reasonably necessary to the normal operation of [the] particular business or enterprise,"[315] but this exception is interpreted very narrowly[316] and one court has stated that "necessary" means an "irresistible demand."[317]

Employers are permitted to have different employment terms "pursuant to a bona fide seniority or merit system, or a system which measures earnings by quantity or quality of production of [for] employees who work in different locations," if such differences are not intended to discriminate on the basis of race, color, religion, sex, or national origin.[318] But the courts have held that where a past seniority system—even one preexisting the enactment of title VII—discriminated against blacks, no present system that fails to rectify the effects of the past discrimination was "bona fide."[319]

Employers may use professionally developed ability tests, but they must not be "designed, intended or used to discriminate."[320] This exception as enacted had great potential for abuse, but the courts have dealt with it quite strictly. In addition to being impermissible if their intent is discriminatory, tests that have the *effect* of excluding blacks are prohibited unless they can be demonstrated to be related to job performance[321] and to be valid as a measure of job performance.[322]

In discussing ability tests, seniority systems, and like matters, the Supreme Court has stated that

> practices, procedures, or tests neutral on their face, and even neutral in terms of intent, cannot be maintained if they operate to "freeze" the status quo of prior discriminatory employment practices,[323]

[315] 42 U.S.C. § 2000e-2(e)(1).

[316] Diaz v. Pan American World Airways, Inc., 442 F. 2d 385 (5 Cir.), *cert. den.*, 404 U.S. 950 (1971).

[317] U.S. v. St. Louis-San Francisco Ry. Co., 464 F. 2d 301, 308 (8 Cir., 1972), *cert. den.*, 409 U.S. 1116 (1973).

[318] 42 U.S.C. § 2000e(h) (Supp. II, 1972).

[319] Local 189, United Paperworkers and Papermakers v. U.S. by Mitchell, 416 F.2d 980 (5 Cir., 1969), *cert. den* 397 U.S. 919 (1970)(where prior racial discrimination had kep blacks in the lowest-paid jobs, court ordered that higher-up positions be filled not on the basis of seniority at the job level immediately below the one to be filled, but on the basis of seniority in the plant as a whole); *cf.*, U.S. v. International Brotherhood of Electrical Workers, Local No. 38, 428 F.2d 144 (6 Cir.), *cert. den.*, 400 U.S. 943 (1970).

[320] 42 U.S.C. § 2000e-2(h).

[321] Griggs v. Duke Power Co., 401 U.S. 424 (1971).

[322] Stevenson v. International Paper Co., 352 F. Supp. 230 (S.D. Ala., 1972).

[323] Griggs v. Duke Power Co., *supra*, at 430.

and that what title VII requires is

> the removal of artificial, arbitrary, and unnecessary barriers to employment when the barriers operate invidiously to discriminate on the basis of racial or other impermissible classification.[324]

The use of *effect,* rather than *intent,* as a criterion is an extremely significant factor in the enforcement of title VII's guarantees. It is very difficult to demonstrate the reasons why an employer acted in a certain way, but relatively easy to demonstrate, say, the number of blacks and whites hired as compared with the number of blacks and whites applying for work. Under most anti-discrimination laws, including those discussed elsewhere in this chapter, the individual claiming to have been the victim of discrimination must prove that the action taken against him was intended to discriminate against him because of his race, color, religion, etc., but under title VII, if a black shows that he was denied a job for which he was qualified and that the employer thereafter continued to seek applicants for that job, the *employer* then bears the burden of demonstrating (1) that he did not intend to discriminate and (2) that the reason for his rejection of the complainant was related to the requirements of the job.[325]

The use of effect as a criterion has led to a number of far-reaching decisions. One company's practice of denying employment to individuals with arrest records (i.e., regardless of whether they had been convicted) was ruled to deny equal employment opportunity to blacks, because they are arrested without cause far more frequently than are whites.[326] Another employer's practice, that of discharging employees whose wages were garnisheed, has been held to be a title VII violation because it subjects a disproportionate number of minority persons to discharge and is not related to the ability of employees to do their jobs.[327]

Similar results have been reached in many cases regarding the discriminatory practices of labor unions. Where the results of the practices at issue were the exclusion or limitation of blacks, unions have been forbidden to limit membership to relatives of members[328] or to condition admission to

---

[324] *Id.* at 431.

[325] McDonnell Douglas Corp. v. Green, 411 U.S. 1972 (1973).

[326] Gregory v. Litton Systems, Inc., 316 F. Supp. 401 (C.D. Calif., 1970), *aff'd,* 472 F. 2d 631 (9 Cir., 1972). Another case has held that denial of employment on the basis of *convictions* is permissible. Richardson v. Hotel Corp. of America, 332 F. Supp. 519 (E.D. La., 1971), *aff'd,* 468 F. 2d 951 (5 Cir. 1971).
327

[327] Wallace v. Debron Corp., ———F. 2d———.42 USLW 2530 (8 Cir., 3/28/74); Johnson v. Pike Corp. of America, 332 F. Supp. 490 (C.D. Calif., 1971).

[328] Local 53, International Assn. of Heat and Frost Insulators and Asbestos Workers v. Vogler, 407 F.2d 1047 (Cir., 1969).

membership on a favorable vote of the present membership.[329] In another instance, a union with a history of discrimination was barred from requiring applicants to demonstrate a full range of abilities or experience in the industry, though it was allowed to require certain minimal qualifications.[330]

In addition to the practices directly related to employment that are outlawed by title VII, it is prohibited to discriminate against an individual because he has been involved in enforcing title VII (e.g., by filing a complaint),[331] and every employer, union or employment agency covered by title VII must post a notice of its nondiscrimination policies on its premises.[332] Also, no party covered by title VII may publish any advertisement for employment or membership "indicating any preference, limitation, specification, or discrimination, based on race, color, religion, sex, or national origin" unless related to a bona fide occupational qualification.[333] Unfortunately, the courts have ruled that the advertising prohibition was not intended to apply to newspapers,[334] though it appears that the First Amendment would not prevent such an application.[335]

In enacting title VII, Congress established the Equal Employment Opportunity Commission (EEOC) to administer it.[336] The EEOC consists of five members, of whom not more than three may be of the same political party, and who are appointed by the President with the advice and consent of the Senate. Except for cases in which the Attorney General brings suit,[337] all complaints of title VII violations must be processed administratively before they may be taken to court.[338] The aggrieved individual[339] files a written complaint, made under oath, with the EEOC, which then notifies the respondent of the charges and makes an investigation to determine whether

---

[329] *Id.*

[330] U.S. v. Local No. 86, International Assn. of Bridge, Structural, Ornamental and Reinforcing Iron Workers, 315 F. Supp. 1202 (W.D. Wash., 1970), *aff'd*, 443 F. 2d 544 (9 Cir.), *cert. den.*, 404 U.S. 984 (1971).

[331] 42 U.S.C. § 2000e-3(a)(Supp. II, 1972).

[332] 42 U.S.C. § 2000e-10.

[333] 42 U.S.C. § 2000e-3(b)(Supp. II, 1972); see also, the discussion of bona fide occupational qualification, *supra.*

[334] Brush v. San Francisco Newspaper Publishing Co., 469 F. 2d 89 (9 Cir., 1972), *cert. den.* 410 U.S. 943 (1973); National Organization for Women v. Gannett Co., Inc., 40 A.D. 2d 107, 338 N.Y.S. 2d 570 (App. Div., 1970), leave to app. granted, 32 N.Y. 2d. 613, 347 N.Y.S. 2d 201, 300 N.E. 2d 733 (1973).

[335] See, Pittsburgh Press Co. v. Pittsburgh Commission on Human Relations, 413 U.S. 376 (1973).

[336] 42 U.S.C. § 2000e-4 (1970; Supp. II, 1973).

[337] 42 U.S.C. § 2000e-6 (1970; Supp. II, 1972).

[338] 42 U.S.C. § 2000e-5(f) (Supp. II, 1972).

[339] Members of the EEOC may also file complaints.

there is "reasonable cause" to proceed further.[340] If reasonable cause is determined to exist, the EEOC then attempts, by means of "informal methods of conference, conciliation, and persuasion," to bring about compliance.[341] If reasonable cause is not found, the EEOC dismisses the case, notifies the complainant, and takes no further action in the matter.[342] All of these informal proceedings are strictly private.[343]

If the relevant state or locality has a law prohibiting the practice complained of and an agency (civil or criminal) empowered to enforce it, no charge may be filed with the EEOC until 60 days after state or local proceedings are commenced.[344]

A complaint must be filed with the EEOC within 180 days after the allegedly unlawful employment practice occurred; if the case is one in which a complaint must first have been filed with a state or local agency, the filing of the complaint with the EEOC must be within 300 days after the practice occurred or within 30 days after notification of the end of the state or local proceedings, whichever is earlier.[345]

If the EEOC is unable to secure voluntary compliance, it may bring a civil action in the federal district court on behalf of the aggrieved person.[346] If the respondent is a state or local government, the EEOC must refer the case to the Attorney General, and he may bring such a lawsuit.[347] In either case, the aggrieved person may intervene in the case.[348] If the EEOC dismisses the charge or fails to bring a lawsuit[349] within 180 days, the aggrieved individual

---

[340] 42 U.S.C. § 2000e-5(b)(Supp. II, 1972).

[341] *Id.*

[342] A finding by the EEOC that reasonable cause is not present does not prevent the aggrieved person from going to court. McDonnell Douglas Corp. v. Green, *supra*.

[343] An EEOC employee who makes public any information about such a proceeding may receive a one year jail term, a fine of $1000, or both. 42 U.S.C. § 2000e-5(b)(Supp. II, 1972).

[344] 120 days during the first year that the state or local law is in operation. In the case of a charge filed by a member of the EEOC which relates to such a state or locality, the EEOC refers the case to the appropriate state or local agency and the 60 (or 120) day period begins to run at the time of referral. 42 U.S.C. ≠2000e-5(c), (d)(Supp. II, 1972). Where an aggrieved person who should have filed his complaint with a state agency mistakenly filed with the EEOC instead, and it hten referred his complaint to the state agency and took back jurisdiction when the state agency failed to act, the administrative procedures required by the statute were held to have been complied with. Love v. Pullman Co., 404 U.S. 522 (1972).

[345] 42 U.S.C. § 2000e-5(e)(Supp. II, 1972).

[346] 42 U.S.C. § 2000e-5(f)(Supp. II, 1972).

[347] *Id.*

[348] *Id.*

[349] Or, if the respondent is a state or local government, the Attorney General fails to bring a suit.

himself has 90 days in which to sue.[350] Once the individual has commenced an action, the EEOC may not bring its own suit.[351] Suit may be brought in the federal district court where the act occurred, where the respondent's relevant employment or membership records are kept, or where the person aggrieved would have worked. If none of these places can be determined, suit may be brought where the respondent's principal place of business is located.[352]

The court may appoint counsel for an aggrieved person suing on his own and may allow him to commence his suit without payment of the usual court fees.[353] Counsel will usually not be appointed unless the complainant has made diligent efforts to find a lawyer.[354] An EEOC finding that no probable cause exists will not automatically bar the court appointment of counsel,[355] but it presumably may be taken into account.

While the statutory administrative procedures must be followed by the aggrieved person before the lawsuit is brought, the fact that the EEOC has failed to conduct any conciliation proceedings does not bar the suit, even if the failure is in no way the fault of the respondent.[356] The complainant is not bound by any agreement reached between the EEOC and the respondent if he did not join in it,[357] nor is he bound by any agreement between the respondent and other individuals in situations similar to his.[358] However, a single individual may sue on behalf of the entire class of which he is a member (e.g., "all black employees of X Co." or "all blacks who have applied for employment with X Co. and have not been hired"),[359] even though the other members have not filed charges with the EEOC.[360] In such an instance, the individual need not allege[361] or prove[362] that he has been the victim of discrimination so long as he alleges and proves that there has been discrimination against the class or some of its members.

[350] 42 U.S.C. § 2000e-5(f)(Supp. II, 1972). If the EEOC retains the case for over 180 days, the 90 day limit by which the complainant may sue does not begin to run until the EEOC notifies him of the end of its administrative proceedings. Cunningham v. Litton Industries, 413 F. 2d 887 (9 Cir., 1969).

[351] EEOC v. Mo. Pacific Ry., – – –F. 2d– – –, 42 USLW 2462 (8 Cir., 2/25/74).

[352] 42 U.S.C. § 2000e-5(f)(Supp. II, 1972).

[353] Id.

[354] Johnson v. Hertz Corp., 316 F. Supp. 961 (S.D. Tex., 1970).

[355] Harris v. Walgreen's Distribution Center, 456 F. 2d 588 (6 Cir., 1972).

[356] Johnson v. Seaboard Airline R.R. Co., 405 F. 2d 645 (4 Cir., 1968), *cert. den.*, 394 U.S. 918 (1969).

[357] Cox v. U.S. Gypsum Co., 409 F. 2d 289 (7 Cir., 1969).

[358] Austin v. Reynolds Metals Co., 327 F. Supp. 1145 (E.D. Va., 1970).

[359] Miller v. International Paper Co., 408 F. 2d 283 (5 Cir., 1969).

[360] Id.

[361] Hadnott v. Laird, 463 F. 2d 304 (D.C. Cir., 1972).

[362] Parham v. Southwestern Bell Telephone Co., 433 F. 2d 421 (8 Cir., 1970).

In many instances, employees have available to them such contract remedies as arbitration. There is no need to resort to such remedies before beginning EEOC or subsequent court proceedings,[363] Even if an employee does resort to a contract arbitration procedure, he may bring a title VII lawsuit after it has been concluded.[364]

If the court finds a favor of the complaining party, it may enjoin the respondent from committing further discriminatory acts and may also order such affirmative action as hiring or reinstatement and/or back pay for a period of up to two years before the original charge was filed.[365] The court may also allow a prevailing party (other than the EEOC) a reasonable attorney's fee.[366]

The EEOC and the Attorney General are permitted to sue against discriminatory employment practices without any individual complaint having been made where either has reasonable cause to believe that a pattern or practice of such behavior exists.[367] Proceedings in such a case are to be expedited, and the Attorney General may request that it be heard by a special three-judge court,[368] with direct review by the Supreme Court.

Equal employment in the Federal Government is covered partly by procedures set forth in Executive Order 11478,[369] promulgated in 1969, and partly by procedures set forth in a new section of title VII, enacted as part of the Equal Employment Opportunity Act of 1972.[370] Both the Executive Order and the new section prohibit discrimination in federal employment on the basis of race, color, religion, sex, or national origin, and the former requires that each department and agency in the executive branch "establish and maintain an affirmative program of equal employment opportunity for all civilian employees and applicants for employment,"[371] and further,

[363] Rios v. Reynolds Metals Co., 467 F. 2d 54 (5 Cir., 1972).

[364] Alexander v. Gardner-Denver Co., ———U.S.———, 42 USLW 4214 (2/19/74).

[365] 42 U.S.C. § 2000e-5(g)(Supp. II, 1972).

[366] Id. Given the experience under similar provisions in other civil rights statutes, this probably means that a successful complainant is entitled to attorney's fees in all but extraordinary cases. See, e.g., Newman v. Piggie Park Enterprises, Inc., 390 U.S. 400 (1968)(public accommodations, 42 U.S.C. § 2000a-3); Northcross v. Board of Education, 412 U.S. 427 (1973)(school desegregation, 20 U.S.C. § 1617 [Supp. II, 1972]).

[367] 42 U.S.C. § 2000e-6 (1970; Supp. II, 1972). The Attorney General's authority under this section expires on March 24, 1974, at which time all suits under the section will be within the sole jurisdiction of the EEOC.

[368] See, 28 U.S.C. § 2284.

[369] 34 Fed. Reg. 12985 (1969), as amended, Exec. Order No. 11590, 36 Fed Reg. 7831 (1971); 42 U.S.C. § 2000e n (1970; Supp. II, 1972).

[370] 86 Stat. 111, § 11.

[371] § 2, Exec. Order No. 11478, 34 Fed. Reg. 12985 (1969); 42 U.S.C. § 2000e n.

to the maximum extent possible, to provide sufficient resources to administer such a program in a positive and effective manner; assure that recruitment activities reach all sources of job candidates; utilize to the fullest extent the present skills of each employee; provide the maximum feasible opportunity to employees to enhance their skills so they may perform at their highest potential and advance in accordance with their abilities; provide training and advice to managers and supervisors to assure their understanding and implementation of the policy expressed in this order; assure participation at the local level with other employers, schools, and public or private groups in cooperative efforts to improve community conditions which affect employability; and provide for a system within the department or agency for periodically evaluating the effectiveness with which the policy of this order is being carried out.[372]

The 1972 provision adds to these requirements a rule that each department or agency have an employee training program.[373]

A complaint by an employee or applicant for employment is made directly to the department or agency involved,[374] with an appeal to the Civil Service Commission.[375] The Civil Service Commission is vested with overall responsibility for the federal program and may enforce the nondiscrimination policy by means of reinstatement, hiring, and back pay.[376] The most significant change regarding federal employment made by the 1972 amendments to title VII is that an aggrieved employee or applicant for employment whose grievance is not settled to his satisfaction by the agency concerned or the Civil Service Commission may now bring a lawsuit in the manner prescribed for title VII actions generally.[377]

## Voting

It will be recalled that almost all of the Reconstruction laws protecting voting rights were held unconstitutional by the courts or repealed by Congress by the early part of this century.[378] The rebuilding process began with the

---

[372] *Id.*

[373] 42 U.S.C. § 2000e-16(b)(Supp. II, 1972).

[374] § 4, Exec. Order No. 11478, 34 Fed. Reg. 12985 (1969); 42 U.S.C. § 2000e n.

[375] *Id.*

[376] 42 U.S.C. § 20004-16(b)(Supp. II, 1972).

[377] 42 U.S.C. § 2000e-16(c)(Supp. II, 1972).

[378] *Supra*; the only provision from this era which has survived is § 1 of the Civil Rights Act of 1870, now cofified as 42 U.S.C. § 1971(a)(1).

Civil Rights Act of 1957,[379] which prohibited intimidation of voters or potential voters, and was continued in the Civil Rights Acts of 1960[380] and 1964[381] and the Voting Rights Acts of 1965[382] and 1970.[383]

Under section 1971 of title 42 of the U.S. Code, all qualified citizens are entitled to vote at any election, state as well as federal,[384] without regard to race, color, or previous condition of servitude. No one acting under color of state law may apply to would-be voters eligibility standards different from those applied to individuals already found qualified to vote[385] or deny anyone's right to vote because of a minor error in registration or other qualification forms.[386] Section 1971 also makes it illegal, whether or not under color of state law, to intimidate anyone for the purpose of interfering with his right to vote in a federal election.[387] An act that is not directly related to voting and that is otherwise legal comes within this section if it is intended to deprive someone of his right to vote.[388] Examples of this are a nonrenewal of a teacher's license[389] and an action taken against one person to discourage a second person from voting.[390]

The Attorney General is authorized to seek injunctive relief in the federal courts against any violation of these rights.[391] In considering any such proceeding, it shall be presumed (in the absence of evidence to the contrary)

---

[379] 71 Stat. 634.

[380] 74 Stat. 86.

[381] 78 Stat. 241.

[382] 79 Stat. 437.

[383] 84 Stat. 315.

[384] This clause probably does not reach action which is wholly private in nature, as neither the Fourteenth nor the Fifteen Amendment reaches such conduct; however, it might reach such conduct on the theory that a denial of the right to vote because of race or color is a "badge or incident" of slavery and therefore violative of the Thirteenth Amendment, which does reach private conduct. See, Civil Rights Cases, 109 U.S. 3 (1883).

[385] The term "vote" includes "all action necessary to make a vote effective," including registration. 42 U.S.C. § 1971(e).

[386] 42 U.S.C. § 1971(a). This provision also forbids the use of any literacy test unless it is wholly in writing and available to an applicant who later requests it. However, the suspension of all literacy tests until 1975 (42 U.S.C. § 1973aa, infra) renders this provision ineffective and unnecessary, at least for the present.

[387] 42 U.S.C. § 1971(b). This provision reaches private action without regard to the three Reconstruction amendments because it relates only to federal elections. U.S. v. Bruce, 353 F. 2d 474 (5 Cir., 1965).

[388] U.S. v. Bruce, supra; U.S.sv. Wood, 295 F. 2d 772 (5 Cir., 1961), cert. den., 369 U.S. 850 (1962).

[389] U.S. v. Bruce, supra.

[390] U.S. v. Wood, supra.

[391] 42 U.S.C. §§ 1971(c), 1971(d).

that anyone who has completed the sixth grade in a public or accredited private school in the United States where instruction is "predominantly" in English is literate.[392] If the court finds that there has been a pattern or practice of denial of the right to vote because of race or color, it must grant court orders entitling individuals to vote if (1) they are of the race or color against which the discrimination has been directed, (2) they possess the qualifications required by state law, and (3) they have been deprived of their right to vote subsequent to the court's finding of discriminatory activity.[393] The court may appoint local voters as referees to hear applications for court voting orders; the referee's report on a voter is sent to the attorney general of the state and made the order of the court if the state does not file a sworn statement challenging it within ten days.[394] In addition to its power to order voting for individuals, the court has broad authority to remedy the effects of present and past discrimination in voting.[395] It may order periodic reports on voting and registration activity from local officials[396] and, at least in an extreme instance, set aside an election.[397]

The procedures in section 1971, which were enacted primarily in the Civil Rights Acts of 1957[398] and 1960,[399] did not prove successful on a large scale, probably due to a combination of cumbersome procedures and a difficult standard of proof for the Government to meet. Accordingly, the Voting Rights Acts of 1965[400] and 1970[401] instituted several different approaches to the problem.

One section of the 1965 act[402] provides that when the Attorney General brings a suit to enforce the right to vote and a finding of discrimination is made, the court "shall authorize" the appointment of federal voting examiners for as long as necessary.[403] If the court finds that any "test

---

[392] 42 U.S.C. § 1971(c); see, note 58, *supra*, see also, 42 U.S.C. § 1973b(e), *infra*, which relates to schools in which the predominant language of instruction is other than English.

[393] 42 U.S.C. § 1971(e).

[394] *Id.*

[395] Louisiana v. U.S., 380 U.S. 145 (1965); U.S. v. McLeod, 385 F. 2d 734 (5 Cir., 1967).

[396] U.S. v. Lynd, 349 F. 2d 785 (5 Cir., 1965).

[397] Bell v. Southwell, 376 F. 2d 659 (5 Cir., 1969).

[398] 71 Stat. 634.

[399] 74 Stat. 86.

[400] 79 Stat. 437.

[401] 84 Stat. 315.

[402] 42 U.S.C. § 1973a.

[403] 42 U.S.C. § 1973a(a). Examiners need not be appointed if the incidents have been few in number and corrected by the state, their effect has been eliminated, and there is no reasonable probability of their future occurence. The procedure for voting registration by these examiners is set forth in 42 U.S.C. § 1973e, discussed *infra*.

or device"[404] has been used in the state or political subdivision in question with the purpose or effect of denying the right to vote because of race or color, it must suspend the use of the tests and devices in the area for as long as is necessary.[405] The court retains jurisdiction over a case of this type for as long as is necessary, during which time no changes in voting procedure may be made unless either the court finds that it does not have the purpose or effect of denying voting rights because of race or color or the change is submitted to the Attorney General and he makes no objection within 60 days. Even if one of these procedures is successfully followed, a private person may bring suit to obtain an independent judicial determination of the legality of the change.[406]

In addition to the subjective method of suspending tests discussed in the preceding paragraph, the 1965 and 1970 Voting Rights Acts[407] instituted an objective method that was effective without any court proceedings; tests or devies are automatically suspended in any state or political subdivision that (1) had a test or device as of November 1, 1964, or November 1, 1968, and (2) had less than half of its voting age residents registered as of November 1, 1964, or November 1, 1968, or had less than half of its voting age residents voting in either the presidential election of 1964 or the presidential election of 1968.[408] A state or subdivision may obtain exemption from this section if it brings a lawsuit in the federal district court in Washington, D.C., and proves

> that no such test or device has been used during the ten years preceding the filing of the action for the purpose or with the effect of denying or abridging the right to vote on account of race or color.[409]

Such a suit is heard by a special three-judge court,[410] with direct appeal to the Supreme Court. If the Attorney General has no reason to believe that the

---

[404] Defined in 42 U.S.C. § 1973b(c) as any requirement that a prospective voter (1) prove his ability to read or write English, (2) demonstrate any educational achievement, (3) possess good moral character, or (4) be vouched for by registered voters or members of any other class.

[405] 42 U.S.C. § 1973a(b).

[406] 42 U.S.C. § 1973a(c).

[407] 79 Stat. 437; 84 Stat. 315.

[408] 42 U.S.C. § § 1973b(a), 1973b(b). The test or device will not be suspended if the incidents have been few in number and corrected by the state, their effect has been eliminated, and there is no reasonable probability of their future occurrence.

[409] 42 U.S.C. § 1973b(a). Note, however, that a provision of the Voting Rights Act of 1970 (42 U.S.C. § 1973aa) outlaws all tests or devices in areas not covered by § 1973b until 1975, so that a successful suit brought before then would not have any immediate effect.

[410] See, 28 U.S.C. § 2284.

state or subdivision bringing suit has used any test or device to deny the right to vote due to race or color during the preceding ten years, he is supposed to consent to a ruling in its favor.[411] In any case, if the court grants judgment for the state or subdivision, it retains jurisdiction over the case for five years, and the Attorney General may move to reopen the judgment if he believes that the state or locality has used a test or device for the prohibited purpose or with the prohibited effect.[412] The Attorney General may, without court order, appoint federal voting examiners for areas covered under this section if (1) he has received complaints from 20 or more residents of the area that they have been denied the right to vote because of their race or color and he believes that the complaints have merit, or (2) he believes the appointment of examiners is necessary to enforce the guarantees of the Fifteenth Amendment.[413]

In addition to the suspension of tests or devices under this section for any state (or subdivision) that falls within its criteria, it may not "enact or seek to administer any voting qualification or prerequisite to voting, or standard, practice, or procedure different from that in force or effect" on the date whose statistics bring the state within the section.[414] As is the case with respect to tests or devices, the state (or subdivision) may sue in the federal court in Washington, D.C., for a determination that the proposed change "does not have the purpose and will not have the effect of denying or abridging the right to vote on account of race or color." Alternatively, the change may be submitted to the Attorney General and placed into effect if he does not object within 60 days. Until either the court has ruled that the change is permissible or the Attorney General has failed to object within the 60-day period, "no person shall be denied the right to vote for failure to comply with [the] qualification, prerequisite, standard, practice, or procedure." As with "test or device" cases, private citizens may sue to challenge the changes notwithstanding the result of either avenue of relief taken by the state. This section has been given an extremely broad interpretation by the courts[415] and has been ruled applicable to such changes as reapportionment,[416] annexation,[417] changes in the location of polling places,[418]

---

[411] 42 U.S.C. § 1973b(a).

[412] *Id.*

[413] 42 U.S.C. § 1973d.

[414] 42 U.S.C. § 1973c. The date is either November 1964 or November 1968.

[415] See, *e.g.*, Allen v. State Board of Elections, 393 U.S. 544 (1969).

[416] Allen v. State Board of Elections, *supra*; Georgia v. U.S., 411 U.S. 693 1702 (1973).

[417] Perkins v. Matthews, 400 U.S. 379, *on remand*, 336 F. Supp. 6 (S.D. Miss., 1971).

[418] *Id.*

changes in campaign spending laws,[419] and changes in the manner in which election challenges are brought in the state courts.[420]

In addition to the presumption of literacy for any individual who has completed the sixth grade in an English-language school previously discussed,[421] the Voting Rights Act of 1965 contained a provision directed at New York State's denial of the franchise to its substantial population of Puerto Rican origin.[422] This section provides that no one who has completed the sixth grade in a school in the United States, including Puerto Rico, in which the "predominant classroom language was other than English" may be denied the right to vote because of his inability to read or write English. This section has been held constitutional as an exercise of Congress' power to enforce the equal protection clause of the Fourteenth Amendment.[423]

The procedure in areas with federal voting examiners is as follows: Anyone who is found by an examiner to possess "the qualifications prescribed by State law not inconsistent with the Constitution and laws of the United States" is placed on a list of eligible voters, which is sent to state officials at least once a month.[424] The state officials responsible for voting registration must place these names on their registration lists and the individuals are then entitled to vote until and unless federal authorities notify the state officials of their loss of eligibility.[425] The lists are made public at the time they are sent to the state officials,[426] and challenges to them must be made within ten days thereafter, supported by the affidavits of two individuals with personal knowledge of the claimed disqualifying facts, and served upon the challenged individual.[427] Challenges are judged by hearing officers appointed by the U.S. Civil Service Commission.[428] They must be decided within 15 days and may be appealed to the U.S. Court of Appeals for the area within 15 days thereafter;[429] the court may overturn the decision of the examiner only if it is "clearly erroneous,"[430] which means that almost all examiners' decisions will be sustained. Note that the use of federal examiners only supercedes state

---

[419] Ladner v. Fisher, 269 So. 2d 633 (Miss., 1972).

[420] Thompson v. Brown, 434 F. 2d 1092 (5 Cir., 1970).

[421] 42 U.S.C. § 1971(c); see note 390, *supra,* and accompanying text.

[422] 42 U.S.C. § 1971b(e).

[423] Katzenbach v. Morgan, 384 U.S. 641 (1966).

[424] 42 U.S.C. § 1973e.

[425] *Id.* To vote in any given election, the individual must have been certified to the state officials at least 45 days before it takes place.

[426] 42 U.S.C. § 1973e(b).

[427] 42 U.S.C. § 1973g.

[428] *Id.*

[429] *Id.*

[430] *Id.*

procedures for voting registration. Such substantive standards as age, residence, and identification are judged under state law unless that law is somehow discriminatory.[431]

In any area in which there are federal examiners, the Attorney General may send observers to watch elections,[432] including primary elections.[433] If a voter is permitted to take a state official into the voting booth to assist him, he may also have a federal observer come in.[434]

The 1965 Voting Rights Act also sought to outlaw poll taxes as prerequisites for voting in state elections.[435] However, before the constitutionality of this provision could be decided, the Supreme Court ruled that poll taxes as a prerequisite for voting violated the equal protection clause,[436] thus making the new section unnecessary.

The method by which federal voting examiners are removed from an area depends upon how they got there in the first place. If they were originally appointed by court order,[437] they may be removed only when the court determines that they are no longer needed.[438] If they were appointed by the Attorney General without court order,[439] they are removed whenever either the Attorney General or the federal district court in Washington, D.C.[440] finds that (1) all persons listed by the federal examiners have been placed on the voting rolls and (2) there is "no longer reasonable cause to believe that persons [in the area] will be deprived of or denied the right to vote on account of race or color."[441]

Criminal penalties relating to the Voting Rights Act of 1965 cover any deprivation of rights secured under it, interference under color of state law with a voter who has qualified under the act in his attempt to vote, destruction or alteration of ballots, and conspiracy to commit any of the acts

---

[431] Perez v. Rhiddlehoover, 186 So. 2d 686 (La.sApp.), *writ refused*, 249 La. 451, 187 So. 2d 438 (1966).

[432] 42 U.S.C. § 1973f.

[433] U.S. v. Executive Committee of the Democratic Party of Greene County, Ala., 254 F. Supp. 543 (N.D. Ala., S.D. Ala., 1966)(2 cases).

[434] U.S. v. Louisiana, 265 F. Supp. 703 (E.D. La., 1966), *aff'd*, 386 U.S. 270 (1967).

[435] 42 U.S.C. § 1973h. The Twenty-fourth Amendment to the Constitution, ratified in the previous year, had outlawed such taxes as prerequisites for voting in federal elections.

[436] Harper v. Virginia Board of Elections, 383 U.S. 663 (1966); *cf.*, U.S. v. Texas, 252 F. Supp. 234 (W.D. Tex.), *aff'd*, 384 U.S. 155 (1966).

[437] 42 U.S.C. § 1973a(a), *supra*.

[438] 42 U.S.C. § 1973k.

[439] 42 U.S.C. § 1973d(b), *supra*.

[440] If removal by the court is sought, there must also be a finding that more than half of the nonwhite residents of voting age are registered. 42 U.S.C. § 1973k.

[441] 42 U.S.C. § 1973k.

listed above.[442] Civilly, the Attorney General may sue for injunctive relief against any violations of the act.[443] Also, upon receipt of allegations, within 48 hours after the polls close in an area with federal examiners, that individuals who were registered under the act and eligible to vote were denied that right, the Attorney General may go to court for orders requiring the casting and counting of the ballots of the complaining individuals.[444]

As has been noted previously, the Voting Rights Act of 1970 went a step further in the area of literacy and other qualifying tests by barring them everywhere in the United States for five years:[445] this prohibition has been found constitutional by the Supreme Court.[446]

The provisions of the Civil Rights Act of 1960, enacted prior to the wholesale federal involvement with elections under the Voting Rights Acts of 1965 and 1970, required state election officials to retain all records of federal elections for a period of twenty-two months and to make them available to the Attorney General upon demand.[447] These provisions remain in force, but appear to have seen very little use since the enactment of the direct intervention provisions of the 1965 and 1970 acts.

## Housing and property

This field is covered by two separate statutory schemes—one dating from 1866,[448] the other from 1968.[449] Despite their substantive similarities, they are wholly independent of one another.[450]

The first, derived from a section of the Civil Rights Act of 1866,[451] relates to property rights generally and provides that

> [a]ll citizens of the United States shall have the same right, in every State and Territory, as is enjoyed by white citizens thereof to inherit, purchase, lease, sell, hold, and convey real and personal property.[452]

[442] 42 U.S.C. § 1973j(a)-(c)($5000 fine or 5 years' imprisonment or both).

[443] 42 U.S.C. § 1973j(d).

[444] 42 U.S.C. § 1973j(e).

[445] I.e., until August 6, 1975. 42 U.S.C. § 1973aa.

[446] U.S. v. Arizona, 400 U.S. 112 (1970).

[447] 42 U.S.C. §§ 1974-1974e.

[448] 42 U.S.C. § 1982.

[449] 42 U.S.C. §§ 3601-19, 3631.

[450] Jones v. Alfred H. Mayer Co., 392 U.S. 409 (1968).

[451] 14 Stat. 27, c. 31, § 1.

[452] 42 U.S.C. § 1982.

This broadly worded provision offers redress for racial discrimination of either a private or a governmental character[453] and covers not just housing, but all property. Yet, unlike the housing provisions of the Civil Rights Act of 1968,[454] it is "not a comprehensive open housing law,"[455] as it does not explicitly cover discrimination in such related areas as services, facilities, advertising, financing, or brokerage, does not authorize assistance to the victim by the Federal Government, and does not expressly provide for money damages.[456] On the other hand, it has been held applicable to such varied situations as racial discrimination in zoning,[457] property insurance,[458] the sale of cemetery lots,[459] and an attempt to bar black visitors to white tenants of a building.[460] Although the availability of money damages for violations of section 1982 has not been settled conclusively,[461] one court has gone so far as to award both compensatory and punitive damages for humiliation suffered in the course of a violation;[462] injunctive relief is definitely within the power of the court to award.[463]

Title VIII of the Civil Rights Act of 1968[464] provided that "[i]t is the policy of the United States to provide, within constitutional limitations, for fair housing throughout the United States."[465] Title VIII specifically makes it unlawful

> (a) To refuse to sell or rent after the making of a bona fide offer, or to refuse to negotiate for the sale or rental of, or otherwise make unavailable or deny, a dwelling to any person because of race, color, religion, or national origin.

> (b) To discriminate against any person in the terms, conditions, or privileges of sale or rental of a dwelling, or in the provision of

[453] Jones V. Alfred H. Mayer Co., *supra*.

[454] 42 U.S.C. § § 3601-19, 3631.

[455] Jones v. Alfred H. Mayer Co., *supra*, at 413.

[456] *Id.; contra*, on the issue of money damages, Brown v. Ballas, 331 F. Supp. 1033 (N.D. Tex., 1971); Walker v. Pointer, 304 F. Supp. 56 (N.D. Tex., 1969).

[457] Park View Heights Corp. v. City of Black Jack, 467 F. 2d 1208 (8 Cir., 1972).

[458] Sims v. Order of United Commerical Travelers of America, 343 F. Supp. 112 (D. Mass., 1972).

[459] Terry V. Elmwood Cemetery, 307 F. Supp. 369 (N.D. Ala., 1969).

[460] Walker v. Pointer, *supra*.

[461] See, note 456, *supra*.

[462] Seaton v. Sky Realty Co., 491 F. 2d. 634 (7 Cir. 1974).

[463] Sullivan v. Little Hunting Park, 396 U.S. 229 (1969).

[464] 82 State. 81; 42 U.S.C. § § 3601-19.

[465] 42 U.S.C. § 3601.

services or facilities in connection therewith, because of race, color, religion, or national origin.

(c) To make, print, or publish, or cause to be made, printed, or published any notice, statement, or advertisement, with respect to the sale or rental of a dwelling that indicates any preference, limitation, or discrimination based on race, color, religion, or national origin, or an intention to make any such preference, limitation, or discrimination.

(d) To represent to any person because of race, color, religion, or national origin that any dwelling is not available for inspection, sale, or rental when such dwelling is in fact so available.

(e) For profit, to induce or attempt to induce any person to sell or rent any dwelling by representations regarding the entry or prospective entry into the neighborhood of a person or persons of a particular race, color, religion, or national origin.[466]

The term "dwelling" includes any residence, any vacant land offered for sale or lease for the construction of a residence,[467] and even a mobile home site.[468] These prohibitions have been held constitutional by the lower courts,[469] with subsection (c) even being construed to apply to newspapers[470] and to prohibit a local Recorder of Deeds from recording deeds containing racially restrictive convenants.[471]

Title VIII also outlaws discrimination in housing financing on the basis of race, color, religion, or national origin[472] and forbids denying any real estate broker access to "multiple listing" or other brokerage services because of his race, color, religion, or national origin, or because he does business with anyone of a particular race, color, religion, or national origin.[473]

As is the case with most civil rights legislation enacted in this century, title VIII contains some exemptions from its prohibitions. Exempt are single-family homes sold or rented by an owner who is not in the real estate

---

[466] 42 U.S.C. § 3604.

[467] 42 U.S.C. § 3602.

[468] U.S. v. Grooms, 348 F. Supp. 1130 (M.D. Fla., 1972).

[469] U.S. v. Hunter, 459 F. 2d 205 (4 Cir.), *cert. den.* 409 U.S. 934 (1972).

[470] *Id.* An interesting aspect of this case is the fact that the person who placed the illegal advertisement was exempt from title VIII, but this was held not go give the defendant newspaper any right to publish his advertisement.

[471] Mayers v. Ridley, 465 F. 2d 630 (D.C. Cir., 1972).

[472] 42 U.S.C. § 3605.

[473] 42 U.S.C. § 3606.

business,[474] rooms or units in dwelling that are owner-occupied and have quarters for four or fewer families,[475] a preference for its own members by a religious organization if membership in the organization is not restricted on account of race, color, or national origin,[476] and a limitation to or preference for its own members by a private club "not in fact open to the public, which as an incident to its primary purpose or purposes provides lodgings which it owns or operates for other than a commercial purpose."[477]

The administration of title VIII is vested in the Department of Housing and Urban Development (HUD), in cooperation with relevant federal, state, and local agencies.[478] HUD is empowered to gain access to the records of those subject to the title and to subpoena individuals or documents, but any lawsuits in which HUD is involved under title VIII are to be conducted by the Attorney General.[479] Three civil enforcement mechanisms are provided, or which two are available to private persons[480] and only one to the Attorney General.[481]

Under the first mechanism, any person aggrieved[482] by a discriminatory housing practice[483] may file a complaint with HUD, which then sends a copy to the respondent.[484] Within 30 days after receiving the complaint,[485] HUD notifies the complainant whether it plans an attempt to resolve it; if it does so

[474] 42 U.S.C. § 3603. The specific terms of this exemption apply to single-family houses sold or rented by an owner not owning or having an interest in more than three such houses. The exemption does not apply where the owner does not reside in the house and it has been previously sold within the last two years, nor does it apply if any broker, agent, or advertisement is used.

[475] 42 U.S.C. § 3603. This exemption protects the legendary (and apocryphal) "Mrs. Murphy's boarding house." A single individual living alone is considered a "family." 42 U.S.C. § 3602.

[476] 42 U.S.C. § 3607.

[477] Id.

[478] 42 U.S.C. § 3608.

[479] 42 U.S.C. § 3611.

[480] 42 U.S.C. §§ 3610, 3612.

[481] 42 U.S.C. § 3613.

[482] The term "person aggrieved" has very broad meaning here, including, e.g., white residents of a discriminatory building who are injured because they are denied the benefits of living in an integrated community. Trafficante v. Metropolitan Life Insurance Co., 409 U.S. 205 (1972).

[483] I.e., a practice forbidden by 42 U.S.C. §§ 3604, 3605, or 3606.

[484] 42 U.S.C. § 3610(a).

[485] If the case is one in which referral to a state or federal agency is required under 42 U.S.C. § 3610(c), within 30 days after the end of the referral period. 42 U.S.C. § 3610(a).

plan, informal and private[486] conciliation efforts are instituted.[487] The original complaint must be filed with HUD within 180 days after the allegedly discriminatory practice occurred.[488] If state or local law provides "substantially equivalent" rights and a state or local agency exists to enforce it, HUD notifies that agency of the complaint and takes no further action on its own unless the agency takes no action in the matter within 30 days and HUD believes that "the protection of the parties or the interests of justice" mandate some action by it.[489] If within 30 days after it takes jurisdiction in the matter,[490] HUD is unable to secure voluntary compliance, and the courts of the relevant state do not provide "substantially equivalent" rights and remedies, the complainant may bring a lawsuit in the federal district court where the act occurred or where the respondent resides or does business.[491] The court may adjourn the case if it believes that conciliation efforts by HUD or a state or local agency are "likely to result in a satisfactory settlement."[492] The court may enjoin an illegal practice and may also order appropriate affirmative action to correct the past results of the practice.[493]

The alternative remedy available to a private individual under title VIII[494] is considerably faster and more direct. Within 180 days after a discriminatory practice occurs, the aggrieved person may bring a lawsuit in the federal district court or in the appropriate state court,[495] though here too the court may adjourn the case pending conciliation efforts at the administrative level.[496] If the suit is brought in federal court, the judge may appoint counsel for the complaining party and permit him to institute the action without paying court fees; if the case is brought in state court, and state law permits, the state court may do likewise.[497] If it finds that discrimination has occurred, the court may award injunctive relief and money damages.[498]

---

[486] Any employee who divulges the content of such proceedings may be fined $1000 or imprisoned for one year. 42 U.S.C. § 3610(a).

[487] 42 U.S.C. § 3610(a).

[488] 42 U.S.C. § 3610(b).

[489] 42 U.S.C. § 3610(c).

[490] Either by deciding to seek resolution of a complaint (42 U.S.C. § 3610[a]) or after a referral period (42 U.S.C. § 3610[c]).

[491] 42 U.S.C. § 3610(d).

[492] 42 U.S.C. § 3612(a).

[493] 42 U.S.C. § 3610(d).

[494] 42 U.S.C. § 3612.

[495] 42 U.S.C. § 3612(a). Note that in this instance, the choice of court is the complainant's. Also, the substantive and remedial rights to be enforced are those of the *federal* law, even if the case is brought in state court. *Cf.*, Testa v. Katt, 330 U.S. 386 (1947).

[496] 42 U.S.C. § 3612(a).

[497] 42 U.S.C. § 3612(b).

[498] 42 U.S.C. § 3612(c).

Punitive damages are also available,[499] even if no actual damages are proven.[500] The court may grant attorney's fees to a successful plaintiff, but unlike the situation in public accommodations[501] and school desegregation[502] cases, may do so only if the plaintiff lacks the financial ability to pay them on his own.[503]

In considering these two remedies available to a private citizen, it must be stressed that they are independent of one another.[504] In fact, it was held in one instance that the plaintiff's beginning his resort to one remedy by filing a complaint with HUD did not prevent him from shifting to the other in midstream by going directly to court.[505]

The Attorney General may sue to enforce title VIII if he finds that there is a pattern or practice of resistance to it or if there is a denial of rights under it[506] which "raises an issue of general public importance."[507] Injunctive or other appropriate relief is available,[508] including requiring action to overcome the effects of past discrimination;[509] a judge who finds that discrimination has occurred should deny injunctive relief, according to one appellate court, only if he is "fully satisfied that the defendant will not continue his unlawful conduct."[510]

In addition to the three remedies for discrimination discussed above, anyone who is threatened or coerced because of his exercise of title VIII rights or his assistance in the exercise of the title VIII rights of anyone else may bring an "appropriate civil action" to prevent the practice,[511] and title IX of the 1968 act[512] provides criminal penalties[513] for anyone who uses force or the threat of force to interfere with the exercise of title VIII rights.

---

[499] Id.

[500] Rogers v. Loether, 467 F. 2d 1110 (7 Cir., 1972), aff'd, subnom. Curtis v. Loether, ———U.S.———, 42 U.S. LW 4259 (2/20%74)(lower court held that punitive damages were available even if no actual damages were proven). See also, Seaton v. Sky Realty Co., 491 F. 2d 634 (7 Cir. 1974).

[501] See, note 216, supra, and accompanying text.

[502] See, notes 251 and 252, supra, and accompanying text.

[503] 42 U.S.C. § 3612(c).

[504] Crim v. Glover, 338 F. Supp. 823 (S.D. Ohio, 1972).

[505] Johnson v. Decker, 333 F. Supp. 88 (N.D. Calif., 1971).

[506] This may be a single, isolated instance. U.S. v. Hunter, supra.

[507] 42 U.S.C. § 3613.

[508] Id.

[509] U.S. v. West Peachtree Tenth Corp. 437 F. 2d 221 (5 Cir., 1971).

[510] U.S. v. Hunter, supra.

[511] 42 U.S.C. § 3617.

[512] 42 U.S.C. § 3631.

[513] A $1000 fine or 1 year in jail or both; if bodily injury results, a $10,000 fine or 10 years in jail or both; and if death results, life imprisonment.

## Civil Rights Commission

The Civil Rights Commission is a purely investigative and fact-finding entity.[514] It neither adjudicates nor enforces violations of law and cannot take any action that will affect the legal rights of an individual.[515] While this may seem rather limited in comparison to some of the statutes, enforcement agencies, and remedies previously discussed, it must be viewed in light of the fact that the Commission was established by the Civil Rights Act of 1957,[516] the first piece of civil rights legislation enacted in over 80 years.

The specific mission of the Commission is to investigate charges of denial of the right to vote because of race, color, religion, sex, or national origin, to study denials of equal protection of the laws, to study federal policies regarding race, color, religion, sex, and national origin, and to serve as a national clearinghouse for information on discrimination in such fields as voting, education, housing, employment, public facilities, transportation, and the administration of justice.[517]

Although the Commission lacks enforcement authority, it does have subpoena power,[518] and its hearings and reports continue to be a valuable source of information on discrimination and the enforcement of the anti-discrimination laws by such agencies as the Department of Justice.

## Community Relations Service

The Community Relations Service, established by the Civil Rights Act of 1964,[519] is situated within the Department of Justice.[520] Its statutory function is to provide assistance to local communities in resolving disputes relating to discriminatory practices based upon race, color, or national origin that impair constitutional rights or affect commerce.[521] It may offer its services of its own volition,[522] or may be asked for assistance by one or more of the parties involved. In addition, it accepts referrals of cases under the

---

[514] 42 U.S.C. §§ 1975-1975e (1970; Supp. II, 1972); *Hannah v. Larche*, 363 U.S. 420 (1960).

[515] *Id.*

[516] 71 Stat. 634, part I.

[517] 42 U.S.C. § 1975c (1970; Supp. II, 1972).

[518] 42 U.S.C. § 1975d (1970; Supp. II, 1972).

[519] 78 Stat. 267, title X; 42 U.S.C. §§ 2000g–2000g-3.

[520] Reorg. Plan No. 1 of 1966, 31 Fed. Reg. 6187 (1966); 42 U.S.C. § 2000g n.

[521] 42 U.S.C. § 2000g-1.

[522] *Id.*

public accommodations statute.[523] All proceedings within the Service are private, and there are criminal penalties for divulging them.[524]

## CONCLUSION

It is often said—usually by those opposing corrective legislation—that "you cannot legislate morality." This is accurate only in the strictest sense, as a change in the law, particularly a major one, does not instantly change the conditions that necessitated its passage.

Our legal system and our social system may move in the same general direction, but they are rarely if ever at precisely the same stage of development. At times, the society and the actuality of its operation are ahead of the law, which must then catch up. Such was the case in the decade or so after the *Dred Scott* decision,[525] which saw the victory of the Union in the Civil War followed by the adoption of the Thirteenth, Fourteenth, and Fifteenth Amendments and various pieces of legislation that seem strong even today. At other times, the converse is true: witness the great step ahead of social reality represented by the decision in *Brown v. Board of Education.*[526]

It may not always be possible to "legislate morality," but it is clear that the law may take a leading role in pointing the way for the development of our morality. Accordingly, those involved in the continuing struggle for equal rights in this country must not overlook the powerful ally they have when "the law" is on their side.

The Constitution and laws of the United States have come a long way from the time when slavery was a recognized and protected institution. All racial discrimination by the federal, state, and local governments and most private discrimination is now prohibited, at least in theory.

The steps necessary to turn that theory into reality must be taken by the victims of discrimination and their allies, not only by challenging individual instances of discriminatory conduct in the administrative agencies and the courts, but by demanding that the responsible government officials, especially those of the Federal Government, exercise their broad powers to enforce the laws. They must also see to it that their legislative representatives enact any further legislation that is needed to eradicate every instance of racial discrimination in our nation. Only when all this is done will the promise of the Declaration, with its "self-evident" principle that "all . . .are created equal," be kept.

[523] 42 U.S.C. § 2000a-3.

[524] 42 U.S.C. § 2000g-2.

[525] Scott v. Sanford, 60 U.S. (19 How.) 394 (1857).

[526] 347 U.S. 483 (1954).

## APPENDIX I

### The 13th, 14th, and 15th Amendments to the Constitution of the United States

*Amendment XIII (Ratified December 6, 1865)*

Section 1. Neither slavery nor involuntary servitude, except as a punishment for crime whereof the party shall have been duly convicted, shall exist within the United States, or any place subject to their jurisdiction.

Section 2. Congress shall have power to enforce this article by appropriate legislation.

*Amendment XIV (Ratified July 9, 1868)*

Section 1. All persons born or naturalized in the United States, and subject to the jurisdiction thereof, are citizens of the United States and of the State wherein they reside. No State shall make or enforce any law which shall abridge the privileges or immunities of citizens of the United States; nor shall any State deprive any person of life, liberty, or property, without due process of law; nor deny to any person within its jurisdiction the equal protection of the laws.

Section 2. Representatives shall be apportioned among the several States according to their respective numbers, counting the whole number of persons in each State, excluding Indians not taxed. But when the right to vote at any election for the choice of electors for President and Vice-President of the United States, Representatives in Congress, the Executive and Judicial officers of a State, or the members of the Legislature thereof, is denied to any of the male inhabitants of such State, being twenty-one years of age, and citizens of the United States, or in any way abridged, except for participation in rebellion, or other crime, the basis of representation therein shall be reduced in the proportion which the number of such male citizens shall bear to the whole number of male citizens twenty-one years of age in such State.

Section 3. No person shall be a Senator or Representative in Congress, or elector of President and Vice-President, or hold any office, civil or military, under the United States, or under any State, who, having previously taken an oath, as a member of Congress, or as an officer of the United States, of any State, to support the Constitution of the United States, shall have engaged in insurrection or rebellion against the same, or given aid or comfort to the enemies thereof. But Congress may by a vote of two-thirds of each House, remove such disability.

Section 4. The validity of the public debt of the United States, authorized by law, including debts incurred for payment of pensions and bounties for services in suppressing insurrection or rebellion, shall not be questioned. But neither the United States nor any State shall assume or pay any debt or obligation incurred in aid of insurrection or rebellion against the United States, or any claim for the loss or emancipation of any slave; but all such debts, obligations and claims shall be held illegal and void.

Section 5. The Congress shall have power to enforce, by appropriate legislation, the provisions of this article.

## Amendment XV (Ratified February 3, 1870)

Section 1. The right of citizens of the United States to vote shall not be denied or abridged by the United States or by any State on account of race, color, or previous condition of servitude.

Section 2. The Congress shall have power to enforce this article by appropriate legislation.

## APPENDIX II

### Sources of assistance in racial discrimination cases

The public and private sources listed below are all national in scope. Many sources—public and private—with a regional, state, or local scope also exist, but they are far too numerous to include here. In many instances the sources that are listed here will be able to supply the names of local sources.

### U.S. Government agencies

1. Equal Employment Opportunity Commission, Washington, D.C. Violations of federal employment statute (title VII) (other than federal employment).

2. Department of Housing and Urban Development, Washington, D.C. Violations of federal housing laws (title VIII).

3. Civil Rights Division, Department of Justice, Washington, D.C., and the local U.S. Attorney, whose office will probably be located near the federal district court for the area. Violations of civil rights laws generally and all violations of criminal law.

4. Federal Bureau of Investigation, Department of Justice, Washington, D.C., and the local office of the F.B.I. Violations of federal criminal laws only.

5. Office of Civil Rights, Department of Health, Education and Welfare, Washington, D.C. All discrimination in public education, including public colleges and universities, and all discrimination in educational institutions receiving federal funds.

6. Office of Federal Contract Compliance, Department of Labor, Washington, D.C. Discrimination by any recipient of federal funds, whether by grant, contract, or loan.

7. Every federal department and agency must have an internal mechanism for handling discrimination complaints regarding employment within that agency, with appeals to the Civil Service Commission and ultimately to the federal courts also available. A federal employee (or applicant for federal employment) must first complain to the appropriate office within the department or agency involved.

*Private agencies*

1. National Association for the Advancement of Colored People (NAACP), 1790 Broadway, New York, N.Y., and local branches and affiliates.

2. NAACP Legal Defense and Educational Fund, Inc. ("Inc. Fund"), 10 Columbus Circle, New York, N.Y.

3. American Civil Liberties Union, 156 Fifth Ave., New York, N.Y., and local affiliates.

4. Lawyers Committee for Civil Rights Under Law, Woodward Building, Washington, D.C.

5. Puerto Rican Legal Defense and Educational Fund, 815 Second Ave., New York, N.Y.

6. National Employment Law Project, 423 West 118 St., New York, N.Y.

7. Native American Rights Fund, 1506 Broadway, Boulder, Colo.

8. National Urban League, 477 Madison Ave., New York, N.Y., and local affiliates.

9. Congress of Racial Equality (CORE), 200 West 135 St., New York, N.Y., and local affiliates.

10. Local legal aid societies and local offices of the Office of Economic Opportunity's Legal Services Program.

# Index

# NEW AND FORTHCOMING BOOKS

## THEME & VARIATIONS: A Behavior Therapy Casebook

Joseph Wolpe, *Temple University and The Eastern Pennsylvania Psychiatric Institute*

Dr. Joseph Wolpe, author of the best seller THE PRACTICE OF BEHAVIOR THERAPY, 2nd Edition, has compiled this important new book as either a companion volume to his textbook, or for independent use in courses utilizing the case study approach.

CONTENTS: I. CONCEPTUAL AND EXPERIMENTAL BASES: The Reciprocal Inhibition Theme and the Emergence of its Role in Psychotherapy. The Case History of a Neurotic Cat. II. BEHAVIOR ANALYSES AND EARLY INTERVENTIONS: Initial Behavior Analysis in Anxiety Neurosis with Depression and Despair. A Demonstration and Discussion of Information-Gathering and Strategy-Planning in an Anxiety Neurosis. Initial Interview in a Case of Depression. Identifying the Antecedents of Agoraphobia. Instigating Assertive Behavior. III. LONGITUDINAL ACCOUNTS OF BEHAVIORAL TREATMENT: Interpersonal Inadequacy and a Separate Insomnia Syndrome: Two Conferences at Different Stages of Treatment. Avoidance of Marital Commitment. An Unusual Syndrome of Indecent Exposure. A Case of Neurodermatitis. The Use of Intercurrent Experiences in the Treatment of a Multi-faceted Psychosomatic Case.

450pp (approx.)    ISBN 0 08 020421 X flexicover  $8.50 (approx.)    ISBN 0 08 020422 8  $17.50 (approx.)
                                                                                      1st quarter 1976

## PHYSICAL DISABILITY AND HUMAN BEHAVIOR, 2nd Edition

J. McDaniel, *University of Colorado*

The new edition provides a more refined, more useful, and somewhat broader base of information for those who have been utilizing the first edition as a textbook and reference. The basic approach remains the same, namely, the choice of psychological processes (perception, learning, motivation, emotions, etc.) as the principal focus, with etiological or diagnostic divisions as incidental to the consideration of the physiological consequences of illness and disability.

270pp (approx.)    ISBN 0 08 019721 3 flexicover  $9.00 (approx.)    ISBN 0 08 019722 1  $15.00 (approx.)
                                                                                      1st quarter 1976

## BEHAVIOR THERAPY AND HEALTH CARE: Principles & Applications

edited by **Roger C. Katz** and **Steven Zlutnick**, *University of Utah College of Medicine*

The central purpose of the text is to highlight important interactions between illness and the environment, and to describe the significant contributions to health care provided by behavior therapists. The book is organized with chapters grouped by organ system. The contents include a combination of recently published articles as well as contributed original papers. Introductions to each chapter are provided by the editors who point out the highlights and the particular significance of the articles. Although the text covers a wide variety of advanced behavioral applications, the editors have written an introductory chapter on basic principles which make the book amenable to a wide cross-section of students and professionals in health education, physical rehabilitation, clinical medicine, psychology, psychiatry, and nursing.

475pp      ISBN 0 08 017828 6 flexicover    $8.75        ISBN 0 08 017829 4  $14.00        March 1975

## EARLY CHILDHOOD AUTISM, 2nd Edition

edited by **Lorna Wing**, *Institute of Psychiatry, London, England*

The second edition of this book, like the first, has contributions from the fields of education, psychology, and psychiatry and has been completely rewritten. In the eight years since the first edition was published, ideas concerning the impairments underlying autistic behavior have become more sophisticated but there has been no fundamental change in emphasis. The present authors all regard early childhood autism and related conditions as resulting from a basic disturbance of cognitive development, the effects of which include abnormalities of language and communication, and a variety of secondary behavioral and emotional problems.

CONTENTS: Part One: CLINICAL AND PSYCHOLOGICAL. Kanner's Syndrome: A Historical Introduction. Diagnosis, Clinical Description and Prognosis. Epidemiology and Theories of Aetiology. Language, Communication, and the Use of Symbols. Motor, Perceptual-Motor and Intellectual Disabilities of Autistic Children. Part Two: EDUCATION, MANAGEMENT OF SERVICES. The Principles of Remedial Education for Autistic Children. An Approach to Teaching Cognitive Skills Underlying Language Development. Towards Reducing Behavior Problems in Autistic Children. The Severely Subnormal Autistic Child. Medical Management. Provision of Services.

314pp (approx.)    ISBN 0 08 017178 8 flexicover  $9.50 (approx.)    ISBN 0 08 017177 X  $15.00 (approx.)
                                                                                      Last quarter 1975

*IMPORTANT BACKLIST TITLE*

## THE PSYCHOLOGY OF LEARNING: An Introduction for Students of Education

Gordon Cross, *King's College London, England*

Discusses some of the practical implications of the classical and more traditional theories of the psychology of learning as well as recent developments. This is an introductory text for student teachers, designed to guide them through the complex theory of contemporary models of learning theory, written in a lively style with a minimum of jargon. Of particular interest is the section which discusses the importance of language in learning.

292pp      ISBN 0 08 018135 X flexicover    $9.50        ISBN 0 08 018136 8  $15.00        1974

 **PERGAMON PRESS**  Maxwell House, Fairview Park, Elmsford, New York 10523
Headington Hill Hall, Oxford OX3 0BW, England ———— PD 565A

# PERGAMON BOOKS FOR PSYCHIATRISTS

## JOB'S ILLNESS: Loss, Grief and Integration

J.H. KAHN, formerly Community Psychiatrist, London Borough of Newham

This book is an examination of the story of Job from the psychiatric point of view. The afflictions of Job are seen as a psychosomatic and depressive reaction to bereavement. The Bible story traces the course of Job's illness and the 'therapy' and emphasises the occasional creative nature of mental illness with subsequent integration of the personality. This unusual book combines together psychiatry, philosophy, literature and the arts in an attempt to use a well-known story as a means of extending and enriching ideas about mental illness and ways of influencing its outcome.

284 pp            April 1975
ISBN 0 08 018087 6 hard $14.00

## METHODS AND EVOLUTION IN CLINICAL AND COUNSELING PSYCHOLOGY

T.C. KAHN, J.T. CAMERON and M.B. GIFFEN, Southern Colorado State College

Two clinical psychologists, one representing the old school, the other the new school of psychology, have combined forces with a psychiatrist teaching at a medical school to produce a textbook in evaluation, counseling, diagnosis, therapy, as well as a review of the entire scope of methods and ideas dealing with techniques used by counselors, psychologists, psychiatrists in evaluating a variety of clients. The book also explores new trends in clinical psychology and counseling.

375 pp        September 1975
ISBN 0 08 017862 6 hard $15.00
ISBN 0 08 017863 4 flexi $ 9.50

## BEHAVIOR THERAPY AND HEALTH CARE: Principles and Applications

ROGER C. KATZ and STEVEN ZLUTNICK, University of Utah College of Medicine

This book covers recent advances in the treatment of physiological dysfunction as well as improvements in patient care resulting from the application of behavioral principles and technology to such problems. The text is organized by systemic disorders and combines previously published articles with original papers specially commissioned for this book. There is an introductory chapter on basic behavioral principles and the book also covers a wide variety of advanced applications which make it suitable for a wide cross section of health care professionals.

475 pp          March 1975
ISBN 0 08 017829 4 hard $14.00
ISBN 0 08 017828 6 flexi $ 8.75

## PERSPECTIVES IN ABNORMAL BEHAVIOR

RICHARD J. MORRIS, Syracuse University, Syracuse, New York

The book presents an overview of the various perspectives currently found in the field of abnormal psychology: it emphasises six major content areas from identification of abnormal behavior through reactions to abnormal behavior. Each section includes readings representing the diversity of contemporary thinking and reflecting the position that abnormal behavior is best understood when approached from an interdisciplinary point of view.

570 pp          March 1975
ISBN 0 08 017738 7 hard $16.00
ISBN 0 08 017739 5 flexi $ 7.95

## BEHAVIORAL INTERVENTION IN HUMAN PROBLEMS

HENRY C. RICKARD, Professor of Psychology, University of Alabama

This volume examines a wide range of successful behavior modification programs geared towards improving the status of individuals with problems in personal and social adjustment. Each article is written by an expert in the field.

"... It is sufficiently academic to be useful as a standard sociological or psychological textbook. It is sufficiently down-to-earth to be of great value to the layman. It deserves to be more than a library shelf dust gatherer."

(Journal of The Institute of Social Welfare, November 1972).

434 pp          1972
ISBN 0 08 016327 0 hard $19.50
ISBN 0 08 017737 9 flexi $ 8.50

## STUDIES IN DYADIC COMMUNI-CATION

ARON WOLFE SIEGMAN, (Editor), University of Maryland, and BENJAMIN POPE, The Sheppard and Enoch Pratt Hospital, Towson, Maryland

The results of a special conference held at the Psychiatric Institute of the University of Maryland, this volume includes a number of diverse studies based on both experimental and naturalistic interviews, experimental dialogues, and free speech samples. The papers cover such topics as the effectiveness of various interviewing styles, the role of the interviewer-interviewee relationship, temporal rhythms of the interview, the role of auditory feedback in the control of spontaneous speech, and speech patterns in patient groups.

346 pp          1972
ISBN 0 08 015867 6 hard $13.50

# PERGAMON PRESS

Fairview Park, Elmsford, New York 10523 & Headington Hill Hall, Oxford OX3 0BW, England

JD/651 A